W9-AOV-620

THE STORY OF
CHRISTIAN HYMNODY

THE STORY OF

Christian Hymnody

~2093

By E. E. RYDEN

AUGUSTANA PRESS
Rock Island, Illinois

THE STORY OF CHRISTIAN HYMNODY

A Revision and Enlargement of the Author's "The Story of Our Hymns," first published in 1930 and appearing in seven subsequent editions.

Copyright 1959
by
AUGUSTANA BOOK CONCERN

Library of Congress Catalog Card Number 59-9242

⟦ PRINTED
IN U·S·A ⟧

AUGUSTANA BOOK CONCERN
ROCK ISLAND, ILLINOIS
1959

To my beloved wife

AGNES ELIZABETH

devoted mother of our children

and faithful companion of many years

whose interest in hymnody and whose

constant encouragement have helped

to inspire this volume.

FOREWORD

A STUDENT of sacred history will find few subjects more fascinating or more rewarding than a study of the hymnody of the Church. To know the story of our hymns is to know something of the spiritual struggles and victories of the people of God through the ages. Henry Ward Beecher has well said: "Hymns are the jewels which the Church has worn, the pearls, the diamonds, the precious stones, formed into amulets more potent against sorrow and sadness than the most famous charm of the wizard or the magician. And he who knows the way that hymns have flowed, knows where the blood of true piety ran, and can trace its veins and arteries to the very heart."

It would be difficult, indeed, to estimate fully the role that sacred song has played in the growth and spread of the Christian faith. It is hardly a coincidence that every great spiritual movement in the history of the Church has been accompanied by a fresh outburst of song. It was so when Ephraim Syrus in the East and St. Ambrose in the West sought to combat the Arian heresy by teaching their followers to sing. It happened again when Luther seized upon this spiritual weapon in his heroic efforts to cleanse the Church of its errors and to lead men back to a saving faith in Christ. Again it was so when the Wesleys sought to arouse their countrymen from their spiritual indifference. Unquestionably, John Wesley was one of the most eloquent preachers the world has ever known, but it is more likely that it was the hymns of Charles that proved the more potent factor in the revival that flamed in England. Nor should it be forgotten that the modern missionary movement which so profoundly stirred the Christian world during the last century had its birth and was carried along on the wings of inspired song.

The power of sacred lyrics in the lives of individual believers has been demonstrated so consistently it hardly needs comment. The memory of a single hymn learned in childhood has often proved decisive in the spiritual crises of later years. As Millar Patrick so well puts it: "The discovery was early made in the Christian era that popular religion is moulded largely by the ideas enshrined in its hymns. Ser-

vii

mons often fly over the people's heads; prayers uttered in their name often fail to carry their hearts and even their intelligence with them; but their songs sink into the memory, color their thought, and fashion their theology much more than any deliberate instruction."

True hymnody reflects the spirit of ecumenicity, revealing the continuity of the Christian Church and the essential oneness of the Christian faith. Catholicity belongs to the very essence of our hymns. Indeed, no more convincing witness to the reality of the *Una Sancta* can be found than that which is borne by the hymnals of Christendom. Here may be discovered true believers of all centuries, climes and communions, though divided by language, customs, doctrines, traditions and many other barriers, worshiping and adoring the same God and Lord with a united voice. And what a paean of praise is heard when their anthems are collected within the covers of one of our church hymnals!

Although this volume is concerned primarily with the hymns themselves and not with the tunes to which they are sung, this is not due to any lack of appreciation of the important role that music fills in the hymnody of the Church. Indeed, the greatness of more than one hymn must be attributed to a large extent to a great tune with which it has had the good fortune of being associated. Even the author of "Lead, kindly Light" attributed the great popularity achieved by that lyric to the fact that John Bacchus Dykes wrote *Lux Benigna* for it.

It is a source of genuine satisfaction, therefore, to note that, along with the steadily rising literary excellence of the hymns that are finding their way into our church hymnals, there is a corresponding concern about the quality of the music. Weak, florid and sentimental tunes of other generations are being replaced by stronger, healthier and more virile compositions that lend dignity, reverence and robustness to the singing of the worshiping congregation.

Here we may mention the growing zeal of hymnal editors to reclaim some of the medieval plainsong melodies that once occupied so large a place in the Western Church, as well as the growing appreciation of the stalwart German chorales, the beautiful French church tunes, the stirring Welsh and Gaelic melodies, and the haunting folk music of Scandinavia and other lands. Nor are today's editors unduly concerned by the fact that the latter often have a secular origin, for they agree with Schweitzer that the real musician knows "by instinct, that all true and deeply felt music, whether secular or sacred, has its home on the heights where art and religion dwell," and they also concur with Ralph Vaughan Williams when he says: "The only 'correct' music is that which is beautiful and noble."

This volume has been inspired by a desire on the part of the author to stimulate a more genuine appreciation and a deeper love for the great lyrics of the Christian Church. In pursuing this purpose an effort has been made to present such facts and circumstances surrounding their authorship and composition as will result in a better understanding of the hymns themselves.

A hymn is a child of the age in which it was written. For this reason the author has followed a chronological arrangement in an endeavor, not only to set forth the historical background of the hymns, but also to trace the spiritual, social, and even political movements in the midst of which they were born. Though a popular style has been adopted to interest the lay reader, every effort has been made to observe historical accuracy.

The materials contained in this volume have been gathered from sources far too numerous to mention. However, the author desires to express a special sense of gratitude to Dr. Richard Beck, the Rev. Sveinbjörn S. Olafsson and Mr. Valdimar Björnson for their aid in the preparation of the chapter on Icelandic hymnody; to the Rev. Toivo Harjunpaa, Dr. Armas K. E. Holmio and Dr. Alvar Rautalahti for valuable information on the hymnody of Finland; to Dr. Laurence N. Field and Dr. F. C. M. Hansen for assistance in gathering biographical material concerning Danish and Norwegian hymn-writers; to Dr. Emil Liedgren, Dr. Conrad Bergendoff, the late Dr. George M. Stephenson, and the Rev. Gösta Hagelin for critical evaluation and historical data relative to certain chapters on Swedish hymnody; and to Dr. F. Eppling Reinartz for information regarding women hymn-writers of the United Lutheran Church in America.

The author also desires to express his indebtedness for valuable source material derived from John Julian's monumental *Dictionary of Hymnology,* as well as helpful information from such scholarly works as Henry Wilder Foote's *Three Centuries of American Hymnody,* Edward S. Ninde's *The Story of the American Hymn,* Louis F. Benson's *The English Hymn,* Albert Edward Bailey's *The Gospel in Hymns,* Alexander MacMillan's *Hymns of the Church,* Moffatt and Patrick's *Handbook to the Church Hymnary,* Percy Dearmer's *Songs of Praise*

Discussed and David R. Breed's *The History and Use of Hymns and Hymn-Tunes.*

Acknowledgments for courtesies granted by publishers and individuals for the use of copyright material will be found on page 641.

Thus we send forth this book with the earnest prayer that it may inspire many devout souls to sing with greater devotion the praises of Him who redeemed us with His blood and made us to be kings and priests unto God.

ERNEST EDWIN RYDEN

Rock Island, Ill., Easter, 1959

TABLE OF CONTENTS

PART III. SCANDINAVIAN HYMNODY

PART IV. ENGLISH HYMNODY

Contents

THE HYMN OF THE REDEEMED

Great and wonderful are thy deeds,
O Lord God the Almighty!
Just and true are thy ways,
O King of the ages!
Who shall not fear and glorify thy name, O Lord?
For thou alone art holy.
All nations shall come and worship thee,
for thy judgments have been revealed.

Revelation 15:3, 4

SINGING GALLERY, CATHEDRAL OF FLORENCE

Sculpture by Luca Della Robbia (1400-1482)
Sketch by Cecile Ryden Johnson

PART I

Early Christian Hymnody

The Gloria in Excelsis

Glory be to God on high, and on earth peace, good will toward men. We praise Thee, we bless Thee, we worship Thee, we glorify Thee, we give thanks to Thee for Thy great glory, O Lord God, Heavenly King, God the Father Almighty.

O Lord, the Only-begotten Son, Jesus Christ; O Lord God, Lamb of God, Son of the Father, that takest away the sin of the world, have mercy upon us. Thou that takest away the sin of the world, receive our prayer. Thou that sittest at the right hand of God the Father, have mercy upon us.

For Thou only art holy; Thou only art the Lord; Thou only, O Christ, with the Holy Ghost, art most high in the glory of God the Father. Amen.

THE PSALMS AND THE CANTICLES

THE PEOPLE of God have always employed song in their worship. In the very midst of the Old Testament Scriptures we find an inspired hymnal — the Book of Psalms. No other hymnbook has reflected so profoundly the hopes and fears, the joys and sorrows, the longings and aspirations of the human soul as does the Psalter. It is the Prayerbook of the Ages.

Our Saviour knew the psalms. He had learned to sing them in the home and synagogue of His childhood. Most assuredly He sang them in the humble home in Nazareth when the family celebrated the Passover Feast. The Jews through the centuries have chanted the Hallel hymns—Psalms 113 to 118—at the paschal table. And our Lord at last went to His Cross with one of these hymns on His lips. The Evangelists Matthew and Mark tell us that the final act of worship in the Upper Room was the singing of a song of praise. "And when they had sung a hymn, they went out to the Mount of Olives." Fraught as they were with Messianic hope, it was fitting that one of these holy hymns should ascend from earth to heaven in the hour when God's own Paschal Lamb was about to be offered.

It was only natural that the New Testament Church should follow the example of Jesus and His disciples in making use of the psalms in the Christian worship. The Jewish Christians could hardly forget the rich tradition of music and song that for centuries had formed a part of the glorious Temple service. Singing also occupied a large place in the national life of the Hebrew people. Moses and the children of Israel had lifted their voices in a song of victorious thanksgiving on the shores of the Red Sea in the day when their nation was born, and there are numerous other instances of patriotic song recorded in the Old Testament.

The structure of the psalms suggests the use of antiphonal singing among the Jews. While this practice may have been confined largely to the great religious festivals in the Temple, it is quite probable that the psalms also formed an important part of the synagogue

3

worship. In any event, every pious Jew must have been familiar with most of the hymns of the Psalter.

How large a place the psalms occupied in the early Christian Church may be deduced from the so-called *Apostolic Constitutions,* a primitive document of uncertain authorship, in which we find such admonitions as these: "Sing the psalms of David, and peruse diligently the Gospel . . . If thou desirest something to sing, thou hast the psalms . . . Assemble yourselves together every day, morning and evening, singing psalms and praying in the Lord's house."

We are also reminded of Paul's specific mention of the psalms in his two almost identical exhortations to the Ephesians and Colossians. To the former he wrote: "Be filled with the Spirit; speaking one to another in psalms and hymns and spiritual songs, singing and making melody with your heart to the Lord." And to the Colossians: "Let the word of Christ dwell in you richly; in all wisdom teaching and admonishing one another with psalms and hymns and spiritual songs, singing with grace in your hearts unto God." It is significant that, in each instance, the psalms are named first.

However, the double reference to "hymns and spiritual songs" also deserves notice, inasmuch as it seems clearly to indicate the introduction of a new element in Christian worship. The psalms had their limitations from the Christian point of view, since the language of the Old Testament was inadequate to describe the glories of a completed redemption. The divine nature of Christ, as well as the whole Christian concept of the Holy Trinity, demanded a new approach to worship. Only by giving expression to their faith in a crucified, risen and glorified Saviour could the first Christians find a form of worship that satisfied their souls. Historical corroboration of this may be found in the famous letter which the younger Pliny wrote to Emperor Trajan from Bithynia in 112 A.D., in which he informed the Roman ruler that the Christians of that province came together on stated days before sunrise and sang hymns alternately (invicem) "to Christ, as to a god."

Eventually the early Church began to draw upon the New Testament writings as the chief source of their distinctive Christian hymns and chants. The canticles of the Gospel of Luke furnished the greater number. Foremost among these was the *Gloria in Excelsis,* or the "Angelic Hymn," so called because its opening lines are taken from the anthem sung by the heavenly choir above the fields of

4

Bethlehem in the night the Saviour was born. Other canticles from the same Gospel are the *Magnificat,* Mary's song of praise at the Annunciation; the *Benedictus,* the exultant utterance of Zacharias when he learned that he was to be the father of the forerunner of the Christ; and the *Nunc Dimittis,* the prayer of thanksgiving that came from the lips of the aged Simeon as he held the Christ-child in his arms in the Temple. All of these have become a permanent part of the liturgies of the Christian Church and have resounded in its sanctuaries through the centuries.

The Church, however, did not confine itself to New Testament source material. It still appropriated language from the Old Testament and gave to it a Christian interpretation. For instance, there is the *Sanctus,* which echoes the song of the seraphim recorded in Isaiah 6:3, "Holy, holy, holy, Lord God of Sabaoth; heaven and earth are full of thy glory." Later these words became associated in the Holy Communion with the *Benedictus Qui Venit,* "Blessed is he that cometh in the name of the Lord: hosanna in the highest!" which is derived from Psalm 118 and occurs anew in Matthew 21:9 as the cry of homage of Christ's followers at the triumphal entry into Jerusalem.

"O all ye works of the Lord, bless ye the Lord; praise him and magnify him for ever," known as the *Benedicite,* is another canticle which had its origin in the Old Testament. It is supposed to have been the song of praise sung by Shadrach, Meshach and Abednego when thrown into the fiery furnace by King Nebuchadnezzar.

The joyous exclamation of praise, *"Hallelujah,"* or *"Alleluia,"* is from the ancient Hebrew worship, and is echoed anew in the 19th chapter of Revelation. Evidently the word was appropriated very early by the Christian Church, and the singing of it became in itself an act of worship. Jerome tells how, in his day, the very ceilings of houses of worship were "shaken with the reverberating Hallelujahs."

The *Trisagion,* a very early canticle which is somewhat similar to the *Sanctus,* has these words: "Holy God, Holy Mighty, Holy Immortal: have mercy on us!"

The *Gloria Patri,* which is sometimes called the "Lesser Doxology" to distinguish it from the *Gloria in Excelsis,* the "Greater Doxology," is an ascription of praise to the Holy Trinity. Based on Matthew 28:19, it may have had its origin in the days of the Apostles. However, the concluding phrase, "As it was in the beginning, is now, and ever shall

5

be, world without end," was not added until after the Arian controversy in the fourth century.

In addition to the early Christian lyrics preserved in the liturgies of the Church, fragments of others may be imbedded in the very text of the New Testament, particularly in the Epistles of Paul and the Apocalypse. For instance, I Timothy 3:16 may be a portion of such a primitive Christian hymn:

> He who was manifested in the flesh,
> Justified in the spirit,
> Seen of angels,
> Preached among the nations,
> Believed on in the world,
> Received up in glory.

The "faithful saying" to which Paul refers in 2 Timothy 2:11 also is believed by some Biblical scholars to be a quotation from one of these hymns, familiarly known and deeply cherished by the first Christians:

> If we died with Him,
> We shall also live with Him:
> If we endure,
> We shall also reign with Him:
> If we shall deny Him,
> He will deny us:
> If we are faithless,
> He abideth faithful;
> For He cannot deny Himself.

It will be noted how well these passages adapt themselves to responsive, or antiphonal, chanting, which was largely the character of ancient Christian singing. Other passages that are possible fragments of such ancient hymns are Ephesians 5:14; 1 Timothy 6:15, 16; James 1:17, and Revelation 1:5-7.

There are strong evidences to support the claim that there was responsive singing in the churches of Asia Minor as early as the latter part of the first century of the Christian era. Credit for introducing this practice is generally ascribed to Ignatius, a pupil of the Apostle John. Ignatius, who was bishop of Antioch, suffered martyrdom about 107 A.D. by being thrown to the lions as a despiser of the pagan gods.

The early Christian worship was sometimes marked by spontaneous outbursts of praise on the part of individual worshipers as they sought to give expression to their gratitude to God and to edify their brethren. Tertullian, who lived in the second century, is

6

authority for the statement that when a believer at a love-feast was invited to sing a song of praise, he might choose "something either taken from the Scriptures, or of his own composition." Both Tertullian and Origen record the fact that, in addition to the public worship, there was rich use of song also in the family circles of Christians.

The corporate worship of the Church during the first three centuries was relatively unadorned. Probably the only written portions of the service were the Holy Scriptures. The responses of the people consisted very largely of such simple expressions as Amen, Hallelujah or Kyrie Eleison. Gradually, however, more definite responses and litanies came into general use, and these, like the psalms and the Lord's Prayer, became established through habit and memory. The New Testament canticles and other liturgical forms were probably introduced in the same manner.

Through this process we may discern how the first written liturgies eventually were evolved. These more elaborate forms of worship had their rise in the fourth century, the most important being the Liturgy of St. James (Jerusalem), St. Mark (Alexandria), St. Clement (Apostolic Constitutions), and St. Chrysostom (Constantinople).

The singing of the early Christians was simple and artless. Augustine describes the singing at Alexandria under Athanasius as "more like speaking than singing." Musical instruments were not used. The pipe, tabret, and harp were associated so intimately with the sensual heathen cults, as well as with the wild revelries and shameless performances of the degenerate theater and circus, it is easy to understand the prejudice against their use in the worship.

"A Christian maiden," says Jerome, "ought not even to know what a lyre or flute is, or what it is used for." Clement of Alexandria writes: "Only one instrument do we use, viz., the word of peace wherewith we honor God: no longer the old psaltery, trumpet, drum, and flute." Chrysostom expresses himself in like vein: "David formerly sang psalms, also we sing today with him; he had a lyre with lifeless strings, the Church has a lyre with living strings. Our tongues are the strings of the lyre, with a different tone, indeed, but with a more accordant piety."

The language of the first Christian hymns, like the language of the New Testament, was Greek. The Syrian tongue was also used in some regions, but Greek gradually attained the ascendancy.

7

The Oldest Christian Hymn

Shepherd of tender youth,
Guiding in love and truth
Through devious ways,
Christ, our triumphant King,
We come Thy Name to sing;
Hither Thy children bring
Tributes of praise.

Thou art our holy Lord,
The all-subduing Word
Healer of strife;
Thou didst Thyself abase,
That from sin's deep disgrace
Thou mightest save our race,
And give us life.

Ever be near our side,
Our Shepherd and our guide,
Our staff and song;
Jesus, Thou Christ of God,
By Thine enduring word
Lead us where Thou hast trod,
Make our faith strong.

So now, and till we die,
Sound we Thy praises high,
And joyful sing;
Let all the holy throng
Who to Thy Church belong,
Unite and swell the song
To Christ, our King.

CLEMENT OF ALEXANDRIA, cir. 200
TR. HENRY MARTIN DEXTER, 1821-90

GREEK AND SYRIAC HYMNS

THERE are historical records to show that very early the post-Apostolic Church began to use hymns that were derived neither from the Psalter nor from the New Testament canticles. In other words, Christians began to sing the praises of the risen and ascended Saviour in lyrics of their own composition. Moreover, they were written in metrical form, and thus we have the beginnings of what is usually designated as Christian hymnody.

Eusebius informs us that in the first half of the third century there existed already a large number of sacred songs. A few of these have been preserved, but the authorship of only one can be determined with any degree of certainty. Usually referred to as "the oldest of all Christian hymns," it is best known by the translation of an American church editor, Henry Martyn Dexter, which begins with the line, "Shepherd of tender youth." In the original Greek, however, the opening line reads, "Bridle of steeds untamed," and it seems to be not so much a children's hymn as one that was aimed to instruct and edify the newly converted pagans who were still "babes in Christ." It is full of metaphors which set forth our Lord under such figures as Shepherd, Fisher of Souls, Everlasting Word, Eternal Light, Teacher, High Priest and King.

The age of this hymn cannot be stated with absolute certainty. However, it is found appended to a very ancient work entitled *The Tutor,* written in Greek by Clement of Alexandria, probably around the year 200 A.D.

This Clement, whose real name was Titus Flavius Clemens, was born approximately 170 A.D. An eager seeker after truth, he studied the religions and philosophical systems of the Greeks, the Assyrians, the Egyptians and the Jews. Eventually he entered the Catechetical School conducted by Pantaenus at Alexandria, Egypt, and there became a convert to Christianity. Some years later Clement himself became the head of the institution, which was the first Christian school of its kind anywhere in the world.

The fame of Clement as a teacher went abroad, and among those who came to receive instruction from him was the famous Origen, who was destined to become the greatest scholar in the ancient Chris-

9

tian church. Another of his pupils was Alexander, afterwards Bishop of Jerusalem, and still later Bishop of Cappadocia.

The Tutor was a work of three volumes. The first described the Tutor, who is Christ; the second contained sundry directions concerning daily life and conduct; the third, after dwelling on the nature of true beauty, condemned extravagance in dress, with men as well as with women.

Appended to this work are two poems, one of which is titled "A Hymn to the Saviour." This is the hymn under discussion. By some critics it is believed that Clement merely quoted it, and that it was written by an earlier poet; others hold the view that it may have been added to Clement's work by a later writer. There is nothing to denote that Clement was not the author, however, and it is generally ascribed to him. A lovely morning hymn, "Sunset to sunrise changes now," is derived from another important work by Clement bearing the title, *Exhortation to the Greeks.*

Clement was forced to leave Alexandria during the persecution of Severus in 202 A.D., and it is thought he found refuge in Palestine. Of his subsequent history practically nothing is known. It is believed he died about 220 A.D.

Another Greek hymn which some authorities believe is as old, or even older than Clement's lyric is the famous "Candlelighting Hymn," of which there are several English translations extant. Robert Bridges, late poet laureate of England, has rendered the one most commonly used. It reads:

> O gladsome Light, O grace
> Of God the Father's face,
> The eternal splendor wearing;
> Celestial, holy, blest,
> Our Saviour Jesus Christ,
> Joyful in Thine appearing.
>
> Now, ere day fadeth quite,
> We see the evening light,
> Our wonted hymn outpouring;
> Father of might unknown,
> Thee, His incarnate Son,
> And Holy Spirit adoring.

Another great poet, Henry Wadsworth Longfellow, rendered the same hymn rather freely into English in "The Golden Legend." Here are his exquisite lines:

O gladsome Light
Of the Father immortal,
And of the celestial
Sacred and blessed
Jesus, our Saviour!
Now to the sunset
Again hast Thou brought us;
And seeing the evening
Twilight, we bless Thee,
Praise Thee, adore Thee,
Father omnipotent!
Son, the Life-giver!
Spirit, the Comforter!
Worthy at all times
Of worship and wonder!

St. Basil, who died in 379 A.D., refers to this hymn as of uncertain date and authorship, but it is a known fact that as early as the second century the Christians gathered to sing hymns at dawn and twilight.

Here it should be stated that these early Greek hymns may have been antedated by a number of lyrics written in the ancient Syriac tongue, which was closely akin to the language of the common people in the Holy Land during the time of Christ. Strange as it may seem, doctrinal controversies gave the first real impetus to hymn-writing in the churches of Syria. As early as the second century, a Gnostic teacher named Bardesanes, born in Edessa in 154 A.D., had succeeded in beguiling many Christians to adopt his heresies by his charming hymns and melodies. His son, Harmonius, followed in the father's footsteps, and the two undoubtedly composed a large number of lyrics. However, only a few fragments of these remain.

The Arians and other heretical teachers, it appears, seized upon the same method to spread their doctrines. It was not until the fourth century, apparently, that any effort was made by orthodox Christians to oppose them with their own weapons. Ephraim Syrus, who has been called "the cithern of the Holy Spirit," was the most influential teacher of his time in the Syrian Church, and the most gifted hymnist as well. This rather extraordinary man was born in northern Mesopotamia about 307 A.D. His zeal for orthodox Christianity was no doubt kindled by his presence at the Council of Nicea in 325 A.D., and thenceforth he was ever an eager champion of the faith.

Ephraim came on the scene almost a century and a half after Bardesanes, but it is evident that the latter's heretical doctrines still held sway in Edessa, the scene of Ephraim's labors. Nothing daunted, Ephraim began to write hymns and to train choirs, not only to counter-

11

act the influence of Bardesanes' teachings, but also the heresies of Marcion, the Manichaeans and the Gnostics of that early day. An ancient record describes him as "a spiritual harper" who, standing in the midst of his choirs, "arranged for them different kinds of songs, and taught them the variation of chants, until the whole city was gathered to him and the party of the adversary was put to shame."

A large number of Ephraim's hymns have survived to the present time, and several have been rendered into English. The only one that seems to have found a place in English hymnody, however, is a baptismal hymn, "Glad sight! the Holy Church." On the other hand, various branches of the ancient Syrian Church, such as the Nestorians, Jacobites, Maronites and the Mar Thomas Christians of the Malabar coast in South India, still make use of Syriac hymns in their liturgies, and some of these are generally ascribed to Ephraim Syrus.

A prayer said by a deacon while the people receive the Lord's Supper in the Liturgy of Malabar, the fifth century Nestorian rite of the Mar Thoma Christians, is the inspiration for a metrical translation which appeared in the *English Hymnal* of 1906 under the title, "Strengthen for service, Lord, the hands." The author of the original Syriac words is unknown, but it is fitting that this beautiful prayer which has been uttered by Christians for more than a thousand years should find a place in our modern hymnals:

> Strengthen for service, Lord, the hands
> That holy things have taken;
> Let ears that now have heard Thy songs
> To clamor never waken.
>
> Lord, may the tongues which "Holy" sang
> Keep free from all deceiving;
> The eyes which saw Thy love be bright,
> Thy blessed hope perceiving.

The first important name among the Greek hymnists was that of Gregory of Nazianzus. Born in 325 A.D., the son of Gregory, Bishop of Nazianzus in Cappadocia, he was compelled by his father to enter the priesthood at the age of thirty-six years. During his student days he had met Basil, with whom he formed a life-long friendship, and also Julian the Apostate, who afterwards became Emperor of the Roman Empire. In 379 A.D. he was called by orthodox Christians to Constantinople, where he was enthroned as Patriarch by the Emperor's own hand. Through the machinations of the Arians, however, he was finally forced to abdicate his office, and returned to his birthplace in Cappadocia. Here he spent the last years of his life in writing sacred poetry of singular beauty and lofty spirit.

To this early period of Greek hymnody belongs also Synesius, Bishop of Ptolemais, a contemporary and friend of St. Augustine. A man of great learning, as well as a statesman and patriot, he was an outstanding figure in his day. When the Goths were knocking at the gates of Rome and the foundations of the ancient Greco-Roman civilization were crumbling, Synesius went to the court of Arcadius and sought to arouse it to a realization of the impending peril; but all in vain. Gibbon writes: "The court of Arcadius indulged the zeal, applauded the eloquence, and neglected the advice of Synesius." His best known hymn, "Lord Jesus, think on me," is the touching prayer of a tired old man who longs for peace. He died in 430 A.D. Some writers have characterized Synesius as more of a Neo-Platonist than a Christian, but there is nothing in this hymn that would support such a charge:

> Lord Jesus, think on me,
>   And purge away my sin;
> From earthborn passions set me free,
>   And make me pure within.
>
> Lord Jesus, think on me,
>   With care and woe opprest;
> Let me Thy loving servant be,
>   And taste Thy promised rest.

Another hymn that comes from the same period is derived from the Liturgy of St. James of Jerusalem, which tradition once attributed to the brother of our Lord. It is known as the Cherubic Hymn, sung in the Mass of the Faithful as the sacred elements are brought into the sanctuary. A prose translation of the Greek runs: "Let us, who mystically represent the Cherubim and sing the holy hymn to the Quickening Trinity, lay by at this time all worldly cares, that we may receive the King of Glory, invisibly attended by the angelic orders. Alleluia, Alleluia, Alleluia!" On the basis of this fifth century sacred lyric, Gerard Moultrie has given the Church the solemnly beautiful communion hymn, "Let all mortal flesh keep silence," which is all the more impressive when sung to the French tune *Picardy*, which in turn is probably based on very ancient plainsong.

Some of the noblest Greek hymns came out of the monastic life of the Eastern Church. This is true particularly of lyrics written at the famous monastery of Mar Saba, located in a desert spot overlooking the Dead Sea, and at the monastery of the Studium in Constantinople. Greatest among the hymn-writers of Mar Saba was John of Damascus, who died about 780 A.D. His two Easter hymns, "Come, ye faithful, raise the strain" and "The day of resurrection," are found today in practically every church hymnal. The latter hymn belongs to the "Golden Canon" series of Easter odes by John, and is traditionally sung in the Greek churches at midnight on Easter morn. At this service the people, upon a given signal, light their candles and transform the darkness into a sudden dramatic blaze of light.

When John of Damascus forsook the world and left behind him his riches and a brilliant career to enter the monastery founded in 520 A.D. by St. Sabas, he took with him his ten-year-old nephew, Stephen. The boy grew up within the walls of the ancient cloister and came to be known as Stephen the Sabaite. Stephen also was a gifted hymnist, and it is he who has given us the hymn made famous by Neale's translation: "Art thou weary, art thou languid?" Stephen died in 794 A.D.

Another famous Greek hymn-writer who seems to have received his inspiration for sacred song at the Mar Saba monastery was St. Andrew of Crete. Born at Damascus about 660 A.D., he entered the cloister at the age of 15. Later he was sent to Constantinople, and in the year 711 A.D. he became archbishop of Crete. The hymn, "Christian, dost thou see them?" is generally ascribed to him, although Neale's English rendering is probably more of a free paraphrase than a faithful translation.

The great Studium monastery in Constantinople, like the Mar Saba monastery, became a spiritual and cultural center where hymnody flourished for several centuries. St. Germanus, patriarch of Constantinople, who died in 780 A.D. at the age of 100 years, was one of the Studium writers. He is believed to have written the lovely Christmas hymn, "A great and mighty wonder." From the pen of St. Anatolius, of whom very little is known except that he lived in the seventh or eighth century, have come the two well-known lyrics, "Fierce was the wild billow" and "The day is past and over."

"Praise ye the Lord, ye servants of the Lord" is another vesper hymn that dates from this early period of the Church. It is derived from the 7th book of the Apostolic Constitutions of the third century, where it follows the *Gloria in Excelsis*.

14

One of the last of the Studium hymnists was Theoctistus, author of what is known as a "Suppliant Canon to Jesus." From this work has been derived the greatly loved "Jesus, Name all names above," which has been called "one of the sweetest hymns of adoration in existence."

A later Greek hymnist, Joseph the Hymnographer, who must not be confused with a lesser writer, Joseph of the Studium, was probably the most prolific of all Greek writers of sacred song. Born in Sicily in the early part of the ninth century, his life was a most eventful one. Once captured by pirates, he spent many years in the Island of Crete as a slave. After regaining his liberty, he went to Constantinople, where he established a monastery. Banished because of his defense of the use of icons, he was recalled by the Empress Theodora and made keeper of the sacred vessels of the Great Church of Constantinople. Banished again because of the icon controversy, he died in 883 A.D. A hymn by Joseph for St. Michael's Day, "Stars of the morning, so gloriously bright," has found a firm place in the Church's hymnody.

Characteristic of nearly all the Greek hymns is the element of pure adoration. The hymnists of the Eastern Church dwell constantly on the glory of the Godhead, the divine perfections, the mystery of the Incarnation, the triumph of the Resurrection. The nature of God and the revelation of His eternal love and divine majesty become the constant theme of adoring rapture and praise. Greek hymnody is nearly always objective. It does not concern itself very often with the response of the human soul to the message of the Gospel. Herein perhaps lies its chief weakness. As pure worship, however, Greek hymnody has never been surpassed. Frequently it rises to sublime heights rarely attained by hymns of the Western Church. In this sense the Eastern Church has left an inheritance of priceless value to all Christendom.

As early as the fourth century the Council of Laodicea had decreed that "besides the appointed singers, who mount the ambo and sing from the book, others shall not sing in the church." How far this rule may have discouraged or suppressed participation of the laity in congregational singing is a subject of dispute among hymnologists. However, it is a matter of record that hymnody suffered a gradual decline in the Eastern Church and eventually assumed more of a liturgical character.

15

An Ancient Morning Hymn

O Splendor of God's glory bright,
O Thou who bringest light from light,
O Light of light, light's living spring,
O Day, all days illumining!

O Thou true Sun, on us Thy glance
Let fall in royal radiance;
The Spirit's sanctifying beam
Upon our earthly senses stream.

The Father, too, our prayers implore,
Father of glory evermore,
The Father of all grace and might,
To banish sin from our delight.

To guide whate'er we nobly do,
With love all envy to subdue,
To make ill-fortune turn to fair,
And give us grace our wrongs to bear.

Rejoicing may this day go hence;
Like virgin dawn our innocence,
Like fiery noon our faith appear,
Nor know the gloom of twilight drear.

Morn in her rosy car is borne:
Let Him come forth, our perfect morn,
The Word in God the Father one,
The Father perfect in the Son.

All laud to God the Father be;
All praise, eternal Son, to Thee;
All glory, as is ever meet,
To God the holy Paraclete.

St. Ambrose, 340-97
Tr. Robert Bridges, 1844-1930

16

THE FATHER OF LATIN HYMNODY

A S THE Christian Church made its triumphant progress westward throughout the Roman Empire, the early Greek hymns and New Testament canticles were introduced into the public worship everywhere. And they were sung, not in Latin, but in their original Greek form. For Latin had not yet come into common use, and the Greek language, or dialects of it, continued to be spoken in Italy, southern Gaul, Germany and North Africa.

Gradually, however, as Latin began to supplant Greek in the worship of the Western Church, the ancient hymns were put into Latin form. And then original hymns began to appear. St. Jerome, who died in 420 A.D., is authority for the statement that it was St. Hilary of Gaul, bishop of Poitiers, who wrote the first Latin hymns, and in this he is supported by Isadore of Seville, who died in 636 A.D. Hilary, it seems, had been banished by Emperor Constantius to Asia Minor in 356 A.D., and during his exile had become profoundly impressed by the singing of Greek hymns in the churches of that region. He himself confirms the fact that when he returned to the West, he brought some of these hymns with him. He also began to write hymns of his own. His most famous hymn is *Lucis Largitor splendide.*

Pope Damasus I, a contemporary of Hilary, is also credited with having written some Latin lyrics.

The "Father of Latin hymnody," however, was none other than the great church father, Aurelius Ambrose, bishop of Milan. It was he who taught the Western Church to glorify the Triune God in sacred song. Concerning this remarkable bishop, Mabillon writes:

"St. Ambrose took care that, after the manner of the Eastern fathers, psalms and hymns should be sung by the people also, when previously they had only been recited by individuals singly, and among the Italians by clerks only."

The father of Ambrose was prefect of the Gauls, and it is believed that the future bishop was born at Treves about 340 A.D. The youthful Ambrose, like his father, was trained for government service, and

17

in 374 A.D. he was appointed Consular of Liguria and Aemilia. During the election of a bishop in Milan, a bitter conflict raged between the orthodox Christians and the Arians, and Ambrose found it necessary to attend the church where the election was taking place in order to calm the excited assembly.

According to tradition, a child's voice was heard to cry out in the church, "Ambrosius!" This was accepted at once by the multitude as an act of divine guidance and the whole assembly began shouting, "Ambrose shall be our bishop!" Ambrose had been attracted to the Christian religion, but as yet had not received baptism. He therefore protested his election and immediately fled from the city. He was induced to return, however, was baptized, and accepted the high office for which he had been chosen.

The story of his subsequent life is one of the most remarkable chapters in the annals of the early Christian Church. Selling all his possessions, he entered upon the duties of his bishopric with such fervent zeal and untiring devotion that his fame spread far and wide.

In like manner as Ephraim Syrus had been moved to write hymns to combat the influence of heretical songs in the East, so Ambrose very early felt constrained to use the same weapon in resisting the popular psalmody of the Arians in the West. Perhaps his most notable achievement was his introduction of congregational singing in Milan. Not only did he write hymns of his own, but he also stimulated others to follow his example. As a result, there developed in the Western Church what came to be known as the Ambrosian cycle of hymns, greatly enriching the Christian worship. Most of the hymns followed a definite metrical pattern, each stanza consisting of four lines of eight syllables each, similar to what is known today as Long Meter. This was also the character of the "office hymns," so called because they were used in monastery worship at various hours during the day. These likewise had their rise under Ambrose.

Ambrose is also credited with having done much to improve and systematize the music of the worship, a task which was later carried to a higher point of perfection by Gregory the Great. As indicated in an earlier chapter, the singing in the post-Apostolic Church was quite simple, probably being confined to the recitation of words in singing tones within the compass of only a few notes. Some of the musical themes were doubtlessly derived from the Old Testament Hebrew worship; others probably were influenced by

18

Greek music, in which the so-called Dorian, Phrygian, Lydian and Mixolydian modes had developed. Out of this background of ancient music was evolved a type of plainsong known as the "Ambrosian chant," which, because of its solemn character, as well as its rhythmical accent and flow, made a powerful appeal to the emotions. Withal, because it was easily mastered by the common people, it quickly sprang into great popularity.

Ambrose also is credited with introducing from the East antiphonal singing, by which device he likewise succeeded in securing the active participation of the congregation in the worship.

Throughout his life Ambrose continued his struggle against the Arian heresy. When Empress Justina, who favored the Arians, sought to induce the Bishop of Milan to open one of the churches of his diocese for their use, Ambrose replied with dignity that it did not behoove the state to interfere in matters of doctrine. When the Council sought to intervene and soldiers were sent to enforce its decree, Ambrose answered: "If you demand my person, I am ready to submit: carry me to prison or to death, I will not resist; but I will never betray the Church of Christ. I will not call upon the people to succor me; I will die at the foot of the altar rather than desert it."

The people of Milan, however, rallied around their beloved bishop, and, when soldiers arrived to surround the church, they found Ambrose and his congregation within, praying and singing. So tremendous was the effect of the song that the soldiers outside of the sanctuary are said to have finally joined in the well-known chants. Every effort to compel Ambrose to yield proved fruitless, and the Empress finally abandoned her plan.

St. Augustine, the most famous of the converts of Ambrose, has left a record of the profound impression made upon his soul when he heard the hymns of Ambrose sung in the Milan basilica. In his *Confessions,* he writes:

> "The days were not long enough as I meditated, and found wonderful delight in meditating, upon the depth of Thy design for the salvation of the human race. I wept at the beauty of Thy hymns and canticles, and was powerfully moved at the sweet sound of Thy Church's singing. Those sounds flowed into my ears, and the truth streamed into my heart: so that my feeling of devotion overflowed, and the tears ran from my eyes, and I was happy in them. It was only a little while before that the church of Milan had begun to practice this kind of consolation and

exultation, to the great joy of the brethren singing together with heart and voice . . . after the manner of the Eastern churches . . . The custom has been retained from that day to this, and has been imitated by many, indeed, in almost all congregations throughout the world."

Ambrose himself has left us this testimony: "They say that people are transported by the singing of my hymns, and I confess that it is true."

Ambrose was no respecter of persons. Although he was a warm friend of the Emperor Theodosius, he denounced the latter's cruel massacre of the people of Thessalonica, and, when Theodosius came to the basilica in Milan to worship, he was met at the door by the brave bishop and denied admittance.

"Do you," he cried, "who have been guilty of shedding innocent blood, dare to enter the sanctuary?"

The emperor for eight months refrained from communion; then he applied for absolution, which was granted him after he had done public penance. He also promised in the future never to execute a death sentence within thirty days of its pronouncement.

It was at Milan that the pious Monica experienced the joy of seeing her tears and prayers answered in the conversion of her famous son, Augustine. The latter, who had come to Milan in the year 384 as a teacher of oratory, was attracted at first by the eloquence of Ambrose's preaching. It was not long, however, before the Word of God began to grip the heart of the skeptical, sensual youth. At length he was induced to begin anew the study of the Scriptures, and his conversion soon followed. It was on Easter Sunday, 387 A.D., that he received the rite of holy baptism at the hands of Bishop Ambrose.

Because so many of the disciples of Ambrose wrote hymns in imitation of their great master, it is quite difficult to determine with absolute certainty which of the Latin lyrics from this period have come from his own hand. The following are generally accepted as Ambrosian in origin: "O Trinity of blessed light" *(O Lux beata Trinitas)*; "O Splendor of God's glory bright *(Splendor Paternae gloriae)*; "O Strength and Stay, upholding all creation" *(Rerum Deus tenax vigor)*; "Creator of the earth and sky" *(Deus Creator omnium)*; "The eternal gifts of Christ the King" *(Aeterna Christi munera)*; and "Come, Thou Saviour of our race" *(Veni, Redemptor gentium)*. The latter was a hymn that Luther prized very highly and one of the first he translated into German.

"That Easter day with joy was bright," "At the Lamb's high feast we sing" and "Now that the daystar glimmers bright" are also sometimes ascribed to Ambrose. However, it is probably more accurate to refer to them as belonging to the "Ambrosian cycle." Other Latin hymns of uncertain authorship from this early period include "Come, Holy Ghost, with God the Son," and "O God of truth, O Lord of might."

The beloved bishop, whose life had been so stormy, passed peacefully to rest on Easter evening, 397 A.D. Thus was fulfilment seemingly granted to the prayer he utters in the hymn, "O Strength and Stay, upholding all creation":

> Grant to life's day a calm unclouded ending,
> An eve untouched by shadows of decay,
> The brightness of a holy deathbed blending
> With dawning glories of the eternal day.

A Triumphant Easter Lyric

"Welcome, happy morning!" age to age shall say,
"Hell today is vanquished, heaven is won today!"
Lo! the dead is living, God for evermore!
Him, their true Creator, all His works adore.
*   "Welcome, happy morning!" age to age shall say.*

Earth with joy confesses, clothing her for spring,
All good gifts return with her returning King;
Bloom in every meadow, leaves on every bough,
Speak His sorrows ended, hail His triumph now.
*   "Hell today is vanquished, heaven is won today!"*

Months in due succession, days of lengthening light,
Hours and passing moments praise Thee in their flight;
Brightness of the morning, sky and fields and sea,
Vanquisher of darkness, bring their praise to Thee:
*   "Welcome, happy morning!" age to age shall say.*

Maker and Redeemer, life and health of all,
Thou from heaven beholding man's abasing fall,
Of the Eternal Father true and only Son,
Manhood to deliver, manhood didst put on:
*   "Hell today is vanquished, heaven is won today!"*

Thou, of life the author, death didst undergo,
Tread the path of darkness, saving strength to show;
Come then, true and faithful, now fulfil Thy word;
'Tis Thine own third morning; rise O buried Lord!
*   "Welcome, happy morning!" age to age shall say.*

Loose the souls long prisoned, bound with Satan's chain;
All that now is fallen raise to life again;
Show Thy face in brightness, bid the nations see;
Bring again our daylight; day returns with Thee;
*   "Hell today is vanquished! heaven is won today!"*

VENANTIUS FORTUNATUS, 530–609
TR. JOHN ELLERTON, 1826–93

A SINGER WHO GLORIFIED THE CROSS

ONE of the last hymnists of the Ambrosian school and the most important Latin poet of the sixth century was Venantius Honorius Fortunatus. He is preeminently the poet of Good Friday and Easter. No one has sung of the Cross with such deep pathos and sublime imagery, or of the triumph of the Resurrection in such joyous and exalted strains, as he.

The early youth of Fortunatus gave little promise of the great contribution he was to make to the Christian Church. Born near Treviso, Italy, about 530 A.D., he seems to have spent his youth devoting his talent to light and frivolous verse for the entertainment of the wealthier circles in which he moved. Someone has described him as "the last of the classical poets and the first of the troubadours."

While a student at Ravenna he almost became blind. Having regained his sight by what he regarded a miracle, he made a pilgrimage to the shrine of St. Martin at Tours, and as a result of this journey the remainder of his life was spent in Gaul. At Poitiers, where St. Hilary, the first Latin hymn-writer, had lived and wrought, he formed the friendship of Queen Rhadegunda, consort of Clothair I, king of the Franks. Rhadegunda, it seems, was the daughter of the king of Thuringia and had been taken captive by Clothair when the latter defeated her father and overran his kingdom. Against her will she had become Clothair's wife, and later they were estranged. She then made her way to Poitiers, where she established a convent called St. Croix. Here she devoted herself to a religious life in association with Agnes, abbess of the cloister. It was through the influence of these two women that Fortunatus was induced to become a priest. Later he became bishop of Poitiers.

Some time before this an event had occurred which inspired two of his most famous hymns. Superstitious veneration of sacred relics had crept into the Church at a very early period, with the result that the churches, convents and monasteries of Europe were flooded with religious objects. Most of these were probably spurious, but the credulous people believed they had been associated in some way with

23

the earthly life of our Lord, His apostles, or early saints of the Church, and therefore regarded them with deep devotion.

It seems that Rhadegunda, in 569 A.D., had obtained from Emperor Justin II what was claimed to be a true fragment of the Cross. The relic had been sent by the Emperor to Euphronius, bishop of Tours, and was to be brought by him to the Convent of St. Croix at Poitiers. In honor of this extraordinary occasion, Fortunatus, at the apparent request of Rhadegunda, wrote the famous Lenten processional hymn, *Vexilla Regis prodeunt,* which has been rendered into English, "The royal banners forward go." On the 19th of November, 569, the relic was brought to Poitiers. A Roman Catholic writer, Abbé E. Briand, in his history of Rhadegunda, has described the journey thus:

"Escorted by a numerous body of clergy and of the faithful holding lighted torches, the Bishop started in the midst of liturgical chants, which ceased not to resound in honor of the hallowed wood of the Redemption. A league from Poitiers the pious cortége found the delegates of Rhadegunda, Fortunatus at their head, rejoicing in the honor which had fallen to them; some carrying censers with perfumed incense, others torches of white wax . . . It was on this occasion that the hymn, *Vexilla Regis,* was heard for the first time, the chant of triumph composed by Fortunatus to salute the arrival of the True Cross."

Fortunatus in this hymn pictures the Cross not as an instrument of torture and shame but rather as an emblem of triumph and victory:

> Fulfilled is all that David told
> In true prophetic song of old;
> How God the nations' King should be,
> For God is reigning from a Tree.
>
> O Tree of beauty, Tree most fair,
> Ordained those holy limbs to bear;
> Gone is thy shame, each crimsoned bough
> Proclaims the King of glory now.

The Latin word *Vexilla* in the opening line of this hymn has reference to the military standard of the Roman cavalry which Emperor Constantine had caused to be surmounted by a cross instead of the traditional Roman eagle. In a sense, even this symbolized the triumph of the Cross, a fact which Fortunatus evidently had not overlooked.

Still more poignant and gripping is the language of the second hymn he composed for the Poitiers festival, *Pange, lingua, gloriosi proelium certaminis.* The common English translation is "Sing, my tongue, the glorious battle." Nowhere in Christian literature can be found a description of the Cross couched in language of such sublime tenderness as this:

> Faithful Cross! above all other,
> One and only noble Tree!
> None in foliage, none in blossom,
> None in fruit thy peer may be;
> Sweetest wood and sweetest iron;
> Sweetest weight is hung on thee!
>
> Bend thy boughs, O Tree of Glory,
> Thy relaxing sinews bend;
> For awhile the ancient rigor
> That thy birth bestowed, suspend;
> And the King of heavenly beauty
> On thy bosom gently tend!

The plainsong tune, *Pange Lingua,* to which this hymn is usually sung, is believed to be as old as the sixth century words.

Another great hymn by Fortunatus, *Salve, festa dies,* is an exultant lyric on the theme of the resurrection. Rendered into English by John Ellerton, "Welcome, happy morning! age to age shall say," this joyous Easter hymn has found its way into practically every hymnal in the English-speaking world. The opening Latin line was subsequently appropriated by various writers for similar hymns for Ascension Day, Whitsunday, Corpus Christi and other festival days of the Church Year.

The hymns of Fortunatus spread to all countries in Europe and eventually were translated into the vernacular. In Sweden, an Easter hymn based on *Pange, lingua, gloriosi* became very popular. An English translation of the Swedish version reads:

> Praise the Saviour, now and ever,
> Praise Him, all beneath the skies;
> Come before Him, and adore Him,
> God's own perfect Sacrifice;
> Victory gaining, life obtaining,
> Now in glory He doth rise.

Almost two centuries before Fortunatus composed his great lyrics in Gaul, another richly-endowed poet of the Ambrosian school was inditing sublime Latin verse far to the West. A contemporary of

Bishop Ambrose, he was the great Spanish bard, Aurelius Clemens Prudentius.

Of his personal history we know very little except that he was born of a distinguished family in northern Spain, probably at Saragossa, about 348 A.D. Having studied law, he occupied important positions of state for many years. At the age of 57, however, he forsook the world and entered a monastery, determined to devote the remainder of his life in the service of the Church. His principal purpose, it seems, was to commend the Christian faith to the cultured and educated classes of his day through the medium of sacred verse. He was preeminently the poet of the Christian martyrs, never ceasing to extol their faith and fortitude. His *Peristephanon* is a work of fourteen lyrics on the "Crowns of the Martyrs." More famous than this, however, is his poetical work entitled *Cathemerinon,* consisting of twelve odes for different hours of the day. Here he sings most beautifully:

> Let me chant in sacred numbers
> As I strike the sounding string,
> Chant in sweet melodious anthems
> Glorious deeds of Christ our King;
> He, my Muse, shall be my story;
> With His praise my lyre shall sing.

From this remarkable work have been derived three imperishable Latin hymn classics: *Corde natus ex Parentis,* the most familiar translation of which begins "Of the Father's Love begotten"; *O sola magnarum urbium,* usually translated "Earth has many a noble city," and *Jam moesta quiesce querela,* a recent translation of which reads, "Despair not, O heart, in thy sorrow."

The latter has been called the finest funeral hymn ever written. Sometimes referred to as the "song of the catacombs," it was regarded by Archbishop Trench of England as "the crowning glory of the poetry of Prudentius." Another archbishop, Johan Olof Wallin, Sweden's greatest sacred poet, made four attempts at translating it before he produced the hymn which is now regarded as the most sublime funeral ode in the Swedish language. Perhaps no Latin hymn has so fascinated English translators as this one. Mrs. Elizabeth Charles rendered it, "Ah, hush now your mournful complainings"; R. F. Littlefield wrote "Be silent, O sad lamentation," and Catherine Winkworth translated it "O weep not, mourn not o'er this bier." In Lutheran lands of Europe it has been a favorite for many generations, and in Germany it has often been sung in its original Latin form, although there are numerous German translations extant. In the ancient Mozarabic Breviary in Spain, it occurs in the Office of the Dead.

Hymnologists of all nations have accorded the highest praise to the lyrics of Prudentius. Bentley calls him the "Horace of the Christians," and Rudelbach declared that his poetry is "like gold set with precious stones." Luther also had the greatest admiration for this ancient Spanish bard, and once expressed the desire that his poetry might be studied in the schools of Germany.

A Tribute to the Crucified King

O Christ, our King, Creator, Lord,
Saviour of all who trust Thy word,
To them who seek Thee ever near,
Now to our praises bend Thine ear.

In Thy dear Cross a grace is found,
It flows from every streaming wound,
Whose power our inbred sin controls,
Breaks the firm bond, and frees our souls.

Thou didst create the stars of night,
Yet Thou hast veiled in flesh Thy light,
Hast deigned a mortal form to wear,
A mortal's painful lot to bear.

When Thou didst hang upon the Tree
The quaking earth acknowledged Thee,
When Thou didst there yield up Thy breath
The world grew dark as shades of death.

Now in the Father's glory high,
Great Conqueror, never more to die,
Us by Thy mighty power defend,
And reign through ages without end.

St. Gregory, 540-604
Tr. Ray Palmer, 1808-87

A POPE WHO REVOLUTIONIZED CHURCH MUSIC

THE JOYOUS, rhythmical church-song introduced by Bishop Ambrose made triumphant progress throughout the Western Church. For almost three centuries it seems to have largely dominated the worship. Its rich melodies and native freshness made a strong appeal to the human emotions, and therefore proved very popular with the people.

However, when Gregory the Great in 590 A.D. ascended the papal chair a reaction had set in. Many of the Ambrosian hymns and chants had become corrupted and secularized and therefore had lost their ecclesiastical dignity. Gregory, to whose severe, ascetic nature the bright and lively style of Ambrosian singing must have seemed almost an abomination, immediately took steps to reform the church music.

Accordingly, a school of music was founded in Rome where the new Gregorian liturgical style, known as "Cantus Romanus," was taught. The Gregorian music was sung in unison. It was slow, uniform and measured, without rhythm and beat, and thus it approached the earlier recitative method of psalm singing.

Although an eminent hymnologist such as the late Louis F. Benson questions the theory that remnants of the ancient Hebrew music may have been preserved in the type of plainsong evolved by the Gregorian school, there are a number of modern musicologists who hold that there is a close relationship between the two. It is generally agreed that the first holy chants employed by the Christians were undoubtedly carried over from the Hebrew worship, and, although these were probably later modified by Greek influences, as noted in the chapter on Ambrosian hymnody, it is not unreasonable to believe that some traces of Hebrew music have survived in Gregorian plainsong. By the same token, they would still later have entered into the Lutheran chorale, which is largely based on plainsong.

In addition to organizing and systematizing the existing plainsong, four additional scales or modes were introduced in the Gregorian chants. Gregory also was instrumental in compiling an anthology of all church music then in use, and this became a nucleus for the whole literature of plainsong.

29

The reform instituted by the Roman pontiff was carried out with great thoroughness. Singers were sent from Rome to all the principal centers of religious life in Europe to introduce the new style of chanting. Deviations from the system were rigorously prohibited, with the result that all local liturgies, such as the Ambrosian in Milan and the Mozarabic in Spain, were soon displaced by the new forms. After the passing of more than thirteen centuries, Gregorian music still reigns supreme in the worship of the Roman Church, an eloquent testimonial to the deeply religious character of plainsong as well as an evidence of its intrinsic worth.

Gregory is easily the greatest figure among the prelates of the Western Church. Like Ambrose, he also came from a distinguished family and at first seemed destined for a political career. He was born in Rome about 540 A.D. His father, Gordianus, was said to have been a grandson of Pope Felix II, and his mother, Silvia, was canonized after her death. Gregory very early achieved great fame in Rome for his piety and learning. After serving in the Roman Senate, he became praeter of the city.

Upon the death of his father, he devoted all of the great fortune he inherited to the work of the Church, founding six monasteries in Sicily and one in Rome. In the year 575 A.D. he entered the latter as a Benedictine monk.

It was at this time that he happened to catch sight of some blue-eyed, fair-haired British children who were being offered for sale in the Roman slave-market. On inquiring about their nationality, he was told that they were Angles.

"Non Angli, sed Angeli" (Not Angles, but angels), exclaimed Gregory.

From that moment he became intensely interested in the idea of Christianizing the British Isles, and he himself volunteered to head a mission of monks. Having obtained permission to do so from Pope Pelagius, he had already gone three days on his journey when he was overtaken and recalled by papal order because of the insistence of the Roman populace. When he became successor to Pelagius in 590 A.D., he commissioned Augustine of Canterbury as Apostle to the British.

Although Gregory probably exercised greater authority in the Church than any Roman prelate up to that time, he ruled with great gentleness and sincere humility. When John the Faster at Constantinople assumed the pretentious title of "Universal Patriarch," Gregory referred to himself as "Servant of God's Servants."

In addition to his epoch-making contribution to the music and liturgy of the Church, Gregory is also believed to have written a number of hymns. Although his authorship cannot be determined with any degree of certainty, he is usually credited with having composed the lovely morning lyric, "Father, we praise thee, now the night is over," as well as the Lenten hymn, "O Christ, our King, Creator, Lord." Other hymns sometimes ascribed to him are "Kind Maker of the world, O hear," "O blest Creator of the light," and "O thou who dost to man accord."

It must be noted here, however, that with the liturgical reforms instituted by Gregory, hymn singing in the worship of the Church became practically a thing of the past. While it is true that the Gregorian chant raised church music to a higher, nobler and more dignified level, its chief weakness lay in the fact that it could be rendered worthily only by trained choirs and clergy. As a result, the common people more and more were reduced to silent, passive worshipers, and the congregational hymn was superseded by a clerical liturgy. What hymns were written were principally office hymns employed by monks in monasteries, and songs for matins, vespers and special religious festivals. The worshiping Church has reason to be truly grateful to God that such inhibitions were removed by the Reformation, and that today in thousands of Christian sanctuaries may be heard even the strains of Gregory's beautiful morning hymn:

> Father, we praise Thee, now the night is over,
> Active and watchful, stand we all before Thee;
> Singing we offer prayer and meditation:
>   Thus we adore Thee.

31

Te Deum Laudamus

We praise Thee, O God;
We acknowledge Thee to be the Lord.
All the earth doth worship Thee, the Father everlasting.
To Thee all angels cry aloud, the heavens and all the powers therein;
To Thee cherubim and seraphim continually do cry:
Holy, holy, holy, Lord God of Sabaoth;
Heaven and earth are full of the majesty of Thy glory.
The glorious company of the Apostles praise Thee.
The goodly fellowship of the prophets praise Thee.
The noble army of Martyrs praise Thee.
The holy Church throughout all the world doth acknowledge Thee:
The Father of an infinite Majesty;
Thine adorable true and only Son;
Also the Holy Ghost, the Comforter.
Thou art the King of Glory, O Christ,
Thou art the everlasting Son of the Father.
When Thou tookest upon Thee to deliver man,
Thou didst humble Thyself to be born of a Virgin.
When Thou hadst overcome the sharpness of death,
Thou didst open the kingdom of heaven to all believers.
Thou sittest at the right hand of God
In the glory of the Father.
We believe that Thou shalt come to be our Judge.
We therefore pray Thee, help Thy servants,
Whom Thou hast redeemed with Thy precious Blood.
Make them to be numbered with Thy saints
In glory everlasting.
O Lord, save Thy people and bless Thine heritage.
Govern them and lift them up forever.
Day by day we magnify Thee;
And we worship Thy Name ever world without end.
Vouchsafe, O Lord,
To keep us this day without sin.
O Lord, have mercy upon us,
Have mercy upon us.
O Lord, let Thy mercy be upon us
As our trust is in Thee.
O Lord, in Thee have I trusted;
Let me never be confounded.

IMMORTAL LATIN LYRICS

THE IMMEDIATE centuries that followed Gregory's historic papal rule produced no outstanding Latin hymnist. However, from time to time a remarkable hymn appeared that was destined for immortality. While the authorship of most of these lyrics is veiled in obscurity, the hymns themselves have survived, and go singing down through the centuries.

One of these, probably dating back to the 7th century, is the inspiring Advent hymn, "Hark, a thrilling voice is sounding." Also from the same period is a remarkable communion hymn, "Draw nigh and take the Body of the Lord."

The latter is found in the *Bangor Antiphoner,* a rare Irish liturgical manuscript now in the Ambrosian Library in Milan. Legend has it that St. Patrick, Apostle to the Irish, may have had something to do with its composition. From this early Latin hymn it is quite evident that Christians of that period received the cup as well as the bread in holy communion, as the first two stanzas reveal:

Draw nigh and take the Body of the Lord,
And drink the holy Blood for you outpoured.

Saved by that Body and that holy Blood,
With souls refreshed, we render thanks to God.

Salvation's giver, Christ the only Son,
By His dear Cross and Blood the victory won.

Offered was He for greatest and for least,
Himself the Victim, and himself the Priest.

Approach ye then with faithful hearts sincere,
And take the pledges of salvation here.

He that His saints in this world rules and shields,
To all believers life eternal yields;

With heavenly bread makes them that hunger whole,
Gives living waters to the thirsty soul.

The Judge Eternal, unto whom shall bow
All nations at the last, is with us now.

33

From *Urbs beata Ierusalem,* which probably dates from the seventh century, two hymns have been derived, namely, "Blessed city, heavenly Salem" and "Christ is made the sure foundation."

Another celebrated hymn of uncertain origin which arose at this time is the deeply cherished Advent lyric, "O come, O come, Emmanuel." The hymn is based on a series of seven Antiphons which were sung on successive days at Vespers from December 17 to December 23. Each of these Antiphons greets the Saviour by one of the many titles ascribed to Him in Holy Writ, such as "Emmanuel," "Rod of Jesse," "Dayspring," "Key of David," etc. Introduced into the Roman liturgy prior to the ninth century, it is believed by some authorities that these Antiphons existed much earlier in the Eastern Church.

The origin of the greatest of all Latin hymns, *Te Deum Laudamus,* is likewise veiled in obscurity. Regarding this noble anthem of praise, which for exalted language must be ranked next to the divinely inspired canticles of Holy Writ, volumes have been written, but with no definite conclusions. It is rather well established, however, that some portions of it existed in Greek form in the early centuries of the Christian era, and it is quite likely that the complete Latin version was not evolved until some time during the fifth century.

There is an interesting legend that the *Te Deum Laudamus* was composed under inspiration and recited responsively by St. Ambrose and St. Augustine immediately after the baptism of the latter in the basilica of Milan, but there is nothing to substantiate the story. Through the centuries it has been the supreme triumphal hymn of the Christian Church, and its use has been invoked on innumerable occasions to celebrate great moments in human history. Paraphrases have also been written in many languages, one of the finest being "Grosser Gott, wir loben dich," which in turn has been rendered into English, "Holy God, we praise Thy Name," and French, "Grand Dieu, nous te bénissons." The English version, by the American, Clarence A. Walworth, is a magnificent hymn of adoration:

> Holy God, we praise Thy Name;
> Lord of all, we bow before Thee!
> All on earth Thy sceptre claim,
> All in heaven above adore Thee;
> Infinite Thy vast domain,
> Everlasting is Thy reign.

Hark! the loud celestial hymn
    Angel choirs above are raising,
Cherubim and seraphim,
    In unceasing chorus praising;
Fill the heavens with sweet accord:
Holy, holy, holy Lord.

Lo! the Apostolic train
    Join the sacred Name to hallow;
Prophets swell the loud refrain,
    And the white-robed martyrs follow;
And from morn to set of sun,
Through the Church the song goes on.

A fine Ascension hymn of unknown authorship from the 7th or 8th century, *Jesu nostra redemptio, amor et desiderium,* has been rendered "O Christ, our hope, our heart's desire" by John Chandler, the British translator who did so much to preserve some of the hymn treasures of the ancient Church.

One of the few Latin hymns of this period to which we may attach a name with certainty is the celebrated Palm Sunday lyric, "All glory, laud, and honor," which was composed by Bishop Theodulph of Orleans, probably in the year 856 A.D. The bishop, it seems, had been suspected by the French monarch, Louis the Pious, of plotting against him, and had been committed to prison in a cloister in Angers. While there he composed the hymn, and on Palm Sunday, as Louis passed the cloister on his way to church, Theodulph, standing at the window of his cell, sang his new song. The emperor, so the story runs, was so deeply affected by the incident he immediately ordered the bishop's release. Through the centuries the hymn has been used liturgically as a processional on Palm Sunday. Theodulph died at Angers in 821 A.D.

The Pentecost hymn, *Veni, Creator Spiritus,* which, next to *Te Deum Laudamus,* is regarded as the greatest Latin hymn ever composed, is believed to have been written some time during the ninth century, or perhaps earlier. Although primarily a hymn for Whitsunday, it came into widespread use in the medieval Church for all solemn occasions when the divine blessing of the Holy Spirit was invoked, such as the ordination of priests, the consecration of bishops, the coronation of kings, the opening of church councils and synods, and the consecration of churches. Its singing was usually attended with the ringing of bells and the use of incense and lights.

Despite the fact that *Veni, Creator Spiritus* was widely known

35

during the Middle Ages, considerable uncertainty exists regarding its authorship. Variously ascribed to St. Ambrose, Gregory the Great, Emperor Charlemagne and Rhabanus Maurus, the weight of modern scholarship favors the latter. Maurus, who was Archbishop of Mainz, died in 856 A.D.

No hymn of the Western Church has been rendered into as many languages as *Veni, Creator Spiritus*. In English alone there are nearly three score known translations. Highly regarded by Martin Luther and other reformers, it came into general use in Protestant liturgical Churches at Pentecost and other occasions of great solemnity. The 1940 *Hymnal* of the Protestant Episcopal Church contains four versions of the hymn: "O come, Creator Spirit, come," "Come, Holy Ghost, our souls inspire," "Come, Holy Ghost, Creator blest," and "Creator Spirit, by whose aid." Two of these—"Come, Holy Ghost, our souls inspire" and "Creator Spirit, by whose aid"—are also included in the 1958 *Service Book and Hymnal* of the Lutheran Church. The former translation is by John Cosin; the latter by John Dryden. The first two stanzas of Dryden's version read:

> Creator Spirit, by whose aid
> The world's foundations first were laid,
> Come, visit every pious mind;
> Come, pour Thy joys on human kind;
> From sin and sorrow set us free,
> And make Thy temples worthy Thee.
>
> O source of uncreated light,
> The Father's promised Paraclete,
> Thrice holy fount, thrice holy fire,
> Our hearts with heavenly love inspire;
> Come, and Thy sacred unction bring
> To sanctify us while we sing.

Another Latin hymn which probably had its origin some time before the eleventh century is *Alleluia, dulce carmen*, which John Mason Neale has translated "Alleluia, song of sweetness." "Hallelujah" or "Alleluia," as explained in an earlier chapter, was very early employed as a simple liturgical response in the Christian worship. Derived from the Hallel psalms, it is a Hebrew word meaning "Praise ye the Lord." In the medieval Church, the use of "Alleluia" was forbidden from Saturday before Septuagesima until Easter. As a result, elaborate services were held in some churches, bidding farewell to "Alleluia." There is an allusion to the practice in this hymn:

Alleluia cannot always
    Be our song while here below;
Alleluia our transgressions
    Make us for a while forego;
For the solemn time is coming
    When our tears for sin must flow.

Therefore in our hymns we pray Thee
    Grant us, blessed Trinity,
At the last to keep Thy Easter
    In our home beyond the sky,
There to Thee forever singing
    Alleluia joyfully!

Here also should be noted the Latin origin of Johann Heermann's gripping German hymn, *Herzliebster Jesu,* to which Robert Bridges gave classical English expression in "Ah, holy Jesus, how hast Thou offended?" It is now definitely known that Heermann's version was based on a Latin prose passage drawn from the writings of Jean de Fécamp, who died in 1078 A.D. For a long time it was believed to have been derived from the 12th century *Orationes* attributed to St. Anselm of Canterbury, but it has been recently established that the French writer was the author of the particular passage in the *Orationes* which inspired Heermann's hymn.

Gratitude to the Dying Saviour

O sacred Head, now wounded,
  With grief and shame weighed down,
Now scornfully surrounded
  With thorns, Thine only crown;
O sacred Head, what glory,
  What bliss till now was Thine!
Yet, though despised and gory,
  I joy to call Thee mine.

How art Thou pale with anguish,
  With sore abuse and scorn;
How does that visage languish
  Which once was bright as morn!
Thy grief and bitter passion
  Were all for sinners' gain;
Mine, mine was the transgression,
  But Thine the deadly pain.

What language shall I borrow
  To thank Thee, dearest Friend,
For this Thy dying sorrow,
  Thy pity without end?
O make me Thine for ever,
  And should I fainting be,
Lord, let me never, never
  Outlive my love to Thee.

Be near when I am dying,
  O show Thy Cross to me!
And, for my succor flying,
  Come, Lord, to set me free.
These eyes, new faith receiving,
  From Thee shall never move;
For He who dies believing
  Dies safely in Thy love.

Ascribed to St. Bernard of Clairvaux, 1090-1153
Paul Gerhardt, 1607-76
Tr. James Waddell Alexander, 1804-59, a.

THE GOLDEN AGE OF LATIN HYMNODY

URING the Middle Ages, when the Church had fallen on evil days, there was very little to inspire sacred song. All over Europe the Gregorian chants, sung in Latin, left no room for congregational singing in the Roman Mass. The barbarian languages were considered too crude for use in worship, and certainly not worthy of being moulded into Christian hymns. Religious poetry was almost invariably written in Latin.

However, in the midst of the spiritual decay and moral depravity which characterized the age there were noble souls whose lives shone like bright stars in the surrounding darkness. Their sacred poetry, a great deal of which was written for private devotion, bears witness to their deep love for the Saviour.

Occasionally one of these poems, or a portion of it, came into use as an office hymn in the monasteries, or as a special hymn for a saint's day, or for one of the great festivals of the Church Year. Invariably, however, they were sung by clergy and choirs, for the voice of the laity was almost completely silenced in the Mass.

The religious fervor inspired by the Crusades, which began in the year 1098 A.D., resulted in the production during the 12th century of Latin poetry of singular lyrical beauty. This may be regarded as the golden age of Latin hymnody, and it was during this period that the most gripping of all Good Friday hymns, "O sacred Head, now wounded," was written. It is generally ascribed to Bernard of Clairvaux, preacher of the Second Crusade, and one of the most brilliant of Latin hymn-writers.

Although composed in the 12th century, the hymn did not achieve unusual fame until five centuries later, when it was rendered into German by the greatest of all Lutheran hymnists, Paul Gerhardt. Lauxmann has well said: "Bernard's original is powerful and searching, but Gerhardt's hymn is still more powerful and profound, as redrawn from the deeper spring of evangelical Lutheran, Scriptural knowledge and fervency of faith."

Gerhardt's version in turn was translated into English by James

W. Alexander of Princeton, a Presbyterian. Thus, as Dr. Philip Schaff puts it, "This classic hymn has shown in three tongues—Latin, German and English—and in three confessions—Roman, Lutheran and Reformed—with equal effect the dying love of our Saviour and our boundless indebtedness to Him."

Yet another Lutheran, none other than John Sebastian Bach, "high priest of church music," has contributed to the fame of the hymn by giving the gripping tune to which it is sung its present form. Strangely enough, this remarkable minor melody was originally a rather frivolous German folksong, and was adapted by Hans Leo Hassler in 1601 to the hymn, "Herzlich thut mich verlangen." It was Bach, however, who moulded the tune into the "Passion Chorale," one of the world's masterpieces of sacred music.

Of Bernard of Clairvaux, volumes might be written. Luther paid him an eloquent tribute, when he said: "If there has ever been a pious monk who feared God it was St. Bernard, whom alone I hold in much higher esteem than all other monks and priests throughout the globe."

Probably no preacher ever exerted a more profound influence over the age in which he lived than did this Cistercian monk. It was the death of his mother, when he was twenty years old, that seemed to have been the turning point in his life. The son of a Burgundian knight, he had planned to become a priest, but now he determined to enter a monastery. He did not go alone, however, but took with him twelve companions, including an uncle and four of his five brothers!

When he was only twenty-four years old, in the year 1115, he founded a monastery of his own, which was destined to become one of the most famous in history. It was situated in a valley in France called Wormwood, a wild region famous as a robber haunt. Bernard changed the name to *Clara Vallis,* or "Beautiful Valley," from which is derived the designation "Clairvaux."

Among his pupils were men who afterwards wielded great influence in the Roman Church. One became a pope, six became cardinals, and thirty were elevated to the office of bishop in the Church.

As abbot of Clairvaux, the fame of Bernard spread through all Christendom. He led such an ascetic life that he was reduced almost to a living skeleton. His haggard appearance alone made a deep impression on his audiences. But he also was gifted with extraordinary eloquence and deep spiritual fervor.

Frequently he would leave his monastery to appear before kings and church councils, always swaying them at will. During the year 1146 he traveled through France and Germany, preaching a second crusade. The effect of his preaching was almost miraculous. In some instances the whole population of cities and villages seemed to rise *en masse,* flocking to the crusade standards.

"In the towns where I have preached," he said, "scarcely one man is left to seven women."

Emperor Conrad and Louis, King of France, were easily won to the cause, and in 1147 the vast horde of crusaders started for the Holy Land. Probably only one-tenth reached Palestine, and the expedition resulted in failure. A miserable remnant returnd home, defeated and disgraced. The blame was thrown on Bernard and it was no doubt this sorrow that hastened his death, in the year 1153.

"O sacred Head, now wounded" *(Salve caput cruentatum)* is derived from an extensive Latin poem which addresses itself to the various members of Christ's body languishing on the Cross, namely, His feet, knees, hands, side, breast, heart and face. The portion of the poem which dwells on His hands *(Salve, Jesu, Pastor bone)* forms the basis of another English hymn translation, "Wide open are Thy hands," which is the work of an eminent American Lutheran theologian, Charles Porterfield Krauth.

"O sacred Head, now wounded" alone would have gained undying fame for Bernard, but we are indebted to this gifted monk for another remarkable poem, *De Nomine Jesu,* from which at least four of our most beautiful English hymns have been derived. One of these is a translation by the Englishman, Edward Caswall:

> Jesus, the very thought of Thee
> With sweetness fills the breast;
> But sweeter far Thy face to see,
> And in Thy presence rest.

A second by the same translator is equally beautiful:

> O Jesus, King most wonderful,
> Thou conqueror renowned,
> Thou sweetness most ineffable,
> In whom all joys are found!

41

A third derived from Bernard's famous lyric has been translated by the American hymnist, Ray Palmer:

> Jesus, Thou Joy of loving hearts,
>> Thou Fount of life, Thou Light of men,
> From the best bliss that earth imparts
>> We turn unfilled to Thee again.

A fourth cento from the same poem has been rendered into English by Robert Campbell. The first two stanzas read:

> Light of the anxious heart,
>> Jesus, Thy suppliants cheer;
> Bid Thou the gloom of guilt depart,
>> And shed Thy sweetness here.

> O happy he whose breast
>> Thou makest Thine abode;
> Sweet light that with the pure wilt rest,
>> For they shall see their God.

Throughout the Middle Ages the verses of Bernard were a source of solace and inspiration to innumerable souls, and it is recorded that even the Crusaders who kept guard over the Holy Sepulcher at Jerusalem sang well-known passages from his *De Nomine Jesu.*

David Livingstone, who took the Latin poem with him into the heart of Africa, also has testified of its influence upon him. He writes: "That hymn of St. Bernard on the Name of Jesus . . . rings in my ears as I wander across the wide, wide wilderness."

A notable contemporary, Bernard of Cluny, shares with Bernard of Clairvaux the distinction of making the 12th century one of the most luminous periods in the history of Latin hymnody. This Bernard was born of English parents in Morlaix of Britanny very early in that century. Having entered the Abbey of Cluny, which at that time was the wealthiest and most luxurious monastery in Europe, he devoted his leisure hours to the composition of a poem of 3,000 lines titled *De contemptu mundi,* or "On the Contemptibleness of the World." The work is a bitter satire on the vices and follies of his age, and neither the Roman hierarchy nor its clergy were spared. In contrast with the dark picture of a sinful world, however, the poet pictured the bliss and the glory of the heavenly Jerusalem, the City of God.

Much of the fame that Bernard of Cluny's poem has achieved is due to four English paraphrases by John Mason Neale which have found their way into practically every standard English hymnal. They are "The world is very evil," "Brief life is here our portion," "Jerusalem the golden," and "For thee, O dear, dear country," all of which are veritable classics of sacred poetry.

Many of the hymns written in this period, like those of Bernard of Cluny, looked forward with longing to the promised joys of the life to come. Undoubtedly this was a reflection of the general feeling of hopelessness shared by many pious souls regarding world conditions during the Dark Ages. Characteristic of these lyrics is Peter Abelard's vivid description of the blessedness of the redeemed:

> O what their joy and their glory must be,
> Those endless Sabbaths the blessed ones see!
> Crown for the valiant, to weary ones rest;
> God shall be all, and in all ever blest.

Abelard is one of the most tragic figures of the 12th century. His secret marriage to Heloise, although he was an ordained priest, and two trials for heresy were sad episodes in a very stormy career. Later in life Abelard entered a monastery and Heloise a convent, but the two never forgot their devotion to each other. After Abelard and his teachings had been condemned by a church council held in Sens in 1140 A.D., at which Bernard of Clairvaux acted as the chief prosecutor, Abelard appealed to Rome and was on his way there when he died at the monastery of Cluny in the year 1142. He was buried by Heloise in the Pere-Lachaise Cemetery in Paris, where she also later was laid at rest—beside him.

A fine Pentecost hymn which evidently also had its origin in the 12th century is "Love of the Father, love of God the Son." It appeared for the first time in a Toulouse manuscript, but its author is not known.

A Prayer to the Holy Spirit

Come, Holy Ghost, in love
Shed on us from above
    Thine own bright ray;
Divinely good Thou art;
Thy sacred gifts impart
To gladden each sad heart;
    O come today.

Come, tenderest friend and best,
Our most delightful guest,
    With soothing power;
Rest, which the weary know,
Shade, 'mid the noontide glow,
Peace, when deep griefs o'erflow;
    Cheer us, this hour.

Come, Light serene, and still
Our inmost bosoms fill;
    Dwell in each breast;
We know no dawn but Thine;
Send forth Thy beams divine,
On our dark souls to shine,
    And make us blest.

Come, all the faithful bless:
Let all who Christ confess
    His praise employ;
Give virtue's rich reward;
Victorious death accord,
And, with our glorious Lord,
    Eternal joy!

Based on Veni, Sancte Spiritus
Tr. Ray Palmer, 1808–87

44

THE ORIGIN OF LATIN SEQUENCES

THE IMPETUS given to sacred song by the two Bernards and other Latin poets of the twelfth century has continued to be felt down to the present time. However, since the Church of Rome continued to frown on congregational singing, very few of the rich devotional lyrics of this period were actually used in worship. What hymns were sung in Latin were confined largely to matins and vespers, and to the various devotional hours observed by clergy and monastic orders. It was not until the dawn of the Reformation that Luther and his German contemporaries began to draw on this vast source of sacred poetry as the basis for hymns in the vernacular.

That an unexpressed universal longing existed during the Middle Ages for some form of hymnody in the corporate worship of the Church may be seen in the rise of a curious type of song known as "sequences." The development of these lyrics is one of the most unusual chapters in the history of Christian hymnody. Very early it became the practice in the Mass for the cantor or the choir to sing a hymn known as the Gradual between the reading of the Epistle and Gospel. The Gradual received its name from the fact that it was usually sung from the altar steps or from a step leading to the ambo, where the Gospel was read.

On festival days the Gradual always ended with an *Alleluia*. In some strange way, perhaps through Byzantine influence from the East, the singers eventually began to embellish the last syllable of *Alleluia* by singing it on a number of additional notes. Since the prolonging of a single syllable tended to become monotonous, words were finally added for the new music, and these eventually were developed into complete hymns. An astonishing number of these medieval lyrics were written. A single collection published in Mainz, Germany, in 1873 contained no less than 895, but the known compositions far exceed this total.

The rapid spread of the use of sequences throughout Europe was probably due to the sanction of local bishops, for there is no evidence that they were ever approved by Rome. In fact, when the

45

Roman liturgy was revised in 1570 by order of the Council of Trent, the Roman hierarchy indicated its displeasure concerning their use by banning all except four. Those retained were *Victimae paschali* for Easter; *Veni, Sancte Spiritus* for Pentecost; *Lauda Sion Salvatorem* for the Feast of Corpus Christi, and *Dies irae, dies illa* for Masses for the dead. *Stabat Mater dolorosa* was added as a fifth sequence in 1727 for use on Friday after Passion Sunday.

Most famous of all of these is *Veni, Sancte Spiritus,* which must not be confused with *Veni, Creator Spiritus,* mentioned in an earlier chapter. Often called the "Golden Sequence," *Veni, Sancte Spiritus* is a deeply moving prayer addressed to the Third Person in the Holy Trinity. It has been characterized by Archbishop Trench as "the loveliest of all hymns in the whole cycle of sacred Latin poetry." And a French hymnologist adds, "I well believe that the author (whoever he was), when he composed this piece, had his soul transfused by a certain heavenly sweetness, by which, the Holy Spirit being its author, he uttered so much sweetness in so few words." John Julian, who rarely uses extravagant phrases, calls it a "magnificent hymn" and refers to its "stately grace" and its "perfect rhythmic melody," and declares that it at once defies comparison with any other hymn in any other language.

The universal interest manifested in this lovely lyric is attested by the vast number of translated versions it has inspired, particularly in the English language. Most commonly used in America is a paraphrase by Ray Palmer, the New England hymnist, entitled "Come, Holy Ghost, in love."

The authorship of *Veni, Sancte Spiritus* is veiled in obscurity. Variously ascribed to Hermannus Contractus, Robert II of France, Stephen Langton, Innocent III and several other medieval writers, the weight of evidence seems to lean toward Pope Innocent. Archbishop Trench dismisses the question with the significant statement that it could have been composed only "by one who had been acquainted with many sorrows and also with many consolations."

Hardly less famous than *Veni, Sancte Spiritus* is another sequence of the 11th or 12th century, *Victimae paschali,* which was authorized by the Roman hierarchy for use on Easter Sunday. The most popular English translation is "Christ, the Lord, is risen today" by Jane Eliza Leeson. Here again we meet with frustration in the effort to determine definite authorship. However, it has generally been ascribed to a

Burgundian priest named Wippo, who was chaplain to Emperors Conrad II and Heinrich III.

This sequence is of more than usual interest, since from it were developed the first liturgical dramas and mystery plays of the Middle Ages. In many of the countries of Europe it was interpolated as the ceremony of the Easter Sepulchre between the Third Lesson and the *Te Deum* at Easter Matins. This became a striking drama in which altar boys took the part of the two angels and three deacons represented the three Marys. In the dialogue which followed, the angels asked, "Whom seek ye?" to which the Marys replied, "Jesus of Nazareth." The angels thereupon removed the white altar-cloth representing the grave clothes, and answered, "He is not here." The Marys then turned toward the choir and sang "Alleluia, the Lord is risen." At this point the officiating bishop or succentor entered the liturgical drama by asking questions, to which the Marys replied by singing in turn various stanzas of *Victimae paschali,* in which the entire choir finally joined. At the conclusion of the rite, the bishop intoned the *Te Deum.*

Martin Luther loved this medieval hymn because of its striking description of the conflict between death and life. He practically incorporated one of its stanzas in his Easter hymn, *Christ lag in Todesbanden.*

Another sequence of this period is *Stabat Mater dolorosa,* which Dr. Philip Schaff characterized as "the most pathetic hymn of the Middle Ages." It is generally attributed to Innocent III. "At the Cross, her station keeping," by Edward Caswell, is the most commonly used English translation. As indicated above, this hymn was one of the five sequences that eventually received the approval of the Church of Rome. It was a favorite processional hymn of the fanatical Flagellants during the 14th century.

The most awe-inspiring Judgment Day hymn ever written, *Dies irae, dies illa,* also is a sequence from this period. It is generally attributed to Thomas of Celano. Concerning this masterpiece of sacred song, Dr. Charles Robinson says: "It stands pre-eminent not only because of the grandeur of the theme, but also from the perfection of its form and rhythm." Sir Walter Scott regarded this hymn as one of the world's greatest poems, and he incorporated it in condensed form with overwhelming effect as the "Hymn for the Dead" in the *Lay of the Last Minstrel.* Scott's version, which begins with the line,

"That day of wrath, that dreadful day," is the most common form in which *Dies irae* appears in modern English hymnals.

Aside from the sequences, a number of other famous Latin hymns date from the Middle Ages. Among these are three impressive communion hymns, "Thee we adore, O hidden Saviour," "O saving Victim, opening wide," and "Very Bread, Good Shepherd, tend us," all of which are believed to have come from the pen of the great medieval scholar, St. Thomas Aquinas, during the 13th century. The latter two were written for the Feast of Corpus Christi by direct commission of Pope Urban IV. Some uncertainty surrounds the authorship of "Thee we adore, O hidden Saviour," but most scholars attribute this beautiful hymn to Aquinas also. "O saving Victim" eventually came to be used in the Roman Mass in the benediction of the Sacrament, and is so employed today.

Thomas à Kempis, the 15th century mystic who wrote the immortal *Imitatio Christi,* is credited with the authorship of a few hymns, the most notable of which is "Light's abode, celestial Salem," an impressive description of the Eternal City. From the same century comes a magnificent Easter hymn, "O sons and daughters, let us sing," which was written by a Franciscan friar, Jean Tisserand, who died in Paris in 1494.

A veil of anonymity rests over a number of fine Latin hymns which appeared about this time. Among these are "Father most holy, merciful and tender," an ode to the Holy Trinity; "Good Christian men, rejoice" *(In dulci jubilo),* a famous macaronic Nativity carol; and "O wondrous type, O vision fair," a Transfiguration hymn.

Here also should be mentioned "Jerusalem, my happy home," which is usually credited to an English writer, F.B.P., whose initials alone are known. However, it has been quite definitely established that the English version was based on a Latin manuscript of the 15th century known as *Meditationes.* Also probably of Latin origin is the exquisite Nativity cradle song, *Joseph, lieber Joseph mein,* which appeared in Germany about this time. Two English translations extant are "Joseph dearest, Joseph mine" and "Long ago, and far away."

One of the last great Latin hymns written before the coming of the Reformation is the immortal Easter carol, "Jesus Christ is risen today. Alleluia!" *(Surrexit Christus hodie).* This hymn seems to have had its rise in Bohemia, but quickly spread to all parts of Europe. The first English version of the lyric was printed in *Lyra Davidica,* which appeared in London in 1708, a year after Isaac Watts' epoch-making *Hymns and Spiritual Songs* was published. Charles Wesley in 1740 added the fourth stanza which is now in general use.

This seems an appropriate place to mention a number of Italian hymns written during the centuries immediately preceding the Reformation. One of the most famous is:

> All creatures of our God and King,
> Lift up your voice and with us sing
> Alleluia, Alleluia!
> Thou burning sun with golden beam,
> Thou silver moon with softer gleam:
> O praise Him, O praise Him,
> Alleluia, Alleluia, Alleluia!

We are not at all surprised to learn that this lovely ode to God's creation was written by the medieval mystic who so fervently loved all of God's creatures—St. Francis of Assisi. The cento is taken from his celebrated hymn of praise known as the Sun Song, which St. Francis composed in the summer of 1225 when sick and nearly blind. The great medieval evangelist drew his inspiration for the poem from the 145th Psalm.

Of considerable interest also is the moving Lenten hymn, "Jesus, refuge of the weary." This was one of a number of spiritual songs written by the famous Florentine preacher and reformer, Girolamo Savonarola, who because of his condemnation of corruption in the Church suffered martyrdom in 1498 at the hands of a mob inspired by the Roman hierarchy of Florence.

"Come down, O Love divine" is another Italian hymn that has won wide favor. A prayer addressed to the Holy Spirit, it is the work of an Augustinian monk, Bianco da Siena, who died in Venice in 1434.

Yet another hymn of Italian origin is the simple but gripping Lenten lyric, "Glory be to Jesus." The author is unknown. However, on October 18, 1815, Pope Pius VII granted "one hundred days of indulgence" to everyone who would "devoutly" repeat the words of the hymn, and it was made clear that the indulgence was also "applicable to the faithful departed." Millions of Protestants have also sung this lovely song—with devout gratitude to God, but without any thought that thereby they were doing aught to merit reward at His hands.

An Invitation to Bethlehem

O come, all ye faithful,
Joyful and triumphant,
O come ye, O come ye to Bethlehem;
Come and behold Him
Born the King of angels:

REFRAIN:

O come, let us adore Him,
O come, let us adore Him,
O come, let us adore Him,
        Christ the Lord!

God of God,
Light of Light,
Lo, He abhors not the Virgin's womb;
Very God,
Begotten not created:

Sing, choirs of angels,
Sing in exultation,
Sing, all ye citizens of heaven above!
Glory to God
In the highest:

Yea, Lord, we greet Thee,
Born this happy morning,
Jesus, to Thee be glory given;
Word of the Father,
Now in flesh appearing:

> *Latin Hymn, XVIII cent.*
> TR. FREDERICK OAKELEY, 1802-80, and others

POST-REFORMATION LATIN LYRICS

THE GOLDEN age of Latin hymnody may be said to have come to an end with the close of the 14th century. More and more the devotional lyrics of the Western Church began to magnify the Virgin Mary and to proclaim the glories of the saints. The number of sequences multiplied to an extraordinary degree, but their quality also rapidly deteriorated.

Then came the Reformation, and following it the Roman Counter-Reformation with an accompanying movement to reform the worship of the Latin Church. In the 16th century a beginning was made under Popes Leo X, Adrian VI and Clement VII to revise the texts of the Church's lyrical poetry generally. Later, in the 17th century, Pope Urban VIII commissioned three Jesuits to continue the reform. As a result of this movement, as noted heretofore, all but five of the Latin sequences were banned from the Mass, and the office hymns in the Roman Breviary lost much of the simple, devotional character which had characterized the lyrics of Ambrose, Hilary and their successors. A great part of the rich treasury of Latin hymnody was thus swept away in the Western Church, and what remained had lost to a large extent its beauty and freshness.

During the four and one-half centuries that have passed since the Reformation, not many new Latin hymns have been written. However, among the few that have appeared are a number of classics that have enriched the worship life of the entire Christian Church.

First in importance perhaps is the glorious Christmas carol, *Adeste, fideles,* "O come, all ye faithful." Recent scholarship has attributed this inspiring lyric to John Francis Wade, a layman who lived in the great Catholic center at Douay, France. This man made his living by teaching Latin and church song, and by copying and selling plain chant and other church music. He died in 1786 at the age of 75 years. There are six manuscript copies of this famous Christmas hymn extant, several of which are signed "Joannes Franciscus Wade scripsit." In one of them, the refrain reads *Venite, adorate* instead of *Venite, adoremus.* The conjecture has been offered that this may have been Wade's original copy, and that he subsequently was induced to change the language of this line to conform with the familiar Invitatory Antiphon.

The beautiful communion hymn, "O bread of life from heaven," is derived from a Latin lyric, *O esca viatorum,* which first appeared in the *Mainz Gesangbuch* of 1661 under the title, "Hymn on the true Bread of Heaven." It is generally believed to have been written by a German Jesuit, although it has sometimes been ascribed to St. Thomas Aquinas. The first two stanzas of the English translation are by the American scholar, Philip Schaff, the third by the English hymnist, Athelstan Riley:

> O Bread of life from heaven,
> To weary pilgrims given,
>   O Manna from above!
> The souls that hunger feed Thou,
> The hearts that seek Thee lead Thou,
>   With Thy most sweet and tender love.
>
> O fount of grace redeeming,
> O river ever streaming
>   From Jesus' holy side!
> Come Thou, Thyself bestowing
> On thirsty souls, and flowing
>   Till all their wants are satisfied.
>
> O Jesus, by Thee bidden,
> We here adore Thee, hidden
>   'Neath forms of bread and wine;
> Grant, when the veil is riven,
> We may behold in heaven
>   Thy glorious countenance divine.

From the 18th century has come a hymn for the Feast of the Circumcision titled *Victis sibi cognomina,* from which we have the English version, "Conquering kings their titles take." The hymn first appeared in the *Paris Breviary* of 1736, but the author is not given. The tune to which this unusual hymn is traditionally sung is known as *Orientis partibus.* This is the popular "Song of the Ass" of medieval times, which ran:

> Out from the lands of Orient
> Was the ass divinely sent;
> Strong and very fair was he,
> Bearing burdens gallantly.
> Heigh, Sir Ass, oh heigh!

The song was sung in French churches as early as the 10th century at the Feast of the Circumcision and other days following Christmas, when a virgin holding a babe rode an ass to the high altar of the church to commemorate the flight of the Holy Family into Egypt.

Charles Coffin, a Latin scholar of some note who become rector of the University of Paris in 1718, was the author of a large number of Latin hymns, 100 of which were published in the *Paris Breviary* of 1736. Two of his Advent hymns, "The advent of our God" and "On Jordan's banks the Baptist's cry," are found in a considerable number of English and American hymnals. Not so well known is a lovely evening hymn by Coffin which John Chandler translated as follows:

> As now the sun's declining rays
>   At eventide descend,
> Even so our years are sinking down
>   To their appointed end.
>
> Lord, on the Cross Thine arms were stretched
>   To draw the nations nigh;
> O grant us then that Cross to love,
>   And in those arms to die.

An exultant English hymn based on the ancient Latin *Te Deum* appeared in a hymnal published by Thomas Cotterill in Staffordshire, England, in 1815. The first stanza reads:

> Thee we adore, eternal Lord!
> We praise Thy Name with one accord;
> Thy saints, who here Thy goodness see,
> Through all the world do worship Thee.

The inspiring Easter hymn, "The strife is o'er," also had a Latin origin. It appeared for the first time anonymously in a Jesuit collection published in Cologne, Germany, in 1695. Its widespread popularity may be accounted for in part to the Palestrina tune with which it has been associated since 1861.

Another post-Reformation hymn which had its birth in the Church of Rome is the gripping devotional lyric, "O God, I love thee; not that my poor love," which is quite evidently of Spanish origin. It is generally believed to have been written by St. Francis Xavier, although it has also been credited to St. Teresa of Spain. The Latin version, *O Deus ego amo Te, Nec amo Te ut salves me*, seems to have been based on an earlier Spanish sonnet, *No me mueve, mi Dios, para quererte*. No date for the hymn can be fixed with certainty, but it appeared as early as 1668 in a German collection by J. Scheffler. The eminent British hymnist, Edward H. Bickersteth, has given us our fine English translation:

O God, I love Thee; not that my poor love
May win me entrance to Thy heaven above,
Nor yet that strangers to Thy love must know
The bitterness of everlasting woe.

But Jesus, Thou art mine, and I am Thine;
Clasped to Thy bosom by Thy arms divine,
Who on the cruel Cross for me hast borne
The nails, the spear, and man's unpitying scorn.

No thought can fathom and no tongue express
Thy griefs, Thy toils, Thy anguish measureless,
Thy death, O Lamb of God the undefiled;
And all for me, Thy wayward sinful child.

How can I choose but love Thee, God's dear Son,
O Jesus, loveliest, and most loving One!
Were there no heaven to gain, no hell to flee,
For what Thou art alone I must love Thee.

Not for the hope of glory or reward,
But even as Thyself hast loved me, Lord,
I love Thee, and will love Thee and adore,
Who art my King, my God, for evermore.

PART II

German Hymnody

The Battle Hymn of the Reformation

A mighty fortress is our God,
A bulwark never failing;
Our helper He amid the flood
Of mortal ills prevailing:
For still our ancient foe
Doth seek to work us woe;
His craft and power are great,
And, armed with cruel hate,
On earth is not his equal.

Did we in our own strength confide,
Our striving would be losing;
Were not the right Man on our side,
The Man of God's own choosing.
Dost ask who that may be?
Christ Jesus, it is He;
Lord Sabaoth His Name,
From age to age the same,
And He must win the battle.

And though this world, with devils filled,
Should threaten to undo us;
We will not fear, for God hath willed
His truth to triumph through us:
The prince of darkness grim,
We tremble not for him;
His rage we can endure,
For lo! his doom is sure,
One little word shall fell him.

That word above all earthly powers,
No thanks to them, abideth;
The Spirit and the gifts are ours
Through Him who with us sideth:
Let goods and kindred go,
This mortal life also;
The body they may kill:
God's truth abideth still,
His Kingdom is forever.

MARTIN LUTHER, 1483-1546
TR. FREDRICK H. HEDGE, 1805-90
Based on Psalm 46

MARTIN LUTHER, FATHER OF EVANGELICAL HYMNODY

THE FATHER of evangelical hymnody was Martin Luther. It was through the efforts of the great Reformer that the lost art of congregational singing was restored and the Christian hymn again given a place in public worship.

Luther was an extraordinary man. To defy the most powerful ecclesiastical hierarchy the world has known, to bring about a cataclysmic upheaval in the religious and political world, and to set in motion spiritual forces that have changed the course of human history—this would have been sufficient to have brought him undying fame. But those who know Luther merely as a Reformer possess only a limited knowledge of the versatile gifts and remarkable achievements of this great prophet of the Church.

Philip Schaff has characterized Martin Luther as "the Ambrose of German hymnody," and adds: "To Luther belongs the extraordinary merit of having given to the German people in their own tongue the Bible, the Catechism, and the hymnbook, so that God might speak *directly* to them in His word, and that they might *directly* answer Him in their songs." He also refers to him as "the father of the modern High German language and literature."

Luther was divinely endowed for his great mission of restoring hymnody to the corporate worship of the Christian Church. From childhood he was passionately fond of music. As a student at Magdeburg, and later at Eisenach, he sang for alms at the windows of wealthy citizens. It was the sweet voice of the boy that attracted the attention of Ursula Cotta and moved that benevolent woman to give him a home during his school days.

The flute and lute were his favorite instruments, and he always used the latter in accompanying his own singing. John Walther, a contemporary composer who later aided Luther in the writing of church music, has left us this testimony: "It is to my certain knowledge that that holy man of God, Luther, prophet and apostle to the German nation, took great delight in music, both in choral and figural composition. I spent many a delightful hour with him in singing; and ofttimes I have seen the dear man wax so happy and merry in heart over the singing that it is well-nigh impossible to weary or content him therewithal. And his discourse concerning music was most noble."

In his *Discourse in Praise of Music,* Luther gives thanks to God for having bestowed the power of song on the "nightingale and the many thousand birds of the air," and again he writes, "I give music the highest and most honorable place; and every one knows how David and all the saints put their divine thoughts into verse, rhyme, and song."

Luther had little patience with the iconoclasts of his day. He wrote in the preface to Walther's collection of hymns, in 1525: "I am not of the opinion that all sciences should be beaten down and made to cease by the Gospel, as some fanatics pretend, but I would fain see all the arts, and music, in particular, used in the service of Him who hath given and created them." At another time he was even more emphatic: "If any man despises music, as all fanatics do, for him I have no liking; for music is a gift and grace of God, not an invention of men. Thus it drives out the devil and makes people cheerful. Then one forgets all wrath, impurity, sycophancy, and other vices."

Luther loved the Latin hymns that glorified Christ. He recognized, however, that many of them were so permeated with Mariolatry and other errors of the Roman Church that a refining process was necessary in order to rid them of their dross and permit the fine gold to appear. Moreover, the Latin hymns, even in their most glorious development, had not grown out of the spiritual life of the congregation. The very genius of the Roman Church had precluded this, for church music and song were regarded as belonging exclusively to the priestly office. Moreover, since the entire worship was conducted in Latin, the congregation was inevitably doomed to passive silence.

Brave efforts by John Huss and his followers to introduce congregational singing in the Bohemian churches had been sternly opposed by the Roman hierarchy. The Council of Constance, which in 1415 burned the heroic Huss at the stake, also sent a solemn warning to Jacob of Misi, his successor as leader of the Hussites, to cease the practice of singing hymns in the churches. It decreed: "If laymen are forbidden to preach and interpret the Scriptures, much more are they forbidden to sing publicly in the churches."

Luther's ringing declaration that all believers constitute a universal priesthood necessarily implied that the laity should also participate in the worship. Congregational singing therefore became inevitable.

Luther also realized that spiritual song could be enlisted as a powerful ally in spreading the evangelical doctrines. During the birth throes of the Reformation he often expressed the wish that some one more gifted than he might give to the German people in their own language some of the beautiful gems of Latin hymnody. He also wanted original hymns in the vernacular, as well as strong, majestic chorales that would reflect the heroic spirit of the age.

"We lack German poets and musicians," he complained, "or they are unknown to us, who are able to make Christian and spiritual songs of such value that they can be used daily in the house of God."

Then something happened that awakened the soul of song in Luther's own bosom. The Reformation had spread from Germany into other parts of Europe, and the Catholic authorities had commenced to adopt stern measures in an effort to stem the revolt. In the Augustinian cloister at Antwerp, the prior of the abbey and two youths, Heinrich Voes and Johannes Esch, had been sentenced to death by the Inquisition for their refusal to surrender their new-born faith.

The prior was strangled to death in his prison cell. The two youths were led to the stake at Brussels on July 1, 1523. Before the faggots were kindled they were told that they might still be freed if they would recant. They replied that they would rather die and be with Christ. Before the fire and smoke smothered their voices, they sang the ancient Latin *Te Deum*, "Lord God, we praise thee."

When news of the Brussels tragedy reached Luther the poetic spark in his soul burst into full flame. Immediately he sat down and wrote a festival hymn commemorating the death of the first Lutheran martyrs. It had been reported to Luther that when the fires began to lick the feet of Voes, witnesses had heard him exclaim, "Behold, blooming roses are strewn around me!" Luther seized upon the words as prophetic and concluded his hymn with the lines:

> Summer is even at the door.
> The winter now hath vanished.
> The tender flowerets spring once more,
> And He who winter banished
> Will send a happy summer.

59

The opening words of the hymn are also significant, "Ein neues Lied wir heben an." Although the poem had more of the character of a ballad than a church hymn, Luther's lyre was tuned, the springtime of evangelical hymnody had indeed come, and before another year had passed a little hymnbook called *The Achtliederbuch* appeared as the first-fruits.

It was in 1524 that this first Protestant hymnal was published. It contained only eight hymns, four by Luther, three by Speratus, and one probably by Justus Jonas. The little hymnbook flew all over Europe, to the consternation of the Romanists. Luther's enemies lamented that "the whole people are singing themselves into his doctrines." So great was the demand for hymns that a second volume known as the *Erfurt Enchiridion* was published in the same year. This contained twenty-five hymns, eighteen of which were Luther's. "The nightingale of Wittenberg" had begun to sing.

This was the beginning of evangelical hymnody, which was to play so large a part in the spread of Luther's teachings. The number of hymnbooks by other compilers increased rapidly and so many unauthorized changes were made in his hymns by critical editors, that Luther was moved to complain of their practice. In a preface to a hymnbook printed by Joseph Klug of Wittenberg, in 1543, Luther writes: "I am fearful that it will fare with this little book as it has ever fared with good books, namely, that through tampering by incompetent hands it may get to be so overlaid and spoiled that the good will be lost out of it, and nothing kept in use but the worthless." Then he adds, rather naively: "Every man may make a hymnbook for himself and let ours alone and not add thereto, as we here beg, wish and assert. For we desire to keep our own coin up to our own standard, preventing no one from making better hymns for himself. Now let God's name alone be praised and our name not sought. Amen."

Of the thirty-six hymns attributed to Luther none has achieved such fame as "A mighty fortress is our God." Of this great hymn, Dr. John Ker has well said, "It breathes the force of battles, faces fearlessly the fire and scaffold, and thrills in every line with unconquerable faith and Christian heroism." It has been translated into practically every language and is regarded as one of the noblest and most classical examples of Christian hymnody. Not only did it become the battle hymn of the Reformation, but it may be regarded as the true national hymn of Germany. Heine called it "the Marseillaise of the Reformation." Frederick the Great referred to it as "God Almighty's grenadier march."

The date of the hymn cannot be fixed with any certainty. Much has been written on the subject, but the arguments do not appear conclusive. D'Aubigné's unqualified statement that Luther composed the hymn and sang it to revive the spirits of his friends at the Diet of Augsburg in 1530 can scarcely be accepted, since it appeared at least a year earlier in a hymnbook published by Joseph Klug.

The magnificent chorale to which the hymn is sung is also Luther's work. Never have words and music been combined to make a more tremendous appeal. Great musical composers have turned to its stirring theme again and again when they have sought to produce a mighty effect. Mendelssohn has used it in the last movement of his Reformation Symphony; Meyerbeer uses it to good advantage in his masterpiece, "Les Huguenots"; and Wagner's "Kaisermarsch," written to celebrate the triumphal return of the German troops from Paris in 1870, reaches a great climax with the whole orchestra thundering forth the sublime chorale. Bach has woven it into a beautiful cantata, while Raff and Nicolai make use of it in overtures.

After Luther's death, when Melanchthon and his friends were compelled to flee from Wittenberg by the approach of the Spanish army, they came to Weimar. As they were entering the city, they heard a little girl singing Luther's great hymn. "Sing on, my child," exclaimed Melanchthon, "thou little knowest how thy song cheers our hearts."

When Gustavus Adolphus, the hero king of Sweden, faced Tilly's hosts at the battlefield of Leipzig, Sept. 7, 1631, he led his army in singing "Ein' feste Burg." Then shouting, "God is with us," he went into battle. It was a bloody fray. Tilly fell, and his army was beaten. When the battle was over, Gustavus Adolphus knelt upon the ground among his soldiers and thanked the Lord of Hosts for victory, saying, "He holds the field forever."

George N. Anderson, a missionary in Tanganyika Province, British East Africa, tells how he once heard an assembly of 2,000 natives sing Luther's great hymn. "I never heard it sung with more spirit; the effect was almost overwhelming," he testifies.

A West African missionary, Christaller, relates how he once sang "Ein' feste Burg" to his native interpreter. "That man, Luther," said the African, "must have been a powerful man, one can feel it in his hymns."

Thomas Carlyle's estimate of "Ein' feste Burg" seems to accord with that of the African native. "It jars upon our ears," he says, "yet there is something in it like the sound of Alpine avalanches, or the first murmur of earthquakes, in the very vastness of which dissonance a higher unison is revealed to us."

Carlyle, who refers to Luther as "perhaps the most inspired of all teachers since the Apostles," has given us the most rugged of all translations of the Reformer's great hymn. There are said to be no less than eighty English translations, but only a few have met with popular favor. In England the version by Carlyle is in general use, while in America the translation by Frederick H. Hedge, a New Englander, has found almost universal acceptance. Carlyle's first stanza closely follows Luther's German:

> A sure stronghold our God is He,
> A trusty Shield and Weapon;
> Our help He'll be, and set us free
> From every ill can happen.
> That old malicious foe
> Intends us deadly woe;
> Arméd with might from hell
> And deepest craft as well,
> On earth is not his fellow.

The greater number of Luther's hymns are not original. Many are paraphrases of Scripture, particularly the psalms, and others are based on Latin, Greek, and German antecedents. In every instance, however, the great Reformer so imbued them with his own fervent faith and militant spirit that they seem to shine with a new luster.

"Come, Holy Spirit, God and Lord" is typical of Luther's treatment of the Latin hymns he cherished so deeply. Based on an 11th century antiphon, *"Veni, Sancte Spiritus, reple tuorum corda fidelium,* which is not to be confused with the Whitsunday sequence, *Veni, Sancte Spiritus,* this hymn had become very popular in Germany, and a German stanza, *Komm, heiliger Geist, Herre Gott,* had appeared in the *Crailsheim Schul-Ordnung* of 1480. Luther adopted this old German version with certain alterations, then added two stanzas to give the hymn its present form. It was published for the first time in the *Erfurt Enchiridion* of 1524 with the pre-Reformation melody to which it is still sung. Luther once remarked that he was convinced the Holy Spirit had inspired both the words and the music of this ancient Latin hymn, and we may add with equal conviction that the Holy Spirit doubtlessly enlightened the mind of the man who created a new hymn out of it.

Luther's lovely Christmas hymn, "All praise to Thee, Eternal Lord," seems to have had its origin much in the same manner. Based on a 11th century Latin sequence, *Grates nunc omnes reddamus,* it had become popular in the vernacular throughout Germany. There is some evidence that it might even have been sung in the services of the church before the Reformation, with the priests doing the singing and the congregation joining at the close of each stanza by chanting "Kyrie Eleison!" Luther likewise added the ancient Greek response to his German words. Something of the beauty of this hymn has been preserved even in translation, as these verses indicate:

> A little child, Thou art our guest,
> That weary ones in Thee may rest;
> Forlorn and lowly is Thy birth,
> That we may rise to heaven from earth.
>
> Thou comest in the darksome night,
> To make us children of the light.
> To make us in the realm divine,
> Like Thine own angels, 'round Thee shine.
>
> All this for us Thy love hath done,
> By this to Thee our love is won,
> For this we tune our cheerful lays,
> And shout our thanks in ceaseless praise.

Again, in "Christ Jesus lay in death's strong bands," we have a hymn based on Latin antecedents. Two of Luther's German stanzas, picturing the conflict between life and death, were practically lifted from the famous Easter sequence, *Victimae paschali,* and other portions of the hymn strongly suggest passages in the equally famous Easter carol, *Surrexit Christus hodie.* In this instance also there was an earlier German version, *Christus ist uperstanden,* with which Luther must have been familiar. However, Luther's treatment of all this source material is quite original, resulting in one of his finest hymns.

"Out of the depths I cry to thee" is one of seven hymns by Luther based on the psalms. This one, which is a paraphrase of the 130th Psalm, appeared in the famous *Achtliederbuch* of 1524.

A Metrical Gloria in Excelsis

All glory be to God on high,
*   Who hath our race befriended;*
To us no harm shall now come nigh,
*   The strife at last is ended;*
God showeth His good will to men,
*   And peace shall reign on earth again;*
O thank Him for His goodness.

We praise, we worship Thee, we trust,
*   And give Thee thanks for ever,*
O Father, that Thy rule is just
*   And wise, and changes never;*
Thy boundless power o'er all thing reigns,
*   Thou dost what'er Thy will ordains:*
'Tis well Thou art our Ruler!

O Jesus Christ, our God and Lord,
*   Begotten of the Father,*
Who hast our fallen race restored
*   And straying sheep dost gather,*
Thou Lamb of God, enthroned on high,
*   Behold our need, and hear our cry:*
Have mercy on us, Jesus!

O Holy Spirit, precious Gift,
*   Thou Comforter unfailing,*
Do Thou our troubled souls uplift,
*   Against the foe prevailing;*
Since Christ for us His Blood hath shed,
*   Avert our woes and calm our dread;*
We trust in Thee to help us!

Ascribed to NIKOLAUS DECIUS, 1541
TR. CATHERINE WINKWORTH, 1829-78, a.

THE HYMN-WRITERS OF THE REFORMATION

THE HYMNS of the Reformation were like a trumpet call, proclaiming to all the world that the day of spiritual emancipation had come. What they sometimes lacked in poetic refinement they more than made up by their tremendous earnestness and spiritual exuberance. Certainly they reflected the spirit of the age in which they were written.

The strident note that often appeared in Luther's hymns can easily be understood in the light of their historical background. The 16th century was a period of religious and political crisis in Europe. The Reformation was being threatened by two powerful foes: the hierarchy of the Church of Rome on the one hand, and the ruthless expansion of Islam on the other. The Pope at Rome, after the Diet of Worms, had fully resolved to crush the spiritual revolt in Germany and to destroy the "Lutheran heresy," and the invasion of the Turks from the East had brought peril to all of Europe.

Luther looked upon the Papacy and Islam as the two greatest enemies of the Christian religion, and expressed himself in his Table Talks as follows: "Antichrist is the Pope and Turk together; a beast full of life must have a body and soul; the spirit or soul of Antichrist is the Pope, his flesh or body the Turk. The latter wastes and assails and persecutes God's Church corporally; the former spiritually and corporally too, with hanging, burning, murdering, etc."

In 1541, when Sultan Suleiman's Turks had over-run all of Hungary and parts of Austria, and were knocking at the gates of Vienna, all of Germany trembled with apprehension. Special days of humiliation and prayer were ordered, with services of intercession in all churches. German parents, remembering the Scriptural promise that out of the mouths of babes and sucklings the Lord ordains strength, brought their children to the sanctuaries that they might add their "Amens" to the prayers for divine aid and deliverance. It was for one of these services in the Wittenberg church that Luther wrote the hymn, "Lord, keep us steadfast in Thy Word." The music had been arranged for the boys of the choir, and the piece bore the title, "A Hymn for the children to sing against the two arch-enemies of Christ and his holy Church, the Pope and the Turks." In its original form, it was more militant than the hymn we now sing:

> Lord, keep us in Thy Word and work,
> Restrain the murderous Pope and Turk,
> Who fain would tear from off Thy throne
> Christ Jesus, Thy beloved Son.

It is quite understandable why this hymn proved particularly distasteful to the Romanists. Following Luther's death, when the Emperor, with the aid of his Spaniards, had all but crushed the Lutheran principalities of Germany, the singing of it was forbidden on pain of death. A Bavarian duke is quoted as having said to his servants: "For aught I care, you may gormandize, get drunk, and profligate, only do not become Lutheran and sing the infamous hymn, *Erhalt uns, Herr, bei deinem Wort.*"

But the note in Luther's hymns was not always militant. When he sang of God's free grace to men through Christ Jesus, or extolled the merits of the Saviour, or gave thanks for the pure Word of God restored to men, there was always such a marvelous blending of childlike trust, victorious faith and spontaneous joy that all Germany thrilled to the message of the "new song."

No better evaluation of Luther's contribution to Christian hymnody and of his influence on Christian worship in general has ever been expressed than that which is given by Merle D'Aubigne in his great work, *The History of the Reformation:*

"The Church was no longer composed of priests and monks; it now was the congregation of believers. All were to take part in worship, and the chanting of the clergy was to be succeeded by the psalmody of the people. Luther, accordingly, in translating the psalms, thought of adapting them to be sung by the Church. Thus a taste for music was diffused throughout the nation. From Luther's time the people sang; the Bible inspired their songs. Poetry received the same impulse. In celebrating the praises of God, the people could not confine themselves to mere translations of ancient anthems. The souls of Luther and of several of his contemporaries, elevated by their faith to thoughts the most sublime, excited to enthusiasm by the struggles and dangers by which the Church at its birth was unceasingly threatened, inspired by the poetic genius of the Old Testament and by the faith of the New, ere long gave vent to their

66

feelings in hymns in which all that is most heavenly in poetry and music was combined and blended . . . Other children of the Reformation followed his footsteps; hymns were multiplied; they spread rapidly among the people and powerfully contributed to rouse it from sleep."

The popularity of the Lutheran hymns was indeed astonishing. Other hymn-writers sprang up in large numbers, printing presses were kept busy, and before Luther's death no less than sixty collections of hymns had been published. Wandering evangelists were often surrounded by excited crowds in the market places, hymns printed on leaflets were distributed, and the whole populace began to sing.

Paul Speratus, Paul Eber, and Justus Jonas were the most gifted co-laborers of Luther. It was Speratus who contributed three hymns to the *Achtliederbuch,* the first hymnbook published by Luther. His most famous hymn, "To us salvation now is come," has been called "the poetic counterpart of Luther's preface to the Epistle to the Romans." It was the great confessional hymn of the Reformation. Luther is said to have wept tears of joy when he heard it sung by a street singer outside his window in Wittenberg.

Speratus is said to have written the hymn in a Moravian prison into which he had been cast because of his bold espousal of the Lutheran teachings. Immediately upon his release he proceeded to Wittenberg, where he joined himself to the Reformers. He later became the leader of the Reformation movement in Prussia and for several years before his death in 1551 served as bishop of Pomerania. His poetic genius may be seen reflected in the beautiful paraphrase of the Lord's Prayer which forms the concluding two stanzas of his celebrated hymn:

> All blessing, honor, thanks, and praise
>   To Father, Son, and Spirit,
> The God who saved us by His grace,
>   All glory to His merit:
> O Father in the heavens above,
> Thy glorious works show forth Thy love,
>   Thy worthy Name be hallowed.

> Thy Kingdom come, Thy will be done
>   In earth, as 'tis in heaven:
> Keep us in life, by grace led on,
>   Forgiving and forgiven;
> Save Thou us in temptation's hour,
> And from all ills; Thine is the power,
>   And all the glory, Amen!

Eber was the sweet singer among the Reformers. As professor of Hebrew at Wittenberg University and assistant to Melanchthon, he had an active part in the stirring events of the Reformation. He possessed more of Melanchthon's gentleness than Luther's ruggedness, and his hymns are tender and appealing in their childlike simplicity. There is wondrous consolation in his hymns for the dying, as witness "I fall asleep in Jesus' arms" and "Lord Jesus Christ, true man and God," both of which breathe a fervent spirit of hope and trust in Christ. A portion of the first stanza of the former lyric was appropriated by Count von Zinzendorf as the beginning of his famous hymn, *Christi Blut und Gerechtigkeit,* which John Wesley translated:

> Jesus, Thy Blood and righteousness
> My beauty are, my glorious dress;
> Midst flaming worlds, in these arrayed,
> With joy shall I lift up my head.

Another of Eber's hymns, "When in the hour of utmost need," is believed to have been written during the bitter days of persecution and suffering following the Reformation, when the forces of Emperor Charles V were over-running the Protestant states and it seemed that the evangelical cause was wholly lost. The singing of this hymn, which is based on the beautiful words of King Jehoshaphat in II Chronicles 20:12, is said to have brought much comfort to Melanchthon and other Reformers during the dark days that followed the death of Luther in 1546.

Justus Jonas, the bosom friend of Luther who spoke the last words of peace and consolation to the dying Reformer and also preached his funeral sermon, has left us the hymn, "If God were not upon our side," based on Psalm 124. This was his sole contribution to the famous *Achtliederbuch* of 1524. As probst of the Schlosskirche in Wittenberg, where Luther posted his 95 theses in 1517, and as professor of church law at the University of Wittenberg from 1521 to 1541, Jonas stood very close to Luther and Melanchthon through all the stirring events of those history-making years.

Here the name of Johann Walther must also be mentioned. A distinguished musician of his day in the service of Frederick the Wise at the latter's court in Torgau, it was Walther who gave Luther invaluable aid in arranging the music for the new Lutheran liturgy. In 1524 he spent three weeks in Luther's home in Wittenberg adapting the old music for the first service in the vernacular. He also wrote five-part harmonies for the tunes in *Geystliche Gesangk Buchleyn,* which was the third hymnbook published by Luther in that year. He returned to Wittenberg the following year to be present when the new service of Holy Communion which Luther and he had rearranged was used for the first time on October 29, 1525.

Walther was pre-eminently a musician and not a hymn-writer, and yet he wrote the text for a number of lyrics. His best known hymns are "Now fain my joyous heart would sing," "O God, my Rock, my heart on Thee," and "Thy Word, O God, declareth." In 1548, Elector Moritz of Saxony made Walther his Kapellmeister at Dresden. He died at Torgau in 1570.

One of the most gifted hymn-writers of the Reformation period was Michael Weisse, who has given to the Church the inspiring Easter hymn,

> Christ, the Lord, is risen again,
> Christ hath broken every chain!
> Hark, angelic voices cry,
> Singing evermore on high,
> Alleluia, Alleluia, Alleluia!
>
> He who gave for us His life,
> Who for us endured the strife,
> Is our Paschal Lamb today;
> We too sing for joy, and say:
> Alleluia, Alleluia, Alleluia!

Weisse, who was born in Silesia in 1480, was a monk at Breslau when the early writings of Luther came into his hands. Together with two other monks he soon fled from the convent and found refuge among the Bohemian Brethren in Bohemia. In 1522 he was sent by Bishop Lucas to Wittenberg to explain to Luther the doctrines and views of the Brethren. Later he was commissioned to edit the first German hymnbook of the Brethren, which appeared in Bohemia in 1531 as *Ein New Gesengbuchlen.* The volume contained 155 hymns, all of which are believed to be either originals or translations by Weisse. No less than 119 of these passed into the Lutheran hymnbooks of Germany during the 16th and 17th centuries, and a number of them are still in use.

From this period also we have the beautiful morning hymn, "My inmost heart now raises," by Johannes Mathesius, pupil and biographer of Luther, and an equally beautiful evening hymn, "Sunk is the sun's last beam of light," by Nicholas Herman. Mathesius was pastor of the church at Joachimsthal, in Bohemia, and Herman was his organist and choirmaster. It is said that whenever Mathesius preached a particularly good sermon, Herman was forthwith inspired to write a hymn on its theme! He was a poet and musician of no mean ability, and his tunes are among the best from the Reformation period. Here are the stanzas of his evening hymn:

> Sunk is the sun's last beam of light,
> And now the world is wrapt in night;
> Christ, light us with Thy heavenly ray,
> Nor let our feet in darkness stray.
>
> Thanks, Lord, that Thou throughout the day
> Hast kept all grief and harm away;
> That angels tarried round about
> Our coming in and going out.
>
> Whatever wrongs we've done or said,
> Let not the charge on us be laid;
> That through Thy free forgiveness blest,
> In peaceful slumber we may rest.
>
> Thy guardian angels round us place,
> All evil from our couch to chase;
> Our soul and body, while we sleep,
> In safety, gracious Father, keep.

The example of the Wittenberg hymnists was quickly followed by evangelicals in other parts of Germany, and hymnbooks began to appear everywhere. As early as 1526 a little volume of hymns was published at Rostock in the Platt-Deutsch dialect. In this collection we find one of the most glorious hymns of the Reformation, "All glory be to God on high," or, as it has also been rendered, "All glory be to Thee, Most High," a metrical version of the ancient canticle, *Gloria in Excelsis.* Five years later another edition was published in which appeared a metrical rendering of *Agnus Dei:*

> O Lamb of God most holy!
> Who on the Cross didst suffer,
> And patient still and lowly,
> Thyself to scorn didst offer;
> Our sins by Thee were taken,
> Or hope had us forsaken:
> Have mercy on us, Jesus!

The author of both of these fine examples of evangelical hymnody was Nikolaus Decius, a Catholic monk in the cloister of Steterburg who had embraced the Lutheran teachings. He later became pastor of St. Nicholas Church in Stettin, where he died under suspicious circumstances in 1541. In addition to being a popular preacher and gifted poet, he also seems to have been a musician of some note. The two magnificent chorales to which his hymns are sung are generally credited to him, although there is a great deal of uncertainty surrounding their composition. Luther prized both hymns very highly and included them in his German liturgy.

A Confirmation Prayer

Let me be Thine forever,
  My gracious God and Lord;
May I forsake Thee never,
  Nor wander from Thy Word:
Preserve me from the mazes
  Of error and distrust,
And I shall sing Thy praises
  Forever with the just.

Lord Jesus, bounteous Giver
  Of light and life divine,
Thou didst my soul deliver;
  To Thee I all resign:
Thou hast in mercy bought me
  With blood and bitter pain;
Let me, since Thou hast sought me,
  Eternal life obtain.

O Holy Ghost, who pourest
  Sweet peace into my heart,
And all my soul restorest,
  Let not Thy grace depart.
And while His Name confessing
  Whom I by faith have known,
Grant me Thy constant blessing;
  Make me for aye Thine own.

NICOLAUS SELNECKER, 1528-92
St. 2, 3, RUDOLSTADT GESANGBUCH, 1688
TR. MATTHIAS LOY, 1828-1915, a.

HYMNS OF THE CONTROVERSIAL PERIOD

MANY of our great Christian hymns were born in troublous times. This is true in a very special sense of the hymns written by Nicolaus Selnecker, a German preacher and theologian who lived during the decades immediately following the Reformation. It was an age marked by doctrinal controversy, not only with the Romanists, but among the Protestants themselves. In these theological struggles, Selnecker will always be remembered as one of the great champions of pure Lutheran doctrine.

The *Formula of Concord,* the last of the Lutheran confessions, was largely the work of Selnecker. Published in 1577, it did more than any other single document to clarify the Lutheran position on many disputed doctrinal points, thus bringing to an end much of the confusion and controversy that had existed up to that time.

Selnecker early in life revealed an artistic temperament. Born in 1532 at Hersbruck, Germany, we find him at the age of twelve years as organist at the chapel in the Kaiserburg, at Nürnberg, where he attended school. Later he entered Wittenberg University to study law. Here he came under the influence of Philip Melanchthon, and was induced to prepare himself for the ministry. It is said that Selnecker was Melanchthon's favorite pupil.

Following his graduation from Wittenberg, he lectured for a while at the university and then received appointment as second court preacher at Dresden and private tutor to Prince Alexander of Saxony. Many of the Saxon theologians at this time were leaning strongly toward the Calvinistic teaching regarding the Lord's Supper, and when Selnecker came out boldly for the Lutheran doctrine he incurred the hostility of those in authority. Later he incurred the displeasure of the Elector August of Saxony and was compelled to leave Dresden.

For three years he taught theology at the University of Jena, but in 1568 he again found favor with the Elector August and was appointed to the chair of theology in the University of Leipzig. Here Selnecker again became involved in bitter doctrinal disputes regarding the Lord's Supper, and in 1576 and 1577 he joined a group of theologians, including Jacob Andreæ and Martin Chemnitz, in working out the *Formula of Concord.*

Upon the death of Elector August the Calvinists again secured ecclesiastical control, and Selnecker once more was compelled to leave Leipzig. After many trials and vicissitudes, he finally returned, May 19, 1592, a worn and weary man, only to die in Leipzig five days later.

During the stormy days of his life, Selnecker often sought solace in musical and poetical pursuits. Many of his hymns reflect his own personal troubles and conflicts. "Let me be Thine forever" is believed to have been written during one of the more grievous experiences of his life. It was a prayer of one stanza originally, but two additional stanzas were added by an unknown author almost a hundred years after Selnecker's death. In its present form it has become a favorite confirmation hymn in the Lutheran Church.

Selnecker's zeal for his Church is revealed in many of his hymns, among them the famous "Abide with us, O Saviour dear." The second stanza of this hymn clearly reflects the distressing controversies in which he was engaged at the time:

> This is a dark and evil day,
> Forsake us not, O Lord, we pray;
> And let us in our grief and pain
> Thy Word and sacraments retain.

In connection with his work as professor in the University of Leipzig, he also served as pastor of the famous St. Thomas Church in that city. It was through his efforts the Motet choir of that church was built up, a choir which afterwards was made famous by John Sebastian Bach.

About 150 hymns in all were written by Selnecker. In addition to these he also was author of some 175 theological and controversial works.

One of the contemporaries of Selnecker was Bartholomäus Ringwalt, pastor of Langfeld, near Sonnenburg, Brandenburg. This man also was a staunch Lutheran and a poet of considerable ability. As such, he became one of the most prolific hymn-writers of the 16th century. His judgment hymn, "The day is surely drawing near," seems to reflect the feeling held by many in those distressing times that the Last Day was near at hand. It was used to a large extent during the Thirty Years' War, and is still found in many hymnbooks. Its final stanza is a gripping prayer to the Saviour for deliverance from the trials and tribulations of those trying days:

> Lord Jesus Christ, do not delay,
>   O hasten our salvation!
> We often tremble on our way,
>   In fear and tribulation.
> Then hear us when we cry to Thee:
> Come, mighty Judge, come, make us free
> From every evil. Amen.

Another hymnist who lived and wrought during these turbulent times was Martin Behm, to whom we are indebted for three beautiful lyrics, "O Jesus, King of glory," "Lord Jesus Christ, my Life, my Light," and "O Holy, blessed Trinity." Behm, who was born in Lauban, Silesia, Sept. 16, 1557, served as Lutheran pastor in his native city during a period of thirty-six years marked by famine, war and pestilence. He was a noted preacher and a gifted poet. His hymn on the Holy Trinity is one of the finest on this theme. It concludes with a splendid paraphrase of the Aaronic benediction:

> Lord, bless and keep Thou me as Thine;
> Lord, make Thy face upon me shine;
> Lord, lift Thy countenance on me,
> And give me peace, sweet peace from Thee.

Valerius Herberger was another heroic evangelical witness during this distressing and turbulent period. While pastor of St. Mary's Lutheran Church at Fraustadt, Posen, he and his flock were expelled from their church in 1604 by King Sigismund III, of Poland, and the property turned over to the Roman Catholics. Nothing daunted, however, Herberger and his people immediately constructed a chapel out of two houses near the gates of the city. They gave the structure the name of "Kripplein Christi," since the first service was held in it on Christmas Eve. Because of his fervent evangelical preaching, the Romanists in derision nicknamed him "the little Luther."

During the great pestilence which raged in 1613, the victims in Fraustadt numbered 2,135. Herberger, however, stuck to his post, comforting the sick and burying the dead. It was during these days that he wrote his famous hymn, *"Valet will ich dir geben,"* which has been translated "Farewell I gladly bid thee." The hymn was published with the title, "'The farewell *(Valet)* of Valerius Herberger that he gave to the world in the autumn of the year 1613, when every hour he saw death before his eyes, but mercifully and also as wonderfully as the three men in the furnace at Babylon was nevertheless spared."

The famous chorale tune, named after the opening German line of the hymn and also known as *St. Theodulph,* was written in 1613 by Melchior Teschner, who was Herberger's precentor.

Other Lutheran hymn-writers of this period were Joachim Magdeburg, Martin Rutilius, Martin Schalling and Philipp Nicolai. The last name in this group is by far the most important and will be given more extensive notice in the following chapter. To Magdeburg, a pastor who saw service in various parts of Germany and Hungary during a stormy career, we owe a single hymn, "Who trusts in God a strong abode." This hymn, which is one of the strongest written during this period, is based on Psalm 73. When originally published in 1572, it contained only one stanza:

> Who trusts in God a strong abode
>   In heaven and earth possesses;
> Who looks in love to Christ above,
>   No fear his heart oppresses;
> In Thee alone, dear Lord, we own
>   Sweet hope and consolation;
> Our shield from foes, our balm for woes,
>   Our great and sure salvation.

Whether or not Magdeburg is author of the remainder of the hymn has not been definitely established.

Martin Rutilius, who was a pastor at Weimar, has been credited with the authorship of the gripping penitential hymn, "Alas, my God! my sins are great." He passed away at Weimar in 1618.

Schalling likewise has bequeathed but a single lyric to the Church, but it is one of the classic hymns of Germany. Its opening line, "O Lord, devoutly love I Thee," reflects the ardent love of the author for the Saviour. It was entitled, "A prayer to Christ, the Consolation of the soul in life and death," and surely its message of confiding trust in God has been a source of comfort and assurance to thousands of pious souls. Its opening stanza reads:

> O Lord, devoutly love I Thee;
> Come, Jesus, and abide with me,
>   And grant me e'er Thy favor.

76

> In this wide world of anxious care,
> Vain-glory find I everywhere,
>   But peace with Thee, my Saviour.
> E'en though, in woeful agony,
> My soul and body pine away,
> Thou art my comfort, ever blest,
> I safely on Thy bosom rest.
> Lord Jesus Christ, my Saviour dear,
> Thy saving hand is ever near.

Although Schalling was a warm friend of Selnecker, he hesitated to subscribe to the *Formula of Concord,* claiming that it dealt too harshly with the followers of Melanchthon. For this reason he was deposed as General Superintendent of Oberpfalz and court preacher at Heidelberg. Five years later, however, he was appointed pastor of St. Mary's church in Nürnberg, where he remained until blindness compelled him to retire. He died in 1608.

A Masterpiece of Hymnody

Wake, awake, for night is flying,
The watchmen on the heights are crying,
Awake, Jerusalem, at last!
Midnight hears the welcome voices
And at the thrilling cry rejoices:
Come forth, ye virgins, night is past!
The Bridegroom comes, awake,
Your lamps with gladness take;
Alleluia!
And for His marriage feast prepare,
For ye must go to meet Him there.

Zion hears the watchmen singing,
And all her heart with joy is springing,
She wakes, she rises from her gloom;
For her Lord comes down all-glorious,
The strong in grace, in truth victorious,
Her Star is risen, her Light is come.
Ah come, Thou blessed One,
God's own beloved Son,
Alleluia!
We follow till the halls we see
Where Thou hast bid us sup with Thee.

Now let all the heavens adore Thee,
And men and angels sing before Thee,
With harp and cymbal's clearest tone;
Of one pearl each shining portal,
Where we are with the choir immortal
Of angels round Thy dazzling throne;
Nor eye hath seen, nor ear
Hath yet attained to hear
What there is ours;
But we rejoice, and sing to Thee
Our hymn of joy eternally.

PHILIPP NICOLAI, 1556-1608
TR. CATHERINE WINKWORTH, 1829-78

THE KING AND QUEEN OF CHORALES

A T RARE intervals in the history of Christian hymnody we meet with a genius who not only possesses the gift of writing sublime poetry but also is a composer of music. During the stirring days of the Reformation such geniuses were revealed in the persons of Martin Luther and Nicolaus Decius. We now encounter another, namely, Philipp Nicolai, writer of the glorious hymn, *"Wachet auf,"* known in English as "Wake, awake, for night is flying."

Nicolai's name would have been gratefully remembered by posterity had he written only the words of this hymn; but, when we learn that he also composed the magnificent chorale to which it is sung, we are led to marvel. It has been called the "King of Chorales," and well does it deserve that distinction.

But our wonder grows when we are told that Nicolai was also the composer of the "Queen of Chorales." That is the title often given to the tune of his other famous hymn, *"Wie schön leuchtet der Morgenstern,"* which in English has been rendered "How brightly beams the morning star."

Both of Nicolai's great tunes have been frequently appropriated for other hymns. The "King of Chorales" has lent inspiration to "Glorious Majesty, before Thee," while the "Queen of Chorales" has helped to glorify such hymns as "All hail to thee, O blessed morn," "Rejoice, rejoice this happy morn," "Our Lord is risen from the dead," and "O Holy Spirit, enter in."

A number of the world's greatest composers also have recognized the beauty and majesty of Nicolai's inspiring chorales and have woven their themes into famous musical masterpieces. The strains of the seventh and eighth lines of *"Wachet auf"* may be heard in the passage, "The kingdoms of this world," of Handel's "Hallelujah Chorus." Mendelssohn introduces the air in his overture to "St. Paul," and the entire chorale occurs in his "Hymn of Praise." He also has made use of the *"Wie schön"* theme in the first chorus of his unpublished oratorio, "Christus."

79

The circumstances that called forth Nicolai's two great hymns and the classic chorales he wrote for them were tragic in nature. A dreadful pestilence was raging in Westphalia. At Unna, where Nicolai was pastor, 1,300 villagers died of the plague between July 1597, and January 1598. During a single week in the month of August no less than 170 victims were claimed by the messenger of death.

From the parsonage which overlooked the churchyard, Nicolai was a sad witness of the burials. On one day thirty graves were dug. In the midst of these days of distress the gifted Lutheran pastor wrote a series of meditations to which he gave the title, *"Freuden Spiegel,"* or "Mirror of Joy." His purpose, as he explains in his preface, dated August 10, 1598, was "to leave it behind me (if God should call me from this world) as the token of my peaceful, joyful, Christian departure, or (if God should spare me in health) to comfort other sufferers whom He should also visit with the pestilence."

"There seemed to me," he writes in the same preface, "nothing more sweet, delightful and agreeable than the contemplation of the noble, sublime doctrine of Eternal Life obtained through the Blood of Christ. This I allowed to dwell in my heart day and night, and searched the Scriptures as to what they revealed on this matter, read also the sweet treatise of the ancient doctor Saint Augustine (*The City of God*) . . . Then day by day I wrote out my meditations, found myself, thank God! wonderfully well, comforted in heart, joyful in spirit, and truly content."

Both of Nicolai's classic hymns appeared for the first time in his *Mirror of Joy.* As a title to *"Wachet auf"* Nicolai wrote, "Of the voice at Midnight, and the Wise Virgins who meet their Heavenly Bridegroom. Mt. 25." The title to *"Wie schön"* reads, "A spiritual bridal song of the believing soul concerning Jesus Christ, her Heavenly Bridegroom, founded on the 45th Psalm of the prophet David."

It is said that the melody to *"Wie schön"* became so popular that numerous church chimes were set to it.

An English translation of Nicolai's exultant words reads:

> How brightly beams the morning star!
> What sudden radiance from afar
> Doth cheer us with its shining!
> Brightness of God, that breaks our night
> And fills the darkened souls with light,
> Who long for truth were pining!

80

Newly, truly, God's Word feeds us,
    Rightly leads us,
    Life bestowing.
Praise, O praise such love o'er-flowing.

Through Thee alone can we be blest;
Then deep be on our hearts imprest
    The love that Thou hast borne us;
So make us ready to fulfill
With ardent zeal Thy holy will,
    Though men may vex or scorn us;
Hold us, fold us, lest we fail Thee,
    Lo, we hail Thee,
    Long to know Thee!
All we are and have we owe Thee.

All praise to Him who came to save,
Who conquered death and scorned the grave;
    Each day new praise resoundeth
To Him, the Life who once was slain,
The Friend whom none shall trust in vain,
    Whose grace for aye aboundeth;
Sing then, ring then, tell the story
    Of His glory,
    Till His praises
Flood with light earth's darkest mazes!

Nicolai's life was filled with stirring events. He was born at Mengerinhausen, August 10, 1556. His father was a Lutheran pastor. After completing studies at the Universities of Erfürt and Wittenberg, Philipp was ordained to the ministry in 1583. His first charge was at Herdecke, but since the town council was composed of Roman Catholic members, he soon was compelled to leave that place. Later he served at Niederwildungen and Altwildungen, and in 1596 he became pastor at Unna. After the dreadful pestilence of 1597 there came an invasion of Spaniards in 1598, and Nicolai was forced to flee.

In 1601 he was chosen chief pastor of St. Katherine's Church in Hamburg. Here he gained fame as a preacher, being hailed as a "second Chrysostom." Throughout a long and bitter controversy with the Calvinists regarding the nature of the Lord's Supper, Nicolai was looked upon as the "pillar" of the Lutheran Church and the guardian of its doctrines. He died October 26, 1608.

Adoration of the Dying Saviour

Ah, holy Jesus, how hast Thou offended,
That man to judge Thee hath in hate pretended?
By foes derided, by Thine own rejected,
　　O most afflicted!

Who was the guilty? Who brought this upon Thee?
Alas, my treason, Jesus, hath undone Thee!
'Twas I, Lord Jesus, I it was denied Thee:
　　I crucified Thee.

Lo, the Good Shepherd for the sheep is offered;
The slave hath sinnèd, and the Son hath suffered;
For man's atonement, while he nothing heedeth,
　　God intercedeth.

For me, kind Jesus, was Thine incarnation,
Thy mortal sorrow, and Thy life's oblation;
Thy death of anguish and Thy bitter Passion,
　　For my salvation.

Therefore, kind Jesus, since I cannot pay Thee,
I do adore Thee, and will ever pray Thee:
Think on Thy pity and Thy love unswerving,
　　Not my deserving.

JOHANN HEERMANN, 1585–1647
Tr. ROBERT BRIDGES, 1844–1930

HYMNS OF THE THIRTY YEARS' WAR

TIMES of suffering and affliction have often brought forth great poets. This was especially true of that bitter period in European history known as the Thirty Years' War. Although it was one of the most distressing eras in the history of the Protestant Church, it gave birth to some of its grandest hymns.

It was during these dreadful decades, when Germany was devastated and depopulated by all the miseries of bloody warfare, that Johann Heermann lived and wrought. He was born at Rauden, Silesia, October 11, 1585, the son of a poverty-stricken furrier. There were five children in the family, but four of them were snatched away by death in early years. Johann, the sole survivor, also became ill, and the despairing mother was torn by fear that he, too, would be taken. Turning to God in her hour of need, she vowed that if He would spare her babe, she would educate him for the ministry.

She did not forget her promise. The child grew to manhood, received his training at several institutions, and in 1611 entered the holy ministry as pastor of the Lutheran church at Koeben, not far from his birthplace.

A few years later the Thirty Years' War broke out, and all of Germany began to feel its horrors. Four times during the period from 1629 to 1634 the town of Koeben was sacked by the armies of Wallenstein, who had been sent by the King of Austria to restore the German principalities to the Catholic faith. Previous to this, in 1616, the city was almost destroyed by fire. In 1631 it was visited by the dread pestilence.

Again and again Heermann was forced to flee from the city, and several times he lost all his earthly possessions. Once, when he was crossing the Oder, he was pursued and nearly captured by enemy soldiers, who shot after him. Twice he was nearly sabered.

It was during this period, in 1630, that his beautiful hymn, *Herzliebster Jesu,* based on a Latin meditation by Jean de Fècamp, was first published. A stanza omitted from Robert Bridges' fine trans-

lation, "Ah, holy Jesus," reflects very clearly the unfaltering faith
of the noble pastor during these hard experiences. It reads:

> Whate'er of earthly good this life may grant me
> I'll risk for Thee; no shame, no cross shall daunt me;
> I shall not fear what man can do to harm me,
>   Nor death alarm me.

The hymn immediately sprang into popularity in Germany, perhaps
through the fact that it reflected the spiritual mood of Protestants
everywhere, and partly because of the gripping tune written for it in
1640 by the great musician, Johann Crüger.

Heermann has been ranked with Luther and Gerhardt as one
of the greatest hymn-writers the Lutheran Church has produced.

One of his hymns, published in 1630 under the group known as
Songs of Tears, is entitled *"Treuer Wächter Israel,"* the English
translation of which begins "Jesus, as a Saviour, aid." It contains
a striking line imploring God to "build a wall around us." A very
interesting story is told concerning this hymn. On January 5, 1814,
the Allied forces were about to enter Schleswig. A poor widow and
her daughter and grandson lived in a little house near the entrance
of the town. The grandson was reading Heermann's hymns written
for times of war, and when he came to this one, he exclaimed, "It
would be a good thing, grandmother, if our Lord would build a wall
around us."

Next day all through the town cries of terror were heard, but
not a soldier molested the widow's home. When on the following
morning they summoned enough courage to open their door, lo, a
snowdrift had concealed them from the view of the enemy! On this
incident Clemens Brentano wrote a beautiful poem, *"Draus vor
Schleswig."*

Another interesting story is recorded concerning Heermann's
great hymn, "O God, eternal source." At Leuthen, in Silesia, on
December 5, 1757, the Prussians under Frederick the Great were
facing an army of Austrians three times their number. Just before
the battle began some of the Prussians began to sing the second stanza
of the hymn. The regimental bands took up the music. One of the com-
manders asked Frederick if it should be silenced. "No," said the king,
"let it be. With such men God will today certainly give me the victory."
When the bloody battle ended with victory for the Prussians, Frederick exclaimed: "My God, what a power there is in religion!"

Other famous hymns by Heermann include, "Ere yet the dawn hath filled the skies," "Zion mourns in fear and anguish," "O Christ, our true and only Light," "Lord, Thy death and passion give" and "Faithful God, I lay before Thee."

Next in importance to Heermann among the hymn-writers of the Thirty Years' War was Johann Rist, pastor, poet and playwright, who spent the greater part of his life at Wedel, close to Hamburg. Rist was recognized as one of the great literary lights of his day, and in 1644 was crowned poet laureate of Germany by Emperor Ferdinand III. Born at Ottensen, March 8, 1607, Rist received his inspiration for hymn-writing while studying at the University of Rinteln under Joshua Stegmann. Later he pursued studies at the University of Rostock until the Thirty Years' War almost emptied that institution of its students. He himself almost succumbed to the pestilence which raged there in 1633. Two years later he was appointed pastor at Wedel, where he led "a patriarchal and happy life" despite the bloodshed, famine, plundering and plague which characterized the era. He died in 1667.

Rist was a prolific writer. Two of his plays depict vividly the times in which he lived. Other secular works also are of considerable historical interest. As a hymn-writer, he was the author of no less than 680 lyrics, for which some of the best musicians of the day composed tunes. As a result, Rist's hymns were soon being sung all over Germany. It is said that even the Romanists became deeply intrigued by them. Invariably they reflect an abiding trust in God and a fervent love to Christ. Still in common use today are "Break forth, O beauteous heavenly light," "O living Bread from heaven," "O darkest woe," "Arise, the kingdom is at hand," "Help us, O Lord, behold we enter," "Rise, O Salem, rise and shine," "Lord Jesus Christ, Thou living Bread," "Arise, sons of the kingdom," and many others.

Michael Schirmer, an educator and poet who lived in Berlin during the Thirty Years' War and for two decades after its close, also found solace in the midst of much suffering, sorrow and hardship by writing spiritual lyrics. Called "the German Job" because of his many afflictions, he left behind him a collection of hymns known as *Biblische Lieder*, published in 1650. Among these is found the beautiful Pentecost hymn, "O Holy Spirit, enter in."

"If thou but suffer God to guide thee," a hymn that breathes a spirit of implicit trust in God, was also born during this period of

German history. It was written by George Neumark under strange circumstances. While on his way to attend the University of Königsberg, he was set on by robbers, who took from him all he possessed. Unable to carry out his plan to study, and completely destitute, he wandered from place to place seeking some kind of employment. Finally he was engaged as a tutor by a wealthy family in Kiel. In spontaneous thanksgiving to God for answered prayers, he thereupon indited his now famous hymn. After having saved enough money to continue his studies, he returned to the university in 1643, pursuing courses in law and poetry. Following graduation, he became court poet, librarian and keeper of archives under Duke Wilhelm II of Saxe-Weimar.

Johann Meyfart also belongs to this period. He was a theological professor at the University of Erfürt, and died at that place in 1642. One of his hymns, "Jerusalem, thou city fair and high," has found its way into many English hymn-books.

The beautiful funeral hymn, "O how blest are ye whose toils are ended," which was translated into English by Henry Wadsworth Longfellow, comes to us from the pen of Simon Dach, another Lutheran theologian who lived during these stirring days. Dach, who was professor of poetry and dean of the philosophical faculty of the University of Königsberg, wrote some 165 hymns. They are marked by fulness of faith and a quiet confidence in God in the midst of a world of turmoil and uncertainty. Dach died in 1659 after a lingering illness. The first stanza of his funeral hymn reads:

> O how blest are ye, whose toils are ended,
> Who through death have unto God ascended!
> Ye have arisen
> From the cares which keep us still in prison.

Two other hymn-writers who belonged to the group of Prussian theologians and poets known as the Königsberg School were Valentin Thilo and Heinrich Albert, both of whom were close friends of Dach, and together with him members of the Poetical Union of that city. Thilo, who was professor of rhetoric at the University of Königsberg, was elected five times as dean of the philosophical faculty and twice as rector of the institution. Most of his hymns were written for the great festivals of the Church Year. Perhaps his best known lyric is the lovely Christmas carol:

> O Jesu so meek, O Jesu so kind,
> Thou hast fulfilled Thy Father's mind;
> Hast come from heaven down to earth,
> In human flesh through human birth.
> O Jesu so meek, O Jesu so kind!
>
> O Jesu so good, O Jesu so meek,
> To do Thy will is all we seek;
> For all we are or have is Thine;
> Do Thou our hearts to Thee incline.
> O Jesu so good, O Jesu so meek!

Heinrich Albert, after having studied law for a while at Leipzig, decided to turn to music and pursued studies at Dresden under his uncle, Heinrich Schütz, the Court Capellmeister. In 1631, when he was appointed organist of the cathedral at Königsberg, he came in contact with Dach and Thilo and soon was writing poetry as well as music. He is credited with 118 secular poems and 74 hymns, as well as 78 sacred tunes. Certain stanzas of his famous hymn, "God who madest earth and heaven," have been used as a morning prayer in Germany probably more extensively than any other sacred verse ever written. The first line is sometimes rendered, "Now the morn new light is pouring." Albert died October 6, 1651.

Matthäus Apelles von Löwenstern, who died in 1648, the year when the Thirty Years' War came to close with the Peace of Westphalia, is one of the few hymn-writers to be created a nobleman. His career was a most unusual one. Born April 20, 1594, at Neustadt, Silesia, the son of a common saddler, he early distinguished himself by his musical gifts, and in 1625 was appointed as music director and treasurer at Bernstadt by Duke Heinrich Wenzel of Münsterberg. The following year he became director of the princely school at that place. Later he served as a councillor to both Emperor Ferdinand II and Ferdinand III, and was raised to the nobility by the latter. Of thirty hymns written by Löwenstern, the best known is a stirring prayer for the Church in perilous times, the first stanza of which reads:

> Lord of our life, and God of our salvation,
> Star of our night, and hope of every nation,
> Hear and receive Thy Church's supplication,
> Lord God Almighty!

Tobias Clausnitzer, who has bequeathed to the Church the hymns, "Look upon us, blessed Lord," and "We all believe in one true God," was chaplain of a Swedish regiment during the Thirty Years' War.

As such he preached the sermon at a service held in St. Thomas Church, Leipzig, on Reminiscere Sunday in 1645, celebrating the accession to the throne of Sweden of Queen Christina, successor to her illustrious father, Gustavus Adolphus. He also preached the thanksgiving sermon at a field service held by command of General Wrangel at Weiden, in the Upper Palatine, on January 1, 1649, after the conclusion of the Peace of Westphalia. Afterwards he became pastor at Weiden, where he remained until his death in 1684.

Other outstanding German hymn-writers who belong to the period of the Thirty Years' War are Martin Opitz, George Weissel, Heinrich Held, Ernst Homburg, Johannes Olearius, Joshua Stegmann, and Wilhelm II, Duke of Saxe-Weimar.

Opitz was somewhat of a diplomat and courtier, as well as a poet. He was a man of vacillating character, and did not hesitate to lend his support to the Romanists whenever it served his personal interests. However, he has left to posterity an imperishable hymn in "Light of Light, O Sun of heaven." He is credited with having reformed the art of verse-writing in Germany. He died during a pestilence in Danzig in 1639.

Homburg and Held were lawyers. Homburg was born near Eisenach in 1605, and later we find him practicing law in Naumburg, Saxony. He was a man of great poetic talent, but at first devoted his gifts to romantic ballads and drinking songs. During the days of the dread pestilence he turned to God, and now he began to write hymns. In 1659 he published a collection of 150 spiritual songs. In a preface he speaks of them as his "Sunday labor," and he tells how he had been led to write them "by the anxious and sore domestic afflictions by which God . . . has for some time laid me aside." The Lenten hymn, "Christ, the Life of all the living," is found in this collection.

Held, who practiced law in his native town of Guhrau, Silesia, also was a man chastened in the school of sorrow and affliction. He is the author of two hymns that have found their way into the English language—"Let the earth now praise the Lord" and "Come, O come, Thou quickening Spirit."

Weissel, a Lutheran pastor at Königsberg, has given us one of the finest Advent hymns in the German language, "Lift up your heads, ye mighty gates."

Olearius, who wrote a commentary on the Bible and compiled one of the most important hymnbooks of the 17th century, has likewise bequeathed to the Church a splendid Advent hymn, "Comfort, comfort, ye My people."

Stegmann, a theological professor at Rinteln who suffered much persecution at the hands of Benedictine monks during the Thirty Years' War, was the author of the beautiful evening hymn, "Abide with us, our Saviour."

Wilhelm II, Duke of Saxe-Weimar, who wrote the inspiring hymn, "Lord Jesus Christ, be present now," was not only a poet and musician, but also a soldier. He was twice wounded in battles with the Imperial forces, and was once left for dead. He was taken prisoner by Tilly, but was released by order of the Emperor. When Gustavus Adolphus came to Germany to save the Protestant cause, Wilhelm after some hesitation joined him. However, when the Duke in 1635 made a separate peace with the Emperor, the Swedish army ravaged his territory.

The Swan-Song of Gustavus Adolphus

Fear not, thou faithful Christian flock;
God is thy shelter and thy rock:
Fear not for thy salvation.
Though fierce the foe and dark the night,
The Lord of hosts shall be thy might,
Christ thine illumination.

Arise, arise, the foe defy!
Call on the Name of God most high,
That He with might endue you.
And Christ, your everlasting Priest,
In all your conflicts shall assist,
From strength to strength renew you.

JOHANN MICHAEL ALTENBURG, 1584-1630
TR. ROBERT BRIDGES, 1844-1930

A HYMN MADE FAMOUS ON A BATTLEFIELD

"FEAR not, thou faithful Christian flock" will always be known as the "swan-song" of the Swedish hero king, Gustavus Adolphus.

No incident in modern history is more dramatic than the sudden appearance in Germany of Gustavus Adolphus and his little Swedish army during the critical days of the Thirty Years' War. It was this victorious crusade that saved Germany, and probably all of northern Europe, for Protestantism.

The untimely death of the Swedish monarch on the battlefield of Lützen, November 6, 1632, while leading his men against Wallenstein's host, not only gained immortal fame for Gustavus, but will always cause the world to remember the hymn that was sung by his army on that historic day.

When Gustavus Adolphus landed in Germany in 1630 with his small but well-trained army, it seemed that the Protestant cause in Europe was lost. All the Protestant princes of Germany had been defeated by Tilly and Wallenstein, leaders of the Imperial armies, and the victors were preparing to crush every vestige of Lutheranism in Germany.

The Margrave of Brandenburg and the Duke of Saxony, however, furnished a few troops to Gustavus, and in a swift, meteoric campaign the Swedish king had routed the army of the Catholic League and had marched all the way across Germany. In the spring of 1632 Gustavus moved into the heart of Bavaria and captured Munich.

The Imperial forces who had sneered at the "Snow King," as they called him, and who had predicted that he would "melt" as he came southward were now filled with dismay. The "Snow King" had proved to be the "Lion of the North."

Wallenstein rallied the Catholic forces for a last stand at Lützen, the battle that was to prove the decisive conflict.

On the morning of November 6, 1632, the two armies faced each other in battle array. Dr. Fabricius, chaplain of the Swedish army, had been commanded by Gustavus to lead his troops in worship. The king himself raised the strains of "Fear not, thou faithful Christian flock," and led the army in singing the stirring hymn. Then he knelt in fervent prayer.

A heavy fog prevented the Protestant forces from moving forward to the attack, and, while they were waiting for the fog to lift, Gustavus ordered the musicians to play Luther's hymn, "A mighty Fortress is our God." The whole army joined with a shout. The king then mounted his charger, and, drawing his sword, rode back and forth in front of the lines, speaking words of encouragement to his men.

As the sun began to break through the fog, Gustavus himself offered a prayer, "Jesus, Jesus, Jesus, help me today to do battle for the glory of Thy holy Name," and then shouted, "Now forward to the attack in the name of our God!" The army answered, "God with us!" and rushed forward, the king galloping in the lead.

When his aid offered him his coat of mail, Gustavus refused to put it on, declaring, "God is my Protector."

The battle raged fiercely. For a time the outcome seemed ominous for the Evangelical forces. At 11 o'clock Gustavus was struck by a bullet and mortally wounded. As he fell from his horse, the word spread quickly through the Swedish lines, "The king is wounded!"

It proved to be the turning point in the battle. Instead of losing heart and fleeing, the Swedish troops charged the foe with a fierceness born of sorrow and despair, and before the day was ended another great victory had been won. The Protestant cause was saved, but the noble Gustavus had made the supreme sacrifice.

The authorship of his famous "battle-hymn" has been the subject of much dispute. The German poet and hymnologist, Albert Knapp, called it "a little feather from the eagle wing of Gustavus Adolphus," and for a long time the Swedish king was regarded as the author. However, the weight of evidence seems to point to Johann Michael Altenberg, a German pastor of Gross Sommern, Thüringen, as the real writer, and Swedish hymnologists, though formerly they clung to the theory that their royal hero had composed it, are now agreed that the hymn is the work of Altenberg. It is generally believed that Altenberg was inspired to write it upon hearing of the victory gained by Gustavus Adolphus at the battle of Leipzig, September 7, 1631, about a year before the battle of Lützen.

In any event, it is a matter of record that the Swedish king adopted it immediately, and that he sang it as his own "swan-song" at the Battle of Lützen. Some one has aptly said, "Whether German or Swede may claim this hymn is a question. They both rightly own it."

The last of the great Lutheran hymn-writers belonging to the period of the Thirty Years' War was Martin Rinkart. Except for the time of the Reformation, these were undoubtedly the most creative decades in the history of Lutheran hymnody, and of all the famous hymns written during this stirring period there is none that surpasses Rinkart's "Now thank we all our God." A magnificent hymn of thanksgiving, its lines as translated by Catherine Winkworth have become familiar throughout the English-speaking world:

> Now thank we all our God
>   With heart and hands and voices,
> Who wondrous things hath done,
>   In whom His world rejoices;
> Who, from our mother's arms,
>   Hath blessed us on our way
> With countless gifts of love,
>   And still is ours today.
>
> O may this bounteous God
>   Through all our life be near us,
> With ever joyful hearts
>   And blessed peace to cheer us;
> And keep us in His grace,
>   And guide us when perplexed,
> And free us from all ills
>   In this world and the next.
>
> All praise and thanks to God
>   The Father now be given,
> The Son, and Him who reigns
>   With them in highest heaven;
> The one eternal God,
>   Whom earth and heaven adore;
> For thus it was, is now,
>   And shall be evermore.

The date of this remarkable hymn is not known definitely. The theory has been advanced that it was written as a hymn of thanksgiving following the Peace of Westphalia, which in 1648 brought to an end the long and cruel war. This claim has been based on the fact that the first two stanzas are a paraphrase of the words of the high priest Simeon, recorded in the Apocryphal book Ecclesiasticus 50: 29—32: "And now let all praise God, who hath done great things, who hath glorified our days, and dealeth with us according to his

93

loving-kindness. He giveth us the joy of our hearts, that we may find peace in Israel as in the days of yore, thus he lets his loving-kindness remain with us, and he will redeem us in our day." Inasmuch as this was the Scripture passage on which all regimental chaplains were ordered to preach in celebration of the conclusion of peace, it has been inferred that Rinkart was inspired to write his hymn at that time.

It is probable, however, that these circumstances were merely a coincidence, and that the hymn was written several years previous to 1648. In Rinkart's own volume, *Jesu Hertz-Buchlein,* it appears under the title *"Tisch-Gebetlein,"* or a short prayer before meals, and many believe that it was originally written for Rinkart's children. It will be noticed that, while the first two stanzas are based on the passage from Ecclesiasticus, the last stanza is derived from the ancient doxology, *Gloria Patri.*

No hymn except Luther's famous "A mighty Fortress is our God" has been used more generally in the Lutheran Church than Rinkart's glorious pæan of praise. In Germany, where it has become the national *Te Deum,* it is sung at all impressive occasions. After the battle of Leuthen, the army of Frederick the Great raised the strains of this noble hymn, and it is said that even the mortally wounded joined in the singing.

In his history of the Franco-Prussian War, Cassel tells of a stirring incident that took place on the day following the battle of Sedan, where the Germans had won a decisive victory. A contingent of Prussian troops marching toward Paris were billeted in the parish church of Augecourt, but found it impossible to sleep because of the extreme excitement of the day. Suddenly a strain of music came from the organ, first very softly but gradually swelling in volume until the whole sanctuary shook. It was the grand old hymn—*"Nun danket alle Gott!"* Instantly men and officers were on their feet, singing the stirring words. Then followed Luther's *"Ein' feste Burg,"* after which the terrible strain seemed relieved, and the tired soldiers lay down to peaceful slumber.

The hymn also has achieved great popularity in England, where it was sung as a *Te Deum* in nearly all churches and chapels at the close of the Boer War in 1902.

Rinkart's life was a tragic one. The greater part of his public service was rendered during the horrors of the Thirty Years' War. Born at Eilenburg, Saxony, April 23, 1586, he attended a Latin school in his home town, and then became a student at the University of Leipzig.

In 1617, by invitation of the town council of Eilenburg, he became pastor of the church in the city of his birth. It was at the beginning of the Thirty Years' War, and, because Eilenburg was a walled city, it became a refuge for thousands who had lost everything in the conflict. Famine and pestilence added to the horror of the situation. Moreover, the other two pastors of the city had died, and Rinkart was left alone to minister to the spiritual needs of the populace.

Twice Eilenburg was saved from the Swedish army through the intercession of Rinkart, first in 1637 and again in 1639. A levy of 30,000 thaler had been made on the city by the Swedish general to aid the Protestant cause. Knowing the impoverished condition of his townsmen, Rinkart went out to the Swedish camp to plead their cause, but to no avail. Turning to those who were with him, Rinkart exclaimed, "Come, my children, we can find no mercy with men, let us take refuge with God." He then fell on his knees and uttered a fervent prayer, after which they sang the hymn of Paul Eber so much used in those trying days, "When in the hour of utmost need." The scene made such an impression on the Swedish commander that he relented and reduced his demand to 2,000 florins or 1,350 thaler.

Rinkart lived only a year after the close of the bloody war. He died, a worn and broken man, in 1649.

A Serene Evening Psalm

The duteous day now closeth,
Each flower and tree reposeth,
*   Shade creeps o'er wild and wood:*
Let us, as night is falling,
On God our Maker calling,
*   Give thanks to Him, the Giver good.*

Now all the heavenly splendor
Breaks forth in starlight tender
*   From myriad worlds unknown;*
And man, the marvel seeing,
Forgets his selfish being,
*   For joy of beauty not his own.*

His care he drowneth yonder,
Lost in the abyss of wonder;
*   To heaven his soul doth steal:*
His life he disesteemeth,
The day it is that dreameth,
*   That doth from truth his vision seal.*

Awhile his mortal blindness
May miss God's loving-kindness,
*   And grope in faithless strife:*
But when life's day is over
Shall death's fair night discover
*   The fields of everlasting life.*

PAUL GERHARDT, 1607–76
TR. ROBERT BRIDGES, 1844–1930

PAUL GERHARDT, PRINCE OF LUTHERAN HYMNISTS

THE greatest German hymnist of the seventeenth century, and perhaps of all time, was Paul Gerhardt. Not even the hymns of Martin Luther are used so generally throughout the Christian world as those of this sweet German singer. More of the beautiful lyrics of Gerhardt have found their way into the English language than those of any other German writer, and with the passing of the years their popularity increases rather than diminishes.

In the Lutheran church at Lübden, in Germany, there hangs a life-size painting of Gerhardt. Beneath it is this inscription: *Theologus in cribro Satanæ versatus* ("A divine sifted in Satan's sieve"). That inscription may be said to epitomize the sad life-story of Germany's great psalmist.

Gerhardt was born March 12, 1607, in Gräfenhaynichen, a village near the celebrated Wittenberg. His father, who was mayor of the village, died before Paul reached maturity. When he was twenty-one years of age he began the study of theology at the University of Wittenberg. The Thirty Years' War was raging, and all Germany was desolate and suffering. Because of the difficulty of securing a parish, Gerhardt served for several years as a tutor in the home of Andreas Barthold, whose daughter Anna Maria became his bride in 1655.

It was during this period that Gerhardt's poetic gifts began to flourish. No doubt he was greatly stimulated by contact with the famous musician, Johann Crüger, who was cantor and director of music in the Church of St. Nicholas in Berlin. In 1648 many of Gerhardt's hymns were published in Crüger's *Praxis Pietatis Melica.*

Through the recommendation of the Berlin clergy, Gerhardt was appointed Lutheran provost at Mittenwalde, and was ordained to this post November 18, 1651. Six years later he accepted the position of third assistant pastor of the Church of St. Nicholas in Berlin. His hymns continued to grow in popularity, and his fame as a preacher drew large audiences to hear him.

The controversy between the Lutherans and Calvinists, which

had continued from the days of the Reformation, flared up again at this time as the result of efforts on the part of Elector Friedrich Wilhelm of Prussia to unite the two parties. Friedrich Wilhelm, who was a Calvinist, sought to compel the clergy to sign a document promising that they would abstain from any references in their sermons to doctrinal differences. Gerhardt was sick at the time, and, although he had always been moderate in his utterances, he felt that to sign such a document would be to compromise the faith. Summoning the other Lutheran clergymen of Berlin to his bedside, he urged them to stand firm and to refuse to surrender to the demands of the Elector.

Soon after this the courageous pastor was deposed from office. He was also prohibited from holding private services in his own home. Though he felt the blow very keenly, he met it with true Christian fortitude.

"This," he said, "is only a small Berlin affliction; but I am also willing and ready to seal with my blood the evangelical truth, and, like my namesake, St. Paul, to offer my neck to the sword."

To add to his sorrows, Gerhardt's wife and a son died in the midst of these troubles. Three other children had died earlier, and now the sorely tried pastor was left with a single child, a boy of six years. In May, 1669, he was called to the church at Lübden, where he labored faithfully and with great success until his death, on June 7, 1676.

The glorious spirit that dwelt in him, and which neither trials nor persecution could quench, is reflected in the lines of his famous hymn, "If God himself be for me," based on the latter part of the eighth chapter of Romans:

> Though earth be rent asunder,
> Thou'rt mine eternally;
> Not fire, nor sword, nor thunder,
> Shall sever me from Thee;
> Not hunger, thirst, nor danger,
> Not pain nor poverty,
> Nor mighty princes' anger,
> Shall ever hinder me.

Catherine Winkworth, who has translated the same hymn in a different meter under the title, "Since Jesus is my Friend," has

probably succeeded best in giving expression to the triumphant faith
and the note of transcendent hope and joy in the final two stanzas:

> My heart for gladness springs;
>   It cannot more be sad;
> For very joy it smiles and sings—
>   Sees naught but sunshine glad.

> The Sun that lights mine eyes
>   Is Christ, the Lord I love;
> I sing for joy of that which lies
>   Stored up for me above.

Because of the warm, confiding faith in God reflected in Gerhardt's hymns, they have become a source of special comfort to
heavy-laden souls. Not only do they breathe a spirit of tender consolation, but also of a "joy unspeakable and full of glory." We have a
beautiful example of this in his Advent hymn, "O how shall I receive
Thee":

> Rejoice then, ye sad-hearted,
>   Who sit in deepest gloom,
> Who mourn o'er joys departed,
>   And tremble at your doom,
> He who alone can cheer you
>   Is standing at the door;
> He brings His pity near you,
>   And bids you weep no more.

In Gerhardt's hymns we find a transition from pure objective faith
to a more subjective note in hymnody. Sixteen of his hymns begin
with the pronoun "I." They are not characterized, however, by the
weak sentimentality so often found in the hymns of our own day,
for Gerhardt never lost sight of the greatest objective truth revealed
to men—justification by faith alone. Nevertheless, because of his
constant emphasis on the love of God, and because his hymns are
truly "songs of the heart," they possess a degree of emotional warmth
that is lacking in the earlier Lutheran hymns.

His lyrics on the glories of nature have never been surpassed.
In contemplating the beauty of created things he is ever praising the
Creator. His famous evening hymn, *"Nun ruhen alle Wälder,"* has
been likened to the beauty and splendor of the evening star. In a
marvelous manner the temporal and the eternal, the terrestrial and
the celestial, are contrasted in every stanza. It was a favorite hymn of
the great German poet, Friedrich von Schiller, who first heard it
sung by his mother as a cradle song. Probably no hymn is more
generally used by the children of Germany as an evening prayer

than this one. The most familiar English translation begins with the line, "Now rest beneath night's shadow." A more recent translation, "The duteous day now closeth," is by the late Robert Bridges, poet laureate of England.

The tune to which this hymn is sung is as famous as the hymn itself. It is ascribed to Heinrich Isaak, one of the first of the great German church musicians, and is believed to have been composed by Isaak in 1490, when he was leaving his native town, Innsbruck, to establish himself at the court of Emperor Maximilian I. It was set to the plaintive words, *"Innsbruck, ich muss dich lassen."* According to tradition, Isaak first heard the beautiful melody sung by a wandering minstrel. Bach and Mozart regarded it as one of the sublimest of all chorales, and each is said to have declared that he would rather have been the composer of this tune than any of his great masterpieces.

Gerhardt wrote 123 hymns in all. In addition to the hymns already mentioned, probably his most famous is "O sacred Head, now wounded," based on the Latin hymn of Bernard of Clairvaux. Other hymns in common use are "Evening and morning," "Jesus, thy boundless love to me," "Put thou thy trust in God," "Immanuel, we sing Thy praise," "Holy Ghost, dispel our sadness," "O enter, Lord, Thy temple," "All my heart this night rejoices," "Beside Thy manger here I stand," "Awake, my heart, and marvel," "Go forth, my heart, and seek delight," "O Saviour dear," and "A pilgrim and a stranger."

Catherine Winkworth, the brilliant English translator of German hymns, has given this estimate of Gerhardt's contribution to the hymnody of the Christian Church:

"As a poet he undoubtedly holds the highest place among the hymn-writers of Germany. His hymns seem to be the spontaneous outpouring of a heart that overflows with love, trust and praise. His language is simple and pure. If it has sometimes a touch of homeliness, it has no vulgarism; and at times it rises to a beauty and grace which always gives the impression of being unstudied, yet could hardly have been improved by art. His tenderness and fervor never degenerate into sentimentality, nor his penitence and sorrow into morbid despondency."

Only the briefest mention can be made concerning several other German hymn-writers of Gerhardt's period who have left lyrics that will never be forgotten.

One of these was Heinrich Theobald Schenk, a pastor at Giessen. Not very much is known regarding this man except that he was the writer of a single hymn, but a hymn that has gained for him the thanks of posterity. Scarcely a hymnbook of any communion can be found today that does not contain "Who are these, like stars appearing?" Schenk died in 1727 at the age of 71 years.

Casper Neumann, another of Gerhardt's contemporaries, has bequeathed to the Church the sublime hymn, "God of Ages, all transcending," the last stanza of which is unusually striking in language:

> Say Amen, O God our Father,
>   To the praise we offer Thee;
> Now, to laud Thy name we gather;
>   Let this to Thy glory be.
> Fill us with Thy love and grace,
> Till we see Thee face to face.

Neumann, who was a celebrated preacher and professor of theology at Breslau from 1678 to 1715, was the author of some thirty hymns, all of which became very popular in Silesia. He was also author of a famous devotional book, *Kern aller Gebete.* He is regarded as a spiritual poet of the first rank.

Another distinguished German educator who wrote hymns during the latter half of the 17th century was Samuel Rodigast, author of the widely used lyric, "Whate'er our God ordains is right." Rodigast, who was born at Groben in 1649, graduated from Jena in 1671 and became adjunct of the philosophical faculty at that university. Four years later, when one of his nearest friends, Severus Gastorius, precentor at Jena, became seriously ill, Rodigast wrote the aforementioned hymn to cheer the sick man and to strengthen his faith. The interesting thing is that when Gastorius recovered, he wrote the equally famous tune, *Was Gott tut,* for Rodigast's words, and since that day the two together have gone singing down through the years. In 1680 Rodigast became conrector of the Greyfriars Gymnasium in Berlin, where he achieved great fame as a scholar and educationist. He died there in 1708 and is buried in the Kloster Kirche in Berlin.

An Exultant Eucharistic Hymn

Deck thyself with joy and gladness,
Dwell no more, my soul, in sadness;
Let the daylight shine upon thee,
Put the wedding garment on thee,
For the Lord of life unending
Unto thee His call is sending:
Come, for now the King most holy
Stoops to thee in likeness lowly.

Hasten, then, my soul, to meet Him,
Eagerly and gladly greet Him.
As without He standeth knocking,
Quickly, thy soul's gate unlocking,
Open wide the fast-closed portal,
Saying to the Lord immortal,
'Come, and leave Thy servant never,
Dwell within my heart forever.'

Jesus, source of life and pleasure
Truest friend and dearest treasure,
Joy, the sweetest man e'er knoweth;
Fount, whence all my being floweth:
Humbly now I bow before Thee,
And in penitence adore Thee;
Worthily let me receive Thee,
Perfect peace and pardon give me.

JOHANN FRANCK, 1618–77
TR. JOHN CASPER MATTES, 1876–1948, a.

GERMAN LAYMEN WHO WROTE HYMNS

AT THIS point in our study of German hymnody we are struck by the large number of laymen of the Church who dedicated their gifts to the writing of sacred lyrics. Men of all walks of life, and particularly those who belonged to the higher cultural and intellectual circles, frequently found inspiration and satisfaction in composing religious verse. Thirty years of bitter religious struggle in Europe had brought people everywhere face to face with the necessity of spiritual commitments. Faith no longer was a matter of speculation or indifference; it demanded steadfastness and conviction.

The universal sorrow and suffering brought on by three decades of uninterrupted warfare had created a sober mood in the hearts of men. They had become other-worldly minded. Many looked for the coming of the millenium. In the midst of a world of uncertainty they sought their solace and peace in the words and promises of Christ. They yearned for His coming to redeem His people.

The hymns written during the latter half of the 17th century, following the Peace of Westphalia, reflected to a large degree this spiritual mood. Often they were subjective and mystical in character. Always they were fervent in their expression of Christian faith and hope. In a sense, they were forerunners of the Pietistic hymns of the following decades.

Johann Franck was the most outstanding lay hymn-writer of this period. Born at Guben, June 1, 1618, the son of an advocate and councillor by the same name, he began the study of law at the University of Konigsberg in 1638. It was his warm friendship here with such hymnists as Simon Dach and Heinrich Held that probably awakened his interests in poetry and hymnody. After returning to his native city, he began the practice of law, and eventually became the mayor of Guben.

To this Lutheran layman we are indebted for what is probably the finest communion hymn in the German language, "Deck thyself with joy and gladness," a hymn which even in its translated form

103

retains something of its note of exultant Christian faith. Franck also was the author of such other gems as "Lord, to thee I make confession," "Light of the Gentile nations," "Praise the Lord, each tribe and nation," and that fervent hymn of devotion to Christ:

> Jesus, priceless Treasure,
> Source of purest pleasure,
>   Truest Friend to me;
> Long my heart hath panted,
> Till it well-nigh fainted,
>   Thirsting after Thee.
> Thine I am, O spotless Lamb,
> I will suffer nought to hide Thee,
> Ask for nought beside Thee.

Franck is ranked next to Gerhardt as the leading hymnist of his period. It was he who began the long series of so-called "Jesus hymns," which reached their fullest development in the later Pietistic school of hymn-writers. Franck held that poetry should be "the nurse of piety, the herald of immortality, the promoter of cheerfulness, the conqueror of sadness, and a foretaste of heavenly glory." His hymns echo his own spirit of Christian cheerfulness and hope. Franck died in 1677.

Next to Franck, the most outstanding lay hymnist of this period was Baron Friedrich R. L. von Canitz, a man who spent all of his life in government service. Born in Berlin in 1654, he studied in the Universities of Leipzig and Leyden. In 1677 he was appointed gentleman of the bed-chamber by Elector Friedrich Wilhelm, and later accompanied the Elector in his military campaigns. At one time he was ambassador to Frankfurt, later he became chief magistrate of Mühlenhoff and Mülenbeck, and then privy counselor to Friedrich III, successor to Friedrich Wilhelm. It was Friedrich III who bestowed on him the title of baron. He died in Berlin in 1699, and his hymns were published posthumously.

From the pen of Canitz we have received the lovely morning hymn, "Come, my soul, thou must be waking," a lyric that has become immensely popular in England and America, as well as in Germany.

In the writings of Dr. Arnold, once headmaster of Rugby School in England, a beautiful story is recorded concerning the death of Canitz. On the last day of his life, so Dr. Arnold relates, Canitz asked to be brought to a window in order that he might look once again upon the rising sun. After gazing in rapt silence at the reddening dawn, he cried out, "Oh, if the appearance of this earthly, created thing is so beautiful and inspiring, how much more shall I not be enraptured at the sight of the unspeakable glory of the Creator himself." No one can read the words of Canitz's morning hymn without understanding what the poet meant.

It was during this period also that the most famous of all German funeral hymns, "Jesus Christ, my sure Defense," was written. Who was the author? None other than a woman of royal birth, Luise Henrietta, Electress of Brandenburg, daughter of Friedrich Heinrich, Prince of Nassau-Orange and Stadtholder of the United Netherlands, wife of Elector Friedrich Wilhelm of Brandenburg, and mother of King Friedrich I of Prussia. In brief, she was the "mother" of the powerful House of Hohenzollern, rulers of modern Germany up until World War I. But neither wealth nor high position offer immunity to sorrow and misfortune, and the Electress of Brandenburg, who was a noble woman in the double sense of that word, found that life's sweetest cup was mingled with much bitterness. Even as she was being married with regal splendor to Friedrich Wilhelm at The Hague on December 7, 1646, her father, the Prince of Nassau-Orange, was lying on his death-bed in the Dutch royal palace. After the wedding Luise Henrietta remained in The Hague to nurse him, while her husband, the Elector, returned to Cleve, where he was residing.

On March 14, 1647, the father died, and three months later the Electress joined her husband at Cleve. A year later she gave birth to her first child, Wilhelm Heinrich. In the fall of 1649 she set out for Berlin with her husband and the little heir to the throne, but on the way the child sickened and died at Wesel. Not until the following April did she finally reach Berlin, more than three years after her marriage to the Elector. According to the hymnologist Lauxmann, it was while mourning the loss of her firstborn son that her famous hymn was written. In the midst of her grief, the 22-year-old Electress gave expression to her unswerving faith in words that Rambach, another hymnologist, has called "an acknowledged masterpiece of Christian poetry":

> Jesus, my Redeemer, lives!
> I, too, unto life must waken;
> He will have me where He is.
> Shall my courage then be shaken?
> Shall I fear? Or could the Head
> Rise, and leave His members dead?

Nay, too closely am I bound
Unto Him by hope for ever;
    Faith's strong hand the Rock hath found,
Grasped it, and will leave it never;
    Not the ban of death can part
    From its Lord the trusting heart.

When her second son, Carl Emil, was born five years later, the Electress founded the Oranienburg orphanage in Berlin as a thank offering to God for having given her an heir to the throne. Carl Emil, however, died at the age of 19, and it was her third son, Friedrich, born in 1657, who finally became the King of Prussia. When another son, Ludwig, was born in 1666, the Electress never regained her strength, and passed away the following year.

Luise of Brandenburg not only was a devout Christian, but a woman who was deeply devoted to the welfare of the German people. Following the ravages of the Thirty Years' War, she sought to help her subjects by establishing model farms, and it was she who introduced the cultivation of potatoes in Germany. She was also instrumental in the establishment of elementary schools. Herself a member of the Reformed Church, she was greatly distressed by the doctrinal controversies raging between the Lutherans and the Calvinists and sought every means to bring about peace. It was she who came to the aid of Paul Gerhardt after he had been deprived of his Berlin parish in 1666.

Among other lay hymn-writers who wrought during this period was Christian Knorr von Rosenroth, a noted Orientalist, scientist and statesman who, in addition to duties of state, edited several Rabbinical writings and works on Oriental mysticism. His best known hymn is "Dayspring of eternity," which has been characterized by one writer as "one of the freshest, most original and spirited of morning hymns, as if born from the dew of the sunrise." Another English version of this hymn is "Come, thou bright and morning star." Rosenroth died at Sulzbach, Bavaria, May 8, 1689, at the very hour, it is said, which he himself had predicted.

Another layman, Ahasuerus Fritsch, chancellor of the University of Jena and president of the consistory of Rudolstadt, was somewhat of an authority in his day on hymnology. Born at Mücheln, December 16, 1629, during the bloodiest period of the Thirty Years' War, he was only two years old when his parents were forced to flee to Voigtland when Mücheln was burned and pillaged. When he was 14,

106

he lost his father. During his youth, Fritsch had many narrow escapes from death at the hands of soldiers, robbers and plunderers. In later years he gained prestige as a statesman, and was the editor of two hymn collections. He is credited with the authorship of "Jesus is my Joy, my All." He died in 1701.

The fine hymn of worship, "Sing praise to God who reigns above," has been ascribed to another layman of this period, Johann J. Schütz, an authority in civil and canon law at Frankfurt am Main. This man, who is described as deeply pious, was a close friend of Philipp J. Spener, and it was at his suggestion that Spener began his *Collegia Pietatis,* or prayer meetings, which were the real beginnings of pietism. After Spener left Frankfurt in 1686, Schütz became a radical separatist, and ceased to attend Lutheran services or to commune. He died on May 22, 1690. He is credited with the authorship of five hymns, but only the one mentioned above has come into common use.

A Glorious Paean of Praise

Praise to the Lord, the Almighty, the King of creation;
O my soul, praise Him, for He is thy health and salvation:
 All ye who hear,
 Now to His temple draw near,
Joining in glad adoration.

Praise to the Lord, who o'er all things so wondrously reigneth,
Shelters thee under His wings, yea, so gently sustaineth:
 Hast thou not seen?
 All that is needful hath been
Granted in what He ordaineth.

Praise to the Lord, who doth prosper thy work and defend thee;
Surely His goodness and mercy here daily attend thee.
 Ponder anew
 What the Almighty can do,
If with His love He befriend thee!

Praise to the Lord, O let all that is in me adore Him;
All that hath life and breath, come now with praises before Him!
 Let the Amen
 Sound from His people again;
Gladly for aye we adore him.

JOACHIM NEANDER, 1650–80
TR. CATHERINE WINKWORTH, 1829–78
Based on Psalms 103 and 150

JOACHIM NEANDER, THE GERHARDT OF THE CALVINISTS

WHILE all Germany during the latter half of the 17th century was singing the sublime lyrics of Paul Gerhardt, prince of Lutheran hymnists, the spirit of song was beginning to stir in the soul of another German poet—Joachim Neander. This man, whose name will always be remembered as the author of one of the most glorious hymns of praise of the Christian Church, was the first German hymn-writer produced by the Reformed, or Calvinistic, branch of the Protestant Church.

Hymnody in the Reformed Church had been seriously retarded by the iconoclastic views of Calvin and Zwingli. These Reformers had frowned on church choirs, organs, and every form of ecclesiastical art. Even hymns, such as those used by the Lutherans, were prohibited because they were the production of men. God could be worshiped in a worthy manner, according to Calvin's principles, only by hymns which were divinely inspired, namely the psalms of the Old Testament Psalter.

This gave rise to the practice of "versifying" the psalms, or putting them into metrical form, in order that they might be sung. Calvin's insistence that there should be the strictest adherence to the original text often resulted in crude paraphrases. The exclusive use of the psalms explains the development of so-called "psalmody" in the Reformed Church as over against "hymnody" in the Lutheran Church.

Psalmody had its inception in France, where Clement Marot, court poet to King Francis I, rendered a number of the psalms into verse. Marot was a gifted and versatile genius, but not inclined to piety or serious religion. However, his psalms became immensely popular with the French Huguenots and exerted a great influence in the struggle between the Protestants and the papal party. When Marot was compelled to flee to Geneva because of Roman persecution, he collaborated with Calvin in publishing the first edition of the famous *Genevan Psalter*, which appeared in 1543.

Following the death of Marot in 1544, Calvin engaged Theodore de Bèze to continue the work, and in 1562 the *Genevan Psalter* was published in completed form, containing all the psalms in metrical dress. The musical editor during the greater part of this period was Louis Bourgeois, to whom is generally ascribed the undying honor of being the composer of probably the most famous of all Christian hymn tunes, "Old Hundredth."

The *Genevan Psalter* was translated into many languages, and became the accepted hymnbook of the Reformed Church in Germany, England, Scotland, and Holland, as well as in France. In Germany the most popular version was a translation by Ambrosius Lobwasser, a professor of law at Königsberg, who, oddly enough, was a Lutheran.

It is quite probable that the *Genevan Psalter* was the first Protestant book of worship brought to American shores. In 1565, when a party of French Huguenots sailed from their homeland to escape persecution and to form a colony in South Carolina and Florida, they found their spiritual consolation in singing the psalm paraphrases of Marot and de Bèze. The expedition, however, came to a tragic end the following year when all the members of the colony were massacred by Spaniards, "not because they were Frenchmen, but because they were Protestants."

For more than 150 years Lutheran hymn-writers in Europe had been pouring forth a mighty stream of inspired song, but the voice of hymnody was stifled in the Reformed Church. Then came Joachim Neander. His life was short—he died at the age of thirty, and many of his hymns seem to have been written in the last few months before his death—but the influence he exerted on the subsequent hymnody of his Church earned for him the title, "the Gerhardt of the Reformed Church."

Neander's hymns are preeminently hymns of praise. Their jubilant tone and smooth rythmical flow are at once an invitation to sing them. They speedily found their way into Lutheran hymnbooks in Germany, and from thence to the entire Protestant world. Neander's most famous hymn, "Praise to the Lord, the Almighty," with its splendid chorale melody, grows in popularity with the passing of years, and promises to live on as one of the truly great lyrics of the Christian Church.

Joachim Neander was born in Bremen, Germany, in 1650. He came from a distinguished line of clergymen, his father, grandfather, great grandfather and great great grandfather having been pastors, and all of them bearing the name Joachim Neander.

Young Joachim entered the Academic Gymnasium of Bremen at the age of sixteen years. It seems that at first he led a careless and profligate life, joining in the sins and follies that characterized student life in his age.

In the year 1670, when Neander was twenty years old, he chanced to attend services in St. Martin's church, Bremen, where Theodore Under-Eyck had recently come as pastor. Two other students accompanied Neander, their main purpose being to criticize the preacher. However, they had not reckoned with the Spirit of God. The burning words of Under-Eyck made a powerful impression on the mind and heart of the youthful Neander, and he who had come to scoff remained to pray.

It proved the turning point in the spiritual life of the young student. Under the guidance of Under-Eyck he was led to embrace Christ as his Saviour, and from that time he and Under-Eyck became life-long friends.

The following year Neander became tutor to five young students, accompanying them to the University of Heidelberg. Three years later he became rector of the Latin school at Düsseldorf. This institution was under the supervision of a Reformed pastor, Sylvester Lürsen, an able man, but of contentious spirit. At first the two men worked together harmoniously, Neander assisting with pastoral duties and preaching occasionally, although he was not ordained as a clergyman. Later, however, he fell under the influence of a group of separatists, and began to imitate their practices. He refused to receive the Lord's Supper on the grounds that he could not partake of it with the unconverted. He induced others to follow his example. He also became less regular in his attendance at regular worship, and began to conduct prayer meetings and services of his own.

In 1676 the church council of Düsseldorf investigated his conduct and dismissed him from his office. Fourteen days after this action was taken, however, Neander signed a declaration in which he promised to abide by the rules of the church and school, whereupon he was reinstated.

There is a legend to the effect that, during the period of his suspension from service, he spent most of his time living in a cave in the beautiful Neanderthal, near Mettmann, on the Rhine, and that he wrote some of his hymns at this place. It is a well-established fact that Neander's great love for nature frequently led him to this place, and a cavern in the picturesque glen still bears the name of "Neander's Cave." One of the hymns which according to tradition was written in this cave bears the title, *"Unbegreiflich Gut, Wahrer Gott alleine."* It is a hymn of transcendent beauty. One of the stanzas reads:

> Thee all the mountains praise;
> The rocks and glens are full of songs of Thee!
> They bid me join my lays,
> And laud the mighty Rock, who, safe from every shock,
> Beneath Thy shadow here doth shelter me.

Many of Neander's hymns are odes to nature, but there is always a note of praise to nature's God. Witness, for instance:

> Heaven and earth, and sea and air,
> All their Maker's praise declare;
> Wake, my soul, awake and sing,
> Now thy grateful praises bring!

"Here behold me, as I cast me," a penitential hymn by Neander, has also found favor throughout Christendom.

In 1679 Neander's spiritual friend, Pastor Under-Eyck, invited him to come to Bremen and to become his assistant in St. Martin's Church. Although his salary was only 40 thalers a year and a free house, Neander joyfully accepted the appointment. The following year, however, he became sick, and after a lingering illness passed away May 31, 1680, at the age of only thirty years.

During his illness he experienced severe spiritual struggles, but he found comfort in the words, "It is better to hope unto death than to die in unbelief." On the day of his death he requested that Hebrews 7:9 be read to him. When asked how he felt, he replied: "The Lord has settled my account. Lord Jesus, make also me ready." A little later he said in a whisper: "It is well with me. The mountains shall be moved, and the hills shall tremble, yet the grace of God shall not depart from me, and His covenant of peace shall not be moved."

In evaluating the hymns of Neander, the English hymnologist James Mearns writes: "Many are of a decided subjective cast, but for this the circumstances of their origin, and the fact that the author did not expect them to be used in public worship, will sufficiently account. . . . But the glow and sweetness of his better hymns, their firm faith, originality, Scripturalness, variety, and mastery of rhythmical forms, and genuine lyric character fully entitle them to the high place they hold."

Another Reformed hymn-writer of this period was Friedrich Adolf Lampe, pastor primarius of St. Stephen's Church in Bremen and later rector and professor of Dogmatics and Church History at the University of Utrecht. Illness compelled him to resign his university post in 1727, and two years later he died at Bremen. Lampe has been called "the most important theologian that had appeared in the German Reformed Church since the Reformation period."

Among Lampe's hymns that have been translated into English are "My life is but a pilgrim-stand," "O healing Rock, O Lamb of God," "O wondrous love of Christ, how bright," and "How swift, O Lord most kind, most bountiful." Although his hymns are Scriptural and marked by a warm piety, they do not match those of Neander in lyric quality.

A Soul's Love for Christ

Thee will I love, my Strength, my Tower,
  Thee will I love, my Joy, my Crown;
Thee will I love with all my power,
  In all Thy works, and Thee alone;
Thee will I love, till the pure fire
Fill all my soul with chaste desire.

I thank Thee, uncreated Sun,
  That Thy bright beams on me have shined;
I thank Thee, who hast overthrown
  My foes, and healed my wounded mind;
I thank Thee, whose enlivening voice;
Bids my freed heart in Thee rejoice.

Uphold me in the doubtful race,
  Nor suffer me again to stray;
Strengthen my feet with steady pace
  Still to press forward in Thy way:
That all my powers, with all their might,
In Thy sole glory may unite.

Thee will I love, my Joy, my Crown;
  Thee will I love, my Lord, my God;
Thee will I love, beneath Thy frown,
  Or smile, Thy sceptre or Thy rod.
What though my flesh and heart decay?
Thee shall I love in endless day.

JOHANN SCHEFFLER, 1624-77
TR. JOHN WESLEY, 1703-91

114

A ROMAN MYSTIC AND HYMN-WRITER

IN JOHANN SCHEFFLER we have the singular example of a man who forsook the Lutheran Church to become a Romanist, but whose hymns have been adopted and sung by the very Church he sought to oppose and confound.

Scheffler was a contemporary of Gerhardt and Neander. He was born in Breslau, Silesia, in 1624. His father, Stanislaus Scheffler, was a Polish nobleman who had been compelled to leave his native land because of his Lutheran convictions. Young Scheffler became a medical student at Strassburg, Leyden and Padua, returning to Oels, Silesia, in 1649 to become the private physician to Duke Sylvius Nimrod of Württemberg-Oels.

During his sojourn in foreign lands he had come in contact with the writings of various mystics and began to lean strongly toward their teachings. At Oels he began to flaunt his separatist views by absenting himself from public worship and the Lord's Supper. When the Lutheran authorities refused to permit the publication of some poems he had written because of their strong mystical tendencies, Scheffler resigned his office and betook himself to Breslau, where he joined himself to a group of Jesuits. Here he pursued the study of the medieval mystics of the Roman Catholic Church, and in 1653 was confirmed as a member of that communion. At this time he took the name of Angelus Silesius, probably after a Spanish mystic named John ab Angelis.

After his ordination as a priest of the Roman Church he became a prolific writer and took special delight in directing bitter polemics against the Church of his childhood. Of these writings, it has well been said: "He certainly became more Roman than the Romans; and in his more than fifty controversial tractates, shows little of the sweetness and repose for which some have thought he left the Lutheran Church."

Scheffler, however, was a poet of the first rank. His verse, always tinged by the spirit of mysticism, sometimes soars to sublime

115

heights, and again descends to a coarse realism, particularly when he describes the terrors of judgment and hell.

His hymns, on the other hand, are almost uniformly of a high order. They are marked by a fervent love for Christ the heavenly Bridegroom, although the imagery, largely based on the Song of Solomon, is sometimes overdrawn, almost approaching the sensual. Few of his hymns reveal his Roman tendencies, and therefore were gladly received by the Protestants. Indeed, they came into more general use among the Lutherans than among the Catholics. They were greatly admired by Count von Zinzendorf, who included no less than 79 in his Moravian collection.

The mysticism of Scheffler often brought him dangerously close to the border-line of pantheism. Vaughn, in his *Hours with the Mystics*, compares Scheffler with Emerson, and declares that both resemble the Persian Sufis. Something of Scheffler's pantheistic ideas may be seen in the following lines:

> God in my nature is involved,
> As I in the divine;
> I help to make His being up,
> As much as He does mine.

And again in this:

> I am as rich as God; no grain of dust
> That is not mine, too: share with me He must.

Duffield, commenting on these astonishing lines, observes, "We need not wonder that this high-flown self-assumption carried him to the door of a Jesuit convent. It is in the very key of much that passes with Romanist theology for heavenly rapture and delight in God."

The pantheistic views of Scheffler may be discerned even in his dying prayer: "Jesus and Christ, God and man, bridegroom and brother, peace and joy, sweetness and delight, refuge and redemption, heaven and earth, eternity and time, love and all, receive my soul."

However, we must agree with Albert Knapp in his judgment of Scheffler's beautiful hymns, that "whencesoever they may come, they are an unfading ornament of the Church of Jesus Christ." The gem among them is "Thee will I love, my Strength, my Tower." Others that have come into general use are "Earth has nothing sweet or fair," "Thy soul, O Jesus, hallow me," "Come follow me, the Saviour spake," "Jesus, Saviour, come to me," "Thou holiest Love, whom most I love," "Loving Shepherd, kind and true," and "O Love, who formest me to wear." The latter has two moving stanzas:

> O Love who formest me to wear
>   The image of Thy Godhead here;
> Who seekest me with tender care
>   Through all my wanderings wild and drear:
> O Love, I give myself to Thee,
> Thine ever, only Thine to be.
>
> O Love, who once in time wast slain,
>   Pierced through and through with bitter woe;
> O Love, who wrestling thus didst gain
>   That we eternal joy might know:
> O Love, I give myself to Thee,
> Thine ever, only Thine to be.

An Early Missionary Hymn

Awake, Thou Spirit of the watchmen
 Who never held their peace by day or night,
Contending from the walls of Sion
 Against the foe, confiding in Thy might.
Throughout the world their cry is ringing still,
And bringing peoples to Thy holy will.

O Lord, now let Thy fire enkindle
 Our hearts, that everywhere its flame may go,
And spread the glory of redemption
 Till all the world Thy saving grace shall know.
O harvest Lord, look down on us and view
How white the field; the laborers, how few!

The prayer Thy Son himself hath taught us
 We offer now to Thee at His command;
Behold and hearken, Lord; Thy children
 Implore Thee for the souls of every land:
With yearning hearts they make their ardent plea;
O hear us, Lord, and say, 'Thus shall it be.'

Send forth, O Lord, Thy strong Evangel
 By many messengers, all hearts to win;
Make haste to help us in our weakness;
 Break down the realm of Satan, death and sin:
The circle of the earth shall then proclaim
Thy Kingdom, and the glory of Thy Name.

KARL HEINRICH VON BOGATZKY, 1690–1774
TR. WINFRED DOUGLAS, 1867–1944, and ARTHUR W. FARLANDER, 1898–

HYMN-WRITERS OF THE PIETIST SCHOOL

SPIRITUAL revivals in the Christian Church have always been accompanied by an outburst of song. This was true of the Reformation, which witnessed the birth of the Lutheran Church, and it was also characteristic of the Pietistic movement, which infused new life and fervor into that communion. The Pietistic revival, which in many respects was similar to the Puritan and Wesleyan movements in England, had its inception in Germany in the latter part of the 17th century and continued during the first half of the 18th century. It quickly spread to other Lutheran countries, particularly Scandinavia, and its influence has been felt even to the present time.

The leader of the movement was Philipp Jacob Spener, pastor of St. Nicolai Church, in Berlin. Spener, although a loyal and zealous son of the Lutheran Church, was not blind to the formalism and dead orthodoxy which had overtaken it following the Thirty Years' War and which threatened to dry up the streams of spiritual life. To stimulate spiritual endeavor and personal piety, Spener and his followers organized Bible study groups. They also encouraged private assemblies for mutual edification. These were known as *Collegia Pietatis,* which gave rise to the name, "Pietists."

August Hermann Francke, the foremost disciple of Spener, succeeded the latter as leader of the movement. The University of Halle, where Francke was called as professor in 1691, became the center of Pietism. Here Francke laid the foundations for the remarkable philanthropic and educational institutions that made his name known throughout the Christian world. It began in 1695 when the greathearted man opened a room in his own house for the instruction of poor children. Within a few years he had established his great orphanage, a high school, and a home for destitute students. The orphans' home was erected on a site where formerly there had been a beer garden.

When Francke began his work he had no money, nor did he receive any support from the state; but as the marvelous work

119

progressed funds poured in from all quarters. In the year of his death, 1727, more than 2,000 children were receiving care and instruction from 170 teachers. Altogether, some 6,000 graduates of theology left Halle during Francke's career, "men imbued with his spirit, good exegetes, and devoted pastors, who spread their doctrines all over Germany, and in the early decades of the 18th century occupied a majority of the pulpits."

Halle also became the cradle of the modern missionary movement. From this place, in 1705, Bartholomew Ziegenbalg and Henry Plütschau were sent forth as the first missionaries to India, nearly a century before William Carey left England for the same field. At Halle the youthful Count von Zinzendorf became a pupil under Francke and received the inspiration that in later years led to the establishment of the far-reaching missions of the Moravians. To Halle, the founder of Methodism, John Wesley, came in 1738, shortly after his conversion in London, in order to become more familiar with the teachings of Luther and the Pietists.

The secret of the marvelous success of Francke's efforts may be read in the simple inscription on the monument erected to his memory in front of the famous orphanage at Halle. It reads: "He trusted in God."

Neither Francke nor Spener were hymn-writers of note, although each composed a few songs. The Pietist movement, however, gave birth to a great revival in hymnody in Germany, both in Lutheran and Reformed circles. At Halle it was Johann Anastasius Freylinghausen who not only became the representative hymnist of the Pietists, but also succeeded Francke as head of the great Halle institutions.

Freylinghausen was a student at the University of Jena when he first heard the preaching of Francke. Shortly afterward he followed him to Halle, and in 1695 became Francke's colleague. He preached at vesper services, conducted midweek meetings, taught classes in the orphanage school, and delivered lectures on homiletics. He served without salary for ten years, since Francke was obliged to use all his income for the support of his institutions of mercy. In 1715 Freylinghausen married Francke's only daughter. At her baptism as an infant he had been her sponsor, and she had received his name, Johanna Anastasia. It was after Francke's death in 1727 that the Halle institutions reached their highest development under the direction of Freylinghausen. When the latter died in 1739, he was buried beside his beloved friend.

Freylinghausen's *Geistreiches Gesangbuch* became the standard hymnbook of the Pietistic movement. The first edition appeared in 1704 and contained 683 hymns. A second hymnbook was published in 1714, when 815 were added. The two collections were combined in 1741 by G. A. Francke, and published as one hymnbook, containing 1,582 hymns and 600 tunes. Freylinghausen was the author of forty-four of these hymns, and is also said to have composed some of the melodies.

The hymns of Freylinghausen are the most worthy of all those produced by the Pietist school. They are marked by genuine piety, depth of feeling, rich Christian experience, and faithfulness in Scriptural expression. The tunes employed, however, were often a distinct departure from the traditional Lutheran chorales, and were not always suited to congregational worship. The so-called "Jesus hymns," which reached their greatest development among the Pietists, find their sweetest expression in Freylinghausen's "Who is there like Thee?" His most famous hymn, "O Jesus, Source of calm repose," was greatly admired by John Wesley, who translated it into English in 1737. Here is Wesley's rendering of the first two stanzas:

> O Jesus, Source of calm repose,
> Thy like no man nor angel knows,
>   Fairest among ten thousand fair!
> E'en those whom death's sad fetters bound,
> Whom thickest darkness compassed round,
>   Find light and life, if Thou appear.
>
> Renew Thine image, Lord, in me,
> Lowly and gentle may I be;
>   No charms but these to Thee are dear;
> No anger may'st Thou ever find,
> No pride, in my unruffled mind,
>   But faith, and heaven-born peace, be there.

It is not strange that from Halle, from whence such mighty missionary influences flowed, should also go forth the first Protestant missionary hymn. It was in 1750 that Karl Heinrich von Bogatzky, while working among the orphans of the Franckean institutions, wrote his famous hymn, "Awake, Thou Spirit of the watchmen."

Bogatzky, who had come from a noble Hungarian family, was disowned by his father when he chose to enroll as a theological student at Halle rather than to prepare for a career as an army officer.

His health failed him, however, and he was unable to enter the ministry. For many years he devoted himself to hymn-writing and devotional literature. He also traveled as a lay preacher. Because of his noble birth he was able to exert a considerable influence in the higher circles of German society. From 1746 until his death in 1774, he lived at the Halle orphanage. He was the author of some 411 hymns, but few of them possess the poetic and spiritual fervor of his missionary hymn.

Johann Jacob Rambach was another important hymn-writer of this period. The son of a cabinet maker of Halle, young Rambach attended the free school established by Francke and came under the direct influence of the great Pietist leader.

Like many a youth, however, he felt that his education was complete at the age of thirteen years, at which time he left school to work in his father's shop. The Lord, on the other hand, seems to have had other plans for the lad, and it was not long before young Rambach suffered a dislocated ankle. Confined to his bed for several weeks, he again turned to his books, and, before he had recovered, the desire to resume his studies took possession of him.

Rambach eventually became one of the outstanding theologians of Halle, as well as preacher at the school church. In 1731 he removed to Giessen to become superintendent and first professor of theology. Here he found conditions vastly different from those at Halle. He was particularly grieved over the fact that his preaching did not seem to bear fruit. Often his efforts to bring about healthier spiritual conditions met with opposition and scoffing on the part of his adversaries. He died in 1735 at the early age of forty-two years—from intense sorrow over the spiritual indifference of his flock, so it has been claimed.

Rambach wrote many splendid hymns, among them two confirmation hymns, "Lord, to Thee I now surrender," and "My Maker, be Thou nigh." Another, "O Thou Love unbounded," has been called the pearl of Rambach's lyrics. It was written on the unusual theme of the patience and long-suffering of God. Rambach's fame, however, rests principally on his work as a hymnologist. During his life-time he published a number of collections from all sources. These hymns were chosen with fine discrimination, and Rambach was the first hymn editor to make a distinction between hymns for congregational worship and those particularly suited for private devotion.

The beautiful Advent hymn, "Rejoice, all ye believers," as well as the Epiphany hymn, "O Saviour of our race," also date from the Pietistic period. Both hymns apparently were written in 1700 by Laurentius Laurentii, cantor and director of music in the Lutheran cathedral at Bremen. Laurentii was not only a splendid musician, but also a hymn-writer of high order, and no less than thirty-four of his hymns were included in the Freylinghausen collections.

Other hymnists of the Pietist school include Christian Scriver, writer of the famous devotional book, *Seelenschatz;* Gottfried Arnold, a noted church historian; Ernst Gottlieb Woltersdorf, founder of an orphanage at Bunzlau, and Christian Richter, a pious physician and an associate of Francke. Few of their hymns, however, are in common use today.

Finally we must mention a German woman of this period to whom we are indebted for a hymn that has grown increasingly popular in recent years. She was Catherina Amalia Dorothea von Schlegel, of whom we know very little except that she contributed a number of lyrics to a collection of spiritual songs published at Wernigerode in 1752. One of these bore the title, *Stille, mein Wille! Dein Jesus hilft siegen,* evidently based on Psalm 46:10, "Be still and know that I am God." It appears from what evidence is available that the writer was a lady attached to the ducal court at Cöthen. The English translation, which appeared for the first time in Jane Borthwick's *Hymns from the Land of Luther,* has these beautiful stanzas:

Be still, my soul; the Lord is on thy side;
  Bear patiently the cross of grief or pain;
Leave to thy God to order and provide;
  In every change He faithful will remain.
Be still, my soul: thy best, thy heavenly Friend
  Through thorny ways leads to a joyful end.

Be still, my soul; thy God doth undertake
  To guide the future as He has the past.
Thy hope, thy confidence, let nothing shake;
  All now mysterious shall be bright at last.
Be still, my soul; the waves and winds still know
  His voice who ruled them while He dwelt below.

A Hymn of Longing for Christ

O Son of God, we wait for Thee,
    We long for Thine appearing;
We know Thou sittest on the throne,
    And we Thy Name are bearing.
Who trusts in Thee may joyful be,
    And see Thee, Lord, descending
    To bring us bliss unending.

We wait for Thee, 'mid toil and pain,
    In weariness and sighing;
But glad that Thou our guilt hast borne,
    And cancelled it by dying.
Hence, cheerfully may we with Thee
    Take up our cross and bear it,
    Till we the crown inherit.

We wait for Thee; here Thou hast won
    Our hearts to hope and duty;
But while our spirits feel Thee near,
    Our eyes would see Thy beauty;
We fain would be at rest with Thee
    In peace and joy supernal,
    In glorious life eternal.

We wait for Thee; soon Thou wilt come,
    The time is swiftly nearing;
In this we also do rejoice,
    And long for Thine appearing.
O bliss 'twill be when Thee we see,
    Homeward Thy people bringing,
    With ecstasy and singing!

PHILIPP FRIEDRICH HILLER, 1699–1769
TR. JOSEPH AUGUSTUS SEISS, 1823–1904

124

THE WÜRTTEMBERG HYMN-WRITERS

THE Pietistic movement quickly made its influence felt in all parts of Germany. In some quarters, especially in the latter stages of the movement, it assumed more radical forms. Sometimes it developed into emotionalism and mysticism. The hymns were often of a subjective type, which led the worshiper to think more about his own spiritual experiences and inner feelings than to direct his thoughts to Him who alone can redeem and sanctify.

Some of the Pietist hymnists, notably Woltersdorf, were given to the use of inordinate language and even sensuous descriptions for the purpose of arousing intense emotion. In one of Woltersdorf's passion hymns, he dwells morbidly on every detail of the physical suffering of Christ, and in another hymn he borrows Scheffler's figure which likens the soul to a bee deriving sustenance from the crimson wounds of Christ.

On the other hand, the Pietistic hymn is exemplified in its highest and noblest form in the writings of the so-called Württemberg school of hymnists, the chief exponent of which was Philipp Friedrich Hiller. Württemberg was blessed with the famous scholar and theologian, Johann Albrecht Bengel, whose sound doctrinal views and profound understanding of human nature not only led to a healthy development of Pietism in southern Germany, but also left a lasting impression on all the theological students who came under his influence at the training schools at Denkendorf. Hiller was one of these.

Hiller's hymns and those of the other Württemberg hymnists never indulge in the weak emotional effusions of which the later Halle hymn-writers were often guilty.

Hiller was a man sorely tried in the school of adversity. Shortly after he began his pastorate at Steinheim, in 1748, he lost his voice and was unable to continue his pulpit duties. However, he believed implicitly in the Pauline teaching that "to them that love God all things work together for good," and, when his voice became silent, his spirit began to sing in tones richer and sweeter than ever. Witness, for example, the note of tenderness in the last stanza of his baptismal hymn, "God, in human flesh appearing":

> Feeble is the love of mother,
>   Father's blessings are as naught,
> When compared, my King and Brother,
>   With the wonders Thou hast wrought;
> Thus it pleased Thy heavenly meekness;
>   Pleasing also be my praise,
> Till my songs of earthly weakness
>   Burst into celestial lays.

Hiller was a prolific writer, his hymns numbering no less than 1,075 in all. Most of these were written for his devotional book, *Geistliches Liederkästlein,* a work that holds an honored place beside the Bible in many pious homes in southern Germany. Indeed, it has been carried by German emigrants to all parts of the world. It is related that when a Germany colony in the Caucasus was attacked by a fierce Circassian tribe about a hundred years ago, the parents cut up their copies of the *Liederkästlein* and distributed its leaves among their children who were being carried off into slavery.

Hiller's hymns, though simple in form and artless in expression, have retained a strong hold on the people of Württemberg, and are extensively used to this day. Among the more popular are "O boundless joy, there is salvation," "Jesus Christ as King is reigning," and "O Son of God, we wait for Thee."

Hiller's rule for hymn-writing, as set forth in one of his prefaces, could be followed with profit by many modern writers of sentimental tendencies. He says: "I have always striven for simplicity. Bombastic expressions of a soaring imagination, a commonplace and too familiar manner of speaking of Christ as a brother, of kisses and embraces, of individual souls as the particular Bride of Christ, of naive and pet images for the Christ-child,—all these I have scrupulously avoided, and serious-minded men will not blame me if, in this respect, I have revered the majesty of our Lord."

Another representative of the Württemberg school was Baron Christoph Carl Ludwig von Pfeil, a diplomat of high attainments and noble, devout character. In September, 1763, he was appointed by Frederick the Great as Prussian ambassador to the Diets of Swabia and Franconia. He was created a baron by Emperor Joseph II shortly afterwards.

Pfeil began writing hymns at the age of eighteen years, at which time he passed through a profound spiritual experience, and he continued the practice as his chief diversion throughout life. He was a prolific writer, his published lyrics numbering about 850. Some of his hymns were written on various phases of civil life. One dealing with the Christian home is typical:

> O blest the house, what'er befall,
> Where Jesus Christ is All in all;
> Yea, if He were not dwelling there,
> How poor and dark and void it were!

The Silesian pastors, Johann Andreas Rothe and Johann Mentzer, also may be regarded as belonging to the more conservative Pietistic hymn-writers. Rothe was pastor at Berthelsdorf, having been brought there through the influence of Count von Zinzendorf, who had heard him preach in Silesia. The Moravian community of Herrnhut formed a part of Rothe's parish, and he took a keen interest in the activities of Zinzendorf and his followers. However, when Rothe, in 1737, found it necessary to report to the ecclesiastical authorities that the Moravians were deviating from sound Lutheran doctrine, the friendship between him and Zinzendorf ceased, and Rothe found it advisable to remove to Thommendorf, where he died in 1758.

Rothe wrote approximately forty hymns, the best known of which is "Now I have found the ground wherein." This hymn was greatly admired by John Wesley and was translated by him in 1740. Because it first appeared in the Moravian hymnbook, the Lutherans suspected that Zinzendorf was the author. Upon discovering that it was written by Rothe, they quickly adopted it.

Mentzer, who has given us the beautiful hymn, "O would, my God, that I could praise Thee," was born at Jahmen, Silesia, in 1658. For thirty-eight years he was pastor at Kemnitz, Saxony, at which place his hymns, about thirty in number, were written. There is an exalted strain in his hymns of praise, as witness:

> O all ye powers that He implanted,
>   Arise, keep silence thus no more,
> Put forth the strength that He hath granted,
>   Your noblest work is to adore;
> O soul and body, be ye meet
> With heartfelt praise your Lord to greet.

This hymn sometimes begins with the line, "O that I had a thousand voices."

A Noble Hymn of Worship

Light of light, enlighten me,
*   Now anew the day is dawning;*
Sun of grace, the shadows flee,
*   Brighten Thou this holy morning;*
With Thy joyous sunshine blest,
Happy is my day of rest!

Fount of all our joy and peace,
*   To Thy living waters lead me;*
Thou from earth my soul release,
*   And with grace and mercy feed me.*
Bless Thy Word, that it may prove
Rich in fruits that Thou dost love.

Hence all care, all vanity,
*   For the day to God is holy;*
Come, Thou glorious Majesty,
*   Deign to fill this temple lowly;*
Naught today my soul shall move,
Simply resting in Thy love.

Let me with my heart today,
*   Holy, holy, holy, singing,*
Rapt awhile from earth away,
*   All my soul to Thee upspringing,*
Have a foretaste inly given,
How they worship Thee in heaven.

BENJAMIN SCHMOLCK, 1672–1737
TR. CATHERINE WINKWORTH, 1829–78a.

HOW A GREAT ORGANIST INSPIRED TWO HYMNISTS

HILE all the hymn-writers of Germany in the early part of the eighteenth century were more or less influenced by the Pietistic movement, there were some who nevertheless refused to be carried away by the emotional extravagances of which some of the Halle song writers were often guilty. In the hymns of these more conservative psalmists we find a happy blending of objective teaching and a warm, personal faith that reminds us of the earlier hymns of Gerhardt.

The chief representatives of this more typical Lutheran school were Benjamin Schmolck, a beloved pastor and a poet of rare ability, and Erdmann Neumeister, creator of the Church Cantata. It was the age in which John Sebastian Bach lived and wrought, and this prince of Lutheran composers, whose title of "high priest of church music" has never been disputed, gave of his musical genius to help make the hymns of Schmolck and Neumeister immortal.

Next to Gerhardt, there is no German hymnist whose name is more frequently found in hymnbooks today than that of Schmolck. Born at Brauchitzdorf, Silesia, where his father was pastor, he was sent to school at Lauban at the age of sixteen. After an absence of five years, the young man returned home and was invited to fill his father's pulpit. The sermon he preached so pleased the father that he determined to send him to the University of Leipzig to study for the ministry. In 1697 he returned to Brauchitzdorf to be ordained as his father's assistant.

In 1702 Schmolck became pastor of Friedenskirche at Schweidnitz, in Silesia. According to the terms of the Peace of Westphalia in 1648, all of the churches in this district had been turned over to the Roman Catholics, and only a "meeting-house," built of timber and clay and without tower or bells, was allowed to the Lutherans. Here Schmolck labored patiently for thirty-five years under the most trying circumstances, not even being permitted to administer communion to the dying except by consent of the Catholic authorities.

129

Schmolck's hymns and spiritual songs, numbering 1,183 in all, brought him fame all over Germany. Many have been translated into English. His fervent love for the Saviour is beautifully reflected in the hymn:

> My Jesus, as Thou wilt,
>   O may Thy will be mine;
> Into Thy hand of love
>   I would my all resign.
> Through sorrow or through joy,
>   Conduct me as Thine own,
> And help me still to say,
>   "My Lord, Thy will be done!"

"Light of light, enlighten me," a noble hymn of praise and adoration, has been happily wedded to a glorious chorale that is usually attributed to Bach. Other hymns that have won renown throughout the Christian world include "Open now thy gates of beauty," "Welcome, Thou Victor in the strife," "Blessed Jesus, here we stand," "What our Father does is well," "My God, I know that I must die," "Hallelujah, lo, He wakes," "My truest Friend abides in heaven," and "Precious Word from God in heaven." The joyous spirit in many of Schmolck's hymns may be seen reflected in the beautiful temple hymn:

> Open now thy gates of beauty,
>   Zion, let me enter there,
> Where my soul in joyful duty
>   Waits on Him who answers prayer:
> O how blessed is this place,
> Filled with solace, light, and grace.

Neumeister followed the example of Schmolck in becoming an ardent champion of the older, conservative Lutheranism. Although he was greatly influenced as a youth by the writings of Francke, he later became convinced that there were dangerous tendencies in the Halle and Herrnhut movements, and he did not hesitate to issue violent polemics against them.

His hymns, on the other hand, offer a curious contrast to his other writings. Often they reveal a warmth and tenderness of feeling that would have merited a place for them in any Pietist hymnbook. This may be seen in the hymn, "Sinners Jesus will receive," which has also been translated "Sinners may to Christ draw near":

Sinners Jesus will receive:
Tell this word of grace to all
Who the heavenly pathway leave,
All who linger, all who fall;
This can bring them back again,
"Christ receiveth sinful men."

Neumeister became pastor of St. James Church in Hamburg in 1715, where he remained for forty-one years until his death in 1756. His fame rests not on his hymns alone, although he wrote 650 in all, but Neumeister will also be remembered as the originator of the Church Cantata. In this new field of musical art he was fortunate in having the co-operation of such a genius as Bach.

Bach belonged to the fifth generation of a remarkable family of musicians. As many as thirty-seven of the family are known to have held important musical positions. John Sebastian, who is by far the greatest musician the Protestant Church has ever produced, was born in Eisenach on March 21, 1685. The greater part of his life was spent in Leipzig, where he labored from 1723 until his death in 1750 as cantor of the Thomas school and director of music at the St. Thomas and St. Nicolai churches.

Bach's devotion to the Lutheran Church has been likened to that of Palestrina to the Church of Rome. There is no loftier example of musical genius dedicated to the service of the Christian religion than we find in the life of the great German musician. Bach felt that his life was consecrated to God, to the honor of his Church, and to the blessing of mankind. Although it was an age when the opera flourished in Europe, Bach gave no attention to it, but devoted all his talent to church music.

As master of organ composition, Bach has never had an equal. His chorales and passion music also belong in a class by themselves. A famous critic has written: "Mozart and Beethoven failed in oratorio, Schubert in opera; the Italian operas of Gluck and Handel have perished. Even in the successful work of these men there is a strange inequality. But upon all that Bach attempted—and the amount of his work is no less a marvel than its quality—he affixed the stamp of final and inimitable perfection."

The twenty-seven years Bach spent in Leipzig were the most productive of his whole career. It was here that he composed most of his immortal organ music. Here also he wrote the *St. Matthew Passion*, the *St. John Passion*, the *St. Mark Passion*, the *B Minor Mass*, as well as numerous other cantatas and masses. It is said that a cantata was sung in St. Thomas Church every Sunday, all of them composed by Bach. In all, he created five different cantatas for each Sunday of the Church Year.

Strangely enough, there is not a single hymn tune that can be credited with absolute certainty to Bach, and yet no composer ever did more for the music of Protestant hymnody than did this great master of composition. Bach chose to take the hymn-tunes of others and to make new arrangements or harmonizations of them. In his hands they invariably became new creations that more rightfully belonged to him than to the original composers; yet he never claimed them.

Commenting on the great contribution that Bach made to Protestant hymnody, Karl Nef says: "As the Gregorian Choral was to Palestrina the framework of his labors, so for Bach was the Protestant church hymn. It fulfilled the high mission of bridging over the gulf between Bach's complicated creations and the emotional life of the masses, and thus making these accessible to the great generality of listeners."

Among the great chorales to which Bach gave their present form may be mentioned *Ach bleib bei uns, Herr Jesu Christ; Christus der ist mein Leben; Herzlich thut mich verlangen; Freu dich sehr, O meine Seele; Jesu, meine Freude; Jesu, meines Herzens Freud; O Gott, du frommer Gott; Schmücke dich, O liebe Seele; Wachet auf! ruft uns die Stimme;* and *Liebster Jesu, wir sind hier.*

During his last years Bach became blind, but even after his vision failed he continued his unceasing labors, revising older compositions and writing new ones. Death ended his extraordinary career on July 28, 1750.

One of the tragic penalties that genius must always pay is the lack of understanding and appreciation by a contemporary generation. Such was the bitter experience of Bach. While an occasional musician who could rise above the feeling of proverbial envy was able to recognize the works of a master, the music of Bach completely passed over the heads of ordinary listeners and critics of his day. The reception given the *St. Matthew Passion* at the first rendition in the St. Thomas Church on Good Friday afternoon, April 15, 1729, was shameful. One of Bach's own pupils has described it in these words:

"Some high officials and well-born ladies in one of the galleries began to sing the first chorale from their hymnbooks. But as the dramatic music proceeded, they were thrown into the greatest wonderment, saying to each other, 'What does it all mean?' While one old lady, a widow, exclaimed, 'Ach Gott! 'Tis surely an opera-comedy!"

Some of Bach's critics even seized upon the occasion to charge that his work was unsatisfactory, and a portion of his salary was withheld until such time as he would listen to the advice of the councilors who lorded it over him! How little he was appreciated in Leipzig may be judged by the fact that his widow, the beloved Magdalena Bach, was permitted to go as a pauper to a public almshouse two years after the death of her husband.

Nearly a hundred years went by, and then a little 11-year-old Jewish lad in Berlin by the name of Felix Mendelssohn heard a strain of the *Passion,* and from that moment he "played Bach, dreamed Bach, and preached Bach in an age that knew the master but little and loved him less." A few days later Felix was baptized as a Christian, and by the time he was confirmed he knew the whole masterpiece by heart. At the age of twenty, when he himself had already achieved world renown, young Mendelssohn resolved to give Bach back to the world. On March 11, 1829, exactly a century after Bach had first given the *St. Matthew Passion,* it was sung by a chorus of four hundred voices, and more than a thousand people who wanted to hear it were turned away. Bach at last had come into his own. "And to think," Mendelssohn afterward jubilantly exclaimed, "that it should be a Jew that gave back to the people this greatest of Christian works!"

With the passing of the years, Bach's genius is being recognized more and more throughout the Church. The performance of his cantatas by the Catholic Schola Cantorum of Paris "is only one of many testimonies to the universality of the art of this son of Lutheranism." There is something in his mighty compositions that touches the deepest springs of religious emotion, regardless of creed or communion.

A Hymn on the Mystical Union

Thou hidden love of God, whose height,
    Whose depth unfathomed no man knows,
I see from far Thy beauteous light,
    Inly I sigh for Thy repose.
My heart is pained, nor can it be
At rest, till it find rest in Thee.

Thy secret voice invites me still
    The sweetness of Thy yoke to prove;
And fain I would; but though my will
    Seem fixed, yet wide my passions rove.
Yet hindrances strew all the way;
I aim at Thee, yet from Thee stray.

Is there a thing beneath the sun
    That strives with Thee my heart to share?
Ah! tear it thence, and reign alone,
    The Lord of every motion there.
Then shall my heart from earth be free,
When it hath found repose in Thee.

Each moment draw from earth away
    My heart that lowly waits Thy call!
Speak to my inmost soul, and say,
    "I am thy Love, thy God, thy All!"
To feel Thy power, to hear Thy voice,
To taste Thy love, be all my choice!

GERHARD TERSTEEGEN, 1697-1769
TR. JOHN WESLEY, 1703-91

GERHARD TERSTEEGEN, HYMN-WRITER AND MYSTIC

WHILE Benjamin Schmolck must be regarded as the greatest of Lutheran hymn-writers in Germany during the eighteenth century, Gerhard Tersteegen holds the same distinction among German Reformed hymnists. Except for the Wesleys in England, no man during his age exerted perhaps so great a spiritual influence in evangelical circles of all lands as did Tersteegen. In some respects his religious views bordered on fanaticism, but no one could question his deep sincerity and his earnest desire to live the life hidden with Christ in God.

Born at Mörs, Rhenish Prussia, November 25, 1697, Tersteegen was only six years old when his father died. It had been the plan of his parents that he should become a Reformed minister, but the death of the father made it impossible for the mother to carry out this purpose. At the age of sixteen he was apprenticed to a merchant, and four years later entered business on his own account.

Although he was only twenty years old at this time, he began to experience seasons of deep spiritual despondency. This lasted for nearly five years, during which time he changed his occupation to that of silk weaving, since he desired more leisure for prayer and meditation. It was not until the year 1724, while on a journey to a neighboring town, that light seemed to dawn on his troubled soul, and he received the assurance that God's grace in Christ Jesus was sufficient to atone for all sin. In the joy and peace which he had found, he immediately wrote the beautiful hymn, "How gracious, kind and good, my great High Priest, art Thou."

From this time until the close of his life, Tersteegen began to devote his energies more and more to religious work and literary activities. An independent religious movement known as *"Stillen im Lande"* had begun about this time, and he soon became known as a leader among these people.

Tersteegen had already ceased to associate with his friends in the Reformed Church, and had gone over to religious mysticism. In one of his strange spiritual moods he wrote what he called "a covenant between myself and God" and signed it with his own blood.

Finally he gave up business pursuits entirely, and his home became the refuge of multitudes of sick and spiritually troubled people. It came to be known as the "Pilgrim's Hut," from the fact that many found a temporary retreat here, as well as spiritual help and guidance. Tersteegen also traveled extensively in his own district, and made frequent visits to Holland to hold meetings there.

Tersteegen never married, and for this reason he was accused of teaching celibacy. Several sects, including the Moravians, sought to induce him to become one of their number, but he steadfastly refused to identify himself with any organized church body. He died at Mülheim, April 30, 1769.

Tersteegen's hymns, as well as his other writings, reflect his spirit of mysticism. His soul was imbued with the sense of the nearness of God, and, through a life of spiritual communion and by renunciation of the world, he developed a simplicity of faith and a child-like trust that found beautiful expression in his hymns.

Two of these, "Thou hidden love of God whose height" and "Lo, God is here, let us adore," made a deep impression on John Wesley, who translated the former during his visit to Georgia in 1736, and the other some time later. Wesley had become familiar with Tersteegen's hymns through contact with Moravian pilgrims who were crossing the Atlantic on the same ship on which he sailed. "Lo, God is here, let us adore" has several English versions, including "God is in His temple" and "God himself is present." Wesley's beautiful translation reads:

> Lo, God is here, let us adore,
> And own how dreadful is this place!
> Let all within us feel His power,
> And silent bow before His face;
> Who knows His power, His grace who prove,
> Serve Him with awe, with reverence love.
>
> Lo, God is here! Him day and night
> United choirs of angels sing;
> To Him enthroned above all height,
> The hosts of heaven their praises bring;
> Disdain not, Lord, our meaner song,
> Who praise Thee with a faltering tongue.
>
> Being of beings, may our praise
> Thy courts with grateful fragrance fill!

> Still may we stand before Thy face,
>   Still hear and do Thy sovereign will;
> To Thee may all our thoughts arise
> A true and ceaseless sacrifice.

Another of Tersteegen's hymns, "God calling yet! shall I not hear?" is one of the most stirring calls to repentance in Christian hymnody. It was rendered into English by Mrs. Sarah Borthwick Findlater in the series of translations known as *Hymns from the Land of Luther*.

Other noted hymns by Tersteegen include "Jesus, whom Thy Church doth own," "O Love divine, all else transcending," and "Triumph, ye heavens," the latter a Christmas lyric of exultant strain.

Tersteegen's conception of the high place which hymnody should occupy in Christian worship is revealed in the following words: "The pious, reverential singing of hymns has something angelic about it and is accompanied by divine blessing. It quiets and subdues the troubled emotions; it drives away cares and anxieties; it strengthens, refreshes and encourages the soul; it draws the mind unconsciously from external things, lifts up the soul to joyful adoration, and thus prepares us to worship in spirit and in truth. We should sing with the spirit of reverence, with sincerity, simplicity and hearty desire. . . . When you sing, O soul, remember that you are as truly communing with the holy and omnipresent God as when you are praying. Consider that you are standing in spirit before the throne of God with countless thousands of angels and spirits of the just, and that you are blending your weak praises with the music of heaven. Serve the Lord with fear, and rejoice with trembling."

Following a Heavenly Leader

Jesus, still lead on,
Till our rest be won;
And although the way be cheerless,
We will follow, calm and fearless;
Guide us by Thy hand
To our Fatherland!

If the way be drear,
If the foe be near,
Let not faithless fear o'ertake us,
Let not faith and hope forsake us;
For through many a foe
To our home we go.

When we seek relief
From a long-felt grief,
When temptations come alluring,
Make us patient and enduring;
Show us that bright shore
Where we weep no more!

Jesus, still lead on,
Till our rest be won;
Heavenly Leader, still direct us,
Still support, console, protect us,
Till we safely stand
In our Fatherland!

NICOLAUS LUDWIG VON ZINZENDORF, 1700-1760
TR. JANE L. BORTHWICK, 1813-1897, a.

138

ZINZENDORF AND MORAVIAN HYMNODY

THE CHURCH of the Moravian Brethren is famous for two things: its missionary zeal and its love for church music. It owes both of these distinguishing characteristics to its great founder and patron leader, Nicolaus Ludwig, Count von Zinzendorf. Not only was this very unusual man a gifted writer of hymns, but he was also an ardent exponent of foreign missions.

Zinzendorf was only ten years old when his soul was fired with a passionate desire to do something to help win the world for Christ. He was a pupil at the famous Pietist school of Francke at Halle, Germany, at the time, and through his endeavors a mission society known as "The Order of the Grain of Mustard Seed," was organized among the lads of his own age.

A few years later he chanced to see a copy of Sternberg's masterpiece, *"Ecce Homo,"* depicting Christ before Pilate and the Jewish mob, wearing His crown of thorns. Beneath the famous picture were inscribed the words:

> This have I done for thee;
> What hast thou done for Me?

From that moment Zinzendorf took as his life motto: "I have but one passion, and that is He and only He." On his wedding day, in 1722, he and his young bride decided to renounce their rank and to dedicate their lives to the task of winning souls for Christ.

The Lord took them at their word. In that same year a number of Protestant refugees from Moravia who had been compelled to leave their homes because of Roman Catholic persecution arrived in Saxony and found refuge on Zinzendorf's large estate. They were a remnant of the Bohemian Brethren, a heroic religious communion which dated back to the days of the noble martyr, John Huss. Though relentlessly hunted and persecuted for more than three centuries, this early evangelical body had continued to maintain its existence in the form of secret religious circles known as "the hidden seed."

Under the protection of Count Zinzendorf, the little band of Moravian refugees established a religious center which they called "Herrnhut." Zinzendorf, who was a Lutheran, induced them to adopt the Augsburg Confession as a statement of their doctrine, but they continued to exist as an independent church body. People from all over Europe, hearing that religious freedom was enjoyed on the Zinzendorf estates, flocked to Herrnhut in large numbers to escape persecution, and it soon became a flourishing colony.

In 1737 Zinzendorf accepted ordination as a bishop of the Brethren, and thus became the real leader of the organization. He immediately began to impart his own missionary zeal to the Moravian movement. Two of the earliest missionaries, David Nitschmann and Leonard Dober, were sent to the island of St. Thomas, in the West Indies, to preach the Gospel to the negro slaves. The blacks were so embittered because of the cruel treatment received at the hands of their white taskmasters that they refused to listen to the missionaries, and very little progress could be made. At last, in order to gain their confidence, Dober sold himself as a slave and shared their hardships with them. He soon died, however, as a result of the privations he suffered. The story of his heroic sacrifice so moved the heart of Prime Minister Wilberforce of England that he forthwith began the movement which eventually led to the emancipation of all slaves in the British Empire.

Missionary zeal continued to flourish among the Moravians, and the little colony of Herrnhut became known as one of the most famous missionary centers of Christendom. Every one of its members felt that he possessed no permanent habitation in this world, and was prepared always to be sent to any part of the globe.

Though still a small organization today, the Moravian Church has never lost its missionary spirit. It is claimed that for every fifty-eight members of the Church at home, there is one missionary in foreign lands. When Carey went to India, the Moravians already had 165 missionaries in non-Christian lands in various parts of the world.

Zinzendorf was a great lover of music. Even as a boy, he wrote hymns. The first was written at the age of twelve, and he was still producing hymns in 1760, the year of his death. Altogether, he is credited with the authorship of more than 2,000 lyrics. His most famous is "Jesus, still lead on," which is also known as "Jesus, lead the way." John Wesley was a great admirer of Zinzendorf's hymns and has given us the beautiful English translation of "Jesus, Thy blood and righteousness," which Zinzendorf based on an earlier hymn by Paul Eber. The last three stanzas, which are the work of the famous Moravian leader, read:

> Bold shall I stand in that great day,
> For who aught to my charge shall lay?
> Fully through Thee absolved I am
> From sin and fear, from guilt and shame.
>
> Lord, I believe Thy precious Blood,
> Which at the mercy-seat of God
> Forever doth for sinners plead,
> For me, e'en for my soul, was shed.
>
> When from the dust of death I rise
> To claim my mansion in the skies,
> E'en then shall this be all my plea,
> "Jesus hath lived, hath died for me."

The Moravian Church in America continues to perpetuate the musical tradition started by Zinzendorf. The city of Bethlehem, Pa., which is one of the important centers of the communion in the United States, has gained national fame for its inspiring festivals of sacred music and song.

141

A Glorious Hymn of Adoration

Beautiful Saviour,
King of Creation,
Son of God and Son of Man!
Truly I'd love Thee,
Truly I'd serve Thee,
Light of my soul, my Joy, my Crown.

Fair are the meadows,
Fair are the woodlands,
Robed in flowers of blooming spring;
Jesus is fairer,
Jesus is purer;
He makes our sorrowing spirit sing.

Fair is the sunshine,
Fair is the moonlight,
Bright the sparkling stars on high;
Jesus shines brighter,
Jesus shines purer
Than all the angels in the sky.

Beautiful Saviour,
Lord of the nations,
Son of God and Son of Man!
Glory and honor,
Praise, adoration,
Now and for evermore be Thine!

MÜNSTER GESANGBUCH, 1677
SCHLESISCHE VOLKSLIEDER, 1842
TR. JOSEPH AUGUSTUS SEISS, 1823-1904

LYRICS FROM ROMAN CATHOLIC SOURCES

OR NEARLY fourteen centuries no congregational singing has been heard during the Mass in Roman Catholic sanctuaries throughout Christendom. However, it is difficult to quench entirely the love of sacred song in a heart that truly adores. This was found to be true particularly of the German people, whose fondness for music is almost a national passion.

Even before the time of Luther, the Germans were wont to sing sacred songs in the vernacular in their private devotions and at festive occasions centering in the home. They also sang them while on pilgrimages, and at Easter and other great festivals of the Church Year they would even join the priests and choirs in the singing of responses in the Mass.

To a certain degree, singing was also permitted in the lesser services, such as matins and vespers. The people likewise developed a love for sacred song through the rise of Christmas and Easter carols which came to play so large a part in the medieval mystery plays.

All of this received a fresh impetus as a result of the Lutheran Reformation. Luther's emphasis on congregational singing and the consequent publication of an unceasing flood of hymnbooks in the German language set all Germany singing. Not even the Church of Rome could escape entirely the contagious enthusiasm created by this great chorus of song. As a result, the Romanists began to publish hymnbooks of their own in the vernacular. In Germany, this practice has continued down to the present time.

Although many of the hymns in these volumes have been permeated with the spirit of Mariolatry and other doctrinal aberrations, an occasional lyrical gem has appeared which has eventually been incorporated into evangelical hymnals. We would mention here four such highly-prized hymns.

Perhaps foremost among these is the greatly cherished *Schönster Herr Jesu*, which is sometimes translated "Beautiful Saviour" and again as "Fairest Lord Jesus." Another is the lovely morning hymn, *Beim frühen Morgenlicht*, known in English as "When morning gilds

143

the skies." A third is the great German paraphrase of the Latin *Te Deum* bearing the title, *Grosser Gott, wir loben dich,* which has been rendered into English as "Holy God, we praise Thy Name." The fourth is the universally loved Christmas carol, *Stille Nacht, heilige Nacht,* which is known throughout the English-speaking world as "Silent night, holy night."

"Beautiful Saviour," or "Fairest Lord Jesus," has in some mysterious way come to be known as "The Crusaders' Hymn." The hymn was first introduced to American worshipers by Richard Storrs Willis, who included it in his *Church Chorals and Choir Studies,* published in 1850. It was accompanied with this explanation: "This hymn, to which the harmony has been added, was lately (1850) discovered in Westphalia. According to the traditionary text by which it is accompanied, it was wont to be sung by the German knights on their way to Jerusalem. The only hymn of the same century which in point of style resembles this is one quoted by Burney from the Chatelaine de Coucy, set about the year 1190, very far inferior, however, to this."

In a London hymnbook, *Heart Melodies,* by Morgan and Chase, the same statement is repeated. There it is referred to as "Crusader's Hymn of the Twelfth Century," to which is added, "This air and hymn used to be sung by the German pilgrims on their way to Jerusalem."

"For these statements," writes James Mearns, "there does not seem to be the shadow of foundation, for the air referred to has not been traced earlier than 1842, nor the words than 1677."

The hymn appeared anonymously in the Roman Catholic *Münster Gesangbuch* of 1677, where it was published as the first of "three beautiful selected new hymns." The tune was entirely different from the one which is now popularly used. During the following century it seems to have moved eastward across Germany until it reached the district of Glaz in Silesia. By this time the text had become somewhat altered, and it had a Silesian folksong as its tune! Hoffman Fallersleben, who heard it for the first time in 1839, recorded the words and music from oral recitation, and published them in his *Schlesische Volkslieder* in 1842. This is the form in which we now know the hymn. From these facts we are compelled to draw the conclusion that this glorious hymn of adoration to the Saviour probably does not go back farther than the 17th century, while the melody is undoubtedly a Silesian folksong of much later origin.

144

It is rather interesting, however, to know that when Franz Liszt made use of the tune in his oratorio, *The Legend of St. Elizabeth,* he states in an appendix to the full score that he had received the tune and text from a cantor named Gottschalg, and adds that it is "an old pilgrim song apparently from the Crusades!"

"When morning gilds the skies" is another German gem with a somewhat similar story. Also the work of an unknown author, it appeared for the first time in 1828 in the Würzburg *Katholisches Gesangbuch.* Slightly different versions, however, have been found in other hymn collections published shortly after that year, which would seem to indicate that the Würzburg hymnbook may not have been the original source. Through a translation by Edward Caswall, which was included in the appendix to the original edition of *Hymns Ancient and Modern,* the hymn quickly achieved popularity in England, and then began to appear in hymnals in America.

The version most commonly used today is one that Robert Bridges, poet laureate of England, prepared for his celebrated *Yattendon Hymnal* in 1899. Bridges not only has captured something of the beauty of the German original, but the last three stanzas of his translation in some respects even surpass it:

No lovelier antiphon
In all high heaven is known
 Than "Jesus Christ be praised."
There to the eternal Word
The eternal psalm is heard,
 "O Jesus Christ be praised!"

Ye nations of mankind,
In this your concord find,
 May Jesus Christ be praised!
Let all the earth around
Ring joyous with the sound,
 May Jesus Christ be praised!

Sing, suns and stars of space,
Sing, ye that see His face,
 Sing, "Jesus Christ be praised!"
God's whole creation o'er,
For aye and evermore
 Shall Jesus Christ be praised!

It is a strange characteristic of hymns derived from Roman Catholic sources that so many of them are anonymous. This is true not only of "Beautiful Saviour" and "When morning gilds the skies," but also of the inspiring hymn of adoration, "Holy God, we praise Thy Name." The first stanza of this German version of the *Te Deum* first appeared in 1774 in the *Katholisches Gesangbuch* of Vienna, dedicated to the Austrian empress, Maria Theresa. The single stanza reads:

> Grosser Gott, wir loben dich
> Herr, wir preisen deine Stärke:
> Vor dir neigt die Erde sich,
> Und bewundert deine Werke.
> Wie du warst vor aller Zeit,
> So bleibst du in Ewigkeit.

In a hymnal published four years later by Ignaz Franz, it appeared in altered form, and since that time has been generally credited to him. There seems to be little justification for this, however. The fine English translation was made by the late Clarence A. Walworth, a Roman Catholic priest of Albany, N. Y., who was one of the founders of the order of Paulists in the United States. He died in 1900. The impressive tune to which this great hymn is sung has been developed from a simple folksong melody to which it was joined in the Vienna hymnbook of 1774.

The last of the four above-mentioned hymns from Roman Catholic sources is undoubtedly the most deeply loved Christmas carol in all of Christendom—"Silent night, holy night." Fortunately, the author of this hymn is known to us. It was Joseph Mohr, an assistant priest at Oberndorf, near Salzburg, Austria. And the composer of the equally sublime music is also known. He was Franz Grüber, organist and choirmaster in the neighboring village of Arnsdorf.

The hymn was written by the 26-year-old Mohr on Christmas eve, in the year 1818. It seems that the young priest had gone to the home of a parishioner that evening. One story has it that he was the guest of a wealthy shipowner at a Christmas party. Another version asserts he had been called to the hut of a poor wood-chopper whose wife had given birth to a child. In any event, it was late that night when Mohr started on his homeward way, and his mind and heart were strangely moved. On the crest of a height called Totenberg, overlooking the village of Oberndorf, he paused in momentary meditation.

The silence of the night, the starry splendor of the winter sky and the murmur of the Salzach River far below thrilled his soul. Quickly he descended to his parish house, and late that night he began to write. It was 4 o'clock on Christmas morning when he finished the lines of *Stille Nacht*. Next morning he hurried to the home of Grüber in Arnsdorf to give him a copy of the hymn. Later in the day Gruber came to Oberndorf with the music he had composed for the text. That night the two, together with the parish choir, sang it for the first time at the village Christmas festival. Grüber accompanied the singing on a guitar, due to the fact that the organ had broken down and could not be used.

It is quite possible that the carol might have passed into oblivion except for the fact that Karl Mauracher of Zillerthal, who had come to repair the organ, heard it sung the following day by the priest and organist. As a result, Mauracher spread the song throughout the Tyrol, and in 1831 Franz Alscher, a Leipzig organist, heard it sung at the Leipzig fair by a quartette from Zillerthal. The following year a Dresden musician named Friese heard it sung by the same group and also copied it down. Thus it was given to the world.

Grüber is the authority for the statement that Mohr wrote a number of other hymns, and he is sometimes credited with the authorship of a little lyric which begins "Holy, Spirit, hear me," but this cannot be established with certainty.

In a memorial on the wall of the church which Mohr served in Oberndorf, he is depicted as leaning from a window of his study listening to a band of children who are singing below. Behind him, with a guitar slung around his shoulder, stands Grüber, playing the accompaniment for the children. In 1897, a memorial tablet was likewise placed on the schoolhouse in Arnsdorf with this inscription:

> Silent night! holy night!
> Who composed this hymn divine?
> Mohr it was who wrote each line,
> Grüber found my tune sublime, —
> Teacher together with priest.

147

A Classical Harvest Hymn

We plough the fields and scatter
The good seed on the land,
But it is fed and watered
By God's almighty hand;
He sends the snow in winter,
The warmth to swell the grain,
The breezes and the sunshine,
And soft, refreshing rain.

REFRAIN:
All good gifts around us
Are sent from heaven above,
Then thank the Lord, O thank the Lord,
For all His love.

He only is the Maker
Of all things near and far;
He paints the wayside flower,
He lights the evening star;
The winds and waves obey Him,
By Him the birds are fed;
Much more to us, His children,
He gives our daily bread.

We thank Thee, then, O Father,
For all things bright and good,
The seed time and the harvest,
Our life, our health, our food;
No gifts have we to offer
For all Thy love imparts,
But that which Thou desirest,
Our humble, thankful hearts.

MATTHIAS CLAUDIUS, 1740-1815
TR. JANE MONTGOMERY CAMPBELL, 1817-78

HYMNODY IN THE AGE OF RATIONALISM

IN religion, as in other things, the pendulum often swings from one extreme to the other. Scarcely had the Pietistic movement run its course before rationalistic tendencies which had thrown religious thought into confusion in France and England began to make their appearance in Germany. Rationalism was an attempt to subject all revealed religion to the test and judgment of the human reason. That which seemed to contradict reason was rejected as superstition.

Strangely enough, the University of Halle, which had been the citadel of Pietism, became the stronghold of Rationalism in Germany. Christian Wolff and Johann Semler, noted philosophers of Halle, were leaders in the new movement. It was not their purpose to establish a new religion of reason, but to "purge" Christianity of the things that seemed unreasonable. But the results of the movement were devastating. The miracles of the Bible that could not be explained by natural causes were rejected as "fables." Christ was robbed of His glory as a divine Saviour and was regarded only as a teacher of morals. Religion became merely the knowledge of God and the pursuit of virtue. What remained of Christianity was a mere shadow: a hypothesis concerning God and immortality, and a teaching of external morality, the attainment of which was largely a matter of man's own efforts.

Rationalism cast its blight over the hymnody of all Europe, but particularly in Germany. It was the golden age of German literature, but such literary geniuses as Goethe, Schiller, Lessing and Wieland possessed none of the Christian zeal of earlier poets, and they wrote no hymns. Most of the hymns that were produced were so tinged with the spirit of the "new theology" they had no permanent value.

The Rationalists were not satisfied with criticizing the Bible: they also sought to "purge" the hymnbooks. The old hymns of Luther, Heermann, Selnecker, and Gerhardt were so completely altered that a noted German hymnologist, Albert Knapp, was moved to observe ironically: "The old hymns were subjected to a kind of transmigration of soul by which their spirits, after having lost their own personality, entered into other bodies." Only a few writers, such as Friedrich

Gottlieb Klopstock, Balthasar Münter, Christian Gellert and Matthias Claudius, wrote hymns of any abiding worth.

Klopstock, the German Milton, whose epic, "Messiah," thrilled Germany as had no other poetic work in centuries, essayed to write a few hymns, but he soared too high. His hymns lacked simplicity of style and were too emotional and subjective to be used for public worship. Only two English translations are familiar—"Blessed are the heirs of heaven," a funeral hymn, and "Grant us, Lord, due preparation," a communion hymn.

Klopstock spent nearly twenty years of his life at the Danish court, having been invited there by King Fredrik V through the influence of Count von Bernstorff, who had become greatly interested in the epic, "Messiah." The Danish monarch gave the poet an annual pension in order to assist him in completing his famous poem without being oppressed by financial worries. In 1770 Klopstock returned to Hamburg, where he died in 1803.

Gellert, who was born in Hainichen, Saxony, July 4, 1715, intended to become a Lutheran pastor. After completing his theological course at the University of Leipzig, however, he found it difficult to deliver sermons without the use of a manuscript, and therefore decided to take up teaching. In 1745 he became a member of the faculty of the University of Leipzig, where he remained until his death in 1769. Among his pupils were many famous men of Germany, including Goethe and Lessing.

Gellert's hymns, although influenced by the age in which he lived, are singular for their genuinely evangelical utterance. It is said that he never attempted to write a hymn except when he was in the proper frame of mind, and only after a season of prayer. His Easter hymn, "Jesus lives! thy terrors now," also translated "Jesus lives! the victory's won," has gained great popularity in England and America.

Matthias Claudius, the author of the splendid hymn, "We plow the fields and scatter," like Gellert, had intended to prepare himself for the Lutheran ministry. While attending the University of Jena, however, the Rationalistic teachings with which he came in contact caused him to lose interest in religion, and he decided to take up journalism instead. In 1777 he became editor of a newspaper at Darmstadt, at which place he became acquainted with Goethe and a group of freethinking philosophers.

Stricken by a serious illness, Claudius began to realize the spiritual emptiness of the life he had been living, and in his hour of need turned again to his childhood faith. When he had recovered, he gave up his position and removed to Wandsbeck, where he edited the *Wandsbecker Bote* in a spirit of Christian faith.

In the life story of Claudius we may discern something of the reaction that was already taking place in many quarters against the deadening influence of Rationalism. Men were hungering for the old evangel of salvation, and there were evidences everywhere of the dawn of a happier day. Although Claudius' poems were not essentially church hymns, they were lyrics that seemed to sound anew some of the tones of Gerhardt's harp. This is seen especially in his surpassingly beautiful ode to evening, "The silent moon is risen," written in the same spirit and meter as Gerhardt's famous evening hymn. One of its stanzas, reflecting something of Claudius' own spiritual groping and, at the same time, confessing the futility of all human efforts to attain moral perfection, reads:

> We, poor, frail mortals, groping,
> Half fearing and half hoping,
>   In darkness seek our way;
> Our airy cobwebs spinning
> With erring and with sinning,
>   Far from the mark we sadly stray.

In the lyrics of Claudius we may observe a transition from the spiritually impoverished hymn production of the rationalistic period to a new type of hymnody, giving expression to the old rugged faith in a more elegant form. Men's souls could no longer be satisfied with the dry husks of philosophical speculation and were turning again to the Bread of God from heaven which gives life to the world.

Balthasar Münter was another faithful Christian witness in this unhappy age of widespread skepticism and unbelief. Born at Lübeck in 1735, he became Lutheran court pastor at Gotha and afterwards of the German Church of St. Peter in Copenhagen. He was the writer of about 100 hymns, many of which were set to tunes composed for them by the greatest musicians of the day. Among the best known of Münter's hymns are "Lord, Thou Source of all perfection," "Full of reverence, at Thy Word," "Behold the man! how heavy lay," and "Woe unto him who says, 'There is no God.' "

A Picture of a Christian Home

O happy home, where Thou art loved the dearest,
 Thou loving Friend and Saviour of our race,
And where among the guests there never cometh
 One who can hold such high and honored place!

O happy home, where two, in heart united,
 In holy faith and blessed hope are one,
Whom death a little while alone divideth,
 And cannot end the union here begun!

O happy home, whose little ones are given
 Early to Thee, in humble faith and prayer,
To Thee, their Friend, who from the heights of heaven
 Dost guide and guard with more than mother's care.

O happy home, where each one serves Thee lowly,
 Whatever his appointed work may be,
Till every common task seems great and holy,
 When it is done, O Lord, as unto Thee!

O happy home, where Thou art not forgotten
 When joy is overflowing, full and free,
O happy home, where every wounded spirit
 Is brought, O great Physician, unto Thee;

And when at last all earthly toil is ended,
 All meet Thee in the blessed home above,
From whence Thou camest, where Thou hast ascended,
 Thine everlasting home of peace and love.

CARL JOHANN PHILIPP SPITTA, 1801-59
TR. SARAH BORTHWICK FINDLATER, 1823-1907

HYMNS OF THE SPIRITUAL RENAISSANCE

IN the early part of the nineteenth century a great spiritual revival swept over Germany and other parts of evangelical Europe. In some respects it resembled the earlier Pietistic movement in Germany and the Wesleyan revival in England, except that it was more conservative than either. In Germany, the old orthodox conservatives and the more radical Pietists joined forces to fight Rationalism, and the union was of benefit to both groups.

There were many influences that contributed to the overthrow of Rationalism. Chief among these was the widespread suffering and distress in Germany, both physical and spiritual, following the Napoleonic wars. Jacobs has well said: "When earthly props fall and temporal foundations crumble, men turn, almost perforce, to God." The downfall of Napoleon and the great empire he had founded was an object lesson to the world of the transitory character of all things material.

The great thinker, Immanuel Kant, also helped to undermine the walls of Rationalism by pointing out the limitations of the human reason. He was followed by the famous theologian, Friedrich Schleiermacher, who taught that the seat of religion is not to be found in either the reason or will, but in feeling—"the feeling of absolute dependence upon God." The way was thus paved for the zealous efforts of Claus Harms, who in 1817, the 300th anniversary of the Reformation, published a new set of ninety-five theses and called upon his countrymen to return again to the pure evangelical teachings of Luther.

Spring-time always brings song-birds and music. It was spring-time in the religious life of Germany, and the sweet notes of evangelical hymnody again were heard throughout the land.

Carl Johann Philipp Spitta was the greatest German hymn-writer of the nineteenth century. He was born August 1, 1801, in Hannover. His father, who was a descendant of a Huguenot family that fled from France during the Catholic persecutions, died when Carl was only four years old. His mother was a Christian Jewess, and it is a beautiful tribute to her fostering care that probably the finest hymn ever

written on the Christian home came from the pen of her son. No
doubt it was the memory of his childhood that led Spitta to write:

> O happy home, whose little ones are given
> Early to Thee in humble faith and prayer,
> To Thee, their Friend, who from the heights of heaven
> Dost guide and guard with more than mother's care.

Spitta began to write verse at the age of eight. It was his mother's
ambition that he should study for the ministry, but, because of his
frail health, it was decided that he should become a watchmaker, and
a younger brother was sent to school instead. The latter died, however,
and now Carl was given his opportunity. He completed his theological
studies in 1824, taught school for four years in Lüne, and in 1828 he
was ordained to the Lutheran ministry.

During his university days, Spitta had become a bosom friend of
Heinrich Heine, the famous poet and prose writer. When the latter
visited Spitta at Lüne, however, and scoffed at holy things in the
presence of Spitta's pupils, the friendship came to an abrupt end. It
was about this time that Spitta passed through a deep spiritual experience, the result of which was the composition of some of his finest
hymns. Writing to a friend in 1826, he says, "In the manner in which
I formerly sang, I sing no more. To the Lord I dedicate my life, my
love, and likewise my song. He gave to me song and melody. I give it
back to Him."

Spitta's hymns aroused unparalleled enthusiasm. His *Psalter und
Harfe,* first published in 1833, appeared in a second and larger edition
the following year. Thereafter a new edition appeared every year, and
by 1889 no less than fifty-five editions had been published. A second
collection of hymns was printed in 1843, and by 1887 it had passed
through forty-two editions. The popularity of Spitta's hymns also
spread to other lands, and a number are found in English and American hymnbooks.

Spitta's child-like faith and his fervent love to the Saviour may
be seen reflected in such a hymn as:

> I know no life divided,
>   O Lord of life, from Thee:
> In Thee is life provided
>   For all mankind and me;
> I know no death, O Jesus,
>   Because I live in Thee;
> Thy death it is that frees us
>   From death eternally.

Other well-known hymns from this gifted writer are "O come, Eternal Spirit," "By the holy hills surrounded," "I place myself in Jesus' hands," "Thou, whose coming seers and sages," "We are the Lord's: His all-sufficient merit," "How blessed from the bonds of sin," "We praise and bless Thee, gracious Lord," "Brethren, called by one vocation," "Withhold not, Lord, the help I crave," "O blessed Sun, whose splendor," and "Say, my soul, what preparation." The beloved German psalmist passed away suddenly while seated at his desk September 28, 1859.

Most noted among the contemporaries of Spitta was Albert Knapp, who, although his hymns never met with the popular favor that attended Spitta's efforts, nevertheless excelled the latter as a poet. Knapp was born at Tübingen, July 25, 1798, and was educated for the Lutheran ministry in the university at that place. His most important post after ordination was at St. Leonard's Church in Stuttgart, where he served from 1845 until his death in 1864.

Knapp was not only a hymnist but also a hymnologist. Perhaps the greatest service he rendered his Church was the editing of a collection of more than 3,000 of the great hymns of Germany. This monumental work, known as *Evangelischer Lieder-Schatz,* is the most comprehensive hymn collection ever published in German, and is a veritable goldmine of the classics of Protestant hymnody. Knapp has been severely criticized, however, for the liberties he took in revising the hymns of some of the older writers. The best known of his own works is a baptismal hymn, "Father, who hast created all." A hymn for church dedication begins with the line, "O God, whom we as Father know."

Carl Bernhard Garve, a Moravian pastor, also contributed a number of compositions to the hymns of this period, the best known of which is the familiar lyric in praise of the Holy Scriptures:

> Thy Word, O Lord, like gentle dews,
> Falls soft on hearts that pine;
> Lord, to Thy garden ne'er refuse
> This heavenly balm of Thine.
> Watered by Thee, let every tree
> Then blossom to Thy praise,
> By grace of Thine bear fruit divine
> Through all the coming days.

An exultant Easter hymn by Garve, "Alleluia! Jesus lives," has also been translated into many languages.

155

Garve served congregations in Amsterdam, Ebersdorf, Berlin, and Neusalz. He spent the last years of his life in Herrnhut, where he died in 1841. He was by far the most important among the later Moravian hymn-writers. Many of his hymns have been adopted by other communions, particularly the Lutheran Church.

To Friedrich Adolph Krummacher, a Reformed pastor, we owe the highly prized hymn:

> Thou art the Way, the Truth, the Life from heaven,
> This blest assurance Thou to us hast given;
> O wilt Thou teach us, Lord, to win Thy pleasure
>   In fullest measure?

Krummacher was a teacher of theology in the Reformed University of Duisburg. After the battle of Jena in 1806 Duisburg was taken from Prussia by Napoleon and the salaries of the professors were cut off. Krummacher continued to lecture, however, until his class consisted of one student! He afterwards served as pastor in a number of cities, finally accepting appointment to St. Ansgarius Church in Bremen. He died in Bremen in 1845.

Another hymnist who lived during the turbulent years of the Napoleonic wars was Jonathan F. Bahnmaier. Born at Oberstenfeld, Württemberg, in 1774, he was appointed professor of education and homiletics at the University of Tübingen in 1815, but shortly afterward was compelled to resign his post. In 1819 he became town preacher at Kirchheim-unter-Teck, where he labored for 21 years. In addition to being a brilliant preacher, he was deeply interested in education, missions, Bible societies and hymnody. He was a member of the committee which compiled the Württemberg *Gesangbuch* of 1842. However, before it could be published, he passed away in 1841. Two of his hymns that have been translated into English are "Spread, O spread, Thou mighty Word" and "Jesu, when Thou once returnest."

It was to this period of war and strife also that Siegfrid August Mahlmann belonged. Mahlmann is chiefly remembered for a patriotic hymn of religious strain which he composed three years after the defeat of Napoleon, namely, *"Gott segne Sachsenland."* First sung November 13, 1815, in the presence of the King of Saxony, it later became the basis for Charles Timothy Brooks' and John S. Dwight's English version, "God bless our native land." Incidentally, it also suggested the tune and meter for Samuel F. Smith's patriotic American hymn, "My country, 'tis of thee." The first stanza of Mahlmann's original German hymn reads:

> *Gott segne Sachsenland,*
> *Wo fest die Treue stand*
>   *In Sturm und Nacht!*
> *Ew'ge Gerechtigkeit,*
> *Hoch über'm Meer der Zeit,*
> *Die jedem Stürm gebeut,*
>   *Schütz uns mit Macht!*

Of the more modern hymn-writers of Germany the most outstanding was Karl von Gerok, chief court preacher at Stuttgart, who died in 1890. An eloquent preacher and an able writer, he attained fame principally through the publication in 1857 of a collection of poems known as *"Palmblätter."* This work had a marvelous circulation in Germany, and by 1916 no less than 130 editions had been printed. Although most of Gerok's compositions are poems rather than hymns, a few have found their way into hymnbooks. One of his devotional lyrics reads:

> Holy, holy, holy, blessed Lord,
>   All the choirs of heaven now adore Thee;
> O that I might join that great white host,
>   Casting down their golden crowns before Thee.
>
> Look on me, a creature of the dust,
>   Pity me, though I have naught of merit;
> Let me bring to Thee for Jesus' sake
>   Humble praises of a contrite spirit.
>
> Bend Thine ear, dear Lord, and hear my prayer;
>   Cleanse me in Thy Blood for sinners given;
> Deck me in the robe of spotless white
>   Thou hast promised to Thy bride in heaven.

One of the most recent hymns from a German source is "O take my hand, dear Father," a moving lyric that comes from the pen of a woman, Julia Hausmann. A heart-breaking tragedy lies behind the hymn. The writer was born of German parents at Mitau, Latvia, where her father was a teacher in the gymnasium, or junior college. Julia had a happy, care-free childhood and made many friends, but she was never seriously in love until she met a young theological graduate who had accepted a call to become a missionary to East Africa. She agreed to marry him, and a few months after he had left for Africa, she also set sail for that continent. However, when she reached the port where she was to meet him, she found that he had been stricken by tropical fever and had died.

Overwhelmed by her sorrow, she sailed for home, and in her hours of loneliness aboard ship she wrote her prayer:

> O take my hand, dear Father,
>   And lead Thou me,
> Till at my journey's ending
>   I dwell with Thee.
> Alone I cannot wander
>   One single day,
> So do Thou guide my footsteps
>   On life's rough way.
>
> O cover with Thy mercy
>   My poor, weak heart,
> Lest I in joy or sorrow
>   From Thee depart.
> Permit Thy child to linger
>   Here at Thy feet,
> Thy goodness blindly trusting
>   With faith complete.

She eventually found herself in St. Petersburg, now Leningrad, Russia, where her sister was the head of St. Ann's boarding school. In later years she succeeded her sister in this position. She also engaged in extensive works of charity. She died in Wösö, Estonia, August 15, 1901.

PART III

Scandinavian Hymnody

A Hymn in Luther's Style

Our Father, merciful and good,
*   Who dost to Thee invite us,*
O cleanse us in our Saviour's blood,
*   And to Thyself unite us!*
Send unto us Thy Holy Word.
*   And let it guide us ever;*
Then in this world of darkness, Lord,
*   Shall naught from Thee us sever:*
*   Grant us, O Lord, this favor!*

O God and man, Christ Jesus blest!
*   Our sorrows Thou didst carry.*
Our wants and cares Thou knowest best,
*   For Thou with us didst tarry.*
O Jesus Christ, our Brother dear,
*   To us and every nation*
Thy Spirit send, let Him draw near
*   With truth and consolation,*
*   That we may see salvation.*

Come, Holy Ghost, Thy grace impart,
*   Tear Satan's snares asunder,*
The Word of God keep in our heart,
*   That we its truth may ponder.*
Then, sanctified, for evermore,
*   In Christ alone confiding,*
We'll sing His praise and Him adore,
*   His precious Word us guiding*
*   To heavenly joys abiding.*

OLAVUS PETRI, 1493–1552
TR. AUGUSTUS NELSON, 1863–1949

160

THE SWEDISH REFORMERS AND THEIR HYMNS

THE REFORMATION fires kindled by Luther and his contemporaries in Wittenberg spread with amazing rapidity to all parts of Europe. In 1516, a year before Luther nailed his famous 95 theses on the door of the castle church in Wittenberg, a 23-year-old Swedish student, Olavus Petri by name, arrived in Wittenberg to continue the studies he had begun earlier in Leipzig. He was a son of Olof Pettersson, a blacksmith in Örebro, Sweden.

Olavus remained at the University of Wittenberg for two or three years until he received his Master's degree. Although he has left no written record of his experiences there, it is quite certain he must have listened to the debate that followed the posting of Luther's bold declarations, and very likely he mingled with the crowd of university students who burned Tetzel's counter-theses.

It seems quite clear that, under the influence of the revolutionary sermons and lectures of Luther and Melanchthon, the blacksmith's son from Örebro experienced a real spiritual awakening. To him, the teachings of Holy Writ became a completely new revelation. According to one historian, in all of Sweden there existed at that time not more than ten manuscript copies of the Holy Bible, and "certainly there could not be found ten laymen who had either heard or read the Sermon on the Mount" (Schück). Now, for the first time, Olavus Petri had come to understand that salvation is the gift of God, freely offered through faith in His Son, Jesus Christ, and not a commodity which could be dispensed by the Pope at Rome or his underlings—for a price.

Full of reforming zeal, the young student, in 1519, hurried back to his native Sweden, where he lost no time entering into the political and spiritual storm that was ready to break over his country.

Soon after his return Olavus became chancellor to the titular head of the diocese of Strängnäs, Bishop Mattias. King Christian II of Denmark had shortly before this laid claim to the crown of Sweden under the terms of the Union of Kalmar, and had sought to enforce it by armed might. The Swedish National party, though first defeated, continued to resist, and Gustavus Vasa eventually emerged as the Swedish leader. The Church of Rome, which possessed probably one-half of the wealth of the nation, was fearful of the establishment of a strong Swedish monarchy, and gave its support to the Danish king. The Stockholm Massacre in 1520, which was aimed at wiping out Swedish resistance, aroused instead the fury of the Swedes and doomed the hopes of Christian II. Within three years Gustavus Vasa had succeeded in driving the Danes out of the country, and the Swedish Estates at an assembly in Strängnäs in June 1523 elected him as king.

It is generally believed that the Stockholm Massacre had been instigated by Roman intrigue in conspiracy with the Danish king. Bishop Mattias, though sympathetic to King Christian, became one of the victims of the infamous "blood bath." Olavus Petri himself almost lost his life when he cried out in protest at the cruel beheading of his friend and superior. Only the intervention of a Wittenberg acquaintance, who asserted that Olavus was a German citizen, saved the young man from a similar fate.

The bold preaching of Olavus against the sale of indulgences, the worship of saints, and other errors and abuses of the papal Church had by this time attracted widespread attention, and Gustavus Vasa recognized in him a valuable ally in his efforts to dispossess the Church. Accordingly, the new monarch appointed Olavus secretary of the Stockholm Council, ordered a pulpit placed in the cathedral church of Stockholm, and gave the young reformer authority to preach to the populace in their native tongue.

Laurentius Andreae, archdeacon of Strängnäs, with whom Olavus had formed a strong friendship and who likewise had espoused the cause of the Reformation, was appointed chancellor to the king. It was largely through his influence that the Lutheran teachings were approved by the Diet of Vesterås in 1527.

A younger brother of Olavus, Laurentius Petri, who had studied in Wittenberg a decade later than Olavus, returned to Sweden during the late 1520s to join in the great task of bringing about a spiritual renaissance in Sweden. Laurentius took holy orders, and by 1531 he had been appointed by the king as the first Lutheran archbishop of the land. As such, he became the spiritual head of the Church during the next forty years.

Although Olavus wisely refrained from advocating radical changes in the life of the Church, the Reformation movement soon encountered violent opposition from the ruling hierarchy. At one time both Olavus and his brother Laurentius were summoned to appear before the papal authorities at Upsala, but neither threats nor bribes could induce them to deviate from their high-minded purpose.

A crisis came in 1525 when Olavus defied the church canon requiring celibacy of the clergy, and married. Although he had been ordained only as a deacon, the church ordinance still applied to him. His marriage created a sensation throughout Sweden, and caused Bishop Brask to address a bitter protest to the king. When this proved futile, Brask appealed to the Archbishop to invoke the inquisition. However, the appeal came too late, for Gustavus Vasa had already broken off relations with Rome and the hierarchy in Sweden had been shorn of its power.

The Swedish reformers were apt pupils of Luther, and quickly made use of the same spiritual weapons in Sweden that Luther had found so effective in Germany. It is significant that the Word of God and a hymnbook in the vernacular were given to the Swedish people in the same year—1526. It seems that Olavus Petri had prepared a partial translation of the New Testament by February of that year, and this probably became the basis of the official version, of which Laurentius Andreae apparently became the final reviser and editor. However, the little hymnbook, which bore the title *Swedish Hymns or Songs,* was undoubtedly the work of Olavus Petri.

This was the beginning of evangelical hymnody in Sweden. The book contained at the most a total of ten hymns, five of which are believed to have been original productions by Petri himself while the others were translations of hymns from Luther's *Achtliederbuch* of 1524. Although no copy of the 1526 hymnal is now known to exist, it is quite possible that Petri's beautiful hymn, "Our Father, merciful and good," was included in this historic collection. In any event, it appeared in a second edition, called *A Few Godly Songs Derived from Holy Writ,* published by the Swedish reformer in 1530. A few fragmentary pages of this hymnbook were discovered in 1871.

How thoroughly Olavus Petri had imbibed the spirit of Luther is reflected not only in the earnestness and zeal with which he proclaimed the doctrines of the Reformation, but also in the character of his hymns. "Our Father, merciful and good" is so strongly suggestive of Luther's style that it was long regarded as a translation of one of his hymns. It is now known that no such hymn of German origin exists.

Most of the hymns in Petri's hymnbooks, however, are translations of German or Latin originals. One of these is Elizabeth Cruciger's glorious Advent hymn:

> Now hail we our Redeemer,
> Eternal Son of God,
> Born in the flesh to save us,
> And cleanse us in His blood;
> The Morning Star ascendeth,
> Light to the world He lendeth,
> Our Guide in grief and gloom.

Another, a translation of an ancient Latin Easter lyric, sounds the Paschal theme of that festival day:

> O Paschal Feast, what joy is thine!
> We praise, dear Lord, Thy Name divine,
> For Thou hast triumphed o'er the tomb;
> No more we need to dread its gloom.

Olavus, like Luther, never ceased praising God for restoring His Word to the Church through the Reformation. This may be seen in one of his more polemic hymns, which is regarded as an original:

> Thy sacred Word, O Lord, of old
> Was veiled about and darkened,
> And in its stead were legends told,
> To which the people harkened;
> Thy Word, for which the people yearned,
> The worldlings kept in hiding,
> And into human fables turned
> Thy truth, the all-abiding.
>
> Now thanks and praise be to our Lord,
> Who boundless grace bestoweth,
> And daily through the sacred Word
> His precious gifts forthshoweth.
> His Word is come to light again,
> A trusty lamp to guide us;
> No strange and divers teachings then
> Bewilder and divide us.

The last hymnbook published by Olavus appeared in 1536. It contained some thirty new hymns, mostly German, and has a close affinity to Sluter's *Gesangbuch* printed in Germany in 1531. How profoundly Olavus Petri influenced the hymnody of his native land may be judged from the fact that no less than nineteen hymns in the 1937 official *Psalmbook* of the Church of Sweden are credited to him as author, translator or paraphraser.

Olavus Petri was also the moving spirit in transforming the Roman Mass into an evangelical service. Oddly enough, however, he did not take his model from Wittenberg but followed the form of the *Neuen Spital* of Nürnberg. The Swedish *Handbook,* or minister's manual, was published in 1529, but the Swedish Mass was not printed until 1531. The new form of worship, however, had already been in use in Stockholm for some time.

The hymnological endeavors of Olavus were continued by his brother Laurentius, who, as archbishop, brought out in 1567, and later in 1572, the most important of all the earlier hymnbooks of the Swedish Church. Laurentius is sometimes given the title, "Father of Swedish hymnody," but it is clear that the honor more rightly belongs to his older brother.

As was the case in Germany, the Reformation movement in Sweden soon gave birth to radical, iconoclastic elements which sought to overturn the Church and cast aside all of its ancient forms of worship. Among these were many Germans, who at that period constituted almost half of the population of Stockholm. Thanks to the conservative policies followed by Olavus, these zealots were finally silenced, but not, however, until some had been summarily dealt with.

In other parts of the country, on the other hand, considerable unrest developed among the common people over the startling changes being made in the worship life of the Church in the nation's capital. It was rumored throughout Sweden that the Mass was being said in Swedish, that even Swedish songs were being sung in the worship, that statues of saints were being removed from the churches, and that the laity was being offered the cup in Holy Communion. Other rumors told of monks being turned out of monasteries and church property being seized by the king.

Led by Church reactionaries, the peasants of the Province of Dalarne rose in rebellion in 1527, but the uprising was quickly put down. Then came a revolt in the Province of Småland in 1529, followed two years later by a repetition of the insurrection in Dalarne. The death throes of the old order were witnessed as late as 1543 in the Dacke uprising in Småland, but again Gustavus Vasa was victorious and all opposition to the reform movement was finally at an end.

The latter years of Olavus were darkened through a growing disagreement with the king over the latter's persistent efforts to usurp authority which rightly belonged to the Church. Both Petri and Laurentius Andreae eventually lost their influence with the monarch. Then a strange thing happened. On the morning of April 20, 1535, the inhabitants of Stockholm were startled to observe six to eight parhelia, or mock suns, surrounding the sun. In that age of superstition, no one doubted that the heavenly phenomenon was an omen of evil days to come. This led Olavus to preach a forceful sermon in which he called for national repentance. To perpetuate the memory of the incident, he even caused the celestial sign to be painted on canvas and placed in the cathedral church, where it hangs to this day.

Gustavus Vasa interpreted the sermon as a personal affront directed against his rule, a conclusion that probably was not incorrect. During the succeeding years his suspicions grew stronger, and his new German advisors, Georg Normann and Konrad von Pyhy, appear to have lost no time in confirming them. When Olavus in 1539, therefore, preached a powerful sermon against the sin of profanity and made it clear that the king was a chief offender, the wrath of Gustavus Vasa knew no bounds. Both Olavus and Laurentius Andreae were brought to trial at Örebro on the charge of being traitors to their country. Both were condemned to die, but the king, having accomplished his purpose, commuted the sentences and imposed heavy fines instead. The people of Stockholm revealed their esteem for Olavus by paying the entire sum for their beloved spiritual leader.

The king eventually seems to have regretted his action, and soon restored both men to favor. Shortly before his trial in 1539, Olavus had been duly ordained, and in 1543 the king named him as pastor of the cathedral church in Stockholm where he had preached for nineteen years. He also made Olavus supervisor of Stockholm's school. The bold reformer could not be silenced, however, and continued to criticize excesses of the government from time to time. Under his wise direction, the Church never experienced a schism in Sweden. Instead, the Reformation in Olavus Petri's native land assumed the character of a return to the Scriptural conception of the Church, a spiritual movement in which the people, the clergy and the hierarchy *en masse* finally accepted the evangelical truths taught by Martin Luther.

Olavus Petri died on April 19, 1552, and ten days later his life-long friend, Laurentius Andreae, followed him. The great Swedish reformer lies buried beneath the pulpit of the cathedral church, and on the stone slab that covers his grave are inscribed these words— undoubtedly suggested by him: "After the darkness, I wait for the light. I am not ashamed of the Gospel of Christ, for it is the power of God unto salvation to every one that believeth."

A Model Hymn of Invocation

O Lord, give heed unto our plea,
O Spirit, grant Thy graces,
That we who put our trust in Thee
May rightly sing Thy praises.
Thy Word, O Christ, unto us give,
That grace and power we may receive
To follow Thee, our Master.

Touch Thou the shepherd's lips, O Lord,
That in this blessed hour
He may proclaim Thy sacred Word
With unction and with power;
What Thou wouldst have Thy servant say,
Put Thou into his heart, we pray,
With grace and strength to say it.

Let heart and ear be opened wide
Unto Thy Word and pleading;
Our minds, O Holy Spirit, guide
By Thine own light and leading.
The law of Christ we would fulfill,
And walk according to His will,
His Word our rule of living.

JESPER SWEDBERG (1653-1735)
Based on a hymn by
JOHANN UTENHOVIUS (c. 1520-1565)

A REJECTED HYMNBOOK

WHEN the Swedish colonists along the Delaware gathered in their temples to worship God in the latter part of the 17th century, they sang songs from a hymnbook, the use of which had been prohibited in Sweden. It was the much disputed work of Bishop Jesper Swedberg. Originally published by the author in 1694 and intended as the official hymnbook of the Church of Sweden, it immediately came under suspicion on the charge that it contained unorthodox teachings, and was promptly confiscated. This, however, did not hinder the authorities from sending the book in large quantities to America, and it was used on this side of the Atlantic by the Delaware colonists for many years.

Swedberg, who was born near Falun, Sweden, in the year 1653, was the first important hymnist of his native land. Since the time of the Reformation no noteworthy advance had been made in Swedish hymnody until Swedberg began to tune his lyre. The official *Psalmbook* had been revised on several occasions, but the Upsala edition of 1645 contained only 182 hymns, far too few to meet the needs of church worship and private devotion.

In 1691, however, Swedberg received a royal commission to prepare a new hymnbook. He was fortunate in having the aid of such gifted poets as Haqvin Spegel, Petrus Lagerlöf, Israel Kolmodin, and Jacob Boethius in the execution of his task.

The new book, containing 482 Swedish hymns and a few in Latin, made its appearance in 1694. A large edition was printed, the financial cost of which was borne largely by Swedberg himself. It met with immediate opposition, particularly from Bishop Carl Carlsson, who charged that the hymnbook contained "innumerable heresies of a theological, anthropological, Christological, soteriological, and eschatological nature."

It was enough. King Karl XI immediately appointed a new commission to revise Swedberg's work, with the result that 75 hymns—mostly those of Swedberg and Spegel—were omitted, and six new hymns added. It was printed in 1696 and remained in use as the

Psalmbook of the Church of Sweden for more than century, until it was succeeded in 1819 by Archbishop Wallin's masterpiece.

The unsold copies of the first edition, about 20,000 in number, were confiscated and stored away. From time to time quantities of these books were sent to the Swedish colonists in America, for whose "preservation in the true faith," as the hymnologist Söderberg ironically remarks, "the Swedish authorities seemed less concerned."

Swedberg felt the slight keenly and often made significant references in his diary to those who had been instrumental in rejecting his work. One of these notations tells how the Cathedral of Upsala was destroyed by fire in 1702, and how the body of Archbishop O. Svebilius, although encased in a copper and stone sarcophagus, was reduced to ashes. "But my hymnbooks," he adds, "which were only of paper, unbound and unprotected, were not even scorched by the flames."

The story of Swedberg's life, though darkened by his one great disappointment, reads almost like romance. It is the story of how a miner's son rose to become the friend of Swedish monarchs and a bishop of the Church. Jesper was only 13 years old when he was sent, in 1666, to begin studies at the University of Upsala. Moral conditions at the institution at this time were deplorable, and the student tutor who had been appointed to instruct the lad was drunk most of the time. "I learned no more during three years," Swedberg wrote in later years, "than another pupil with a conscientious teacher could have learned in three weeks."

His father eventually removed him to the University of Lund, where he had the good fortune of being received into the home of a professor who was a friend of the Swedberg family. Five years later he returned to Upsala to complete his theological education, and in 1683, at the age of 30 years, he was ordained as a pastor of the Church of Sweden.

While serving as a chaplain of the royal cavalry regiment in Stockholm, he attracted the attention of King Karl XI. He soon became a court preacher. Nine years after his ordination he was appointed a professor at the University of Upsala, and he had hardly been installed in his new office before the king designated him as *Rector Magnificus* of the institution. Swedberg's preferment over other professors at the university, as well as his efforts to exercise discipline and improve moral conditions among teachers and students, accounted for much of the opposition and enmity which he later encountered. To him, piety was of far greater importance than the mere possession of knowledge. He once wrote: "Should I chance to meet a doctor of profound learning but worldly-minded and ungodly, and a poverty-stricken but pious peasant, I will lift my hat and honor the latter but not the former." And again, "There are many who possess only a faith of the head and not of the heart; a ghost without a body." While he decried the emotional excesses and unchurchly tendencies that manifested themselves among the Pietists, he nevertheless sympathized with their efforts to bring about a moral and spiritual renewal within the Church.

"Let no one be surprised or take me to task," he wrote, "that in my zeal and eagerness in emphasizing the doctrine concerning faith I should likewise stress good works as the necessary fruits of a true and living faith. From such teaching I shall not cease as long as a warm drop of blood flows in my body, nor as long as I can use my tongue, my hand and my pen."

But Swedberg's enemies accused him of heresy, and charged that he was attempting to introduce "a new religion." Here it might be mentioned that the most zealous of these "defenders" of orthodoxy, Bishop Carlsson, was the man who a few years earlier, during witchcraft trials in Stockholm, and urged that certain women who had been condemned to die should be given "a foretaste of the tortures of hell-fire" before they were beheaded.

"The treatment given Swedberg's Psalmbook," writes Emil Liedgren, Sweden's foremost living hymnologist, "is probably the greatest literary scandal in the history of our country. It leaves one astounded over the implacable spirit revealed by the bishops and theologians in their treatment of many of the most beautiful and gripping hymns of Spegel, Swedberg and Brask."

Nevertheless, the final form in which Swedberg's hymnbook was published was still so impregnated by his spirit that a noted critic has called it "the most precious heritage he left his native land." The fact that the latest Swedish *Psalmbook* (1937) contains no less than thirty-three hymns and translations credited to Swedberg in part or in whole testifies eloquently to the enduring mark he has left on Swedish hymnody. It was Swedberg who wrote the sublime stanza that has become the most deeply cherished doxology of the Church of Sweden. Archbishop Wallin incorporated it as the con-

cluding stanza of his famous lyric, "O my soul, on wings ascending,"
which for nearly a century and a half has been the final hymn in
the Swedish *Psalmbook*. It reads:

> Bless us, Father, and protect us
> From all harm in all our ways;
> Patiently, O Lord, direct us
> Safely through these fleeting days;
> Let Thy face upon us shine,
> Fill us with Thy peace divine;
> Praise the Father, Son, and Spirit,
> Praise Him, all that life inherit.

Haqvin Spegel, one of those who collaborated with Swedberg in
the preparation of the rejected hymnbook, was the more gifted poet
of the two. It was he who, by his hymns, fixed the language forms
that subsequently became the model for Swedish hymnody. Although
Spegel never stooped to subjective sentimentality, his hymns breathe
a spirit of personal faith and fervent devotion. A sweet pastoral
fragrance permeates the hymn, "We Christians should ever consider,"
as witness the following stanza:

> The lilies, nor toiling nor spinning,
> Their clothing how gorgeous and fair!
> What tints in their tiny orbs woven,
> What wondrous devices are there!
> All Solomon's stores could not render
> One festival robe of such splendor
> As modest field lilies do wear.

His communion hymn, "The death of Jesus Christ, our Lord,"
is a classic example of how effectively Spegel could set forth in lyrical
form some of the objective truths of the Christian faith.

Although both Swedberg and Spegel suffered intense humiliation
as a result of the treatment accorded their dedicated efforts, both
men lived to receive high honors at the hands of their countrymen
and Church. Spegel was elevated to the foremost ecclesiastical office
in the Church when he was created archbishop in 1711. He died
three years later. Swedberg was consecrated bishop of Skara in 1702,
a position he held for thirty-three years. He died in 1735, universally
mourned by the Swedish people. Emmanuel Swedenborg, the famous
mystic and philosopher, was a son of the distinguished hymnist.

Among other hymn-writers who contributed lyrics to Swedberg's
book was Jacob Arrhenius, professor of history at the University of

Upsala. This man, though he devoted a great deal of his time to the financial affairs of the university, was a richly endowed spiritual poet. The intimate tenderness with which he sang of the Saviour's love sounded a new note in Swedish hymnody. It was he who wrote:

> Jesus is my Friend most precious,
>   Never friend did love as He;
> Can I leave this Friend so gracious,
>   Spurn His wondrous love for me?
> No! nor friend nor foe shall sever
>   Me from Him who loves me so;
> His shall be my will forever,
>   There above, and here below.

The Swedish Te Deum

We worship Thee, almighty Lord,
Our hearts revere Thy gracious word
    When it goes forth
    From heaven o'er all the earth.
Holy, holy, holy art Thou, O God!

Upon a mountain builded high,
Thy Church doth in Thy strength rely,
    And standeth sure
    While earth and time endure.
Holy, holy, holy art Thou, O God!

Through her shall every land proclaim
The sacred might of Jesus' Name,
    And all rejoice
    With Christian heart and voice.
Holy, holy, holy art Thou, O God!

All nations to Thy throne shall throng,
And raise on high the victory song,
    While cherubim
    Reply to seraphim,
Holy, holy, holy art Thou, O God!

JOHAN OLOF WALLIN, 1779–1839
TR. CHARLES WHARTON STORK, 1881–

DAVID'S HARP IN THE NORTHLAND

W HEN Longfellow translated Tegnér's Swedish poem, "Children of the Lord's Supper," he introduced Johan Olof Wallin to the English-speaking world in the following lines:

> And with one voice
> Chimed in the congregation, and sang an anthem immortal
> Of the sublime Wallin, of David's harp in the Northland.

Wallin is Scandinavia's greatest hymnist and one of the foremost in the entire Christian Church. The Swedish *Psalmbook* of 1819, which was cherished for more than a century as the hymnbook of the Swedish people, was in large measure the work of one man. Of the 500 hymns in the volume, 128 were original hymns, 178 revisions, twenty-three translations, and thirteen semi-originals—all from his pen. In brief, no less than 342 of the hymns of the *Psalmbook* of 1819 reflected the genius of this remarkable writer.

Early in life Wallin began to reveal poetic talent. Born at Stora Tuna, Dalarne province, in 1779, he overcame the handicaps of both poverty and poor health and at the age of twenty-four had gained the degree of Doctor of Philosophy at the University of Upsala. In 1805, and again in 1809, he won the chief prize for poetry at the university.

In 1806 he was ordained to the Lutheran ministry. Very early he attracted attention by his able preaching. In 1812 he was transferred to Stockholm, and in 1816 he became dean of Västerås. In 1824 he was elevated to the bishopric, and thirteen years later became Primate of the Church of Sweden when he was made Archbishop of Upsala. He died in 1839.

As early as 1807 Wallin had begun to publish collections of old and new hymns. He possessed the rare ability of translating sacred poetry of other lands in such a way that not infrequently the translation excelled the original in beauty and virility.

In 1811 a commission was appointed by the Swedish parliament to prepare a new hymnbook. The "revised" hymnal of Jesper Swedberg had then been in use for more than a century. Wallin was made

175

a member of this body. Within three years the commission presented its labors in the form of a first draft. However, it did not meet with universal favor, nor was Wallin himself satisfied with the result. By this time Wallin's genius had been revealed so clearly that the commission was moved to entrust to him the entire task of completing the book. He gladly undertook the work, and on November 28, 1816, was able to report that he had finished his labors. A few minor changes were subsequently made, but on January 29, 1819, the new hymn-book was officially authorized by King Karl XIV.

Unfortunately, Wallin's hymns have not become generally known outside of his own native land. It is only in recent years that a number have been translated into English. One of these is his famous Christmas hymn, which for more than a century has been sung in every sanctuary in Sweden to greet the dawn of Christmas day. The first stanza reflects something of the glory of the Christmas evangel:

> All hail to thee, O blessed morn,
> To tidings long by prophets borne
> Hast thou fulfilment given.
> O sacred and immortal day,
> When unto earth, in glorious ray,
> Descends the grace of heaven!
> Young and old their voices blending,
> Praise are sending
> Unto heaven
> For the Saviour to us given.

The old, traditional hymns of the Church, despite defects in language and form, were regarded by Wallin with deep reverence. However, he was unrelenting in his demand that every new hymn adopted by the Church should be tested by the severest classical standards. "A new hymn," he declared, "aside from the spiritual considerations, which must never be compromised in any way, should be so correct, simple and lyrical in form, and so free from inversions and other imperfections in style, that after the lapse of a hundred years a father may be able to say to his son, 'Read the Psalmbook, my boy, and you will learn your mother tongue!' "

The profound influence which Wallin's hymns have exerted over the Swedish language and its literature for more than a century is eloquent testimony not only to his poetic genius, but also to the faithfulness with which he adhered to the high standards he had imposed on himself.

The charge has been made that some of Wallin's hymns are tinged with the spirit of Rationalism. It is true that in his earlier years the great Swedish hymnist was strongly influenced by the so-called "New Theology" which had swept over Europe at that time. His poems and hymns from this period bear unmistakable marks of rationalizing tendencies. Even some of the hymns in the first part of the *Psalmbook,* dealing with the person and attributes of God, are not entirely free from suspicion.

However, as Wallin became more and more absorbed in his great task, his own spiritual life seems to have been deepened and a new and richer note began to be heard in his hymns. In 1816 this change was made manifest in an address Wallin delivered before the Swedish Bible Society, in which he declared war on the "New Theology," and took his stand squarely upon the confessions of the Lutheran Church. He said:

"So far had we traveled in what our age termed 'enlightenment' and another age shall call 'darkness,' that the very Word of God . . . was regarded as a sort of contribution to ancient history which had already served its purpose and was needed no more."

The atonement of Christ now became the central theme in his hymnbook, the pure evangelical note of which may be heard in one of his hymns:

> There is a truth so dear to me,
> I'll hold it fast eternally,
> It is my soul's chief treasure:
> That Jesus for the world hath died,
> He for my sins was crucified—
> O love beyond all measure!
> O blessed tidings of God's grace,
> That He, who gave the thief a place,
> To paradise will take me,
> And God's own child will make me!
>
> Kind Shepherd, Son of God, to Thee
> Mine eyes, my heart, in silent plea
> And humble prayer, are lifted.
> From Thee I strayed; ah, leave me not,
> But cleanse my soul from each dark blot,
> For I am sore afflicted.
> A wandering sheep, but now restored,
> Ah, bear me to Thy fold, dear Lord,
> And let me leave Thee never,
> O Thou who lovest ever!

Again we find him giving expression to faith's certainty in one of his other hymns, a two-stanza cento of which reads:

177

By Thy Cross, O Christ, and passion
　　Thou hast brought us full salvation;
Thou hast stooped in great compassion
　　To redeem a lost creation.
Like a shepherd Thou hast sought us,
　　In Thy heavenly fold to gather;
With Thy precious Blood hast bought us
　　To restore us to the Father.

Ah, how blest is he who knoweth
　　That his faith on Thee is founded
Whom the Father's love bestoweth
　　Through eternal grace unbounded.
Thou, O Christ, to every nation
　　Art a Saviour freely given,
In whose Name is our salvation,
　　And none else in earth or heaven.

Wallin is described as a strange personality whose life was full of contradictions. Two unhappy romances seem to have left their mark on him. Usually melancholy in spirit, it is said that he very rarely smiled. He seemed to derive little satisfaction from life, and even his closest friends found it difficult to comprehend his moods. The tremendous drive that brought such prodigious achievements was undoubtedly a manifestation of his inner restlessness. It also revealed itself in the frequent references to the future life found in his hymns. No one has written more beautifully of heaven and of its spiritual joys than Wallin. This may be seen in the final hymn that completed his collection:

"O my soul, on wings ascending,
　　On the holy mount seek rest,
Where sweet angel-harps are blending
　　With the anthems of the blest.
Let thy fervent praise and prayer
Come before thy Maker there,
Knowing that, while yet a mortal,
Thou art near the Father's portal.

It was during the cholera epidemic of 1834 that Wallin began his monumental work, "The Angel of Death," an epic poem that was not completed until a few weeks before his passing in 1839. While somber and solemn in tone, it nevertheless reflects an unshaken faith in the certainty of the resurrection and the life beyond the grave. The day of his own death—it was a Sunday morning—seemed like a festal home-coming. Shortly before breathing his last, he cried, "My Lord, I am coming! My country, my King, my God!" And thus Wallin's restless soul found peace at last.

The lyrical quality and exalted language in Wallin's hymns made them particularly appropriate on festival days. "We worship Thee, almighty Lord," which is a metrical version of the *Te Deum Laudamus,* is an impressive example of the poetic genius of this master psalmist.

Although a hymn usually loses much in the process of translation, something of the rare beauty in Wallin's poetry is still apparent in another of his lyrics:

> Where is the Friend for whom I'm ever yearning?
> My longing grows when day to night is turning;
> And though I find Him not as day recedeth,
>   My heart still pleadeth.
>
> His hand I see in every force and power,
> Where waves the harvest and where blooms the flower;
> In every breath I draw, my spirit burneth:
>   His love discerneth.
>
> When summer winds blow gently, then I hear Him;
> Where sing the birds, where rush the streams, I'm near Him;
> But nearer still when in my heart He blesses
>   Me with caresses.
>
> O where such beauty is itself revealing
> In all that lives, through all creation stealing,
> What must the Source be whence it comes, the Giver?
>   Beauty forever!

Other great hymns of the Swedish archbishop that have been translated into English include "A voice, a heavenly voice I hear," "I know in whom I trust," "Again Thy glorious sun doth rise," and "He lives, O fainting heart, anew!"

Wallin's *Psalmbook* aroused tremendous interest throughout the Christian world. Mohnike, Knapp, Weiss and other German hymnologists gave it undivided praise. Mohnike declared, "This is undoubtedly the most excellent hymnbook in the entire Evangelical Church, and, if translated, it would become the hymnbook for all Christian people." Knapp concurred by saying, "The Scriptural content of this book is clothed in the most beautiful classical language; there is nothing in Evangelical Germany to equal it."

Something of the enduring quality of Wallin's hymns is reflected in the fact that the Church of Sweden did not make a single change in his hymnbook for 101 years. The first move for a revision was made in 1920 when an appendix of 173 hymns was tentatively added, but the 500 hymns of the 1819 *Psalmbook* were left intact. The first permanent change was made in 1937 when a new *Psalmbook* containing 600 hymns and a number of canticles was published. The new hymnbook, however, still bears the marks of Wallin's extraordinary genius, since more than one-third of all the hymns in the collection are either originals, translations or revisions by him.

The 1937 *Psalmbook* clearly reflects something of the enthusiasm with which the Church of Sweden has followed the leadership of their late great Primate, Archbishop Nathan Söderblom, in becoming a significant part of the ecumenical movement. For the first time in the history of Swedish hymnody, the *Psalmbook* contains hymns from Anglican and Reformed sources. Among these are Toplady's "Rock of Ages," Watts' "O God, our help in ages past," Adams' "Nearer, my God, to Thee," Heber's "Holy, holy, holy, Lord God almighty," Lyte's "Abide with me," Stone's "The Church's one Foundation," and How's "For all the saints who from their labors rest."

We also find hymns by Roman Catholic writers such as "Lead, kindly Light" by Newman, "Thee will I love, my Strength, my Tower" by Scheffler, and "Silent night, holy night" by Mohr.

Greater recognition has also been given to Lutheran writers of other Scandinavian countries, including Denmark's Grundtvig and Ingemann, Norway's Landstad, Wexels and Johannes Johnson, and Finland's Runeberg, Topelius and Tolpo.

American hymnody has not been given as large a place in the 1937 *Psalmbook* as it deserves. The hymns of Whittier, Palmer, Coxe, van Dyke, North, Gladden and Hosmer have been completely ignored. Included, however, are Benson's "O Thou whose feet have climbed life's hill," Bliss' "More holiness give me," and Baxter's "There is a gate that stands ajar." The latter two are of the Gospel song type, and are currently found in very few standard American hymnals. Be it said to the credit of the Swedish translators, however, that their translations are superior to the originals.

The moving spirit in the creation of the 1937 *Psalmbook* was the late Bishop Johan Alfred Eklund of Karlstad. As early as 1934 he had edited a tentative collection, and this became the basis of the new book. He himself contributed no less than forty-two original hymns, revisions or translations to the book. Among the translations are a number of the finest evangelical hymns of Germany. Karl G. E. Liedgren of Västerås, Sweden's leading hymnologist, and Fredrik Natanael Beskow, noted educator, sociologist and writer, also played a prominent role in the preparation of the new *Psalmbook*. Liedgren, in addition to writing a number of impressive original hymns, did much through his volume, *Spiritual Song on Anglo-Saxon Soil*, to direct attention to Anglican hymnody.

Others who made significant contributions to the new hymnbook were Edvard Evers, late pastor in Norrköping, who is credited with seven original lyrics and a number of translations; Lars Johan Paul Nilsson, pastor and occasional court preacher, who has eight hymns of unusual merit; Anders Frostenson, a pastor and poet of evident promise, who is the author of nine original lyrics in the collection, and Erik Natanael Söderberg, writer and publisher, who contributed five.

An Advent Triumph Song

Prepare the way, O Zion!
    Ye awful deeps, rise high;
Sink low, ye lofty mountains,
    The Lord is drawing nigh;
The righteous King of glory,
Foretold in sacred story.

REFRAIN:
    O blest is He that came
    In God the Father's Name!

O Zion, He approaches,
    Your Lord and King for aye;
Strew palms where He advances,
    Spread garments in His way;
God's promise faileth never,
Hosanna sound forever.

Fling wide your portals, Zion,
    And hail your glorious King;
His tidings of salvation
    To every people bring,
Who, waiting still in sadness,
Would sing His praise with gladness.

The throne which He ascended
    Is fixed in heaven above;
His everlasting Kingdom
    Is light and joy and love;
Let us His praise be sounding
For grace and peace abounding.

FRANS MIKAEL FRANZEN, 1772-1847
TR. AUGUSTUS NELSON, 1863-1949

THE GOLDEN AGE OF SWEDISH HYMNODY

ARCHBISHOP WALLIN was not alone in the preparation of that hymnic masterpiece known as the *Psalmbook* of 1819. Although the lion's share of the task unquestionably fell to him, Wallin was aided by a number of the greatest spiritual poets in Scandinavian history. It was the golden age of Swedish hymnody, when such men as Franzèn, Hedborn, Geijer, Åström, Afzelius and Nyström were singing "the glories of the Lamb."

Foremost in this unusual group was the beloved Frans Mikael Franzèn, a lyric poet of singular talent who is claimed by both Sweden and Finland. He was born in Uleaborg, Finland, in 1772, and rightly could call Finland his native land. However, his parents were of Swedish lineage, and when Sweden lost Finland to Russia at the close of the Napoleonic wars, many of the Swedes living in Finland at that time returned to the land of their forebears.

Franzèn was a professor at the University of Åbo at the time, and found the decision a difficult one to make. He was intensely loyal to Finland, but his native language was Swedish, and all of his poetry was written in that tongue. Indeed, his lyrics were being read with delight on both sides of the Gulf of Bothnia, and he was already being hailed as a rising star on the firmament of Swedish literature. Accordingly, Franzèn in 1812 accepted a call to become the pastor of Kumla parish in Sweden.

The change from the stimulating academic life of Åbo to the dull monotony of a quiet country parish proved almost more than the gifted poet could endure at first, but it was during the first years at Kumla that Franzèn wrote some of his finest hymns. After thirteen years of faithful service in that rural community, his fame had reached Stockholm, and in 1825 he was called to become pastor of St. Clara Church in the nation's capital. He also was named secretary of the Swedish Academy. Though usually mild in personality and warmly evangelical in his preaching, the new pastor in St. Clara parish soon began to create a stir in Stockholm by the boldness with which he berated the burghers for such prevalent sins as drunkenness, immorality, gambling, gluttony and frivolity. At one time, in the midst of a sermon, he pointed through the window toward the adjoining churchyard and exclaimed: "Out there is a congregation of those who are dead and yet alive; but in here, I fear, there are many who are said to be alive, and yet are dead in sin and unbelief."

After ten years of service in St. Clara Church, Franzèn was appointed Bishop of Härnösand, with jurisdiction over the Province of Norrland. Although he was 62 years old at the time, he gladly accepted the difficult post. Lappland was included in his far-stretching ecclesiastical domain, and one of his greatest concerns was to check the spread of intemperance that threatened to demoralize the lives of the nomads of the North. Whisky, it was said by a contemporary, flowed into Lappland in a volume that equalled all the water that flowed out of that region through its many torrents. For thirteen years Franzèn labored untiringly for the spiritual uplift of his diocese, and when death came in the summer of 1847, it found the beloved 75-year-old bishop still faithfully discharging the duties of his arduous office.

Work on the 1819 *Psalmbook* had already begun when Franzèn moved to Sweden in 1812, but he was soon closely associated with Wallin in the project. It is claimed that he exerted a strong spiritual influence over the latter. Though not as prolific a writer as Wallin, the hymns of Franzèn are rich in content and finished in form. Because of their artless simplicity it has been said that "the cultured man will appreciate them and the unlettered man can understand them." Among the more popular are two evening hymns—"The day departs, yet Thou art near" and "When vesper bells are calling." The latter is a hymn of solemn beauty:

> When vesper bells are calling
>   The hour of rest and prayer,
> When evening shades are falling,
>   And I must hence repair,
> I seek my chamber narrow,
>   Nor my brief day deplore,
> For I shall see the morrow,
>   When night shall be no more.

"Prepare the way, O Zion," an Advent hymn of great power and beauty, is considered by many as Franzèn's finest lyric. Another outstanding one is his communion hymn, "Thine own, O loving Saviour," which has called thousands of hungering souls to the Lord's Supper. The first stanza reads:

> Thine own, O loving Saviour,
>   Are bidden here by Thee;
> Thy passion's fruits, Thy favor,
>   Thyself Thou givest free
> To all who by Thy grace and love
>   Are members of Thy Kingdom,
> Now here, and then above.

His hymn for the first communion of catechumens, "Come, O Jesus, and prepare me," is also regarded as one of the most appealing of its kind in Swedish hymnody.

When we add to these such hymns as "Ajar the temple gates are swinging," "Thy scepter, Jesus, shall extend," "Awake, the watchman crieth" and "The little while I linger here," it is easy to understand why Franzèn ranks so high among the hymnists of the North. The 1819 *Psalmbook* contained no less than twenty-nine contributions from his pen, and of these twenty-three have been retained in the 1937 *Psalmbook*. And yet, this humble man who left so large a spiritual heritage to his countrymen always spoke very modestly about his work. "I greatly fear," he once said, "that I failed to measure up to Wallin's faith in me." The Swedish people, however, seem to think otherwise.

To Samuel Johan Hedborn, another of Wallin's contemporaries, posterity will ever be grateful for "Glorious Majesty, before Thee," a magnificent hymn of praise that for loftiness of poetic sentiment and pure spiritual exaltation has probably never been excelled. The first stanza suggests something of the celestial beauty of this noble hymn:

> Glorious Majesty, before Thee
> We bow to worship and adore Thee;
>   With grateful hearts to Thee we sing.
> Earth and heaven tell the story
> Of Thine eternal might and glory,
>   And all Thy works their incense bring.
> Lo, hosts of Cherubim
> And countless Seraphim
>   Sing, Hosanna,
> Holy is God, almighty God,
> All-merciful and all-wise God!

Hedborn, the son of a poverty-stricken Swedish soldier, was born in Heda, Sweden, in the year 1783. He began his career as a school teacher, served for a while as court preacher, and finally became pastor at Åskeryd, where he died in 1849. He was a gifted writer, and his lyric poetry and folk-songs struck a responsive chord in Swedish hearts. In 1812 he published a collection of hymns, and in the following year a second volume appeared. It is claimed that the Christocentric note in Hedborn's hymns profoundly influenced Wallin and helped to establish the latter in the orthodox Lutheran teaching.

In addition to the sublime anthem mentioned above, two other hymns of Hedborn have been given English dress. One of these is the beautiful Epiphany hymn, "Now Israel's hope in triumph ends"; the other a communion hymn, "With holy joy my heart doth beat."

Erik Gustav Geijer, professor of history in Upsala University, was another of the poetic geniuses of this golden age in Swedish hymnody. He was born at Ransäter, Värmland, Sweden, in the same year that Hedborn first saw the light of day, namely 1783. Like Hedborn, he also published a little collection of hymns in 1812 which immediately focused attention upon him as a poet of unusual ability. Although his hymns do not rise to the artistic heights attained by his other poems, it is believed that Geijer purposely avoided high-sounding phrases as unworthy of the dignity and spirit that should be found in hymnody.

His passion hymn, "Thy Cross, O Jesus, Thou didst bear," is a gripping portrayal of the conquering power of the Saviour's sacrificial love. There is likewise a glorious note of victory heard in his Easter hymn:

> In triumph our Redeemer
> Is now to life returned.
> All praise to Him who, dying,
> Hath our salvation earned!
> No more death's fetter galls us,
> The grave no more appalls us,
> For Jesus lives again.

In the preparation of the *Psalmbook* there was no one on whom Wallin leaned so heavily for help and counsel as Johan Åström, parish priest in Simtuna and Altuna. This man, who was born in 1767, was a lyric poet of unusual ability, and Wallin valued his judgment very highly, even to the extent of seeking his criticism of his own hymns. Eighteen of the hymns in the *Psalmbook* are from Åström's pen. Some of them, unfortunately, show traces of the spirit of Rationalism, from which influence Åström had not quite been able to free himself.

We are immeasurably indebted to Åström for the present form of the glorious All Saints' Day hymn, "In heaven above, in heaven above." This hymn, in which we may discern something of the celestial radiance and beauty of the heavenly country itself, is ranked as one of the finest of Swedish sacred lyrics. More than three centuries old, it dates back in its original form to 1620. It was written by L. Laurentii Laurinus, parish pastor in Häradshammar, at the time of his wife's death, and was appended to the funeral sermon preached by another pastor. Åström recognized the rare beauty of the hymn and used his poetic genius to clothe it in immortal language. William Maccall, a Scotchman, has in turn rendered it into English so successfully that much of its original beauty is preserved.

> In heaven above, in heaven above,
> Where God our Father dwells,
> How boundless there the blessedness!
> No tongue its greatness tells;
> There face to face, and full and free,
> Ever and evermore we see—
> We see the Lord of hosts!

Arvid Afzelius, court chaplain and pastor at Enköping, was another member of this remarkable group of Swedish hymnists. It was he who wrote the inspiring hymn of praise beginning:

> Unto the Lord of all creation
> Thy voice, my soul, in anthems raise.
> Let every heart a fit oblation
> Bring unto Him with songs of praise.
> O contemplate in humbleness
> The power and riches of His grace.

Johan Hjertèn, an obscure country pastor at Hellstad, was the author of six hymns in the *Psalmbook,* among them the devotional hymn, "Jesus, in my walk and living." It is said that the artless simplicity of his hymns provided an excellent pattern for the other writers of his day, many of whom were fond of the grandiloquent phrases so characteristic of the hymnody of Rationalism.

The last of this group whose name we would mention was a layman, Per Olof Nyström. This man, who was a high naval officer, wrote many excellent hymns, among them a devotional lyric that for more than a hundred years has been cherished almost as a universal prayer by the pious folk of Sweden. Its first stanza reads:

> O Fount of truth and mercy,
> Thy promise cannot fail;
> What Thou hast said must ever
> In heaven and earth prevail;
> "Call upon Me in trouble,
> And I will help afford."
> Yea, to my latest moment,
> I'll call upon Thee, Lord.

A Hymn Born of a Broken Heart

Children of the heavenly Father
Safely in His bosom gather;
Nestling bird nor star in heaven,
Such a refuge e'er was given.

God His own doth tend and nourish,
In His holy courts they flourish,
From all evil things he spares them,
In His mighty arms He bears them.

Neither life nor death shall ever
From the Lord His children sever;
Unto them His grace He showeth,
And their sorrows all He knoweth.

Though He giveth or He taketh,
God His children ne'er forsaketh,
His the loving purpose solely
To preserve them pure and holy.

CAROLINE V. SANDELL BERG, 1832–1903
TR. ERNST WILLIAM OLSON, 1870–1958

THE FANNY CROSBY OF SWEDEN AND THE PIETISTS

AS will be noted in a subsequent chapter, the 19th century witnessed the phenomenon of gifted Christian women assuming a place of primary importance among the foremost hymn-writers of the Church. Just as England had its Charlotte Elliott and Frances Havergal, and America had its Fanny Crosby, so Sweden had its Lina Sandell.

The rise of women hymn-writers came simultaneously with the great spiritual revival which swept over evangelical Europe and America in successive tidal waves from 1800 to 1875. In Sweden, the religious renaissance received its first impulse, no doubt, from Lutheran Germany. However, the Wesleyan movement in England also began to make its influence felt in wider circles, and the coming to Stockholm of such a man as George Scott, an English Methodist, gave added impetus to the evangelical revival which was already under way. Carl Olof Rosenius, Sweden's greatest lay preacher and the most prominent leader in the Pietistic movement in that country, was one of Scott's disciples, although he remained faithful to the Lutheran doctrine and a member of the Established Church to the end of his life.

It was in the midst of the Rosenius movement that Lina Sandell became known to her countrymen as a great song-writer. She was born October 3, 1832, at Fröderyd, her father being the parish pastor at that place. Frail during her youth, she usually preferred to spend her time in her father's study rather than join her comrades in play. When she was twenty-six years old, she accompanied him on a journey to Gothenburg, but they never reached their destination. At Hästholmen the vessel on which they had sailed gave a sudden lurch and the father fell overboard, drowning before the eyes of his devoted daughter.

The tragedy proved a turning point in Lina Sandell's life. In the midst of her grief she sought comfort in writing hymns. Her songs seemed to pour forth in a steady stream from the depths of a broken heart. Fourteen of her lyrics were published anonymously the same year in a Christian periodical, *Budbäraren*. Although she lived to write 650 hymns in all, these fourteen from the pen of the grief-stricken young woman have retained a stronger hold on the hearts of her countrymen than most of her later productions. Among these "first-fruits" born of sorrow are such hymns as: "Saviour, O hide not Thy loving face from me," "Others He hath succored," and "Children of the heavenly Father." Other hymns that have come to be deeply loved are "Thy holy wings, dear Saviour," "Strait is the gate to all that come," and "Day by day Thy mercies, Lord, attend me."

The remarkable popularity attained by her hymns has been due to a large extent, no doubt, to the music written for them by Oskar Ahnfelt, a "spiritual troubadour" of his day. Ahnfelt not only possessed the gift of composing pleasing melodies that caught the fancy of the Swedish people, but he traveled from place to place throughout the Scandinavian countries singing them to the accompaniment of a guitar. Miss Sandell once said: "Ahnfelt has sung my songs into the hearts of the people."

The inspiration for her songs came at sundry times and places. Sometimes in the midst of the noise and confusion of the city's streets, she would hear the words of a new song. Sometimes she awoke in the still hours of the night with the words of a new hymn ringing in her ears. She always kept a slate by her bedside on which to record instantly these heaven-born thoughts.

In 1867 Miss Sandell was married to a Stockholm merchant, C. O. Berg, but she continued to sign her hymns with the initials, "L. S.", by which she was familiarly known throughout Sweden. She died on July 27, 1903.

Not only Ahnfelt, but also Jenny Lind helped to make Lina Sandell's hymns known. The "Swedish Nightingale" was herself a Pietist and found great spiritual inspiration in listening to the preaching of Rosenius and the singing of Ahnfelt. At these conventicles the marvelous singer who had gained the homage of two continents sat with common workingmen on crude benches and joined her sweet voice in the singing of the Pietist hymns. Ahnfelt, in visiting the home of the great singer, once told her of his desire to publish these songs. When Jenny Lind learned that financial difficulties stood in the way, she quickly provided the necessary funds, and so the first edition of *Ahnfelt's Songs*, which in reality consisted mostly of the hymns of Lina Sandell and Rosenius, was made possible.

Rosenius and Ahnfelt encountered much opposition in their evangelism efforts. At one time King Karl XV was petitioned to forbid Ahnfelt's preaching and singing. The monarch refused until he had had an opportunity to hear the "spiritual troubadour." Ahnfelt was commanded to appear at the royal palace. Being considerably perturbed in mind as to what he should sing to his monarch, he besought Lina Sandell to write a special hymn. She was equal to the occasion and within a few days the song was ready. With his guitar under his arm and the hymn in his pocket, Ahnfelt repaired to the palace and sang:

> Who is it that knocketh upon your heart's door
>   In peaceful eve?
> Who is it that brings to the wounded and sore
>   The balm that can heal and relieve?
> Your heart is still restless, it findeth no peace
>   In earth's pleasures;
> Your soul is still yearning, it seeketh release
>   To rise to the heavenly treasures.

The king listened with moist eyes. When Ahnfelt had finished, the monarch gripped him by the hand and exclaimed: "You may sing as much as you desire in both of my kingdoms!"

Mention has already been made of the hymns of Rosenius. These, like the songs of Lina Sandell, were likewise a powerful factor in the spread of the evangelical movement in Sweden.

Rosenius was the son of a parish pastor in Norrland, Sweden. From the time of his birth, February 3, 1816, he was dedicated by his pious parents for the holy ministry. After having pursued studies for a short time at Upsala University, however, he became appalled at the low moral and spiritual standards he found among the students, and for a while his own faith was severely shaken. During these spiritual difficulties he came in contact with George Scott, the Methodist evangelist in Stockholm, and eventually he began to hold meetings as a "lay preacher."

In 1842 Scott and Rosenius began the publication of *Pietisten*, a religious monthly that was destined to play a most important part in the spiritual revival in Sweden. When Scott was constrained the same year to leave Sweden because of violent opposition to his movement, Rosenius became his successor, both as editor of *Pietisten* and as the leader of those who were trying to bring about the dawn of a new spiritual day.

Rosenius centered his activity in the Swedish capital, preaching and writing. He also traveled extensively throughout the country, and so the movement spread. Numerous lay preachers, known as "läsare," sprang up everywhere, holding private meetings in homes and in so-called "mission houses" built near the parish churches.

Agitation for separation from the Established Church found no sympathy with Rosenius, who stood firmly on the Lutheran doctrine and regularly took communion at the hands of its ordained ministers.

"How long do you intend to remain within the Church?" he once was asked.

"As long as Jesus is there," was the answer of Rosenius.

"But how long do you think He will be there?"

"As long as men are born anew, for that is not the work of the devil."

In 1856 Rosenius, together with many earnest-minded ecclesiasts and leaders in the Established Church, organized the National Evangelical Foundation, which originally was intended to promote home and inner mission activities. It subsequently embraced the cause of foreign missions also and became one of the greatest spiritual influences emanating from Scandinavia. Rosenius died in 1868 at the age of fifty-two.

His hymns, like those of Lina Sandell, became known largely through the musical genius of Ahnfelt. Everywhere Ahnfelt's songs were on the lips of the so-called "believers." Emigrants leaving Sweden for America brought them with them to the New World, where they became a source of solace and strength in the midst of the many troubles and difficulties that beset them. Perhaps no song was heard more often in their humble gatherings than the concluding stanza of Rosenius' hymn, "With God and His mercy, His Spirit, and Word":

> O Shepherd, abide with us, care for us still
> And feed us and lead us and teach us Thy will;
> And when in Thy heavenly fold we shall be,
>   Our thanks and our praises,
> Our thanks and our praises we'll render to Thee.

Although the songs of Lina Sandell and Rosenius do not rise to the lofty poetic expression of the noble hymns of Wallin's *Psalm-*

book, their strong spiritual appeal found a warm response in the hearts of the Swedish people, and it is significant that when a revision of the *Psalmbook* was published in 1937, eleven of Lina Sandell's and three of Rosenius' lyrics were included in the new hymnal.

Incidentally, the new *Psalmbook* of 1937 was unique for the interest it revealed in children's hymns. Whereas Wallin's collection of 1819 contained only one lyric for those of tender years, the revised 1937 volume devoted an entire section to hymns of this character. Included here were Lina Sandell's "Children of the heavenly Father" and two others by her. Here also we find contributions by a number of other Swedish women who wrote hymns for children, such as Charlotta Lindblom, Jeanna Oterdahl, Siri Dahlquist and Elizabeth Ehrenborg-Posse.

The latter, who lived during the same period as Lina Sandell, has been credited with having started the Sunday school movement in Sweden. A daughter of Swedish aristocracy, "Betty" Ehrenborg found herself in Stockholm after the death of her father, and here she came under the influence of Rosenius and other Pietists. Her interest in children led her to invite three little girls from poverty-stricken homes to come to her own home on a Sunday morning in 1851. Soon the number of children multiplied, and it was necessary to find larger quarters for the class.

The following year Miss Ehrenborg went to England to study the Sunday school movement there. When she returned to Stockholm she established her Sunday school in the Kungsholm district, where much poverty reigned. Eventually she found it necessary to train other teachers in order to care for the increasing number of children who were attracted to the school. In 1856 she married Baron J. A. Posse, a man of strong religious convictions, who gave enthusiastic support to the movement.

While in England, the baroness had become familiar with many hymns written for children, and because of the scarcity of such lyrics in her native tongue, she began to translate some of these. Among others, she even transformed Cowper's "There is a fountain filled with blood" into a charming song for children! Perhaps her most popular hymn is the lovely Christmas carol, "When Christmas morn is dawning," which may have had a German antecedent but is more probably an original composition. Baroness Ehrenborg-Posse died in 1880.

A Child Looks to God

I lift my eyes unto heaven above,
And fold my hands to draw near Thee;
For Thou, dear Lord, dost Thy children love,
And Thou hast promised to hear me.

How sweet to bless Thee and praise Thy Name,
For Thou, O Christ, art my Saviour;
Kind Shepherd, guard me from sin and shame,
And let me love Thee forever.

A little flower in Thy garden fair,
My life to Thee has been given;
O Saviour, keep me in Thy dear care,
And bring me safely to heaven.

Dear Lord, I thank Thee for all Thy love
And gifts divine beyond measure;
A sweeter song I will raise above
To Thee, my heart's dearest treasure.

JOHAN LUDVIG RUNEBERG, 1804-77
PARAPHRASE, ERNEST EDWIN RYDEN, 1886-
BASED ON TR. BY IDA MARIE KAARTO-KASKINEN, 1903-

THE HYMNS OF HEROIC FINLAND

IN THE British Museum may be seen a priceless volume of Latin lyrics bearing the name, *Piae Cantiones*. It contains a famous collection of medieval sacred and secular songs, many of them of Finnish and Swedish origin, published in Greifswald, Pomerania, in 1582. The copy in the British Museum, which is one of the very few original volumes in existence, was presented in 1852 to the British Minister in Stockholm, who brought it with him to London. It was hailed there as a discovery of major importance, bringing to the attention of the English-speaking world for the first time a rich store of medieval Latin lyrics hitherto unknown.

The story of *Piae Cantiones* is very fascinating. According to information given in the first edition, the collection was made and edited "by a prominent person in the cathedral church and school at Åbo (Turku) in Finland." The Finnish edition, which was published in 1616, informs us that this Åbo editor was Magister Jacob Finno. Editing of the lyrics was quite necessary, since many of these contained Romish errors prevalent throughout Europe before the Reformation. Finno was evidently aided by other scholars at Åbo in this work, among whom may have been a young student named Theodoricus Petri Ruutha, son of a landed proprietor in Borgå, Finland.

There was no printing press in Finland at that time, and, since Ruutha was leaving Åbo to continue his studies at the University of Rostock, he was commissioned to have the collection printed in Germany. Ruutha found a printing press at Greifswald, not far from Rostock, and here the "pious songs" were published in 1582.

The Finnish edition of 1616 informs us that many of these Latin lyrics were written by medieval bishops and churchmen in Finland. Some of the latter were undoubtedly Swedish ecclesiasts, since Sweden and Finland were one kingdom at this time. The Finnish hymnologist, P. J. I. Kurvinen, after exhaustive research, has determined that about one-third of the 74 songs in the collection are found in earlier sources, principally from central Europe and France, but *Piae Cantiones* is the only known source for the large majority. The unique book also contains many plainsong tunes and other medieval music which would have been irretrievably lost to posterity except for the zeal of the Finnish scholars. Among the gems found in this priceless volume may be mentioned the spring carol, "Spring has now unwrapped the flowers," with its lovely tune, *Tempus adest floridum,* which John Mason Neale unfortunately adapted to "Good King Wenceslas"; the charming dialogue Christmas carol, "Joseph dearest, Joseph mine," which has also been translated "Long ago and far away"; and the tune, *Divinum Mysterium,* to which Prudentius' hymn, "Of the Father's love begotten," is usually sung.

The Latin songs in *Piae Cantiones* are typical of the kind of lyrics that were sung in Finland and all other countries in Europe for centuries before the Reformation. Though not used in the stated worship of the Church, they were often translated into the vernacular and were popularly sung in social gatherings and in the home on festive occasions. As such, they paved the way for the great outburst of evangelical hymnody that accompanied the triumphant progress of the Reformation in Germany and throughout northern Europe.

To Bishop Michael Agricola, the "Martin Luther of Finland," goes the credit for having laid the foundation for congregational singing in his native land. The first Finnish Mass in the vernacular, published by him in 1549, followed very closely the Mass of Olavus Petri, the Swedish reformer. Its rubrics provided for the singing of hymns and psalms, but only one hymn appears with the printed Mass. This is Decius' well-known paraphrase of the *Agnus Dei,* and is based on Olavus Petri's Swedish version, *"O rene gudz lamb."* Agricola did not write any hymns of his own, but he was the translator of some thirty, chiefly Latin office hymns, sequences, antiphons and canticles, all of which were printed in his *Prayerbook* of 1544.

In 1551 Agricola published another volume containing a number of the Old Testament canticles in prose translation, and followed it by translating the entire Psalter into Finnish.

It remained for the above-mentioned Jacob Finno, however, to become the creator of Finland's first real hymnal. This volume, which was printed in 1583, contained 101 hymns, most of them translations from the Latin, the German and the Swedish, but also a few originals, presumably the work of Finno.

In 1614, Hemming of Masku published a greatly enlarged hymnbook containing 242 hymns. Of these, no less than 135 were originals or translations by Hemming himself. Hemming was also the translator and publisher of the 1616 Finnish edition of *Piae Cantiones*. It is interesting to note that the latest Finnish hymnal, which appeared in 1938, still retained seven of Finno's hymns and twenty of Hemming's.

The third Finnish hymnbook, which was published in 1701, followed very closely the pattern of the Swedish *Psalmbook* of 1695, even to the extent of having the same number of hymns, namely, 413. In addition to the hymns of the two foregoing Finnish hymn-writers, it contained translations of new German and Swedish hymns.

The commemoration of the 300th anniversary of the Reformation in 1817 gave the impetus for the creation of a new and more comprehensive hymnbook. For some six centuries Finland and Sweden had been united politically, and the closest cultural and religious ties existed between the two countries. Although the political union came to an end during the Napoleonic wars, when Finland became an independent duchy of Russia, Swedish as well as Finnish continued to be spoken in Finland, and many congregations employed the former language in their worship. It became necessary, therefore, to appoint two hymnal committees, the one to prepare the Finnish hymnal and the other to edit the Swedish book. During the ensuing years a number of tentative drafts were submitted by the two groups, but it was not until 1886 that the General Church Council gave final approval to their work. The Finnish hymnal of 1701 had then been in official use for 185 years!

The complete political independence which came to Finland at the close of World War I greatly stimulated the upsurge of national consciousness which had begun to manifest itself in that country nearly a century earlier. There had also taken place marked changes in the Finnish language. These basic causes, together with the need of more hymns for special occasions, brought on an insistent demand for a more distinctive Finnish hymnbook. As a result, a new official book of worship was published in 1938 containing 633 hymns. Five years later a revised version of the official Swedish hymnbook was also authorized.

Unfortunately, not many Finnish hymns have been rendered into English. However, when the *Service Book and Hymnal* of the Lutheran Church of America was published in 1958, it was found to contain four lyrics that are fairly representative of Finnish hymnody.

Of unusual interest is a very tender children's hymn, "I lift my eyes unto heaven above," which comes from the pen of Johan Ludvig Runeberg. Though he wrote in Swedish, Runeberg was Finland's national poet. He first gained renown in the middle of the 19th century through his patriotic verse and particularly as the author of Finland's national anthem, *"Maamme Laula,"* or *"Vårt Land."* His collection of *Ensign Ståhl's Songs,* in which the anthem first appeared, aroused great enthusiasm throughout Scandinavia.

An indescribable charm and a warm devotional spirit in Runeberg's hymns have made them deeply cherished, both in Finland and Sweden. Nor do they seem to lose their popularity with the passing of time. The Finnish hymnal of 1938 contains twenty-three of his lyrics, while the Swedish hymnal of 1943 has fifty. The recent *Psalmbook* of the Church of Sweden also honored the Finnish poet of Swedish ancestry by including eight of his hymns. Among these is the hymn mentioned above, which every child in Finland and Sweden knows as an evening prayer. One could wish that the children of America also might learn to love it.

The sweet tune to which "I lift my eyes unto heaven above" is sung is the composition of Rudolf Lagi, who before his death in 1868 was organist of the Great Church in Helsinki, originally called the Nicholai Church after the ruling Russian czar. Lagi was regarded as the leading musician in Finland during the middle of the last century.

Another hymn included in the 1958 American hymnal is known in Finland as the "Pilgrim Song." It was written by Wilhelmi Malmivaara, a Lutheran provost in Ostrobothnia, who was a leader of a Pietistic movement in that region during the latter part of the 19th century. It reads:

> Lord, as a pilgrim on earth I roam,
> By foes surrounded, far from my home;
> Whate'er betide me,
> Walk Thou beside me,
> Shepherd divine!
>
> Though friends forsake me, Thou art the same,
> Faithful forever is Thy blest Name,
> Thou wilt not leave me,
> Oft though I grieve Thee,
> Thou Friend divine!
>
> Thou art my refuge; grant me, I pray,
> Strength for each burden, light on my way,
> Balm in my sorrow,
> Grace for tomorrow,
> Saviour divine!

198

Lord, let Thy presence lead all the way,
Until the dawning of that great day
When I shall see Thee
Throned in Thy glory,
God blest for aye!

Concerning this hymn, which was written by Malmivaara during a period of great sorrow following the death of his wife and two children within a space of two weeks, his biographer has written: "This is one of the few religious songs that has found its way to every corner of our Fatherland. It breathes the yearning of a Finnish soul and the longings of a Christian . . . who humbly and prayerfully trusts in God. The Finnish Christian piety which is characterized by a spirit of quiet sorrow and sadness has found in this hymn its most beautiful expression."

During the dreadful days of the 1940 Russo-Finnish conflict, which was one of the tragic episodes of World War II, Malmivaara's beautiful hymn became a source of hope and consolation to thousands of bereaved homes throughout Finland. An American pastor who visited the ravaged country on a mission of mercy at the close of the war reported that he heard it sung wherever he went in Finland. Although he was unable to understand the words, the tune continued to haunt him for months after his return to the United States. This tune, which had been composed for secular words by Ernest August Hagfors, a music instructor in Finland's oldest Teachers' College at Jyväskylä, was already well known when Malmivaara wrote his hymn. The latter, it is said, appropriated it because he wanted to give the Pietists a song they would love to sing.

"Jesus, hear my humble pleading," another Finnish hymn included in 1958 in the *Service Book and Hymnal* of the Lutheran Church of America, is the work of a contemporary woman hymnist, Jenny Pohjola-Salmio, of Orivesi, Finland. Written during her youth, the hymn first appeared in a collection of choir anthems called *Zion's Tunes*. The final stanza of the hymn reads:

Near the mercy-seat abiding,
Let my soul Thy glory see;
In Thy grace alone confiding,
Perfect peace I find in Thee.
Tune my heart to sing Thy praises
Till I join the heavenly throng
Which through endless ages raises
Sweetest praise with harp and song.

199

The fine tune accompanying the hymn was written by Armas Toivi Maasalo, director of the Helsinki Institute of Church Music and organist of St. John's Church in the Finnish capital. Known as one of the foremost musicians of Finland, Maasalo has won fame for his orchestra compositions and piano concertos, as well as for the large contribution he has made to the music of the Church.

Another hymn introduced into the *Service Book and Hymnal* from Finnish sources, though its author was a Swedish hymn-writer, bears the title, "Arise, my soul, arise!" It was written around the year 1745 by a pious layman, Johan Kahl, who hailed from the ancient Hanseatic city of Visby, situated on the island of Gotland in the Baltic Sea. Composed in a most unusual meter, the hymn is a singularly inspiring anthem of praise to the ascended and victorious Christ:

> Arise, my soul, arise!
> Stretch forth to things eternal,
> And haste thee to the feet of thy Redeemer God.
> Though hid from mortal eyes,
> He dwell in light supernal,
> Yet worship Him in humbleness and own Him Lord.
> His banquet of love
> Awaits thee above;
> Behold, the marriage festal of the Lamb is come!
> Rejoice, my soul, rejoice,
> To heaven lift up thy voice:
> Alleluia, Alleluia, Alleluia!
>
> List to the harps of heaven!
> Hark to the song victorious,
> The never-ending anthem sounding through the sky.
> To mortals is not given
> To chant its strains all-glorious;
> Yet sing, my soul, the praise of Him who reigns on high,
> Who bought with His Blood
> The ransomed of God;
> To Him be everlasting power and victory.
> And let the great Amen
> Resound through heaven again.
> Alleluia, Alleluia, Alleluia!

Kahl wrote a large number of hymns, but for some unaccountable reason they did not find a place in the authorized hymnbooks of his homeland. The Swedish *Psalmbook* of 1819 included only one of his lyrics, as did the more recent *Psalmbook* of 1937. However, no less than 60 of a total 223 lyrics which appeared in 1743 in *Zions Sånger* were from his pen. This collection was translated into Finnish in 1790 by Elias Lagus and became the favorite songbook of the conservative Pietists in Southwest Finland known as the *Rukoile-*

vaiset, or "Praying People." When two other revival movements arose in Finland during the 19th century—"The Awakened" in north and central Finland and the Laestadians in the far north and in Lapland— these also adopted *Zions Sånger* as their favorite hymnbook. How deeply the hymns of Kahl have left their impress on the spiritual life of the people of Finland is evidenced by the fact that the 1938 official hymnbook of the Church of Finland contains no less than nine of his lyrics, including the one given above.

Something also needs to be said concerning the stirring tune to which "Arise, my soul, arise!" is sung. In the summer of 1890, two young Finnish students, Berndt Mikael Nyberg and Ilmari Krohn, who were engaged in collecting secular melodies and folksongs in central Finland, encountered an old church sexton from southwest Finland who belonged to the "Praying People" of that region. From his lips they heard for the first time the tune to which the Pietists apparently for many generations had sung Kahl's grand hymn.

This led Nyberg the following summer to visit that section of Finland, where he discovered a remarkable number of choice folk melodies wholly unknown up to that time among music lovers in other parts of the country. These were subsequently published by Nyberg and Krohn in a volume titled *People's Gift to the Church.* Through this collection the tune of Kahl's hymn found its way into several hymnals, including the Finnish hymnbook of 1938. It is significant that, whereas practically no religious folk tunes were known in official church circles previous to the happy discovery of Nyberg and Krohn, the present authorized hymnal contains no less than 124 of these native melodies.

Another hymn-writer that Finland may justly claim as one of its own sons is Frans Mikael Franzèn, previously referred to under Swedish hymnody. Although he came from Swedish forebears, Franzèn was born in Finland and received his education there. He was a professor at Åbo University and already a writer of renown when he decided to leave his native land for Sweden. This occurred in 1812, three years after the long political union between that country and Finland had come to an end as a result of Russian conquest. In Sweden, Franzèn not only became a bishop of the Church, but also one of the principal contributors to Archbishop Wallin's famous *Psalmbook* of 1819. Franzèn's hymns are deeply cherished, both in Sweden and in Finland.

Kingo's Hymn of Praise

Praise to Thee and adoration,
Blessed Jesus, Son of God,
Who, to serve Thine own creation,
Didst assume our flesh and blood.
Grant that I may never stray
From Thy sacred fold away,
But with zeal and holy favor
Follow Thee, O blessed Saviour.

Let me never, Lord, forsake Thee
E'en though bitter pain and strife
On my way should overtake me;
But may I through all my life
Walk in fervent love to Thee,
In all woes for comfort flee
To Thy birth, Thy death and passion,
Till I see Thy full salvation.

THOMAS HANSEN KINGO, 1634-1703
TR. KRISTEN KVAMME, 1866-1938a.

KINGO, THE POET OF EASTERTIDE

DENMARK'S first great hymnist, Thomas Kingo, hailed from the land of Robert Burns. His grandfather, who also bore the name of Thomas, emigrated from Scotland to Denmark near the end of the 17th century to become a tapestry weaver for Christian IV.

Because of the large number of hymns written by Kingo on the theme of Christ's resurrection, he came to be known as the "Poet of Eastertide." In trying to find an explanation for the remarkable genius of this early Danish spiritual poet, Nikolai Grundtvig, another Danish hymn-writer, wrote two hundred years later: "Kingo's hymns represent not only the greatest miracle of the 17th century, but such an exceptional phenomenon in the realm of poetry that it is explainable only by the fates who in their wisdom preserved the seed of an Easter lily for a thousand years, and then returned it across the sea that it might flower in its original soil." This was an obvious reference to the fact that Kingo's grandfather came from that part of Scotland which once had been settled by Viking sea rovers, and a suggestion that Kingo's poetic command of the Danish language may have harked back to ancestors who lived many centuries before him!

The boy who was destined to become one of Denmark's most famous spiritual bards was born in Slangerup, December 15, 1634. At the age of six years he entered the Latin school of his native city, and ten years later became a student of the school in Frederiksborg. The principal of this institution, Albert Bartholin, discovered unusual gifts in the lad and took him into his own home. After completing theological studies at the university, he returned in 1668 to his native city of Slangerup as Lutheran parish pastor.

About this time Kingo began to attract attention as a writer of secular poetry. It was not until 1673, however, that his first collection of hymns appeared under the title, "Spiritual Songs, First Part." The profound impression created by this production is evidenced by the fact that in 1677 he was elevated from an obscure parish to the bishopric of the diocese of Fyen.

Kingo had dedicated his "Spiritual Songs" to Christian V, and thus had attracted the attention of the Danish monarch. In his "address" to the king, Kingo deplored the fact that the Danish people in their worship had depended so largely upon hymns of foreign origin.

"The soul of the Danes," he added significantly, "is not so bound and improverished but that it can soar as high toward heaven as that of other peoples, even if it be not borne upward by strange and foreign wings."

The Second Part of his "Spiritual Songs" appeared in 1681, this collection being dedicated to the Danish queen. Many of Kingo's hymns were written to be sung to popular folk melodies. In justification of this practice, the poet wrote:

"If a pleasing melody set to a song of Sodom delights your ear, how much more, if you are a true child of God, should not that same melody delight your soul when sung to a song of Zion!"

In his dedicatory address to Queen Charlotte, the poet of Scotch forebears gave expression to his great love for the Danish language, praised her for her heroic efforts to master the language before coming to Denmark as its queen, and ironically flayed certain foreign courtiers who for "thirty years had eaten the bread of the Fatherland in the service of the king without making an effort to learn thirty Danish words."

By this time the Danish people had come to a full realization that a poet of the first magnitude had risen in their midst. In June, 1679, Kingo was created a member of the nobility, and in 1682 he received the honorary degree of doctor of theology. The following year came the royal appointment to prepare a hymnbook for the Church of Denmark. The king's decree specifically stated that Kingo should include a number of his own hymns, but he was directed to make few changes in the old, traditional hymns, and "under no circumstances to alter the meaning of Luther's hymns."

Here it should be noted that Kingo was not the first creator of a Danish hymnbook. As early as 1528, Claus Martensön Tönderbinder, an evangelical pastor at Malmö, published at that place a manual called *Det kristelige Messe-embede paa Danske,* or "The Christian Mass in Danish," in which were found ten hymns, some translated from the Latin, and others from the German of Luther and the

Swedish of Olavus Petri. The following year Tönderbinder, with the aid of his friends, Arvid Petersen and Hans Spendemager, published a second volume of the same character containing additional hymns, a few of which had been written by Petersen. It is possible that these three men were also responsible for a third book published in 1533, known as *Malmö Psalmebogen*, which, in revised form and with additions from time to time, remained the hymnbook of the Danish and Norwegian Lutherans for more than a century.

The first part of Kingo's new book appeared in 1689. It met with a storm of disapproval not altogether unmerited. Of the 267 hymns in this book, 136 were by Kingo himself. Members of the Danish court who had been objects of Kingo's merciless satire now found an opportunity to secure revenge. Kingo's book, which had been published at his own expense, was rejected, and Soren Jonassen, dean of Roskilde, was appointed to take over the task. His work, which was completed in 1693, did not contain a single one of Kingo's hymns! It too was promptly disapproved. A commission was then appointed by the king to supervise the work, and again Kingo came into favor. The new hymnbook, which was officially approved in 1699, was based largely on Kingo's work, and contained 85 of his original hymns.

Although Kingo lived to see his life-work crowned with success, he never fully recovered from the indignity and humiliation he had suffered. His death occurred on October 14, 1703. The day before he died, he is said to have exclaimed: "Tomorrow, Lord, we shall hear glorious music."

A biographer declares that Kingo was "in love with the sun," and that he regarded light as the "true element." This is reflected in his morning hymns, which are among the finest songs of praise ever written. Here is the opening stanza of one of these:

> The sun arises now
> In light and glory,
> And gilds the rugged brow
> Of mountains hoary,
> Rejoice, my soul, and lift
> Thy voice in singing
> To God from earth below,
> Thy song with joy aglow
> And praises ringing.

Even in his celebrated Easter hymn, Kingo reverts to his favorite theme of the sun:

> Like the golden sun ascending
> In the darkly clouded sky,
> And on earth its glory spending
> Until clouds and darkness fly,
> So my Jesus from the grave,
> From death's dark, abysmal cave,
> Rose triumphant Easter morning,
> Brighter than the sun returning.

Nor could he forget the same theme even when he dwelt with gripping pathos on the subject of Christ's passion:

> Such a night was ne'er before,
> Even heaven has shut its door;
> Jesus, Thou our Sun and Light,
> Now must bear the shame of night.

When the commission appointed by the Danish king was revising his hymnbook, Kingo pleaded that his Lenten hymns might be retained. Among the most soul-stirring of these is the hymn, "Over Kedron Jesus treadeth." Kingo's hymns, though objective in character, never fail to make a strong personal appeal. Witness, for example, the following from his Good Friday hymn:

> Print Thine image, pure and holy,
> On my heart, O Lord of grace;
> So that nothing high or lowly
> Thy blest likeness can efface.
> Let the clear inscription be:
> Jesus crucified for me,
> And the Lord of all creation,
> Be my refuge and salvation.

Other hymns of Kingo that have been translated into English include "Praise to Thee and adoration," "Dearest Jesus, draw Thou near me," "He that believes and is baptized," "I come, invited by Thy word," and "Softly now the day is ending." His post-communion hymn, which has become very popular in Lutheran circles in America, reflects something of the spiritual fervor with which Kingo could dwell on the thought of the mystical union between Christ and the believer:

> O Jesus, blessed Lord, to Thee
> My heartfelt thanks forever be,
> Who hast so lovingly bestowed
> On me Thy Body and Thy Blood.
>
> Break forth, my soul, for joy and say,
> "What wealth is come to me this day,
> My Saviour dwells within me now,
> How blest am I, how good art Thou!"

When Kingo died, his remains were laid at rest in a small village church near Odense. On the slab is an inscription which likens the great Danish psalmist to a sun which, although it has set, still lights the way for the pilgrim who seeks the way of life.

Grundtvig pays Kingo this tribute: "He effected a combination of sublimity and simplicity, a union of splendor and fervent devotion, a powerful and musical play of words and imagery that reminds one of Shakespeare." And on Kingo's monument at Odense is this beautiful epitaph, also written by Grundtvig:

> Thomas Kingo is the psalmist
>   Of the Danish temple choir.
> This his people will remember
>   As long as song their hearts inspire.

The Great White Host

Behold a host like mountains bright!
Lo! who are these, arrayed in white,
A glorious band, with palms in hand
  Around the throne of light?
Lo, these are they who overcame
Great tribulation in His Name,
And with His Blood the Lamb of God
  Hath washed away their shame.
Before God's face they sing and pray,
Their voices blend with angels' lay,
And all conspire, a joyous choir,
  To laud Him night and day.

Then sing, ye conquering legions white,
Let myriad voices hail His might,
And praise the Lord, who by His word
  Hath stablished you in light.
Ye, who all earthly lure did flee,
Who sowed and toiled, but tears to see,
With rapture bring your sheaves and sing
  A heavenly melody.
Lift up your palms, your voices raise
Through heaven's vault and endless days.
To God and to the Lamb is due
  Eternity of praise.

HANS ADOLF BRORSON, 1694-1764
Composite Version, 1955

BRORSON, THE POET OF CHRISTMAS

NO SCANDINAVIAN hymn perhaps has attained such popularity in recent years in American circles as "Behold a host." This sublime "glory song" was first given to the world after its writer, Hans Adolph Brorson, had gone to join the "host, arrayed in white" singing "before the throne of light."

It was published by his son in a collection entitled *Hans Adolph Brorson's Swan-Song*, which appeared in 1765, a year after the famous Danish hymn-writer had gone to his final rest. The collection contained seventy hymns, all written in the last year of the poet's life.

Brorson was a product of the Pietistic movement emanating from Halle, in Germany. Born June 20, 1694, at Randrup, Denmark, he early came under the influence of the great spiritual awakening which was then sweeping through the Lutheran Church.

Brorson's father was a Lutheran pastor, all of whose three sons, including the hymn-writer, entered the service of the Church. Brorson's first pastorate was in his native city of Randrup, a place he dearly loved and to which he often returned in later life when he found himself oppressed by manifold cares.

It was during his ministry in Randrup that Brorson began writing his first hymns. He speaks of the eight years spent at this place as the happiest in his life. In 1729 he was called to become Danish preacher at Tonder, where he labored side by side with Johan Herman Schrader, a German pastor, who also was a Pietist and a hymnist of some note. Because of the mixed Danish and German population of Tonder, a curious situation existed in the church worship. Although Brorson preached in Danish, the congregation sang in German! To remedy this, Brorson, in 1732, wrote a number of his famous Christmas hymns, among them *"Den yndigste Rose er funden,"* a most exquisite gem of sacred poetry. A free rendering of four of its eleven stanzas by the late August W. Kjellstrand follows:

> The sweetest, the fairest of roses
> I've found. Among thorns it reposes:
> 'Tis Jesus, my soul's dearest Treasure,
> Of sinners a Friend above measure.

E'er since the sad day when frail mortals
Were thrust from fair Eden's bright portals,
The world has been dark, full of terror,
And man dead in sin, lost in error.

Then mindful of promises given,
God sent from the gardens of heaven
A Rose, 'mid the thorns brightly blowing,
And freely its fragrance bestowing.

Wherever this Rose Tree is grounded,
The kingdom of God there is founded;
And where its sweet fragrance is wafted,
There peace in the heart is engrafted.

As Kingo was known among the Danes as the "Poet of Easter," so Brorson from this time was hailed as the "Poet of Christmas."

In 1747, Brorson was appointed by Christian VI to become bishop of the diocese of Ribe. It is said that the Danish monarch upon meeting Brorson at a certain occasion inquired of him if he was the author of the hymn, "Awake, all things that God has made." When the poet modestly answered in the affirmative, so the story runs, the king promised him a bishopric.

When Erik Pontoppidan, later bishop of Bergen, was appointed to revise Kingo's hymnal, which for forty years had served the churches of Denmark and Norway, he found his task a comparatively simple one because of the valuable assistance rendered by Brorson. Kingo's hymns were changed only slightly, and the greater part of the new material was from Brorson's pen.

The later years of the poet were darkened by sad experiences. In the year that Brorson was elevated to the bishopric, his beloved wife died while giving birth to their thirteenth child. This and other troubles served to make him melancholy in spirit, but he continued to compose poems of rare beauty. His thoughts, however, turned more and more toward heaven and the blessedness of the life hereafter. A celestial radiance is reflected in the hymns contained in the "Swan-Song" collection. This is particularly true of "Behold, a host arrayed in white," a lyric that has become a universal favorite through its association with Edvard Grieg's famous adaptation of a Norwegian folksong.

Brorson's earnest character and pious nature made him deeply concerned about the salvation of souls. Many of his poems and hymns contain solemn warnings touching on the uncertainty of life and the need of seeking salvation. His gripping hymn, "Jeg gaar i Fare, hvor jeg gaar," which undoubtedly gave Archbishop Wallin, the great Swedish hymnist, the inspiration for a similar lyric, is typical of these hymns. Two of its stanzas read:

> Death walks beside me everywhere;
> Its shadows oft appall me.
> I know not when the hour is here
> When God from earth shall call me.
> A moment's failing breath,
> And I am cold in death,
> Faced with eternity fore'er;
> Death walks beside me everywhere.
>
> I walk to heaven everywhere,
> Preparing for the morrow
> When God shall hear my anxious prayer,
> And banish all my sorrow.
> Be quiet then, my soul,
> Press onward to thy goal;
> All earthly things do thou forswear,
> And walk to heaven everywhere.

Other well-known hymns by Brorson are "Thy little ones, dear Lord, are we," "O Father, may Thy Word prevail," "O watch and pray," "Life's day is ended," "My heart, prepare to give account," "By faith we are divinely sure," "Children of God, born again of His Spirit," "O seek the Lord today," "I see Thee standing, Lamb of God," "Stand fast, my soul, stand fast," "Jesus, Name of wondrous grace," "My heart remains in wonder," and "O Thou blest Immanuel." Brorson's childlike spirit may be seen reflected in the first of these, a children's Christmas hymn:

> Thy little ones, dear Lord, are we,
> And come Thy lowly bed to see;
> Enlighten every soul and mind,
> That we the way to Thee may find.
>
> With songs we hasten Thee to greet,
> And kiss the dust before Thy feet;
> O blessed hour, O sweetest night,
> That gave Thee birth, our soul's delight.
>
> O draw us wholly to Thee, Lord,
> Do Thou to us Thy grace accord,
> True faith and love to us impart,
> That we may hold Thee in our heart.
>
> Until at last we too proclaim
> With all Thy saints Thy glorious Name;
> In paradise our songs renew,
> And praise Thee as the angels do.

211

The Church on the Rock

Built on a Rock the Church doth stand,
    Even when steeples are falling;
Crumbled have spires in every land,
    Bells still are chiming and calling;
        Calling the young and old to rest,
        Calling the souls of men distressed,
          Longing for life everlasting.

Not in our temples made with hands
    God, the almighty, is dwelling;
High in the heavens His temple stands,
    All earthly temples excelling;
        Yet He who dwells in heaven above
        Deigns to abide with us in love,
          Making our bodies His temple.

We are God's house of living stones,
    Built for His own habitation;
He fills our hearts, His humble thrones,
    Granting us life and salvation;
        Were two or three to seek His face,
        He in their midst would show His grace,
          Blessings upon them bestowing.

Yet in this house, an earthly frame,
    Jesus the children is blessing;
Hither we come to praise His Name,
    Faith in our Saviour confessing;
        Jesus to us His Spirit sent,
        Making with us His covenant,
          Granting His children the Kingdom.

Through all the passing years, O Lord,
    Grant that, when church bells are ringing,
Many may come to hear God's Word
    Where He this promise is bringing:
        I know Mine own, Mine own know me,
        Ye, not the world, My face shall see;
          My peace I leave with you, amen.

NIKOLAI F. S. GRUNDTVIG, 1783-1872; TR. CARL DOVING, 1867-1937
Revised, FRED C. M. HANSEN, 1888-

GRUNDTVIG, THE POET OF WHITSUNTIDE

NIKOLAI F. S. GRUNDTVIG was the last and greatest of the celebrated triumvirate of Danish hymn-writers. As Kingo was the bright star of the 17th century and Brorson of the 18th century, so Grundtvig shone with a luster all his own in the 19th century. The "Poet of Easter" and the "Poet of Christmas" were succeeded by the "Poet of Whitsuntide."

The appellation given to Grundtvig was not without reason, for it was he, above all others, who strove mightily in Denmark against the deadening spirit of Rationalism which had dried up the streams of spirituality in the Church. No one labored with more amazing courage and zeal to bring about the dawn of a new day than did the "Poet of Whitsuntide."

Nor did Grundtvig strive in vain. Before his life-work was ended, fresh Pentecostal breezes began to blow, the dry bones began to stir, and the Church of Denmark, moved by the Spirit of God, experienced a new spiritual birth.

Rationalism had worked havoc with the most sacred truths of the Christian religion. As some one has said, "It converted the banner of the Lamb into a bluestriped kerchief, the Christian religion into a philosophy of happiness, and the temple dome into an umbrella."

Under the influence of the "New Theology," ministers of the Gospel had prostituted the church worship into lectures on science and domestic economy. It is said that one minister, in preaching on the theme of the Christ-child and the manger, developed it into a lecture on the proper care of stables, and another, moved by the story of the coming of the holy women to the sepulcher on the first Easter morning, delivered a peroration on the advantages of getting up early! God was referred to as "Providence" or "the Deity," Christ as "the founder of Christianity," sin as "error," salvation as "happiness," and the essence of the Christian life as "morality."

Grundtvig's father was one of the few Lutheran pastors in Denmark who had remained faithful to evangelical truth. The future poet, who was born in Udby, September 8, 1783, had the advantage, therefore, of being brought up in a household where reigned the spirit of true Christian piety. It was not long, however, before young Grundtvig, as a student at the University of Copenhagen, came under the influence of the "New Theology." Although he planned to become a minister, he lost all interest in religion during his final year at school, and finished his academic career "without spirit and without faith."

A number of circumstances, however, began to open his eyes to the spiritual poverty of the people. Morality was at a low ebb, and a spirit of indifference and frivolity banished all serious thoughts from their minds. It was a rude shock to his sensitive and patriotic soul to observe, in 1807, how the populace of Copenhagen laughed and danced while the Danish fleet was being destroyed by English warships and the capital city itself was being bombarded by the enemy. His satirical poem, "The Masquerade Ball of Denmark," written at the time, was one of the first evidences of Grundtvig's ability to use biting scorn in exposing the spiritual laxity of his day.

While teaching history in a school for boys in Copenhagen in 1810, Grundtvig received a request from his old father to become his assistant in the parish of Udby. He had already gained recognition by this time for his literary work, and he was loathe to leave the Danish capital. Moreover, he had no special desire to enter the ministry. Not wishing to disappoint his father, however, he applied for ordination, and then began the preparation of his probation sermon, which had to be preached before censors. In this sermon, which was delivered before church officials on March 17, 1810, young Grundtvig attacked the prevailing spirit of rationalism among the Danish clergy.

"The Word of God," said he, "has departed from His house, and that which is preached there is not the Word of God, but the materialistic speculations of men. Holy men of old believed in the message they were called to preach, but the human spirit has now become so proud that it feels itself capable of discovering the truth without the light of the Gospel, and so faith has died. My brethren! let us not, if we share this blindness and contempt for the heavenly light, be false and shameless enough to desecrate the Holy Place by appearing there as preachers of a Christianity which we ourselves do not believe."

This was the beginning of a long and bitter controversy with the clergy and ecclesiastical authorities of the Church of Denmark, a struggle which was destined to continue almost to the end of Grundtvig's career. Needless to say, the bishop of the diocese vetoed his assignment to Udby. Grundtvig was found guilty of having "wilfully insulted the Danish clergy, both individually and as a body," and was sentenced to be reprimanded by the dean of the theological faculty.

Jens Christian Aaberg, in his fascinating book on *Hymns and Hymnwriters of Denmark,* describes in a gripping manner the spiritual crisis through which Grundtvig passed during the ensuing year, and how he finally came to conviction and faith. In reading the *Early History of Prussia* by A. von Kotzebue, he came to a passage where the author ridiculed the "missionary zeal that, like a fire on the steppes, caught the kings of Poland and Scandinavia and moved them to frantic efforts for the conversion of neighboring peoples," and then went on to state proudly, "But while her neighbors all accepted Christianity and the withered Cross drew steadily nearer to the green oak, Prussia remained faithful to her ancient gods."

"The withered Cross!" Grundtvig felt stung to the depth of his soul by the contemptuous words, and, throwing the book aside, he sprang to his feet and vowed that henceforth he would dedicate his life in proclaiming the glory of that despised emblem. And so he wrote:

"On the rim of the bottomless abyss toward which our age is blindly hastening, I will stand and confront it with a picture illumined by two shining lights, the Word of God and the testimony of history. As long as God gives me strength to lift up my voice, I will call on my people, and admonish them in His Name."

A great change now came into Grundtvig's life, and he informed his father that he would willingly become his assistant. Thus, more than a year after having preached the sermon which had created such a sensation throughout Denmark, young Grundtvig was duly ordained in Copenhagen on May 11, 1811, and a few days later was installed at Udby, the old church of his childhood.

This proved to be but the beginning of a long and stormy career which found Grundtvig continually in conflict with the constituted authority of the Church. For many years he was a pastor without a church. He was not permitted even to confirm his own children. In order to find an effective means of arming the laity against the confusing claims and contradictory teachings of the theologians, Grundtvig finally was led to place the main emphasis on the Apostles' Creed. He contended that Jesus had taught the Creed to His disciples during the forty days after His resurrection when He appeared to them from

215

time to time, "speaking of the things pertaining to the kingdom of God." The Creed, he insisted, had been transmitted orally through the early centuries, and constituted, with the words of institution of the two sacraments and the Lord's Prayer, in a special sense "The living Word of God."

Some charged that Grundtvig placed the Apostles' Creed above the Bible, but it is probably more correct to say that he placed them side by side. He did insist, however, that the Bible must be understood in the light of the Creed.

Regardless of how we may view his theological position, it must be conceded that no one strove more mightily to infuse new spiritual life into the Church of his day than did Grundtvig.

He also became a principal champion of a movement to raise the intellectual standards of the Danish people through folk schools. The first of these so-called Grundtvigian schools was opened at Rödding in 1844, and quickly the movement for popular education spread, not only through Denmark, but also to Sweden, Norway and Finland. He has rightly, therefore, been called "the father of the public school in Scandinavia."

Although Grundtvig always attracted large audiences by his powerful preaching, he probably exerted an even greater influence over his age by his literary activities. His poetry and hymns alone attracted so much attention, it became a popular saying that "Kingo's harp has been strung afresh."

Grundtvig's strongest hymns are those that deal with the Church and the sacraments. The divine character of the Church is continually stressed, for Christ not only founded it, but, as the Living Word, He is present in it and in the sacraments to the end of time. "Built on a Rock, the Church doth stand" is probably his most famous hymn. Among Danes and Norwegians there are few hymns sung more often than this one, and it is also beginning to appear in American hymnals, including the *Service Book and Hymnal* of 1958 and the *Pilgrim Hymnal* of 1959.

Grundtvig was more concerned about the thought he was trying to convey than the mode of expression; therefore his hymns are often characterized by strength rather than poetic beauty. They also are so deeply tinged with national spirit and feeling they lose much of the color and fragrance of their native heath when translated. That Grundtvig could rise to lyrical heights is revealed especially in his festival hymns. There is a charming freshness in these stanzas of his Christmas hymn:

> The happy Christmas comes once more,
> The heavenly Guest is at the door,
> The blessed words the shepherd thrill,
> The joyous tidings, "Peace, good-will."
>
> O wake, our hearts, in gladness sing,
> And keep our Christmas with our King,
> Till living song, from loving souls,
> Like sound of mighty water rolls.
>
> O holy Child, Thy manger gleams
> Till earth and heaven glow with its beams,
> Till midnight noon's broad light hath won,
> And Jacob's star outshines the sun.
>
> Thou patriarchs' joy, Thou prophets' song,
> Thou heavenly Dayspring, looked for long,
> Thou Son of Man, incarnate Word,
> Great David's Son, great David's Lord:
>
> Come, Jesus, glorious heavenly guest,
> Keep Thine own Christmas in our breast,
> Then David's harpstrings, hushed so long,
> Shall swell our jubilee of song.

The Danish hymnologist Brandt has pointed out the distinctive characteristics of his country's three great hymnists by calling attention to their favorite symbols. That of Kingo was the sun, Brorson's the rose, and Grundtvig's the bird. Kingo extols Christ as the risen, victorious Saviour — the Sun that breaks through the dark shades of sin and death. Brorson glorifies Christ as the Friend of the spiritually poor and needy. They learn to know Him in the secret prayer chamber as the Rose that spreads its quiet fragrance. Grundtvig's hymns are primarily hymns of the Spirit. They laud the Holy Spirit, the Giver and Renewer of life, who bears us up on mighty wings toward the mansions of light.

Grundtvig's constant emphasis on the Word of God as the one and only rule and guide for the believer is reflected in another of his great hymns:

> God's Word is our great heritage,
>   And shall be ours forever;
> To spread its light from age to age
>   Be this our chief endeavor.
> Through life it guides our way,
> In death it is our stay;
> Lord, grant while time shall last,
> Thy Church may hold it fast
>   Throughout all generations.

217

Other noted hymns by Grundtvig include "Love, the fount of light from heaven," "As the rose shall blossom here," "My Lord, I hear Thee pleading," "Bright and glorious is the sky," "A Babe is born in Bethlehem," "From the grave remove dark crosses," "O let Thy Spirit with us tarry," "Fair beyond telling," "This is the day that our Father hath given," "The peace of God protects our hearts," "O wondrous kingdom here on earth," "With gladness we hail this blessed day," "He who has helped me hitherto" and "Peace to soothe our bitter woes." The last named hymn is typical of Grundtvig's consistent emphasis on the Church as a divinely established institution, through which the Gospel is proclaimed and the sacraments administered to bring the blessings of redemption to mankind. Here is the comforting message it contains:

> Peace to soothe our bitter woes
> God in Christ on us bestows;
> Jesus bought our peace with God
> With His holy, precious Blood;
> Peace in Him for sinners found
> Is the Gospel's joyful sound.
>
> Peace to us the Church doth tell,
> 'Tis her welcome and farewell;
> Peace was our baptismal dower,
> Peace shall bless our dying hour;
> Peace be with you, full and free,
> Now and through eternity.

In contrast with the greater part of his stormy career, the latter years of Gruntdvig's life were serene and happy. At long last the people of Denmark came to recognize that a great prophet had risen in their midst, and they became eager to make compensation for the calumny and indignity heaped upon him in former years by bestowing one honor after another upon him. When Denmark became a constitutional monarchy in 1848, Grundtvig was a member of the constitutional assembly. He also was elected several times to the Riksdag. In 1861, when he celebrated his golden jubilee as a pastor, representatives of all departments of Church and State were present, as well as a great assembly of outstanding persons from the other Scandinavian countries. The King at this time bestowed upon him the title of Bishop, and the Mother Queen Carolina Amalia presented him with a seven-branched golden candlestick from the women of Norway, Sweden and Denmark.

On Sept. 1, 1872, when nearly 89 years old, he conducted services in his church at Vartov as usual, preaching a sermon full of warmth and feeling. On the following day he passed away while sitting in his chair and listening to his son as the latter read to him. Thus ended the remarkable career of the sage of Denmark who once was the loneliest man in all the land, but who always will be remembered as the greatest historian, poet, educator, religious philosopher, hymn-writer and folk leader that nation has produced.

The March of Pilgrims

Through the night of doubt and sorrow
Onward goes the pilgrim band,
Singing songs of expectation,
Marching to the promised land.
Clear before us through the darkness
Gleams and burns the guiding light;
Brother clasps the hand of brother,
Stepping fearless through the night.

One the light of God's own presence
O'er His ransomed people shed,
Chasing far the gloom and terror,
Brightening all the path we tread:
One the object of our journey,
One the faith which never tires,
One the earnest looking forward,
One the hope our God inspires;

One the strain that lips of thousands
Lift as from the heart of one;
One the conflict, one the peril,
One the march in God begun:
One the gladness of rejoicing
On the far eternal shore,
Where the one almighty Father
Reigns in love for evermore.

Onward, therefore, pilgrim brothers,
Onward with the Cross our aid!
Bear its shame and fight its battle,
Till we rest beneath its shade;
Soon shall come the great awakening,
Soon the rending of the tomb;
Then the scattering of all shadows,
And the end of toil and gloom.

BERNHARDT SEVERIN INGEMANN, 1789–1862
TR. SABINE BARING-GOULD, 1834–1924

A WRITER OF PILGRIM SONGS

IN A country which produced such a triumvirate of hymn-writers as Kingo, Brorson and Grundtvig, it was not easy for another man to gain recognition as a spiritual poet of the first rank. And yet, Bernhard Severin Ingemann achieved such distinction. Still more remarkable, he lived and wrought as a contemporary of the great Grundtvig, and won the acclaim of his countrymen during the very years when the "Poet of Whitsuntide" was stirring the hearts of the Danish people as they had never been moved before.

Like Grundtvig and Brorson, Ingemann was the son of a pastor. His father, Soren Ingemann, was serving the parish of Falster in 1789, when Bernhard was born. The father died when the lad was only 11 years old, but Bernhard could never forget him and often wrote feelingly concerning him.

It was his mother's wish that Bernhard should follow in the footsteps of the father, wherefore she made it possible for him in 1806 to enter the University of Copenhagen. When the English attacked the Danish capital in the following year, young Bernhard joined a volunteer corps of students to help defend the city.

Like many other students of his day, Ingemann soon began to feel the deadening effects of Rationalism, and lost all interest in preparing for the ministry. The death of his mother, followed in quick succession by the loss of his four brothers, now brought him close to the verge of mental collapse, and he even contemplated ending his own life. All of his brothers had died of tuberculosis, and his own health was very frail.

However, as a result of a profound spiritual experience, Ingemann was brought back to his childhood faith, and now for the first time he found a new joy and purpose in life. In the words of a Swedish hymnologist, "The nearness of death drove him into the arms of the Lord of life. Sorrow taught him to pray. He found once more the God of his childhood years, and he himself became in spirit almost as a child again."

221

Soon he revealed unusual gifts as a lyrical poet of a highly idealistic type, and his literary efforts began to win wide acclaim. Receiving a stipend from the government to encourage him in his studies, he visited Germany, France, Italy and Switzerland, and on his return in 1822 was appointed a professor of literature in the famous academy at Sorö, on the island of Sjaelland. It was in the atmosphere of this ancient center of Scandinavian religion and culture, and under the shadow of Sorö's famous 12th century cathedral where the great Valdemar Atterdag and other famous Viking kings were sleeping, that Ingemann spent the remainder of his life, writing epic poems and historical novels that contributed mightily in arousing the national spirit of Denmark, a work which Grundtvig had already so ably begun.

Although Ingemann's secular writings gained for him national fame, the passing of time has made it evident that he will be chiefly remembered because of his work as a hymnist. In 1822 he published a small collection of morning and evening hymns. This was followed in 1825 by a volume of church hymns, which was reprinted in enlarged form in 1843. Because of his success in these ventures, he now was commissioned to prepare a new hymnal for the Church of Denmark, a task which he successfully completed in 1855. Ingemann was one of Grundtvig's closest friends and admirers, and therefore some of the latter's hymns found their way into the official hymnal of the Church for the first time. Ingemann also included a few of his own.

The relative stature of Denmark's various spiritual poets in the judgment of present-day Danish hymnologists is reflected in the latest authorized hymnbook of the Church of Denmark, which contains 173 hymns by Grundtvig, 107 by Brorson, 96 by Kingo and 29 by Ingemann.

Ingemann's fame as a hymn-writer rests primarily on two lyrics, both of them pilgrim songs. One of these, *"Igjennem Nat og Traengsel,"* because of Baring-Gould's translation, "Through the night of doubt and sorrow," has come into widespread use in the English-speaking world. It was first published in the *People's Hymn-book* in England in England in 1867, after which it was included in the famous *Hymns Ancient and Modern* edition of 1875.

His other pilgrim song, *"Dejlig er Jorden,"* is the most beloved of all of Ingemann's lyrics. It was written to be sung to the tune of

222

"Beautiful Saviour," which had been brought to his notice by a neighboring pastor who had discovered it in a German hymn collection. There it was noted as a marching song the Crusaders had sung on their pilgrimage to the Holy City. Ingemann accepted this as a fact, although it has since been disputed, but he changed its theme to dwell instead on the thought of the age-long pilgrimage of God's people toward the New Jerusalem. In the striking words of the German hymnologist Koch:

"The crusaders' pilgrimage to the holy city in the East has in Ingemann's hymn been lifted to a higher plane: it becomes the pilgrimage of the entire human race toward the City built on the Everlasting Hills . . . It is not the march of sin-burdened mortals who, with drooping heads, drag themselves forward through the dreary deserts of a fallen world. Rather, it is a joyous, ransomed multitude, with faces lifted toward heaven, marching through the lovely kingdoms of the earth."

The lyrical beauty of Ingemann's original is difficult to translate, but here is its opening stanza:

> Fair is creation,
> Fairer God's heaven,
> Happy the marching pilgrim throng.
> Onward through regions
> Fragrant with beauty,
> Go we to Paradise with song.

Ingemann was a sensitive soul. Serene and gentle by nature, he loved the peaceful, idyllic things of life. He saw something of God's eternal love in everything about him, and to the last he retained a childlike trust in his Maker. Perhaps that is one reason why he was particularly successful in writing children's hymns. It is doubtful if a lovelier or a more imaginative Christmas carol for children has ever been written than "Christmas brings joy to every heart." Even in its translation it retains much of its beauty:

> Christmas brings joy to every heart,
>   Sets old and young rejoicing,
> What angels sang once to all on earth
>   Oh, hear the children voicing.
> Bright is the tree with lights aglow,
>   Like birds that perch together.
> The child that holdeth Christmas dear
>   Shall keep these joys forever.

Joy comes to all the world today,
To hall and cottage hasting.
Come, sparrow and dove, from roof-tree tall,
And share our Christmas feasting.
Dance, little child, on mother's knee,
The lovely day is dawning;
The road to Paradise is found
This blessed Christmas morning.

Once to this earth our Saviour came,
An infant poor and lowly,
To open for us those gardens fair
Where dwell His angels holy.
Christmas joy He bringeth us,
The Christ-child King of heaven,
"To every little child," He saith,
"Shall angel wings be given."

Other of Ingemann's hymns that have been rendered into English are: "As wide as the skies is thy mercy, O God," "The sun is rising in the East," and "Jesus, my Saviour, my Shepherd blest."

Ingemann died on February 24, 1862, at Sorö, the scene of most of his labors.

Among other hymn-writers of this period should be mentioned Birgitte Catherine Boye, who was born in Gentofte, Denmark, March 7, 1742. Married to a forester at the age of 19, within five years she had become the mother of four children. Despite her many household cares, however, she employed her spare time in diligent study of German, French and English, and soon became proficient as a translator, rendering numerous hymns of Klopstock, Gellert and Rambach into Danish.

She also began to write original hymns, and, when the Society for the Advancement of Liberal Arts in 1773 sent out a call soliciting contributions from all who had "a desire and talent for writing sacred poetry," she submitted twenty of her lyrics. Eighteen were accepted.

When Guldberg's Hymnal was published in 1778, it was found to contain no less than 124 original hymns and 24 translations from the pen of this unusual woman. Many of them, however, reflected something of the stilted, bombastic style that characterized hymnody in the age of Rationalism, and few have proved to be of enduring value. Two exceptions are "Rejoice, rejoice this happy morn" and "Our Lord is risen from the dead," both of which are sung to the tune of *Wie schön leuchtet der Morgenstern.* In Denmark and Norway, as well as in many Lutheran churches in America, it has become a tradition to use the former hymn at Christmas and the latter on Easter Sunday.

With the coming of evangelical revival throughout Scandinavia during the middle of the 19th century, a number of gifted Danish hymn-writers appeared. Casper J. Boye was one of the foremost of these. Born of Danish parents at Kongsberg, Norway, in 1791, he was sent to the University of Copenhagen to receive his education. After teaching for some years in a Latin school, he became a pastor of the Garrison Church in Copenhagen, a position he held until his death in 1851. Boye was a prolific writer of hymns, many of which were published under the title, *Spiritual Songs.* An evening hymn, "Abide with us, the day is waning," and a morning hymn, "Day is breaking, night is ended," are among the most popular.

Herman Andreas Timm and Theodore Vilhelm Oldenburg were other spiritual poets of this period. The former will be remembered chiefly for his hymn, "Dost thou know the living fountain?" and the latter, an ardent advocate of foreign missions, for his very fine lyric, "Thine, O Jesus, thine forever."

A Triumphant Funeral Hymn

I know of a sleep in Jesus' Name,
A rest from all toil and sorrow;
Earth folds in her arms my weary frame,
And shelters it till the morrow;
The soul is in heaven at home with God,
And sorrow is gone forever.

I know of a blessed eventide;
And when I am faint and weary,
At times with the journey sorely tried
Through hours that are long and dreary,
Then often I yearn to lay me down
And sink into peaceful slumber.

I know of a morning bright and fair
When tidings of joy shall wake us,
When songs from on high shall fill the air
And God to His glory take us,
When Jesus shall bid us rise from sleep;
How joyous that hour of waking!

O Jesus, draw near my dying bed
And take me into Thy keeping,
And say, when my spirit hence is fled,
"This child is not dead but sleeping,"
And leave me not, Saviour, till I rise
To praise Thee in life eternal.

MAGNUS BROSTRUP LANDSTAD, 1802–1880
Tr. Service Book and Hymnal, 1958

LANDSTAD, A BARD OF THE FROZEN FJORDS

THIS is the story of a man whose chance purchase of two books at an auction sale for the sum of four cents was probably the means of inspiring him to become one of the foremost Christian poets of the North.

Magnus Brostrup Landstad was a poverty-stricken student at the University of Christiania (now Oslo), Norway, when he happened to pass a house in which a sale of books was being conducted. Moved by curiosity, he entered the place just as a package of old books was being offered. We will let him tell the remainder of the story:

"I made a bid of four cents, the deal was made, and I walked home with my package. It contained two volumes in leather binding. One was *Freuden-Spiegel des ewigen Lebens* by Philipp Nicolai. On the last few pages of this book four of Nicolai's hymns were printed. The other book was Bishop A. Arrebo's *Hexaemeron, The Glorious and Mighty Works of the Creation Day.* In this manner two splendid hymn collections, one German and the other Danish-Norwegian, unexpectedly came into my possession. I was not acquainted with either of these works before. Nicolai's hymns made a deep impression on me, and I at once attempted to translate them . . . My experience with these hymn collections, I believe, gave me the first impetus in the direction of hymn writing. Furthermore, it gave me a deeper insight into the life and spirit of the old church hymns."

Two of the hymns of Nicolai that Landstad attempted to translate were *"Wachet auf, ruft uns die Stimme"* and *"Wie schön leuchtet der Morgenstern,"* noble classics that have never been excelled. The young student was so successful in his rendering of the former hymn that it subsequently found a place in the hymnbook of the Church of Norway.

Landstad was born October 7, 1802, in Maaso, Finnmarken, Norway, where his father was pastor of the Lutheran church. This parish is at the extreme northern point of Norway. Therefore Landstad once could write, "I was baptized in the northernmost church in the world."

227

Later the family moved to Oksnes, another parish among the frozen fjords of the Norse seacoast.

"The waves of the icy Arctic," he writes poetically, "sang my cradle lullaby; but the bosom of a loving mother warmed my body and soul."

The stern character of the relentless North, with its solitude, its frozen wastes, its stormy waters and its long months of winter darkness, no doubt left a profound and lasting impression upon the lad whose early years were spent in such environments. The Napoleonic wars also were raging, and it was a period of much sorrow and suffering among the common people. When the boy was nine years old the family removed to Vinje. Although they continued to suffer many hardships, the natural surroundings at this place were more congenial, and in summer the landscape was transformed into a magic beauty that must have warmed the heart and fired the childish imagination of the future hymnist.

Magnus was the third of ten children. Although the family was sorely pressed by poverty, the father recognized unusual talent in the boy, and at the age of twenty years he was sent to the university in Christiania. During his first year at the institution two of his brothers died. Young Landstad was greatly cast down in spirit, but out of the bitterness of this early bereavement came two memorial poems that are believed to represent his first attempt at verse-writing.

In 1827 he completed his theological studies at the university and the following year he was appointed resident vicar of the Lutheran church at Gausdal. During his pastorate at this place he wrote his first hymn. In 1834 he became pastor at Kviteseid, where he continued the writing of hymns and other poems. Five years later he became his father's successor as pastor of the parish at Seljord. It was here, in 1841, that he published his first work, a book of daily devotions highly prized by his countrymen. In 1849 he was called to Fredrikshald, where he was given an assistant in order that he might have more time for hymnological endeavors. Ten years later he was appointed to the parish of Sandeherred, and he continued to labor at this place until his retirement in 1876.

For centuries Norway and Denmark had been closely connected politically and culturally. The Lutheran Church was, moreover, the state Church of both countries. As a consequence of this relationship, Norway had always looked to Denmark for its hymn literature, and no hymnist of note had thus far appeared in the northern country.

Now, however, it began to dawn on the Norwegian people that a native singer had risen in their own midst. The political ties with Denmark having been broken as a result of the Napoleonic wars, the spirit of nationalism began to assert itself, and the demand for a new hymnbook for the Church of Norway constantly grew stronger. In 1848 the Norwegian ecclesiastical authorities requested Landstad to undertake the task, but not until four years later could he be prevailed upon to assume the arduous duties involved in so great an endeavor.

In 1861 the first draft of his *Kirke-Salmebog* was published. It did not meet with complete approval. In defense of his work, Landstad wrote: "We must, above all, demand that our hymns possess the elements of poetic diction and true song. We must consider the historical and churchly elements and the orthodox objectivity which shows respect for church tradition and which appreciates the purity, clearness, and force of confession. But the sickly subjectivity, which 'rests' in the varying moods of pious feelings and godly longings, and yet does not possess any of the boldness and power of true faith such as we find in Luther's and Kingo's hymns — this type of church hymn must be excluded. Finally, we must also emphasize the aesthetic feature. Art must be made to serve the Church, to glorify the name of God, and to edify the congregation of worshipers. But it must always be remembered that art itself is to be the servant and not the master."

Landstad continued for several years to revise his own work, and in 1869 the hymnbook was finally published and authorized for use in the Church of Norway. Within a year it had been introduced into 648 of the 923 parishes of the country.

An early interest in the folk lore of his native land undoubtedly contributed much to Landstad's later success as a hymn-writer. During the sixteen years he served as pastor among the majestic fjords of Telemark, he began to record the many legends that were told of trolls and goblins and little people who inhabited the forests and the mountains. He also listened to kitchen maids and hired hands and simple peasants as they sang their primitive folksongs. It is said he became as happy as a child whenever he discovered a new one, and he jotted down faithfully the words and music he had heard.

"Our folksongs," he once complained, "have retreated farther and farther into the fjords and hidden valleys, and there they sit like frightened birds, or chirp and sing to themselves. Our new, strange music has frightened them away from the people. With the help of God, let us seek to liberate them from their prison, and bring them back again to our poets and musicians."

Landstad's views, however, were not always accepted without criticism. In some learned circles it was charged that his language was altogether too common-place and "folksy." Indeed, it was this criticism that was largely responsible for delaying the publication of his *Kirke-Psalmebog* for all of eight years. Pietists also attacked him because he had published a collection of Telemark folksongs twenty years earlier. "It is unworthy," they charged, "for a minister of the Gospel to devote himself to such secular things." But the deepest hurt of all came to Landstad when his congregation at Sandeherred, which was dominated by a group of Pietists, refused to permit their pastor to use his hymnbook in his own church!

The note of melancholy that persists in many of Landstad's hymns is undoubtedly the fruit of the sorrow and privation experienced during the earlier part of his ministry. With twelve children to feed and clothe, the Norwegian psalmist found himself constantly in straitened circumstances. It was partly to relieve this situation that he left his beloved Telemark to serve the parish of Fredrikshald. Here, however, he had no parsonage, and the large family was compelled to live in crowded rented quarters. Sickness soon followed, and in 1851 two of Landstad's children died of typhus. The following year a third child was taken.

It was during these heart-breaking experiences, however, that Landstad wrote some of his finest hymns. One of them, "I know of a sleep in Jesus' Name," a hymn that has brought solace and peace to thousands of bereaved souls, is said to have been composed as dawn was breaking one morning after a whole night spent in prayer. Another hymn that speaks of the blessedness of those who have died in faith, "Full many shall come from the East and the West," has this stanza:

> Then ended will be, like a dream that is past,
>   All trial and trouble and sorrow;
> All questions and doubts will be answered at last,
>   When dawneth eternity's morrow.
> Have mercy upon us, O Jesus!

A penitential hymn, written much in the style of Luther's *"Aus tiefer Noth,"* echoes the cry of the contrite publican:

> To Thee, O Lord, the God of all,
> With contrite heart I humbly call,
> And view my sins against Thee, Lord,
> The sins of thought and deed and word;
> In my distress I cry to Thee,
> O God, be merciful to me.

Landstad has sometimes been called the "Psalmist of Advent," and certainly he lived and wrote as though he were constantly watching and waiting for the coming of Christ and of His Kingdom. This longing is beautifully expressed in a hymn beginning with the line, "To God above I raise my song."

When Landstad retired from active service in 1876, the Norwegian parliament voted him an annual pension of 4,000 crowns, the largest amount ever given a pastor, for the great service he had rendered his country. He died four years later, greatly lamented by the whole Norwegian nation.

Landstad's hymns can hardly be considered apart from the work of Ludwig Mathias Lindeman, a Norwegian organist who ranks among the world's foremost writers of hymn-tunes. Lindeman, who was born November 28, 1812, in Trondhjem, Norway, received his first instruction from his father, who was organist in Our Lady's Church of that city. After pursuing theological studies for a time, his love of music led him finally to decide to become an organist. In 1839 he was appointed to this position in Our Saviour's Church in Christiania (Oslo). Here he found a kindred spirit in Wilhelm Andreas Wexels, pastor and hymnist, who will be considered in the following chapter.

With the adoption of Landstad's *Kirke-Psalmbog* in 1869, Lindeman began to work on a book of melodies for the new hymns. By 1872 he had completed his labors, and by 1877 it had received the approval of a special commission and ordered published under the title, *Koralbog for den Norske Kirke*. Bishop Skaar, who was a member of the commission which approved the work of both Landstad and Lindeman, once wrote: "Landstad's hymns and Lindeman's tunes have given to church song a new life in our country." And at Lindeman's funeral, it was said: "He taught the Norwegian people to sing."

Among Lindeman's better known tunes are *Holy Mountain, Easter Glory, Spring of Souls, Our Lady-Trondhjem,* and *Lindeman.* But he will be chiefly remembered for his magnificent chorale, *Kirken,* which has made Grundtvig's "Built on a Rock" second only to Luther's "A Mighty Fortress" among the great hymns of the Church.

Out of Every Tribe and Nation

O happy day, when we shall stand
 Amid the heavenly throng,
And sing with hosts from every land
 The new celestial song.

O blessed day! From far and near
 The servants of the Lord
Shall meet His ransomed children there
 Who heard God's saving Word.

O what a mighty, rushing flood
 Of love without surcease
Shall surge about the throne of God,
 In joy and endless peace!

Lord, may Thy bounteous grace inspire
 Our hearts to watch and pray,
That we may join the heavenly choir
 Upon that glorious day.

WILHELM ANDREAS WEXELS, 1797-1866
TR. GEORGE ALFRED TAYLOR RYGH, 1860-1943

A HYMNIST OF THE HEAVENLY HOME

THE MIDDLE of the 19th century was undoubtedly the most productive period in the history of Norwegian hymnody. Landstad was not alone in his efforts to give to his countrymen a hymnbook they could call their own. For nearly two decades before Landstad began his epochal task, another Norwegian pastor had been dreaming and working on a similar project. Indeed, he seems to have been moved by the conviction that God had called him to perform this mission. His name was Wilhelm Andreas Wexels.

It was in 1818 that Wexels was appointed catechist in Our Saviour's Church in Christiania (Oslo). Twenty-eight years later he became the residing curate of the congregation, a position he held until his death in 1866. His entire ministry, therefore, was confined to the one church in the Norwegian capital.

Wexels was one of the most controversial figures of his day in Norway. By some he was called "a servant of the devil" and "anti-Christ." Others mockingly referred to him as "the holy preacher." Still others regarded him as a saint of God, a modern prophet, divinely sent to lead his people out of the wilderness of Rationalism and back again to faith in Christ the Redeemer.

There were several reasons perhaps why Wexels aroused such mingled emotions. The spiritual blight which Rationalism had cast over all of Europe had not left Norway untouched. The preaching of Christ crucified no longer appealed to people who were supposed to be enlightened, especially the intelligentsia of the nation's capital. The need of a spiritual awakening, the theme of much of Wexels' preaching and praying, was particularly distasteful to these classes.

Even the Pietists were displeased with him. Wexels, though his father was Norwegian, had been born in Copenhagen, where during his youth he had come under the influence of Nicolai Grundtvig. The latter, because of his emphasis on the Church, its ministry and the sacraments, was considered too "high church" for the Pietists, who regarded Wexels with suspicion for the same reason. Nor did Wexels have too much faith in the methods of the Pietists. Although he, like

233

them, longed and prayed for spiritual renewal within the Church, the disastrous results he had witnessed among the followers of the separatists had made him fearful of a subjective, emotional type of religion.

And there was a third reason why Wexels found it difficult to obtain a following. The death of his beloved wife in 1830, just seven years after their happy marriage, had left him melancholy and crushed in spirit. It was a blow from which he never fully recovered. From that time his mind turned more and more to thoughts of the life beyond the grave. Would those who had not accepted salvation in Christ in this life be given a second chance after death? The more he pondered the question, the more firmly convinced he became of such a possibility. Though ridiculed for his views and even accused of heresy, the idea had now become a matter of conscientious conviction with him, and, wisely or otherwise, he sometimes preached it publicly.

However, the earnestness with which he proclaimed the need of accepting the grace of God in Christ had begun to attract listeners. Whereas for many years he had been compelled to preach to an almost empty church, he finally had the joy of seeing a large congregation growing up around him. The crowds that thronged Our Saviour's Church to hear him—both young and old—became larger and larger year by year. While the Rationalists scoffed at the great verities of the Christian religion and while scarcely anything but lectures on morality were heard from many pulpits throughout Norway, Wexels preached on such themes as the resurrection of the dead and the life everlasting. And the people heard him gladly. Even to old age, no minister exerted so great an influence over his countrymen as he. Said a contemporary: "Wexels is not an eloquent preacher, but the Holy Spirit seems to have touched his lips."

Church historians claim that Wexels' ministry proved to be a turningpoint in the Church of Norway, marking a return to conservative Lutheran teaching. Eventually he had as many friends as once he had had enemies. He was even offered the bishopric of Bergen, but refused to accept the honor, preferring to remain with his beloved congregation in the nation's capital.

But Wexels' influence was not confined to his preaching. He was also an author and hymn-writer of considerable ability. For several years he edited a theological magazine, and between 1837 and 1854 his *Commentary on the New Testament* appeared in four parts. He was also the author of a *Bible History* and a *Book of Devotions for the Common People,* both of which passed through many editions.

More important than these, however, were his efforts to give to the Church of Norway an official hymnbook. Eighteen years before Landstad received his commission to create such a book, Wexels published a volume under the title, *Hymn Verses, Selected from Old Hymns, for Use in the Home and the School.* This was in 1834. Six years later he published a large volume called *Christian Hymns.* It contained 714 hymns, of which fifteen were original, fifty translations from Wallin's Swedish *Psalmbook* of 1819, and several others borrowed from the German. A second edition in 1844 contained 747 hymns. Then followed two other hymnbooks in rapid succession, one of them a collection of mission hymns, and finally, in 1849, Wexels brought out a *Hymnbook* of 504 hymns, concerning which he wrote: "And let it be considered as a proposal for a general church hymnal, submitted to the gracious judgment of Christians."

The collection, however, met with severe criticism and was not adopted. Nevertheless, Wexels tried again in 1859, when he published yet another edition of *Christian Hymns.* This time the collection contained no less than 850 hymns. But it also failed to win approval, and so it remained for Landstad ten years later to produce the hymnbook for which the Norwegian people had so long waited.

Many of Wexels' hymns, however, have survived through the years and "will be sung in Norway," says Bishop Skaar, "as long as Christ is confessed." Especially will he be remembered for the missionary hymn, "O happy day when we shall stand," written for a general convention of the Norwegian Mission Society in 1846. As one who preached so often on the theme of the Christian's eternal hope and who looked forward with such intense longing to the glories of heaven, Wexels' memory will likewise be cherished by thousands who have found comfort in his beautiful song:

> O precious thought! Some day the mist shall vanish;
> Some day the web of gloom shall be unspun.
> A day shall break whose beams the night shall banish,
> For Christ the Lord shall rise, the Eternal Sun.
>
> O precious thought! All sinless, pure, and holy,
> By flesh and Satan nevermore oppressed,
> My thoughts and deeds shall glorify Him solely,
> Who brought my soul unto His perfect rest.

> The saints of God, all clad in spotless raiment,
>   Before the Lamb shall lift victorious palms;
> For bliss eternal Christ has rendered payment,
>   Earth's tearful strains give way to joyous psalms.
>
> I pray Thee, O my precious Saviour, waken
>   These hallowed thoughts of Paradise in me,
> And let them solace me, till I am taken
>   To dwell in Salem evermore with Thee.

Poetic genius sometimes seems to be inherited, and it is interesting to note that Marie Wexelsen, whose mother was a sister of Wexels and whose father was his cousin, also became a hymn-writer. Born September 20, 1832, at Ostre Toten, Norway, she began writing at the age of twenty. A greatly loved Christmas lyric which has come from her pen reads in part:

> I am so glad each Christmas Eve,
>   The night of Jesus' birth!
> Then like the sun the Star shone forth,
>   And angels sang on earth.
>
> The little Child in Bethlehem,
>   He was a King indeed!
> For He came down from heaven above
>   To help a world in need.
>
> He dwells again in heaven's realm,
>   The Son of God today;
> And still He loves His little ones,
>   And hears them when they pray.

Miss Wexelsen lived for a number of years at Trondhjem, where she passed away in 1911.

Johan Nordahl Brun, who, like both Wexels and Landstad, was a sturdy defender of the evangelical faith against the desolating onslaughts of the Rationalists of his day, was likewise a hymn-writer of considerable ability. Brun, who came on the scene somewhat earlier than either Wexels or Landstad, was born March 21, 1745, at Bynesset, Norway, the son of a merchant. Early in childhood he conceived from a pious mother an abiding love for the Word of God. Before he was eleven years old, he had read through the Scriptures twice, and it was undoubtedly this experience that made him the great champion of the Christian faith that he proved to be in later years.

After attending Latin school and the university at Trondhjem, Brun went to Copenhagen, where he studied theology. Then followed three years in Trondhjem as instructor, preacher and writer. During a second visit to Copenhagen he wrote a drama entitled *Zarine* which created a sensation in the Danish capital.

In 1773 he was appointed assistant pastor in his home parish of Bynesset, and the following year he became rector at Bergen. He held this position for thirty years, acquitting himself with great distinction as a powerful preacher and an able defender of conservative Christianity. In 1804 he was elevated to the bishopric of the diocese of Bergen. He passed away in 1816.

Brun possessed unusual literary gifts and was intensely interested in hymnody. In 1786 he published a collection of sixty-five original lyrics. These were intended to supplement the hymns in *Guldberg's Hymnbook,* which was then in use. Brun's best known hymn is one in praise of the Scriptures. Perhaps it was the memory of the great heritage he received in childhood that caused him to write:

> How blest are they who hear God's Word,
> Who keep in faith what they have heard,
>   Who daily grow in learning;
> From light to light they shall increase,
> And tread life's weary path in peace,
>   The balm of joy discerning
>   To soothe the spirit's yearning.
>
> Through sorrow's night my sun shall be
> God's Word — a treasure dear to me,
>   My shield and buckler ever.
> My title as His child and heir
> The Father's hand hath written there,
>   His promise failing never:
>   "Thou shalt be mine forever."
>
> Today His voice with joy I heard,
> And nourished by His holy Word,
>   That bread so freely given,
> May stronger faith through grace prevail,
> And may its fruits for me avail,
>   That, after I have striven,
>   I rest with Him in heaven.

A Hymn That Welcomes Death

The Lord our great Redeemer
  Lives crowned upon the throne;
As King of earth and heaven,
  He saves, and He alone;
He conquered death by dying
  Upon the accursed tree,
And from His death sprang glorious
  Eternal life for me.

Christ is my Rock, my Refuge,
  He is my soul's true life;
In Him, I fear no shadows,
  Nor yet the final strife.
O grave, where is thy triumph?
  O death, where is thy power?
In Christ, I'm more than victor —
  Then come, thou glorious hour!

HALLGRIM PETURSSON, 1614-1674

CHRISTIAN SINGERS OF ICELAND

OR AT least eleven centuries Iceland has been a virtual out-post of Scandinavia. It was about the year 850 A.D. that venturesome Vikings from Norway discovered the little island lying in the icy waters of the North Atlantic just below the Arctic Circle. It seems, however, that they found it already inhabited by a small group of monks who had come from Ireland known as Culdees.

Successive waves of migration from Norway began in 870, being led by Norwegian noblemen and chieftains, and before fifty years had passed a considerable population had settled in the island. Other groups came from the "Western Islands," which was the designation employed for England, Scotland and Ireland. Many of these were descendants of Vikings who had settled much earlier in the British Isles, having fled from Norway to escape the rule of despotic kings. Perhaps the greater number came from Ireland, and there is abundant evidence that considerable Celtic blood was thus infused into the veins of the early Icelanders.

The greatest influx, however, came from the Scandinavian penin-sula, and the close kinship between the Icelanders and the Scandina-vians becomes at once apparent by a comparison of their respective languages. A Norwegian, Dane or Swede today would have little difficulty in comprehending Icelandic. Due to centuries of isolation, however, the Icelandic tongue has been much less influenced by the changes that result from contact and intercourse with other peoples. Consequently, the language spoken in Iceland today is probably much closer to that used by the roving Vikings of a thousand years ago than the speech now employed by Scandinavians on the continent.

Christianity probably first came to Iceland with the Irish Culdees to whom reference has been made. It is believed, however, that it was completely wiped out with the advent of the pagan Norsemen settlers in 870. About a century and a half later it was re-introduced by mis-sionaries sent from Norway by King Olaf Trygvesson. In 1020 it was formally made the state religion.

With the coming of Christianity, the Roman Mass soon replaced the ancient Norse mythological cult. That traditional Gregorian chants with Latin text were used very early in Iceland by the clergy is clearly indicated in the Saga of Bishop Laurentius of Holar, written in the years following the bishop's death in 1323. Here we find an account of how that churchman objected vigorously to *tripla* and *tvisyngja,* that is, three- and two-part singing of the Mass. The good bishop considered such practice as *leikaraskapur,* or frivolity, and advocated instead the employment of *slettan song,* or plainsong, which was the character of all medieval liturgical music of the Church.

Iceland very early came under the sovereignty of the Norwegian kings, but by the terms of the Union of Kalmar of 1397, which linked together Sweden, Norway, Denmark and Iceland, the Icelanders eventually gave their allegiance to the ruling house of Denmark. When the Reformation came to Denmark during the rule of Frederik I and his son, Christian III, it was only natural, therefore, that it should spread to Iceland. It was introduced there by Gizur Einarssen, who had studied in Wittenberg under Luther and Melanchthon. Einarssen in 1540 was made bishop of Skalholt although he was only 25 years old at the time, and through his vigorous efforts the Church Order that Bugenhagen had prepared for the evangelical worship in Denmark soon replaced the Roman form of the Mass.

Oddur Gottskalksson, another Iceland youth who likewise had studied in Denmark and Germany, aided the Reformation movement in his homeland by secretly translating the New Testament into his mother tongue and bringing it to Roskild for printing. It is said that, for nobility of expression, this version of the New Testament Scriptures has never been excelled in the Icelandic language.

The Reformation was not carried out in Iceland without opposition, however. In fact, Jon Arasen, bishop of Holar, who headed the Roman party, sought to stir up armed rebellion. For this he was executed in 1550.

As in all other lands where Luther's teachings were embraced, congregational singing soon became a part of the public worship. It is believed that the first hymnbook consisted of a few Icelandic translations of hymns derived from the Danish-Norwegian hymnal of Claus Martensön Tönderbinder which appeared in 1528. The Icelandic counterpart was printed in Reykjavik under the title, *Graduale, or Messusaungs bök,* which means "Songbook of the Mass." A final edition of this book was published by Bishop Magnussen as late as 1773. In

1861 Iceland got its first comprehensive hymnal when Thordersen published *Nyr vidbaetir vid hina evangelisku sälmabök,* or "New Contributions to the Evangelical Psalmbook." Like the 1855 *Psalmebog* of Denmark, it was based largely on the old Kingo hymnal, but contained numerous new hymns by Brorson, Grundtvig, Ingemann and Boye, Denmark's foremost hymnists.

Iceland, however, could not remain satisfied indefinitely with hymns adopted from the other Scandinavian countries. Poetry had always flourished to a remarkable degree in the little island, having had its origin in the Eddic and Skaldic verse of ancient Nordic bards. Even during the five hundred years between the 14th and 19th centuries, when prose-writing in Iceland was almost non-existent, poetry of singular beauty and great virility continued to be produced in an amazing quantity.

Hymn-writing began to form an important part of this native lyric literature soon after the Reformation. Among the earliest and greatest of all Icelandic hymn-writers was Hallgrim Petursson, who during the 17th century won immortal fame by his "Passion Hymns." Born in 1614, the son of an humble church sexton in the Holar Cathedral, Hallgrimur began to reveal unusual gifts during his childhood, but he received only a very limited education. In fact, he was expelled from school when it was discovered that he had written stinging satire in verse, ridiculing his schoolmaster! A few years later he went to Copenhagen, where he disappeared from sight, and apparently the world was to hear no more of the church sexton's son.

However, God had other plans for the young man. It chanced one day that a certain Brynjolf Sveinsson, a theological student from Iceland who was destined later to become one of his country's greatest bishops, passed by a blacksmith shop in the Danish capital. From within came the sounds of a violent quarrel, and suddenly a young man ran into the street, heaping abuse upon his employer in unrefined Icelandic. His words were profane, but his mastery of the language was unmistakable. The young man was Hallgrim Petursson.

Through the friendship thus formed between the two, Sveinsson came to recognize unusual gifts in the blacksmith apprentice, and finally persuaded him to resume his studies. Petursson did so for a period of four years, and then something happened that cast a shadow over his whole life. It seems that in the year 1627 a fleet of four pirate ships from North Africa had made an attack on the defenseless coast of Iceland in the region of Heimaey, among the so-called Irishmen's Isles. Jon Thorsteinsson, pastor of the island parish and himself a hymn-writer, was one of those killed in the raid. Some 350 others were taken captive and carried off to Africa, where most of them were sold on the slave-market at Algiers. Here for many years they suffered great cruelties, principally because of their Christian faith, and many died. At length, however, the Moslem pirate-city offered to accept a ransom from the Danish government in exchange for the survivors.

Thirty-four were thus brought to Copenhagen, where the Danish authorities concluded it would be necessary to instruct them anew in the Christian faith. During their sojourn of ten years in a Moslem environment, it seems, they had become greatly confused in spiritual matters. Hallgrim Petursson was one of those who received a commission to teach them, and he accepted the task gladly.

Among the captives was a certain Gudrid, a woman of alluring beauty. An unfortunate infatuation soon developed between teacher and pupil, and, although the woman had been married before she was carried off in the pirate raid, and although her husband presumably was still alive, Petursson ignored these facts. Together they returned to Iceland, where, after the husband died a few years later, the two were married. During the years that followed, Petursson experienced deep remorse. His sorrow was made the more bitter when he discovered that his wife still clung to some of her Mohammedan beliefs. They also suffered from abject poverty and the evident scorn of their fellow men. Petursson's sincere repentance is clearly reflected in one of his Passion Hymns written in later years.

At this critical point of his life, it was Brynjolf Sveinsson who again came to his aid. The latter, who was now Bishop of Skalholt, after satisfying himself that Petursson was a truly penitent man and had experienced a genuine change of heart, ordained him in 1644 as a Lutheran pastor and assigned him to the barren region where he had spent his years of shame and rejection. Later he was transferred to another small parish at Sourby on the Whalefirth. It was on the shores of this picturesque fjord that Petursson was moved to sing the praises of the Man of Sorrows who by His sufferings and death had so wonderfully redeemed him. The Passion Hymns, fifty in number, are a poignant portrayal of our Lord's last conflict, from the moment when he sang the Paschal hymn with His disciples in the Upper Room until the seal was made fast on His tomb. Each hymn

242

is introduced by a Scripture passage descriptive of an incident in the Passion history. The first one is in the nature of an invocation, and concludes with the prayer:

> Thy Spirit, gracious Lord, bestow;
> Anoint Thy servant's lips, that so
> His song may to Thy glory be,
> And fire men's hearts with love to Thee.

And Hallgrim Petursson's prayer was literally answered, for no hymn-writer of Iceland has so gripped the hearts of his countrymen as did this humble pastor poet of three centuries ago. His Passion Hymns have been called "the flower of Icelandic poetry." First published in 1666, they have been reprinted again and again, and in 1943 the 52nd edition was issued in Reykjavik.

In one of these poetic meditations, Petursson describes the Apostle Peter's bitter tears of repentance when Jesus during the trial in the high priest's palace turned and looked on him. Undoubtedly the poet was led to think of his own sad mistakes in earlier years, for he goes on to say:

> Lord Jesus, look on me,
>   Thy kind face turning;
> My soul with agony
>   Of sin is burning.
>
> The way is long, I find
>   My weak steps falling;
> O turn, to my dark mind
>   Thy grace recalling.
>
> Oft, oft with contrite eyes
>   I gaze to heaven;
> Then, at Thy look, arise
>   In tears, forgiven.

Another fine example of Petursson's lyric poetry may be found in his moving funeral hymn, *"Alt Eins og Blomstrid Eina,"* from which the cento, "The Lord our great Redeemer," has been derived.

Petursson's hymns have been likened to spring flowers, hidden under the snow, unknown to the outside world for nearly 300 years. But then it happened that Charles Venn Pilcher, professor of Old Testament Literature at Wycliffe College, Toronto, and later Anglican bishop in Sydney, Australia, translated them in 1913, and thus gave them to the whole Church. Concerning Iceland's great hymnist, Pilcher has written:

"He raised, as it were, a mighty crucifix of song over Iceland, and thither, for two centuries and a half, the weary and the heavy laden have turned their eyes. He sang the theme of the ages, and his song has become immortal . . . It has been the custom in Iceland, in the scattered farm-houses, to sing the Passion Hymns through during Lent. The implements of work would be laid down, and then, the spinning-wheels being hushed, the father would lead the household in sacred song. Thus the Story of the Cross, in Hallgrim's deathless setting, has for centuries sounded forth beneath the Northern Lights and the Arctic stars. Our poet has become the more-than David of his people, for he sang, not a coming, but a present Christ . . . He lived long ago, in at least relative poverty and isolation, far away, 'at the gates of the world.' He knew nothing of the aspirations, international, industrial, social, which make our twentieth century so unquiet. But he sang one theme which can never become old, because it is the divine response to a universal need. 'Godly meditation on the Passion and Death of the Lord Jesus is indeed precious.' So Hallgrim wrote in his own foreword, and the Christian Church of our land and day can still reply 'Amen.' "

The Passion poet of Iceland came to the end of his earthly journey under sad and tragic circumstances. Stricken with the dread disease of leprosy at the age of 53, he suffered for seven long years "with singular patience and unswerving faith," until death brought release in the year 1674.

For a long time after Petursson's death, no important hymnist arose to succeed him, and Iceland became more or less dependent on Denmark for leadership in this aspect of its worship. With the dawn of the 19th century, however, a number of native hymn-writers began to appear. One of the earliest and most prolific writers of this period was Helgi Halfdanarson, a pastor's son in northern Iceland, who was born in 1826. After receiving his degree in theology in Copenhagen in 1854, he taught for a number of years at the Theological Seminary in Reykjavik, and in 1885 he became its president, a position he held until his death in 1894.

Halfdanarson was an unusually successful teacher, but he exerted an even greater influence through his literary work, particularly by his catechism and his labors on the Icelandic hymnbook of 1886. To the latter he contributed no less than 211 original and translated hymns.

First rank among Iceland's 19th century spiritual poets, however, is generally accorded to Matthias Jochumsson. This man, who was born on a farm in western Iceland in 1835, rose to become one of the foremost thinkers of his day. He seems to have passed through many difficult spiritual conflicts, but out of these struggles were born hymns of strong conviction and rare insight.

Another of the hymn-writers of the late 19th century was Pall Jonsson, whose calm and worshipful evening hymn may be considered fairly representative of Icelandic hymnody of that period. It reads:

On the wings of light declining,
  Sinks the westering sun to sleep:
Lord, alike in dark or shining,
  Thy pure eyes their vigil keep.
Let Thy light, which faileth never,
  Round me shine, though day depart;
And, though night prevaileth, ever
  Flood the chambers of my heart.

Among the more recent hymn-writers of Iceland, Valdimar Briem is unquestionably the most outstanding. This man, who died in 1930 at the age of 82 years, was the richly endowed scion of a distinguished family in northern Iceland. For thirty-eight years he served as pastor of Stori-Napur parish, during which period he also held the office of district superintendent. From 1909 until his death he was vice-bishop of the Skalholt diocese.

To the Iceland hymnbook of 1886 Briem contributed no less than 102 original hymns and thirty-nine translations. Deeply cherished by his countrymen, many of his lyrics continue to grace the pages of the recent 1945 Icelandic hymnal. He was also accorded an unusual distinction in 1958, when two of his hymns were included in the *Service Book and Hymnal* of the Lutheran Church of America. Even in their translated form, a suggestion of their poetic beauty is easily apparent. In one of these, a nature hymn titled "How marvelous God's greatness," Briem pictures something of the awe-inspiring grandeur of the tempestuous waves of winter that beat against the rockbound shores of his Arctic homeland:

The ocean's vast abysses
  In one grand psalm record
The deep mysterious counsels
  And mercies of the Lord;
The icy waves of winter
  Are thundering on the strand;
E'en grief's chill stream is guided
  By God's all-gracious hand.

245

Briem's other hymn in the above mentioned hymnal is the moving prayer of a soul yearning to be conformed to the likeness of Christ through the transforming power of God's Spirit:

> Lord, let Thy Spirit, from earthly passion weaning,
>   Lead me along Thy will's all-holy way,
> To find by faith, on Jesus' bosom leaning,
>   'Mid trial, doubt and need, in Him my stay.
>
> Lord, let Thy Spirit, new love and life bestowing,
>   Create a holy heart my breast within;
> That I, into my Saviour's likeness growing,
>   May bear His image through a world of sin.
>
> Lord, let Thy Spirit, Thy Word's deep wealth unsealing,
>   Lighten mine eyes with truth's celestial fire;
> In life, in death, the narrow path revealing
>   Unto the Promised Land of our desire.

Another recent Icelandic hymn-writer who received recognition when one of his hymns was included in the *Service Book and Hymnal* mentioned above is the late Steingrimur Thorsteinsson. A philologist by training, he was for years a teacher of classics and modern languages in the State College of Iceland at Reykjavik, and later became rector of the institution.

Thorsteinsson, who died in 1913 at the age of 82, has given his Church a number of fine hymns. The 1945 hymnbook of Iceland contained four originals and two translations from his pen. One of the originals, an evening hymn of serene beauty, has retained even in its translated form something of its native charm. The English version is the work of Jakobina Johnson, a Seattle poet of no mean ability:

> The fading day adorns the west
> And calls our waiting world to rest;
> Thou Lord of light and all we know,
> Thy calm and peace on us bestow.
>
> O Lord, as silent shadows fall,
> Thy loving kindness shield us all;
> And for thy children near and far
> Set out o'er each a golden star.
>
> Of thy protecting hand aware,
> May all in sleep invite Thy care;
> And, strength renewed and darkness gone,
> Behold with joy the light of dawn.

246

PART IV

English Hymnody

A Lyric by an Ancient British Bard

A hymn of glory let us sing,
New hymns throughout the world shall ring;
By a new way none ever trod
Christ mounteth to the throne of God.

May our affections thither tend,
And thither constantly ascend,
Where, seated on the Father's throne,
Thee, reigning in the heavens, we own!

Be Thou our present joy, O Lord,
Who wilt be ever our reward;
So shall the light that springs from Thee
Be ours through all eternity.

O risen Christ, ascended Lord,
All praise to Thee let earth accord,
Who art, while endless ages run,
With Father and with Spirit, One.

THE VENERABLE BEDE, 673-735
TR. ST. 1-3, ELIZABETH RUNDLE CHARLES, 1820-96
TR. ST. 4, BENJAMIN WEBB, 1820-85

THE IRON RULE OF PSALMODY IN ENGLAND

PERHAPS the first Christian hymns written on English soil came from the pen of the Venerable Bede in the early part of the 8th century. Inasmuch as all worship throughout Europe at that time was conducted in Latin, Bede's lyrics were not written in the language of the Angles, but in the universal language of the Church.

Almost a legendary figure of the dim past, the Venerable Bede was nevertheless an historical character whose name looms large in the story of the early Church in England. Born in the year 673 A.D. near the place where Benedict Biscop afterwards founded the monasteries of Wearmouth and Jarrow, he received his education in one of these cloisters under the direction of Benedict. About the year 702 he was ordained as a priest. He spent his entire life in one or the other of the two monasteries, and died on May 26, 735. Cuthbert records the fact that he sang a hymn on his deathbed. He was buried at Jarrow, but in the 11th century his remains were removed to Durham, where they were re-interred in the same sarcophagus where rests the dust of Cuthbert.

Bede was one of the great scholars of his age and a prolific writer on almost every subject, including grammar, philosophy, poetry, biography, and ecclesiastical history. His contribution to early English history has been of extraordinary value. He also was interested in hymnody, and his *Liber Hymnorum* contains a dozen original Latin hymns. It is here we find this first of English bards intoning his famous Ascension Day hymn, *Hymnum canamus gloriae,* the first stanza of which is almost prophetic of the great chorus of song which was destined to resound throughout the world during the succeeding centuries:

> A hymn of glory let us sing,
> New hymns throughout the world shall ring;
> By a new way none ever trod
> Christ mounteth to the throne of God.

England, however, was slow in heeding the admonition of its earliest hymnist to sing "new hymns." During the Reformation, when

249

hymnody began to flourish in many countries of northern Europe through the inspiration and example of Martin Luther, England failed to follow suit, and this despite the fact that most of the changes that had been made in the liturgy of the Church of England had followed closely the lines indicated by Luther and the German Reformers. Perhaps the primary blame for this failure rests at the door of Archbishop Cranmer, who hesitated for a long time before deciding whether he should adopt Luther's idea of making free use of hymns in the stated worship of the Church, or if he should follow Calvin in restricting sacred song to paraphrases of the psalms.

In the first enthusiasm of the Reformation movement in England it had appeared for a while that Luther's views would be triumphant. The first significant hymnal to be published in English was Miles Coverdale's famous *Goostly Psalmes and Spiritual Songs.* This volume not only followed the pattern set by Luther's hymnbooks by including Latin translations, original hymns and psalm paraphrases, but revealed throughout the closest affinity to the hymns of the German Reformers. Coverdale's version of the 46th Psalm was written in exactly the same meter as Luther's *Ein' feste Burg,* and there were numerous other meters employed that were clearly of German origin. Two other English Reformers, Robert Wisdome and Thomas Becon, who likewise composed psalm paraphrases during this period, also copied the German patterns.

A curious letter which Archbishop Cranmer in 1544 addressed to King Henry VIII gives an insight into the thinking of the English Primate at this time. Enclosing a rough translation of the Latin hymn, *Salve festa dies,* Cranmer wrote to his monarch:

"I have travailed to make the verses in English. . . . I made them only for a proof to see how English would do in song. But by cause my English verses want the grace and facility that I would wish they had, your majesty may cause some other to make them again, that can do the same in more pleasant English and phrase."

Since it is quite doubtful that a man of Cranmer's learning and with his mastery of the English language was incapable of rendering Latin verse into acceptable English, it is far more likely that his lack of enthusiasm for the task was motivated by a desire to delay the whole question of whether any hymns in English, except paraphrases of the psalms, should be sanctioned in the public worship. Hesitating between Luther's and Calvin's views on the subject, he eventually came out on the side of Calvin, and when the Prayer Book of 1559 was published, it was found to contain no hymns at all. After that year few traces of Lutheran hymnody can be found in English books of worship, and the Church of England became more and more committed to the use of psalmody.

A more unfortunate decision for the worship life of the British people could hardly have been conceived. It virtually placed an ecclesiastical ban on all hymnody of a definite New Testament content, and doomed the greater part of the English-speaking world for more than two centuries to the exclusive use of metrical versions of the psalms. These paraphrases were often the wretched work of incompetent "versifiers," and usually devoid of a truly evangelical message. Moreover, since no lyrics of "human composure" were sanctioned, there was nothing to challenge the great English poets of those days to employ their genius in writing Christian hymns.

Equally unfortunate was the fact that psalmody did little to inspire British musicians to compose new tunes. In course of time, common meter and long meter became almost the invariable mold for the versified psalms, and most of them had their traditional tunes, largely imported from the continent. Thus, while the floodgates of hymnody were being opened in Germany and other lands where Luther's views were accepted, and while musicians on the continent vied with one another in composing chorales in a great variety of meters for the new hymns, neither poets nor musicians in England found any incentive for creative effort on behalf of the worship of the Church.

The first "versifier" of the psalms in England was not a poet, but "groom of the robes" under both Henry VIII and Edward VI. It was during the latter's brief reign that Thomas Sternhold, who undoubtedly was a devout man but limited in poetical ability, published a volume of nineteen psalms in metrical form under the title, *Certayne Psalms*. This was in 1549, the very year that Parliament authorized the first *Prayer Book* of Edward VI. It was followed shortly by a second collection of thirty-seven paraphrases. When a new edition was published in 1551, it had been augmented by seven psalm versions from the pen of John Hopkins, who was hardly any better qualified to write poetry than Sternhold. Henceforth the official hymnal of the Church of England came to be known as the *Sternhhold and Hopkins Psalter,* or simply the "Old Version." In its final form, it contained an appendix in which a few hymns had been included, including Luther's "Lord, keep us steadfast in thy Word" and an English translation of his paraphrase of the Lord's Prayer. Here, however, ended the influence of Lutheran hymnody in British worship until it was revived by translations from the German by John Wesley nearly 200 years later. Says H. Leigh Bennet, an English hymnologist:

"The narrower canons of Calvin, admitting nothing but paraphrases of Scripture, and even of Scripture little outside the psalms, became the stern rule of our hymnody for the next century and a half."

Despite the shortcomings of the "Old Version," however, so firmly did it retain its hold on the British people that when an attempt was made by Nahum Tate and Nicholas Brady in 1696, nearly a century and a half later, to introduce a "New Version," it met with widespread popular resistance. Percy Dearmer, in his *Songs of Praise Discussed,* illustrates this prejudice against change by relating two incidents that occurred at the time. A pastor who asked a villager why he no longer joined in the singing in church received the answer: "Well, Sir, David speaks so plain that us cannot mistake 'un; but as for Mr. Tate and Brady, they have taken the Lord away." And Tate himself tells how, when he was present at family prayers at the home of a friend, one of the maids explained her refusal to sing by saying, "If you must know the plain truth, Sir, as long as you sung Jesus Christ's psalms, I sung along with ye; but now that you sing psalms of your own invention, ye may sing by yourselves!"

Though the *Tate and Brady Psalter* lacked something of the rugged quality of its predecessor and to some extent used the florid style which was characteristic of literature of the latter part of the 17th century, it nevertheless was an improvement over Sternhold and Hopkins. From its contents have been derived a number of classic paraphrases found in modern hymnals, such as "Through all the changing scenes of life," a version of Psalm 34, and "As pants the hart for cooling streams," a rendering of Psalm 42.

A clamor for hymns of a distinctive New Testament content may have been responsible for the printing of a supplement to the "New Version" in 1698. This addition contained English translations of the

252

Latin *Te Deum* and *Veni, Creator Spiritus,* as well as the New Testament canticles, the *Nunc Dimittis,* the *Benedictus,* and the *Magnificat.* It also included paraphrases of the Creed, the Ten Commandments, and the Lord's Prayer. Most interesting of all, it contained six original hymns of "human composure!" Three of these were for Holy Communion, namely, "Thou God, all glory, honor, power," "All ye who faithful servants are," and "To God be glory, peace on earth"; two for Easter, "Since Christ, our Passover, is slain" and "Christ from the dead is raised and made," and the well-known Christmas carol, "While shepherds watched their sheep by night." The last named is credited to Nahum Tate.

Public singing in the English worship ceased entirely during the reign of "bloody Mary," but the use of psalms received a new impetus when English and Scotch refugees who fled from Roman Catholic persecution found sanctuary in Geneva. Here, under the powerful influence of Calvin and his associates, the English exiles became deeply impressed by the Reformed worship, and ere long they set to work to prepare a psalmbook of their own. The result was a collection which had as its title, *One and Fiftie Psalmes.* In a subsequent edition of this volume, William Kethe, one of the refugees, introduced twenty-five additional paraphrases of his own, among them a version of Psalm 100. Set to Louis Bourgeois' famous tune, *Old Hundredth,* this paraphrase became immensely popular both in England and Scotland, and today is regarded as one of the classics of psalmody. Despite its crudeness of expression, it possesses a quaint charm that is very appealing:

> All people that on earth do dwell,
> Sing to the Lord with cheerful voice;
> Him serve with mirth, His praise forth tell.
> Come ye before Him, and rejoice.

Another example of psalmody from this period is an anonymous paraphrase of the Twenty-third Psalm from the *Scottish Psalter.* This historic book of worship, which was first published by returning exiles from Geneva in 1564 and which found its final form almost a hundred years later, contained a picturesque rendering of the Shepherd Psalm sometimes ascribed to Francis Rous. It begins:

> The Lord's my Shepherd, I'll not want.
> He makes me down to lie
> In pastures green; He leadeth me
> To quiet waters by.

An Invitation to Song

Let all the world in every corner sing,
"My God and King!"
The heavens are not too high,
His praise may thither fly;
The earth is not too low,
His praises there may grow.
Let all the world in every corner sing,
"My God and King!"

Let all the world in every corner sing,
"My God and King!"
The Church with psalms must shout;
No door can keep them out;
But, above all, the heart
Must bear the longest part.
Let all the world in every corner sing,
"My God and King!"

GEORGE HERBERT, 1593–1633

EARLY HERALDS OF ENGLISH HYMNODY

DESPITE the prohibitions placed on the use of hymns in public worship, there was nothing to prevent pious souls whose spiritual aspirations could not be suppressed from rising on the wings of song to give expression to their Christian faith and love. As a consequence, a number of exquisite lyrics were written in England during the 17th century. Most of these were intended merely for private devotion and edification, and it was not until later years that they found their way into hymn collections.

Some of these have only recently been recovered from forgotten volumes, and are being eagerly welcomed into modern hymnals.

Earliest among these spiritual poets was George Herbert. A member of a distinguished noble family, Herbert was born in Montgomery Castle, April 31, 1593. Following his education at Cambridge, he became a favorite in the court of James I, and was likewise an intimate friend of Lord Bacon and Bishop Andrewes. Although he originally had ambitions to enter the service of the government, he later decided to take holy orders and was ordained by the Established Church. He died as rector of Bemerton parish in 1632 at the age of 39 years.

All evidence points to Herbert as a very devout soul. Oddly enough, his biography was written by none other than Izaak Walton, author of the famous book, *The Compleat Angler*. Walton states that even as a child Herbert "seemed to be marked out for piety, and to become the care of Heaven, and of a particular good angel to guard and guide him." Reference is made to him even in *The Compleat Angler*, where he is called "the holy Herbert." It is said that Herbert, like Martin Luther, was a musician, and that he often accompanied his own singing on the viol or the lute.

About three weeks before his death, he delivered a sheaf of poems into the hands of a friend with the request that they be published "if he can think it may turn to the advantage of any dejected soul." It is from this collection, which was published the following year under the title, *The Temple*, that we have received such hymns

255

as "Let all the world in every corner sing," "Teach me, my God and King," "Sweet day, so cool, so calm, so bright," "King of glory, King of peace," and "The God of love my shepherd is."

A contemporary author and divine, the noted Richard Baxter, bears Herbert this testimony: "I must confess that next to the Scripture poems, there is none so savory to me as Mr. George Herbert's. Herbert speaks to God like one that really believeth in a God, and whose business in the world is most with God." Modern critics also agree with this high estimate of Herbert's hymns. The eminent British hymnologist, Percy Dearmer, ranks him "second only to Henry Vaughan as a religious poet," and asserts that his hymn, "The God of love my shepherd is," which he calls "an exquisite version" of the Twenty-third Psalm, "may safely be crowned as the best ever made."

The Wesleys also regarded Herbert's hymns very highly and included some of them in their hymnbooks. The first of these Wesley collections was published by John Wesley during his visit in Georgia in 1737. Printed in "Charles-town" as a volume of 76 pages, it is interesting to note that it contained six hymns by Herbert, whereas Charles Wesley, "the Bard of Methodism," was not represented by a single one!

Incidentally, it might be added that John Wesley was summoned before the grand jury in Savannah, Ga., in 1737 on the charge that he had made alterations in the *Metrical Psalms* and that he was "introducing into the church and service at the Altar compositions of psalms and hymns not authorized by any proper judicature!" To such an extent had the Calvinistic prejudice against hymnody spread even to the New World.

Herbert referred to "Let all the world in every corner sing" as an antiphon, and he intended that a chorus should sing the words, "My God and King!"

Henry Vaughan, whom Dearmer ranks so high among the English spiritual poets of this period, was eleven years old when Herbert died. He was born in Skethiog, Wales, in 1621, and belonged to an old and honored family of South Wales. He was a staunch royalist, for which he suffered imprisonment and the loss of his property during the days of the Commonwealth. He received his education at Jesus College, Oxford, and at the age of 24 published a volume of poems. Later he became a physician. However, he continued to write poems of a high order throughout his life. One of them, bearing the title, *"Retreat,"* is said to have offered a number of ideas to Wordsworth for his *Intimations of Immortality.* Vaughan's poems were largely forgotten for nearly two centuries until Henry Francis Lyte edited them in 1847. Choicest among his hymns are "Up to those bright and gladsome hills," "My soul, there is a country," and "They are all gone into the world of light."

While Herbert and Vaughan were writing hymns, the great John Milton was engaged in producing such immortal verses as *L'allegro, Il Penseroso,* and *Comus,* and later such masterpieces as *Paradise Lost, Paradise Regained,* and *Samson Agonistes.* However, Milton also at times devoted himself to writing paraphrases of the psalms. He was only 16 years old when he produced "Let us, with a gladsome mind," a rendering of Psalm 136. In all, he wrote nineteen metrical versions of the psalms, but not many of them have come into common use. In addition to the one already mentioned, the more popular are "How lovely are thy dwellings fair," "Ring out, ye crystal spheres," and "The Lord will come and not be slow." Milton, who was born in London in 1608, died in that city in 1674.

Other famous literary lights who produced hymns during the 17th century were Richard Baxter, John Bunyan, and Joseph Addison.

That a hymn of such beautiful Christian resignation as "Lord, it belongs not to my care" should have its birth in a life as stormy and turbulent as that of Richard Baxter is one of the miracles of divine grace. This hymn is a cento from a longer poem by the sorely afflicted man, bearing the title, "The Covenant and Confidence of Faith," the opening line of which reads, "My whole, though broken heart, O Lord." It was dated "London, at the Door of Eternity: Richard Baxter, August 7, 1671."

Although the notorious Chief Justice Jeffreys branded this noble Christian warrior as "an old rogue, an old schismatical knave, a hypocritical villain, a conceited, stubborn, fanatical dog, a snivelling Presbyterian," and sent him to jail for eighteen months at the age of 70 years, Christians throughout the world will never cease to thank God when they sing Baxter's beautiful words:

> Christ leads me through no darker rooms
> Than He went through before;
> He that into God's Kingdom comes
> Must enter by this door.

> Come, Lord, when grace has made me meet
>   Thy blessed face to see;
> For if Thy work on earth be sweet,
>   What will Thy glory be?
>
> My knowledge of that life is small,
>   The eye of faith is dim;
> But 'tis enough that Christ knows all,
>   And I shall be with Him.

From Baxter we have also received the lovely lyric, "Ye holy angels bright." His best known work is the devotional book, *The Saints' Everlasting Rest.*

Although Baxter was ordained by the Church of England, he questioned the episcopacy as it was then constituted. Though siding with Cromwell, he did not hesitate to rebuke the latter when he assumed supreme power in the State. For a brief time after the Restoration he served as chaplain to the King. Later he participated in the Savoy Conference in an unsuccessful attempt to amend the *Book of Common Prayer.*

It would be difficult to imagine a greater contrast than that presented by the personalities of Baxter and Herbert. The life of the former was stormy and full of conflict; that of the latter was idyllic and peaceful. And yet, a noted British author has referred to them as "the two great model pastors of the 17th century." Baxter died in 1691, four years after his release from the prison sentence imposed by Jeffreys.

John Bunyan's name is so familiar that he needs no introduction. As the author of *The Pilgrim's Progress,* he is known throughout the Christian world. Not so well known, however, is the fact that he was also the author of a number of hymns, two of which, "He who would valiant be" and "He that is down need fear no fall," are in most common use.

"He who would valiant be" is a revision of the poem, "Who would true valour see," taken from the chapter in *The Pilgrim's Progress* entitled "Mr. Valiant for Truth." Although the revision is not as vigorous as the original, the last line, "To be a pilgrim," which comes as a refrain at the close of each stanza, will be a perpetual reminder of the source of the hymn and of its heroic writer.

Bunyan, who was the son of a tinker, was born in Elstow, England, in 1628. At the age of 16 he was drafted into the forces of Cromwell and served for three years. After joining a religious sect founded by John Giffort, he became an itinerant preacher and was cast into jail after the Restoration for disregarding the Act of Uniformity. He remained there for twelve years, during which time he wrote nine books, including *Grace Abounding,* an autobiographical account of his early life and spiritual struggles. The adoption of the Declaration of Indulgence in 1672 brought about his release, but when it was revoked three years later, he was again imprisoned. It was at this time that he began *The Pilgrim's Progress,* a work which by many is considered as second only to the Bible. He died in 1688 and is buried in Bunhill Fields.

It was during the time of Bunyan's prison experiences that one of England's great literary geniuses was born. He was the famous poet and essayist, Joseph Addison. Besides being one of the leading literary lights of his time, Addison was a devout Christian as well. From time to time he appended a poem to the charming essays which appeared in *The Spectator,* and from this source have been derived five hymns of rare beauty. They are the so-called "Creation" hymn, "The spacious firmament on high," which Haydn included in his celebrated oratorio; the Traveler's hymn, beginning with the line, "How are Thy servants blest, O Lord"; and three other hymns, almost equally well-known, "The Lord my pasture shall prepare," "When rising from the bed of death," and "When all Thy mercies, O my God." The latter contains one of the most striking expressions in all the realm of hymnody:

> Through all eternity to Thee
> A joyful song I'll raise:
> But oh, eternity's too short
> To utter all Thy praise!

In the essay introducing this hymn, Addison writes: "If gratitude is due from man to man, how much more from man to his Maker. The Supreme Being does not only confer upon us those bounties which proceed immediately from His hand, but even those benefits which are conveyed to us by others. Any blessing which we enjoy, by what means soever derived, is the gift of Him who is the great Author of Good and the Father of Mercies."

The Traveler's hymn, "How are Thy servants blessed, O Lord," was written after Addison's return from a perilous voyage on the Mediterranean.

In addition to his literary pursuits, Addison also occupied several important positions of state with the English government. He died on June 17, 1719, at the age of forty-seven. When he was breathing his last, he called for the Earl of Warwick and exclaimed: "See in what peace a Christian can die!"

Another devout soul who has won an imperishable place among the English hymn-writers of the 17th century was Samuel Crossman. Although he does not rank with such literary geniuses as Addison, Milton, Bunyan or Baxter, he will always be remembered for his Lenten lyric, "My song is love unknown," which is undoubtedly one of the finest hymns on the Passion in the English language. Here are three of its stanzas:

> My song is love unknown,
> My Saviour's love to me;
> Love to the loveless shown
> That they might lovely be.
> O who am I,
> That for my sake
> My Lord should take
> Frail flesh and die?
>
> He came from His blest throne
> Salvation to bestow;
> But men made strange, and none
> The longed-for Christ would know.
> But O, my Friend,
> My Friend indeed,
> Who at my need
> His life did spend!
>
> Here might I stay and sing,
> No story so divine;
> Never was love, dear King,
> Never was grief like Thine.
> This is my Friend,
> In whose sweet praise
> I all my days
> Could gladly spend.

Crossman is believed to have been born in the year 1624. He received his education at Cambridge, where he graduated in 1660. He leaned toward the Puritan cause and was deposed from the ministry in 1662, but afterwards conformed and became one of the King's chaplains. He was appointed prebendary of Bristol in 1667, and later, in 1683, a few weeks before he died, he became dean of Bristol. Among his published sermons are two preached in the Cathedral of Bristol on January 30, 1679, and January 30, 1680, which had been set aside as days of humiliation "for the execrable murder of Charles I."

In addition to the above hymn, Crossman also wrote another in the same unusual meter, the title of which is "Jerusalem on high." Both hymns appeared in a small pamphlet, *The Young Man's Meditation,* which was published in London in 1664, the year of the great plague. Leigh Bennett, commenting on the latter hymn, writes: "The vision of the heavenly city and the delight and sadness which it inspires are portrayed with equal delicacy; and the crisp rhythm, the longing refrain, and a trace of Puritan feeling add to its charm." Here is the final stanza:

> Ah me! ah me! that I
>   In Kedar's tents here stay;
> No place like that on high;
>   Lord, thither guide my way:
> O happy place!
>   When shall I be,
>   My God, with Thee,
> To see Thy face!

Another hymn-writer of the 17th century was John Quarles, son of the renowned essayist, Francis Quarles. John was born in Essex in 1624. Educated at Oxford, he joined the military garrison at that place in behalf of King Charles I against the Parliamentary forces. He was promoted to the rank of captain in the King's service, but when the latter was murdered, he went to London to follow literary pursuits. Most of his writings were religious in character, and it is from these that two hymns have been derived, "O King of kings, before whose throne" and "Long did I toil, and knew no earthly rest."

A hymnist who is said to have exerted a profound influence over John Wesley also belongs to this period. He was Henry More, who, while studying at Cambridge, became the leader of a select group of high-minded scholars who called themselves the Cambridge Platonists. More refused a number of opportunities of high preferment in order to teach and to pursue the study of philosophy. He was the author in 1640 of *Psychozoia,* described as "the first part of the song of the soul." His best known hymn is "The holy Son of God most high."

261

Ken's Immortal Evening Hymn

All praise to Thee, my God, this night,
For all the blessings of the light;
Keep me, O keep me, King of Kings,
Beneath Thine own almighty wings!

Forgive me, Lord, for Thy dear Son,
The ill that I this day have done,
That with the world, myself, and Thee,
I, ere I sleep, at peace may be.

Teach me to live, that I may dread
The grave as little as my bed;
Teach me to die, that so I may
Rise glorious at the aweful day.

O when shall I, in endless day,
For ever chase dark sleep away,
And hymns divine with angels sing
In endless praise to Thee, my King?

Praise God, from whom all blessings flow;
Praise Him, all creatures here below;
Praise Him above, ye heavenly host;
Praise Father, Son, and Holy Ghost.   Amen.

THOMAS KEN, 1637-1711a

A BRAVE BISHOP AND HIS HYMNS

IT IS always true of history that very few recognize a significant event when it is in the making. In a very definite sense this was so during the transition from psalmody to hymnody in England. It was evident at the beginning of the 17th century that a change was impending, but changes are not easily wrought in the worship life of the Church, and many discouraging setbacks were experienced by those who sought to bring about reform.

The earliest attempt to create a hymnbook for use in the Established Church was made by George Wither, a rather strange character, the story of whose life reads almost like fiction. Vacillating between loyalty to his royal master and love for his native land, he found himself caught in the bitter civil war that brought untold misery and suffering to England. Captured at one time by the royalists, he was saved from hanging only through a jest by Sir John Denham, who insisted that "his majesty really must not hang George Wither, for so long as he lives no one will account me the worst poet in England!" He was twice imprisoned for offending the king and the nobility, and once for making a heroic plea for the rights and liberties of the common man.

It was in 1623 that Wither published a volume which he called *The Hymnes and Songs of the Church,* and received a patent from the King to have it bound up with every copy of the metrical Psalms. There are many who believe that, except for the Puritan reaction which set in soon thereafter, this might easily have proved the introduction of hymnody in the Established Church. Instead, Wither suffered naught but financial loss and persecution for his brave effort. The famous organist and composer, Orlando Gibbons, had written some of the tunes for the hymnbook. In 1641 a part of the volume was republished, but seems to have met with the same fate.

This apparently was the last time any serious effort was made from within the Church of England to break the iron rule of psalmody. It now remained for the non-conformists and Independents to bring about the dawn of a new day.

263

Modern hymnologists, even those of the Reformed Church, find it difficult to understand the reluctance of a large segment of Protestantism to break away from the unhappy dictum of Calvin. Millar Patrick of Edinburgh, Scotland, writing the introduction of the *Handbook to the Church Hymnody,* which reviews the contents of the official hymnal of all the Presbyterian Churches in the British Commonwealth with the exception of Canada, expresses his wonder in this wise:

"It seems extraordinary now that the Reformed Churches should so long have been content, as Watts puts it, to pray and preach in Christ's name, but to sing in terms of the Law, and above all to be inhibited entirely from using the name of Christ in their worship-song. Religion could not fail to suffer from such an unnatural restriction. Notoriously, it did suffer. The severity of thought and austerity of life which long characterized the Churches of this order were undoubtedly traceable in part at least to the compulsion laid upon the people to praise God only in terms of pre-Christian categories of thought. The discovery was early made in the Christian era that popular religion is moulded largely by the ideas enshrined in its hymns. Sermons often fly over the people's heads; prayers uttered in their name often fail to carry their hearts and even their intelligence with them; but their songs sink into the memory, color their thought, and fashion their theology, much more than any deliberate instruction."

But the saintly Bishop Thomas Ken was tuning his harp, and before the end of the 17th century he had begun to sing. And his song began to echo throughout all of England. Although Ken apparently wrote only three hymns, they have won for him an imperishable place in the hearts of all Christians. His sublime evening prayer, "All praise to thee, my God, this night," is ranked as one of the four masterpieces of English hymnody. His beautiful morning hymn, "Awake, my soul, and with the sun," is scarcely less deserving of high distinction. His midnight hymn, "My God, now I from sleep awake," although it has never attained the popularity of the other two, nevertheless shares something of the heavenly aura that seems to rest over them. All three hymns end with the so-called "long meter" doxology, the most famous stanza of its kind ever written:

Praise God, from whom all blessings flow;
Praise Him, all creatures here below;
Praise Him above, ye heavenly host;
Praise Father, Son, and Holy Ghost.

Nothing similar to this doxology is found in any Ambrosian or other Latin hymns, wherefore it is believed to be an entirely original composition by Ken. It has sometimes been called "the Protestant *Te Deum laudamus.*"

Another stanza that has endeared itself to Christians throughout the English-speaking world is from his evening hymn:

Teach me to live, that I may dread
The grave as little as my bed;
Teach me to die, that so I may
Rise glorious at the aweful day.

Born at Berkhampstead, England, in 1637, Ken looms as a heroic figure during turbulent times in English history. Left an orphan in early childhood, he was brought up by his brother-in-law, the famous angler, Izaak Walton. Ken's name has been found cut in one of the stone pillars at Winchester, where he went to school as a boy.

When, in 1679, the wife of William of Orange, the niece of the English monarch, asked Charles II to send an English chaplain to the royal court at The Hague, Ken was selected for the position. However, he was so outspoken in denouncing the corrupt lives of those in authority in the Dutch capital that he was compelled to leave the following year. Charles thereupon appointed him one of his own chaplains.

Ken continued to reveal the same spirit of boldness, however, in rebuking the sins of the dissolute English monarch. On one occasion, when Charles asked the courageous pastor to give up his own dwelling temporarily in order that Nell Gwynne, a notorious character, might be housed, Ken answered promptly: "Not for the King's kingdom."

Instead of punishing the bold and faithful minister, Charles so admired his courage that he appointed him Bishop of Bath and Wells. When some of the King's counselors advised against the appointment, Charles is said to have broken off the argument by exclaiming: "Odd's fish! Who shall have Bath and Wells but little Ken, who would not give poor Nelly a lodging!"

Charles always referred to Ken as "the good little man" and, when it was chapel time, he would usually say: "I must go in and hear Ken tell me of my faults." Bishop Burnet, in his *History of His Own Times,* bears testimony to the faithfulness with which Ken discharged his duties as the spiritual adviser of his monarch. He records the fact that, as the king lay dying, Ken "applied himself to the awakening of the king's conscience," but evidently with little success.

When Charles died, and the papist James II came to the throne, Ken, together with six other bishops, was imprisoned in the Tower of London. Although he was acquitted, he was later removed from his bishopric by William III.

The last years of his life were spent in a quiet retreat, and he died in 1711 at the age of seventy-four years. He had requested that "six of the poorest men in the parish" should carry him to his grave, and this was done. It was also at his request that he was buried under the east window of the chancel of Frome church, the service being held at sunrise. As his body was lowered into its last resting-place, and the first light of dawn came through the chancel window, his friends sang his immortal morning hymn:

> Awake, my soul, and with the sun
> Thy daily stage of duty run.
> Shake off dull sloth, and joyful rise
> To pay thy morning sacrifice.
>
> All praise to Thee, who safe hast kept,
> And hast refreshed me while I slept:
> Grant, Lord, when I from death shall wake
> I may of endless life partake.

It is said that after Bishop Ken had written this hymn, he sang it to his own accompaniment on the lute every morning as a part of his private devotion. This and the evening hymn were first published in a devotional manual he had prepared for the students of Winchester College. In this work Bishop Ken urged the students to sing the hymns devoutly in their rooms every morning and evening.

The historian Macaulay paid Ken a beautiful tribute when he said that he came as near to the ideal of Christian perfection "as human weakness permits."

Lord Houghton, in writing on Ken's request to be buried "under the east window of the chancel of Frome church," has left this touching tribute to the humble and beloved bishop:

266

Let other thoughts, where'er I roam,
    Ne'er from my memory cancel
The coffin-fashioned tomb at Frome
    That lies beneath the chancel;
A basket-work where bars are bent,
    Iron in place of osier,
And shapes above that represent
    A mitre and a crozier.

These signs of him that slumbers there
    The dignity betoken;
These iron bars a heart declare
    Hard bent, but never broken;
This form portrays how souls like his,
    Their pride and passion quelling,
Preferred to earth's high palaces
    This calm and narrow dwelling.

There with the churchyard's common dust
    He loved his own to mingle;
The faith in which he placed his trust
    Was nothing rare or single;
Yet laid he to the sacred wall
    As close as he was able,—
The blessed crumbs might almost fall
    Upon him from God's table.

Who was this father of the Church,
    So secret in his glory?
In vain might antiquarians search
    For record of his story;
But preciously tradition keeps
    The fame of holy men;
So here the Christian smiles or weeps
    For love of Bishop Ken.

The Pearl of English Hymnody

When I survey the wondrous Cross
  On which the Prince of Glory died,
My richest gain I count but loss,
  And pour contempt on all my pride.

Forbid it, Lord, that I should boast,
  Save in the death of Christ, my God;
All the vain things that charm me most,
  I sacrifice them to His Blood.

See, from His head, His hands, His feet,
  Sorrow and love flow mingled down!
Did e'er such love and sorrow meet,
  Or thorns compose so rich a crown?

Were the whole realm of nature mine,
  That were an offering far too small;
Love so amazing, so divine,
  Demands my soul, my life, my all.

ISAAC WATTS, 1674-1748

ISAAC WATTS, FATHER OF ENGLISH HYMNODY

B Y UNIVERSAL consent the title, "Father of English Hymnody," is bestowed upon Isaac Watts. English hymns had been written before the time of Watts, notably the beautiful classics of Herbert, Crossman, Baxter, Ken and Addison; but it remained for the genius of Watts to break the paralyzing reign of psalmody in the Reformed Church which had continued uninterrupted since the days of Calvin.

Watts was born in Southampton, England, July 17, 1674. His father was a "dissenter," and twice was imprisoned for his religious views. This was during the time when Isaac was still a baby, and the mother often carried the future poet in her arms when she went to visit her husband in prison.

When Isaac grew up, a wealthy man offered to give him a university education if he would consent to take holy orders in the Established Church. This he refused to do, but prepared instead for the Independent ministry.

Early in life young Watts had revealed signs of poetic genius. As a boy of seven years he had amused his parents with his rhymes. As he grew older he became impatient with the wretched paraphrases of the psalms then in use throughout England and Scotland. These views were shared generally by those who possessed a discriminating taste in poetry. "Scandalous doggerel" was the term applied by Samuel Wesley, father of the famous Wesley brothers, to the versified psalms of Sternhold and Hopkins.

When young Watts ventured to voice his displeasure with the psalm-singing in his father's church in Southampton, one of the church officers retorted: "Give us something better, young man." Although he was only eighteen years old at the time, he accepted the challenge and his first hymn was sung at the following Sunday evening service. There was a note of prophecy in its first stanza, proclaiming, as it did, the dawn of a new day in the worship life of England:

> Behold the glories of the Lamb
> Amidst His Father's throne;
> Prepare new honors for His Name,
> And songs before unknown.

269

The hymn met with such favorable reception that the youthful poet was encouraged to write others, and within the next two years he had produced nearly all of the 210 hymns that constituted his famous collection, *Hymns and Spiritual Songs,* published in 1707. This was the first real hymnbook in the English language.

Twelve years later he published his *Psalms of David,* a metrical version of the Psalter, but, as he himself stated, rendered "in the language of the New Testament, and applied to the Christian state and worship." Indeed, the psalms were given such a distinctively Christian flavor that their Old Testament origin is often overlooked. Witness, for example, the opening lines of his version of Psalm 72:

> Jesus shall reign where'er the sun
> Does his successive journeys run;
> His Kingdom stretch from shore to shore,
> Till moons shall wax and wane no more.

Note, also, how in his rendering of Psalm 117 he not only refers to God the Creator, but also calls on the worshiper to praise "the Redeemer's Name":

> From all that dwell below the skies
> Let the Creator's praise arise;
> Let the Redeemer's Name be sung
> Through every land, by every tongue.

But if Watts could "Christianize" the psalms and make them glorify Christ, his spirit was even more on fire as he paraphrased the message of the New Testament and its victories of faith:

> Give me the wings of faith to rise
>   Within the veil and see
> The saints above, how great their joys,
>   How great their glories be.
>
> Once they were mourning here below,
>   And wet their couch with tears;
> They wrestled hard, as we do now,
>   With sins and doubts and fears.
>
> I ask them whence their victory came;
>   They, with united breath,
> Ascribe their conquest to the Lamb,
>   Their triumph to His death.
>
> They marked the footsteps that He trod,
>   His zeal inspired their breast,
> And, following their incarnate God,
>   Possess the promised rest.

In addition to being a preacher and a poet, Watts was an ardent student of theology and philosophy, and wrote several notable books. Always frail in health from childhood, his intense studies finally resulted in completely shattering his constitution, and he was compelled to give up his parish.

During this period of physical distress, the stricken poet was invited to become a guest for a week in the home of Sir Thomas Abney, an intimate friend and admirer. The friendship continued to grow, and inasmuch as Watts did not improve in health, he was urged to remain. He finally so endeared himself to the Abney family that they refused to let him go, and he who had come to spend a week remained for the rest of his life—thirty-six years!

The great hymnist died on November 25, 1748, and was buried at Bunhill Fields, London, near the graves of John Bunyan and Daniel Defoe. A monument to his memory was placed in Westminster Abbey, the highest honor that can be bestowed upon an Englishman.

To Isaac Watts we are indebted for some of our noblest Christian hymns. "When I survey the wondrous Cross" has been named by Matthew Arnold as the finest hymn in the English language, and most critics concur in the judgment. Certainly it is one of the most beautiful. John Julian, the noted hymnologist, declares that it must be classified with the four lyrics that stand at the head of all English hymns.

Other hymns of Watts continue to hold their grip on the Christian Church after the passing of two centuries. No Christmas service seems complete without singing his beautiful paraphrase of Psalm 98, "Joy to the world, the Lord is come!" Another hymn, "O God, our help in ages past," based on Psalm 90, is indispensable at New Year's time, reminding us in language, both solemn and sublime, of the contrast between the brevity of human existence and the eternity of God. There is something majestic in the very simplicity of words like these:

> Before the hills in order stood,
>   Or earth received her frame,
> From everlasting Thou art God,
>   To endless years the same.
>
> A thousand ages in Thy sight
>   Are like an evening gone,
> Short as the watch that ends the night
>   Before the rising sun.

Time, like an ever-rolling stream,
Bears all its sons away;
They fly forgotten, as a dream
Dies at the opening day.

Nor can we omit mention of that ascription of praise to the Saviour that bears the title, "Join all the glorious names," in which these triumphant lines occur:

Great Prophet of my God,
My tongue would bless Thy Name;
By Thee the joyful news
Of our salvation came,
The joyful news of sins forgiven,
Of hell subdued, and peace with heaven.

O Thou Almighty Lord,
My Conqueror and my King,
Thy sceptre and Thy sword,
Thy reigning grace I sing:
Thine is the power, behold I sit
In willing bonds before Thy feet.

Something of that same exultant spiritual joy is also voiced in another magnificent hymn of praise:

Come, we that love the Lord,
And let our joys be known;
Join in a song with sweet accord,
And thus surround the throne.

Let those refuse to sing
That never knew our God;
But children of the heavenly King
Must speak their joys abroad.

Then there is the majestic hymn of worship, "Before Jehovah's aweful throne," as well as the appealing Lenten hymn, "Alas, and did my Saviour bleed?" And who has not been stirred by the challenge in "Am I a soldier of the Cross?"

Other hymns by Watts include such favorites as "There is a land of pure delight," "Sweet is the work, my God," "Come, let us join our cheerful songs," "Give to the Lord immortal praise," "Come, Holy Spirit, Heavenly Dove," "O that the Lord would guide my ways," "My dear Redeemer and my Lord," "How beauteous are their feet," "Come, sound His praise abroad," "My soul, repeat His praise," "O bless the Lord, my soul," "Lord of the worlds above," "Lord, we confess our numerous faults," "In vain we seek for peace with God,"

"Not all the blood of beasts," "So let our lips and lives express," "The Lord my Shepherd is," and "When I can read my title clear."

Although Watts never married, he deeply loved little children, and he is the author of some of the most famous nursery rhymes in the English language. The profound genius that produced "O God, our help in ages past" also understood how to appeal to the childish mind by means of such happy little jingles as "How doth the little busy bee" and "Let dogs delight to bark and bite," as well as by the exquisite cradle-song:

> Hush, my dear, lie still and slumber;
>   Holy angels guard thy bed;
> Heavenly blessings without number
>   Gently falling on thy head.
>
> Sleep, my babe, thy food and raiment,
>   House and home, thy friends provide;
> All without thy care or payment,
>   All thy wants are well supplied.
>
> How much better thou'rt attended
>   Than the Son of God could be,
> When from heaven He descended,
>   And became a child like thee.
>
> Soft and easy is thy cradle,
>   Coarse and hard thy Saviour lay,
> When His birthplace was a stable,
>   And His softest bed the hay.

Seeking the Heavenly Prize

Awake, my soul, stretch every nerve,
  And press with vigor on;
A heavenly race demands thy zeal,
  And an immortal crown.

A cloud of witnesses around
  Hold thee in full survey:
Forget the steps already trod,
  And onward urge thy way.

'Tis God's all-animating voice
  That calls thee from on high;
'Tis His own hand presents the prize
  To thine aspiring eye:

That prize with peerless glories bright
  Which shall new luster boast,
When victors' wreaths and monarchs' gems
  Shall blend in common dust.

Then, wake, my soul, stretch every nerve,
  And press with vigor on;
A heavenly race demands thy zeal,
  And an immortal crown.

PHILIP DODDRIDGE, 1702-1751

DODDRIDGE: PREACHER, TEACHER, HYMNIST

IT IS significant that hymnody in England had its rise among the Nonconformists. As indicated earlier, the effort of George Wither in 1623 to introduce a hymnbook within the Church of England proved abortive. Toward the end of the 17th century, however, there are evidences that hymns were being introduced in some Independent congregations. A small Independent hymnal bearing the name, *A Collection of Divine Hymns,* containing contributions by six different authors, including Baxter, appeared in 1694, but probably did not have widespread use.

There is also a record that Benjamin Keach, a Baptist minister, sought to introduce hymn singing in his congregation. In a little book written in 1691 bearing the name, *The Breach Repaired,* he defends the practice and reveals that for a period of eighteen years his congregation had sung a hymn each time they observed the Lord's Supper.

Then came Isaac Watts, an Independent, with his epoch-making *Hymns and Spiritual Songs* in 1707, to be followed closely by another Independent clergyman and hymn-writer, Philip Doddridge, who in many respects might be called Watts' spiritual progeny. Then came the Wesleys with another soul-stirring revival of song. But all this took place outside the Established Church, and a whole century passed by before the soul of hymnody was awakened within the Church of England.

Philip Doddridge, who was born in London on June 26, 1702, was the son of an oil merchant. Like the Wesley brothers, he came from a large family. While there were nineteen children in the Wesley family, Philip was the last of twenty in the Doddridge household.

The religious background of Doddridge was significant. His maternal grandfather was a Lutheran pastor who had fled Bohemia to escape Roman Catholic persecution, and his paternal grandfather was a clergyman who had been ejected from his Church of England parish because he refused to obey the mandate of the Act of Uniformity.

Both of Philip's parents were devout people, and the boy was brought up in a home where piety was the rule.

Physically, he was such a delicate child that his life was despaired of almost from birth. His parents died while he was yet quite young, but kind friends cared for the orphan boy and sent him to school.

Because he revealed such unusual gifts as a student, the Duchess of Bedford offered to give him a university training on condition that he would become a minister of the Church of England. This, however, Philip declined to do, and he entered a nonconformist seminary instead.

At the age of twenty-one years he was ordained as pastor of the Independent congregation at Kibworth, England. Six years later he began his real life work at Northampton, where he served as the head of a theological training school and preached in the local congregation.

To this school came young men from all parts of the British Isles and even from the continent. Most of them prepared to become ministers in the Independent Church. Doddridge himself was practically the whole faculty. Among his subjects were Hebrew, Greek, Algebra, Philosophy, Trigonometry, Logic, and theological branches.

As a hymn-writer Doddridge ranks among the foremost in England. He was a friend and admirer of Isaac Watts, whose hymns at this time had set all England singing. In some respects his lyrics resemble those of Watts. Although they do not possess the strength and majesty found in the latter's hymns, they have more personal warmth and tenderness. Witness, for instance, the children's hymn:

> See Israel's gentle Shepherd stand
> With all-engaging charms;
> Hark! how He calls the tender lambs,
> And folds them in His arms.

Note also the spiritual joy that is reflected in the hymn so often used at confirmation:

> O happy day, that stays my choice
> On Thee, my Saviour and my God!
> Well may this glowing heart rejoice,
> And tell its raptures all abroad.

276

Something of Doddridge's own confiding trust in God is expressed in the beautiful lines:

> Shine on our souls, eternal God!
>   With rays of beauty shine;
> O let Thy favor crown our days,
>   And all their round be Thine.
>
> Did we not raise our hands to Thee,
>   Our hands might toil in vain;
> Small joy success itself could give,
>   If Thou Thy love restrain.

Other hymns by Doddridge include such gems as "Hark, the glad sound, the Saviour comes," "O God of Bethel, by whose hand," "Great God, we sing that mighty hand," "O Fount of good, to own Thy love," "Father of all, Thy care we bless," and "My God, and is Thy table spread?"

Doddridge wrote about four hundred hymns. Most of them were composed for use in his own congregation in connection with sermons. It was customary in those days to "line out" hymns, that is, to repeat them from the pulpit line by line, with the congregation singing them in like fashion.

Doddridge's hymns were not published during his life-time, but manuscript copies were widely circulated among the Independent congregations in England. The fact that about one-third of his hymns are still in common use on both sides of the Atlantic bears witness of their unusual merit.

Though Doddridge struggled under the burden of feeble health, his life was filled with arduous duties. When he was only forty-eight years old it became apparent that he had fallen a victim to tubercular infection. He was advised to leave England for Lisbon, Portugal. He lacked funds for the voyage, but friends throughout England came to his aid. The journey was undertaken, but on October 26, 1751, he died at Lisbon.

A Hymn of the Ages

Jesus, Lover of my soul,
  Let me to Thy bosom fly,
While the nearer waters roll,
  While the tempest still is high.
Hide me, O my Saviour, hide,
  Till the storm of life is past;
Safe into the haven guide:
  O receive my soul at last!

Other refuge have I none;
  Hangs my helpless soul on Thee;
Leave, ah, leave me not alone,
  Still support and comfort me.
All my trust on Thee is stayed,
  All my help from Thee I bring:
Cover my defenseless head
  With the shadow of Thy wing.

Thou, O Christ, art all I want;
  More than all in Thee I find.
Raise the fallen, cheer the faint,
  Heal the sick, and lead the blind.
Just and holy is Thy name,
  I am all unrighteousness;
False and full of sin I am,
  Thou art full of truth and grace.

Plenteous grace with Thee is found,
  Grace to cover all my sin;
Let the healing streams abound,
  Make and keep me pure within.
Thou of life the Fountain art,
  Freely let me take of Thee;
Spring Thou up within my heart,
  Rise to all eternity.

CHARLES WESLEY, 1707-1788

278

WESLEY, THE SWEET BARD OF METHODISM

EVERY great religious movement has witnessed an outburst of song. This was particularly true of the Lutheran Reformation in Germany and other lands, and of the Methodist revival in England. John and Charles Wesley, like Martin Luther, understood something of the value of sacred song in impressing religious truths upon the hearts and minds of men. While John Wesley was undoubtedly a preacher of marvelous spiritual power, the real secret of the success of the Wesleyan movement more likely must be sought in the sublime hymns written by his brother Charles.

With Isaac Watts, Charles Wesley shares the pre-eminent place in English hymnody. No less than 6,500 hymns are said to have been written by this "sweet bard of Methodism." Naturally they are not all of the highest order, but it is surprising how many rise to real poetic heights. Of the 770 hymns in the *Wesleyan Hymn Book,* 612 are from the pen of Charles Wesley!

Wesley did not write hymns merely as a duty, nor yet as a pastime. His soul seemed filled with music and poetry, and when his genius became touched by the divine spark of Christ's Spirit, it burst into full flame. It has been said of Franz Schubert that "he had to write music." The same was true of Charles Wesley. Because his soul was full of song, he had to give expression to it in immortal lyrics. The inspiration for these came to him under all sorts of conditions. Some were composed on horseback, others in a stagecoach or on the deck of a vessel. Even as he was lying on his deathbed, at the age of eighty years, he dictated his last hymn to his faithful and devoted wife. It begins with the words, "In age and feebleness extreme."

Charles was next to the youngest of nineteen children born to Samuel Wesley and his remarkable wife Susanna. The father, who was a clergyman in the Church of England, possessed more than ordinary literary gifts. He was the author of at least one hymn that has survived the passing of time, "Behold, the Saviour of mankind." The mother presided over the rectory at Epworth, where both of her distinguished sons were born, and also looked after the education of the younger children of her large family. Concerning this very unusual mother and the spiritual influence she exerted over her children, volumes have been written.

Poverty and other tribulations descended upon the Epworth rectory like the afflictions of Job. The climactic disaster came in 1709, when the Wesley home was completely destroyed by fire. John, who was only six years old at the time, was left behind in the confusion, and when the entire house was aflame he was seen to appear at a second-story window. The agonized father fell upon his knees and implored God to save his child. Immediately a neighbor mounted the shoulders of another man and managed to seize the boy just as the roof fell in. Thus was spared the child who was destined to become the leader of one of the greatest spiritual movements in the history of the Christian Church.

While John and Charles were students at Oxford University, they became dissatisfied with spiritual conditions among the students. Soon they formed an organization devoted to religious exercises. Because of their strict rules and precise methods, they were nicknamed "the Methodists," a name that afterwards became attached to their reform movement.

The hymns of Charles Wesley are so numerous that only a few of the more outstanding can be mentioned here. "Hark! the herald angels sing," "Love divine, all loves excelling" and "Jesus, Lover of my soul" form a triumvirate of hymns never surpassed by a single author. Add to these such hymns as "A charge to keep I have," "Arise, my soul, arise," "Christ, whose glory fills the sky," "Come, Thou long-expected Jesus," "Soldiers of Christ, arise," "Hail the day that sees Him rise," "Christ the Lord is risen today," "Lo, He comes with clouds descending," "Rejoice, the Lord is King," "Ye servants of God, your Master proclaim," "Come, O Thou Traveler unknown," "O for a thousand tongues to sing," "Forth in Thy Name, O Lord, I go," "Author of life divine," and "Victim Divine, Thy grace we claim," and it will readily be understood why the name of Charles Wesley is graven in such large letters in the hymnody of the Christian Church.

While hymns of many other writers gradually disappear from modern hymnals, those of Charles Wesley continue to reveal a remarkable hold on the worship life of the Church, and a new appreciation is sometimes shown for lyrics once forgotten but again recovered. One such is his communion hymn, "Victim Divine, Thy grace we claim," in which Wesley emphasizes the doctrine of the real presence of Christ in the Lord's Supper:

> We need not now go up to heaven
>> To bring the Saviour down;
> Thou art to all already given,
>> Thou dost e'en now Thy banquet crown:
> To every faithful soul appear,
> And show Thy real presence here.

"Jesus, Lover of my soul" is generally recognized as the finest hymn of Wesley. This is all the more remarkable since it was one of the earliest written by him. It was first published in 1740 in a collection of 139 hymns known as *Hymns and Sacred Poems*. This was at the beginning of the Wesleyan movement, which soon began to spread like a fire on the steppes all over England.

There are several stories extant as to the origin of the hymn. The most trustworthy of these tells how the author was deeply perplexed by spiritual difficulties one day, when he noticed through his open study window a little song bird pursued by a hungry hawk. Presently the bird fluttered exhausted through the window and straight into the arms of Wesley, where it found a safe refuge. Pondering this unusual incident, the thought came to Wesley that, in like manner, the soul of man must flee to Christ in seasons of doubts and fears. Then he took up his pen and wrote:

> Jesus, Lover of my soul,
> Let me to Thy bosom fly.

The reference to the "tempest" and the "storm of life" may have been prompted by the memory of an earlier experience in 1735 when he and his brother John were on their way to the colony of Georgia. On this journey the brothers formed a friendship with a band of Moravians who were sailing on the same ship for America. During the crossing a terrible tempest arose and for a while it was feared the ship would go down. While all other passengers were filled with terror, the Wesleys were impressed by the calmness and courage of the Moravians, who sang hymns in the midst of the raging storm.

Seeking for a reason for their spiritual fortitude, the brothers found that the Moravians seemed to possess complete assurance of salvation through faith in Christ. Also they made the disconcerting discovery that they themselves did not have the same feeling of certainty, but had been trying to work out their salvation by methods of their own. John Wesley later made the humble confession that he and his brother had gone to Georgia to convert the people there, whereas they themselves had need to be converted!

Upon their return to London the brothers fell in with other Moravians, and through them became familiar with Luther's teachings. Charles came to a saving faith in Christ during a severe illness, and a week later his brother had a similar spiritual experience. It was on May 24, 1738, that John Wesley attended a meeting in Aldersgate Street, where some one was reading Luther's preface to the Epistle to the Romans. Then for the first time light dawned on his soul, and he found peace with God through Christ.

Soon afterwards John Wesley left for Halle, Germany, the seat of the Pietist movement, in order to become more familiar with the teachings of Luther and the evangelical methods of the Pietists. At Halle he also became deeply imbued with missionary zeal. Upon his return to England he launched, with John Whitefield, the greatest spiritual movement his country had ever known. Revivals flamed everywhere. No buildings were large enough to house the crowds that gathered to hear the evangelists, and, because the English clergy were hostile to the movement, most of the meetings were held in the open air.

Charles at first aided in preaching, but eventually devoted his time mainly to hymns. It is estimated that John Wesley held no less than forty thousand preaching services, and traveled nearly a quarter of a million miles. It was he who said, "The world is my parish." John wrote some original hymns, but his translations of German hymns are more important. We are indebted to him for the English versions of Paul Gerhardt's "Put thou thy trust in God" and "Jesus, Thy boundless love to me"; Tersteegen's "Thou hidden love of God whose height" and "Lo, God is here, let us adore"; Freylinghausen's "O Jesus, Source of calm repose," Zinzendorf's "Jesus, Thy blood and righteousness," and Scheffler's "Thee will I love, my Strength, my Tower."

Charles Wesley died March 29, 1788, after spending fifty years in the service of the Lord he loved. The day before he was taken ill, he preached in City Road Chapel, London. The hymn before the sermon was Watts' "I'll praise my Maker, while I've breath." The following evening, although very sick, he amazed his friends by singing the entire hymn with a strong voice. On the night of his death he tried several times to repeat the hymn, but could only say, "I'll praise—I'll praise—," and with the praise of his Maker on his lips, he went home to God. John Wesley survived his brother three years, entering his eternal rest on March 2, 1791. The text of his last sermon was, "Seek ye the Lord while he may be found."

Whether Charles Wesley or Isaac Watts should be accorded first place among English hymnists has been a subject of much dispute. The fact is that each occupies a unique position, and the one complements the other. While Watts dwells on the aweful majesty and glory of God in sublime phrases, Wesley touches the very hem of Christ's garment in loving adoration and praise. Dr. Breed compares the two in the following striking manner:

"Watts is more reverential; Wesley more loving. Watts is stronger; Wesley sweeter. Watts appeals profoundly to the intellect; Wesley takes hold of the heart. Watts will continue to sing for the Pauls and Peters of the Church; Wesley for the Thomases and the Johns. Where both are so great it would be idle to attempt to settle their priority. Let us only be grateful that God in His gracious providence has given both to the Church to voice the praises of various classes."

Henry Ward Beecher uttered one of the most beautiful of all tributes to "Jesus, Lover of my soul" when he said: "I would rather have written that hymn of Wesley's than to have the fame of all the kings that ever sat on the earth. It is more glorious. It has more power in it. I would rather be the author of that hymn than to hold the wealth of the richest man in New York. He will die. He *is* dead, and does not know it. . . . But that hymn will go singing until the last trump brings forth the angel band; and then, I think, it will mount up on some lip to the very presence of God."

A Noble Hymn of Praise

The God of Abraham praise,
Who reigns enthroned above;
Ancient of everlasting days,
And God of love;
To Him uplift your voice,
At whose supreme command
From earth we rise, and seek the joys
At His right hand.

The God who reigns on high
The great archangels sing,
And "Holy, holy, holy," cry,
"Almighty King,
Who was, and is, the same,
And evermore shall be:
Eternal Father, great I AM,
We worship Thee."

Before the Saviour's face
The ransomed nations bow,
O'erwhelmed at His almighty grace,
Forever new;
He shows His prints of love:
They kindle to a flame,
And sound through all the worlds above,
"Worthy the Lamb."

The whole triumphant host
Give thanks to God on high:
"Hail, Father, Son and Holy Ghost!"
They ever cry;
Hail, Abraham's God, and mine!
I join the heavenly lays.
All might and majesty are Thine,
And endless praise.

THOMAS OLIVERS, 1725–1799
Based on the Yigdal

AN IMMORTAL HYMN BY A SHOEMAKER

AS THE Wesleyan revival swept over the British Isles on the wings of inspired song, many of its followers began to imitate the example of its two great leaders by composing hymns. Some of these came from the educated classes, and not a few were clergymen who forsook the Established Church for the new movement. Still others were from the ranks of the common people, among them numerous "down and outs" who were converted by the fiery preaching of John Wesley, or the heart-moving hymns of his brother Charles.

Thomas Olivers is a typical example of the latter type—men who had been caught up by the movement and whose lives had been radically changed by the Gospel. Olivers, who was born in Tregonan, England, in 1725, lost his parents when he was only four years old. Becoming an apprentice to a shoemaker, he began to lead a dissolute life and became notorious for wickedness in a parish where "sin abounded."

Finally he was driven out of his native village. By mere chance he came to Bristol, where he heard George Whitefield preach on the text, "Is not this a brand plucked out of the fire?"

"When the sermon began," Olivers afterwards wrote, "I was certainly a dreadful enemy of God and to all that is good; and one of the most profligate and abandoned young men living." But the sermon brought him under the deepest conviction of sin, and for days afterward he wrestled in prayer until he finally found peace with God.

After he had joined the Methodist Society at Bradford-on-Avon, Olivers had planned to continue in his vocation as a shoemaker. But John Wesley recognized unusual possibilities in the young man, and persuaded him to become one of his evangelists. He is said to have travelled at least 100,000 miles in England and Ireland, preaching the Gospel, and often encountering violent opposition. When he died in London in 1799, he was buried in Wesley's tomb in City Road Chapel burying-ground.

Olivers wrote a number of hymns, but only one, "The God of Abraham praise," has survived. This one, however, possesses such extraordinary qualities that critics have judged it among the finest and noblest of English hymns. James Montgomery, one of England's foremost hymn-writers, placed it above any he knew for majesty and elevation of thought, and many others have testified to the profound impression created when they first heard it.

Olivers relates that he wrote the hymn after listening to the preaching of a Jewish rabbi in a London synagogue, at which time a cantor sang an ancient Hebrew melody. Olivers composed his hymn in the meter of this tune, which is now known as *Leoni*. Here is one stanza of the magnificent hymn:

> The God who reigns on high
> The great archangels sing,
> And "Holy, holy, holy," cry,
> "Almighty King,
> Who was, and is, the same,
> And evermore shall be:
> Eternal Father, great I AM,
> We worship Thee."

How an unlettered man who was a novice at writing poetry could compose sublime lines like these is one of those mysteries that will always defy comprehension. It can be explained only as an evidence of divine inspiration.

At the time the hymn was written, Olivers was visiting in the home of John Bakewell, who, like Olivers, also has given the Church a great hymn. Bakewell was born at Brailsford, England in 1721, and from his youth was deeply interested in religion. At the age of 23 he began to preach in his own neighborhood, and five years later, in London, he met the Wesleys and others who awakened his interest in hymnody. He is said to have composed a number of hymns, but only one, "Hail, Thou once despised Jesus," has survived. After turning to Methodism, Bakewell was appointed head of the Greenwich Royal Park Academy, but afterwards became an evangelist. He died in 1819 and was buried in the Wesleyan cemetery connnected with the City Road Chapel in London.

Two other hymn-writers who were associated with the Wesleyan movement were John Cennick and William Williams, each of whom, like Olivers and Bakewell, won fame chiefly by a single great hymn.

Cennick, who was of Bohemian ancestry, first met John Wesley in 1739. Of that meeting Wesley has the following notation in his diary: "On Friday, March 1739, I came to Reading, where I found a young man who had in some measure known the powers of the world to come. I spent the evening with him and a few of his serious friends, and it pleased God much to strengthen and comfort them."

For a while Cennick assisted Wesley as a lay preacher, but in 1741 he forsook the Methodist movement on account of Wesley's "free grace" doctrines and organized a society of his own along Calvinistic lines. Later he joined himself to John Whitefield as an evangelist, but finally he went over to the Moravians, in which communion he labored abundantly until his death in 1755 at the early age of thirty-seven years

To Cennick we are indebted for the original form of the majestic hymn on Christ's second coming, "Lo! He comes, with clouds descending." Charles Wesley later improved the original text, but the meter of the poem and the basic ideas were Cennick's. James King, in his *Anglican Hymnology,* gives this lyric third place among English hymns, it being excelled in his estimation only by Bishop Ken's "All praise to Thee, my God, this night" and Wesley's "Hark! the herald angels sing."

Williams, a Welshman by birth, has also left a hymn that has gone singing down through the years. It is the rugged and stirring hymn that sets forth in such striking imagery the experiences of the Israelites in the wilderness, "Guide me, O Thou great Jehovah."

Williams, who earned the title of the "Watts of Wales," wrote the hymn originally in Welsh. Of him it has been said that "He did for Wales what Wesley and Watts did for England, or what Luther did for Germany." His first hymnbook, *Hallelujah,* was published in 1744, when he was only twenty-seven years old.

The Welsh hymnist originally intended to enter the medical profession, but, after passing through a spiritual crisis, was ordained as a deacon in the Church of England. Because of his free methods of evangelism, he was denied full ordination, and later identified himself with the Wesleyan revival. Like Cennick, however, he soon forsook the Wesleys, and now we find him a Calvinistic Methodist, having adopted Wales as his parish. He was a powerful preacher and an unusual singer, and for forty-five years carried on a blessed work

287

until, on January 11, 1791, he passed through "the swelling current" and, as we may believe, landed "safe on Canaan's side."

Here also we must mention another hymnist of this period who came in contact with the Wesleys in a rather peculiar way. He was John Byrom, who will always be remembered, not only as the author of the glorious Christmas anthem, "Christians, awake! salute the happy morn," but also as the man who taught both John and Charles to write shorthand!

Byrom, who was born at Kersall Cell, England, February 29, 1692, was a brilliant student at Cambridge, where he won a fellowship in 1714. Instead of continuing at Cambridge, however, he went to France to study medicine. Upon his return to England in 1718 he invented a system of shorthand. Among his friends and pupils were the Wesleys. John's journals and private papers were largely written in this manner.

Many of Byrom's poems were published in *The Spectator,* and in 1773 they were collected in two volumes. From these have been derived a number of hymns, but only his Christmas composition has come into general use. Byrom died September 28, 1763.

Yet another Nonconformist hymn-writer of this period, though not a follower of the Wesleys, was James Allen. Born at Gayle, England, June 24, 1734, he received his education at Cambridge with the purpose of taking holy orders, but left the University in 1752 to become a follower of Benjamin Ingham. Eventually he joined the Sandemanians and carried on a ministry in a chapel he erected on his own estate. He died in 1804.

In addition to publishing a small volume of seventeen hymns, Allen became the editor and chief contributor to the *Kendal Hymn Book* of 1757. It was in this volume that his hymn, "While my Jesus I'm possessing," first appeared. The hymn was subsequently revised by Walter Shirley as "Sweet the moments, rich in blessing," and has found its way into many modern hymnals. As originally written, it closely resembles some of the Moravian hymns of the period in dwelling with almost morbid interest on every detail of the Saviour's physical sufferings on the Cross. Here are two of Allen's verses:

> O how happy are the moments
>   Which I here in transport spend!
> Life deriving from his torments
>   Who remains the sinner's Friend.

288

> Here I'll sit, forever viewing
>   How the blood streams from each vein;
> Every stream, my soul bedewing,
>   Mortifies the carnal flame.

Another Independent minister who wrote hymns at this period was Simon Browne, from whom we have received the well-known hymn for Whitsunday, "Come, gracious Spirit, heavenly Dove." As pastor of Independent Chapel, Old Jewry, London, he was a near neighbor of Watts, and the two became close friends. Browne was a prolific writer on many subjects, and in 1720 published a volume of hymns.

Brooding over the death of his wife and son, and also over the tragedy of having accidentally killed a highwayman who had attacked him, he became emotionally unbalanced. He imagined that he was forsaken of God and that he possessed neither reason nor soul. Retiring from the ministry, he spent his time in translating classical authors, writing books for children, and compiling a dictionary. Toplady, writer of "Rock of Ages," said of him, "Instead of having no soul, he wrote and reasoned and prayed as if he had two." He died at Shepton Mallet in 1732.

To this early period of English hymnody also belong the two familiar hymns, "Jesus, and shall it ever be?" and "Behold a Stranger at the door." Both were written by Joseph Grigg, who was born in London of poverty-stricken parents about the year 1720. He was trained to work as a mechanic, but at the age of 25 became assistant minister in the Silver Street Presbyterian Church in London. In 1747 he retired from the ministry, married a woman of wealth, and thenceforth devoted himself to the writing of devotional literature.

Grigg composed some forty hymns in all, but is chiefly known for the two mentioned above. "Jesus, and shall it ever be?" is said to have been written when Grigg was 10 years old. It was extensively revised, being put into its present form by Benjamin Francis in 1787, about twenty years after the death of Grigg.

Another Hymn of the Ages

Rock of Ages, cleft for me,
Let me hide myself in Thee:
Let the water and the blood
From Thy riven side which flowed
Be of sin the double cure,
Cleanse me from its guilt and power.

Not the labors of my hands
Can fulfil Thy law's demands;
Could my zeal no respite know,
Could my tears forever flow,
All for sin could not atone;
Thou must save, and Thou alone.

Nothing in my hand I bring,
Simply to Thy Cross I cling;
Naked, come to Thee for dress;
Helpless, look to Thee for grace;
Foul, I to the Fountain fly:
Wash me, Saviour, or I die!

When I draw this fleeting breath,
When my eyelids close in death,
When I soar to worlds unknown,
See Thee on Thy judgment throne,
Rock of Ages, cleft for me,
Let me hide myself in Thee.

AUGUSTUS MONTAGUE TOPLADY, 1740-1778

A HYMN THAT GREW OUT OF A QUARREL

ALTHOUGH Isaac Watts' beautiful hymn, "When I survey the wondrous Cross," is regarded by most critics as the finest hymn in the English language, Toplady's "Rock of Ages," holds the distinction of being the most popular. Perhaps no hymn ever written has so gripped the hearts of Christians of all communions as this noble hymn.

A British magazine once invited its readers to submit a list of the hundred English hymns that stood highest in their esteem. A total of 3,500 persons responded, and "Rock of Ages" was named first by 3,215.

We have tried the same experiment with a group of Bible students, and "Rock of Ages" easily headed the list.

Augustus Montague Toplady, the writer of this hymn, was born on November 4, 1740, at Farnham, England. His father, a major in the English army, was killed the following year at the siege of Carthagena. The widowed mother later removed to Ireland, where her son was educated at Trinity College, Dublin. It was during this period of his life that Augustus, then sixteen years of age, chanced to attend an evangelistic service held in a barn. The preacher was an unlettered layman, but his message so gripped the heart of the lad he determined then and there to give his heart to God. Of this experience Toplady afterward wrote:

"Strange that I who had so long sat under the means of grace in England should be brought right unto God in an obscure part of Ireland, amidst a handful of people met together in a barn, and by the ministry of one who could hardly spell his own name. Surely it was the Lord's doing and is marvelous."

Toplady was ordained at the age of twenty-two as a minister of the Church of England. He was frail of body, and after some years he was stricken with tuberculosis. It was while fighting the ravages of this disease that he wrote his famous hymn, two years before his death.

The hymn first appeared in the *Gospel Magazine,* of which Top-

291

lady was editor, in the year 1776. It was appended to a curious article in which the author attempted to show by mathematical computation how dreadful is the sum total of sins committed by a man during his lifetime, and how impossible it is for a sinner to atone for this debt of guilt. But Christ, who is the sinner's refuge, has paid the entire debt. It was this glorious thought that inspired him to sing:

> Rock of Ages, cleft for me,
> Let me hide myself in Thee.

For some years John Wesley, the founder of Methodism, and Toplady had been engaged in a theological dispute. Toplady was a confirmed Calvinist and intolerant of Wesley's Arminian views. Both men were intemperate in their language and hurled unseemly and sometimes bitter invectives at each other. Wesley characterized Toplady as a "chimney-sweep" and "a lively coxcomb." Toplady retorted by calling Wesley "Pope John" and declaring that his forehead was "petrified" and "impervious to a blush." There are reasons for believing that the article in the *Gospel Magazine* by Toplady was for the purpose of refuting Wesley's teachings, and that "Rock of Ages" was written at the conclusion of the article as an effective way of clinching the argument.

In our day, when we find "Rock of Ages" on one page of our hymnals and John Wesley's translation of "Jesus, Thy Blood and righteousness" on the next, it is hard to understand the uncharitable spirit that existed between these two servants of Christ. Perhaps, had they really understood each other, they would have found that they were more in accord than ever they suspected.

Nevertheless, God is able to use the most imperfect of human instruments for His praise, and "Rock of Ages" has undoubtedly been the means of bringing many souls to Christ. Its strength lies in the clear and simple manner in which it sets forth the truth that salvation is by grace alone, through the merits of Christ. Even a child can understand the meaning of the words,

> Nothing in my hand I bring,
> Simply to Thy Cross I cling.

Or these,

> Not the labors of my hands
> Can fulfil Thy law's demands;
> Could my zeal no respite know,

292

Could my tears forever flow,
All for sin could not atone;
Thou must save, and Thou alone.

In this comforting and triumphant faith Toplady himself passed into glory in his thirty-eighth year. A few hours before his death he exclaimed: "My heart beats every day stronger and stronger for glory. Sickness is no affliction, pain no curse, death itself no dissolution." His last words were: "My prayers are all converted into praises."

During his illness some friends had expressed the hope that he might soon be restored. Toplady shook his head.

"No mortal man can live," he said, "after the glories which God has manifested to my soul."

At another time he told how he "enjoyed a heaven already in his soul," and that his spiritual experiences were so exalted he could ask for nothing except a continuation of them.

Toplady had requested that he be buried beneath the gallery over against the pulpit of Totenham Court Chapel. Strangely enough, this building was intimately associated with the early history of Methodism. It was built by Whitefield, and here also Wesley preached Whitefield's funeral sermon. Perhaps it was Toplady's way of expressing the hope that all the bitterness and rancor attending his controversy with Wesley might be buried with him.

Also significant is the fact that, in the very year that Toplady wrote "Rock of Ages," he brought out a collection of psalms and hymns which, according to the title, was intended "for public and private worship." Evidently his earlier association with the Wesleys had borne fruit, and he now had become an ardent exponent of the use of hymns in the worship of the Established Church. It is likewise interesting to note that, despite his bitter controversy with John Wesley, he included in his hymnbook a large number of hymns of the Wesleys, whether by their permission or not, we cannot say!

The Coronation Hymn

All hail the power of Jesus' Name!
    Let angels prostrate fall;
Bring forth the royal diadem,
    And crown Him Lord of all.

Crown Him, ye martyrs of your God
    Who from His altar call;
Extol the Stem of Jesse's rod,
    And crown Him Lord of all.

Ye seed of Israel's chosen race,
    Ye ransomed from the fall,
Hail Him who saves you by His grace,
    And crown Him Lord of all.

Sinners, whose love can ne'er forget
    The wormwood and the gall;
Go, spread your trophies at His feet,
    And crown Him Lord of all.

Let every kindred, every tribe,
    On this terrestrial ball,
To Him all majesty ascribe,
    And crown Him Lord of all.

O that with yonder sacred throng
    We at His feet may fall;
We'll join the everlasting song
    And crown Him Lord of all.

EDWARD PERRONET, 1726–92
JOHN RIPPON, 1751–1836

THE BIRD OF A SINGLE SONG

SOME men gain fame through a long life of work and achievement; others through a single notable deed. The latter is true in a very remarkable sense of Edward Perronet, author of the Church's great coronation hymn, "All hail the power of Jesus' Name."

"Perronet, bird of a single song, but O how sweet!" is the charming tribute of Bishop Fess in referring to this inspired hymn and its author.

Although Perronet was a man of more than ordinary ability, his name probably would have been lost to posterity had he not written the coronation hymn. An associate of the Wesleys for many years, Perronet also wrote three volumes of sacred poems, some of unusual merit. All of them, however, have been practically forgotten except his one immortal hymn. So long as there are Christians on earth, it will continue to be sung, and after that—in heaven!

Perronet came from a distinguished line of French Protestants who had found refuge in England during times of religious persecution in their homeland. His father, Vincent Perronet, was vicar of Shoreham. Both father and son, though ardent supporters of the Established Church, became intensely interested in the great evangelical revival under Whitefield and the Wesleys. At one time young Perronet traveled with John Wesley. Much opposition had been stirred up against the Wesleyan movement, and in some places the preachers were threatened by mobs. Concerning these experiences, Wesley makes the following notation in his diary:

"From Rockdale we went to Bolton, and soon found that the Rockdale lions were lambs in comparison with those of Bolton. Edward Perronet was thrown down and rolled in mud and mire. Stones were hurled and windows broken."

On another occasion it is recorded that Wesley wanted to hear Perronet preach. The author of our hymn, however, seems to have been somewhat reluctant about preaching in the presence of the great reformer. Wesley, nevertheless, without consulting Perronet, made the announcement that the young man would occupy the pulpit on the following morning. Perronet said nothing, but on the morrow he mounted the pulpit and explained that he had not consented to preach. "However," he added, "I shall deliver the best sermon that has ever been preached on earth," whereupon he read the Sermon on the Mount from beginning to end, adding not a word of comment!

"All hail the power of Jesus' Name" has been translated into almost every language where Christianity is known, and wherever it is sung it seems to grip human hearts. One of the most remarkable stories of the power of this hymn is related by E. P. Scott, a missionary to India. Having learned of a distant tribe in the interior to whom the Gospel had not yet been preached, this missionary, despite the warnings of his friends, packed his baggage and, taking his violin, set out on his perilous venture. After traveling several days, he suddenly came upon a large party of the tribesmen, who surrounded him and pointed their spears at him.

Believing death to be near, the missionary nevertheless took out his violin and with a prayer to God began to sing "All hail the power of Jesus' Name!" He closed his eyes as he sang, expecting every moment to be pierced through with the threatening spears. When he reached the stanza, "Let every kindred, every tribe," he opened his eyes. What was his surprise to see every spear lowered, and many of the tribesmen moved to tears!

He remained for two years and a half, preaching the story of redemption and leading many of the natives to Jesus. When he was about to return to America on furlough, they pleaded, "O missionary, come back to us again!" He did so, and finally passed away in the midst of the people who had learned to love the man who had brought them the Gospel of Christ.

It is interesting to know that, while the people of both England and America prize this hymn very highly, they sing it to different melodies. The English tune, known as *Miles Lane,* was written by William Shrubsole. The tune used in America, on the other hand, is called "Coronation" and was composed by a carpenter of Charlestown, Mass., by the name of Oliver Holden. This man was very fond of music and spent his spare time in playing a little organ on which he composed his tunes. The organ may still be seen in Boston.

Perronet died January 2, 1792. His last words were:

> "Glory to God in the height of His divinity!
> Glory to God in the depth of His humanity!
> Glory to God in His all-sufficiency!
> Into His hands I commend my spirit."

By this time other members of the Church of England clergy likewise had begun to feel the contagious influence of hymnody among the Nonconformists and were imitating their example. Even before Perronet and Toplady wrote their lyrics, Martin Madan, chaplain of Lock Hospital, London, had published a hymnbook containing 170 hymns, to which he added twenty-four three years later. Here again most of the hymns were by Watts and Charles Wesley, and hardly a single one by the clergy of the Established Church. Most of Wesley's hymns, however, were in the form in which George Whitefield had revised them, their new Calvinistic tone being more agreeable to Madan than Wesley's Arminian views. This was bitterly resented by Wesley in the preface to his own hymnbook of 1780. Incidentally, Madan had appropriated the Wesley hymns for his collection without the permission of the author.

Yet another Church of England clergyman who published a hymnbook at this time was R. Conyers, vicar of Hemsley and a friend of William Cowper. In a collection of psalms and hymns which appeared in 1767, Conyers followed the example of Madan in making use primarily of Nonconformist hymns, although he included a few originals by John Newton and Cowper.

It was now becoming quite evident that the spiritual fervor of the evangelical movement was stirring all of England, and not even the Established Church could escape the enthusiasm aroused by hymns that were on everyone's lips. Here and there throughout the Church, poets, scholars, clergymen and musicians were tuning their harps for an outburst of spiritual song that had been suppressed for nearly 300 years. It came in the 19th century, resulting in the rise of an imposing array of gifted, dedicated poets and composers such as no other nation had ever produced.

In Praise of the Word of God

Father of mercies, in Thy Word
  What endless glory shines!
Forever be Thy Name adored
  For these celestial lines.

Here the Redeemer's welcome voice
  Spreads heavenly peace around;
And life and everlasting joys
  Attend the blissful sound.

O may these heavenly pages be
  My ever dear delight;
And still new beauties may I see,
  And still increasing light.

Divine Instructor, gracious Lord,
  Be Thou for ever near;
Teach me to love Thy sacred Word,
  And view my Saviour there.

ANNE STEELE, 1716-78

ENGLAND'S FIRST WOMAN HYMNIST

WHILE Isaac Watts was working on his immortal version of *Psalms of David*, a baby girl was born to a Baptist minister at Broughton, fifteen miles away. The child was Anne Steele, destined to become England's first woman hymn-writer. This was in 1716.

Her father, who was a merchant as well as a minister, served the church at Broughton for sixty years, the greater part without pay. The mother died when Anne was only a babe of three years. From childhood the future hymnist was delicate in health, and in 1735 she suffered a hip injury which made her practically an invalid for life.

The hardest blow, however, came in 1737, when her lover, Robert Elscourt, was drowned on the day before he and Anne were to have been married. The grief-stricken young woman with heroic faith nevertheless rose above her afflictions and found solace in sacred song. It is believed that her first hymn, a poem of beautiful resignation, was written at this time:

> Father, whate'er of earthly bliss
> Thy sovereign will denies,
> Accepted at Thy throne, let this
> My humble prayer arise:
>
> Give me a calm and thankful heart,
> From every murmur free;
> The blessings of Thy grace impart,
> And make me live to Thee.

That the Lord heard her prayer may be attested by the fact that she became the greatest hymn-writer the Baptist Church has produced. Throughout her life she remained unmarried, living with her father and writing noble hymns. In 1760 her first poems appeared in print under the pen name of "Theodosia." Her father at this time makes the following notation in his diary: "This day Nanny sent part of her composition to London to be printed. I entreat a gracious God, who enabled and stirred her up to such a work, to direct it and bless it for the good of many. I pray God to make it useful, and keep her humble." The book proved immensely popular, and the author devoted the profits from its sale to charity.

Among the more famous hymns from her pen are: "Father of Mercies, in Thy Word," "How helpless guilty nature lies," "Dear Refuge of my weary soul," "O Thou whose tender mercy hears," "Thou only Sovereign of my heart," and "Thou lovely source of true delight."

England's pioneer woman hymnist fell asleep in November, 1788, her last words, "I know that my Redeemer liveth." Her epitaph reads:

> Silent the lyre, and dumb the tuneful tongue,
>   That sung on earth her great Redeemer's praise;
> But now in heaven she joins the angelic song,
>   In more harmonious, more exalted lays.

The decades during which Miss Steele lived and wrought were remarkable for the large number of hymn-writers of her own communion who flourished in England. In addition to Miss Steele, the Baptist Church produced such hymnists as Samuel Medley, Samuel Stennett, Benjamin Francis, Johnson Fawcett and John Rippon.

Medley lived a dissipated life in the British navy until he was severely wounded in a sea fight off Cape Lagos in 1759. While he was convalescing in the home of his grandfather, the latter read to him a sermon by Isaac Watts. This was the first step in his conversion. When he was restored to health he went to London, where he opened a school. Later he became a Baptist minister. In 1772 he was called to Liverpool, where he achieved great success as a preacher to sailors. He passed away in 1799. He was the author of a large number of hymns, most of which were written for his own services. His best known are "I know that my Redeemer lives," "O could I speak the matchless worth," and "Awake, my soul, to joyful lays."

Rippon gained fame more as a hymn compiler than as a writer of hymns. Born at Tiverton, England, in 1751, he became pastor of the Baptist congregation in Carter's Lane, London, at the age of 22 years, continuing there until his death in 1836. He was one of the most influential dissenting ministers of his time. In 1787 he issued a large collection of hymns, mainly based on the works of Watts. This was followed in 1791 by another collection. In 1800 he printed the 10th edition of this work, increasing the number of hymns by sixty. It was enlarged again in 1827, and after Rippon's death, *The Comprehensive Rippon* was published with no less than 1,170 hymns in 100 meters! Needless to say, Rippon's collections became the

300

standard hymnbook of the Baptist Church and enjoyed a tremendous circulation.

Stennett was an outstanding scholar who in 1758 succeeded his father as pastor of the Baptist church in Little Wild Street, London, where he preached for thirty-seven years. He was an ardent exponent of social reforms, and is said to have been a friend of the reigning monarch, George III. He is known to have been the author of some 39 hymns, five of which were contributed to *Rippon's Selection* of 1787. Three of the best known are "On Jordan's rugged banks I stand," " 'Tis finished, so the Saviour cried," and "Majestic sweetness sits enthroned." The latter, which is based on Song of Solomon 5: 10-16, has lines of rare beauty:

> Majestic sweetness sits enthroned
> Upon the Saviour's brow;
> His head with radiant glories crowned,
> His lips with grace o'erflow.

Benjamin Francis was another Baptist hymnist of this period. Born in Wales, it was not until he was twenty years old that he learned to speak English. After receiving his education at Bristol, he became pastor at Horsley, in Gloucestershire, where he spent forty-two successful and happy years. He excelled in the writing of Welsh hymns, and contributed 194 of his own to a collection he published. Many of these are still in common use in Wales. He also wrote five hymns for *Rippon's Selection,* including "Before Thy throne, eternal King" and "In sweet exalted strains." He also wrote a revision of Joseph Grigg's "Jesus, and shall it ever be?"

John Fawcett was the last in a long line of Baptist hymn-writers during the 18th century. Fawcett was the pastor of a small congregation at Waingate when, in 1772, he received a call to succeed Dr. J. Gill in a large London church. He had preached his farewell sermon and had loaded his household goods on a number of wagons when the tears of his parishioners caused his wife to exclaim:

"Oh, John, John, I cannot bear this! I know not how to go."

"Nor I, either," replied her husband. "Nor will we go. Unload the wagons, and put everything in the place where it was before."

It was this moving experience that caused him a few days later to write the well-known hymn, "Blest be the tie that binds." Among his other hymns are "How precious is the Book divine," "Lord, dismiss us with Thy blessing," and "Praise to Thee, Thou great Creator."

The Name Above All Names

How sweet the Name of Jesus sounds
In a believer's ear!
It soothes his sorrows, heals his wounds,
And drives away his fear.

It makes the wounded spirit whole,
And calms the troubled breast;
'Tis Manna to the hungry soul,
And to the weary rest.

Dear Name! the Rock on which I build,
My Shield and Hiding-place;
My never-failing Treasury, filled
With boundless stores of grace.

Weak is the effort of my heart,
And cold my warmest thought;
But when I see Thee as Thou art,
I'll praise Thee as I ought.

Till then I would Thy love proclaim
With every fleeting breath;
And may the music of Thy Name
Refresh my soul in death

JOHN NEWTON, 1725-1807

A SLAVE-TRADER WHO WROTE CHRISTIAN LYRICS

IN one of England's famous old churches there is a tablet marking the last resting-place of one of its rectors, and on the tablet this epitaph:

"JOHN NEWTON, *clerk, once an Infidel and Libertine, a servant of slavers in Africa, was, by the rich Mercy of our Lord and Saviour Jesus Christ, preserved, restored, pardoned, and appointed to preach the Faith he had long labored to destroy.*"

This inscription, written by Newton himself before his death, tells the strange story of the life of the man who wrote "How sweet the Name of Jesus sounds" and scores of other beautiful hymns.

Newton was born in London, July 24, 1725. His father was a sea captain. His mother, a deeply pious woman, though frail in health, found her greatest joy in teaching her boy Scripture passages and hymns. When he was only four years old he was able to read the Catechism.

The faithful mother often expressed the hope to her son that he might become a minister. However, when the lad was only seven years of age, she died, and he was left to shift largely for himself. On his 11th birthday he joined his father at sea, and made five voyages to the Mediterranean. Through the influence of evil companions and the reading of infidel literature, he began to live a godless and abandoned life.

Being pressed into the navy when a war seemed imminent, young Newton deserted. He was captured, however, and flogged at the mast, after which he was degraded.

At this point his life teems with reckless adventures and strange escapes. Falling into the hands of an unscrupulous slave-dealer in Africa, he himself was reduced practically to the abject condition of a slave. In his misery he gave himself up to nameless sins. The memory of his mother, however, and the religious truths she had implanted in his soul as a child gave his conscience no peace.

The reading of *The Imitation of Christ,* by Thomas à Kempis, also exerted a profound influence over him, and a terrifying experience in a storm at sea, together with his deliverance from a malignant fever in Africa, served to bring the prodigal as a penitent to the throne of mercy.

After six years as the captain of a slaveship, during which time he passed through many severe struggles in trying to find peace with God through the observance of a strict moral life, Newton, on his last voyage, met a pious captain who helped to bring him to faith in Christ.

For nine years at Liverpool he was closely associated with Whitefield and the Wesleys, studying the Scriptures in Hebrew and Greek, and occasionally preaching at religious gatherings of the dissenters. In 1764 he was ordained as curate of Olney, where he formed the famous friendship with the poet William Cowper that gave to the world so many beautiful hymns.

It was at Newton's suggestion that the two undertook to write a hymnbook. The famous collection known as *The Olney Hymns* was the result of this endeavor. Of the 349 hymns in the book, Cowper is credited with sixty-six, while Newton wrote the remainder. "How sweet the Name of Jesus sounds" appeared for the first time in this collection. It is a hymn of surpassing tenderness, and ranks among the finest in the English language.

Other notable hymns by Newton are: "Come, my soul, thy suit prepare," "Approach, my soul, the mercy-seat," "While with ceaseless course the sun," "One there is above all others," "For a season called to part," "Safely through another week," "On what has now been sown," "May the grace of Christ our Saviour," "Though troubles assail us, and dangers affright," "Day of judgment, day of wonders," and "Glorious things of thee are spoken."

Newton's life came to a close in London in 1807, after he had served for twenty-eight years as rector of St. Mary Woolnoth. Among his converts were numbered Claudius Buchanan, missionary to the East Indies, and Thomas Scott, the Bible commentator. In 1805, when his eyesight began to fail and he could no longer read his text, his friends advised him to cease preaching. His answer was: "What! shall the old African blasphemer stop while he can speak?"

When he was nearly eighty years old it was necessary for an assistant to stand in the pulpit to help him read his manuscript sermons. One Sunday Newton had twice read the words, "Jesus Christ is precious." "You have already said that twice," whispered his helper; "go on." "John," said Newton, turning to the man, "I said that twice, and I am going to say it again." Then the rafters rang as the old preacher shouted, *"Jesus Christ is precious!"* Newton's whole life may be said to be summed up in the words of one of his appealing hymns:

> Amazing grace! how sweet the sound
> That saved a wretch like me!
> I once was lost, but now am found —
> Was blind, but now I see.

A Hymn on God's Providence

God moves in a mysterious way
    His wonders to perform;
He plants His footsteps in the sea,
    And rides upon the storm.

Deep in unfathomable mines
    Of never-failing skill,
He treasures up His bright designs,
    And works His sovereign will.

Ye fearful saints, fresh courage take;
    The clouds ye so much dread
Are big with mercy, and shall break
    In blessings on your head.

Judge not the Lord by feeble sense,
    But trust Him for His grace;
Behind a frowning Providence
    He hides a smiling face.

His purposes will ripen fast,
    Unfolding every hour;
The bud may have a bitter taste,
    But sweet will be the flower.

Blind unbelief is sure to err,
    And scan His works in vain.
God is His own interpreter,
    And He will make it plain.

WILLIAM COWPER, 1731–1800

AN AFFLICTED POET WHO GLORIFIED GOD

P AUL once wrote to the Corinthians: "God chose the weak things of the world, that he might put to shame the things that are strong."

In a very special sense this truth was exemplified in the life of the poet William Cowper. If God ever made use of a frail instrument through which to glorify himself, He did it in this man. Feeble in health from childhood, with a sensitive, high-strung mind that ever was on the point of breaking, he still labored in such a way that his sad and feverish life certainly was not lived in vain.

Cowper was born at Great Berkhamstead, England, in 1731. His father was an English clergyman. His mother died when the child was only six years old. Even as a youth, he was distressed by frequent mental attacks. He once wrote pathetically: "The meshes of that fine network, the brain, are composed of such mere spinner's threads in me that when a long thought finds its way into them it buzzes, and twangs, and bustles about at such a rate as seems to threaten the whole contexture."

In the previous sketch we have related how the famous friendship between the poet and John Newton led to the joint publication of *The Olney Hymns*. Newton's idea in suggesting this project was not merely "to perpetuate the remembrance of an intimate and endeared friendship," as he states in the preface of the noted collection, but also to occupy Cowper's mind, which already had revealed signs of approaching madness.

In 1773, two years after the two friends had begun *The Olney Hymns,* Cowper passed through a mental crisis that almost ended in tragedy. Obsessed with the idea that it was the divine will that he should offer up his life by drowning himself in the Ouse river, the afflicted poet ordered a post chaise, and instructed the driver to proceed to a certain spot near Olney, where he planned to leap into the river. When he reached the place, Cowper was diverted from his purpose when he found a man seated at the exact place where he had intended to end his life. Returning home, he is said to have thrown himself on his knife, but the blade broke. His next attempt was to hang himself, but the rope parted.

After his recovery from this harrowing experience, he was so impressed by the realization of God's overruling providence that he was led to write the hymn, "God moves in a mysterious way." It is regarded by many critics as the finest hymn ever written on the theme. James T. Fields declares that to be the author of such a hymn is an achievement that "angels themselves might envy."

That God had a purpose in sparing the life of the sorely tried man is made clear when we learn that Cowper lived for twenty-seven years after passing through this crisis. Although he continued to experience some distressing periods, it was during these years that he wrote some of his most beautiful hymns. Among them are "O for a closer walk with God," "Sometimes a light surprises," "Jesus, where'er Thy people meet," and "There is a fountain filled with blood."

The latter hymn has often been criticized because of its strong figurative language. The expression, "a fountain filled with blood," has proved so offensive to modern taste that many hymnbooks have omitted the hymn entirely. Dr. Ray Palmer, writer of "My faith looks up to Thee," opposed these views vigorously. He once wrote:

"Such criticism seems to us superficial. It takes the words as if they were intended to be a literal prosaic statement. It forgets that what they express is not only poetry, but the poetry of intense and impassioned feeling, which naturally embodies itself in the boldest metaphors. The inner sense of the soul, when its deepest affections are moved, infallibly takes these metaphors in their true significance, while a cold critic of the letter misses that significance entirely. He merely demonstrates his own lack of the spiritual sympathies of which, for fervent Christian hearts, the hymn referred to is an admirable expression."

Cowper also wrote a number of secular poems that achieved great fame. "The Task" has been called "one of the wisest books ever written, and one of the most charming." Another poem, "John Gilpin," is a very happy and mirthful narrative.

Although Cowper's mother died in his early childhood, he never forgot her. When he was fifty-six years old, a cousin sent him a miniature of her. In acknowledging the gift, he wrote: "I had rather possess my mother's picture than the richest jewel in the British crown; for

I loved her with an affection that her death, fifty years since, has not in the least abated."

Cowper died in 1800. Three years before his death, he lost his lifelong comforter and friend, Mrs. Morley Unwin, who had cared for him with the solicitude of a mother. The sorrow was almost too great for his feeble nature, and he again sank into deepest gloom. At times he thought God had forsaken him. Only at intervals was he able to resume his literary work. His last poem was "The Castaway," written March 20, 1799. Through all his spiritual and mental depression, however, he was ever submissive to the will of God. But the time of release for this chastened Christian was at hand.

Bishop Moule tells the story of his departure thus: "About half an hour before his death, his face, which had been wearing a sad and hopeless expression, suddenly lighted up with a look of wonder and inexpressible delight. It was as if he saw his Saviour, and as if he realized the blessed fact, 'I am not shut out of Heaven after all!' This look of holy surprise and of joyful adoration remained until he had passed away, and even as he lay in his coffin the expression was still there. One who saw him after death wrote that 'with the composure and calmness of the face, there mingled also a holy surprise.' "

Mrs. Browning, in her poem entitled "Cowper's Grave," concludes with these lines:

> "O poets, from a maniac's tongue was poured the deathless singing!
> O Christians, at your Cross of hope a hopeless hand was clinging!
> O men, this man in brotherhood your weary paths beguiling,
> Groaned inly while he taught you peace, and died while you were
>   smiling."

It is a noble tribute to the deathless work of an afflicted man, and reminds us that Cowper is still singing his wondrous theme of "redeeming love," although his

> "poor lisping, stammering tongue
> Lies silent in the grave."

Worshiping the Ascended Saviour

Look, ye saints, the sight is glorious,
    See the Man of Sorrows now;
From the fight returned victorious,
    Every knee to Him shall bow;
        Crown Him! Crown Him!
        Crown Him! Crown Him!
Crowns become the victor's brow.

Crown the Saviour, angels crown Him!
    Rich the trophies Jesus brings;
In the seat of power enthrone Him,
    While the vault of heaven rings;
        Crown Him! Crown Him!
        Crown Him! Crown Him!
Crown the Saviour King of kings.

Sinners in derision crowned Him,
    Mocking thus the Saviour's claim;
Saints and angels crowd around Him,
    Own His title, praise His Name;
        Crown Him! Crown Him!
        Crown Him! Crown Him!
Spread abroad the victor's fame.

Hark, those bursts of acclamation,
    Hark, those loud triumphant chords!
Jesus takes the highest station;
    O what joy the sight affords!
        Crown Him! Crown Him!
        Crown Him! Crown Him!
King of kings, and Lord of lords.

THOMAS KELLY, 1769-1854

310

A GREAT IRISH HYMN-WRITER

IRELAND would not ordinarily be regarded as a likely place to look for an evangelical hymn-writer, and yet one of the most distinguished spiritual poets of the 19th century had his birthplace in the "Emerald Isle." He was Thomas Kelly, the writer of such magnificent hymns as "Look, ye saints, the sight is glorious," "The head that once was crowned with thorns," "Through the day Thy love has spared us," "We sing the praise of Him who died," "Of Thy love some gracious token," "Come, see the place where Jesus lay," and "On the mountain's top appearing."

Nor does this begin to exhaust the list. In all, Kelly wrote 765 hymns over a period of 51 years, and for many of them he also composed the music! He was an accomplished musician as well as a poet.

The English hymnologist, John Julian, laments the fact that hymn editors apparently are averse to original investigation, and suggests that a more careful study of Kelly's hymnbooks would yield many more lyrics of great merit. It is quite significant that Duffield's *English Hymns* reviews thirty of Kelly's hymns, the largest number of any author except Watts, Wesley, Doddridge, Newton and Montgomery.

"Look, ye saints, the sight is glorious" is undoubtedly the finest Ascension Day hymn in the English language. Sung to the Welsh tune *Bryn Calfaria,* it makes a powerful appeal. "The head that once was crowned with thorns" is likewise an Ascension Day hymn of unusual excellence.

Kelly was born in Dublin, July 13, 1769, the son of an Irish jurist. He entered Trinity College, Dublin, with the purpose of studying for the bar. Through the reading of the works of Romaine, however, he developed strong religious convictions and decided to prepare for the ministry. His earnestness of mind and spiritual anxiety at one time led him close to fanaticism, and his ascetic practices even endangered his health. It was only after he had come to comprehend the Pauline doctrine of justification by faith alone that he found peace of mind and soul.

311

In 1792 he was ordained by the Anglican Church. Evangelical religion was not held in high esteem in Ireland in those days, and when Kelly's preaching in St. Luke's Church in Dublin proved too fervent in the opinion of the rector of that parish, he was told to desist. Rowland Hill, who shared Kelly's views, was likewise silenced. Both of the men were further inhibited when Archbishop Fowler of Dublin issued a decree closing all of the pulpits in his diocese to the two zealous preachers.

Having no other alternative, Kelly thereupon became a Dissenter, erecting places of worship at Athy, Portarlington, Wexford and other places. He was a magnetic preacher, and this, together with his extraordinary gifts as a hymnist and his humble, friendly personality, brought him great popularity. Possessing considerable means, his abounding liberality made him beloved of the poor of Dublin and of the whole country during the great Irish famine. Indeed, it was said of him that he was a friend of every worthy cause.

Kelly was the author of a number of hymnbooks, all of which passed through several editions. When the seventh and last edition of his principal hymnal was published in 1853, Kelly was then 84 years old. As the aged pastor and hymn-writer scanned the volume, he remarked that the 767 hymns contained in it covered a span of sixty years, but he added, "There is no difference in the doctrine of the verses, no matter what difference there may be in their age."

Another Irish poet who was writing deathless verse at this time was Thomas Moore, who, like Kelly, was also born in Dublin, May 28, 1779. Very few Protestants, perhaps, when they sing "Come, ye disconsolate, where'er ye languish," are aware of the fact that the words were written by a Roman Catholic, but such was the religious persuasion of Moore. Like Kelly, he also received his education at Trinity College, Dublin, but was not permitted to graduate because he was a Romanist.

Although he was the writer of thirty-two sacred songs, Moore is better known for his ballads and other poems. Lovers of English lyric poetry will always remember him as the writer of "The last rose of summer," "Believe me, if all those endearing young charms," "The harp that once through Tara's halls," "Oft in the stilly night," and a number of other ballads that have lived through the years to make the name of Thomas Moore famous.

Moore was a man of curious make-up. True to his Celtic nature, he possessed a fiery temper that often brought him into embarrassing situations. Jeffrey, the famous critic, once aroused his ire by saying unkind things about his poetry. Moore promptly challenged Jeffrey to a duel. The authorities interfered before any blood was shed. It was then discovered that one of the pistols contained no bullet, whereupon the two men became fast friends.

Moore was one of the few men who ever made a financial success of writing poetry. For *Lalla Rookh* he received $15,000 before a single copy had been sold. However, like most men of poetic gifts, he had no natural bent for business. At one time he accepted a government position in the revenue service at Bermuda. He did not enjoy his tasks, and so he placed his duties in the hands of a deputy, while he went on a tour of America. The deputy, however, absconded with the proceeds of a ship's cargo, whereupon Moore found himself liable for the loss of $30,000.

Moore's hymns first appeared in his volume of *Sacred Songs,* published in 1816. Most of them were written to popular airs of various nations. They have attained greater popularity in America than in Great Britain. One of the most famous is "Sound the loud timbrel o'er Egypt's dark sea."

"Come, ye disconsolate" was so changed by Thomas Hastings, the American hymnist, it became practically a new hymn. The second line of the first stanza, as Moore originally wrote it, was:

> Come, at the shrine of God fervently kneel.

But the greatest change was made in the third stanza, which departed very radically from true hymn style. It originally read:

> Come, ask the infidel what boon he brings us,
> What charm for aching hearts he can reveal,
> Sweet is that heavenly promise Hope sings us—
> Earth has no sorrow that God cannot heal.

Hastings changed it to read:

> Here see the Bread of Life; see waters flowing
> Forth from the throne of God, pure from above,
> Come to the feast of love; come, ever knowing
> Earth has no sorrow but Heaven can remove.

The last three years of Moore's life were very unhappy. A nervous affliction rendered him practically helpless. His death occurred on February 26, 1852, at the age of seventy-three years.

The Christian's Eternal Destiny

For ever with the Lord!
Amen, so let it be;
Life from the dead is in that word,
'Tis immortality.

Here in the body pent,
Absent from Him I roam,
Yet nightly pitch my moving tent
A day's march nearer home.

My father's house on high,
Home of my soul, how near
At times to faith's foreseeing eye
Thy golden gates appear!

Ah, then my spirit faints
To reach the land I love,
The bright inheritance of saints,
Jerusalem above!

For ever with the Lord!
Father, if 'tis Thy will,
The promise of that faithful word
E'en here to me fulfill

Be Thou at my right hand,
Then can I never fail;
Uphold Thou me, and I shall stand;
Fight, and I must prevail.

So when my latest breath
Shall rend the veil in twain,
By death I shall escape from death,
And life eternal gain.

Knowing as I am known,
How shall I love that word,
And oft repeat before the throne,
"For ever with the Lord!"

JAMES MONTGOMERY, 1771-1854

THE HYMN LEGACY OF A MORAVIAN EDITOR

NEXT to Charles Wesley and Isaac Watts, no man has made a larger contribution to English hymnody than James Montgomery. Perhaps no layman in the entire history of the Christian Church has left a richer legacy of sacred song to succeeding generations than he. And with the passing years, his hymns reveal extraordinary vitality, strengthening rather than losing their hold on the worshiping Church.

Shortly before he died, Montgomery was asked by a friend, "Which of your poems will live?" He answered, "None, sir; nothing, except perhaps a few of my hymns."

Montgomery was right. Although he wrote a number of pretentious poems, they have been almost forgotten. But his hymns live on. No modern hymnal would seem complete without such classics as "Angels from the realms of glory," "Hail to the Lord's Anointed," "Prayer is the soul's sincere desire," "Go to dark Gethsemane," "Shepherd of souls, refresh and bless," "O pour Thy Spirit from on high," "O Spirit of the the living God," "Songs of praise the angels sang," "In the hour of trial," "Forever with the Lord," "Come to Calvary's holy mountain," "According to Thy gracious word," "Lift up your heads, ye gates of brass," "Lord, teach us how to pray aright," and "Jerusalem, my happy home."

Montgomery wrote some 400 hymns in all, and nearly one-fourth of these are still enjoying widespread use. John Julian brings him this tribute:

"His poetic genius was of a high order, higher than most who stand with him in the front rank of poets. His ear for rhythm was exceedingly accurate and refined. His knowledge of Holy Scripture was most extensive. His religious views were broad and charitable. His devotional spirit was of the holiest type. With the faith of a strong man he united the beauty and simplicity of a child. Richly poetic without exuberance, dogmatic without uncharitableness, tender without sentimentality, elaborate without diffusiveness, richly musical without apparent effort, he has bequeathed to the Church of Christ

315

wealth which could only have come from a true genius and a sanctified heart."

Montgomery began writing hymns as a little boy. He was born at Irvine, Ayrshire, Scotland, November 4, 1771. His father was a Moravian minister, and it had been determined that the son James should also be trained for the same calling. Accordingly he was enrolled in the Moravian seminary at Fulneck, Yorkshire, England. The parents, however, were sent to the West Indies as missionaries, and when they soon died there, it became necessary for James to discontinue his schooling.

For a while he worked as a clerk in a store, but this was entirely distasteful to one who possessed the literary gifts of Montgomery. At the age of nineteen he went to London with a few of his poems in manuscript form, trying to find a publisher who would print them. In this he was unsuccessful. Two years later we find him in Sheffield, where he became associated with Robert Gales, editor of the *Sheffield Register*.

Gales was a radical, and, because he displeased the authorities by some of his articles, he found it convenient in 1794 to leave England for America. Montgomery, then only twenty-three years old, took over the publication of the paper and changed its name to the *Sheffield Iris*. Montgomery, however, proved as indiscreet as Gales had been, and during the first two years of his editorship was twice imprisoned by the government, the first time for publishing a poem entitled "The Fall of Bastille," and the second time for an account of a riot in Sheffield.

In 1797 he published a volume of poems called *Prison Amusements,* so named from the fact that some of them had been written during his imprisonment. In later years the British government granted him a pension of $1,000 per year in recognition of his achievements, perhaps by way of making amends for the indignity offered him by his two prison experiences.

In Montgomery's hymns we may hear for the first time the missionary note in English hymnody, reflecting the newly-awakened zeal for the evangelization of the world which had gripped the English people. The Baptist Missionary Society had been organized in 1792; Carey had gone to India as its apostle; and in 1799 the English Church Missionary Society had been formed.

In the fervor aroused for foreign missions in England we may discern a continuation of the impulses which went forth from the Pietistic movement at Halle, Germany, nearly a century earlier, when Bartholomew Ziegenbalg and Henry Plütschau were sent from that cradle of the modern missionary movement as the first missionaries to India. We may also see something of the influences emanating from the great Moravian missionary center at Herrnhut. John Wesley visited both these places before he began his great revival in England, and became deeply imbued with zeal for missions.

Moravian contact with England had resulted in the formation of many Moravian societies, and it was one of these that had sent Montgomery's parents as missionaries to the West Indies. It was not without reason, therefore, that Montgomery became the first English hymnist to sound the missionary trumpet. He could never forget that his own parents had given their lives in bringing the Gospel to the wretched blacks of the West Indies. His father's grave was at Barbadoes and his mother was sleeping on the island of Tobago. For the same reason, Montgomery became a bitter opponent of slavery.

The missionary note was first heard in his great Advent hymn, "Hail to the Lord's Anointed," written in 1821. One of the stanzas not usually found in hymnbooks reads:

> Kings shall fall down before Him,
>   And gold and incense bring;
> All nations shall adore Him,
>   His praise all people sing;
> For He shall have dominion
>   O'er river, sea, and shore,
> Far as the eagle's pinion
>   Or dove's light wing can soar.

Two other missionary hymns are "Lift up your heads, ye gates of brass" and "Hark! the song of jubilee." The latter sweeps along in triumphant measures:

> He shall reign from pole to pole,
>   With illimitable sway;
> He shall reign, when like a scroll
>   Yonder heavens have passed away;
> Then the end: beneath His rod
>   Man's last enemy shall fall:
> Hallelujah! Christ in God,
>   God in Christ, is all in all!

Although it probably does not enjoy the popularity of some of his other hymns, "For ever with the Lord" has aroused great enthusiasm among literary critics. Julian says that "it is full of lyric fire and deep feeling," and Dr. Theodore Cuyler declares that it contains four lines that are as fine as anything in hymnody. This beautiful verse reads:

> Here, in the body pent,
>   Absent from Thee I roam,
> Yet nightly pitch my moving tent
>   A day's march nearer home.

Montgomery's last words were words of prayer. After his usual evening devotion on April 30, 1854, he fell into a sleep from which he never woke on earth. And so was fulfilled in his own experience the beautiful thought contained in his glorious hymn on prayer:

> Prayer is the Christian's vital breath,
>   The Christian's native air,
> His watchword at the gates of death—
>   He enters heaven with prayer.

Closely associated with Montgomery was another man who was deeply interested in hymnology. He was Thomas Cotterill, a clergyman of the Church of England who had been profoundly affected by the evangelical movement and who had not failed to note the tremendous part played by hymn-singing in its success. Cotterill, who was born in Cannock, England, in 1779, became a Fellow at Cambridge during his studies there. He was ordained in 1803, and soon we find him at the Staffordshire potteries, where he labored for nine years among a poverty-stricken and ignorant class of people.

In 1817 he became perpetual curate of St. Paul's in Sheffield, where his interest in hymnody soon brought him in contact with Montgomery. Cotterill was more of a hymn compiler than a writer, and had already, in 1810, brought out a collection of hymns that had passed through eight editions. In 1819 he induced Montgomery to collaborate with him in the publication of a greatly enlarged ninth edition. This volume contained 150 psalms and 367 hymns, 50 of which were by Montgomery and 25 by Cotterill.

Inasmuch as hymns had not yet been authorized in public worship, some bishops forbade their use in their dioceses, and many people looked upon their increasing use with considerable dismay. A storm of opposition broke with the publication of the new edition, and Cotterill gained little by trying to force it on his own Sheffield congregation. Suit was finally brought against Cotterill in the Consistory Court of the York archdiocese.

Through the intervention of Archbishop Harcourt, the case was finally compromised, Cotterill agreeing to withdraw the book and to prepare a new one under the Primate's guidance. This was done, and the number of hymns was reduced from 367 to 146, selected principally by Cotterill. The suppressed book, however, "did more than any other collection to mold the hymnbooks of the next period; and nearly nine-tenths of the hymns therein . . . usually in the altered form given them by Cotterill or James Montgomery . . . are still in common use in Great Britain and America."

It was at Cotterill's death in 1823 that Montgomery wrote his lament, "Friend after friend departs." Another writer has said of Cotterill that he combined "the piety of a saint, the tastes of a scholar, the aspect and demeanor of an unaffected Christian gentleman." His best known hymns are "Awake, ye saints, awake," "Great God of Abraham, hear our prayer," and the greatly loved

> Our God is love, and all his saints
> His image bear below;
> The heart with love to God inspired
> With love to man will glow.

The Scriptural warning, "Let him that thinketh he standeth take heed lest he fall," is exemplified in the life of another English hymn-writer who lived at this time. He was George Heath, an Independent clergyman who in 1770 became pastor of a Presbyterian church at Honiton, Devonshire. Proving himself unworthy of the office, he was deprived of his parish "for cause." And this was the man who wrote "My soul, be on thy guard!" It appears that later he became a Unitarian minister. His well-known hymn appeared in a volume he published in 1781 containing hymns and poetic essays "sacred to the worship of the Deity." He died in 1822.

A Sublime Hymn of Adoration

Holy, Holy, Holy, Lord God Almighty!
 Early in the morning our song shall rise to Thee;
Holy, Holy, Holy! merciful and mighty;
 God in three Persons, blessed Trinity!

Holy, Holy, Holy! all the saints adore Thee,
 Casting down their golden crowns around the glassy sea,
Cherubim and Seraphim falling down before Thee,
 Which wert, and art, and evermore shalt be.

Holy, Holy, Holy! though the darkness hide Thee,
 Though the eyes of sinful man Thy glory may not see,
Only Thou art holy: there is none beside Thee,
 Perfect in power, in love, in purity.

Holy, Holy, Holy, Lord God Almighty!
 All Thy works shall praise Thy Name, in earth, and sky,
  and sea;
Holy, Holy, Holy! merciful and mighty;
 God in three Persons, blessed Trinity!

REGINALD HEBER, 1783–1826

HEBER, MISSIONARY BISHOP AND HYMNIST

IN the glorious hymns of Reginald Heber, missionary bishop to India, we find not only the noblest expression of the missionary fervor which in his day was stirring the Church, but also the purest poetry in English hymnody. Christians of all ages will gratefully remember the name of the man who wrote the most stirring of all missionary hymns, "From Greenland's icy mountains," as well as that sublime hymn of adoration, "Holy, holy, holy, Lord God Almighty!"

Heber had the good fortune of beginning his work in the early part of the 19th century, just as the age of romanticism in English literature began to dawn. Wordsworth's *Lyrical Ballads* had appeared in 1798. Then came Coleridge with his *Ancient Mariner,* Southey with *Lodore,* and Byron with *Childe Harold,* followed quickly by Shelley and Keats and their beautiful classics. It was inevitable that religious poetry also should find wings to express itself in language that possessed imagination as well as fervency and reverence. Nor could it continue to confine itself to the rigid molds of common meter, long meter and short meter, in which the greater part of psalmody and hymnody up to that time had been enshrined.

Heber apparently realized this, and immediately adopted forms that imparted a new spirit of joy and exultation to his hymns. In a sense, therefore, the age of true hymnody in the Church of England had its beginnings with him. Indeed, it is a matter of record that Heber made a valiant effort to produce a hymnal that would receive the official sanction of his Church, but in this, unfortunately, he failed.

The psalm-singing in his congregation, he once wrote to a friend, "continues bad," and he begged for advice how he might obtain something better than the *Old Version* of Sternhold and Hopkins. Being unable to find anything satisfactory, he finally set to work himself to create a new hymnbook, and in this task he tried to enlist the aid of Walter Scott, Southey, Henry Hart Milman and others.

Milman alone responded, but Heber persisted in his endeavor until the collection was completed in 1820. It was not published until after Heber's death, however, inasmuch as Archbishop Sutton of London thought the time "was not ripe" for such a book of worship!

Heber was born at Malpas, Cheshire, April 21, 1783, the scion of an ancient Yorkshire family. He was educated at Oxford, where he formed the friendship of Sir Walter Scott. His gift for writing poetry revealed itself while he was still a student, when he won a prize for a remarkable poem on Palestine. It is said that Heber, who was only seventeen years old at the time, read the poem to Scott at the breakfast table, and that the latter suggested one of its most striking lines.

Following the awarding of the prize, for which young Heber had been earnestly striving, his parents found him on his knees in grateful prayer.

Following his ordination, Heber served in an obscure parish at Hodnet for sixteen years, and it was here that all of his hymns were written. He also engaged in other literary activities that brought him some fame. All the while, however, he cherished a secret longing to go to India. It is said that he would work out imaginary journeys on the map, while he hoped that some day he might become bishop of Calcutta.

His missionary fervor at this time is also reflected in the famous hymn, "From Greenland's icy mountains," written in 1819. The allusions to "India's coral strand" and "Ceylon's isle" are an indication of the longings that were running through his mind.

His earnest prayer was answered in 1822, when at the age of forty years he was called to the episcopate as bishop of Calcutta. After three years of arduous work in India, the life of the gifted bishop was cut short. During this period he ordained the first native pastor of the Episcopal Church—Christian David.

A man of rare refinement and noble Christian personality, Heber was greatly beloved by all who knew him. "One of the best of English gentlemen," was the tribute accorded him by Thackeray. It was not until after his death, however, that he leaped into fame through his hymns.

The story of how "From Greenland's icy mountains" was written reveals something of the poetic genius of Heber. It seems that he was visiting his father-in-law, Dr. Shipley, vicar and dean of Wrexham, on the Saturday before Whitsunday, 1819. The dean, who was planning to preach a missionary sermon the following morning, asked young Heber to write a missionary hymn that might be sung at the service. The latter immediately withdrew from the circle of friends to another part of the room. After a while the dean asked, "What have you written?" Heber replied by reading the first three stanzas of the hymn. The dean expressed satisfaction, but the poet replied, "No, no, the sense is not complete." And so he added the fourth verse—"Waft, waft, ye winds, His story"—and the greatest missionary hymn of all time had been born.

The story of the tune to which the hymn is sung is equally interesting. A Christian woman in Savannah, Georgia, had come into possession of a copy of Heber's words. The meter was unusual, and she was unable to find music to fit the words. Learning of a young bank clerk who was said to be gifted as a composer, she sent the poem to him. Within a half hour it was returned to her with the beautiful tune, *Missionary Hymn,* to which it is now universally sung. The young bank clerk was none other than Lowell Mason, who afterwards achieved fame as one of America's greatest hymn-tune composers. The marvel is that both words and music were written almost in a moment—by real inspiration, it would seem.

Bishop Heber's hymns are characterized chiefly by their lyrical quality. They are unusually rich in imagery. This may be seen particularly in his beautiful Epiphany hymn, "Brightest and best of the sons of the morning." In some respects the hymns of Heber resemble the later lyrics of Henry Francis Lyte, writer of "Abide with me, fast falls the eventide." They sound, however, a much more joyous note than the hymns of Lyte, in which are always heard strains of sadness.

Lord Tennyson called "Holy, holy, holy, Lord God Almighty" the world's greatest hymn, and there are many who would agree with him. It should be observed that this noble anthem is a hymn of pure adoration, and perhaps herein lies the secret of its power. There should be more hymns of this character in Christian worship. The tune to which it is always sung, *Nicaea,* was written by the great English composer, John B. Dykes, and is comparable in majesty to the hymn itself.

Other fine hymns by Heber include "The Son of God goes forth to war," "God that madest earth and heaven," "O Thou, whose infant feet were found," "When through the torn sail," "Bread of the world in mercy broken," "Brightest and best of the sons of the morning," "By cool Siloam's shady rill," and "Hosanna to the living Lord."

Altogether Heber wrote fifty-seven hymns, and it is said that every one is still in use, a rare tribute to the genius of this consecrated writer.

We have already referred to the fact that Henry Hart Milman was the only poet who responded to Heber's appeal for aid in the preparation of his new hymnal. Milman's contribution to this collection, which was eventually published by Heber's widow in 1827, consisted of thirteen hymns, including his magnificent Palm Sunday hymn, "Ride on, ride on in majesty."

Milman at the time the hymns were written was professor of poetry at Oxford, at which institution he had left a record of unusual brilliance as a student. In 1849 he became dean of St. Paul's Cathedral, London. In addition to his accomplishments as a poet and dramatist, he achieved considerable fame as a church historian. His *History of the Jews* in 1830 aroused a storm of criticism because of his use of the modern historical method in the treatment of the subject, and sale of the book was stopped. Milman died at Sunninghill, Ascot, in 1868.

Heber's life was closely paralleled in many respects by another great hymn-writer who lived in the same period, namely, Sir Robert Grant. Born two years later than the gifted missionary bishop, he, like Heber, died in India. Although he did not enter the service of the Church but engaged in secular pursuits, Grant was a deeply spiritual man and his hymns bear testimony of an earnest, confiding faith in Christ. Between his hymns and those of Heber there is a striking similarity. The language is chaste and exalted. The rhythm is faultless. The lines are chiseled as perfectly as a cameo. The imagery is almost startling in its grandeur. Take, for example, a stanza from his magnificent hymn, "O worship the King":

> O tell of His might, O sing of His grace,
> Whose robe is the light, whose canopy space;
> His chariots of wrath the deep thunder-clouds form,
> And dark is His path on the wings of the storm.

There is something beautifully tender in that other hymn of Grant's in which he reveals childlike trust in Christ:

> When gathering clouds around I view,
> And days are dark, and friends are few,
> On Him I lean, who, not in vain,

Experienced every human pain;
He sees my wants, allays my fears,
And counts and treasures up my tears.

Nor would we forget his other famous hymn, "Saviour, when in dust to Thee," based on the Litany. When we learn that the man who wrote these hymns was never engaged in religious pursuits, and that his whole life was crowded with arduous tasks and great responsibilities in high government positions, we have reason to marvel.

Sir Robert Grant was born in the county of Inverness, Scotland, in 1785. His father was a member of Parliament and a director of the East India Company. Robert also was trained for political life, and, after graduating from Cambridge University in 1806, began the practice of law. In 1826 he was elected to Parliament, five years later became privy counselor, and in 1834 was named governor of Bombay. He died at Dapoorie, in western India, in 1838.

While a member of Parliament, Sir Robert introduced a bill to remove the restrictions imposed upon the Jews. The historian Macaulay made his maiden speech in Parliament in support of this measure.

Mention should be made here also of another of Bishop Heber's contemporaries, John Marriott, who likewise was deeply interested in the missionary movement and who, incidentally, gained undying fame as the author of a single hymn. Considered one of the finest Christian lyrics in the English language, "Thou, whose almighty word" has found a permanent place among the great missionary hymns of the Church. Marriott was born at Cottesbach, England, September 11, 1780, and at one time was chaplain to the Duke of Buccleuch. He was a close friend of Sir Walter Scott, who dedicated the opening lines of *Marmion* to him. Some of Marriott's poems and hymns appeared in print during his lifetime, a circumstance which, because of his modesty, caused him much dismay. He died in 1825.

Sir Walter Scott is not usually thought of as belonging in the category of hymn-writers, and yet it is to him that we are indebted for one of the most moving English versions of *Dies Irae*. This famous Latin hymn on the final judgment, it would appear, has captured the imagination of more English poets than any other hymn, and there are at least 150 translations extant. Scott often confessed that

325

no hymn moved him more profoundly than this one, and that is probably why he introduced a condensed form of it into his *Lay of the Last Minstrel.* "That day of wrath, that dreadful day," as sung in Melrose Abbey at the conclusion of the *Lay,* is called "Hymn for the Dead."

Scott's fame as a poet and novelist is such that it is quite unnecessary to add anything here concerning his life and works. His place as a lyric poet and as the writer of ballads and metrical romances is very high, but it was principally by his novels that he gained undying fame. In recognition of his literary achievements he was made a baronet in 1820. His later life was filled with tragedy, brought on by financial failure, but his heroic struggle in the face of adversity has been characterized as a story of "moral grandeur." He died in 1832, mourned by the whole literary world.

William Wordsworth was another famous English poet of this period who has bequeathed to the Church a hymn that will always be deeply cherished. It is the lovely noon-day lyric, "Blest are the moments, doubly blest." As printed in modern hymnals, the hymn has five stanzas, but the original poem contained these three additional opening verses:

> Up to the throne of God is borne
> The voice of praise at early morn,
> And He accepts the punctual hymn
> Sung as the light of day grows dim:
>
> Nor will He turn his ear aside
> From holy offerings at noontide.
> Then here reposing let us raise
> A song of gratitude and praise.
>
> What though our burthen be not light,
> We need not toil from morn to night;
> The respite of the mid-day hour
> Is in the thankful creature's power.

In an introduction to the hymn, the great English poet writes: "Bishop Ken's Morning and Evening Hymns are, as they deserve to be, familiarly known. Many other hymns have also been written on the same subject; but, not being aware of any being designed for noon-day, I was induced to compose these verses. Often one has occasion to observe cottage children carrying, in their baskets, dinner to their fathers engaged with their daily labors in the fields and woods. How gratifying would it be to me could I be assured that any portion of these stanzas had been sung by such a domestic concert under such circumstances. A friend of mine has told me that she introduced this hymn into a village school which she superintended, and the stanzas in succession furnished her with texts to comment upon in a way which without difficulty was made intelligible to the children, and in which they obviously took delight, and they were taught to sing it to the tune of the old 100th Psalm."

What a beautiful and child-like sentiment from the man who wrote "Intimations of Immortality"! It almost sounds like an apology for having written a hymn, and it suggests the thought that Wordsworth might have written many more had he been urged to do so.

Wordsworth began his great career when, in 1798, he collaborated with Coleridge in publishing *Lyrical Ballads*. It is said that he was deeply stirred in his early life by the French Revolution, and this event, together with his well-known love of nature, provided the first inspiration for his poetry. His works are too well-known to need recounting here. He succeeded Southey as Poet Laureate of England in 1843, and died seven years later.

A Hymn That Wins Souls

Just as I am, without one plea,
But that Thy blood was shed for me,
And that Thou bidd'st me come to Thee,
O Lamb of God, I come, I come.

Just as I am, and waiting not
To rid my soul of one dark blot,
To Thee whose Blood can cleanse each spot,
O Lamb of God, I come, I come.

Just as I am, though tossed about
With many a conflict, many a doubt,
Fightings and fears, within, without,
O Lamb of God, I come, I come.

Just as I am, poor, wretched, blind;
Sight, riches, healing of the mind,
Yea, all I need, in Thee I find,
O Lamb of God, I come, I come.

Just as I am, Thou wilt receive,
Wilt welcome, pardon, cleanse, relieve;
Because Thy promise I believe,
O Lamb of God, I come, I come.

Just as I am; Thy love unknown
Hath broken every barrier down;
Now to be Thine, yea, Thine alone,
O Lamb of God, I come, I come.

CHARLOTTE ELLIOTT, 1789-1871

AN INVALID WHO BLESSED THE WORLD

" JUST as I am" will doubtlessly be sung to the end of time and as often as Christians sing it they will praise God and bless the memory of the woman who wrote it—Charlotte Elliott.

This hymn will have a greater value, too, when we know something of the pain and effort it cost the writer to produce it. Miss Elliott was one of those afflicted souls who scarcely know of real surcease from suffering. Though she lived to be eighty-two years old, she was never well, and often endured seasons of great physical distress. She could well understand the sacrifice made by one who

> Strikes the strings
> With fingers that ache and bleed.

Of her own afflictions she once wrote: "He knows, and He alone, what it is, day after day, hour after hour, to fight against bodily feeling of almost overpowering weakness, languor and exhaustion, to resolve not to yield to slothfulness, depression and instability, such as the body causes me to long to indulge, but to rise every morning determined to take for my motto: 'If a man will come after Me, let him deny himself, take up his cross daily, and follow Me.' "

But God seemed to have had a purpose in placing a heavy cross upon her, for her afflictions made her think of other sufferers like herself and made her the better fitted for the work that He had prepared for her — the ministry of comfort and consolation. How beautifully she resigned herself to the will of God may be seen in her words: "God sees, God guides, God guards me. His grace surrounds me, and His voice continually bids me to be happy and holy in His service, just where I am."

"Just as I am" was written in 1836, and appeared for the first time in the second edition of *The Invalid's Hymn Book,* which was published that year and to which Miss Elliott had contributed 115 pieces.

The great American evangelist, Dwight L. Moody, once said that this hymn had probably touched more hearts and brought more souls to Christ than any other ever written. Miss Elliott's own brother, who was a minister in the Church of England, himself wrote:

"In the course of a long ministry, I hope to have been permitted to see some fruit of my labors; but I feel far more has been done by a single hymn of my sister's."

It is said that after the death of Miss Elliott, more than a thousand letters were found among her papers, in which the writers expressed their gratitude to her for the help the hymn had brought them.

The secret power of this marvelous hymn must be found in its true evangelical spirit. It sets forth in very simple but gripping words the all-important truth that we are not saved through any merit or worthiness in ourselves, but by the sovereign grace of God through faith in Jesus Christ. It also pictures the utter helplessness and wretchedness of the human soul, and its inability to rise above its own sins; but very lovingly it invites the soul to come to Him "whose blood can cleanse each spot."

The hymn was born out of the author's personal spiritual experiences. Though a daughter of the Church, brought up in a pious home, it seems that Miss Elliott had never found true peace with God. Like so many other seeking souls in all ages, she felt that men must do something themselves to win salvation, instead of coming to Christ as helpless sinners and finding complete redemption in Him.

When Dr. Caesar Malan, the noted preacher of Geneva, came to visit the Elliott home in Brighton, England, in 1822, he soon discovered the cause of her spiritual perplexity, and became a real evangelical guide and counsellor. "You have nothing of merit to bring to God," he told her. "You must come just as you are, a sinner, to the Lamb of God that taketh away the sin of the world."

Throughout the remainder of her life, Miss Elliott celebrated every year the day on which her friend had led her to Christ, for she considered it to be her spiritual birthday. Although it was fourteen years later that she wrote her immortal hymn, it is apparent that she never forgot the words of Dr. Malan, for they form the very core and essence of it.

The inspiration for the hymn came one day when the frail invalid had been left alone at the home of her brother. She was lying on a couch and pondering the words spoken by Dr. Malan many years before, when suddenly she seemed to comprehend as never before the glorious truth that salvation is altogether the gift of God's grace in Christ. Then came the heavenly inspiration. Rising from her couch, she wrote:

> Just as I am, without one plea,
> But that Thy blood was shed for me,
> And that Thou bidd'st me come to Thee,
> O Lamb of God, I come, I come.

By common consent, Miss Elliott is given the foremost place among English women hymn-writers. She was the author of some 150 hymns in all. Next to "Just as I am," perhaps her finest lyric is the beautiful hymn of Christian resignation:

> My God and Father, while I stray
> Far from my home, in life's rough way,
> O teach me from my heart to say,
>   "Thy will be done."
>
> If but my fainting heart be blest
> With Thy sweet Spirit for its guest,
> My God, to Thee I leave the rest,
>   "Thy will be done."
>
> Renew my will from day to day,
> Blend it with Thine, and take away
> All that now makes it hard to say,
>   "Thy will be done."
>
> Then when on earth I breathe no more
> The prayer oft mixed with tears before,
> I'll sing upon a happier shore,
>   "Thy will be done."

The Sun That Ne'er Goes Down

Sun of my soul, Thou Saviour dear,
It is not night if Thou be near;
O may no earthborn cloud arise
To hide Thee from Thy servant's eyes.

When the soft dews of kindly sleep
My wearied eyelids gently steep,
Be my last thought, how sweet to rest
Forever on my Saviour's breast.

Abide with me from morn till eve,
For without Thee I cannot live;
Abide with me when night is nigh,
For without Thee I dare not die.

If some poor wandering child of Thine
Have spurned today the voice divine,
Now, Lord, the gracious work begin;
Let him no more lie down in sin.

Watch by the sick; enrich the poor
With blessings from Thy boundless store;
Be every mourner's sleep tonight,
Like infant's slumber, pure and light.

Come near and bless us when we wake,
Ere through the world our way we take;
Till in the ocean of Thy love
We lose ourselves in heaven above.

JOHN KEBLE, 1792–1866

HOW HYMNS HELPED BUILD A CHURCH

MANY of the classic hymns of the Christian Church have been derived from devotional poems that were never intended as hymns by their writers. This is true of the beautiful morning hymn, "New every morning is the love," and the equally beautiful evening hymn, "Sun of my soul, Thou Saviour dear." Both of these gems of hymnody have been taken from one of the most famous devotional books ever written — John Keble's *The Christian Year*.

Keble was born at Fairford, England, April 25, 1792, the son of a country vicar. The only elementary training he received was at the hands of his gifted father, but at the age of fifteen years he was ready to enter Oxford University. Here he distinguished himself as a brilliant scholar, and at the age of twenty-three he was ordained as a clergyman of the Church of England. He remained as a tutor at Oxford for a number of year, but when his mother died he returned to Fairford to assist his father. Although he received a number of tempting offers at this time, he preferred to labor in this obscure parish, where he might be of help and comfort to his father and his two sisters.

It was not until 1835, when his father died and the home was broken up, that Keble accepted the vicarage of Hursley, another humble and scattered parish, with a population of 1,500 people. He married in the same year, and here he and his devoted wife labored until 1866, when they passed away within six weeks of each other.

It was in 1827, when Keble was only twenty-seven, that he yielded to the strong entreaties of his father and his friends and consented to publish the volume of poems known as *The Christian Year*. The verses follow the church calendar, and it was the author's desire that the book should be a devotional companion to the *Book of Common Prayer*. For this reason it has been called "The Prayer Book in Poetry."

Keble was so modest concerning his work that he refused to permit the volume to bear his name, and so it was given to the world anonymously. The work was a marvelous success. From 1827 to 1867, a year after the author's death, the book had passed through one hundred and nine editions. Keble used a large part of the proceeds derived from the sale of his book in helping to rebuild the church at Hursley. He also was instrumental in having churches built at Otterbourne and Amplifield, hamlets that belonged to his parish.

Religious leaders, as well as literary critics, have been unanimous in rendering high tribute to this remarkable volume. Dr. Arnold, the great schoolmaster of Rugby, speaking of Keble's poems, says: "Nothing equal to them exists in our language. The knowledge of Scripture, the purity of heart, and the richness of poetry, I never saw equaled." "It is a book," says Canon Barry, "which leads the soul up to God, not through one, but through all of the various faculties which He has implanted in it." And Dr. Pusey adds: "It taught, because his own soul was moved so deeply; the stream burst forth, because the heart that poured it out was full; it was fresh, deep, tender, loving, because he himself was such; he was true, and thought aloud, and conscience everywhere responded to the voice of conscience."

The publication of *The Christian Year* brought Keble such fame that, in 1831, he was elected professor of poetry at Oxford. He did not remove thither, but in 1833 he preached at Oxford his famous sermon on "National Apostasy" which is credited with having started the so-called Oxford Movement.

This movement had its inception in the earnest desire on the part of many prominent leaders of the Church of England, including John Newman, to bring about a spiritual awakening in the Church. They looked askance at the evangelistic methods of the Wesleyan leaders and turned to the other extreme of high church ritualism. All England was profoundly stirred by a series of "Tracts for the Times," written by Newman and his friends, among them Keble. A disastrous result of the movement was the desertion of Newman and a large number of others to the Church of Rome; but Keble shrank from this final step and remained a high church Anglican.

Although a great part of his later life was occupied with religious controversy, we would like to remember Keble as a consecrated Christian poet and an humble parish pastor. For more than thirty years he labored faithfully among his people, visiting from house to house. If it was difficult for a catechumen to attend confirmation instruction during the day, Keble would go to his house at night, armed with cloak and lantern. He gave each candidate a Bible, in which he had marked the passages that were to be learned. These Bibles were highly prized, and some of them are to be found in Hursley to this day. It was noticed that, whenever the vicar prepared to read and explain a passage of Scripture, he would first bow his head and close his eyes while he asked for the guidance of the Holy Spirit.

Keble's famous morning hymn, "New every morning is the love," is taken from a poem of sixteen verses. The first line reads, "O timely happy, timely wise." It contains four oft-quoted stanzas that ought to be treasured in the heart of every Christian:

> New mercies, each returning day,
> Hover around us while we pray;
> New perils past, new sins forgiven,
> New thoughts of God, new hopes of heaven.

> Old friends, old scenes, will lovelier be,
> As more of heaven in each we see:
> Some softening gleam of love and prayer
> Shall dawn on every cross and care.

> The trivial round, the common task,
> Will furnish all we ought to ask;
> Room to deny ourselves, a road
> To bring us daily nearer God.

> Only, O Lord, in Thy dear love,
> Fit us for perfect rest above;
> And help us this, and every day,
> To live more nearly as we pray.

The evening hymn is also taken from a longer poem, in which the author first describes in graphic words the setting of the sun:

> 'Tis gone! that bright and orbéd blaze,
> Fast fading from our wistful gaze;
> Yon mantling cloud has hid from sight
> The last faint pulse of quivering light.

> In darkness and in weariness
> The traveler on his way must press,
> No gleam to watch on tree or tower,
> Whiling away the lonesome hour.

Then comes the beautiful and reassuring thought:

> Sun of my soul! Thou Saviour dear,
> It is not night if Thou be near!
> O may no earthborn cloud arise
> To hide Thee from Thy servant's eyes.

Other familiar hymns by Keble are "The Voice that breathed o'er Eden," "Blest are the pure in heart," and "Lord, in Thy Name Thy servants plead."

Two other Church of England clergymen who wrote unforgettable hymns at this period were John Cawood and Richard Mant.

Cawood, the son of a poor farmer, was born at Matlock, England, March 18, 1775. During his youth he passed through a profound religious experience which caused him to choose the ministry as a life calling. After four years at Oxford, he became perpetual curate at Bewdley, where he remained from 1814 until his death in 1852. Cawood wrote a number of hymns, of which at least two have come into general use, namely, "Almighty God, Thy Word is cast" and "Hark! what mean those holy voices?"

Mant came from a more distinguished family. He was born February 12, 1776, at Southampton, the birthplace of Isaac Watts, where his father was rector of All Saints' Church. Following his graduation from Oxford, young Mant served for a while as domestic chaplain to the Archbishop of Canterbury. Then he became the successor to his father in his home parish in Southampton. Later we find him as rector of St. Botolph's in London. In 1820 he was appointed Bishop of Kellaloe and Kilfenoragh in Ireland, and three years later was transferred to the see of Down and Conner. In 1833 the see of Dromore was added to his diocese. He passed away in 1848.

Bishop Mant was a voluminous writer. Among the works that came from his "unresting pen" was a *History of the Church in Ireland*. In 1837 he published a volume on the ancient hymns of the Church, to which he added a few of his own lyrics. His splendid hymn, "For all thy saints, O Lord," first appeared in this work. "Round the Lord in glory seated" is another of his better known hymns.

Another man who lived and wrought during the years when Keble was writing *The Christian Year* was Richard Whately. He possessed a brilliant mind and became a Fellow of Oriel at Oxford. After a varied career as a minister and professor at Oxford, he was appointed Archbishop of Dublin. He did much to promote elementary education in Ireland and to alleviate suffering among the poor. Whately was a strong opponent of the Oxford Movement, and yet Newman confessed that it was he who had taught him how to think and reason! He died in 1863 after a distinguished career.

Whately never aspired to be a poet, but it is from his pen we have received the beautiful second stanza to Heber's "God that madest earth and heaven." It is based on the Latin antiphon used at Compline, which is the last liturgical service of the day, said after nightfall, or, in monasteries, just before retiring. The verse reads:

> Guard us waking, guard us sleeping,
> And, when we die,
> May we in Thy mighty keeping
> All peaceful lie.
> When the last dread call shall wake us,
> Do not Thou, our Lord, forsake us,
> But to reign in glory take us
> With Thee on high.

The Hymn of a Perplexed Soul

Lead, kindly Light, amid th' encircling gloom,
  Lead Thou me on!
The night is dark, and I am far from home;
  Lead Thou me on!
Keep Thou my feet; I do not ask to see
The distant scene; one step enough for me.

I was not ever thus, nor prayed that Thou
  Shouldst lead me on;
I loved to choose and see my path; but now
  Lead Thou me on!
I loved the garish day, and, spite of fears,
Pride ruled my will. Remember not past years.

So long Thy power hath blest me, sure it still
  Will lead me on
O'er moor and fen, o'er crag and torrent, till
  The night is gone,
And with the morn those angel faces smile,
Which I have loved long since, and lost awhile.

JOHN HENRY NEWMAN, 1801-90

A FAMOUS HYMN BY A PROSELYTE OF ROME

WHEN the children of Israel were about to resume the march from Mount Sinai and Moses had received the command to lead the people into the unknown wilderness, we are told in the Book of Exodus that Moses hesitated.

"See," said the great leader, "Thou sayest unto me, 'Bring up this people': and Thou hast not let me know whom Thou wilt send with me." And God answered, "My presence shall go with thee, and I will give thee rest."

It was the sublime thought of the guiding presence of God that gave to John Henry Newman the inspiration for "Lead, kindly Light."

There was much of tragedy in the strange life of Newman. He was born in London, the son of a banker, February 21, 1801. It is said that he was extremely superstitious as a boy, and that he would cross himself, after the custom of Roman Catholics, whenever he entered a dark place. He also came to the conclusion that it was the will of God that he should never marry.

Newman graduated from Trinity College, Oxford, at the age of nineteen, and four years later was ordained by the Church of England. He soon began to be attracted by Roman Catholic teachings and to associate with leaders of that communion. In 1833 he was in poor health, and determined to go to Italy. This was the year of the famous Oxford Movement, which was destined to carry so many high Anglicans into the Roman communion. While in Rome Newman was brought still further under the influence of the Romanists, who lost no opportunity to take advantage of his perplexed state of mind. Leaving Rome, he went down to Sicily, where he was stricken with fever and was near death. After his recovery, his one thought was to return to his native shores. He writes:

"I was aching to get home; yet for want of a vessel was kept at Palermo for three weeks. At last I got an orange-boat bound for Marseilles. We were becalmed a whole week on the Mediterranean Sea. Then it was (June 16, 1833) that I wrote the lines: 'Lead, kindly Light.'"

The hymn, therefore, may be said to be the work of a man who found himself in deep mental, physical, and spiritual distress. Newman was greatly dissatisfied with conditions within his own Church. In his perplexity he scarcely knew where to turn, but he had no intention at this time, as he himself states, to forsake the Church of England for the Roman Catholic communion. This step was not taken by him until in 1855.

"Lead, kindly Light" was published for the first time in *"The British Magazine,* in March, 1834. It bore the title, "Faith—Heavenly Leadings." Two years later he printed it with the title, "Light in the Darkness," and the motto, "Unto the godly there ariseth up light in the darkness." At a later date he published it under the title, "The Pillar of the Cloud."

Newman ascribed its popularity as a hymn to the appealing tune written for it in 1865 by John B. Dykes. As to its poetic qualities there has been the widest divergence of opinion. While one critic has called it "one of the outstanding lyrics of the nineteenth century," William T. Stead observes, caustically, that "It is somewhat hard for the staunch Protestant to wax enthusiastic over the invocation of a 'Kindly Light' which led the author straight into the arms of the Scarlet Woman of the Seven Hills."

The hymn has often been attacked on the ground that it is not definitely Christian in character. In this respect it is similar to Mrs. Adams' famous hymn, "Nearer, my God, to Thee." When the Parliament of Religions convened in Chicago a few years ago, Newman's hymn was the only one sung by representatives of all creeds from every part of the world. Bishop Bickersteth of England, feeling the need of a Christian note in the hymn, added the following stanza:

> Meantime along the narrow rugged path
> Thyself hast trod,
> Lead, Saviour, lead me home in childlike faith,
> Home to my God
> To rest for ever after earthly strife
> In the calm light of everlasting life.

This was done, said Bishop Bickersteth, "from a deep conviction that the heart of the belated pilgrim can only find rest in the Light of Light." The additional stanza, however, has not come into general use.

340

Many interpretations have been given to the closing lines,

> And with the morn those angel faces smile,
> Which I have loved long since, and lost awhile.

Some have believed that Newman by "angel faces" had in mind loved ones lost through death. Yet others are convinced that the author had reference to actual visions of angels said to have come to him in youth, and the loss of which greatly grieved him in later life. The author himself, in a letter written January 18, 1879, refused to throw further light on the lines, pleading that he had forgotten the meaning he had in mind when the hymn was written forty-six years before.

Newman is also the author of "Praise to the Holiest in the height," as well as the translator of "Now that the daystar glimmers bright," a Latin hymn of the 5th century.

Rome honored its distinguished proselyte by making him a cardinal. It is said, however, that Newman was never again a happy man after having surrendered the faith of his fathers. He died at Birmingham, England, August 11, 1890, at the age of eighty-nine years.

A disciple of Newman's, Frederick William Faber, may be mentioned in this connection, for the lives of the two men were strangely intertwined. Faber, who was the son of an English clergyman, was born at Yorkshire, June 28, 1814. He was graduated from Oxford in 1836, and became a minister of the Anglican Church at Elton in 1843.

While at Oxford he came under the influence of the Oxford Movement and formed a deep attachment for Newman. It was inevitable, therefore, that he too should be carried into the Roman Church, which communion he joined in 1846. For some years he labored with Newman in the Catholic church of St. Philip Neri in London. He died in 1863 at the age of forty-nine years.

Faber wrote a large number of hymns, many of them before his desertion to the Church of Rome. Others, written after his defection, containing eulogies of Mary and petitions addressed to the saints, have been purged by hymnal editors in order to make them suitable for Protestant hymnbooks. His inordinate use of the word "sweet" and his familiar manner of addressing Christ as "sweet Saviour" has called down harsh criticism on his hymns as sentimental and effeminate.

However, such hymns of Faber's as "There's a wideness in God's mercy," "Hark, hark, my soul! angelic songs are swelling," "O Saviour, bless us ere we go," "O Paradise, O Paradise," "O come and mourn with me awhile," "Most ancient of all mysteries," "My God, how wonderful Thou art," and "Faith of our fathers, living still" have probably found a permanent place in the hymnbooks of the Church Universal, and will be loved and cherished both for their devotional spirit and their poetic beauty.

Faber wrote "Faith of our fathers" after his defection to the Church of Rome. In its original form the author expressed the hope that England would be brought back to the papal fold. The opening lines, as Faber wrote them, were:

> Faith of our fathers! Mary's prayers
> Shall win our country back to thee.

Matthew Bridges was another distinguished proselyte of Rome, and this despite the fact that in earlier years he wrote a book entitled *The Roman Empire under Constantine the Great,* the avowed purpose of which, as he himself stated, was "to examine the real origin of certain papal superstitions whose antiquity has been so often urged against Protestants, with no little triumph and presumption." But Bridges was a man of strange contradictions, and the influence of John Henry Newman proved too strong, and in 1848 he took the fateful step. The latter years of his life were spent in Canada, where he died in 1894.

Bridges was richly endowed as a poet and writer. In 1847 he published *Hymns of the Heart* and followed this in 1852 with a second collection of hymns titled *In the Passion of Jesus.* A number of splendid hymns have been derived from these volumes, including such classics as "Behold the Lamb of God," "O God, accept my heart this day," and "Crown Him with many crowns."

In the same category as Faber and Bridges was Henry Collins, an Oxford graduate who was ordained by the Church of England in 1853 but who four years later went over to the Church of Rome. Becoming a Trappist monk, he spent many years as chaplain to nuns of the Cistercian Order at Staplehill, Dorset. He is the author of two hymns, one of which, "Jesus, my Lord, my God, my all," has come into widespread use.

Another disciple of Newman who followed him into the Church of Rome was Frederick Oakely, who won fame chiefly by his English translation of the famous Latin hymn, *Adeste fideles*. His rendering, beginning with "O come, all ye faithful," has found almost universal acceptance throughout the English-speaking world. The son of Charles Oakeley, at one time governor of Madras, Frederick received his education at Oxford and was ordained as a minister of the Church of England. While serving Margaret Chapel in London, he became deeply interested in the Oxford Movement and soon introduced an ultra-ritualistic service. He also issued a pamphlet in which he asserted his right "to hold, as distinct from teaching, all Roman doctrine."

This led to a suspension of his license to preach until he would agree to retract his errors. Instead of so doing, he resigned all appointments in the Church of England and joined Newman. When the new Roman hierarchy was established in England in 1852, he was made a canon of Westminster.

Yet another hymn-writer of the Church of England who forsook his Church to become a member of the Roman communion was Robert Stephen Hawker. Educated at Oxford, Hawker in 1834 became vicar of Morwenstow in Cornwall. An eccentric individual, but highly gifted, he was the author of two volumes of poetry, including a number of hymns for children. Two of these are "Sing to the Lord the children's hymn" and "Welcome, that star in Judah's sky." He was received into the Church of Rome on his deathbed. He died the following day, on August 15, 1873.

The Name Above All Names

Jesus, Name all names above;
 Jesus, best and dearest;
Jesus fount of perfect love,
 Holiest, tenderest, nearest;
Thou the source of grace completest,
 Thou the purest, Thou the sweetest,
Thou the well of power divine,
 Make me, keep me, seal me Thine!

Jesus, crowned with bitter thorn,
 By mankind forsaken,
Jesus, who through scourge and scorn
 Held Thy faith unshaken,
Jesus, clad in purple raiment,
 For man's evils making payment:
Let not all Thy woe and pain,
 Let not Calvary be in vain!

Jesus, open me the gate
 That of old he entered
Who, in that most lost estate,
 Wholly on Thee ventured;
Jesus, leave me not to languish:
 Helpless, hopeless, full of anguish!
Jesus, let me hear Thee say,
 "Thou shalt be with me today!"

THEOCTISTUS OF THE STUDIUM, cir. 890
Tr. JOHN MASON NEALE, 1818-66a.

THE OXFORD MOVEMENT AND ANCIENT HYMNS

ALMOST a century and a half ago—in the year 1818, to be exact—there was born in the great city of London a child who was destined to become an unusual scholar. He was christened John Mason Neale, a name that may be found today on many pages of the world's best hymnbooks.

When he was only five years old, John's father died, and, like so many other men who have achieved fame, he received the greater part of his elementary training from a gifted mother.

At Cambridge University, which he entered at an early age, he soon became a brilliant student, leading his classes and winning numerous prizes. After his graduation he was ordained by the Church of England.

In two previous chapters—on John Keble and John Henry Newman—we have made reference to the strange spiritual phenomenon known as the Oxford Movement, which carried so many gifted scholars out of the Church of England and into the waiting arms of Rome. Neale was one of those who was caught up by the movement, but fortunately, like Keble, remained faithful to his own Church to the end of life.

The causes behind the Oxford Movement were deep and profound. The Church of England was spiritually sick, perilously nigh unto death. Headmaster Thomas Arnold of Rugby has been quoted as saying that nothing could save the Established Church as it was then constituted.

It was an age of great social and political unrest, brought on largely by the poverty and economic distress of the masses. The industrial revolution precipitated by the age of the steam machine had thrown multitudes out of work, and riots flared in all parts of England. Soon the Church became the scapegoat in the eyes of a large segment of the population, who saw in it a symbol of intrenched vested interests. The defection from the Established Church to the Dissenters at this time was very great, and it was estimated that by

1800 one-fourth of the people of England had severed their connection with it. Nevertheless they were compelled to continue paying taxes for its support.

Enemies of the Church charged the clergy with worldliness and lack of spirituality. They resented the Church's hostility to social and political reforms which were designed to grant the new industrial cities proper representation in Parliament, to repeal inhuman criminal laws, to reduce the working hours of women and children, and to abolish the slave trade. They also were angered by the refusal of the Church to give up any of its special privileges, or to reduce the number of high ecclesiastical dignitaries who were drawing enormous salaries while the people starved.

Although the Oxford Movement, in its initial phases, sought to revitalize the Church spiritually, it gradually developed a definite "high church" trend with almost exclusive emphasis on liturgical practices carried over from the Church of Rome. It also strongly insisted on maintaining the privileged position of the Church. It vigorously defended the essential divine character of the episcopacy, which it claimed has been preserved by "Apostolic Succession" from the Apostle Peter, the alleged first bishop of Rome, and through him to all succeeding popes and bishops in an unbroken line to the present. This, Newman and his followers insisted, was the only source and basis for a continuing revelation of truth and of religious authority.

The whole tendency of the movement was to exalt the clergy as a sacerdotal class and to bring the laity under the rule of the priesthood. Many of its leaders also cherished the idea of a reunion of all Christendom in one Church, presumably under the authority of the pope. The outcome was inevitably disastrous. Many of the leaders, to the consternation of all England, went over to Rome, and those who remained in the Church of England chose to be known as a "high church" party who called themselves Anglican Catholics.

The movement, however, was not without some happier consequences for which all Christians will have reason to be forever grateful. For one thing, because of the stimulus it gave to research into Greek and Latin liturgy and hymnody, it may be said to have completely revolutionized Christian worship in England. It created a deeper reverence for the sanctuary, it enriched and embellished every part of its service, it raised the standards of church music, and, above all, it finally broke the tyrannical rule of psalmody which a Calvinistic

346

Puritanism had imposed on the worship life of the English people. The publication in 1861 of the great hymnal, *Hymns Ancient and Modern,* was an epoch-making event for the whole Church and particularly for the English-speaking world. For the first time in its history, England had an ecumenical hymnbook to take the place of the outmoded *Metrical Psalter.*

More than that, the Oxford Movement sent its poets and scholars back to those pristine springs from which flowed the first offerings of praise to the Triune God, namely the Greek and Latin liturgies and lyrics, to recover some of their choicest hymns and to give them to the Christian world in the most widely used of all modern languages.

During the first sixteen years of the Oxford Movement its literary leaders, such as Neale, Edward Caswell and John Chandler, wrote very few original hymns, but devoted their efforts almost exclusively to the work of translating these ancient classics.

Neale's interest in the early hymns of the Christian Church led him to the morning lands of history, particularly Greece. To him, more than any one else, we owe some of the most successful translations from the classical languages. By his sojourn in eastern lands, he seems to have been enabled particularly to catch the spirit of the Greek hymns, and often his translations read almost like original poems. For instance, in order to do justice to the famous Easter hymn of John of Damascus, written some time during the eighth century, Neale celebrated Easter in Athens and heard the "glorious old hymn of victory," as he called it, sung by a great throng of worshipers at midnight. The result is his sublime translation:

> The Day of Resurrection!
>   Earth, tell it out abroad!
> The Passover of gladness,
>   The Passover of God!
> From death to life eternal,
>   From earth unto the sky,
> Our Christ hath brought us over,
>   With hymns of victory.

Another very famous translation from the Greek by Neale is the hymn:

> Art thou weary, art thou languid,
>   Art thou sore distressed?
> "Come to me," saith One, "and, coming,
>   Be at rest."

347

This hymn is often regarded as an original by Neale, but the author was St. Stephen the Sabaite, an 8th century monk who spent his life in the monastery of St. Sabas, near Bethlehem.

Neale was equally successful in the translation of ancient Latin hymns. Perhaps the most notable is his rendering of Bernard of Cluny's immortal hymn:

> Jerusalem, the golden,
>   With milk and honey blest,
> Beneath thy contemplation
>   Sink heart and voice oppressed:
> I know not, O I know not
>   What joys await us there,
> What radiancy of glory,
>   What light beyond compare.

So facile was Neale in the art of writing either English or Latin verse, that he often astounded his friends. It is said that on one occasion John Keble, author of *The Christian Year,* was a visitor in Neale's home. Absenting himself from the room for a few minutes, Neale returned shortly and exclaimed: "I thought, Keble, that all your poems in *The Christian Year* were original; but one of them, at least, seems to be a translation." Thereupon he handed Keble, to the latter's amazement, a very fine Latin rendering of one of Keble's own poems. He had made the translation during his absence from the room.

Neale's translations are too numerous to give a complete list. Certainly our hymnals have been marvelously enriched by such hymns as "Jesus, Name all names above," "O come, O come, Emmanuel," "Good Christian men, rejoice," "All glory, laud and honor," "The day is past and over," "Of the Father's love begotten," and scores of others that might be mentioned.

But Neale did not confine himself to translations. He also is the author of a number of splendid original hymns. He was particularly fond of writing hymns for holy days and festivals of the Church Year. "O very God of very God," for Advent; "O Thou, who by a star didst guide," for Epiphany, and "Blessed Saviour, who hast taught me," for confirmation, are among these.

Because of his "high church" tendencies, as well as his interest in the Oxford Movement, Neale was suspected by some of leaning toward the Church of Rome. However, there is nothing of Roman error to be found in his hymns. The evangelical note rings pure and clear, and for this reason they will no doubt continue to be loved and sung through centuries yet to come. Neale died August 6, 1866, at the age of forty-eight years, trusting in the atoning blood of Christ, and with the glorious assurance expressed in his version of St. Stephen's hymn:

> If I still hold closely to Him,
>   What hath He at last?
> "Sorrow vanquished, labor ended,
>   Jordan passed."
>
> If I ask Him to receive me,
>   Will He say me nay?
> "Not till earth and not till heaven
>   Pass away."

Another Englishman who gained renown by translations of the old classical hymns of the Church was Edward Caswall. He was a contemporary of Neale, and, like the latter, came under the influence of the Oxford Movement. While Neale, however, remained faithful to his own communion, Caswall turned Romanist. He was made a priest in the Congregation of the Oratory, which Cardinal Newman had established in Birmingham, a position he continued to hold until his death in 1878.

Two of the most beautiful hymns in the English language— "Jesus, the very thought of Thee" and "O Jesus, King most wonderful"—were derived by Caswall from the famous Latin poem, *De Nomine Jesu,* by Bernard of Clairvaux. Of the former hymn Dr. Robinson has said: "One might call this poem the finest in the world and still be within the limits of all extravagance."

Among other fine translations from the Latin by Caswall are "Hark! a thrilling voice is sounding" and "Glory be to Jesus." He also has given us some hymns from the German.

Another of the successful translators of classical hymns was John Chandler, who in 1837 published a volume entitled *Hymns of the Primitive Church.* One of his best translations is "O Christ, our hope, our heart's desire," a Latin hymn of the 8th century. It is said that Chandler mistook the *Paris Breviary* for an ancient collection of Latin hymns. Many of the hymns which he designated as "primitive," such as "Conquering kings their titles take," "The advent of our God" and "On Jordan's banks the Baptist's cry," were actually written in the 18th century. Chandler, who succeeded his father as Anglican vicar of Witley, died in 1876.

A Woman's Gift to the Church

Nearer, my God, to Thee,
Nearer to Thee,
E'en though it be a cross
That raiseth me,
Still all my song shall be,
Nearer, my God, to Thee,
Nearer to Thee.

Though, like a wanderer,
The sun gone down,
Darkness be over me,
My rest a stone,
Yet in my dreams I'd be
Nearer, my God, to Thee,
Nearer to Thee.

Then let my way appear
Steps unto heaven;
All that Thou sendest me
In mercy given;
Angels to beckon me
Nearer, my God, to Thee,
Nearer to Thee.

Then with my waking thoughts,
Bright with Thy praise,
Out of my stony griefs
Bethel I'll raise,
So by my woes to be
Nearer, my God, to Thee,
Nearer to Thee.

Or, if on joyful wing,
Cleaving the sky,
Sun, moon, and stars forgot,
Upwards I fly;
Still all my song shall be,
Nearer, my God to Thee,
Nearer to Thee.

SARAH FLOWER ADAMS, 1805-48

350

SARAH ADAMS AND THE RISE OF WOMEN HYMN-WRITERS

NINETEENTH century hymnody was characterized by an extraordinary number of women hymn-writers. It is significant that this development came, as we have noted in a previous chapter, with the great spiritual revivals which stirred evangelical Europe and America from 1800 to 1875. It was also coincident with the general movement that resulted in the enlargement of women's influence and activity in all spheres of human endeavor.

Dr. Breed has suggested that the remarkable increase in women hymnists, as well as the unusual number of hymn translations, may be indicative of a period of decadence in sacred song. While this was probably true of the latter half of the 19th century, which saw the rise of the so-called "Gospel song," we must cheerfully recognize the fact that such women as Charlotte Elliott, Sarah Adams, Cecil Alexander and Frances Havergal in England and Mary Lathbury, Anna Warner, Catherine Esling, Harriet Beecher Stowe, Phoebe Cary, Elizabeth Prentiss and Fanny Crosby in America have made a genuine contribution to the treasure-store of Christian hymns. Indeed, the hymnody of the Church would have been immeasurably poorer had these consecrated women failed to make use of their heaven-born talent.

And, although we must deplore the apparent fact that "original utterance in sacred song is departing from the Church," we must be forever grateful to such gifted women as Catherine Winkworth, the Borthwick sisters and other English women, who, through their excellent translations, gave to the English-speaking world some of the finest gems in German hymnody.

Charlotte Elliott was the forerunner of this long line of women hymnists. Then came Sarah Flower Adams, the writer of "Nearer, my God, to Thee," one of the greatest sacred lyrics ever given to the Church, and certainly one of the noblest ever written by a woman.

Sarah Flower was born at Harlow, England, February 22, 1805, the daughter of Benjamin Flower, editor of the *Cambridge Intelligencer*. The mother died when Sarah was only five years old. A sister,

Eliza, was a gifted musician, while Sarah early showed talent along literary lines. In later years Eliza wrote music for the hymns of her sister.

Sarah was fond of the stage. She believed that it, as well as the pulpit, could be made to teach great moral truths. Her dreams of becoming an actress, however, never materialized because of poor health. In 1834 she became the wife of John Bridges Adams, a civil engineer, after which she made her home in London. Her health was seriously impaired through caring for her sister, who died a consumptive in 1846, and Sarah survived her by less than two years.

Her great hymn was written in 1840. It was published the following year in a volume of hymns and anthems edited by her pastor, William Johnson Fox. This man was a Unitarian, and for this reason Mrs. Adams has also been classified with that sect. It is said, however, that she became a Baptist near the close of her life. Other hymns written by her indicate that she had arrived at a living faith in Christ. Perhaps the many trials that came to her proved in the end to be the means of bringing her to the Saviour. And thus was fulfilled in her own life the beautiful lines:

> E'en though it be a cross
> That raiseth me.

"Nearer, my God, to Thee" has probably aroused more discussion than any other hymn. Because it is based entirely on the story of Jacob at Bethel and omits reference to Christ, it has been called more Unitarian than Christian. Many efforts have been made, but without much success, to write a substitute hymn with a definite Christian note. In 1864 Bishop How of London wrote a hymn, the first stanza of which reads:

> Nearer, O God, to Thee!
> Hear Thou our prayer;
> E'en though a heavy cross
> Fainting we bear.
> Still all our prayer shall be
> Nearer, O God, to Thee,
> Nearer to Thee!

Prof. Henry Eyster Jacobs of Philadelphia, in 1887, also wrote a version:

> Nearer, my God, to Thee,
> Nearer to Thee!
> Through Word and Sacrament
> Thou com'st to me.

Thy grace is ever near,
Thy Spirit ever here
  Drawing to Thee.

Ages on ages rolled,
    Ere earth appeared,
Yet Thine unmeasured love
    The way prepared;
Long hast Thou yearned for me
That I might nearer be,
    Nearer to Thee!

Thou, Christ, hast come to earth,
    My sin to bear,
My every wound to heal,
    My pain to share.
"God in the flesh" for me
Now brings me nearer Thee,
    Nearer to Thee!

Mrs. Adams' hymn was a favorite of William McKinley, the martyred president. When he was dying, his attending physician heard him murmur, " 'Nearer, my God, to Thee, E'en though it be a cross,' has been my constant prayer."

A Hymn Written in the Shadows

Abide with me! fast falls the eventide;
The darkness deepens, Lord, with me abide!
When other helpers fail and comforts flee,
Help of the helpless, O abide with me!

Swift to its close ebbs out life's little day;
Earth's joys grow dim, its glories pass away;
Change and decay in all around I see;
O Thou who changest not, abide with me!

I need Thy presence every passing hour;
What but Thy grace can foil the tempter's power?
Who like Thyself my guide and stay can be?
Through cloud and sunshine, O abide with me!

I fear no foe, with Thee at hand to bless;
Ills have no weight, and tears no bitterness.
Where is death's sting? Where, grave, thy victory?
I triumph still, if Thou abide with me!

Hold Thou Thy Cross before my closing eyes,
Shine through the gloom, and point me to the skies;
Heaven's morning breaks, and earth's vain shadows flee;
In life, in death, O Lord, abide with me.

HENRY FRANCIS LYTE, 1793-1847

HENRY FRANCIS LYTE AND HIS SWAN SONG

MANY a man who has labored in obscure places, practically unnoticed and unpraised by his own generation, has achieved a fame after his death that grows in magnitude with the passing years.

When Henry Francis Lyte died in 1847, he was little known beyond his humble seashore parish at Lower Brixham, England; but today, wherever his beautiful hymns are sung he is gratefully remembered throughout the Christian world as the man who wrote "Abide with me."

In response to a questionnaire sent to American readers some years ago by *The Etude,* a musical magazine, 7,500 out of nearly 32,000 persons who replied named "Abide with me" as their favorite hymn. It easily took first rank, displacing such older favorites as "Rock of Ages" and "Jesus, Lover of my soul."

Innumerable Christians have sung this hymn at the close of vespers, and a settled peace has come into their hearts as they have sensed the nearness of Him who said, "And lo! I am with you always." Yet, this is not in reality an evening hymn. Its theme is the evening of life, and it was written when Lyte felt the shadows gathering about his own head. We catch his meaning in the second stanza:

Swift to its close ebbs out life's little day;
Earth's joys grow dim, its glories pass away.

Lyte was always frail in health. He was born in Scotland, June 1, 1793, and was early left an orphan. Nevertheless, despite the handicap of poverty, he struggled through college, and on three occasions won prizes in poetry.

His first ambition was to become a physician, but during college days he determined to enter the ministry. The death of a young friend, a brother clergyman, brought about a profound change in the spiritual life of Lyte. Called to the bedside of his friend to give him consolation, he discovered to his sorrow that both he and the dying man were blind guides who were still groping for light. Through a prayerful search of the Scriptures, however, they both came to a firm faith in Christ. Lyte wrote of his friend:

"He died happy under the belief that though he had deeply erred, there was *One* whose death and sufferings would atone for his delinquencies, and that he was forgiven and accepted for His sake."

Concerning the change that came into his own life, he added: "I was greatly affected by the whole matter, and brought to look at life and its issue with a different eye than before; and I began to study my Bible and preach in another manner than I had previously done."

For nearly twenty-five years after this incident Lyte labored among humble fisherfolk and sailors of the parish at Lower Brixham, but his consuming spiritual fervor led him to overtax his physical powers, and from time to time he was obliged to spend the winters in more friendly climes.

In the autumn of 1847 he wrote a friend that the swallows were flying southward, and he observed, "They are inviting me to accompany them; and yet alas; while I am talking of flying, I am just able to crawl."

The Sunday for his farewell service came. His family and friends admonished him not to preach a sermon, but the conscientious minister insisted. "It is better," he said, "to *wear* out than to *rust* out."

He did preach, and the hearts of his hearers were full that day, for they seemed to realize that it was probably the last time they would hear him. The faithful pastor, too, seemed to have a premonition that it would be his last message. The service closed with the Lord's Supper, administered by Lyte.

"Though necessarily much exhausted by the exertion and excitement of this effort," his daughter afterward wrote, "yet his friends had no reason to believe that it had been hurtful to him."

This was September 4, 1847. That afternoon he walked out along the shore to watch the sun as it was setting in a glory of crimson and gold. It was a peaceful, beautiful Sunday evening. Returning to his home, he shut himself up in his study for the brief space of an hour, and when he came out, he handed a near relative the manuscript containing the famous hymn, "Abide with me." He also had composed a tune of his own for the words, but this never came into general use.

During the following week Lyte left his beloved England for Italy. However, he got no farther than Nice, in France, where he was obliged to discontinue his journey. Here he passed away November 20 of the same year. His last words were, "Joy! Peace!" and then he fell asleep.

A little cross marks his grave in the English cemetery at Nice, for he was buried there. Every year hundreds of pilgrims visit his grave and many tell touching stories of how Lyte's hymn brought them to faith in Christ Jesus.

It was Lyte's life-long wish that he might leave behind him such a hymn as this. In an earlier poem he had voiced the longing that he might write

> Some simple strain, some spirit-moving lay,
> Some sparklet of the soul that still might live
> When I was passed to clay. . . .

> O Thou! whose touch can lend
> Life to the dead, Thy quick'ning grace supply,
> And grant me, swanlike, my last breath to spend
> In song that may not die!

His prayer was fulfilled. As long as men shall worship the crucified and risen Lord, so long will they continue to sing the sad and beautiful words of Lyte's swan song.

In Lyte we have a hymn-writer of the first rank. Indeed, he is comparable to any of England's greatest hymnists, not excepting Watts, Wesley or Montgomery. His hymns are real lyrics, Scriptural in language, rich in imagery, and exalted in poetic conception. "In no other author," says an eminent authority, "is poetry and religion more exquisitely united."

Aside from the sublime hymn we have mentioned, Lyte has given to the Church such noble lyrics as "Jesus, I my cross have taken," "Pleasant are Thy courts above," "Praise, my soul, the King of heaven," "God of mercy, God of grace," "My spirit on Thy care," "As pants the hart for cooling streams" and "O that the Lord's salvation." The latter hymn is one of the few ever written that voice a prayer for the salvation of Israel.

Another clergyman hymn-writer of this period was Samuel John Stone, who spent most of his life ministering to the poor and underprivileged populace in the East End of London. Born in Whitmore, Staffordshire, in 1839, he became, following his graduation from Oxford, his father's curate at St. Paul's, Haggerston, London. Later he succeeded him as rector of the parish. After twenty years, he changed his field of labor to All-Hallows-on-the-Wall, London, another parish consisting of impoverished people, where, it has been said, "He created a beautiful place of worship for the humble folk, and made it a center of light in the dark places."

The one hymn for which Stone will always be gratefully remembered is "The Church's one foundation," which was written in the midst of a controversy between Bishop Gray of Capetown and Bishop Colenso of Natal in which the former had accused the latter of liberal and heretical tendencies in an expository work on *The Pentateuch*. Stone believed that the Church was in danger of schism as a result of Colenso's writings, and wrote his hymn in support of Gray's position. A second hymn by Stone that is found in many hymnals is a prayer of repentance, "Weary of earth, and laden with my sin." It was written to illustrate the clause in the Apostles' Creed, "I believe in the forgiveness of sins." Stone passed away in 1900.

Another outstanding hymnist of this period was John Samuel Bewley Monsell, from whom we have received such hymns as "Fight the good fight with all thy might," "On our way rejoicing," "Lord of the living harvest," "Holy offerings, rich and rare," and "O worship the Lord in the beauty of holiness."

Monsell, the son of the Archdeacon of Londonderry, was born in 1811, and after his graduation from Trinity College, Dublin, took holy orders in 1834, becoming chaplain to Bishop Mant. Later he became rector of St. Nicholas, Guildford, England. His home life at this place has been described as "full of the beauty of holiness, with genial brightness and gaiety playing like sunshine over all the troubles of life." His life had a tragic ending in 1875 when he fell from the roof of his church while supervising repairs.

While these clerics were inditing their hymns, two British laymen were also writing sacred verse. One was Bernard Barton, who came to be known as the "Quaker Poet" of England; the other was James Edmeston, an eminent London architect and surveyor.

Barton was in many respects an unusual person. Although he never rose above the position of a bank clerk, in which vocation he served faithfully at Woodbridge for forty years, he was a man of letters and attracted many literary lights of his day by his poetry, including Charles Lamb, Southey, Scott and Byron. Late in life he was given a government pension of 100 pounds per year on the recommendation of Sir Robert Peel. He passed away at Woodbridge in 1849.

It is Barton from whom we have received the hymn, "Walk in the light, so shalt thou know" and "Lamp of our feet, whereby we trace."

Edmeston, the other layman hymnist, was the author of no less than two thousand hymns! Not many of them have survived, but our Christian hymnbooks are the richer for the vesper song,

Saviour, breathe an evening blessing,
    Ere repose our spirits seal;
Sin and want we come confessing;
    Thou canst save, and Thou canst heal.

Another of Edmeston's well-known hymns is "Lead us, heavenly Father, lead us." It is said that he was an ardent lover of children and that he visited the London Orphan Asylum regularly. It was there he got the inspiration for many of his children's hymns. One of his diversions was to write a new hymn every Sunday, reading it at family worship on the day it was composed. He died at the age of 76 in 1867.

That Sweet Story of Old

I think, when I read that sweet story of old,
  When Jesus was here among men,
How He called little children as lambs to His fold,
  I should like to have been with them then.

I wish that His hand had been placed on my head,
  That His arm had been thrown around me,
And that I might have seen His kind look when He said,
  "Let the little ones come unto Me."

Yet still to His footstool in prayer I may go,
  And ask for a share in His love;
And if I now earnestly seek Him below,
  I shall see Him and hear Him above.

In that beautiful place He has gone to prepare
  For all who are washed and forgiven;
Full many dear children are gathering there,
  "For of such is the kingdom of heaven."

But thousands and thousands who wander and fall
  Never heard of that heavenly home;
I should like them to know there is room for them all,
  And that Jesus has bid them to come.

I long for the joy of that glorious time,
  The sweetest and brightest and best,
When the dear little children of every clime
  Shall crowd to His arms and be blest.

JEMIMA LUKE, 1813-1906

A HYMN WRITTEN IN A STAGE-COACH

SOMEONE has said, "Let me write the songs of a nation, and I care not who may write its laws." It is a wise saying; for who can estimate the influence of the songs we sing, especially the songs we sing in childhood? Certainly there is no more effective way of instilling Christian truths into the hearts of children than through the instrumentality of hymns.

When Jemima Luke sat in an English stage-coach in 1841 composing the lines of a little poem that had been ringing in her mind, she could hardly have known that her labor of love would gladden the hearts of thousands of children in the years to come. But that is how the hymn, "I think when I read that sweet story of old," had its birth, and surely there are few lyrics that are more deeply cherished by childish hearts today than this one.

The poet's maiden name was Jemima Thompson. Her father was a missionary enthusiast, and she herself was filled with ardent zeal for the cause of missions. That accounts for the missionary note heard in her hymn.

Jemima started writing at the age of thirteen, when she made anonymous contributions to *The Juvenile Magazine*. In later years, after she had become a teacher, it happened that she visited a school where she heard the children singing a fine old marching song.

"What a lovely children's hymn it would make," she mused, "if only that tune had suitable religious words.'

She hunted through many books for the words she desired, but could find none that satisfied her. Some time later, as she was riding in a stage-coach with nothing to occupy her, she thought of the tune again. Taking an old envelope from her pocket, she recorded on the back of it the words that have come to be loved on both sides of the Atlantic.

When she returned home, she taught the words and the melody to her Sunday school class. Her father, who was superintendent of the school, chanced to hear them one day.

"Where did that hymn come from?" he asked.

"Jemima made it!" was the proud answer of the youngsters.

The last stanza of the hymn, which begins with the words, "But thousands and thousands who wander and fall," was added subsequently by the author, who desired to make it suitable for missionary gatherings. Her interest in foreign missions continued unabated throughout life. At one time she was accepted as a missionary to the women of India, but poor health prevented her from carrying out her purpose. However, for several years she edited *The Missionary Repository,* the first missionary magazine in England for children, and numbered among her contributors such famous missionaries as David Livingstone, Robert Moffatt and James Montgomery.

In 1843 she married a minister, Samuel Luke. After his death in 1868 she devoted much of her time in promoting the erection of parsonages in parishes that were too poor to provide them for their pastors.

When an international convention of the Christian Endeavor Society was held in Baltimore in 1904, Mrs. Luke sent the following message to the young people:

"Dear children, you will be men and women soon, and it is for you and the children of England to carry the message of a Saviour's love to every nation of this sin-stricken world. It is a blessed message to carry, and it is a happy work to do. The Lord make you ever faithful to Him, and unspeakably happy in His service! I came to Him at ten years of age, and at ninety-one can testify to His care and faithfulness."

At the time Jemima Luke was writing her famous hymn for her Sunday school class another English woman was also composing songs for children. She was Dorothy Ann Thrupp, who began her career by contributing poems to two London religious weeklies under the pen-name of "Iota." In 1830 she edited a songbook bearing the title, *Hymns for the Young.* Miss Thrupp is credited with the authorship of a large number of the hymns which appeared in this volume, although all were printed anonymously. Most of her hymns have been forgotten, but tens of thousands of children throughout the world will bless her memory when they sing what is undoubtedly one of the loveliest children's lyrics ever written:

> Saviour, like a shepherd lead us,
>   Much we need Thy tender care;
> In Thy pleasant pastures feed us,

For our use Thy folds prepare:
Blessed Jesus, blessed Jesus,
Thou hast bought us; Thine we are.

Here we would also mention Adelaide Ann Procter, the writer of another beautiful hymn usually sung by children, "My God, I thank Thee, who hast made the earth so bright." Miss Procter was the daughter of Bryan Waller Procter, a barrister of London who himself was highly regarded as a poet and dramatist of his day, and who numbered among his close friends such literary geniuses as Dickens, Charles Lamb and Leigh Hunt.

Born in London in 1825, Adelaide very early began to write verse. Her first poems were sent anonymously to Dickens as editor of *Household Words,* and it was not until he had been publishing them for two years that he learned from her mother who the real writer was. Two volumes of verse came from her pen, and some of her songs became immensely popular. One of these was "The Lost Chord." She died at the early age of 39 years after having given much of her time and strength to works of benevolence. Dickens pays her this rare tribute:

"Now it was the visitation of the sick that had possession of her; now it was the sheltering of the homeless; now it was the elementary teaching of the densely ignorant; now it was the raising up of those who had wandered and got trodden underfoot; now it was the wider employment of her own sex in the general business of life; now it was all these things at once. Perfectly unselfish, swift to sympathize and eager to relieve, she wrought at such designs with a flushed earnestness that disregarded season, weather, time of day or night, food, rest."

Another woman hymn-writer of this period whose name will be gratefully remembered is Anna Letitia Waring, from whom we have received the beautiful lyric, "In heavenly love abiding." Miss Waring, who was born at Plas-y-Velin, England, in 1823, belonged originally to the Society of Friends, but eventually joined the Church of England because of her desire to receive the sacrament. She was an assiduous student, and mastered Hebrew in order to study Old Testament poetry in the original. In later life she spent much time in visiting the prisons in Bristol. James Martineau at one time acknowledged a "long-standing spiritual obligation" to her. She died in 1910.

363

Redemption's Story in Song

There is a green hill far away,
 Without a city wall,
Where the dear Lord was crucified,
 Who died to save us all.

We may not know, we cannot tell,
 What pains He had to bear,
But we believe it was for us
 He hung and suffered there.

He died that we might be forgiven,
 He died to make us good;
That we might go at last to heaven,
 Saved by His precious Blood.

There was no other good enough
 To pay the price of sin;
He only could unlock the gate
 Of heaven, and let us in.

O dearly, dearly has He loved,
 And we must love Him too,
And trust in His redeeming blood,
 And try His works to do.

CECIL FRANCES ALEXANDER, 1823-95

AN ARCHBISHOP'S WIFE WHO WROTE HYMNS

SHORTLY before the death in 1911 of Archbishop William Alexander, primate of the Anglican Church in Ireland, he remarked that he would be chiefly remembered as the husband of the woman who wrote "The roseate hues of early dawn" and "There is a green hill far away."

The humble prelate was right. Although he occupied an exalted position in the Church less than half a century ago, few people today are familiar with his name. But who has not heard the name of Cecil Frances Humphreys Alexander, who, in spite of multitudinous duties as wife and mother, found time to be a parish worker among the poor and to write hymns that shall never die?

When Cecil Frances was only a little girl, she began to reveal poetic talent. Because her father was an officer in the Royal Marines and rather a stern man, she was not sure that he would be pleased with her efforts, and therefore hid her poems under a carpet! When the father finally discovered what his nine-year-old daughter was busying herself with, he set aside a certain hour every Saturday evening, at which time he read aloud the poems she had written.

The family numbered among its friends none other than John Keble, writer of the famous collection of devotional poems known as *The Christian Year,* and he, too, gave encouragement to the youthful poet.

In 1848, at the age of twenty-five, she published a volume of hymns for little children that probably has never been excelled by a similar collection. Two years later she became the bride of a parish minister, William Alexander, afterwards Bishop of Derry and Raphoe, and later Archbishop of Armaugh. Alexander was rector of a country church in the county of Tyrone at the time, and there was much poverty in his flock. Among these needy folk the young minister's wife moved about like a ministering angel. A beautiful tribute to her memory from the pen of her husband reads: "From one poor home to another, from one bed of sickness to another, from one sorrow to

365

another, she went. Christ was ever with her, and in her, and all felt her influence."

But the poetic spark that glowed within her soul was not permitted to die. Even when children began to bless this unusual household and the cares of the mother increased, her harp was tuned anew and sweeter songs than ever began to well up from her joyous, thankful heart.

Practically all of the four hundred hymns and poems written by Mrs. Alexander were intended for children and for this reason their language is very simple. Nevertheless, her lyrics set forth some of the most profound truths of the Christian faith. Witness, for example, the simple language of "There is a green hill far away." A child has no difficulty in comprehending it, and yet this precious hymn expounds in a most touching way the whole story of the Atonement:

> He died that we might be forgiven,
> He died to make us good;
> That we might go at last to heaven,
> Saved by His precious Blood.

Again, the infinite worth of the sacrifice which Christ made when He, the Sinless One, died for sinners is expressed in these simple words:

> There was no other good enough
> To pay the price of sin,
> He only could unlock the gate
> Of heaven, and let us in.

Archbishop Alexander mentioned two hymns by which his wife's name, and incidentally his own, would be remembered. He might have added several others, such as the challenging hymn, "Jesus calls us; o'er the tumult," or the two beautiful children's hymns, "Once in royal David's city" and "All things bright and beautiful." And among her splendid poems he might have mentioned the sublime verse entitled "The Burial of Moses." Her own confiding trust in God is reflected in the lines:

> O lonely tomb in Moab's land!
> O dark Beth-peor's hill!
> Speak to these curious hearts of ours,
> And teach them to be still;
>
> God has His mysteries of grace,
> Ways that we cannot tell;
> He hides them deep, like the secret sleep
> Of him He loved so well.

366

Mrs. Alexander died in 1895 at the age of seventy-two years. She was buried in Londonderry, Ireland. At Archbishop Alexander's funeral sixteen years later "The roseate hues of early dawn" was sung in Londonderry cathedral, and when the body was lowered into the grave the mourners sang "There is a green hill far away." A more appropriate hymn for a Christian's funeral than the former could scarcely be chosen:

> The highest hopes we cherish here,
>   How fast they tire and faint!
> How many a spot defiles the robe
>   That wraps an earthly saint!
> O for a heart that never sins,
>   O for a soul washed white,
> O for a voice to praise our King,
>   Nor weary day or night!
>
> Here faith is ours, and heavenly hopes,
>   And grace to lead us higher;
> But there are perfectness and peace
>   Beyond our best desire.
> O by Thy love and anguish, Lord,
>   O by Thy life laid down,
> Grant that we fall not from Thy grace,
>   Nor cast away our crown!

A Joyous Christmas Carol

All my heart this night rejoices
    As I hear,
    Far and near,
Sweetest angel voices;
"Christ is born," their choirs are singing,
    Till the air
    Everywhere
Now with joy is ringing.

Hark! a voice from yonder manger,
    Soft and sweet,
    Doth entreat,
"Flee from woe and danger;
Brethren, come; from all that grieves you
    You are freed;
    All you need
I will surely give you."

Come then, let us hasten yonder;
    Here let all,
    Great and small,
Kneel in awe and wonder,
Love Him who with love is yearning;
    Hail the star
    That from far
Bright with hope is burning.

PAUL GERHARDT, 1607-76
TR. CATHERINE WINKWORTH, 1829-78

BRILLIANT ENGLISH WOMEN WHO TRANSLATED HYMNS

I N PAYING tribute to the many English women who have given the Church immortal hymns, it also is necessary to acknowledge the debt of gratitude posterity owes to a number of brilliant women whose translations of hymns from other languages, chiefly German, have greatly enriched the hymnody of the entire English-speaking world.

Foremost among these translators was Catherine Winkworth, but also of great importance were the consecrated efforts of two gifted sisters, Jane Borthwick and Sarah Borthwick Findlater, as well as the work of Francis Elizabeth Cox and Elizabeth Rundle Charles. All of these, it seems, conceived a deep love for the marvelous hymns of Germany and spent many years of their lives in giving them to their own countrymen in their native tongue.

John Wesley, more than a century earlier, had given the English people a glimpse into the rich treasure-store of Germany hymnody when he translated such classics as "Lo, God is here, let us adore," "Jesus, Thy Blood and righteousness," "Thou hidden love of God whose height," "Jesus, Thy boundless love to me," "Thee will I love, my Strength, my Tower," and "Put thou thy trust in God." However, no further serious effort, it seems, was made to carry on the work he had so ably begun until Catherine Winkworth appeared.

Born in London, September 13, 1829, she spent most of her life in the vicinity of Manchester, and it was here her famous *Lyra Germanica* was written. When published in 1855, it met with an extraordinary reception and went through twenty-three editions. A second series under the same name, issued three years later, ran into twelve editions. These translations of German hymns are ranked with the foremost English devotional classics of the 19th century, and Dr. Martineau said of them that they are "only a little short of native music."

In 1863 she published the *Chorale Book for England,* containing a number of fine chorale tunes from Germany, and in 1869 yet another volume under the title, *Christian Singers of Germany.*

Miss Winkworth possessed the marvelous ability of preserving the spirit of the great German hymns while clothing them in another language. It is she who has given us in English dress, to mention only a few, such German classics as Rinkart's "Now thank we all our God," Luther's "Out of the depths I cry to Thee," Decius' "All glory be to God on high," Neander's "Praise to the Lord, the Almighty," Schmolck's "Open now thy gates of beauty," Franck's "Deck thyself in joy and gladness," Nicolai's "Wake, awake, for night is flying," and Gerhardt's "All my heart this night rejoices."

In 1826 she moved with her family to Clifton, England, where she became secretary of an association for the promotion of higher education for women, a supporter of Clifton High School for Girls, and a member of Cheltenham Ladies' College. She died suddenly at Monnetier, in Savoy, July 1, 1878. Bishop Percival, then headmaster of Clifton College, said of her:

"She was a person of remarkable intellectual and social gifts and very unusual attainments; but what specially distinguished her was her combination of rare ability and great knowledge with a certain tender and sympathetic refinement which constitutes the special charm of the womanly character."

The Borthwick sisters also cherished a deep love for German hymnody. Members of an old Scotch family, Jane Laurie was born in Edinburgh in 1813 and Sarah in 1823. Sarah became the bride of a Scotch minister named Eric Findlater, and lived for a time in Perthshire.

The two sisters always worked closely together and collaborated in the preparation of a volume of translations entitled *Hymns from the Land of Luther.* This book was the first in a series of four which began in 1854 and ended in 1862. Although it is difficult to distinguish the individual work of the two, Jane is generally credited with the rendering into English of such hymns as Spitta's "How blessed from the bonds of sin," Zinzendorf's "Jesus, still lead on," and Schmolck's "My Jesus, as Thou wilt," while Sarah is believed to be the translator of Tersteegen's "God calling yet," Spitta's "O happy home, where Thou art loved the dearest," Schmolck's "My God, I know that I must die," Laurenti's "Rejoice, all ye believers," and a large number of other German hymns.

Jane Borthwick died in 1897, and her younger sister followed her ten years later.

Elizabeth Rundle Charles was another gifted writer and translator of the 19th century. Born at Tavistock, England, January 2, 1828, she was the daughter of John Rundle, a member of Parliament. Evidently it was a family of means, inasmuch as Elizabeth received all of her education at home from tutors. She became the author of a number of popular works with historical settings, including her famous book, *The Schonberg-Cotta Family,* depicting the life and times of Martin Luther. She also wrote a number of original hymns and rendered a few translations from the German and Latin. These were published in the volume, *Voice of Christian Life in Song,* which appeared in 1864, and *Songs Old and New,* which came out in 1882.

Mrs. Charles' finest original hymn is "Praise ye the Father for His loving-kindness." She also is remembered as the translator of the first three stanzas of the Venerable Bede's famous Ascension Day hymn, "A hymn of glory let us sing."

Frances Elizabeth Cox, the last of this remarkable line of women hymnists, has been called "one of the most felicitous of translators of German hymns." Her first translations, numbering 49 hymns, appeared in 1841 in *Sacred Hymns from the German.* They were subsequently revised in 1862. Her best known renderings are "Jesus lives! thy terrors now" and "Who are these like stars appearing?" It is said that Baron Bunsen assisted her in the choice of German hymns most worthy of translation. Miss Cox passed away in 1897 at the age of 85 years.

371

A Hymn to the Ascended Lord

See the Conqueror mounts in triumph,
See the King in royal state,
Riding on the clouds his chariot
To His heavenly palace gate!
Hark! the choir of angel voices
Joyful alleluias sing,
And the portals high are lifted
To receive their heavenly King.

Who is this that comes in glory
With the trump of jubilee?
Lord of battles, God of armies,
He has gained the victory!
He who on the Cross did suffer,
He who from the grave arose,
He has vanquished sin and Satan,
He by death has spoiled His foes.

Thou hast raised our human nature
On the clouds to God's right hand;
There we sit in heavenly places,
There with Thee in glory stand;
Jesus reigns, adored by angels;
Man with God is on the throne;
Mighty Lord, in Thine Ascension
We by faith behold our own.

Glory be to God the Father;
Glory be to God the Son,
Dying, risen, ascending for us,
Who the heavenly realm has won;
Glory to the Holy Spirit;
To One God, in Persons Three;
Glory both in earth and heaven,
Glory, endless glory, be.

CHRISTOPHER WORDSWORTH, 1807–85

372

A BISHOP WHO USED HYMNS TO TEACH

WHEN John Keble wrote his poetic companion to the *Book of Common Prayer* known as *The Christian Year*, he intended it for personal edification and family devotion; when Christopher Wordsworth some thirty years later published *The Holy Year*, he made it clear that the hymns therein had been written for use in public worship. As such, he made them as artless and simple in language as possible, in order that the meaning might not be mistaken. Also he made them objective rather than subjective in content. His definition of a hymn, as set forth in the preface of the volume, is very instructive. He wrote:

"A hymn in public worship is the collective voice of the congregation speaking to God, and singing His praise, or supplicating His grace. The Church triumphant thanks God for His great glory, and while she duly remembers what the Lamb who has been slain has done for her, it is not by decomposing herself into individuals that she glorifies Him; but by an universal chorus of praise for the salvation He has wrought for the whole company of faithful people in every nation under heaven."

Wordsworth also believed that hymns constituted one of the most effective vehicles by which to teach spiritual truths. Quoting Paul's admonition to the Colossians to teach and admonish one another "in psalms and hymns and spiritual songs," he once wrote:

"A Church which forgoes the use of hymns in her office of teaching neglects one of the most efficacious instruments for correcting error and for disseminating truth, as well as for ministering comfort and edification." At another time he declared it to be "the first duty of a hymn to teach sound doctrine, and thus to save souls."

Consistent with this principle, Wordsworth made his own hymns thoroughly Scriptural, sometimes almost to the point of paraphrasing portions of Holy Writ. Witness, for example, his metrical rendering of Paul's immortal ode to love:

> Gracious Spirit, Holy Ghost,
> Taught by Thee, we covet most
> Of the gifts at Pentecost,
>   Holy, heavenly love.

373

Faith that mountains could remove,
Tongues of earth or heaven above,
Knowledge, all things, empty prove
    Without heavenly love.

Love is kind, and suffers long;
Love is meek, and thinks no wrong,
Love than death itself more strong;
    Therefore give us love.

Faith and hope and love we see,
Joining hand in hand, agree;
But the greatest of the three,
    And the best, is love.

Wordsworth came from a distinguished English family. His uncle was none other than William Wordsworth, the celebrated poet. His father, for whom he was named, was rector of Lambeth and then Master of Trinity College, Cambridge. Christopher himself had an extraordinarily brilliant career as a student at Cambridge, and following his graduation became Classical Lecturer and Public Orator at the university.

In 1836 he was appointed headmaster of Harrow, one of England's famous schools for boys. He took his responsibility seriously, and sought to bring about a thorough moral and spiritual reform at the institution. "It will be my earnest endeavor," he told his young, headstrong students, "to make all of you, first, Christians; secondly, gentlemen, and thirdly, scholars." Whether his students wanted to become gentlemen and scholars or no, is debatable, but it soon developed that they had little desire to become Christians. In any event, attendance dropped from 190 to 69, and soon Wordsworth found himself conveniently transferred to become canon of Westminster Abbey.

Two years later, in 1850, he began a nineteen years' ministry in the humble country parish of Stanford-in-the-Vale-cum-Goosey. It was here he wrote *The Holy Year,* containing hymns for every season and festival of the Church Year, and it is in this volume we find such well-known lyrics as "O day of rest and gladness," "O Lord of heaven and earth and sea," "Songs of thankfulness and praise," "Alleluia! Alleluia! Hearts to heaven," "See the Conqueror mounts in triumph," "Holy, holy, holy Lord," "Hark! the sound of holy voices," as well as the Pentecost hymn quoted above.

In 1869 Wordsworth was elevated to the bishopric of Lincoln, a position be held until he resigned a few months before his death in 1885. Canon Ellerton has borne him this beautiful tribute:

"He was a most holy, humble, loving, self-denying man. And the man is reflected in his verse. To read one of his best hymns is like looking into a plain face, without one striking feature, but with an irresistible charm of honesty, intelligence, and affection."

One of Wordsworth's contemporaries was John Hampden Gurney, from whom we have received such splendid hymns as "Lord, as to Thy dear Cross we flee," "Great King of nations, hear our prayer," "We saw Thee not when Thou didst come," and a revised version of Richard Baxter's "Ye holy angels bright." Gurney was educated at Cambridge with the intention of entering the legal profession, but turned to the Church instead. He became curate of Lutterworth, a parish once held by Wycliff, and served there for seventeen years. It was here he compiled his first hymn collection in 1838. Later he became rector of St. Mary's, Marylebone, London, where he issued a second collection in 1851. He also was author of several historical works. He died in 1862.

Other Church of England hymn-writers who lived during this period were William H. Bathurst, John E. Bode, Richard Massie and Arthur Russell.

William Hiley Bathurst will be remembered chiefly for two hymns, "O for a faith that will not shrink" and "How blest are they whose hearts are pure." Following his graduation from Oxford in 1819, he became rector of Barwick-in-Elmet, Yorkshire, a position he held for thirty-three years. Conscientious scruples about certain portions of the *Book of Common Prayer,* particularly concerning the baptismal and burial rites, caused him to resign in 1852, after which he retired to private life. He was the author of a volume of lyrics titled *Psalms and Hymns for Public and Private Use,* published at Leeds in 1830.

John Ernest Bode has perpetuated his name in modern hymn-books by his confirmation hymn, "O Jesus, I have promised." The hymn will have additional significance when we learn that it was written by Bode for a confirmation service in which his own daughter and two sons made their vows to serve their Master "to the end." Bode, who had been an outstanding scholar at Oxford, was rector at Cambridgeshire at the time. Although he published an entire volume

375

of hymns for the Church Year, this is the only one that has survived. He died in 1874.

While Oxford Movement translators were primarily interested at this period in preserving the classical heritage of Greek and Latin hymns, two other Church of England poets were devoting themselves to the study of the great treasury of German hymnody. One of these was Arthur Tozer Russell, the other Richard Massie.

Russell was ordained by Bishop Wordsworth in 1829. At first an extreme high churchman, he changed his views in later years and became one of the most effective critics of the flood of tracts issued by Newman and his followers. He became deeply interested in German Lutheran hymns, and in 1851 published a hymnbook which contained not only numerous hymns from the German but also followed the very arrangement of the old Lutheran hymn collections.

From Russell's pen have come English translations of Decius' metrical *Agnus Dei*, "O Lamb of God, most holy"; one of the stanzas of Johann Rist's "Break forth, O beauteous heavenly light," and a portion of Heinrich Albert's "God, who madest earth and heaven." Russell wrote some 140 original hymns, but they have not shown the same vitality as his translations.

Massie, the other poet who became an ardent student of German Lutheran hymnody, was the scion of a wealthy Cheshire family. Born in Chester, England, in 1800, he devoted his entire life to literature, and published two volumes of translations from the German. One was titled *Martin Luther's Spiritual Songs* and the other *Lyra Domestica*, an English rendering of Spitta's *Psalter und Harfe*. Massie has given us in English dress Luther's "Christ Jesus lay in death's strong bands"; Christian Knorr von Rosenroth's "Come, thou bright and morning star"; Gerhardt's "Evening and morning," and Spitta's "O blessed Sun whose splendor."

John Burton was another English layman who, like Massie, was deeply interested in hymnody. Unlike Massie, however, who was born in a family of wealth and culture, Burton came from humble antecedents. Born in Stratford, Essex, in 1803, he was in poor health from his fifteenth to his twenty-fifth year. Apparently miraculously restored, he was able for fifty years to earn his livelihood as a cooper and basket-maker. A deacon in a Congregational church, he taught Sunday school for twenty-seven years, and wrote a large number of hymns for children. Four hymn collections were published, and from one of these has been derived the consecration hymn, "Saviour, Thee my heart I tender."

Burton died of smallpox in 1877, contracted while visiting a poor chimney-sweep who was suffering from the disease. Following his death, all of his papers were burned, among them many of his hymns which he was engaged in revising for publication at the time he was stricken.

Two Baptist ministers who composed hymns during this period were Cornelius Elven and Edward Mote. Elven served a Baptist congregation in his native town of Bury St. Edmunds for almost half a century. He was a close friend of the great Baptist preacher, Charles H. Spurgeon, who wrote at his death in 1873: "Mr. Elven was a man of homely attainments, pre-eminently practical as a preacher, full of faith and the Holy Ghost." He will be remembered chiefly for his gripping hymn based on our Lord's parable of the Pharisee and the Publican, "With broken heart and contrite sigh."

Mote, who ministered for twenty-six years to a Baptist congregation at Horsham, England, wrote some 100 original hymns. The Christian world will be forever grateful to him principally for one of these, "My hope is built on nothing less." He died at Horsham in 1874.

The Symbol That Survives

In the Cross of Christ I glory,
　　Towering o'er the wrecks of time;
All the light of sacred story
　　Gathers round its head sublime.

When the woes of life o'ertake me,
　　Hopes deceive, and fears annoy,
Never shall the Cross forsake me;
　　Lo! it glows with peace and joy.

When the sun of bliss is beaming
　　Light and love upon my way,
From the Cross the radiance streaming
　　Adds new luster to the day.

Bane and blessing, pain and pleasure,
　　By the Cross are sanctified;
Peace is there that knows no measure,
　　Joys that through all time abide.

JOHN BOWRING, 1792-1872

A UNITARIAN WHO GLORIED IN THE CROSS

AMONG the great hymns of the Cross, Sir John Bowring's classic, "In the Cross of Christ I glory," occupies a foremost place. This is all the more remarkable when we are reminded that Bowring was known as a Unitarian, a communion which not only denies the deity of Christ, but ignores the true significance of the Cross. Yet here is a hymn that every evangelical Christian rejoices to sing, for it is one that magnifies the Cross and makes it the very center of the Christian religion.

There was a great deal of strange contradiction in the life of Bowring. Although in early years he was a strong champion of social progress in Great Britain, such as abolition of the corn laws, popular education, prison reform, abolition of flogging in the Navy and a number of other movements for the uplift of the poor and under-privileged, he seems to have forgotten many of his high ideals in later life.

It is significant that Bowring's best hymns were written in the years when his conscience was most sensitive, before political expediency was permitted to supersede principle.

Bowring was a learned man. As a linguist he was virtually a genius. It is said that he could speak twenty-two languages fluently, and was able to converse in at least one hundred different tongues. He found special delight in translating poems from other languages, and his published works contain renditions from Bohemian, Slavonic, Russian, Serbian, Polish, Slovakin, Illyrian, Teutonic, Esthonian, Dutch, Frisian, Lettish, Finnish, Hungarian, Biscayan, French, Provencal, Gascon, Italian, Spanish, Portuguese, Cathalonian and Galician sources.

In addition to his other accomplishments, Bowring had a very distinguished career in English politics. He was twice a member of the British parliament. Later he became consul general for the English government at Hong Kong, China. During this period he chanced to sail down the Chinese coast to Macao, where nearly 400 years earlier the Portuguese explorer, Vasco da Gama, had built an imposing cathedral. The structure had been wrecked by a typhoon, but the tower still remained, and surmounting it a great bronze cross, sharply outlined against the sky. Far above the wreckage surrounding it, the cross seemed to Bowring to be a symbol of Christ's Kingdom, glorious and eternal, living through the centuries while other kingdoms have come and gone. Instantly the words of the hymn seemed to suggest themselves to him, and in a short while a famous lyric had been written.

The structure of the hymn is interesting. The first stanza declares the Cross of Christ to be the central fact in divine revelation and the one theme in which the Christian never ceases to glory. The second stanza pictures the Cross as the Christian's refuge and comfort in time of affliction, while the third tells how it even adds luster to the days of joy and sunshine. The final stanza summarizes these two ideas, and the hymn closes by proclaiming the eternal character of the peace and joy that flow from the Cross.

Bowring eventually became governor of Hong Kong, in which position he was vested with supreme naval and military power. Now again the strange contradictions in his life appear. While some claim that he was a benevolent ruler and did much to promote the welfare of the peoples of the Far East, there are others who accuse him of gross abuse of his authority as well as singular indifference to the physical and moral welfare of the Chinese. For one thing, it is charged that his high-handed methods and his insolence in dealing with the Chinese were directly responsible for the second Opium War in 1856. The war ended disastrously for the Chinese, and a continuance of the opium trade was forced upon them, besides being compelled to grant numerous other commercial concessions to the British.

This failure on the part of so-called Christian nations to practice Christian principles in their dealings with the peoples of Asia and Africa is no doubt responsible to a large extent for the antagonism revealed toward the West in the upsurge of nationalism in many parts of the world today.

Bowring is said to have been frequently surprised and gratified to hear his hymns sung at unexpected times and in unusual places. In 1825 he wrote a poem titled "Watchman, tell us of the night." He did not know until ten years later that it was being used as a hymn until he heard it sung by Christian missionaries in Turkey. Another of Bowring's hymns that has had wide use is one that emphasizes the wisdom and love of God:

> God is Love; His mercy brightens
> All the path in which we rove;
> Bliss He wakes, and woe He lightens:
> God is Wisdom, God is Love.

At the age of 80 years, Bowring is said to have begun every day with a song of thanksgiving on his lips. Some one has also asserted that he was "a devoted and evangelical believer," and that his connection with the Unitarian Church was merely nominal and accidental. Unitarian or Christian? A benevolent humanitarian and lover of his fellow men, or an unscrupulous politician and a ruthless oppressor of the weak and defenseless? Who will give the answer?

John Bowring was knighted by the British government before he died, but that honor seems quite empty now. Much more important is the fact that on his tombstone there is inscribed in bold letters:

IN THE CROSS OF CHRIST I GLORY

Did he ask to have those words inscribed there, and do they reflect his hope for eternity?

A Vision of the Final Triumph

Ten thousand times ten thousand
In sparkling raiment bright,
The armies of the ransomed saints
Throng up the steeps of light;
'Tis finished, all is finished,
Their fight with death and sin;
Fling open wide the golden gates,
And let the victors in!

What rush of alleluias
Fills all the earth and sky;
What ringing of a thousand harps
Bespeaks the triumph high;
O day, for which creation
And all its tribes were made;
O joy, for all its former woes
A thousandfold repaid!

O then what raptured greetings
On Canaan's happy shore,
What knitting severed friendships up,
Where partings are no more!
Then eyes with joy shall sparkle
That brimmed with tears of late;
Orphans no longer fatherless,
Nor widows desolate.

Bring near Thy great salvation,
Thou Lamb for sinners slain;
Fill up the roll of Thine elect,
Then take Thy power and reign;
Appear, Desire of Nations,
Thine exiles long for home;
Show in the heavens Thy promised sign,
Thou Prince and Saviour, come!

HENRY ALFORD, 1810–71

382

A BELOVED DEAN AND HIS HYMNS

'TIS said that Henry Alford, the great English New Testament scholar and dean of Canterbury, cherished a desire throughout his life to visit the Holy Land. His wish was never fulfilled. But when he died, they inscribed on his tomb the beautiful Latin words, *Deversorium viatoris proficientis Hierosolymam,* "The inn of a pilgrim traveling to Jerusalem."

In a sense, the words were symbolic of the whole life of the beloved dean. No churchman probably ever applied himself to his work more assiduously than he, and yet, despite his strenuous duties, he never permitted earthly tasks or cares to rob him of the sense of God's daily care and guidance, or to obscure the heavenly goal. It is said that at the end of a day's hard work, as well as after every meal, he would stand up and thank God for the blessings he had received. Something of this perpetual spirit of gratitude may be seen in his famous harvest hymn:

> Come, ye thankful people, come,
> Raise the song of harvest-home;
> All is safely gathered in
> Ere the winter storms begin;
> God our Maker doth provide
> For our wants to be supplied;
> Come to God's own temple, come,
> Raise the song of harvest-home.

Alford was born in London in 1810, the son of an Anglican clergyman. Following his graduation from Cambridge he became curate to his father, and then rose rapidly from one position to another until he was named dean of Canterbury. Even as a student he gave promise of rare literary ability and unusual scholarship. He was the author of a volume on *English Descriptive Poetry,* another on *The Queen's English,* and several volumes of sermons. He also wrote considerable poetry and a number of hymns. *The Contemporary Review* was launched by him, and for some time he was its editor.

In a book titled *A Dissuasive Against Rome,* Alford definitely took issue with the "high church" movement which had resulted in the defection of Newman to the Church of Rome.

It was as a Greek scholar, however, that Alford attained greatest distinction. His four-volume edition of the *Greek Testament* on which he labored for twenty years became the standard critical commentary of the later 19th century. He also was a member of the New Testament Revision Committee.

In addition to the harvest hymn noted above, Alford has left two other hymns that are found in most modern hymnals, namely, "Ten thousand times ten thousand," and the processional, "Forward! be our watchword." When he died in 1871, "Ten thousand times ten thousand" was sung with great feeling at the last rites in Canterbury Cathedral. His passing was mourned throughout the Christian world, but the beloved dean's wish to see the Holy City had been fulfilled at last.

Another Biblical scholar and hymn-writer whose career in many respects closely paralleled that of Alford's was Edward Hayes Plumptre. Born in London, like Alford, he also developed into one of England's most distinguished churchmen and scholars. Ordained in 1846, he became successively chaplain of King's College, London; dean of Queen's College, Oxford; prebentary of St. Paul's and professor of New Testament Exegesis, King's College; rector of Pluckley; vicar of Bickley, and, in 1881, dean of Wells.

While Alford was a member of the New Testament Revision Committee, Plumptre became a member of the Old Testament Committee. He was author of a number of volumes, including the standard work on the life of Bishop Ken, as well as several collections of poems and hymns. Perhaps his best known lyric is the fine processional which has grown very popular on both sides of the Atlantic:

> Rejoice, ye pure in heart,
> Rejoice, give thanks, and sing;
> Your festal banner wave on high,
> The Cross of Christ your King.
> Rejoice, rejoice!
> Rejoice, give thanks, and sing!

Other hymns by Plumptre that have come into general use are: "Thine arm, O Lord, in days of old," "Thy hand, O God, has guided," and "O Light, whose beams illumine all."

He also was the translator of a number of Latin hymns. He passed away at Wells February 1, 1891.

One of the most beautiful hymn prayers in our hymnals, "At

384

even when the sun was set," came from the pen of another English clergyman at this time. The writer was Henry Twells, a man who had learned in the school of affliction to know something of the comfort and strength to be found in prayer. Its lines reflect not only a feeling of deep human need, but also the confiding faith of the soul who composed them:

> O Saviour Christ, our woes dispel;
>   For some are sick, and some are sad,
> And some have never loved Thee well,
>   And some have lost the love they had.
>
> O Saviour Christ, Thou too art Man;
>   Thou hast been troubled, tempted, tried;
> Thy kind but searching glance can scan
>   The very wounds that shame would hide.
>
> Thy touch has still its ancient power;
>   No words from Thee can fruitless fall;
> Hear, in this solemn evening hour,
>   And in Thy mercy heal us all.

Twells was born in Birmingham in 1823 and was educated in King Edward's School of that city. Among his schoolmates were the future noted churchmen, Archbishop Benson, Bishop Lightfoot and Bishop Westcott. Later he attended Cambridge. Ordained in 1849, he spent most of his life in serving parishes and as a schoolman. At one time he was sub-vicar of Holy Trinity, Stratford-on-Avon. In 1884 he was made honorary canon of Peterborough Cathedral, but resigned this position because of ill health. He then moved to Bournemouth, on the Channel. Here he built and partly endowed with his own funds the Church of Augustine, and served it until his death in 1900.

It was at the request of Sir Henry W. Baker, chairman of the committee which created *Hymns Ancient and Modern,* that Twells wrote "At even when the sun had set" for the 1868 Appendix to that famous hymn collection. Twells at the time was headmaster of the Godolphin School for Boys, and the hymn, so he states, was written one afternoon while he was trying to supervise an examination.

"I am afraid," he writes, "I could not have been very energetic or lynx-eyed in my duties that day, but I little anticipated the popularity the hymn would attain . . . Copies have been kindly sent to me in Greek, Latin, German, French, Welsh and Irish. I like to think that I have brought souls nearer Christ, and if so I heartily thank God for it."

Another hymn that has gained wide acceptance in hymnals, "Breathe on me, Breath of God," was likewise written by a schoolman during this period. The author was Edwin Hatch, a graduate of Oxford, who came to be recognized as a man of profound learning. After his ordination he worked for a while in an East End parish in London, but in 1860 he accepted a call to become Professor of Classics in Trinity College, Toronto, Canada. On his return to England three years later he became Vice-principal of St. Mary's Hall, Oxford, and later Bampton Lecturer, University Reader in Ecclesiastical History and finally Hibbert Lecturer.

The great German theologian, Harnack, translated Hatch's Bampton Lectures into German, and after the latter's death in 1889, he wrote of him, "In his learning that of England's great old theologians, Ussher and Pearson, lived to me again." Despite his scholarly attainments, however, Hatch is said to have possessed a faith "as simple and unaffected as a child's." This is beautifully reflected in the one hymn he has left us:

> Breathe on me, Breath of God,
> So shall I never die,
> But live with Thee the perfect life
> Of Thine eternity.

"Spirit of God, descend upon my heart," one of the finest of all hymns for Pentecost, likewise belongs to this period. It was the work of George Croly, a London clergyman who gained considerable notice during his day by his literary activities. Born and educated in Dublin, he moved to London in 1810 to become rector of two churches—St. Benet and St. Stephen's—the latter in one of the poorest and most degraded sections of the city. Here he re-established a pulpit in which there had been no preaching for a century, and attracted large congregations.

It is said that when Croly's flock wanted a hymnbook, he prepared one of his own. It was known as Psalms and Hymns for Public Worship. The hymn named above, which is the only one of Croly's that has survived, is from that collection. Though strongly subjective in language, it has a universal appeal. Two of its stanzas are unusually moving:

Spirit of God, descend upon my heart;
  Wean it from earth, through all its pulses move;
Stoop to my weakness, mighty as Thou art,
  And make me love Thee as I ought to love.

I ask no dream, no prophet ecstasies,
  No sudden rending of the veil of clay,
No angel visitant, no opening skies;
  But take the dimness of my soul away.

Another London minister, Charles Edward Oakley, who became rector of St. Paul's, Covent Garden, in 1863, just three years after Croly died, has given the Church a missionary hymn that has been finding its way into many hymnals in recent years, namely, "Hills of the North, rejoice!" It is of high poetic quality, calling on all the four corners of the earth to hearken to the glad tidings of redemption.

Oakley, who was born in Rhyl, North Wales, in 1832, was educated at Oxford. He lived to be only 33 years old, passing away two years after assuming charge of his London parish, greatly mourned by his people. A memorial to him in St. Paul's Church reads in part: "He bore witness not only with his lips but in his life to Divine grace . . . Although his pastoral charge over this parish lasted only for two years, yet the great work which in that short time he was enabled to effect will long be gratefully remembered by those who could appreciate the worth of his loving spirit, devotedness of life, and eminently Christian character."

The King of Love as a Shepherd

The King of love my shepherd is,
 Whose goodness faileth never;
I nothing lack if I am His,
 And He is mine for ever.

Where streams of living water flow
 My ransomed soul He leadeth,
And where the verdant pastures grow
 With food celestial feedeth.

Perverse and foolish oft I strayed,
 But yet in love He sought me,
And on His shoulder gently laid,
 And home, rejoicing, brought me.

In death's dark vale I fear no ill
 With Thee, dear Lord, beside me,
Thy rod and staff my comfort still,
 Thy Cross before to guide me.

Thou spread'st a table in my sight;
 Thy unction grace bestoweth;
And O what transport and delight
 From Thy pure chalice floweth!

And so through all the length of days
 Thy goodness faileth never;
Good Shepherd, may I sing Thy praise
 Within Thy house for ever.

HENRY WILLIAMS BAKER, 1821-1877
Psalm 23

HE HELPED CREATE A GREAT HYMNBOOK

IN the autumn of 1857 five ministers of the Church of England met in the vicarage of St. Barnabas, Pimlico, and decided that the time was ripe for the publication of a representative church hymnbook. The prejudice against "hymns of human composure" had largely disappeared within the Established Church, and unauthorized hymnbooks of varying quality were being introduced in congregations everywhere.

The flood-gates had been opened, and scores of able hymn-writers were springing up in a genuine national revival of song. From the "free lance" hymnals already published, as well as from the vast treasury of hymnody translated from classical and German sources, material for a comprehensive hymnbook had become available in abundance.

The meeting in the St. Barnabas vicarage, therefore, proved an epoch-making event in the annals of worship in the English-speaking world. The committee of five, which decided to proceed with the undertaking on its own responsibility, was subsequently enlarged, and Sir Henry Williams Baker, vicar of Monkland in Herefordshire, a man deeply interested in hymnology, became chairman of the group. William Henry Monk, director of the choir of King's College, London, was named as editor of music. It was he who suggested that the new hymnbook be called *Hymns Ancient and Modern.*

Baker, who was the son of Vice-Admiral Sir Henry Loraine Baker, had been educated at Cambridge, and soon revealed unusual gifts as a hymn editor. However, he exercised his editorial rights so freely that one contributor, who evidently smarted under the changes made in his hymns, caustically remarked that H. A. and M. (the name of the new volume) should be interpreted to mean "Hymns asked for and mutilated!"

Hymns Ancient and Modern was published in 1861 and sprang into instant popularity. James Moffatt calls this a tribute to Baker's "accurate diagnosis of the needs of the Anglican Church and the masterly skill with which he provided for them." It is significant that

389

132 of the total number of 273 hymns in the collection were translations from the Latin, indicating the strong influence exerted by the Oxford Movement. Chief among the translators were Neale, Caswall, Chandler and Isaac Williams. No Greek hymns were included inasmuch as Neale did not complete his work on Greek translations until the following year. Only ten translations from the German were adopted for the first edition. A total of 131 English hymns in the collection embraced such authors as Bishop Ken, Watts, Charles Wesley, Toplady, Cowper, Newton and Montgomery.

Much of the popularity of the famous volume must be ascribed to the new tunes it contained. In addition to ancient plainsong and French church tunes, it included a number of stalwart German chorales and also traditional English and Scottish psalm tunes. In addition to Monk, outstanding composers who contributed original music included Sir Frederick Ouseley, professor of music at Oxford, and John Bacchus Dykes, precentor of Durham Cathedral. Such tunes by Dykes as *Nicaea, Hollingside, St. Cross, St. Cuthbert* and *Melita* appeared in this hymnbook for the first time.

An appendix of 113 hymns was added to the volume in 1868, the additions consisting chiefly of modern hymns and a few of Neale's Greek translations. At this time also was added Baker's original lyric, "The King of Love my Shepherd is." Subsequent additions and revisions were made in 1875, in 1889 and in 1904, and now, for almost a century *Hymns Ancient and Modern* has been the most widely used hymnbook in the English-speaking world.

Other hymns contributed by Baker are "I am not worthy, holy Lord," "Lord, Thy word abideth," "O God of love, O King of peace," "O perfect life of love," "Praise, O praise our God and King," and a number of translations from the Latin. He also greatly revised the highly-prized hymn of worship, "We love the place, O God." The original of this hymn was written by William Bullock, a member of the Royal Navy who became a missionary to Nova Scotia and served there for thirty-two years under the Society for Propagating the Gospel. The hymn was first published at Halifax in 1854 in Bullock's *Songs of the Church.*

Baker succeeded to the baronetcy on the death of his father in 1859, but remained as vicar at Monkland until his death in 1877. His most enduring monument is the hymnbook he left behind him.

Closely associated with Baker in the preparation of *Hymns*

Ancient and Modern was Francis Pott, rector of Northill, Bedfordshire. Pott was deeply interested in hymnody, and a member of the original committee that launched the epoch-making hymnal. He himself, in 1861, published *Hymns Fitted to the Order of Common Prayer,* and in 1898 his desire to see a reform in chanting led him to issue *The Free Rhythm Psalter,* which, however, met with an indifferent reception. Pott will be remembered chiefly for two original hymns, "Angel voices, ever singing" and "Forty days and forty nights," as well as for his translation of the Latin hymn, "The strife is o'er, the battle done."

Another churchman who for a time was a member of the *Hymns Ancient and Modern* committee was Thomas Benson Pollock, creator of the metrical litany. Pollock, who was born on the Isle of Man in 1836, was educated at Trinity College, Dublin. He began the study of medicine in London, but afterwards decided to enter the ministry and became curate to his brother, J. S. Pollock, who was vicar of the famous mission known as St. Alban's in Birmingham.

It was a poverty-stricken district, but the two brothers labored with intense devotion and gathered a large congregation. The total salary offered as a "living" was only 150 pounds per year, or approximately $750. Nevertheless, they built one of the finest churches in Birmingham and added three assistant ministers, six lay readers and four sisters to their staff of workers. Because of their "high church" tendencies, the brothers at first were threatened with mob violence, but eventually they won the love and admiration of the people in their district, who always referred to Thomas Pollock as "Father Tom." After thirty years as curate, he succeeded his brother as vicar, but his health had become undermined by his strenuous labors, and he died a year later in 1896. Of the two brothers, it has been said:

"They lived and died for St. Alban's Mission. They gave it their prospects, their hopes of preferment, their money, their patrimony, and their health, for the anxieties of their work and their unceasing and almost incredible exertions undoubtedly hastened the day of their departure."

Thomas Pollock will be chiefly remembered for three of his metrical litanies: "Jesus, in Thy dying woes," based on the Saviour's Seven Words on the Cross; "Jesus, from Thy throne on high," and "Jesus, with Thy Church abide."

A Vesper Hymn of Rare Beauty

The radiant morn hath passed away,
    And spent too soon her golden store;
The shadows of departing day
    Creep on once more.

Our life is but an autumn sun,
    Its glorious noon how quickly past!
Lead us, O Christ, our lifework done,
    Safe home at last.

O by Thy soul-inspiring grace
    Uplift our hearts to realms on high;
Help us to look to that bright place
    Beyond the sky,

Where light, and life, and joy, and peace
    In undivided empire reign,
And thronging angels never cease
    Their deathless strain;

Where saints are clothed in spotless white,
    And evening shadows never fall,
Where thou, eternal Light of light,
    Art Lord of all.

GODFREY THRING, 1823-1903

A COUNTRY PARSON AND HIS HYMNS

H AD Godfrey Thring not written hymns, it is quite evident that his name would never have become known to posterity. As rector of Alford-with-Hornblotton, he was the spiritual shepherd of two obscure parishes in rural south-central England near Glastonbury, which once had been the ancient seat of King Arthur's rule. Nothing very remarkable ever happened in these pastoral surroundings, and the world passed by the humble rector.

All Saints' Church in Alford was built in the 14th century, and its people have been described as "fighting farmers" and "milkmen, rough and quarrelsome." St. Peter's Church in Hornblotton stands in the midst of cow-pastures and quite close to the manorhouse of the squire of the district. The Alford congregation today has only 50 parishioners, and that of Hornblotton barely more than 75.

But Godfrey Thring was not a man to sit indolently in his rural rectory and twiddle his thumbs. He had been born in that very house in 1823, for his father had been the rector of Alford-with-Hornblotton before him. In fact, when Godfrey expressed a desire to become a clergyman like his father, the latter sought in every way to dissuade him. However, the mother proved to be stronger-willed than her husband, and that settled the matter. Godfrey was ordained as soon as he had graduated at Oxford, and ultimately he took over his father's double parish.

His duties as rector were not sufficient to occupy his work-week, wherefore Thring devoted much of his time to writing hymns and compiling hymnals. Something of his ability as a spiritual poet was revealed when his beautiful vesper hymn, "The radiant morn hath passed away," was included in the 1868 Appendix to *Hymns Ancient and Modern*. Two years earlier he had already prepared a hymnbook of his own, titled *Hymns Congregational and Others*. In the same year he issued a second volume, *Hymns and Verses*. This was followed in 1874 by *Hymns and Sacred Lyrics*.

Most of the hymnbooks in England at this time were partisan in spirit, reflecting various divisive doctrinal emphases or prejudices that often deprived the worshiper of some of the best hymns. With these Thring was deeply dissatisfied, wherefore he set to work to prepare an ecumenical hymnal which would be representative of the whole Church. It appeared in 1880 under the name, *A Church of England Hymn Book,* with the explanation that it was "adapted to the daily services of the Church throughout the year." In literary excellence, this book even surpassed *Hymns Ancient and Modern,* setting a standard that has continued to challenge all future hymnal compilers. An improved edition of this work was published in 1882 under the title, *The Church of England Hymn Book.*

Following the publication of the latter volume, Thring's brother Edward, the distinguished educator and headmaster of Uppingham, wrote him as follows: "Be sure that no painting, no art work you could have done, could have been so powerful for good. . . . As long as the English language lasts, sundry of your hymns will be read and sung . . . and many a soul of God's best creatures will thrill at your words. What more can a man want?"

His brother was right. Few, indeed, are the worshipers in the English-speaking world who have not been deeply moved in spirit as they have sung Thring's surpassingly lovely evening prayer in verse, or that other gripping hymn that bids us give to our needy brethren the cup of cold water in Christ's name:

O God of mercy, God of might,
In love and pity infinite,
Teach us, as ever in Thy sight,
    To live our life to Thee.

Teach us the lesson Thou hast taught,
To feel for those Thy Blood hath bought,
That every word and deed and thought
    May work a work for Thee.

For all are brethren, far and wide;
Since Thou, O Lord, for all hast died;
Then teach us, whatso'er betide,
    To love them all in Thee.

In sickness, sorrow, want, or care,
Whate'er it be, 'tis ours to share;
May we, where help is needed, there
    Give help as unto Thee.

And may Thy Holy Spirit move
All those who live, to live in love,
Till Thou shalt greet in heaven above
    All those who live to Thee.

394

In recognition of the service he had rendered the Church, the rector of the obscure Alford-with-Hornblotton parish was named prebendary of Wells Cathedral, a sanctuary which is also associated with the names of two other hymn-writers, Ken and Plumptre. Thring died at Shanley Green, Surrey, September 13, 1903.

In addition to the mentioned hymns, he was the author of such well-known lyrics as "From the eastern mountains," "Saviour, blessed Saviour," "Thou to whom the sick and dying," "I heard a sound of voices," "To Thee, O God, we render thanks," and certain stanzas of "Crown Him with many crowns," of "Lord, who at Cana's wedding feast," and of "Saviour, breathe an evening blessing."

A distinguished contemporary of Thring's, and likewise a hymn-writer, was William Bright, from whom we have received the impressive communion hymn, "And now, O Father, mindful of the love," as well as two others in common use, "And now the wants are told that brought," and "At Thy feet, O Christ, we lay." The latter hymn has a stanza that every Christian might well make his daily prayer:

> Fain would we Thy Word embrace,
> Live each moment on Thy grace,
> All our selves to Thee consign,
> Fold up all our wills in Thine,
> Think, and speak, and do, and be
> Simply that which pleases Thee.

Bright was born in Doncast in 1824, and was educated at Oxford. After his ordination in 1848, he held various posts and in 1868 became canon of Christ Church, Oxford, and Regius Professor of Ecclesiastical History. He was the author of a number of historical works on the Early Church and also made a collection of ancient collects selected from various rituals. In 1866 he published *Hymns and Other Poems,* in which the above hymns first appeared. He died at Oxford in 1901.

Stopford Augustus Brooke, a clergyman who in 1872 was appointed Chaplain in Ordinary to Queen Victoria, will also be remembered as a hymn-writer of great ability. Seceding from the Church of England in 1881, he became the minister of an Independent congregation in London, where he soon became known as one of the most brilliant preachers in that metropolis. For use in his own church he published a hymnbook titled *Christian Hymns* in which he included a number of original lyrics. Of unusual merit is "Let the whole creation cry," a hymn of praise that has come into widespread use. Ill health finally forced his retirement, after which he devoted himself exclusively to literary work. He died in 1916.

Charles Kingsley was another distinguished churchman and author of this period, but it is only through accident that his name has gotten into the hymnbooks of Christendom. In 1871, four years before he died, Kingsley was asked to compose a hymn to be sung by a choir of 1,000 voices at the cornerstone laying for a working men's block in Queen's Hospital in Birmingham. Kingsley responded with a poem which began:

> Accept this building, gracious Lord,
> No temple though it be;
> We raised it for our suffering kin,
> And so, good Lord, for Thee.
>
> Accept our little gift, and give
> To all who here may dwell,
> The will and power to do their work,
> Or bear their sorrows well.

Then followed the words that have since found their way into many hymnals: "From Thee all skill and science flow, all pity, care, and love," a hymn with a modern flavor and emphasis on the subject of Christian concern for the sick and afflicted.

Kingsley was born in 1819 in Holne vicarage, Devonshire, the son of a country gentleman who became a clergyman. As a schoolboy in Bristol, Charles witnessed the workers' riots there in which the bishop's palace was burned and many rioters shot down by soldiers. "That sight made me a radical," he afterwards said. After graduating from Cambridge, he took holy orders and began his ministry at Eversley, on the edge of Windsor Forest. Here he shared all the trials and vicissitudes of his humble parishioners, and even worked with them in the fields. In times of epidemics, he went from house to house to bring medicine and to render help to the sick. From this time forward his consuming passion was "to rehabilitate Christianity as the poor man's religion and the workingman's friend."

A friendship with F. D. Maurice, the social reformer, intensified Kingsley's sympathies for the under-privileged, and soon he joined himself with a group of churchmen who sought to turn the Socialist movement, then in its beginning, into Christian channels. From his facile pen there came such gripping social novels as *Yeast* and *Alton Locke,* as well as the dramatic poem, *Saint's Tragedy.* Because of

396

these writings he was suspected in some circles of harboring revolutionary ideas. The Bishop of London even prohibited him from preaching in his diocese. Despite this, Kingsley continued to write, and soon his famous historical novels, *Hypatia* and *Westward, Ho,* appeared.

Ere long, honors began to be heaped on him. He became professor of History at Cambridge Universary; Queen Victoria made him her private chaplain, and he was appointed canon of Westminster Abbey, where he preached to great congregations. And when this remarkable poet, novelist, nature-lover, preacher, historian and humanitarian died in 1875 at the age of 56 years, a whole nation mourned him. He was buried in his own parish churchyard in Eversley, where his devoted wife rests beside him. Their tomb bears the famous inscription in Latin: "We have loved, we love, we shall love."

In a very definite sense it can be said of Charles Kingsley, that in his life and work he did what he could to bring about the fulfilment of the prayer expressed in his beautiful hymn:

> And hasten, Lord, that perfect day
> When pain and death shall cease,
> And Thy just rule shall fill the earth
> With health, and light, and peace;
>
> When ever blue the sky shall gleam,
> And ever green the sod,
> And man's rude work deface no more
> The paradise of God.

The Voice of Jesus

I heard the voice of Jesus say,
  "Come unto me and rest;
Lay down, thou weary one, lay down
  Thy head upon my breast."
I came to Jesus as I was,
  Weary, and worn, and sad;
I found in Him a resting place,
  And He hath made me glad.

I heard the voice of Jesus say,
  "Behold, I freely give
The living water, thirsty one,
  Stoop down, and drink, and live."
I came to Jesus and I drank
  Of that life-giving stream;
My thirst was quenched, my soul revived,
  And now I live in Him.

I heard the voice of Jesus say,
  "I am this dark world's light;
Look unto me, thy morn shall rise,
  And all thy day be bright."
I looked to Jesus, and I found
  In Him my star, my sun;
And in that light of life I'll walk
  Till traveling days are done.

HORATIUS BONAR, 1808-1889

BONAR, THE SWEET SINGER OF SCOTLAND

ONE of Scotland's most earnest soul-winners was also its greatest hymnist. He was Horatius Bonar, a name that will be forever cherished by all who find something of their own love for the Saviour expressed in the spiritual songs of this noble Scotchman.

Like Cecil Frances Alexander, Dr. Bonar wrote his songs for children; but they are spiritually so profound they will always satisfy the most mature Christian mind, despite their simplicity. No matter how old we may become, our hearts will ever be stirred as we sing the tender words:

> I long to be like Jesus,
>   Meek, loving, lowly, mild;
> I long to be like Jesus,
>   The Father's holy child.
> I long to be with Jesus,
>   Amid the heavenly throng,
> To sing with saints His praises,
>   To learn the angels' song.

The subjective, emotional element is strongly present in the hymns of Bonar. In this respect there is a striking resemblance to the lyrics of the great German writer, Benjamin Schmolck. Both used the name "Jesus" freely, and both became almost daringly intimate, yet the hymns of neither are weak or sentimental.

In Bonar we behold the strange paradox of a man with a strong physique and powerful intellect combined with the gentle, sympathetic nature of a woman and the simple, confiding faith of a child. The warmth and sincerity of his personal faith in Christ may be seen reflected in all his hymns. "I try to fill my hymns with the love and light of Christ," he once said, and certainly he has drawn many souls to Him by the tenderness of their appeal.

Bonar is ever pointing in his hymns to Christ as an all-sufficient Saviour, dwelling in simple language on the blessings of the Atonement and the willingness of God to accept all who come to Him through Christ. In these days of liberal theology, when practically all stress is placed on "living the Christ-life" while the meritorious work of Christ on behalf of the sinner is largely ignored or forgotten, it would be most salutary for the Church to listen anew to such words as these:

> Upon a Life I have not lived,
>> Upon a Death I did not die,
> Another's Life; Another's Death:
>> I stake my whole eternity.
>
> Not on the tears which I have shed;
> Not on the sorrows I have known;
> Another's tears; Another's griefs:
>> On them I rest, on them alone.
>
> Jesus, O Son of God, I build
>> On what Thy Cross has done for me;
> There both my death and life I read;
>> My guilt, my pardon there I see.
>
> Lord, I believe; O deal with me
>> As one who has Thy Word believed!
> I take the gift, Lord, look on me
>> As one who has Thy gift received.

Many stories are related of Bonar's methods of dealing with seeking souls. A young man who was troubled by a grievous sin once came to him for help. The Scotch pastor assured him that God was willing to forgive and that the blood of Jesus His Son had atoned for all sin. The despairing young man found it difficult to believe the Gospel message, however, and continually reminded Bonar of the greatness of his transgression. Finally an inspiration came to Bonar. "Tell me," he demanded, "which is of greater weight in the eyes of God — your sin, black as it is, or the blood of Jesus, shed for sinners?" Light dawned on the soul of the troubled young man, and he cried joyfully, "Oh, I am sure the blood of Jesus weighs more heavily in God's sight than even my sin!" And so he found peace.

Bonar was a man of boundless energy. When he was not preaching, he was writing hymns or tracts or books. One of his tracts, *Believe and Live,* was printed in more than a million copies, and the late Queen Victoria of England was much blessed by it. His hymns number about 600, and the fact that at least 100 are in common use today testifies to their enduring worth. Dr. Bonar never used his hymns in his own church worship, but when, on a certain occasion near the close of his life, he broke the rule, two of his elders showed their emphatic disapproval by walking out of church!

Perhaps the finest hymn Bonar ever wrote is "I heard the voice of Jesus say." Other familiar hymns are "Thy works, not mine, O Christ," "Not what my hands have done," "Blessing, and honor, and glory, and power," "All that I was, my sin, my guilt," "Thy way, not mine, O Lord" "Glory be to God the Father," "A few more years shall roll," and "Here, O my Lord, I see Thee face to face." The latter is a communion hymn of rare beauty, setting forth the Lord's Supper as the Christian's "love feast" in the fellowship of the Saviour. Here is a stanza:

> This is the hour of banquet and of song:
> This is the heavenly table spread for me;
> Here let me feast, and, feasting, still prolong
> The brief bright hour of fellowship with Thee.

Bonar was born in Edinburgh, December 19, 1808. His father was a lawyer, following a long line of eminent Scottish ministers. His mother was a gentle, pious woman, and it was largely through her influence that her three sons, John, Horatius and Andrew, entered the ministry of the Church of Scotland. Andrew became a noted Bible commentator.

After completing his course at the University of Edinburgh, Horatius began mission work in Leith. In one of the most squalid parts of the city services and Sunday school were held in a hall. The children seemed to find little relish in singing the psalm paraphrases, which were still exclusively used by the Church of Scotland at that late date, wherefore Bonar decided to write songs of his own. Like Luther he chose happy tunes familiar to the children, and composed words to fit them. His first two hymns were "I lay my sins on Jesus" and "The morning, the bright and beautiful morning." Another was "I was a wandering sheep." Needless to say, the children sang and enjoyed them.

At this time, also, he wrote his first hymn for adults, "Go, labor on! Spend and be spent!" It was intended to encourage those who were working with him among the poor of his district.

After four years Bonar was ordained as a minister of the Church of Scotland, assuming charge of a new church at Kelso. He was a man of prayer, and his first sermon to his people was an exhortation to prayer. It is said that a young servant in his home was converted by his prayers. Hearing the earnest supplications that came from his locked study, she thought: "If he needs to pray so much, what will become of me, if I do not pray!"

In 1843 Dr. Bonar married Miss Jane Lundie, and for forty years they shared joy and sorrow. She, too, was a gifted writer, and it is she who has given us the moving hymn, "Fade, fade, each earthly joy."

Sorrow was one of the means used by the Lord to enrich and mellow the life of Bonar. Five of his children died in early years. It required much of divine grace in such experiences to write lines like these:

> Spare not the stroke; do with us as Thou wilt;
> Let there be naught unfinished, broken, marred.
> Complete Thy purpose, that we may become
> Thy perfect image, O our God and Lord.

Bonar himself was sorely afflicted during the last two years of his life. He died in 1889, deeply mourned by all Scotland as well as by Christians throughout the world who had come to know him through his tracts and hymns. At his funeral one of his own hymns was sung. It was written on the theme of his family motto, "Heaven at Last."

> What a city! what a glory!
> Far beyond the brightest story
> Of the ages old and hoary:
> Ah, 'tis heaven at last!
>
> Broken death's dread bands that bound us,
> Life and victory around us;
> Christ, the King, himself hath crowned us;
> Ah, 'tis heaven at last!

Another distinguished Scotchman who was writing hymns at this time was William Dalrymple Maclagen, Archbishop of York. Maclagen, who was born in Edinburgh in 1826, came from an outstanding Scottish family. At first, he intended to enter the legal profession, and to that end studied law at the University of Edinburgh. However, after serving as a lieutenant in the British army in India, he became physically incapacitated and resigned his commission, having decided to take holy orders. After graduating from Cambridge, he was ordained by the Church of England. After serving as curate in a number of parishes, he became successively rector of Newington, vicar of Kensington, prebendary of Reculverland in St. Paul's Cathedral, Bishop of Lichfield, and in 1891 Archbishop of York. In

402

the latter capacity, he crowned Alexandra as Queen at the coronation of King Edward VII.

Archbishop Maclagen was the founder of the Poor Benefices Fund. He also established a Training College for Clergy at York, in which he discouraged "high church" practices, particularly in liturgical matters. He is represented in our hymnals by three splendid hymns, "The saints of God! their conflict past," "Be still, my soul, for God is near," and "Lord, when Thy Kingdom comes, remember me."

A Great Marching Song

Onward, Christian soldiers,
Marching as to war,
With the Cross of Jesus
Going on before.
Christ the royal Master
Leads against the foe;
Forward into battle,
See, His banners go!

At the sign of triumph
Satan's legions flee;
On, then, Christian soldiers,
On to victory!
Hell's foundations quiver
At the shout of praise;
Brothers, lift your voices,
Loud your anthems raise.

Crowns and thrones may perish.
Kingdoms rise and wane,
But the Church of Jesus
Constant will remain;
Gates of hell can never
'Gainst that Church prevail;
We have Christ's own promise,
And that cannot fail.

Onward, then, ye faithful,
Join our happy throng;
Blend with ours your voices
In the triumph-song;
Glory, laud, and honor,
Unto Christ the King;
This through countless ages
Men and angels sing.

SABINE BARING-GOULD, 1834-1924

BARING-GOULD AND HIS MARCHING HYMN

WHEN Sabine Baring-Gould, on Whitsunday, 1865, sat up a greater portion of the night to compose a hymn, he did not realize he was writing words that some day would be sung throughout the English-speaking world. The hymn he was writing was "Onward, Christian soliders."

The story is an interesting one. At that time Baring-Gould was minister of the Established Church at Lew-Trenchard, England. On Whitmonday the children of his village were to march to an adjoining village for a Sunday school rally.

"If only there was something they could sing as they marched," the pastor thought, "the way would not seem so long." He searched diligently for something suitable, but failed to find what he wanted. Finally he decided to write a marching song. It took the greater part of the night to do it, but the next morning the children's pilgrimage was made the lighter and happier by "Onward, Christian soldiers."

Commenting on the hymn some thirty years later, the author said: "It was written in great haste, and I am afraid some of the rhymes are faulty. Certainly, nothing has surprised me more than its popularity."

In this instance, as in many others that might be mentioned, the tune to which it is inseparably wedded has no doubt contributed much to make it popular. Sir Arthur Seymour Sullivan, the great English organist who wrote "The Lost Chord," in 1872 composed the stirring music now used for Baring-Gould's hymn.

Objection has sometimes been voiced against the hymn because of its martial spirit. However, it should be noted that this hymn gives not the slightest hint of warfare with carnal weapons. The allusion is to spiritual warfare, and the warrior is the Christian soldier.

We are reminded throughout this hymn of Paul's military imagery in the sixth chapter of Ephesians, where he tells us that "our wrestling is not against flesh and blood, but against the principalities, against the powers, against the world-rulers of this darkness, against the spiritual hosts of wickedness in the heavenly places," and admonishes us to put on "the whole armor of God." We also recall the same apostle's exhortation to Timothy to "war the good warfare," and to "fight the good fight of faith."

It is salutary to be reminded by such a hymn as this of the heroic character of the Christian life. The follower of Jesus is not to sit with folded hands and sing his way into Paradise. A sickly, sentimental religion has no more place in the Christian Church today than it had in those early days when apostles and martyrs sealed their faith with their life-blood. Baring-Gould's hymn seems almost an exultant answer to Isaac Watts' challenging stanza:

> Must I be carried to the skies
> On flowery beds of ease,
> While others fought to win the prize,
> And sailed through bloody seas?

We sometimes hear it said that the Church of Christ has fallen on evil days, and more than one faithful soul fears for the future. Baring-Gould has reminded us here of Christ's "own promise" that, though kingdoms may rise and fall, His kingdom shall ever remain, for the gates of hell shall not prevail against it.

During a desperate battle between the French and Austrians in the Napoleonic wars, a French officer rushed to his commander and exclaimed, "The battle is lost!" Quietly the general answered, "One battle is lost, but there is time to win another." Inspired by the commander's unconquerable optimism, the French army renewed the struggle and snatched victory out of the jaws of defeat. That has ever been the history of the Church of Christ.

Baring-Gould was one of England's most versatile ministers. In addition to his hymn-writing, he was a novelist of considerable reputation. For many years he regularly produced a novel every year. His *Lives of the Saints* in fifteen volumes, his *Curious Myths of the Middle Ages* and his *Legends of the Old Testament* are all notable works. It is said that he did all his writing in long hand without the aid of a secretary. He once declared that he often did his best work when he felt least inclined to apply himself to his task. He never waited for an "inspiration," but plunged into his work and then stuck to it until it was finished.

The beautiful evening hymn, "Now the day is over," is also from Baring-Gould's pen, and, to show his versatility, he also composed the tune for it. This hymn, like "Onward, Christian soldiers," was also evidently written for children, as some of its stanzas would indicate. But old and young alike seem to love to sing:

> Now the day is over,
>   Night is drawing night,
> Shadows of the evening
>   Steal across the sky.
>
> Now the darkness gathers,
>   Stars begin to peep,
> Birds and bees and flowers
>   Soon will be asleep.
>
> Jesus, give the weary
>   Calm and sweet repose;
> With Thy tenderest blessing
>   May mine eyelids close.
>
> Grant to little children
>   Visions bright of Thee;
> Guard the sailors tossing
>   On the deep blue sea.
>
> Through the long night-watches
>   May Thine angels spread
> Their white wings above me,
>   Watching round my bed.

Baring-Gould was also a translator of no mean ability. His version of Bernhardt Severin Ingemann's famous Danish hymn, "Through the night of doubt and sorrow," has helped to make this fine lyric known throughout the English-speaking world.

Despite his arduous and unceasing labors, Baring-Gould lived to the ripe old age of ninety years. He died in 1924, but his "Onward, Christian soldiers" goes marching on.

A Parting Hymn of Praise

Saviour, again to Thy dear Name we raise
With one accord our parting hymn of praise;
Once more we bless Thee ere our worship cease,
Then, lowly bending, wait Thy word of peace.

Grant us Thy peace upon our homeward way;
With Thee began, with Thee shall end the day;
Guard Thou the lips from sin, the hearts from shame,
That in this house have called upon Thy Name.

Grant us Thy peace, Lord, through the coming night,
Turn Thou for us its darkness into light;
From harm and danger keep Thy children free,
For dark and light are both alike to Thee.

Grant us Thy peace throughout our earthly life,
Our balm in sorrow, and our stay in strife;
Then, when Thy voice shall bid our conflict cease,
Call us, O Lord, to Thine eternal peace.

JOHN ELLERTON, 1826-93

HYMNS THAT HELPED THE COMMON MAN

JOHN ELLERTON received few honors during his life-time. The English parishes in which he labored as a faithful spiritual shepherd were humble and obscure. His parishioners for the most part were common folk—workers in shop and factory; toilers who strained under heavy burdens; laborers with gnarled hands and bent backs; "hewers of wood and bearers of water" whose lives often were drab and empty and hopeless; "ordinary" people to whom poverty was a familiar specter.

But into the lives of these people came John Ellerton with his understanding sympathy, his comforting ministrations, and, above all, with his inspiring song, and all at once the daily round was lightened and a new hope dawned on their weary world.

Ellerton was one of England's greatest hymnists, deserving to rank with Watts and Wesley, Montgomery and Newton, Keble and Heber. Born in London, December 16, 1826, he was brought up in a home that was radiant with Christian joy. He once wrote of his parents, "I used to feel how happy my father and mother were, even more than how good they were."

Following his education at Cambridge, Ellerton served a number of parishes as curate. In 1860 he became vicar at Crewe Green, not far from Liverpool, where he found a parish composed of some 500 mechanics in the steel works of a railroad, besides the farmers and laborers who worked on the estate of Lord Crewe. It was not long before he became deeply concerned about the deplorable condition of the many poor in the district, and he also began to devote himself to the task of raising educational standards among the workers. He himself received a wretched income, and he found it necessary to supplement it by holding services in a hall in Crewe each Sunday, for which he received an additional pound each week.

There was a mechanics' school at Crewe, and this Ellerton reorganized to become one of the most successful in England. He was made chairman of the education committee, and he himself taught English and Bible History in the school. More important, he began to write hymns, and ere long he organized one of the first choral associations to be found in that part of England. It was for a music festival at Nantwich, sponsored by this association, that Ellerton composed "Saviour, again to thy dear Name we raise," which has been called "one of the greatest evening hymns of the Church."

A study of the hymn reveals how very helpful its message must have been to the people among whom Ellerton labored. Albert Edward Bailey, in his stimulating volume, *The Gospel in Hymns,* writes: "In stanza 1 we must picture the closing session of the Nantwich Festival; its dozen or so choirs robed in their variously-colored gowns and together singing their final prayer, then kneeling for the benediction. In the remaining three stanzas are three prayers for peace: peace of mind for the journeys to the several towns whence the singers have come, peace during the night, peace through the various vicissitudes of life until we attain the peace of eternity. Simple and heartfelt, universal in its application, it emphasized that frame of mind which is essential for successful work — absence from worry. Because we all need this serenity, all hymnbooks contain this perfect expression of that need."

From the above, it is quite clear that the Christian Church and its servants have been proclaiming "the peace of God which passeth all understanding" to troubled and burdened humanity long before our modern "peace of mind" cults came into existence.

Ellerton wrote some fifty hymns in all, in addition to ten Latin translations, which is not a large number when compared to the prolific works of Watts, Wesley and other great hymn-writers. However, Ellerton's hymns were mostly pure gold, and a large number of them are still in universal use throughout the English-speaking world. It has been pointed out by James Moffatt "that his hand may be traced and his voice heard in every hymnbook of importance during the last thirty years of his life." Among other important achievements, he was the joint compiler of the last and greatest of all editions of *Hymns Ancient and Modern.*

"The day Thou gavest, Lord, is ended" is another of Ellerton's hymns that has won world-wide fame. Originally written as a missionary hymn, it has come to be used more often as an evening prayer. When Queen Victoria in 1897 celebrated the 60th anniversary of her accession to the throne of the British Empire, she chose this hymn to be sung on the day when Jubilee services were held in tens of thousands of churches throughout the British Empire. Its final stanza is particularly significant in view of what has happened to that Empire in recent years. Here are three of them:

> We thank Thee that Thy Church, unsleeping
> While earth rolls onward into light,
> Through all the world her watch is keeping,
> And rests not now by day or night.
>
> As o'er each continent and island
> The dawn leads on another day,
> The voice of prayer is never silent,
> Nor dies the strain of praise away.
>
> So be it, Lord; Thy throne shall never,
> Like earth's proud empires, pass away;
> Thy Kingdom stands, and grows for ever,
> Till all Thy creatures own Thy sway.

The long-forgotten Scriptural truth which Luther brought to light during the Reformation, namely, the "universal priesthood of all believers," is emphasized in another of Ellerton's great hymns, "Behold us, Lord, a little space." As Ellerton saw the humble people of his parishes go about their daily tasks, he began to comprehend, with Luther, how all honest work, if it be done as unto the Lord, is as sacred an act and as acceptable a service in God's eyes as that which is rendered by priest or prelate standing before a holy altar. And so he wrote:

> Yet these are not the only walls
> Wherein Thou mayst be sought;
> On homeliest work Thy blessing falls,
> In truth and patience wrought.
>
> Work shall be prayer, if all be wrought
> As Thou wouldst have it done;
> And prayer, by Thee inspired and taught,
> Itself with work be one.

Other notable hymns by Ellerton are "Throned upon the awful Tree," "This is the day of light," "Now the laborer's task is o'er," "O Father all creating," and a portion of "God the Omnipotent! King, who ordainest." He will also be remembered for three of his Latin translations, "Welcome, happy morning! age to age shall say," "From East to West, from shore to shore," and "O Strength and Stay, upholding all creation."

Ellerton never secured a copyright on his hymns, declaring that if they were "counted worthy to contribute to Christ's praise in the congregation, one ought to feel very thankful and humble." He continued to serve humble parishes until his death in 1893, and the only honor that ever came to him from the Church of England was during his last illness when he was made an honorary canon of St. Alban's Cathedral, a position, however, in which he was never installed.

Also writing hymns at this time was another rare soul, whose exalted position in the Church contrasted greatly, however, with the humble parishes served by Ellerton. He was Edward Henry Bickersteth, Bishop of Exeter. Bickersteth, who was born in Islington, London, in 1825, was the son of a Church of England clergyman who at one time had been a missionary to West Africa and later became the first secretary of the Church Missionary Society. The Bickersteths belonged to the so-called evangelical, or low, wing of the Anglican Church, and the father had edited *Christian Psalmody*, which was accounted the best evangelical hymnbook of that day.

Edward inherited something of his father's poetic gifts, as well as his love for hymnody. For years it had been the father's custom on Sundays to require the children in the household to repeat a hymn at tea as a part of the family devotions. The only exception to the rule was when the father had written a hymn of his own, in which case he would read it for the first time to his children.

Following his graduation from Cambridge, Edward was ordained by the Church of England and served three parishes successively as curate. He then rose from one position to another until he was appointed Bishop of Exeter in 1885. Although he published several collections of sermons and no less than twelve volumes of poems, his most important work was probably performed as editor of *The Hymnal Companion to the Book of Common Prayer*, published in 1870. This hymnbook, like that of his father's, became immensely popular in evangelical circles of the Church of England, and within three years had been adopted by almost 1,500 parishes.

Bickersteth's hymns are far more subjective than those of other Church of England writers. Although this is usually a weakness in a hymn intended for corporate worship, there is nevertheless a quality in most of Bickersteth's lyrics that lends to them a universal appeal. This personal approach of the believer to his Lord may be seen in the poet's frequent use of the first person singular pronouns. Here is a stanza from his fine communion hymn, "Not worthy, Lord, to gather up the crumbs":

I hear Thy voice: Thou bidd'st me come and rest;
I come, I kneel, I clasp Thy pierced feet;
Thou bidd'st me take my place, a welcome guest
Among Thy saints, and of Thy banquet eat.

Other popular hymns by the good Bishop of Exeter are "O God, the Rock of Ages," "Peace, perfect peace, in this dark world of sin," and his marvelous translation of an old Spanish hymn of unknown date, which has become almost an English classic in the exquisite language in which Bickersteth clothed it. Here are two stanzas:

O God, I love Thee; not that my poor love
May win me entrance to Thy heaven above,
Nor yet that strangers to Thy love must know
The bitterness of everlasting woe.

How can I choose but love Thee, God's dear Son,
O Jesus, loveliest, and most loving One!
Were there no heaven to gain, no hell to flee,
For what Thou art alone I must love Thee.

Few hymns, perhaps, have brought as much comfort and assurance to sad and troubled souls as Bickersteth's "Peace, perfect peace." Probably there is a reason for this, inasmuch as it was written at the bedside of an aged, dying relative, Archdeacon Hill of Liverpool. When Bickersteth called to see the sick man, he found him deeply depressed spiritually. The Bishop thereupon opened his Bible and read the passage from Isaiah 23:3: "Thou wilt keep him in perfect peace, whose mind is stayed on thee: because he trusteth in thee." Then, in a few moments, he composed the comforting lines of the hymn and read them to the dying man, concluding with the stanza:

It is enough; earth's struggles soon shall cease,
And Jesus calls us to heaven's perfect peace.

Bickersteth himself entered into that perfect peace of heaven in 1906. Concerning the life and character of this saintly man, his biographer has written: "As he went in and out amongst clergy and laity, there was the impression left everywhere which is best expressed in the words of the Shunammite respecting Elisha, 'Behold, now, I perceive that this is an holy man of God which passeth by us continually.' "

413

The Stranger at the Door

O Jesus, Thou art standing
  Outside the fast-closed door,
In lowly patience waiting
  To pass the threshold o'er.
Shame on us, Christian brethren,
  His Name and sign who bear,
O shame, thrice shame upon us,
  To keep Him standing there!

O Jesus, Thou art knocking;
  And lo, that hand is scarred,
And thorns Thy brow encircle,
  And tears Thy face have marred.
O love that passeth knowledge,
  So patiently to wait;
O sin that hath no equal,
  So fast to bar the gate!

O Jesus, Thou art pleading
  In accents meek and low,
"I died for you, my children,
  And will ye treat me so?"
O Lord, with shame and sorrow
  We open now the door;
Dear Saviour, enter, enter
  And leave us nevermore.

WILLIAM WALSHAM HOW, 1823-97

A GREAT HYMN AND A GREAT PAINTING

I T IS significant that many of the great hymns of the Church have been written by clergymen who have been known for their zeal as soul-winners. They have evidently made the discovery that sacred song is a powerful instrument in the hands of the Holy Spirit to melt cold and hardened hearts and to woo men to Christ. Bishop William Walsham How, one of the last of the outstanding English hymnists of the 19th century, undoubtedly owed much of his success, both as a pastor and as a church leader, to the moving lyrics that came, first from his heart, and then from his pen.

Bishop How once gave a striking description of the characteristics he believed should be found in an ideal minister of the Gospel. "Such a minister," he said, "should be a man pure, holy, and spotless in his life; a man of much prayer; in character meek, lowly, and infinitely compassionate; of tenderest love to all; full of sympathy for every pain and sorrow, and devoting his days and nights to lightening the burdens of humanity; utterly patient of insult and enmity; utterly fearless in speaking the truth and rebuking sin; ever ready to answer every call, to go wherever bidden, in order to do good; wholly without thought of self; making himself the servant of all; patient, gentle, and untiring in dealing with the souls he would save; bearing with ignorance, wilfulness, slowness, cowardice, in those of whom he expects most; sacrificing all, even life itself, if need be, to save some."

Those who knew How best said it was almost a perfect description of his own life and character.

When Queen Victoria, in 1879, made him Bishop of Bedford, with East London as his diocese, How was tireless in his efforts to alleviate conditions in that poverty-stricken district. When he first began his work in the slums, people would point to him and say, "There goes a bishop." But as they came to know him better, they said, "There goes *the* bishop." And finally, when they learned to love him, they exclaimed, "There goes *our* bishop."

"O Jesus, Thou art standing," is Bishop How's most celebrated hymn. It is based on the beautifully moving words of the Saviour in

415

the Book of Revelation, "Behold, I stand at the door, and knock: If any man hear my voice, and open the door, I will come in to him, and will sup with him, and he with me."

Though the language of the hymn is commonplace, there are striking expressions here, as in How's other hymns, that immediately arrest the attention of the worshiper. In the first stanza we are reminded that there are nominal Christians who bear "His Name and sign" and yet are keeping the Saviour patiently waiting outside a "fast-closed door." In the succeeding verse we are told that it is sin that keeps the door so tightly shut. Then comes the concluding stanza with its gripping picture of the surrender of a human heart to the pleading Christ.

The imagery in the hymn, no doubt, was suggested by Holman Hunt's celebrated painting, "The Light of the World." This was executed by Hunt in 1855, while the hymn by How was written twelve years later. It will be recalled that the Hunt masterpiece pictures the Saviour patiently standing and knocking at a closed door. The high weeds, the tangled growth of vines, as well as the unpicked fruit lying on the ground before the door, suggest that it has not been opened for a long time. A bat is hovering in the vines overhead, a further suggestion of isolation and inhospitable seclusion.

Ruskin tells us that the white robe worn by the heavenly Stranger shows us that He is a Prophet, the jeweled robe and breatplate indicate a Priest, and the crown of gold a King. The crown of thorns is now bearing leaves "for the healing of the nations." In His scarred hand He carries a lighted lantern, signifying "the Light of the world."

When Holman Hunt's picture was first exhibited, it excited considerable comment. Some one, however, ventured the criticism that there was a fault in the painting inasmuch as Hunt had forgotten to indicate a latch on the door.

"There is no mistake," said the great artist. "I did not put a latch on the outside of the door because there is none. That door can only be opened from within." How true! Even God cannot enter an unwilling heart; it must be opened to Him, or He will never come in and make it His abode.

Bishop How's hymn pictures in language what Holman Hunt expressed on canvas, and perhaps it has helped to open even more hearts to the Saviour than the artist's famous masterpiece.

But this is not How's only great hymn. The good bishop was a

416

close friend of John Ellerton and collaborated with the latter in the creation of *Church Hymns*. To this volume he contributed the majestic and thrilling All Saints' Day hymn, "For all the saints who from their labors rest," to say nothing of "O Word of God Incarnate," "O one with God the Father," "O holy Lord, content to fill," and "Summer suns are glowing." Two others, "We give Thee but Thine own" and "Jesus, Name of wondrous love," have likewise won an imperishable place in English hymnody.

The talented bishop died in the year 1897, mourned not only by those who had learned to love him because of his noble Christian character, but also by those who had come to know him through his beautiful hymns. With the passing of more than six decades since his death, there is increasing evidence that Bishop How will be numbered among the great hymn-writers of the Christian Church.

Another Anglican clergyman who was writing hymns at this time was Henry John Pye, who has bequeathed to the Church a hymn for the Festival of the Presentation titled "In His temple now behold Him." After serving the Clifton-Campville parish in Staffordshire for a number of years, Pye and his wife, who was the only daughter of Bishop S. Wilberforce, were caught up by the Oxford Movement, and were among those who unfortunately defected to the Church of Rome. He was the compiler of a book of hymns which appeared in 1851 for use in his own congregation.

Here it seems appropriate to mention a series of independent hymnals published somewhat earlier in the region of Staffordshire which came to be known as the "Staffordshire Hymnbooks." Among Anglican clergymen who contributed to these collections was Edward Cooper, rector of Hamstall-Ridware and later of Yoxall, Staffordshire, until his death in 1833. His well-known hymn, "Father of heaven, whose love profound," first appeared in the Uttoxeter Collection of 1805, and afterwards in a collection of his own published in 1811 for use in his congregations at Hamstall-Ridware and Yoxall. Another of his hymns that came into widespread use was "This is the day the Lord hath blest."

A Rapturous Hymn of Adoration

O Saviour, precious Saviour,
    Whom, yet unseen, we love;
O Name of might and favor,
    All other names above:
We worship Thee, we bless Thee,
    To Thee alone we sing;
We praise Thee and confess Thee,
    Our holy Lord and King.

O Bringer of salvation,
    Who wondrously hast wrought,
Thyself the revelation
    Of love beyond our thought;
We worship Thee, we bless Thee,
    To Thee alone we sing;
We praise Thee and confess Thee,
    Our gracious Lord and King.

In Thee all fulness dwelleth,
    All grace and power divine;
The glory that excelleth,
    O Son of God, is Thine.
We worship Thee, we bless Thee,
    To Thee alone we sing;
We praise Thee and confess Thee,
    Our glorious Lord and King.

O grant the consummation
    Of this our song above,
In endless adoration
    And everlasting love;
Then shall we praise and bless Thee
    Where perfect praises ring,
And evermore confess Thee,
    Our Saviour and our King.

FRANCES RIDLEY HAVERGAL, 1836-79

418

FRANCES RIDLEY HAVERGAL, THE CONSECRATION POET

THE beauty of a consecrated Christian life has probably never been more perfectly revealed than in the life of Frances Ridley Havergal. To read the story of her life is not only an inspiration, but it discloses at once the secret of her beautiful hymns. She *lived* her hymns before she wrote them.

This sweetest of all English singers was born at Astley, Worcestershire, December 14, 1836. Because she was such a bright, happy and vivacious child, her father, who was a minister of the Church of England and himself a hymn-writer of no mean ability, called her "Little Quicksilver." She was a brilliant pianist and passionately fond of singing. However, because she looked upon her talent as a gift from God to be used only in His service, she would sing naught but sacred songs.

Her sunshiny nature became even more radiant following a deep religious experience at the age of fourteen. Of this she afterwards wrote:

"I committed my soul to the Saviour, and earth and heaven seemed brighter from that moment."

At the age of eighteen she was confirmed. It is evident that she looked upon her confirmation as one of the most blessed experiences of her life, for when she returned home she wrote in her manuscript book of poems:

> Oh! Thine for ever, what a blessed thing
> To be for ever His who died for me!
> My Saviour, all my life Thy praise I'll sing,
> Nor cease my song throughout eternity.

Four years later, while pursuing studies in Düsseldorf, Germany, Miss Havergal chanced to see Sternberg's celebrated painting, *Ecce Homo,* with the inscription beneath it:

> This I have done for thee;
> What hast thou done for me?

419

This was the painting that once had made such a profound impression on the youthful mind of Count Zinzendorf. Miss Havergal was likewise deeply moved, and immediately she seized a piece of scrap paper and a pencil, and wrote the famous hymn:

> Thy life was given for me,
>   Thy Blood, O Lord, was shed,
> That I might ransomed be,
>   And quickened from the dead.
> Thy life was given for me,
> What have I given for Thee?

She felt the verses were so poor after she had read them over that she tossed them into a stove. The piece of paper, however, fell out untouched by the flames. When she showed the words to her father a few months later, he was so moved by them he immediately composed a tune to which they could be sung.

She is often referred to as "the consecration poet." This is an allusion to her consecration hymn, written in 1874:

> Take my life, and let it be
> Consecrated, Lord, to Thee;
> Take my moments and my days;
> Let them flow in ceaseless praise.

The circumstances that led to the writing of this hymn are interesting. Miss Havergal was spending a few days in a home where there were ten persons, some of them unconverted, while the others were rather half-hearted Christians who seemed to derive no joy from their religion. A great desire came upon her that she might be instrumental in bringing them all to a living faith in Christ. Her prayer was strangely answered, and on the last night of her stay her heart was so filled with gratitude she could not sleep. Instead, she spent the night writing the consecration hymn.

Her prayer, "Take my silver and my gold; not a mite would I withhold," was not an idle petition with her. In August, 1878, she wrote to a friend: "The Lord has shown me another little step, and of course I have taken it with extreme delight. 'Take my silver and my gold,' now means shipping off all my ornaments to the Church Missionary House (including a jewel cabinet that is really fit for a countess), where all will be accepted and disposed of for me. I retain a brooch or two for daily wear, which are memorials of my dear parents, also a locket containing a portrait of my dear niece in heaven, my Evelyn, and her two rings; but these I redeem, so that the whole value goes to the Church Missionary Society. Nearly fifty articles are being packed up. I don't think I ever packed a box with such pleasure."

Miss Havergal was only forty-two at the time of her death, on June 3, 1879. When her attending physician told her that her condition was serious, she replied, "If I am really going, it is too good to be true!" At the bottom of her bed she had her favorite text placed where she could see it: "The blood of Jesus Christ His Son cleanseth us from all sin." She also asked that these words be inscribed upon her coffin and on her tombstone. Once she exclaimed: "Splendid! To be so near the gates of heaven!" And again, "So beautiful to go! So beautiful to go!" She died while singing:

> Jesus, I will trust Thee,
>   Trust Thee with my soul;
> Guilty, lost, and helpless,
>   Thou hast made me whole:
> There is none in heaven
>   Or on earth like Thee;
> Thou has died for sinners,
>   Therefore, Lord, for me!

Some of the more popular hymns by Miss Havergal, aside from those already mentioned, are: "O Saviour, precious Saviour," "I am trusting Thee, Lord Jesus," "Golden harps are sounding," "Jesus, Master, whose I am," "Lord, speak to me that I may speak," and "Singing for Jesus, our Saviour and King." While she was writing the hymns destined to make her famous, another remarkable young woman, "Fanny" Crosby, America's blind hymn-writer, was also achieving renown by her songs. Miss Havergal and Miss Crosby never met, but each was an ardent admirer of the other, and on one occasion the English poet sent a touching greeting to her American friend:

> Dear blind sister over the sea,
> An English heart goes forth to thee.
> We are linked by a cable of faith and song,
> Flashing bright sympathy swift along:
> One in the East and one in the West
> Singing for Him whom our souls love best;
> "Singing for Jesus," telling His love
> All the way to our home above,
> Where the severing sea, with its restless tide,
> Never shall hinder and never divide.
> Sister! What shall our meeting be,
> When our hearts shall sing, and our eyes shall see!

The Steadfast Love of God

O Love that wilt not let me go,
 I rest my weary soul in Thee;
I give Thee back the life I owe,
That in Thine ocean depths its flow
 May richer, fuller be.

O Light that followest all my way,
 I yield my flickering torch to Thee;
My heart restores its borrowed ray,
That in Thy sunshine's blaze its day
 May brighter, fairer be.

O Joy that seekest me through pain,
 I cannot close my heart to Thee;
I trace the rainbow through the rain,
And feel the promise is not vain
 That morn shall tearless be.

O Cross that liftest up my head,
 I dare not ask to fly from Thee;
I lay in dust life's glory dead,
And from the ground there blossoms red
 Life that shall endless be.

GEORGE MATHESON, 1842-1906

MATHESON AND HIS SONG IN THE NIGHT

NO HYMN of the latter part of the 19th century has achieved greater popularity or is found in more church hymnals than "O Love that wilt not let me go." Written on a summer evening in 1882, it has brought undying fame to its author, the Scotchman, George Matheson.

A deeper appreciation will be felt for this hymn when we know that it may truly be called a "song in the night," for Matheson was blind when he wrote it.

Born in Glasgow, Scotland, March 27, 1842, Matheson enjoyed partial vision as a boy. However, after entering Glasgow University at the age of fifteen, his sight began to fail and he became totally blind. Despite this handicap, he was a brilliant scholar and graduated with honor in 1861. Having decided to enter the ministry, he remained four additional years for theological studies.

The famous hymn was written seventeen years later at Innellan, a seaport summer resort in Scotland, where Matheson was serving as minister. He tells the story in his own words:

"It was written in the manse of my former parish (Innellan) one summer evening in 1882. It was composed with extreme rapidity; it seemed to me that its construction occupied only a few minutes, and I felt myself rather in the position of one who was being dictated to than an original artist. I was suffering from extreme mental distress, and the hymn was the fruit of pain."

Many conjectures have been made regarding the cause of the "mental distress" from which the author was suffering. Because of the opening line, "O Love that wilt not let me go," it has been suggested that Matheson had been bitterly disappointed in his hopes of marrying a young woman to whom he had become deeply attached. It is said her refusal to marry him was due to his blindness.

Although this story cannot be vouched for, there are many significant hints in the hymn to his sad affliction, such as the "flickering torch" and the "borrowed ray" in the second stanza, the beautiful thought of tracing "the rainbow through the rain" in the third stanza, and the "cross" referred to in the final stanza. The hymn is so artistically constructed and is so rich in poetic thought and symbolic meaning, it will well repay careful study.

Despite his handicap, Matheson was blessed with a fruitful ministry. A devoted sister, who had learned Greek, Latin and Hebrew in order to aid him in his theological studies, remained his co-worker and helper throughout life. In all his pastoral calls she was his constant guide.

After a ministry at Innellan lasting for eighteen years he was called as pastor of St. Bernard's Church in Edinburgh. Here he remained for thirteen years, attracting large congregations by his preaching.

The later years of his life were spent in literary work. He was the author of several volumes in prose, among them a very fine devotional book called *Moments on the Mount*. He fell asleep on August 28, 1906, to await the break of eternity's dawn, confident in the assurance that

> . . . the promise is not vain
> That morn shall tearless be.

Matheson wrote a number of other very splendid hymns. Among the best is "Make me a captive, Lord."

Another Scottish hymn-writer of this period who will be remembered because of a great hymn is Walter Chalmers Smith. Here is the opening stanza of the lyric:

> Immortal, invisible, God only wise,
> In light inaccessible hid from our eyes,
> Most blessed, most glorious, the Ancient of Days,
> Almighty, victorious, Thy great Name we praise.

Born in Aberdeen, Scotland, in 1824, Smith received his education in Aberdeen and Edinburgh, and was ordained in 1850 to become pastor of a congregation in Islington, London. Later he served Free Church congregations in Milnathort, Glasgow and Edinburgh, Scotland, and during the jubilee year of the Free Church of Scotland in 1893 he was Moderator of its Assembly. He was the author of a number of works and of a collection of lyrics to which he gave the title, *Hymns of Christ and the Christian Life*. It was in this volume, published in 1876, the above hymn first appeared. It is based on the words written by Paul to Timothy, as recorded in I Timothy 1:17.

Hymns by members of the nobility are rather rare, but John Campbell, Marquis of Lorne and later ninth Duke of Argyll, has given the Church a beautiful paraphrase of the 121st Psalm, "Unto the hills around do I lift up." It was written in 1877, a year before Campbell sailed for Canada to become its Governor General, and is found in a collection of psalm versions issued by him under the title, *Book of Psalms*.

Needless to say, the people of Canada became very fond of the hymn written by the man who governed them from 1878 to 1883, and it eventually found its way into the *Hymnary* of the United Church Canada. During World War II it was a favorite among Canadian soldiers, and at the request of a Canadian chaplain it was included in 1958 in the *Service Book and Hymnal* of the Lutheran Church of America. Campbell died in Scotland in 1914.

Another Scottish hymnist, Archibald H. Charteris, founder of the Young Men's Guild of the Church of Scotland, while on a steamer on Lake Como in 1889, wrote "Believing fathers oft have told" for use by that youth organization. Concerning the hymn, he once said, "Poor as it is, it is in sympathy with the young men choosing to stand on Christ's side in the life-long battle."

Elizabeth Cecilia Douglas Clephane, one of the few women hymn-writers of Scotland, has given the Church two hymns that will not soon be forgotten. The one is "The Ninety and Nine," the other "Beneath the Cross of Jesus." The former, which is more of a spiritual song than a hymn, was made famous by Ira Sankey, the great Gospel singer and composer who accompanied Dwight L. Moody on his evangelistic tours of the United States and Great Britain.

Sankey and Mr. Moody had boarded a train for Edinburgh to hold a series of services there, when the former chanced to see a poem in a newspaper he had purchased. It was Miss Clephane's "Ninety and Nine." Two days later in Edinburgh, after Moody had preached on the theme of "The Good Shepherd," he turned to Sankey to ask if he had an appropriate hymn to sing. The latter thought of the newspaper clipping, and, placing it on the reed organ in front of him, he sat down and began to sing. The music, it seems, came to him as though by inspiration. "Note by note," writes Sankey, "the tune was given, which has not been changed from that day to this."

425

Following a Star

As with gladness men of old
Did the guiding star behold;
As with joy they hailed its light,
Leading onward, beaming bright;
So, most gracious God, may we
Evermore be led to Thee.

As with joyful steps they sped
To that lowly manger bed,
There to bend the knee before
Him whom heaven and earth adore;
So may we with willing feet
Ever seek Thy mercy seat.

As they offered gifts most rare
At that manger rude and bare;
So may we with holy joy,
Pure and free from sin's alloy,
All our costliest treasures bring,
Christ, to Thee, our heavenly King.

Holy Jesus, every day
Keep us in the narrow way;
And, when earthly things are past,
Bring our ransomed souls at last
Where they need no star to guide,
Where no clouds Thy glory hide.

In the heavenly country bright
Need they no created light;
Thou its Light, its Joy, its Crown,
Thou its Sun which goes not down;
There for ever may we sing
Alleluias to our King.

WILLIAM CHATTERTON DIX, 1837-98

426

ENGLISH LAYMEN WHO WROTE HYMNS

HE nation-wide interest in sacred song awakened in England when Christian hymnody came into its own in the 19th century challenged the poetic genius not only of clergymen but of laymen of the Church as well.

We have already noted the number of consecrated women who not only composed original lyrics of the first rank, but also led the way in translations from Germany's rich hymn treasury. But men of the Church were also active. Perhaps the most outstanding lay hymnist of the century was William Chatterton Dix, to whom we are indebted for such splendid hymns as "Alleluia! sing to Jesus," "As with gladness men of old," "What child is this, who, laid to rest?" "To Thee, O Lord, our hearts we raise," and "Come unto me, ye weary."

There was nothing of the spectacular or unusual in the life of Dix. Born in Bristol in 1837, the son of a surgeon, he was educated in the Grammar School of Bristol for a commercial career. He became, in fact, the manager of a marine insurance company in Glasgow, a vocation which he followed to the end of his life.

Here it should be noted, however, that he came from a family with a marked literary bent. His father, who had a fondness for poetry, was the author of *The Life of Thomas Chatterton,* the poet, who, incidentally, was a Bristol boy. This also accounts for the middle name the elder Dix gave to his son.

With such a background, it is not difficult to understand why William Chatterton Dix in early years revealed an aptitude for writing verse, and particularly hymns. Of him it has been said, "Few modern writers have shown so signal a gift as his for the difficult art of hymn-writing." In 1861 he published *Hymns of Love and Joy.* This was followed six years later by *Altar Songs, Verses on the Holy Eucharist.* Then came *A Vision of All Saints* in 1871, and *Seekers of a City* in 1878.

"As with gladness men of old" was set to a fine German tune, *Treuer Heiland,* by Conrad Kocher, but the tune has so long been

427

associated with Dix's hymn it has finally come to be known as *Dix*. No modern hymnal seems complete without this lovely Epiphany lyric.

The inspiring Thanksgiving hymn, "For the beauty of the earth," is the work of another layman of this period, namely, Folliott Sandford Pierpoint. This man, who was born in Bath in 1835 and received his education at Cambridge, afterwards devoted himself to educational work. At one time he was classical master at Somersetshire College. He was deeply interested in sacred poetry, and made contributions to a number of collections, including *Lyra Eucharistica*, in which the above popular hymn first appeared in 1864.

The name of Henry Fothergil Chorley, who also lived and wrought during this stirring period in English hymnody, will be remembered for a single hymn he wrote — "God the Omnipotent! King, who ordainest." Born in 1808 at Blackley, Lancashire, he had no formal education, but early began to reveal literary ability and was given a post on the staff of *The Athenaeum,* where he wrote musical criticisms and book reviews. Although he was the author of a number of novels and dramas, they have long since been forgotten. His one hymn alone has survived. He was on the staff of the *London Times* when he passed away in 1872.

Next to Dix, one of the best known lay hymn-writers of the 19th century was Edward Osler, who was first a physician and then an editor. Collaborating with W. Hall in the production of a hymnbook, he contributed fifty hymns and fifteen psalm versions of his own. His best known hymn is a prayer for consecrated pastors, the first stanza of which reads:

> Lord of the Church, we humbly pray
> For those who guide us in Thy way,
> And speak Thy holy word;
> With love divine their hearts inspire,
> And touch their lips with hallowed fire,
> And needful grace afford.

In addition to this hymn, two others that have come into common use are "O God unseen, yet ever near" and "Worship, honor, glory, blessing."

Osler, who at one time was associated with the Society for Promoting Christian Knowledge in London and in Bath, moved to Truro in 1841, where he became editor of the *Royal Cornwall Gazette*.

William Whiting, another layman who wrote hymns at this time, will be remembered for his "Eternal Father! strong to save," probably the most popular hymn for travellers in the English language. It had the good fortune of being included in the first edition of *Hymns Ancient and Modern,* where it was set to the stirring tune *Melita,* composed by John B. Dykes. The hymn and tune have been associated together ever since. Whiting was born in Kensington in 1825, and for more than two decades was master of the Winchester College Choristers' School. He died there in 1878.

From the pen of Thomas Briarly Browne of Wellington, England, has come a paraphrase of Psalm 114, "Praise the Lord of heaven, praise Him in the height," which has found its way into many standard hymnals. It is taken from a volume titled *National Bankruptcy and Other Poems.* Browne was also the author of some other works, but very little concerning his life has been recorded. He was born in 1805 and died in 1874.

The beautiful lyric, "There's a Friend for little children," is the work of a man who was engaged in business as an ironmonger on the Isle of Wight during the greater part of his life. His name was Albert Midlane, and he was born at Newport, on that island, in the year 1825. His father died shortly before Albert saw the light of day, and the boy was brought up by a pious mother.

Midlane credits a Sunday school teacher of the sect of the Strict Brethren, to which he belonged, with having inspired him to write poetry. His first printed hymn, "Hark! in the presence of our God," was written at the age of 17 and published in *Youth's Magazine* in November, 1842. In the succeeding years he composed a total of 300 hymns, many of which came into common use. John Julian lists no less than 83 in his monumental *Dictionary.* Evangelistic in content, they may be regarded as forerunners of the so-called Gospel songs. Spurgeon included many of them in his hymnbook of 1866, prizing them highly because of their Scriptural content.

Midlane retained a life-long interest in Sunday school work, and published a number of hymn collections for children and for the promotion of evangelism. He died at Newport in 1909.

A Happy Morning Hymn

When morning gilds the skies,
My heart awaking cries,
        May Jesus Christ be praised.
When evening shadows fall,
This rings my curfew call,
        May Jesus Christ be praised.

When mirth for music longs,
This is my song of songs,
        May Jesus Christ be praised.
God's holy house of prayer
Hath none that can compare
        With "Jesus Christ be praised."

To Him, my highest and best,
Sing I, when love-possest,
        May Jesus Christ be praised.
What'er my hands begin,
This blessing breaketh in,
        May Jesus Christ be praised.

No lovelier antiphon
In all high heaven is known
        Than "Jesus Christ be praised."
Thereto the eternal Word
The eternal psalm is heard,
        "O Jesus Christ be praised."

Ye nations of mankind,
In this your concord find,
        May Jesus Christ be praised.
Let all the earth around
Ring joyous with the sound,
        May Jesus Christ be praised.

Sing, suns and stars of space,
Sing, ye that see His face,
        Sing, "Jesus Christ be praised."
God's whole creation o'er,
For aye and evermore
        Shall Jesus Christ be praised.

German Hymn, XIX cent.
Tr. ROBERT BRIDGES, 1844–1930

A POET LAUREATE AND HIS HYMNAL

AS WE come to the threshold of the 20th century, we make the interesting discovery that England, where once the use of hymns in worship was not only frowned on but even prohibited, has actually become Christendom's foremost exponent of sacred music and song. Once the flood-gates were opened during the 19th century, a veritable host of church poets and musicians began to vie with one another in the production of hymnal after hymnal. As a result, creative leadership in the realm of Christian hymnody passed from the continent to the British Isles.

Robert Seymour Bridges, poet laureate of England, and his *Yattendon Hymnal* were symbols of this revolutionary change. Where once the great poets of England paid little heed to sacred song, here, as the 20th century was dawning, was the leading writer of verse in the British Empire undertaking on his own initiative the preparation of a collection of hymns!

Bridges had a most interesting career. Born at Walmer, Kent, in 1844, the son of a Kentish squire, he received his education at Oxford. Curiously enough, he had determined to be a physician, wherefore he studied medicine at St. Bartholomew's Hospital in London and eventually became casualty physician there. He also engaged in general practice. Having revealed unusual gifts as a poet, however, he finally gave up the practice of medicine in 1882 and moved to Yattendon in Berkshire to devote himself entirely to literary pursuits. His *Eros and Psyche* and *The Christian Captives,* as well as other writings, brought him national recognition, and in 1913 he was appointed poet laureate.

In addition to being a distinguished scholar, Bridges was also an accomplished musician. His interest in music and hymnody led him eventually to take over the direction of the village choir, a position he held for nine years. It was at this time he conceived the idea of preparing a small selection of 100 of the choicest Christian hymns for use in the Yattendon services. Enlisting the aid of Harry Ellis Wooldridge, professor of Fine Art at Oxford University, the two set to work on the project, which was published in 1899 as the *Yattendon Hymnal*. Of the 100 hymns in the volume, Bridges himself wrote or translated forty-four, and selected the others with scrupulous care, thus assuring the highest standard of literary excellence.

The same emphasis was placed on the music. For Bridges' fine translations of German hymns, the noble chorales that originally accompanied them were likewise introduced. Other treasures of older church music, including strong French Protestant tunes of the 16th century, were also recovered. As a result, the *Yattendon Hymnal* became, in the words of James Moffatt, "easily the most distinguished of individual pioneer contributions to modern hymnody."

It is through this hymnal that Bridges has given to the English-speaking world such splendid translations as "Ah, holy Jesus, how hast Thou offended," "When morning gilds the skies," "Love of the Father, love of God the Son," "Fear not, thou faithful Christian flock," "O Splendor of God's glory bright," "O gladsome light, O grace," "The duteous day now closeth," "All my hope on God is founded," and "Come, O Creator Spirit, come."

Among Bridges' original hymns in the volume are "Enter Thy courts, Thou Word of life," "Eternal Father, who didst all create," "Rejoice, O land, in God thy might," "Thee will I love, my God and King," and "Gird on thy sword, O man, thy strength endue." The latter hymn has an impressive final stanza:

> Thy work with beauty crown, thy life with love;
> Thy mind with truth uplift to God above:
> For whom all is, from whom was all begun,
> In whom all Beauty, Truth and Love are one.

While Bridges was working on his *Yattendon Hymnal*, Rudyard Kipling, another great English literary genius who has been called "the unofficial Poet Laureate of the Empire," had begun to produce his famous stories and his inimitable verse. It is claimed that the only reason why he was never named Poet Laureate was because he offended Queen Victoria by calling her "the Widow of Windsor." However, Kipling received world-wide recognition and innumerable honors, including the coveted Nobel Prize for Literature.

Born in Bombay, India, in 1865, the son of an artist and curator of the museum at Lahore, Kipling received his education in England and then returned to India to become a journalist. When his first barracks stories began to appear, the world began to realize that a

432

star of the first magnitude was rising on the literary firmament. A born story-teller, his adept use of slang caught the ear of the public. *Plain Tales from the Hills* was soon followed by *Barrack Room Ballads.*

Then came his sojourn in America, where he found a bride in Vermont, and wrote *Captains Courageous* and other stories with an American flavor.

But Kipling also knew how to write for children, and his *Jungle Books, Just-So Stories, Puck of Pook's Hill* and *Rewards and Fairies* captured the hearts and imaginations of youngsters everywhere. One of his two hymns, *Land of our birth, we pledge to thee,* was a challenge addressed to the children of the British Empire to be loyal and true to their native land, but also a prayer to God that He might direct them in the paths of steadfastness and truth. Here are the prayer stanzas:

> Father in heaven who lovest all,
> O help Thy children when they call,
> That they may build from age to age
> An undefilèd heritage.
>
> Teach us to bear the yoke in youth,
> With steadfastness and careful truth;
> That in our time Thy grace may give
> The truth whereby the nations live.
>
> Teach us to rule ourselves alway,
> Controlled and cleanly night and day;
> That we may bring, if need arise,
> No maimed or worthless sacrifice.
>
> Teach us to look in all our ends
> On Thee for judge, and not our friends;
> That we, with Thee, may walk uncowed
> By fear or favor of the crowd.
>
> Teach us the strength that cannot seek,
> By deed or thought, to hurt the weak;
> That, under Thee, we may possess
> Man's strength to comfort man's distress.
>
> Teach us delight in simple things,
> And mirth that has no bitter springs;
> Forgiveness free of evil done,
> And love to all men 'neath the sun.

Kipling was fiercely patriotic, and his writings are credited with having done more than any other single factor in arousing the spirit of imperialism in England. Yet, no one was more aware than he of the dangers of "an over-weening consciousness of national greatness,"

433

and never has a poet spoken more prophetically of his country than he in his famous "Recessional" of 1897. It was the year of Queen Victoria's "Diamond Jubilee," completing sixty years of her reign, the longest rule in British history. The event was marked with unequaled pomp and pageantry, climaxed by huge military and naval reviews intended to impress the world with England's vast power and might.

Kipling, however, found little satisfaction in the great military spectacle. Because he was not England's Poet Laureate, he had not been asked to write a poem in honor of the Jubilee. However, the *London Times* had importuned him to write some appropriate verses, and they finally came just as the Jubilee reached its end. When published, they created a sensation throughout England, and Kipling was both commended and condemned. However, with the passing of half a century, and with two World Wars a part of history, the poet and patriot now stands forth as a prophet. England's pomp and greatness of yesterday is already become much like the forgotten glory and pride of Tyre and Nineveh. Will America heed the lesson contained in lines such as these?

God of our fathers, known of old,
  Lord of our far-flung battle-line,
Beneath whose awful hand we hold
  Dominion over palm and pine—
Lord God of Hosts, be with us yet,
Lest we forget—lest we forget!

The tumult and the shouting dies;
  The captains and the kings depart:
Still stands Thine ancient sacrifice,
  An humble and a contrite heart.
Lord God of Hosts, be with us yet,
Lest we forget—lest we forget!

Far-called, our navies melt away;
  On dune and headland sinks the fire:
Lo, all our pomp of yesterday
  Is one with Nineveh and Tyre!
Judge of the Nations, spare us yet,
Lest we forget — lest we forget!

If drunk with sight of power, we loose
  Wild tongues that have not Thee in awe,
Such boastings as the Gentiles use,
  Or lesser breeds without the Law—
Lord God of Hosts, be with us yet,
Lest we forget—lest we forget!

434

> For heathen heart that puts her trust
>   In reeking tube and iron shard,
> All valiant dust that builds on dust,
>   And guarding, calls not Thee to guard,
> For frantic boast and foolish word—
> Thy mercy on Thy people, Lord!

When Kipling passed away in London, January 18, 1936, he not only had won the Nobel Prize for literature, but the adulation of the entire literary world.

Adoration of the Holy Trinity

Ye watchers and ye holy ones,
Bright seraphs, cherubim, and thrones,
 Raise the glad strain, Alleluia!
Cry out, dominions, princedoms, powers,
Virtues, archangels, angels' choirs,
 Alleluia!

O higher than the cherubim
More glorious than the seraphim,
 Lead their praises, Alleluia!
Thou bearer of the eternal Word,
Most gracious, magnify the Lord,
 Alleluia!

Respond, ye souls in endless rest,
Ye patriarchs and prophets blest,
 Alleluia, Alleluia!
Ye holy twelve, ye martyrs strong,
All saints triumphant, raise the song,
 Alleluia!

O friends, in gladness let us sing,
Supernal anthems echoing,
 Alleluia, Alleluia!
To God the Father, God the Son,
And God the Spirit, Three in One,
 Alleluia!

JOHN ATHELSTAN RILEY, 1858–1945

A COMPANION TO THE BOOK OF COMMON PRAYER

WHILE Robert Bridges was working on his *Yattendon Hymnal,* a group of seven distinguished scholars who belonged to the so-called High Church party in the Church of England conceived the idea of compiling a hymnbook which they hoped might become "a humble companion to the Book of Common Prayer for use in the Church." Leaders in the project were Percy Dearmer, T. A. Lacey and John Athelstan Riley.

A young musician who even then was giving evidence of possessing unusual genius as a composer was chosen as the musical editor. His name was Ralph Vaughan Williams, who at the time of his death in 1958 at the age of 86 years was still creating magnificent symphonies and sacred chorals, and receiving the homage of the world as its greatest contemporary composer.

The result of their combined labors was published in 1906 under the title, *The English Hymnal.* By the Anglo-Catholics it was hailed as an artistic and literary triumph, but the evangelical party in the Church of England received it with marked coolness. As a rival of *Hymns Ancient and Modern,* it failed completely.

The inclusion of 161 translations from the Latin at once betrayed the Anglo-Catholic leanings of some of its compilers, who, not content with Latin hymns of unquestioned evangelical content such as the translations of John Mason Neale, introduced a dozen or more other hymns that reflected distinctive Roman Catholic doctrines. Some of these invoked the supplications of the saints and martyrs. Others contained prayers for the dead. Still others were tinged with Mariolatry. Typical of these is this stanza from a hymn addressed to a patron saint:

> Another year completed,
> The day comes round once more
> Which with our patron's radiance
> Is bright as heretofore.
> Now, strong in hope, united
> His festival we greet;
> He will present our troubles
> Before the mercy-seat.

437

Another hymn, addressed largely to the Virgin Mary, reads:

> Jesu's tender Mother,
>   Make thy supplication
> Unto Him who chose thee
>   At His incarnation;
> That, O matchless Maiden,
>   Passing meek and lowly,
> Thy dear Son may make us
>   Blameless, chaste and holy.

Yet another, which is a prayer for the departed, invokes the prayers of Mary and the saints in these words:

> When, O kind and radiant Jesu,
>   Kneels the Queen Thy throne before,
> Let the court of Saints attending,
>   Mercy for the dead implore;
> Hearken, loving Friend of sinners,
>   Whom the Cross exalted bore.

Because of the storm of criticism which met *The English Hymnal,* an abridged edition was published a year after its first appearance, in which five of the more objectionable hymns were eliminated and four others revised. However, even with these alterations the book failed to win the support of the evangelical wing of the Church.

Despite all this, *The English Hymnal* contained one of the finest collections of sacred verse ever published in the English language. By this time Christian hymnody had come to full flower in England, and all of the choicest compositions of such spiritual poets as Heber, Montgomery, Newton, Cowper, Lyte, How, Keble, Ellerton, Baker, Bonar, Wordsworth, Alford, Faber, Dix, and Robert Bridges, to say nothing of the treasures of Watts, Doddridge and Charles Wesley, were available to the compilers. Then, too, translations from the Greek and Latin by Neale, Caswall, Chandler and others had brought to light the rich classical hymn heritage of the Church. Added to these were the fine English translations of Germany's great hymns by Catherine Winkworth, the Borthwick sisters, Frances Cox, John Wesley and Bridges. From the German alone, twenty-two hymns were included in the collection.

And now, for the first time, an English hymnbook had reached across the Atlantic to appropriate sacred lyrics by American poets! No less than four centos from the poems of John Greenleaf Whittier were included, and one each by William Cullen Bryant, Oliver Wendell Holmes, James Russell Lowell and Samuel Johnson. Other Americans who were recognized were Frederick Lucian Hosmer, Samuel Longfellow, Bishop Arthur Cleveland Coxe, Bishop Phillips Brooks, Bishop George Washington Doane and Philipp Bliss. The latter's contribution was a typical American "gospel hymn," and, strangely enough, one of a very inferior type.

Among the principal English contributors were two members of the editorial committee—Riley and Dearmer. The former was the translator of nine Latin and Greek hymns and the author of three original lyrics. One of Riley's originals, "Ye watchers and ye holy ones," written for the magnificent German tune, *Lasst uns erfreuen herzlich sehr,* which is said to be based on the musical notes of the bells of Cologne Cathedral, has already become one of the great hymn classics in the English language. His other two hymns—"Come, let us join the Church above" and "Saints of God, lo Jesu's people"—are less familiar.

Riley, who was born in London, August 10, 1858, received his education at Oxford, and was a member of the House of Laymen of the Province of Canterbury during most of his life. Besides being interested in hymnody, he was the author of *Athos, or the Mountain of the Monks; Prayer Book Revision,* and a work on hymn tunes and Latin sequences. He died November 17, 1945.

It was Percy Dearmer, however, who was the moving spirit in the creation of *The English Hymnal.* In addition to serving as editor of this epoch-making volume, his personal contribution consisted of six original hymns and twelve translations, eleven of which are from the Latin. His original lyrics in the book are "A brighter dawn is breaking," "The winter's sweep was long and deep," "God, we thank Thee; not in vain," "Father, who on man dost shower," "Lord, the wind and sea obey Thee," "Jesu, good above all other," and "Holy God, we offer here." The last named is a communion hymn which approaches very closely the Roman Catholic concept of the Mass as a reenactment of the sacrifice of Christ, offered unto God anew as a propitiation for man's sin.

Dearmer's eleven Latin translations are generally done so well they easily give the impression of being original English hymns. This is particularly true of the 10th century office hymn, *O Pater sancte,* and Gregory the Great's *Nocte surgentes.* The former, in Dearmer's hands, becomes "Father most holy, merciful and tender," and the latter is rendered "Father, we praise Thee, now the night is over." Unfortunately, other translations by Dearmer often reflect his Anglican "high church" tendencies, particularly in reference to the Virgin Mary, the invocation of saints, and the suggestion of the sacrificial character of the Mass.

An unusual hymn in the collection, in the translation of which Dearmer collaborated, is "Strengthen for service, Lord," from the Syriac *Liturgy of Malabar* used by the Thoma Church in India. Its opening stanza reads:

> Strengthen for service, Lord, the hands
> That holy things have taken;
> Let ears that now have heard Thy songs
> To clamor never waken.

Dearmer must be regarded as the most important English hymnodist of the 20th century. Born in London, February 27, 1867, he was educated at Oxford and was ordained by the Church of England in 1892. After serving as curate in a number of parishes, he became vicar of St. Mary's, Primrose Hill, London, where he served from 1901 to 1915. A poet by nature, Dearmer had the good fortune of having a great musician, Martin Shaw, as his organist, and undoubtedly the two artists found mutual inspiration in each other. It was during this period too that *The English Hymnal* was being produced with the aid of that other great musician and composer, Ralph Vaughan Williams, a circumstance that must have offered an additional creative incentive to Dearmer.

In Dearmer we find a man in whom a fine artistic temperament was combined with a strong sense of social justice. For many years he was one of the outstanding leaders in the London Christian Social Union, and many of his finer hymns, notably those written in later years, deal with modern social problems. These will be noted in another chapter, in which his subsequent labors, including his epochal work on *Songs of Praise*, will be presented. Suffice to state here that he served as a chaplain with the British Red Cross in Serbia during World War I, and at the close of that conflict was made professor of ecclesiastical art at King's College, Oxford. In 1931 he became canon of Westminster.

In addition to the hymnbooks already mentioned, Dearmer also edited the *Oxford Book of Carols* in 1928, *Songs of Praise for Boys and Girls* in 1929, and *Songs of Praise for Little Children* in 1933, as well as the handbook, *Songs of Praise Discussed.* He likewise was the author of a number of works dealing with the ecclesiastical arts and social questions.

Dearmer contended that the failure of the Church to retain its hold on the intellectual classes in England was due to the low standards reflected in its hymnody, both from a literary and musical point of view. He insisted, therefore, that nothing but the finest sacred poetry should be included in *The English Hymnal.* As a result, the book set a new standard for literary excellence.

From the pen of William Romanis (1824-1899), a British clergyman who was classical headmaster at Cheltenham College from 1846 to 1856, we find in *The English Hymnal* the lovely evening hymn:

> Round me falls the night;
> Saviour, be my light;
> Through the hours in darkness shrouded
> Let me see Thy face unclouded;
> Let Thy glory shine
> In this heart of mine.

The growing social note in English hymnody is heard in another hymn, "Thy Kingdom come, O God," which cries out in words like these:

> When comes the promised time
> That war shall be no more,
> And lust, oppression, crime
> Shall flee Thy face before?

The writer of this was another British clergyman, Lewis Hensley (1824-1905), who, after serving as vicar of a rural parish at Hitchin, was appointed honorary canon of St. Alban's Cathedral in 1881. He was the author of two small hymn collections. He died in 1905.

A Classic Marriage Hymn

O perfect Love, all human thought transcending
    Lowly we kneel in prayer before Thy throne,
That theirs may be the love which knows no ending,
    Whom Thou for evermore dost join in one.

O perfect Life, be Thou their full assurance
    Of tender charity and steadfast faith,
Of patient hope, and quiet, brave endurance,
    With childlike trust that fears nor pain nor death.

Grant them the joy which brightens earthly sorrow;
    Grant them the peace which calms all earthly strife,
And to life's day the glorious unknown morrow
    That dawns upon eternal love and life.

DOROTHY FRANCES GURNEY, 1858-1932

WOMEN WHO WON FAME BY A SINGLE HYMN

IN THE foregoing chapter we have noted something of the epochal character of *The English Hymnal* of 1906. The lasting influence of this hymn collection in raising both the literary and musical standards of English hymnody can scarcely be over-estimated. The volume was also remarkable for the number of contemporary women hymn-writers it brought to light. Some of these are known today solely because of a single hymn included in this book.

It was to be expected, of course, that such gifted hymnists as Charlotte Elliott, Frances Havergal and Sarah Adams would be represented, and no further reference to these need be given here. However, we now encounter such names as Katherine Hankey, Mrs. Dorothy Frances Gurney, Caroline Noel, Isabel Stephenson, Emily Steele Elliott, Jane Eliza Leeson, Mrs. Mary Lundlie Duncan, Christina Rossetti and Mary Fowler Maude, all of whom contributed lyrics to the famous collection.

Dorothy Frances Gurney (1858-1932) will long be remembered as the author of "O perfect love, all human thought transcending," probably the finest and most impressive wedding hymn ever written. The daughter of the Rev. Frederick G. Blomfield and the granddaughter of Bishop Blomfield of London, she grew up in the atmosphere of a devout home marked by refinement and culture. All this is clearly reflected in her hymn. Her unusual gifts were revealed early in life in two volumes of verse, as well as in a devotional work titled *A Little Book of Quiet.* One of her best known poems is "God's Garden," from which these lines are often quoted:

> The kiss of the sun for pardon,
> The song of the birds for mirth:
> One is nearer God's heart in a garden
> Than anywhere else on earth.

Isabella Stephenson (1843-1890) wrote only one hymn during her life-time, and that hymn found its way into *The English Hymnal.* "Holy Father, in Thy mercy" is a prayer for travelers. Miss Stephenson, who was the daughter of a British army officer, was an invalid for many years. She lived all of her life at Cheltenham, England. Her hymn is said to have been composed at a time "when her faith and affection were under the stress of a special need to find some such mode of expression." However, when the crisis had passed, she never wrote verse again. Nevertheless, her one hymn continues to enshrine a prayer that has brought strength and assurance to innumerable anxious souls in hours of darkness and distress.

Katherine Hankey (1834-1911) contributed two hymns to *The English Hymnal,* but only one of them, "I love to tell the story," has survived the passing of time. There are few hymnbooks today that do not include it. Although it is highly subjective and can hardly be considered poetry of a high order, it breathes a confession of faith that finds a deep response in believing hearts.

Miss Hankey, the daughter of a banker at Clapham, England, belonged to an evangelical group known as the Clapham Sect. While still a young girl she began teaching Sunday school, and at 18 conducted a large Bible class for shop girls in London. Her influence over this group was remarkable, and the members of the class could never forget her. Five of them, it is said, came together again at her funeral, fifty years after the class had ceased to exist. As a result of a trip to South Africa to bring home an invalid brother, she became intensely interested in foreign missions. In later years she devoted the income from all her writings to this cause. Among her books is one on confirmation. Her last years were spent in hospital visitation work in London.

The life story of another contributor, Carolina Maria Noel (1817-1877), is a strange one. The daughter of Canon Gerard Thomas Noel, an Anglican clergyman and himself a writer of hymns, Carolina wrote her first spiritual song at the age of 17. However, for some unknown reason, she ceased entirely to compose hymns after she reached the age of 20. Then, after the lapse of two decades, with the coming of sickness and suffering, her harp was tuned again, and the last twenty years of her life were spent in writing hymns of comfort and encouragement for other sufferers like herself. Her best known hymn, "At the Name of Jesus," was first published in a volume titled *The Name of Jesus, and Other Verses for the Sick and Lonely.*

Also included in *The English Hymnal* was a children's hymn prayer considered by many to be the most appealing in the English

444

language. There probably are few children, at least in Britain and America, who have not lisped these sweet verses before falling asleep at night:

> Jesus, tender Shepherd, hear me,
>   Bless Thy little lamb tonight;
> Through the darkness be Thou near me,
>   Keep me safe till morning light.
>
> Through this day Thy hand has led me,
>   And I thank Thee for Thy care;
> Thou hast warmed me, clothed and fed me,
>   Listen to my evening prayer.
>
> Let my sins be all forgiven;
>   Bless the friends I love so well;
> Take me, Lord, at last to heaven,
>   Happy there with Thee to dwell.

Mary Lundlie Duncan, a young mother who died at the age of 25, was the author of this tender little hymn. She intended it only for her own children, but it became her gift to all the children of the world. The writer, who was born at Kelso in 1814, was the daughter of a parish minister, Robert Lundlie, and she herself married a minister of the Scottish Free Church, William Wallace Duncan. A younger sister became the wife of the greatest of all Scottish hymnists, Horatius Bonar. Mrs. Duncan is described as "a rare spirit, amiable, accomplished and beautiful." She was fond of writing verse, and during the last year of her life composed twenty-three poems, among them her lovely children's prayer. They were published a year after she died by her mother under the title, *Rhymes for My Children.*

Emily Steele Elliott (1836-1897) likewise will be remembered by posterity for a single hymn that appeared in *The English Hymnal.* There is something strangely moving about "Thou didst leave Thy throne, and Thy kingly crown," a lyric which seems to be growing in the affections of Christians on both sides of the Atlantic. Miss Elliott came by her gifts as a poet honestly, being a niece of Charlotte Elliott, author of "Just as I am" and other famous hymns. Two hymn collections came from her pen, and she also edited *The Church Missionary Juvenile Instructor* for a number of years.

Jane Eliza Leeson (1807-1882) was another woman hymn-writer who received recognition from the editors of *The English Hymnal.* Included in that celebrated volume was her lovely children's hymn, "Loving Shepherd of Thy sheep." Miss Leeson, who spent all of her life in London, was the author of a number of hymn collections, principally for children. Her better known hymns, in addition to the one mentioned, are "Saviour, teach me day by day," "Gracious Saviour, gentle Shepherd," "Sweet the lesson Jesus taught," and "Dear Saviour, to Thy little lambs." For many years she was a member of the Catholic Apostolic Church, and contributed a number of original hymns, as well as translations from the Latin, to the hymnbook of that communion. Among her translations is "Christ the Lord is risen today" from the Latin sequence, *Victimae Paschali.*

Miss Leeson is said to have composed some of her hymns, supposedly by divine prompting, at public services in Bishopsgate Church in London. One who witnessed the production of such a hymn has recorded that "it was delivered slowly, with short pauses between the verses, a pause three times as long as any one would ordinarily make in reading."

A contemporary hymn-writer, Mrs. Mary Fowler Maude, whose confirmation hymn, "Thine for ever, God of love," reminds us very much of Miss Havergal's lyrics, was the wife of Joseph Maude, a vicar on the Isle of Wight. Here she taught a Sunday school class of girls, all of whom were being prepared for confirmation. During an absence of twelve weeks, Mrs. Maude wrote a series of weekly letters to these girls, and to one of these she appended the hymn she had composed.

When her husband was transferred to the parish of Chirk in Wales, Mrs. Maude became the teacher of a class of miners, and after her husband's death she taught a class of young men at Overton. In 1911, when she was dying at the age of 93, the members of her class gathered outside her door and sang "Thine for ever." Then followed another favorite song of hers, "Will the anchor hold?" The dying woman smiled and told those about her, "Tell them that it does not fail — it holds!"

Mrs. Maude's famous confirmation hymn, which was given an honored place in *The English Hymnal,* reads in part:

> Thine for ever! God of love,
> Hear us from Thy throne above;
> Thine for ever may we be
> Here and in eternity.
>
> Thine for ever! O how blest
> They who find in Thee their rest!
> Saviour, Guardian, heavenly Friend,
> O defend us to the end.

Thine for ever! Lord of life,
Shield us through our earthly strife;
Thou the Life, the Truth, the Way,
Guide us to the realms of day.

We have already noted in a previous chapter that *The English Hymnal* included a score or more hymns by outstanding American poets and hymnists. It should be added that two American women were likewise honored. One was the famous blind composer of "gospel songs," Fanny Crosby, whose work will be noted in a later chapter; the other was Mrs. Julia A. Carney, a Boston schoolteacher.

Of the 8,000 or more hymns written by Fanny Crosby, "Safe in the arms of Jesus" was chosen for inclusion in the English collection. Mrs. Carney's contribution was the delightful children's song, "Little drops of water." In 1848 an English clergyman by the name of Dr. E. C. Brewer published a poem which had an identical opening stanza, and for years it was generally supposed that he was the original writer. Later it developed that Mrs. Carney had printed it three years earlier in a *Reader* prepared for use in a primary school which she taught in the vestry of Hollis Street Church in Boston. Evidently the English clergyman had appropriated Mrs. Carney's first stanza, and then added four inferior verses of his own. Here is the little hymn as the American woman wrote it:

Little drops of water,
Little grains of sand,
Make the mighty ocean
And the beauteous land.

And the little moments,
Humble though they be,
Make the mighty ages
Of eternity.

Little deeds of kindness,
Little words of love,
Make our earth an Eden,
Like the heaven above.

So our little errors
Lead the soul away,
From the paths of virtue
Into sin to stray.

Little seeds of mercy
Sown by youthful hands,
Grow to bless the nations
Far in heathen lands.

447

Two distinguished British hymnists, Bishop Bickersteth and Godfrey Thring, feeling that the American text was not quite complete, essayed to add certain stanzas. The former wrote:

> Little ones in glory
>> Swell the angels' song:
> Make us meet, dear Saviour,
>> For their holy throng.

And Thring added three additional verses, including a doxology:

> Little children's angels,
>> Happy in the sky,
> See their heavenly Father
>> On His throne on high.
>
> Little children's voices,
>> Heavenly choirs among,
> Swell the angel-chorus
>> With their simple song.
>
> Glory then for ever
>> Be to Father, Son,
> With the Holy Spirit,
>> Blessed Three in One.

The doxology is now generally added to Mrs. Carney's famous little primary hymn. Mrs. Carney died in Galesburg, Ill., November 2, 1908, at the age of 85 years.

The last of the gifted women hymn-writers whose poetic talents were recognized by the discriminating editors of *The English Hymnal* was Christina Rossetti (1830-1894). This remarkable woman belonged to a brilliant Italian family who had come to England as refugees. Her father became professor of Italian at King's College, London, and a brother, Dante Gabriel, gained fame as an artist. The latter immortalized the classical features of Christina as the Virgin Mary in two of his paintings, "Ecce Ancilla Domini" and "Girlhood of the Virgin." Holman Hunt and other famous artists also used her as a model.

The one romance in Christina's life resulted unhappily when she broke off her engagement to the man she intended to marry when he embraced the Roman Catholic faith. Her deeply sensitive nature never fully recovered from this disappointment, which was intensified when her health also began to fail. She revealed poetic talent very early in life, and now she found solace in writing religious verse of rare beauty. She also gave much of her time to charity work in

London. One of her biographers has written: "Hers was a cloistral spirit, timid, nun-like, bowed down by suffering and humility; her character was so retiring as to be almost invisible. All that we really need to know about her, save that she was a great saint, is that she was a great poet." She was the author of several devotional books, both in prose and poetry, such as *Called to Be Saints, Seek and Find, The Face of the Deep,* and *The Prince's Progress, and Other Poems.*

Two of Miss Rosetti's hymns were published in *The English Hymnal,* namely, her exquisite Christmas carol, "In the bleak midwinter," and an All Saints' Day lyric of rare poetic imagination, "What are these that glow from afar?" For the former, the noted English musician, Gustav Holst, wrote the tune *Cranham.* Among Miss Rossetti's hymns that have gained wide circulation in later hymnbooks are "Love came down at Christmas," "Spring bursts today," and "The shepherds had an angel."

Because many of the earlier hymnal editors failed to note carefully the authorship of the lyrics they published, a veil of anonymity has been thrown about numerous hymns. Such is the case with the well-known marriage hymn, "Lord, who at Cana's wedding feast." The hymn first appeared in a volume published in 1853 titled *Psalms and Hymns,* where it was signed "A. T." The editor of the collection was Joseph Francis Thrupp, vicar of the Anglican church at Barrington, Cambridge, and it is generally supposed that the initials "A. T." stand for Adelaide Thrupp, his daughter.

Joseph Francis Thrupp was himself a hymnist of no mean ability. Of 329 psalms and hymns that appear in his collection, no less than 46 bear his own initials. However, none of these is in common use today. Apparently, the only one that is destined to survive is the wedding hymn which bears the initials of his daughter Adelaide.

Another English woman who will probably be remembered because of a single lyric is Sarah Doudney, who has given us the lovely evening hymn, "Saviour, now the day is ending," each stanza of which closes with the prayer:

> Set Thy seal on every heart,
> Jesus, bless us e'er we part.

Miss Doudney, who spent the greater part of her life in a remote village in Hampshire, England, passed away in 1926. She was chiefly known as a novelist, but published a volume called *Psalms of Life* in 1871. Among her works of fiction are *A Woman's Glory* and *Stepping Stones.*

A Prayer for Peace and Brotherhood

Son of God, eternal Saviour
    Source of life and truth and grace,
Son of Man, whose birth incarnate
    Hallows all our human race,
Thou, our Head, who, throned in glory,
    For Thine own dost ever plead,
Fill us with Thy love and pity,
    Heal our wrongs, and help our need.

As Thou, Lord, hast lived for others,
    So may we for others live;
Freely have Thy gifts been granted,
    Freely may Thy servants give.
Thine the gold and Thine the silver,
    Thine the wealth of land and sea,
We but stewards of Thy bounty,
    Held in solemn trust for Thee.

Come, O Christ, and reign among us,
    King of Love, and Prince of Peace;
Hush the storm of strife and passion,
    Bid its cruel discords cease;
By Thy patient years of toiling,
    By Thy silent hours of pain,
Quench our fevered thirst of pleasure,
    Shame our selfish greed of gain.

Dark the path that lies behind us,
    Strewn with wrecks and stained with blood;
But before us gleams the vision
    Of the coming brotherhood.
Thou who prayedst, Thou who willest
    That Thy people should be one,
Grant, O grant our hope's fruition:
    Here on earth Thy will be done.

SOMERSET CORRY LOWRY, 1855-1932

450

A WAR-WEARY WORLD SINGS OF PEACE

WHEN the church bells proclaimed the dawn of the 20th century, a war-weary world prayed that it might be a century of peace. The Hague Peace Conference initiated by Nicholas II of Russia in 1899 had reflected the universal longing of mankind for a cessation of human bloodshed. The International Court of Arbitration, established at the Hague in the same year, was hailed by some as the dawn of a new day when the law of the tooth and the nail of the jungle would at last be supplanted by a rule of justice and righteousness.

But there were many disturbing signs on the horizon. Even while the nations were discussing peace in the Dutch capital, Englishmen and Dutch settlers in South Africa were locked in deadly combat, and a dark suspicion lurked in the minds of many that the discovery of fabulous diamond deposits and vast gold fields in that region had been a basic cause of the conflict.

Europe itself resembled an armed camp. All of the great Powers, riding the crest of colonialism, were greedily seeking to exploit the backward races of the earth while jealously watching each other's moves in an intense rivalry to gain a greater place in the sun. Still, nobody wanted war, and to make sure that none would occur, they had formed two great military alliances in Europe in order to maintain a "balance of power."

And there was social unrest. Rumblings of discontent were growing ever louder among the masses. The widespread uprisings in Europe in 1848 had indeed proved abortive, but Karl Marx, by his *Das Kapital* of 1867, had not only continued to fan the flames of revolt, but had actually provided the proletariat with a textbook on social and political revolution.

Despite all this, there were many intellectuals who believed that mankind had become "too civilized" to resort to war, and few were the prophets who were bold enough to predict that the world was standing on the brink of a catastrophic conflict, or that a social revolu-

451

tion was impending, the magnitude of which had never before been witnessed.

Nevertheless, before half the century was gone, the world was destined to witness two of the most bloody conflicts in history, accompanied by unparalleled material destruction and indescribable human misery and suffering. It was also to see the fall of several of the mightiest dynasties in Europe and the seizure of power by ruthless fascist dictators or atheistic Communists. It was likewise to experience a world-wide economic depression of unprecedented severity, bringing increased demands in many countries that the State assume far greater responsibilty for the welfare of its people. And as these revolutionary movements swept around the world, they were to create social and political ferment everywhere, particularly among the exploited peoples of Africa, Asia and the islands of the sea, resulting in the rise of intense nationalism, as well as insistent demands for political freedom, racial equality, economic opportunity and social justice.

Except for the solemn warnings sounded by Kipling in his famous "Recessional" and by Tennyson in his "Ring out, wild bells, to the wild sky," there was little in English hymnody during the latter part of the 19th century to arouse the Church to a realization of how close was the impending crisis. However, a few prophetic souls who seem to have been able to read the signs of the times more clearly than their fellows had come together in London in 1896 to found the Christian Social Union. Its avowed purpose was to challenge the Church to champion the rights of the common man, to work for more humane laws, to oppose injustice and oppression, to cleanse the body politic of dishonesty and corruption, and to seek to instill Christian ideals and principles into international relations. A leader of the movement and editor of the organization's magazine, *The Commonwealth*, was Henry Scott Holland, from 1884 to 1910 canon of St. Paul's in London.

As Holland looked out upon the far-flung British Empire and the many troubles that were beginning to beset it on all sides, not least of all the Boer conflict, there came from his pen in 1902 this passionate hymn prayer:

> Judge eternal, throned in splendor,
> Lord of lords and King of kings,
> With Thy living fire of judgment
> Purge this realm of bitter things;
> Solace all its wide dominion,
> With the healing of Thy wings.

Gilbert Keith Chesterton, the noted journalist and critic, was another Englishman who was profoundly disturbed by the role his country had played in the Boer War. Called "one of the most vivacious, versatile and provocative figures" of his day, Chesterton was convinced that the conflict had been brought on by British greed, and he was unsparing in his criticism of Cecil Rhodes' policies. His scorn for British political leadership and for contemporary civilization in general is bitterly reflected in a hymn he contributed to *The English Hymnal* in 1906, the first stanza of which reads:

> O God of earth and altar,
> Bow down and hear our cry,
> Our earthly rulers falter,
> Our people drift and die;
> The walls of gold entomb us,
> The swords of scorn divide,
> Take not Thy thunder from us,
> But take away our pride.

"Thy thunder" was undoubtedly intended to denote God's warning of an approaching storm. Chesterton lived to witness the coming of World War I, but he passed away in 1936, three years before the storm of World War II broke, an agonizing conflict of "blood and sweat and tears" that brought the British Empire close to the brink of disaster.

Another hymn in *The English Hymnal* that cried out against the sacrifice of human lives to promote British imperialism came from the pen of Arthur Christopher Benson, a Fellow of Magdalene College, Cambridge. It bore the title, "O Lord of hosts, who didst upraise." Written in 1899, during the Boer conflict, it pleaded for peace in burning words like these:

> And must we battle yet? Must we,
> Who bear the tender Name divine,
> Still barter life for victory,
> Still glory in the crimson sign?
> The Crucified between us stands,
> And lifts on high His wounded hands.
>
> As rains that weep the clouds away,
> As winds that leave a calm in heaven,
> So let the slayer cease to slay;
> The passion healed, the wrath forgiven,
> Draw nearer, bid the tumult cease,
> Redeemer, Saviour, Prince of Peace!

453

With the turn of the century a new note began to be heard in English hymnody. As hymn-writers pleaded with the nations to beat their swords into plowshares and their spears into pruning-hooks, they also emphasized the essential oneness of the human race. They were not carried away by an easy optimism, however, but seem to have seen clearly that only as men become one in Christ can they become one with each other. Peace and brotherhood will forever remain an unrealized dream until mankind is willing to submit to the rule of the Prince of Peace. Thus we find John Oxenham singing:

> In Christ there is no East or West,
>   In Him no South or North,
> But one great fellowship of love
>   Throughout the whole wide earth.
>
> In Him shall true hearts everywhere
>   Their high communion find;
> His service is the golden cord
>   Close-binding all mankind.
>
> Join hands, then, brothers of the faith,
>   Whate'er your race may be:
> Who serves my Father as a son
>   Is surely kin to me.
>
> In Christ now meet both East and West,
>   In Him meet South and North;
> All Christly souls are one in Him
>   Throughout the whole wide earth.

Oxenham, whose real name was William A. Dunkerley, had an unusual career. Born in England in 1852, he engaged in business for many years, traveling extensively in Europe and America. To relieve the tedium of long journeys, he took up writing, and soon decided to make it his career. When publishers hesitated to accept his manuscript, *Bees in Amber*, he printed it himself and sold 285,000 copies. During World War I he became deeply interested in the spiritual welfare of those in military service. His *Hymns for Men at the Front* had a circulation of 8,000,000 copies, and were sung round the world. Among the finer hymns of Oxenham in this collection is his "Lord God of hosts, whose mighty hand." He died in 1941, two years after the outbreak of World War II, at the age of 89.

Another Englishman who joined the chorus of those who were pleading the cause of peace and Christian brotherhood was Somerset

Corry Lowry. This man, who was ordained by the Church of England in 1879 and who served a number of parishes until he retired at Bournemouth to devote all his time to the writing of devotional books and a hymn collection, will be gratefully remembered for his lyric, "Son of God, eternal Saviour." A hymn of deep feeling, it was written in 1893 and published in *Goodwill* magazine the following year. It subsequently found a place in *The English Hymnal*, and lately has been incorporated in many hymn collections. No prayer for peace in all of Christian hymnody is more moving than that expressed in the following lines:

> Come, O Christ, and reign among us,
>   King of Love, and Prince of Peace;
> Hush the storm of strife and passion,
>   Bid its cruel discords cease;
> By Thy patient years of toiling,
>   By Thy silent hours of pain,
> Quench our fevered thirst of pleasure,
>   Shame our selfish greed of gain.

Lowry wrote some sixty hymns in all, but this is the only one that has come into general use. He died in 1932.

Though it became unpopular to be a "pacifist" during the patriotic hysteria of the first World War, there were some brave souls who refused to be silenced. Appalled and shocked by the hatreds and cruelties engendered by that dread conflict, they did not hesitate to characterize the resort to war's savagery as a denial of Christian teaching and a reproach to our civilization. Thus we find Clifford Bax, an English poet and dramatist who gained considerable fame in the 1920's by his musical plays, coming out boldly in the very midst of the war with a hymn that startled England. He wrote:

> Turn back, O man, forswear thy foolish ways.
> Old now is earth, and none may count her days,
> Yet thou, her child, whose head is crowned with flame
> Still wilt not hear thine inner God proclaim,
> "Turn back, O man, forswear thy foolish ways."
>
> Earth might be fair, and all men glad and wise.
> Age after age their tragic empires rise,
> Built while they dream, and in that dreaming weep:
> Would man but wake from out his haunted sleep,
> Earth might be fair, and all men glad and wise.
>
> Earth shall be fair, and all her people one;
> Nor till that hour shall God's whole will be done.
> Now, even now, once more from earth to sky,
> Peals forth in joy man's old, undaunted cry,
> "Earth shall be fair, and all her folk be one!"

455

As the weary war years dragged on and the daily casualties mounted, English hearts grew heavy. Hardly a British home knew escape from sorrow, and as the tragedy deepened they looked to the Church for hope and consolation. Commemoration services were frequent, and for one of these William Charter Piggott (1872-1943), a Congregational pastor in London, wrote a hymn that came into widespread use. It reads in part:

> For those we love within the veil
> Who once were comrades of our way,
> We thank Thee, Lord, for they have won
> To cloudless day.
>
> Not as we knew them any more,
> Toil-worn, and sad with burdened care:
> Erect, clear-eyed, upon their brows
> Thy Name they bear.
>
> There are no tears within their eyes;
> With love they keep perpetual tryst;
> And praise and work and rest are one,
> With Thee, O Christ.

Still other hymnists, as they pondered the mystery of life and death and human suffering, sought to find meaning in the sacrificial devotion and heroism of those who bled and died. Some found comfort in the conviction that, despite the wild passions of war and the spiritual blindness of men, God was working out His eternal plans and purposes. One of these was Edward Grubb (1854-1939), editor of a monthly periodical, *The British Friend*. In a volume titled *The Light of Life: Hymns of Faith and Consolation*, Grubb expressed his faith in words like these:

> Our God, to whom we turn
> When weary with illusion,
> Whose stars serenely burn
> Above this world's confusion,
> Thine is the mighty plan,
> The steadfast order sure,
> In which the world began,
> Endures, and shall endure.

As might be expected, hymns on the theme of the resurrection and the life everlasting appeared in England in considerable numbers following the war. One of these was written by Frederick B. Macnutt (1873-1949), a Church of England clergyman who served as a chaplain

456

with the British forces in Flanders and France from 1915 to 1918. Author of a number of publications, including *The Reproach of War, Classics of the Inner Life,* and *From Chaos to God,* Macnutt was asked to contribute a hymn to *Songs of Praise* of 1925. Recalling his war experiences when day after day he had laid fallen soldiers to rest among the poppies blooming in the midst of countless crosses "row on row," he responded with a beautiful Easter lyric:

> Let all the multitudes of light,
>   Their songs in concert raising,
> With earth's triumphal hymns unite,
>   The risen Saviour praising.
> Ye heavens, His festival proclaim!
> Our King returneth whence He came,
>   With victory amazing.
>
> For us He bore the bitter Tree,
>   To death's dark realm descending,
> Our foe He slew, and set us free,
>   Man's ancient bondage ending.
> No more the tyrant's chains oppress;
> O conquering Love, Thy Name we bless,
>   With Thee to heaven ascending.
>
> Jesus, to Thee be endless praise
>   For this Thy great salvation!
> O Holy Father, Thine always
>   Be thanks and adoration!
> Spirit of life and light, to Thee
> Eternal praise and glory be:
>   One God of all creation!

Incidentally, it was set to the German tune, *Es ist das Heil,* one of the chorales which appeared in Luther's historic *Achtliederbuch* of 1524 and later harmonized by Bach.

Cyril A. Alington, head master of Eton College, later dean of Durham, and at one time chaplain to King George, was the author of another triumphant Easter hymn. Titled "Good Christian men, rejoice and sing," it concludes with these stanzas:

> Praise we in songs of victory
> That love, that life which cannot die,
> And sing with hearts uplifted high:
>   Alleluia!
>
> Thy Name we bless, O risen Lord,
> And sing today with one accord
> The life laid down, the life restored:
>   Alleluia!

457

Yet another new Easter hymn which appeared in the 1931 edition of *Songs of Praise* came from the pen of none other than John Masefield, who had become poet laureate of England upon the death of Robert Bridges in 1930. This hymn, bearing the title, "Sing, men and angels, sing," was taken from Masefield's play, *Easter,* published in 1929. One of its stanzas reads:

> After the winter's snows
> A wind of healing blows,
> And thorns put forth a rose
> And lilies cheer us;
> Life's everlasting spring
> Hath robbed death of his sting,
> Henceforth a cry can bring
> Our Master near us.

Masefield is represented in the same hymnal by two other lyrics, "By weary stages the old world ages," derived from his mystery play, *The Coming of Christ,* and "O Christ who holds the open gate," which is taken from *The Everlasting Mercy.*

As the warring nations came to their senses at least temporarily at the close of World War I and began to survey the awful wreckage their unbridled passions and folly had wrought, the revulsion against future international conflicts was felt throughout the world. In Britain this was reflected in a very significant way when the Privy Council drew up and duly authorized a "Peace Version" of the national anthem. This famous hymn, the origin of which is veiled in obscurity, first appeared in *Harmonia Anglicana* about the year 1745. At that time the second stanza, which refers to the king and is a prayer for him, ran:

> O Lord our God, arise,
> Scatter his enemies,
> And make them fall!
> Confound their politics,
> Frustrate their knavish tricks,
> On him our hopes we fix,
> O save us all!

The official "Peace Version" of the anthem, now shorn of all of its original belligerent spirit, reads:

> God save our gracious King,
> Long live our noble King,
> God save the King!
> Send him victorious,
> Happy and glorious,
> Long to reign over us;
> God save the King!

One realm of races four,
Blest more and ever more,
    God save our land!
Home of the brave and free,
Set in the silver sea,
True nurse of chivalry,
    God save our land!

Of many a race and birth
From utmost ends of earth,
    God save us all!
Bid strife and hatred cease,
Bid hope and joy increase,
Spread universal peace,
    God save us all!

An Ode to the Scriptures

Book of books, our people's strength,
　　Statesman's, teacher's, hero's treasure,
Bringing freedom, spreading truth,
　　Shedding light that none can measure—
　　　　Wisdom comes to those who know thee,
　　　　All the best we have we owe thee.

Thank we those who toiled in thought,
　　Many divers scrolls completing,
Poets, prophets, scholars, saints,
　　Each his word from God repeating;
　　　　Till they came who told the story
　　　　Of the Word, and showed His glory.

Praise we God, who hath inspired
　　Those whose wisdom still directs us;
Praise Him for the Word made flesh,
　　For the Spirit which protects us.
　　　　Light of Knowledge, ever burning,
　　　　Shed on us thy deathless learning.

PERCY DEARMER, 1867–1936

460

AN ECUMENICAL ENGLISH HYMNAL

IN THE foregoing chapter mention was made of certain Easter lyrics written expressly for *Songs of Praise*. Here we must give a fuller account concerning this latest and most remarkable of all English hymnbooks. The editor of this splendid hymn collection, which came out during the interlude between World War I and World War II, was the noted hymnodist, Percy Dearmer, who already had won renown as the guiding genius of the group that created *The English Hymnal* two decades earlier. At that time Dearmer had the skillful assistance of Ralph Vaughan Williams as musical editor; in 1925 he had both Williams and Martin Shaw.

Although some of the same "high church" tendencies that appeared in the earlier volume were also revealed in *Songs of Praise*, Dearmer carefully avoided the doctrinal aberrations that provoked such a storm of criticism against *The English Hymnal*.

In producing *Songs of Praise* it was Dearmer's purpose to create a hymnal which represented not only the finest and best in poetry and music, but also one that was truly ecumenical in content. How well he succeeded is attested by the enthusiasm with which it was received throughout the English-speaking world, not only by Anglicans but by other communions as well. Its great popularity resulted in a second enlarged edition in 1931.

Dearmer was severe in his condemnation of what he termed "the debased hymnody" of an earlier period, and he contended that the inferior verse and music in use in both the Anglican and Free Churches of England during the latter half of the 19th century had alienated "the strongest character and intelligence of the nation." He expressed the hope, however, that in the future "intelligent men will be able to take up a hymnbook and read it with as much interest and appreciation as any other collection of poetry or music."

As intimated in an earlier chapter, *Songs of Praise* was unique because of its emphasis on social justice. It also sounded a definite international note of brotherhood and peace. The newly awakened

461

social consciousness of British hymn-writers was reflected in such hymns as this one by Charles Kingsley:

> The day of the Lord is at hand, at hand;
>   Its storms roll up the sky;
> The nations sleep starving on heaps of gold;
>   All dreamers toss and sigh;
> The night is darkest before the morn;
> When the pain is sorest the child is born,
>   And the day of the Lord is at hand.

Other hymns of the same type are Shelley's "The world's great age begins anew," Walt Whitman's "All the past we leave behind," J. A. Symond's "These things shall be! A loftier race," and Gerald Massey's "Through all the long dark night of years." While one is moved to sympathize with the lofty ideals and aspirations expressed in these hymns, it is unfortunate that a definite Christian note is so often missing. The impression is usually left that a new and better world is slowly evolving without a corresponding regeneration of society or the individual.

This criticism, however, can hardly be directed at the hymns of Dearmer, who contributed no less than twenty-three original lyrics to his now famous collection. A prolific writer, Dearmer dwelt on almost every conceivable subject. Many of his hymns picture the blessedness of the saints of God who have entered into glory. From its earthly side, he viewed the Christian religion as something intensely practical, and the Christian life as a constant warfare against sin and evil, cruelty and oppression, selfishness and greed, falsehood and hypocrisy, injustice and inhumanity, or in whatever other form man's lack of love for his fellow man might manifest itself. No matter what his theme might be, therefore, an insistent social note is always sounded. Take, for instance, his Lenten hymn, "Now quit your care," in which these lines occur:

> To bow the head
>   In sackcloth and in ashes,
>   Or rend the soul,
>   Such grief is not Lent's goal;
> But to be led
>   To where God's glory flashes,
>   His beauty to come nigh,
>   To fly, to fly
>   To fly where truth and light do lie.
>
> For righteousness
>   And peace will show their faces
>   To those who feed
>   The hungry in their need,

462

> And wrongs redress,
> Who build the old waste places
> And in the darkness shine.
> Divine, divine,
> Divine it is when all combine!

Dearmer possessed the happy faculty of being able to write for the unlettered as well as for the learned, for children as well as for their elders. There is a peculiar charm in his delightful lyrics for children, due in part, perhaps, to the vivid language he uses. Witness, for instance, this stanza from his missionary hymn, "Remember all the people":

> Some work in sultry forests
> Where apes swing to and fro,
> Some fish in mighty rivers,
> Some hunt across the snow.
> Remember all God's children,
> Who yet have never heard
> The truth that comes from Jesus,
> The glory of His word.

We have already noted how *The English Hymnal* of 1906 set a precedent by including a number of hymns by America's great poets. In collecting material for *Songs of Praise,* Dearmer continued to look across the Atlantic for additional hymns that emphasized what had come to be known in America as "the social gospel." He found a large number of these in the lyrics of Frederick Lucian Hosmer, Samuel Longfellow, Samuel Johnson and James Russell Lowell. He also was deeply intrigued with the warm note of human sympathy he discovered in the poems of John Greenleaf Whittier, and included no less than eleven centos from the latter's works, an extraordinary tribute to the beloved Quaker poet.

Next to Dearmer himself, no contemporary British hymn-writer made so great a contribution to *Songs of Praise* as did George Wallace Briggs, a Church of England clergyman who served as a chaplain in the Royal Navy during World War I. Briggs was unusually gifted, not only as a poet but also as a musician, and no less than sixteen original hymns and seven hymn tunes in *Songs of Praise* are the product of his genius. Among his lyrics are "The Spirit of the Lord revealed," "Our Father, by whose servants," "Christ is the world's true Light," and "Lord, who thyself hast bidden us to pray." In the latter occur these stanzas:

463

Not for tomorrow, its uncharted road,
  Shall be our prayer;
Sufficient for each day our daily load,
  Thy daily care.

Thine is the burden for the coming years;
  Their weal or woe,
Their joys and griefs, their laughter and their tears
  We would not know.

We would not bear to hear complete the tale,
  If it were told;
Enough to know Thy mercies cannot fail,
  Nor love grow cold.

Katherine Emily Roberts, author of the very tender baptismal hymn, "O Lord, Thy people gathered here," was one of the very few contemporary women hymn-writers of England represented in *Songs of Praise*. Before her marriage in 1913 to Richard Ellis Roberts, a London editor, she had launched on a career as a professional singer. In collaboration with her husband Mrs. Roberts in 1923 published *Carol Stories*. She also was the author of a number of plays and a book of historical pageants.

Another contemporary woman hymn-writer in England is Miss Margaret Cropper of Kendal, Westmoreland, whose hymn, "O Christ, whom we may love and know," has found its way into hymnals on both sides of the Atlantic. Written for the Girls' Friendly Society of Townsend House, London, its glowing lines reflect the kind of virtues for which every Christian young woman should earnestly seek and pray:

O Christ, whom we may love and know
  And follow to the end,
We who are friends together come
  To Thee, our heavenly Friend.

Thou who didst share our daily toil
  To make us good and free,
Help us to share Thy fiery love
  And shining purity.

Give us Thy love that loves us all
  And dared the glorious Cross,
That we may love to share and know
  Each other's joy and loss.

Give us Thy purity to shield
  Our souls in each dark place,
To give us wings to rise to Thee,
  And power to see Thy face.

PART V

American Hymnody

The First American Hymn

I love Thy Kingdom, Lord,
    The house of Thine abode,
The Church our blest Redeemer saved
    With His own precious blood.

I love Thy Church, O God;
    Her walls before Thee stand,
Dear as the apple of Thine eye,
    And graven on Thy hand.

For her my tears shall fall;
    For her my prayers ascend:
To her my cares and toils be given,
    Till toils and cares shall end.

Beyond my highest joy
    I prize her heavenly ways,
Her sweet communion, solemn vows,
    Her hymns of love and praise.

Jesus, Thou Friend divine,
    Our Saviour and our King,
Thy hand from every snare and foe
    Shall great deliverance bring.

Sure as Thy truth shall last,
    To Zion shall be given
The brightest glories earth can yield,
    And brighter bliss of heaven.

TIMOTHY DWIGHT, 1752–1817

THE BEGINNINGS OF HYMNODY IN AMERICA

THE rise of hymnody in America ran parallel with the development of hymn-singing in England. The Puritans who came from Holland in the Mayflower in 1620 were "separatists" from the Church of England, hence they used a psalmbook of their own, published by Henry Ainsworth at Amsterdam in 1612. This was the book that cheered their souls on the perilous crossing of the Atlantic and during the hard and trying years that followed their landing at Plymouth.

> Amid the storm they sang,
> And the stars heard and the sea;
> And the sounding aisles of the dim woods rang
> With the anthems of the free.

This was also the book that comforted Priscilla, when John Alden stole in and found that

> Open wide on her lap lay the well-worn psalmbook of Ainsworth.

The later Puritans who came directly from England, on the other hand, were not "separatists," hence they brought with them the psalmbook of Sternhold and Hopkins, which was the version of the Psalter approved at that time by the Established Church.

The wretched paraphrases of the psalms in both the Ainsworth and the "orthodox" Sternhold and Hopkins psalmbooks eventually led to an insistent demand among the New England Puritans for an entirely new psalmbook which should also adhere more closely to the Hebrew original. The result was the famous *Bay Psalmist* of 1640, which was the first book of any kind printed in British America.

The Puritan editors of this early attempt at American psalmody cared no more for poetic effect than did their brother versifiers across the waters. This they made quite plain in the concluding words of the preface to the *Bay Psalmist*: "If therefore the verses are not always so smooth and elegant as some may desire or expect; let them consider that God's Altar needs not our polishings: Ex. 20, for wee have respected rather a plaine translation, than to smooth our verses with the sweetness of any paraphrase, and soe have attended to Conscience rather than Elegance, fidelity rather than poetry, in translating the hebrew words into english language, and David's poetry into english meetre: that soe wee may sing in Sion the Lords songs of praise according to his own will; untill hee take us from hence, and wipe away all our tears, and bid us enter into our masters joye to sing eternall Halleluiahs."

The editors scarcely needed to apprise the worshiper that he should not look for artistic verse, for a glimpse within its pages was sufficient to disillusion any one who expected to find sacred poetry of a high order. The metrical form given Psalm 137 is an example of the Puritan theologians' contempt for polished language:

> The rivers on of Babilon
>   there when wee did sit downe;
>   yea even then wee mourned, when
>   wee remembred Sion.
>
> Our Harps wee did hang it amid,
>   upon the willow tree.
>   Because there they that us away
>   led in captivitee,
>
> Required of us a song, & thus
>   askt mirth: us waste who laid,
>   sing us among a Sions song,
>   unto us then they said.

Nevertheless, strange as it may seem, the *Bay Psalmist* passed through twenty-seven editions, and was even reprinted several times abroad, being used extensively in England and Scotland. Gradually, however, psalmody began to lose its hold on the Reformed churches, both in Europe and America, and hymnody gained the ascendancy. The publication in 1707 of the epoch-making work of Isaac Watts, *Hymns and Spiritual Songs,* was the first step in breaking down the prejudice in the Calvinistic churches against "hymns of human composure." In America the Great Awakening under Jonathan Edwards, which began in 1734 and which received added impetus from the visit of John Whitefield in 1740, also brought about a demand for a happier form of congregational singing. Then came the influence of the Wesleyan revival with its glorious outburst of song.

Jonathan Edwards himself, stern Puritan that he was, was finally forced to confess that it was "really needful that we should have some other songs than the Psalms of David." Accordingly, hymn singing grew rapidly in favor among the people.

The first attempt to introduce hymns in the authorized psalm-books was made by Joel Barlow, a chaplain in the Revolutionary War. Instructed by the General Association of Congregational Churches of Connecticut to revise Watts' *Psalms of David* in order to purge them of their British flavor, he was likewise authorized to append to the psalms a collection of hymns. He made a selection of seventy hymns, and the new book was published in 1786.

It was received with delight by the Presbyterians, but the Congregationalists who had sponsored it were thoroughly dissatisfied. As an example of the morbid character of Puritan theology, Edward S. Ninde has called attention to the fact that while Barlow failed to include Wesley's "Jesus, Lover of my soul" or Watts' "When I survey the wondrous Cross," he did select such a hymn by Watts as "Hark, from the tombs, a doleful sound," and another which begins:

My thoughts on awful subjects roll,
Damnation and the dead.

A second attempt to make a complete revision of Watts' *Psalms of David* was decided upon by the Congregational churches, and this time the task was entrusted to Timothy Dwight, president of Yale College. Dwight, who was a grandson of Jonathan Edwards, was born in 1752. He entered Yale at the age of thirteen and graduated with highest honors in 1769. At the outbreak of the Revolutionary War he was commissioned a chaplain and throughout the conflict he wrote songs to enthuse the American troops. In 1795 he was elected president of Yale College, a position he held for twenty years.

Dwight exhibited a spirit of bold independence when he added to the revised "Psalms" by Watts a collection of two hundred and sixty-three hymns. Of these hymns, one hundred and sixty-eight also were by Watts, indicating the hold which that great hymnist retained on the English-speaking world. Other hymn-writers represented in Dwight's book include Stennett, Doddridge, Cowper, Newton, Toplady, and Charles Wesley. Only one of the latter's hymns was chosen, however, and Toplady's "Rock of Ages" was not included!

Dwight himself wrote thirty-three paraphrases of the Psalms, but they were so freely rendered they are usually classified as original hymns. Among these is his splendid version of Psalm 137, "I love Thy Kingdom, Lord," which may be regarded as the earliest hymn of American origin still in common use today. It is usually dated 1800, which is the year when Dwight's work was published.

The Hymn of a Wounded Spirit

I love to steal awhile away
From every cumbering care,
And spend the hour of setting day
In humble, grateful prayer.

I love in solitude to shed
The penitential tear,
And all His promises to plead
Where none but God can hear.

I love to think of mercies past,
And future good implore,
And all my cares and sorrows cast
On Him whom I adore.

I love by faith to take a view
Of brighter scenes in heaven;
The prospect doth my strength renew,
While here by tempests driven.

Thus when life's toilsome day is o'er,
May its departing ray
Be calm as this impressive hour
And lead to endless day.

PHOEBE HINSDALE BROWN, 1818

470

AMERICA'S FIRST WOMAN HYMNIST

LESS than twenty years after the hymns of Timothy Dwight had been published, a devout, humble, poverty-stricken American woman began to write lyrics that will not soon be forgotten. Her name was Phoebe Hinsdale Brown, and the story of her life is perhaps the most pathetic in the annals of American hymnody.

"As to my history," she wrote near the end of her life, "it is soon told; a sinner saved by grace and sanctified by trials."

She was born at Canaan, N. Y., May 1, 1783. Both parents died before she was two years old and the greater part of her childhood was spent in the home of an older sister who was married to the keeper of a county jail. The cruelties and privations suffered by the orphaned child during these years were such that her son in later years declared it broke his heart to read of them in his mother's diary. She was not permitted to attend school, and could neither read nor write. She was eighteen years old before she escaped from this bondage and found opportunity to attend school for three months. This was the extent of her education within school walls.

In 1805, at the age of twenty-two, she married Timothy H. Brown, a house painter. He was a good man, but extremely poor. Moving to Ellington, Mass., they lived in a small, unfinished frame house at the edge of the village. Four little children and a sick sister who occupied the only finished room in the home added to the domestic burdens of Mrs. Brown.

In the summer of 1818 a strange incident led to the writing of her famous hymn. There being no place in her crowded home for a few moments of quiet prayer and meditation, she would steal away at twilight to the edge of a neighboring estate, where there was a magnificent home surrounded by a beautiful garden.

"As there was seldom any one passing that way after dark," she afterwards wrote, "I felt quite retired and alone with God. I often walked quite up to that beautiful garden . . . and felt that I could have the privilege of those few moments of uninterrupted communion with God without encroaching upon any one."

But her movements had been watched, and one day the mistress of the mansion turned on her in the presence of others and rudely demanded: "Mrs. Brown, why do you come up at evening so near our house, and then go back without coming in? If you want anything, why don't you come in and ask for it?"

Mrs. Brown tells how she went home, crushed in spirit. "After my children were all in bed, except my baby," she continues, "I sat down in the kitchen, with my child in my arms, when the grief of my heart burst forth in a flood of tears. I took pen and paper, and gave vent to my oppressed heart in what I called 'My Apology for my Twilight Rambles, addressed to a Lady.'" The "Apology," which was sent to the woman who had so cruelly wounded her began with the lines:

> Yes, when the toilsome day is gone,
> And night, with banners gray,
> Steals silently the glade along
> In twilight's soft array.

Then continued the beautiful verses of her now famous "Twilight Hymn:"

> I love to steal awhile away
> From little ones and care.
> And spend the hours of setting day
> In gratitude and prayer.

Seven years later, when Dr. Nettleton was preparing his volume of *Village Hymns,* he was told that Mrs. Brown had written some verses. At his request she brought forth her "Twilight Hymn" and three other lyrics, and they were promptly given a place in the collection. Only a few slight changes were made in the lines of the "Twilight Hymn," including the second line, which was made to read "From every cumbering care," and the fourth line, which was changed to "In humble, grateful prayer." Four stanzas were omitted, otherwise the hymn remains almost exactly in the form of the "Apology."

One of the omitted stanzas reveals a beautiful Christian attitude toward death. Mrs. Brown wrote:

> I love to meditate on death!
> When shall his message come
> With friendly smiles to steal my breath
> And take an exile home?

472

One of the other hymns by Mrs. Brown included in *Village Hymns* is a missionary lyric, "Go, messenger of love, and bear." This was written a year earlier than her "Twilight Hymn." Her little son Samuel was seven years old at the time, and the pious mother's prayer was that he might be used of the Lord in His service. This was the period when the English-speaking world was experiencing a tremendous revival of interest in foreign missions, and in her heart she cherished the fond hope that her own boy might become a messenger of the gospel. Then came the inspiration for the hymn:

> Go, messenger of love, and bear
>   Upon thy gentle wing
> The song which seraphs love to hear,
>   The angels joy to sing.
>
> Go to the heart with sin oppressed,
>   And dry the sorrowing tear;
> Extract the thorn that wounds the breast,
>   The drooping spirit cheer.
>
> Go, say to Zion, "Jesus reigns" —
>   By His resistless power
> He binds His enemies with chains;
>   They fall to rise no more.
>
> Tell how the Holy Spirit flies,
>   As He from heaven descends;
> Arrests His proudest enemies,
>   And changes them to friends.

Her prayer was answered. The son, Samuel R. Brown, in 1838 sailed as a missionary to China, and eleven years later, when Japan was opened to foreigners, was transferred to that field. He was the first American missionary to the Japanese.

Mrs. Brown died at Henry, Illinois, October 10, 1861. She was buried at Monson, Mass., where some thirty years of her life had been spent. Her son, the missionary, has written this beautiful tribute to her memory:

"Her record is on high, and she is with the Lord, whom she loved and served as faithfully as any person I ever knew; nay, more than any other. To her I owe all I am; and if I have done any good in the world, to her, under God, it is due. She seems even now to have me in her hands, holding me up to work for Christ and His cause with a grasp that I can feel. I ought to have been and to be a far better man than I am, having had such a mother."

473

A Triumphant Missionary Hymn

Hail to the brightness of Zion's glad morning,
    Joy to the lands that in darkness have lain!
Hushed be the accents of sorrow and mourning,
    Zion in triumph begins her mild reign.

Hail to the brightness of Zion's glad morning,
    Long by the prophets of Israel foretold;
Hail to the millions from bondage returning,
    Gentiles and Jews the blest vision behold.

Lo, in the desert rich flowers are springing,
    Streams ever copious are gliding along;
Loud from the mountaintops echoes are ringing,
    Wastes rise in verdure, and mingle in song.

Hark, from all lands, from the isles of the ocean,
    Praise to Jehovah ascending on high;
Fallen the engines of war and commotion,
    Shouts of salvation are rending the sky.

THOMAS HASTINGS, 1784–1872a.

474

THOMAS HASTINGS, POET AND MUSICIAN

HIGH among those who in the early days of America labored to raise the standards of hymnody must be inscribed the name of Thomas Hastings, Doctor of Music. Poet and musician by nature, Hastings will be gratefully remembered as the first American hymnist to dedicate his entire life in the task of elevating and ennobling the worship of the Christian Church.

The story of his life is typical of the struggles and hardships of many American pioneers who conquered in spite of the most adverse circumstances. Born at Washington, Conn., October 15, 1784, young Hastings removed with his parents to Clinton, N. Y., when only twelve years old. The journey was made in ox-sleds through unbroken wilderness in the dead of winter.

The frontier schools of those days offered little opportunity for education, but the eager lad trudged six miles a day to receive the instruction that was given. A passionate fondness for music was first satisfied when he secured a musical primer of four pages costing six pence. The proudest moment in his life came when he was named leader of the village choir.

It was not until he was thirty-two years old that Hastings was able to secure employment as a music teacher, but from that time until his death, in 1872, he devoted all his energies to the work he loved.

Hastings was tireless in contending that good music should have a recognized place in religious worship. He once wrote: "The homage that we owe Almighty God calls for the noblest and most reverential tribute that music can render."

In 1822 his "Dissertation on Musical Taste" attracted widespread attention and exerted great influence in ecclesiastical and musical circles. The following year he became editor of the *Western Recorder* of Utica, N. Y., which gave him added opportunity to spread his views on church music. Nine years later twelve churches in New York City joined in engaging his services as choir director, and for the remainder of his life Hastings made the great American metro-

475

polis his home. His *History of Forty Choirs* summarizes many of his experiences during this period. By the time he founded his *Musical Magazine* in 1836, his reputation as an authority in church music had been firmly established.

Hastings was an albino, and was seriously afflicted with eye trouble. Despite this handicap, he accomplished a prodigious amount of work. No less than fifty volumes of church music came from his pen. It is also claimed that he wrote more than 1,000 hymn tunes, among them some of the finest in our American hymnals. Who has not found inspiration in singing that sweet and haunting melody know as *Ortonville* to the lovely hymn, "Majestic sweetness sits enthroned," or the tune *Retreat* to the hymn, "From every stormy wind that blows"? And how can we ever be sufficiently grateful for the tune called *Toplady,* which has endeared "Rock of Ages" to millions of Christians?

Through the composing of tunes, Hastings was led to write hymns also. The text of more than 600 are attributed to him, although many of them appeared anonymously. "Hail to the brightness of Zion's glad morning" is generally regarded as his best hymn. It reflects in striking language the spirit of the missionary age in which Hastings lived and wrought. Another stirring missionary lyric, written by Hastings in 1831, is only a bit less popular:

> Now be the gospel banner
>   In every land unfurled;
> And be the shout, Hosannah!
>   Reechoed through the world;
> Till every isle and nation,
>   Till every tribe and tongue,
> Receive the great salvation,
>   And join the happy throng.

A hymn with the title, "Pilgrimage of Life," though very simple, is singularly beautiful and very tender in its appeal. The first stanza reads:

> Gently, Lord, O gently lead us,
>   Pilgrims in this vale of tears,
> Through the trials yet decreed us,
>   Till our last great change appears.

Hastings also added a third stanza to Thomas Moore's "Come, ye disconsolate," which greatly improved the lyric:

476

Here see the Bread of Life; see waters flowing
   Forth from the throne of God, pure from above;
Come to the feast of love; come, ever knowing
   Earth has no sorrow but heaven can remove.

Shortly after removing to New York City, Hastings began to collaborate with another great pioneer American composer, Lowell Mason, and the two eventually brought forth a hymn collection called *Spiritual Songs for Social Worship.* In 1858 the University of the City of New York conferred upon the man who was self-trained in music and hymnody the degree of Doctor of Music. Hastings did not cease writing hymns and composing tunes until three days before his death, which occurred on May 15, 1872.

477

Key's Hymn of Praise

Lord, with glowing heart I'd praise thee
For the bliss Thy love bestows,
For the pardoning grace that saves me,
And the peace that from it flows.
Help, O God, my weak endeavor;
This dull soul to rapture raise;
Thou must light the flame, or never
Can my love be warmed to praise.

Praise, my soul, the God that sought thee,
Wretched wanderer, far astray;
Found thee lost, and kindly brought thee
From the paths of death away.
Praise, with love's devoutest feeling,
Him who saw thy guilt-born fear,
And, the light of hope revealing,
Bade the blood-stained Cross appear.

Lord, this bosom's ardent feeling
Vainly would my lips express;
Low before Thy footstool kneeling,
Deign Thy suppliant's prayer to bless;
Let Thy grace, my soul's chief treasure,
Love's pure flame within me raise;
And, since words can never measure,
Let my life show forth Thy praise.

FRANCIS SCOTT KEY, 1779-1843

FRANCIS SCOTT KEY, PATRIOT AND HYMNIST

FRANCIS SCOTT KEY is known to every American as the author of our national anthem, "The Star-Spangled Banner"; but his fame as a Christian hymnist has not gone abroad to the same degree. And yet, as the author of "Lord, with glowing heart I'd praise Thee," he ranks among the foremost of American hymn-writers.

Key lived during the stirring days of America's birth as a nation. His father was an officer in the Continental army who fought with distinction during the Revolutionary War. Francis was born at Frederick, Maryland, August 1, 1779. After receiving a legal education he began to practice law in Washington, and served as United States district attorney for three terms, holding that office at the time of his death.

The story of how he came to write "Star-Spangled Banner" scarcely needs to be repeated. During the War of 1812 Key was authorized by President Madison to visit the British fleet near the mouth of the Potomac in order to obtain the release of a physician friend who had been taken prisoner by the invaders.

The British admiral granted the American's request, but owing to the fact that an attack was about to be made on Fort McHenry, which guarded the harbor of Baltimore, Key and his party were detained all night aboard the truce-boat on which they had come.

It was a night of great anxiety. A fierce bombardment continued during the hours of darkness, and as long as the shore fortifications replied to the cannonading, Key and his friends were certain that all was well. Toward morning the firing ceased, and they were filled with dark forebodings. The others went below to obtain some sleep, but Key continued to pace the deck until the first streaks of dawn showed that the "flag was still there."

His joy was so unbounded that he seized a piece of paper, and hastily wrote the words of his famous anthem. It was not completed until later in the day, when he reached Baltimore and joined in the victorious joy that filled the city.

While "Star-Spangled Banner" is not a Christian hymn, there

are noble sentiments in it that reveal the writer at once as a devout Christian, and this was eminently true of Key.

As a member of the Protestant Episcopal Church he held a lay reader's license, and for many years read the service and visited the sick. He also conducted a Bible class in Sunday school. Although he lived in a slave state, he was finally moved by conscientious scruples to free his slaves. He also did much to alleviate conditions among other unfortunate Negroes.

When the Protestant Episcopal Church in 1823 appointed a committee to prepare a new hymnbook for that body, Key was made a lay member of it. Another member of the committee was Dr. William Muhlenberg, who in that same year had published a little hymnal for use in his own congregation. It was in this hymnal, known as *Church Poetry,* that Key's beautiful hymn, "Lord, with glowing heart I'd praise Thee," was first published.

In Dr. Muhlenberg's hymnbook the hymn had only three stanzas, and that is the form in which it has since appeared in all other hymnals. In 1900, however, Key's autograph copy of the hymn was discovered, and it was found that the hymn originally had four stanzas. The missing one reads:

> Praise thy Saviour God that drew thee
> To that Cross, new life to give,
> Held a blood-sealed pardon to thee,
> Bade thee look to Him and live.
> Praise the grace whose threats alarmed thee,
> Roused thee from thy fatal ease,
> Praise the grace whose promise warmed thee,
> Praise the grace that whispered peace.

Another excellent hymn, "Before the Lord we bow," was written by Key in 1832 for a Fourth of July celebration. There is a strong patriotic strain that runs through its stanzas, as witness:

> Before the Lord we bow,
> The God who reigns above,
> And rules the world below,
> Boundless in power and love.
> Our thanks we bring
> In joy and praise,
> Our hearts we raise
> To heaven's high King.

The nation Thou hast blest
  May well Thy love declare,
From foes and fears at rest,
  Protected by Thy care.
    For this fair land,
      For this bright day,
      Our thanks we pay—
    Gifts of Thy hand.

Earth, hear thy Maker's voice,
  Thy great Redeemer own;
Believe, obey, rejoice,
  And worship Him alone.
    Cast down thy pride,
      Thy sin deplore
      And bow before
    The Crucified.

A bronze statue of Key, placed over his grave at Frederick, Md., shows him with his hand outstretched at the moment when he discovered that the flag was "still there," while his other hand is waving his hat exultantly.

An Exquisite Baptismal Hymn

Saviour, who Thy flock art feeding
With the Shepherd's kindest care,
All the feeble gently leading,
While the lambs Thy bosom share.

Now, these little ones receiving,
Fold them in Thy gracious arm;
There, we know, Thy word believing,
Only there secure from harm.

Never, from Thy pasture roving,
Let them be the lion's prey;
Let Thy tenderness, so loving,
Keep them through life's dangerous way.

Then, within Thy fold eternal,
Let them find a resting place,
Feed in pastures ever vernal,
Drink the rivers of Thy grace.

WILLIAM AUGUSTUS MUHLENBERG, 1796–1877

THE HYMN-WRITER OF THE MUHLENBERGS

WILLIAM Augustus Muhlenberg, one of America's early hymn-writers, came from a distinguished colonial family. His great grandfather, Henry Melchior Muhlenberg, was the "patriarch of the Lutheran Church in America," having come to these shores from Germany in 1742, in which year he founded the first permanent Lutheran organization in the new world.

A son of the patriarch and grandfather of the hymn-writer bore the name of Frederick Augustus Muhlenberg. He, too, was a Lutheran minister, but during the stirring days of the Revolutionary period he became identified with the independence movement of the struggling colonies. He was president of the convention which ratified the Consitution of the United States and also served as first speaker of the new House of Representatives. His brother, Peter Muhlenberg, was also a distinguished patriot. When the Revolution broke out, he was pastor of a congregation at Woodstock, Va. It was he who stood in the pulpit of his church and, throwing aside his clerical robe, was disclosed wearing the uniform of a Continental colonel.

"There is a time to preach and a time to pray," he cried, "but these times have passed away. There is a time to fight, and that time has come!"

Thereupon he called upon the men of his congregation to enlist in his regiment. Before the war ended he had risen to the rank of major general.

William Augustus Muhlenberg, the hymn-writer, was born in Philadelphia in 1796. Since the German language was then being used exclusively in the German Lutheran churches, he and his younger sister were allowed to attend Christ Episcopal Church. In this way William Augustus drifted away from the Church of his great forebears, and when he grew up he became a clergyman in the Episcopal communion.

It is evident that Muhlenberg brought something of the spirit of the "Singing Church" into the Church of his adoption, for in 1821 he issued a tract with the title, "A Plea for Christian Hymns." It appears that the Episcopal Church at this time was using a prayer-book that included only fifty-seven hymns, and no one felt the poverty of his Church in this respect more keenly than did Muhlenberg.

Two years later the General Convention of the Episcopal body voted to prepare a hymnbook, and Muhlenberg was made a member of the committee. One of his associates was Francis Scott Key, author of "Star-Spangled Banner."

As a member of the committee Muhlenberg contributed four original hymns to the new collection. They were "I would not live alway," "Like Noah's weary dove," "Shout the glad tidings, triumphantly sing," and "Saviour, who Thy flock art leading." The latter is a baptism hymn and is regarded as one of the finest ever written on that theme. Although Muhlenberg never married, he had a very deep love for children. No service seemed so hallowed to him as the baptism of a little child. It is said that shortly after his ordination, when asked to officiate at such a rite, Muhlenberg flushed and hesitated, and then asked a bishop who was present to baptize the babe. The latter, however, insisted that the young clergyman should carry out the holy ordinance and from that day there was no duty that afforded Muhlenberg greater joy.

Muhlenberg often expressed regret that he had written "I would not live alway." It seems that the poem was called into being in 1824, following a "heart-breaking disappointment in the matter of love." Muhlenberg was a young man at the time, and in his later years he sought to alter it in such a way that it would breathe more of the hopeful spirit of the New Testament. He contended that Paul's words, "For me to live is Christ" reflected a more Christian sentiment than Job's lament, "I would not live alway." However, the hymn as originally written had become so fixed in the consciousness of the Church, that all efforts of the author to revise it were in vain.

Nearly all of Muhlenberg's hymns that have survived were written during his earlier years. His later ministry centered in New York City, where he became the head of a boys' school and then rector of the Church of the Holy Communion. He soon was recognized as an outstanding leader in the great metropolis. After having founded St. Luke's Hospital, the first church institution of its kind in New York City, he spent the last twenty years of his life as its superintendent.

His death occurred when he was past eighty years. It is said that when the end was drawing near, the hospital chaplain came to his bedside to pray for his recovery.

"Let us have an understanding about this," said the dying Muhlenberg. "You are asking God to restore me and I am asking God to take me home. There must not be a contradiction in our prayers, for it is evident that He cannot answer them both."

The Way, the Truth, and the Life

Thou art the Way; to Thee alone
From sin and death we flee;
And he who would the Father seek,
Must seek Him, Lord, by Thee.

Thou art the Truth; Thy Word alone
True wisdom can impart;
Thou only canst inform the mind,
And purify the heart.

Thou art the Life; the rending tomb
Proclaims Thy conquering arm;
And those who put their trust in Thee
Nor death nor hell shall harm.

Thou art the Way, the Truth, the Life;
Grant us that Way to know,
That Truth to keep, that Life to win
Whose joys eternal flow.

GEORGE WASHINGTON DOANE, 1799–1859

THE LYRICS OF BISHOP DOANE

CRITICS will forever disagree on the subject of the relative merits of great hymns. Bishop George Washington Doane's fine hymn, "Thou art the Way; to Thee alone," has been declared by some to be the foremost of all hymns written by American authors. Dr. Breed, on the other hand, declares that it is "by no means the equal" of other hymns by Doane. Another authority observes that it "rather stiffly and mechanically paraphrases" the passage on which it is founded, while Edward S. Ninde rejects this conclusion by contending that although "metrical expositions of Scriptures are apt to be stilted and spiritless . . . this one is a success."

Ninde, however, does not agree that it is "the first of American hymns," reserving this honor, as do most critics, for Ray Palmer's "My faith looks up to Thee."

Bishop Doane was born in Trenton, N. J., May 27, 1799. This was the year in which George Washington died, wherefore the future hymn-writer was named after the great patriot. At the age of nineteen he was graduated by Union College with the highest scholastic honors. After teaching for a season, he became pastor of Trinity Episcopal Church, Boston, Mass., the church afterwards made famous by Phillips Brooks.

When only thirty-three years old he was elevated to the bishopric of New Jersey, which position he held until his death in 1859. By this time he had already won fame as a hymn-writer. It was in 1824, at the age of twenty-five, that Doane published a little volume of lyrics entitled *Songs by the Way*. One of the hymns in this collection was the beautiful paraphrase, "Thou art the Way; to Thee alone."

This hymn alone would have been sufficient to have perpetuated the name of the young poet, but there was another gem in the same collection that will always be treasured by those who love Christian song. It is the exquisite evening hymn:

> Softly now the light of day
> Fades upon my sight away;
> Free from care, from labor free,
> Lord, I would commune with Thee.

Among the many achievements of this versatile bishop was the founding of Saint Mary's Hall, a school for young women, at Burlington, N. J. Doane lies buried in the neighboring churchyard, and it is said that the students on every Wednesday evening at chapel services sing "Softly now the light of day" as a memorial tribute to the founder of the institution.

Both of these hymns were quickly recognized as possessing unusual merit, and almost immediately found their way into hymnbooks. Today there is scarcely a hymnal published in the English language that does not contain them.

But Bishop Doane's fame does not rest on these two hymns alone. He was destined to write a third one, equally great but of a very different character from the other two. It is the stirring missionary hymn:

> Fling out the banner! let it float
> Skyward and seaward, high and wide;
> The sun that lights its shining folds,
> The Cross, on which the Saviour died.

It was written in 1848 in response to a request from the young women of St. Mary's Hall for a hymn to be used at a flag-raising. The third stanza is one of rare beauty:

> Fling out the banner! heathen lands
> Shall see from far the glorious sight,
> And nations, crowding to be born,
> Baptize their spirits in its light.

The hymn, as may be surmised, is based on the passage from the Psalter: "Thou has given a banner to them that fear thee, that it may be displayed because of the truth."

Bishop Doane was a zealous advocate of missions. It was during his childhood that the modern missionary movement had its inception and swept like a tidal wave over the Christian world. "Fling out the banner" is a reflection of the remarkable enthusiasm that filled his own soul, revealing itself in his aggressive missionary leadership. Indeed, he became known in his own Church as "the missionary bishop of America."

A son, William Croswell Doane, also became a distinguished bishop of the Episcopal Church. Writing of his father's rare gifts as a hymnist, he declares that his heart was "full of song. It oozed out in his conversation, in his sermons, in everything that he did. Sometimes in a steamboat, often when the back of a letter was his only paper, the sweetest things came."

Incidentally, seldom has a son followed so closely in the footsteps of his sire as did the younger Doane. Besides rising as did his father to a bishopric in the Episcopal Church, he also was known as a brilliant scholar and a poet of no mean ability. He will probably be chiefly remembered for his hymn of adoration addressed to the Holy Trinity:

> Ancient of Days, who sittest throned in glory,
> To Thee all knees are bent, all voices pray;
> Thy love has blessed the wide world's wondrous story
> With light and life since Eden's dawning day.

This hymn was written in 1886 in connection with the 200th anniversary observance of the founding of Albany, N. Y., as the first American city. Later, when the Episcopal Hymnal committee expressed a desire to include it in the official church collection, Bishop Doane revised it for worship purposes.

Doane was born in Boston in 1832, and received his education at Burlington College, which had been founded by his father. After his ordination, he served as assistant to his father in Burlington, N. J., and later became rector at Hartford and Albany. In 1869 he was elected Bishop of the Albany diocese, a position he held for forty-four years until his death in 1913.

489

Bryant's Home Mission Hymn

Look from Thy sphere of endless day,
    O God of mercy and of might;
In pity look on those who stray
    Benighted in this land of light.

In peopled vale, in lonely glen,
    In crowded mart, by stream or sea,
How many of the sons of men
    Hear not the message sent from Thee.

Send forth Thy heralds, Lord, to call
    The thoughtless young, the hardened old,
A wandering flock, and bring them all
    To the Good Shepherd's peaceful fold.

Send them Thy mighty Word, to speak
    Till faith shall dawn, and doubt depart,
To awe the bold, to stay the weak,
    And bind and heal the broken heart.

Then all these wastes, a dreary scene
    On which with sorrowing eyes we gaze,
Shall grow with living waters green,
    And lift to heaven the voice of praise.

                    WILLIAM CULLEN BRYANT, 1794-1878a.

AMERICA'S FIRST POET AND HIS HYMNS

WILLIAM Cullen Bryant, America's first great poet, was also a hymn-writer. Although he did not devote much of his thought and genius to sacred lyrics, he wrote at least two splendid hymns that merit a place in every hymn collection. The one, "Thou, whose unmeasured temple stands," is a church dedication hymn of rare beauty; the other, "Look from Thy sphere of endless day," is unquestionably one of the finest home mission hymns ever written.

Born at Cummington, Mass., November 3, 1794, he was educated at Williams College to be a lawyer. It was his writing of "Thanatopsis" as a boy of seventeen years that gave the first notice to the world that America had produced a great poet.

It is said that when the lines of "Thanatopsis" were submitted to Richard H. Dana, editor of the *North American Review,* he was skeptical.

"No one on this side of the Atlantic," he declared, "is capable of writing such verses."

Bryant was brought up in a New England Puritan home. Family worship and strict attendance at public worship was the rule in the Bryant household. Every little while the children of the community would also gather in the district schoolhouse, where they would be examined in the Catechism by the parish minister, a venerable man who was loved by old and young alike.

While yet a little child Bryant began to pray that he might receive the gift of writing poetry. No doubt he had been influenced to a large degree in this desire by the fact that his father was a lover of verse and possessed a splendid library of the great English poets. The youthful Bryant was taught to memorize the noble hymns of Isaac Watts, and when he was only five years old he would stand on a chair and recite them to imaginary audiences.

Early in life Bryant came under the influence of the Unitarian doctrines which were then sweeping through New England as a reaction against the stern, harsh teachings of Puritanism. When he was only 26 years old he was invited to contribute lyrics to a volume of hymns then in course of preparation by the Unitarians. He responded by writing five hymns. Six years later he wrote "Thou, whose unmeasured temple stands" for the dedication of the Second Unitarian Church of New York City. He usually attended the First Congregational Unitarian Church of that city.

About thirty years later, however, when Bryant was sixty-four years old, a profound change occurred in his religious convictions. During a trip abroad his wife became critically ill in Naples. At first her life was despaired of, but when she finally was on the road to recovery Bryant sent for a warm friend of the family, the Rev. R. C. Waterston, who was in Naples at the time. The latter tells of his meeting with the aged poet in the following words:

"On the following day, the weather being delightful, we walked in the royal park or garden overlooking the Bay of Naples. Never can I forget the beautiful spirit that breathed through every word he (Bryant) uttered, the reverent love, the confiding trust, the aspiring hope, the rooted faith . . . He said that he had never united himself with the Church, which, with his present feeling, he would most gladly do. He then asked if it would be agreeable to me to come to his room on the morrow and administer the communion, adding that, as he had never been baptized, he desired that ordinance at the same time.

"The day following was the Sabbath, and a most heavenly day. In fulfilment of his wishes, in his own quiet room, a company of seven persons celebrated together the Lord's Supper . . . Previous to the breaking of bread, William Cullen Bryant was baptized. With snow-white head and flowing beard, he stood like one of the ancient prophets, and perhaps never, since the days of the apostles, has a truer disciple professed allegiance to the divine Master."

Twenty years after this experience, in the last year of the poet's life, he made some contributions to the Methodist Episcopal hymnal. A revision of one of the hymns which he had written in 1820 for the Unitarian hymnal reveals his changed attitude toward the Lord Jesus Christ. For the Unitarian book he had written:

> Deem not that they are blest alone
> Whose days a peaceful tenor keep;
> The God who loves our race has shown
> A blessing for the eyes that weep.

492

For the Methodist hymnbook he changed the third line to read:

The anointed Son of God makes known.

The hymn was sung in its changed form at the poet's funeral, as well as another beautiful hymn entitled "The Star of Bethlehem," written in 1875 for the semi-centennial of the Church of the Messiah in Boston.

493

The Challenge of Eternal Truth

Once to every man and nation
Comes the moment to decide,
In the strife of truth with falsehood,
For the good or evil side;
Some great cause, God's new messiah,
Offering each the bloom or blight,
And the choice goes by for ever
'Twixt that darkness and that light.

Then to side with truth is noble,
When we share her wretched crust,
Ere her cause bring fame and profit,
And 'tis prosperous to be just;
Then it is the brave man chooses,
While the coward stands aside,
Till the multitude make virtue
Of the faith they had denied.

By the light of burning martyrs,
Christ, Thy bleeding feet we track,
Toiling up new Calvaries ever
With the Cross that turns not back.
New occasions teach new duties;
Time makes ancient good uncouth;
They must upward still and onward
Who would keep abreast of truth.

Though the cause of evil prosper,
Yet 'tis truth alone is strong,
Though her portion be the scaffold
And upon the throne be wrong,
Yet that scaffold sways the future,
And, behind the dim unknown,
Standeth God within the shadow,
Keeping watch above His own.

JAMES RUSSELL LOWELL, 1819-1891

THE NEW ENGLAND POETS AS HYMNISTS

THE RENOWNED British hymnodist, Percy Dearmer, often expressed regret in his writings that the great poets of England were rarely importuned to compose hymns for their fellow countrymen. For two centuries after the Reformation the only songs the British people sang in worship were Psalms paraphrased by versifiers who possessed little or no poetic genius. Even when hymns finally were accepted, no effort apparently was made to inspire the masters of English verse to employ their gifts in the creation of original Christian lyrics.

The situation was quite different when the young Republic on this side of the Atlantic was born. The decades following the Revolutionary War witnessed the dawn of a remarkable period in American literature. New England particularly seemed to provide fertile soil for literary genius, and before many years had passed the names of Bryant, Longfellow, Lowell, Holmes and Whittier were familiarly known throughout the English-speaking world. And all of them wrote some hymns!

However, not all were uniformly successful in this area. In the preceding chapter we have already noted the work of William Cullen Bryant as a hymnist, and in a following chapter we will deal with the hymns of Whittier. Here we would review the achievements of the other three.

Henry Wadsworth Longfellow, though a deeply religious man and one who sounded a Christian note in many of his poems, was not essentially a hymnist. When his brother Samuel, who afterwards won considerable distinction as a hymn-writer, was ordained as a minister, Longfellow wrote a hymn for the occasion beginning with the line, "Christ to the young man said." It has never come into general use, however, and John White Chadwick afterwards observed rather facetiously, "It must have troubled Samuel's sense of what a hymn should be!"

Undoubtedly the best hymn that Longfellow ever wrote, and one that has found its way into numerous hymnals, is the well-known Christmas lyric:

> I heard the bells of Christmas day
> Their old familiar carols play,
> And wild and sweet the words repeat
> Of peace on earth, good will to men.
>
> And in despair I bowed my head:
> "There is no peace on earth," I said,
> "For hate is strong, and mocks the song
> Of peace on earth, good will to men."
>
> Then pealed the bells more loud and deep:
> "God is not dead, nor doth He sleep;
> The wrong shall fail, the right prevail,
> With peace on earth, good will to men."

Among the shorter poems of Longfellow, there is none more deeply cherished than his "Psalm of Life." Although this lyric can hardly be said to reveal the qualities required in a hymn, our spiritual poetry would be much the poorer if we did not possess the inspired lines,

> Tell me not in mournful numbers,
> Life is but an empty dream.

However, since it expresses only in a general way the author's faith in the immortality of the soul rather than pointing to Christ's victory over death as the basis of our hope of eternal life, it falls short of being a hymn with a Christian message.

More definitely Christian in tone are some of Longfellow's hymn translations. In an earlier chapter reference has already been made to his beautiful English rendering of the ancient Greek candlelighting hymn, "O gladsome Light," which he included in "The Golden Legend." In a work titled *The Poets and Poetry of Europe* published in 1845, Longfellow likewise translated a number of fine German hymns. Among these is one by Simon Dach, reading in part:

> Oh, how blest are ye whose toils are ended,
> Who through death have unto God ascended!
> Ye have arisen
> From the cares which keep us still in prison.
>
> Christ has wiped away your tears forever;
> Ye have that for which we still endeavor;
> To you are chanted
> Songs that ne'er to mortal ears were granted.

Two tragic events that cast a shadow over the poet's life and for a time interrupted his writing occurred in 1861. The one was the outbreak of the Civil War and the other, the death of his wife when her dress caught fire in their beautiful Craigie House in Cambridge, Mass. However, when he began to write again, he gives us a glimpse in "The Children's Hour" of the beauty of his home life, even as a widower, with his two sons, Ernest and Charles, and his three daughters,

> "Grave Alice, and laughing Allegra,
> And Edith with golden hair."

Born in Portland, Maine, in 1807, Longfellow graduated from Bowdoin College at the age of 18, and was given the degree of LL.D. by the same institution when he was 21. Nathaniel Hawthorne was a classmate. He taught at his alma mater from 1829 to 1835, and in the latter year was chosen as Professor of Belle Lettres at Harvard, a position he held until 1854. He was honored with the degree of LL.D. by Harvard and Cambridge (England), and in 1869 Oxford University bestowed on him the degree of D.C.L. He died in 1882, and two years later a bust was placed to his memory in the Poets' Corner in Westminster Abbey.

James Russell Lowell, like Longfellow, never essayed to be a hymn-writer, and yet he has given to the world unforgettable lines that have thrilled Christian hearts, notably his "Vision of Sir Launfal." Born February 22, 1819, in Cambridge, he was a descendant of Perceval Lowle, who had emigrated from Somersetshire, England, to Massachusetts in 1639 to found one of the most famous New England families. Incidentally, the Lowells became intermarried with the Cabots, another great name in New England. The poet's father, who was pastor of West Congregational Church in Boston for 55 years, is described as a person of rare sweetness and charm, qualities which reappeared in his youngest son, James Russell.

The latter, after graduating from Harvard "without special honors" in 1838, vacillated for a time between business, the ministry, medicine and law, and finally decided on the last-named profession. His first literary efforts were mainly due to the necessity of supplementing his meager income. Like most literary lights in New England at the time, he soon became an ardent champion of Abolition. The writing of *The Bigelow Papers,* couched in rustic New England dialect, brought him sudden fame, and from this time forward he became one of the nation's most powerful foes of slavery.

In 1876 he was appointed by President Hayes as American minister to the court of Spain, and in 1880 he was transferred to the court of St. James as minister to Great Britain. His reputation as a man of letters had already preceded him to England, and he immediately found himself in great demand as a public speaker. By this time he had become a world figure, and his utterances were widely quoted.

As early as 1842, Lowell wrote a hymn for the dedication of a church in Watertown, Mass. Twenty-four years later, apparently by request, he composed a beautiful Christmas carol for the children of the Church of the Disciples in Boston, a stanza of which reads:

"What means this glory round our feet,"
    The Magi mused, "more bright than morn?"
And voices chanted clear and sweet,
    "Today the Prince of Peace is born."

His greatest hymn, however, is an adaptation of various lines from his great anti-slavery poem, "The Present Crisis," resulting in a challenging plea for national righteousness. This hymn, "Once to every man and nation," when sung to the Welsh tune, *Ton-y-Botel,* makes a powerful appeal to the emotions.

The third of the New England literary lights who wrote hymns was Oliver Wendell Holmes. Holmes, like Lowell, started on a law career, but soon gave it up for medicine. He suddenly sprang into fame, following his graduation from Harvard, by his poem, "Old Ironsides," which saved the frigate *Constitution* from being scrapped. After medical studies in Paris, he returned to become Professor of Anatomy in Harvard's medical school. His success as a teacher was extraordinary, particularly in stimulating his students in scientific research.

His fame as a physician and teacher, however, was soon eclipsed by his success as an essayist, novelist and poet. One of the founders of the *Atlantic Monthly,* he eventually became one of its principal contributors. *The Autocrat of the Breakfast Table* attracted widespread attention on both sides of the ocean by its tangy, sparkling wit and humor. Published in serial form in *The Atlantic Monthly,* it is credited with having saved that magazine from disaster during the financial crisis of 1857. Then followed *The Professor of the Breakfast*

Table and *The Poet of the Breakfast Table,* both of which helped to make his place secure in American literature.

It was at the conclusion of the first of these that he wrote his finest hymn:

> Lord of all being, throned afar,
> Thy glory flames from sun and star;
> Center and soul of every sphere,
> Yet to each loving heart how near.

He introduced the beautiful lyric with these words: "Peace to all such as may have been vexed in spirit by any utterance these pages may have repeated! They will doubtless forget for the moment the difference in the hues of truth we look at through our human prisms, and join in singing (inwardly) this hymn to the Source of the light we all need to lead us, and warmth which alone can make us brothers."

Holmes was a liberal in religion. However, he could never get away from the influence left on him by his clergyman father, though he rebelled against the latter's stern Calvinistic theology. His constant emphasis was on the love of God. In his novel, *Elsie Venner,* he puts on the lips of Helen the words: "It is all trust in God and in His Word. These are enough for me." That he looked upon Christ as the perfect revelation of God may be seen in his "Hymn of Trust," which also appeared among the poems of *The Professor of the Breakfast Table:*

> O Love Divine, that stooped to share
> Our sharpest pang, our bitterest tear,
> On Thee we cast each earthborn care;
> We smile at pain while Thou art near.

Two of his other poems, "Robinson of Leyden" and "The Chambered Nautilus," also reflect something of Holmes' religious philosophy. In the midst of the popularity he enjoyed following the publication of his *Autocrat of the Breakfast Table* and other writings, he is quoted as having said concerning his hymns, "It would be one of the most agreeable reflections to me if I could feel that I had left a few worthy to be remembered after me."

The beloved poet-physician died in 1894 at the age of 85 years. His last appearance was at a meeting of the Boston Young Men's Christian Union, at which time he brought a message in verse, closing with this prayer:

> Our prayers accept; our sins forgive;
> Our youthful zeal renew;
> Shape for us holier lives to live
> And noble work to do.

The Quaker Poet's Prayer

Dear Lord and Father of mankind,
  Forgive our feverish ways;
Reclothe us in our rightful mind,
In purer lives Thy service find,
  In deeper reverence praise.

In simple trust like theirs who heard,
  Beside the Syrian sea,
The gracious calling of the Lord,
Let us, like them, without a word
  Rise up and follow Thee.

O Sabbath rest by Galilee,
  O calm of hills above,
Where Jesus knelt to share with Thee
The silence of eternity
  Interpreted by love!

Drop Thy still dews of quietness,
  Till all our strivings cease;
Take from our souls the strain and stress,
And let our ordered lives confess
  The beauty of Thy peace.

Breathe through the heats of our desire
  Thy coolness and Thy balm;
Let sense be dumb, let flesh retire;
Speak through the earthquake, wind, and fire,
  O still small voice of calm.

JOHN GREENLEAF WHITTIER, 1807-92

THE QUAKER POET WRITES HYMNS

OF all American poets, there is none who is more genuinely loved than John Greenleaf Whittier. A man of the people, a true American, and full of the milk of human kindness, Whittier put so much of his own character into his poetry it will never lose its singular charm and appeal.

Whittier's life is a story of struggle. He was born of humble Quaker parents at Haverhill, Mass., December 17, 1807. He knew of nothing but drudgery and hard work throughout his childhood, and received a very meager education. But the poetic spark was in him even as a child. One day, when a small boy, he sat before the kitchen fire and wrote on his slate:

> And must I always swing the flail
> And help to fill the milking pail?
> I wish to go away to school;
> I do not wish to be a fool.

No doubt it was the memory of these childhood experiences that later inspired him to write with such depth of feeling and understanding the lines of "The Barefoot Boy":

> Blessings on thee, little man,
> Barefoot boy, with cheek of tan!
> With thy turned-up pantaloons,
> And thy merry whistled tunes;
> With thy red lips, redder still
> Kissed by strawberries on the hill;
> With the sunshine on thy face,
> Through thy torn brim's jaunty grace:
> From my heart I give thee joy—
> I was once a barefoot boy!

Through hard work he managed to save enough to attend Haverhill Academy two seasons. Though this was the extent of his scholastic training, he never ceased to be a student.

A wandering Scotchman who chanced to visit the quiet Quaker home and sang such lyrics as "Bonny Doon," "Highland Mary," and "Auld Lang Syne" kindled the boy's imagination. He immediately borrowed a copy of Burns' poems from the village schoolmaster, and now for the first time he seriously began to think of becoming a poet.

When he was only twenty-five years old he had already begun to attract attention by his verse. He had also achieved some success in politics and was planning to run for Congress. Soon, however, came the call of the Abolition movement, and Whittier, always true to his Quaker conception of "the inner voice," determined to sacrifice all of his political ambitions to become a champion of the slaves.

It was not long before he was recognized as pre-eminently the *poet* of anti-slavery, as Phillips was its *orator,* Mrs. Stowe its *novelist,* and Sumner its *statesman.* The fervor with which he threw himself into the cause may be seen reflected in the stirring lines of verse written in those days, notably "The Star of Bethlehem."

While some of Whittier's anti-slavery poems were more vehement than inspiring, there were others that were written in his more characteristic pleading strain by which he sought to awaken the spirit of human kindness and compassion in his fellow men, not only for the slaves but for all who suffer from injustice and oppression. Thus he concluded his poem on "Worship," written in 1848, with three stanzas that are included in almost every standard hymnbook of our day:

> O brother man, fold to thy heart thy brother!
>> Where pity dwells, the peace of God is there;
> To worship rightly is to love each other,
>> Each smile a hymn, each kindly deed a prayer.
>
> Follow with reverent steps the great example
>> Of Him whose holy work was doing good;
> So shall the wide earth seem our Father's temple,
>> Each loving life a psalm of gratitude.
>
> Then shall all shackles fall; the stormy clangor
>> Of wild war-music o'er the earth shall cease;
> Love shall tread out the baleful fire of anger,
>> And in its ashes plant the tree of peace.

The vigor with which he espoused the Abolition cause stirred up deep resentment among his enemies. At Philadelphia, where he published *The Pennsylvania Freeman,* the office of the paper was attacked by a mob and burned. But Whittier was not dismayed. When Daniel Webster in 1850 made his notable defense of the Fugitive Slave law in the United States Senate, Whittier wrote "Ichabod" in reply.

At a time when the Abolition movement seemed to be losing

ground rather than gaining, the poet gave expression to his faith in God in the beautiful poem, "Seed-Time and Harvest." His duty, as he saw it, was to sow the seed; God would take care of the harvest.

Because the Quakers do not sing in their services, Whittier knew little of music. However, he once wrote: "A good hymn is the best use to which poetry can be devoted, but I do not claim that I have succeeded in composing one." At another time he observed that two hundred years of silence had taken all of the "sing" out of the Quakers.

Nevertheless, more than fifty of Whittier's lyrics are found in modern hymnals, and they are constantly growing in popularity among hymnal editors. Indeed, recent collections contain a larger number of the Quaker poet's hymns than those of any other American writer.

Most of Whittier's hymns are centos derived from his longer poems. For instance, "Immortal Love, for ever full" and "O Lord, and Master of us all" consist of selected stanzas from "Our Master," a poem which first appeared in 1867. His poem, "The Eternal Goodness," published the same year, has yielded the moving hymn of repentance, "I bow my forehead to the dust," as well as the beautiful hymn of child-like trust:

> I know not what the future hath
>   Of marvel or surprise,
> Assured alone that life and death
>   His mercy underlies.
>
> I know not where His islands lift
>   Their fronded palms in air;
> I only know I cannot drift
>   Beyond His love and care.
>
> And so beside the silent sea
>   I wait the muffled oar;
> No harm from Him can come to me
>   On ocean or on shore.
>
> And Thou, O Lord, by whom are seen
>   Thy creatures as they be,
> Forgive me if too close I lean
>   My human heart on Thee!

Perhaps the most loved of all of Whittier's hymns is "Dear Lord and Father of mankind." This is another example of how hymnal editors have chosen portions of a longer poem, in this instance "The

503

Brewing of the Soma," to form an impressive worship hymn. In his original poem Whittier describes how a certain sect in India drink an intoxicating liquor brewed from the plant called soma, and while in this excited state imagine that they have partaken of the drink of gods and thus have entered into union with the Divine. He then goes on to declare that many a worshiper in a Christian fane still mistakes emotional excitement for a spiritual experience. Then come the lines in which the poet sets forth the true approach to God in worship and prayer:

> Dear Lord and Father of mankind,
>   Forgive our foolish ways;
> Reclothe us in our rightful mind,
> In purer lives Thy service find,
>   In deeper reverence praise.

Only a few of Whittier's lyrics were purposely written to be used as hymns. One of these is "All things are Thine; no gift have we," which was composed in 1872 for the dedication of Plymouth Church in St. Paul, Minn.

Whittier's best poems were written after he was 50 years old. As the years multiplied, his verses reflected more and more his simple, unfaltering trust in the goodness of God. When accused of being a Universalist, he denied this, but stated that he had a very strong *hope* that in God's long years "life's broken circle" would be made whole and that all men would be saved.

No one has written with greater conviction or more sublime faith concerning the future life than he. Only once did he seem to seek for greater assurance. "The awful mysteries of life and nature," he wrote, "sometimes almost overwhelm me. 'What, Where, Whither?' These questions sometimes hold me breathless." But near the end of life—he died in 1892 at the age of 85—there came from the depth of his trustful heart this moving prayer:

> When on my day of life the night is falling,
>   And, in the winds from unsunned spaces blown,
> I hear far voices out of darkness calling
>   My feet to paths unknown;
>
> Thou, who hast made my home of life so pleasant,
>   Leave not its tenant when its walls decay;
> O Love Divine, O Helper ever present,
>   Be Thou my strength and stay!

As Whittier mellowed with the years, the fierce ardor with which he had espoused the cause of the downtrodden slaves was replaced by a gentler note in which love and brotherhood became the constantly recurring theme. His very appearance reflected his inner serenity, and those who knew him best described him as a saintly character. Phoebe Cary, in one of her last poems, has given us in a single verse what may be described as the perfect epitaph:

> But not thy strains, with courage rife,
> Nor holiest hymn, shall rank above
> The rhythmic beauty of thy life,
> Itself a canticle of love.

Palmer's Famous Hymn

My faith looks up to Thee,
Thou Lamb of Calvary,
  Saviour divine!
Now hear me while I pray,
Take all my guilt away,
O let me from this day
  Be wholly Thine.

May Thy rich grace impart
Strength to my fainting heart,
  My zeal inspire;
As Thou hast died for me,
O may my love for Thee
Pure, warm, and changeless be,
  A living fire.

When life's dark maze I tread,
And griefs around me spread,
  Be Thou my Guide;
Bid darkness turn to day,
Wipe sorrow's tears away,
Nor let me ever stray
  From Thee aside.

When ends life's transient dream,
When death's cold, sullen stream
  Shall o'er me roll,
Blest Saviour, then, in love,
Fear and distrust remove;
O bear me safe above,
  A ransomed soul.

RAY PALMER, 1808–87

AMERICA'S GREATEST HYMN AND ITS AUTHOR

ALTHOUGH a number of America's great poets wrote hymns, it was not given to any one of them to compose America's finest Christian lyric. Bryant wrote "Look from Thy sphere of endless day," Whittier was the author of "Dear Lord and Father of mankind." Holmes composed "Lord of all being, throned afar," and Longfellow has given us "I heard the bells of Christmas day;" but, beautiful as these hymns are, none of them can compare with "My faith looks up to Thee." This, "the most precious contribution which American genius has yet made to the hymnody of the Christian Church," came from the pen of a very humble but gifted minister, Ray Palmer.

Palmer, who was born at Little Compton, R. I., November 12, 1808, was a direct descendant of John Alden and his good wife, Priscilla. One of his forebears was William Palmer, who came to Plymouth in 1621.

Through pressure of poverty Ray found it necessary to leave home at the age of thirteen, after having received only a grammar school education. For two years he clerked in a Boston dry goods store, during which time he passed through some deep spiritual experiences, with the result that he gave his heart to God.

His pastor, who recognized unusual gifts in the young man, urged him to attend school. Eventually he graduated from Phillips Andover Academy and from Yale. For a while he taught in New York and New Haven, but in 1835 he was ordained as a Congregational minister. He served a congregation in Bath, Maine, for fifteen years, and another at Albany, N. Y., for a like period, after which he became corresponding secretary of the American Congregational Union, a position he held until 1878, when he was compelled to retire because of failing health.

It was while he was teaching in New York City that "My faith looks up to Thee" was written. He was only twenty-two years old, and he had no thought at the time that he was composing a hymn for general use. He tells in his own account of the hymn how he had

507

been reading a little German poem of two stanzas, picturing a penitent sinner before the Cross. Deeply moved by the lines, he translated them into English, and then added the four stanzas that form his own hymn. The words of the hymn, he tells us, were born out of his own spiritual experience.

"I gave form to what I felt, by writing, with little effort, the stanzas," he said. "I recollect I wrote them with very tender emotion, and ended the last lines with tears."

"A ransomed soul!" Who would not have been moved to deep emotion after having written a poem with such a sublime closing line!

Palmer copied the poem into a little note-book which he constantly carried in his pocket. Frequently he would read it as a part of his private devotion. It never seemed to occur to him that it might some day be used as a hymn.

But God was watching over that little poem. One day as Palmer was walking along the busy streets of Boston, he chanced to meet Lowell Mason, the famous composer of Savannah, Ga. Mason was compiling a hymnbook at the time and asked Palmer, who had gained somewhat of a reputation as a poet, if he would give him some verses for which he could compose music. Palmer remembered the poem in his note-book, and, while the two men stepped into a nearby store, a copy of the poem was made and given to Mason.

When the two men met again a few days later, Mason exclaimed: "Dr. Palmer, you may live many years and do many good things, but I think you will be best known to posterity as the author of 'My faith looks up to Thee.'"

Mason wrote the beautiful tune known as *Olivet* for the hymn, and perhaps the music contributed as much as the words to endear it to the hearts of millions. Certainly here is an instance where words and music are perfectly wedded, and should never be separated.

Palmer's whole life was characterized by a warm, almost passionate, devotion to Christ. Something of this love is beautifully reflected in his hymn, "Jesus, these eyes have never seen," which was his own favorite and which many regard as second only to "My faith looks up to Thee." It is a lyric of such tender appeal, it deserves to be quoted in full:

> Jesus, these eyes have never seen
> That radiant form of Thine;
> The veil of sense hangs dark between
> Thy blessed face and mine.

I see Thee not, I hear Thee not,
    Yet art Thou oft with me;
And earth hath ne'er so dear a spot
    As where I meet with Thee.

Like some bright dream that comes unsought
    When slumbers o'er me roll,
Thine image ever fills my thought,
    And charms my ravished soul.

Yet though I have not seen, and still
    Must rest in faith alone,
I love Thee, dearest Lord, and will,
    Unseen, but not unknown.

When death these mortal eyes shall seal,
    And still this throbbing heart,
The rending veil shall Thee reveal,
    All glorious as Thou art.

Palmer wrote the best of his original hymns—he was the author of thirty-eight in all—while he was still a young man. As he grew older he became deeply interested in the translation of Latin hymns, and to him belongs the distinction of being the first American to introduce this type of hymnody on this side of the Atlantic. No doubt he was inspired by the example of John Mason Neale and other gifted English translators who at this time were engaged in similar efforts. Nor was Palmer one whit behind them in the excellence of his renditions. Says Albert Edward Bailey: "We have reason to be proud of him, for he matched the best of the High Churchmen in the beauty and inspirational power of his translations."

One of his translations is of the hymn *Rex Christi, factor omnium,* generally ascribed to Gregory the Great. Palmer's opening line reads, "O Christ, our King, Creator, Lord." Another of his translations, "Come, Holy Ghost, in love," is based on the famous medieval hymn, *Veni Sancte Spiritus.* His most famous translation from the Latin, however, is "Jesus, Thou Joy of loving hearts," which is a very free rendering of a portion of *De Nomine Jesu* by Bernard of Clairvaux. This greatly beloved lyric, which has become a favorite communion hymn in many Christian bodies, is a gem of rare beauty.

Palmer died in 1887. On the day before he breathed his last, he was heard repeating feebly the last stanza of his favorite hymn:

When death these mortal eyes shall seal,
    And still this throbbing heart,
The rending veil shall Thee reveal,
    All glorious as Thou art.

A Hopeful Missionary Lyric

The morning light is breaking,
The darkness disappears;
The sons of earth are waking
To penitential tears;
Each breeze that sweeps the ocean
Brings tidings from afar
Of nations in commotion,
Prepared for Zion's war.

See heathen nations bending
Before the God we love,
And thousand hearts ascending
In gratitude above;
While sinners, now confessing,
The gospel call obey,
And seek the Saviour's blessing,
A nation in a day.

Blest river of salvation,
Pursue thine onward way;
Flow thou to every nation,
Nor in thy richness stay;
Stay not till all the lowly
Triumphant reach their home;
Stay not till all the holy
Proclaim: "The Lord is come!"

SAMUEL FRANCIS SMITH, 1808-95

SAMUEL SMITH, A PATRIOTIC HYMN-WRITER

THE NAME of Samuel Francis Smith will always be remembered as long as Americans sing "My country, 'tis of thee," and that will probably be as long as the Republic lives. Although "Star-Spangled Banner" has been officially designated by Congress as our national anthem, it has not succeeded in displacing "America" in the affections of the American people, and the latter is still regarded as our national *hymn*.

But the New England pastor who gave to his country its most deeply cherished patriotic song has a further claim to fame, for it was he who likewise gave to the Church one of its most stirring missionary hymns, "The morning light is breaking." These two hymns are not only the finest of Smith's lyrics, but, strange as it may seem, they are the first he ever wrote. Both were composed in the winter of 1832, when, at the age of 24 years, he was a student at Andover Theological Seminary.

Smith's interest in foreign missions was not accidental. The famous "Haystack Prayer-meeting," which marked the beginning of the modern missionary movement in America, had occurred at Williams College just two years before Smith was born. By the time he became a theological student at Andover, missionary fervor in this country had reached a white heat, and Smith himself had been seized with a desire to become a messenger of the Gospel to foreign lands.

A cheering message had just come from Adoniram Judson in far-off Burma. After years of painful disappointment and failure, Judson was able to report that light was breaking and that multitudes were turning in faith to Christ. Smith was fired with hopeful enthusiasm, and in a moment of spiritual exaltation the immortal missionary hymn was born:

> The morning light is breaking,
>> The darkness disappears;
> The sons of earth are waking
>> To penitential tears;
> Each breeze that sweeps the ocean
>> Brings tidings from afar
> Of nations in commotion,
>> Prepared for Zion's war.

While Smith was still a student at Andover, another hymn that came from his pen, "The Missionary's Farewell," had this interesting stanza:

Yes, my native land, I love thee;
   All thy scenes, I love them well;
Friends, connections, happy country,
   Can I bid you all farewell?
   Can I leave you,
Far in heathen lands to dwell?

Following his graduation from school, Smith continued to reveal his interest in the cause of missions by accepting a position as editor of a missionary magazine, through which he wielded great influence. When the "Lone Star" mission in India appeared to be in danger because of lack of funds, Smith did much to save it by a fervent poem entitled "Lone Star." At this time he also wrote a third missionary hymn, "Onward speed thy conquering flight." This, however, failed to reach the lyrical heights attained by "The morning light is breaking," which has been compared in poetic excellence to Heber's "From Greenland's icy mountains."

Although Smith never carried out his earlier resolve to become a missionary, his zeal for missions was so intense that in 1860 he left the church he was serving as pastor in Waterville, Maine, to become secretary of the Baptist Missionary Union. In this capacity he spent two years visiting foreign fields, and had the satisfaction of hearing his own hymns sung in many tongues. Referring to "The morning light is breaking," he once wrote:

"It has been a great favorite at missionary gatherings, and I have myself heard it sung in five or six different languages in Europe and Asia. It is a favorite with the Burmans, Karens and Telugus in Asia, from whose lips I have heard it repeatedly."

A son of the distinguished hymn-writer became a missionary to the Burmans.

Smith filled many important pulpits in New England during his long and illustrious career. At one time he was a professor in modern languages. He was an unusual linguist, being familiar with fifteen tongues. In 1894, a year before his death, he was still vigorous in mind and body, writing and preaching. Although he was eighty-six years old at the time, he sought diligently for a textbook that would enable him to begin the study of Russian! It was in this year, too, that he wrote a splendid hymn for a church dedication:

> Founded on Thee, our only Lord,
>> On Thee, the everlasting Rock,
> Thy Church shall stand as stands Thy Word,
>> Nor fear the storm, nor dread the shock.
>
> For Thee our waiting spirits yearn,
>> For Thee this house of praise we rear;
> To Thee with longing hearts we turn;
>> Come, fix Thy glorious presence here.
>
> Come, with Thy Spirit and Thy power,
>> The Conqueror, once the Crucified;
> Our God, our Strength, our King, our Tower,
>> Here plant Thy throne, and here abide.
>
> Accept the work our hands have wrought;
>> Accept, O God, this earthly shrine;
> Be Thou our Rock, our Life, our Thought,
>> And we, as living temples, Thine.

Fortunately, the celebrated hymnist has left us a personal account of how he wrote "America." Lowell Mason, the composer, had given him a collection of German books containing songs for children with the request that Smith examine them and translate anything of merit.

"One dismal day in February, 1832," he wrote long afterward, "about half an hour before sunset, I was turning over the leaves of one of the music books when my eye rested on the tune which is now known as 'America.' I liked the spirited movement of it, not knowing it at that time to be 'God save the King.' I glanced at the German words and saw that they were patriotic, and instantly felt the impulse to write a patriotic hymn of my own, adapted to the tune. Picking up a scrap of waste paper which lay near me, I wrote at once, probably within half an hour, the hymn 'America' as it is now known everywhere. The whole hymn stands today as it stood on the bit of waste paper, five or six inches long and two and a half wide."

The story is told that Smith once visited the Board of Trade in Chicago, and, while he was sitting in the gallery, the traders suddenly became aware of his presence. All at once trading on the floor ceased and from the wheat pit came the song, "My country, 'tis of thee." The author acknowledged the tribute by rising and bowing, whereupon he was escorted to the floor, where the entire assembly, with uncovered heads, joined in singing the remaining stanzas.

The hymn as Smith originally wrote it contained five verses, but the third was dropped at an early date by the author because of its anti-British sentiment. This stanza had been inspired, no doubt, by the fact that Smith grew up in the North End of Boston under the very shadow of Copp's Hill and of North Church, where Paul Revere's lanterns had flashed their message of the movements of the Red Coats. War animosities are never productive of exalted sentiments, and Smith often expressed the fervent wish that the stanza might be forgotten.

The German hymn which gave Smith the inspiration for "America" is known as "Sachsenlied," written by Siegfried A. Mahlmann as a tribute to the King of Saxony in 1815. Smith did not learn until some time later that the tune the Germans used for *Gott segne Sachsenland* was the same as that used by the British in singing "God save the King!" The source of the tune is wrapped in obscurity, and whether it is English or German in origin will probably never be determined. In any event, this is how it came about that the English national anthem and America's favorite patriotic hymn are sung to the same tune!

Before entering Andover Seminary, Smith had graduated from Harvard in the celebrated class of 1829, of which Oliver Wendell Holmes and other distinguished Americans also were members. Holmes once wrote a poem for a class reunion in which he referred to his classmate in the following lines:

> And there's a nice youngster of excellent pith—
> Fate tried to conceal him by naming him Smith;
> But he shouted a song for the brave and the free—
> Just read on his medal, "My country," "of thee."

On November 19, 1895, the venerable pastor and poet was called suddenly to his eternal home. He died as he was taking a train from Boston to preach in a neighboring town.

Here it should be mentioned that Mahlmann's "Sachsenlied" not only furnished the inspiration for "America," but also provided the model for another patriotic song which is somewhat more devotional in character:

> God bless our native land;
> Firm may she ever stand
>   Through storm and night:
> When the wild tempests rage,

Ruler of wind and wave,
Do Thou our country save
    By Thy great might.

For her our prayers shall rise
To God above the skies;
    On Him we wait.
Thou who art ever nigh,
Guarding with watchful eye,
To Thee aloud we cry,
    God save the state!

The above translation of Mahlmann's German hymn is the work of two New England pastors, Charles Timothy Brooks and John Sullivan Dwight. Brooks made the first translation about the year 1834. Some time later Dwight made slight changes in the first stanza and completely re-wrote the second.

"The Blessed Angels Sing"

It came upon the midnight clear,
  That glorious song of old,
From angels bending near the earth
  To touch their harps of gold:
"Peace on the earth, good will to men,
  From heaven's all gracious King;"
The world in solemn stillness lay
  To hear the angels sing.

Still through the cloven skies they come
  With peaceful wings unfurled,
And still their heavenly music floats
  O'er all the weary world;
Above its sad and lowly plains
  They bend on hovering wing,
And ever o'er its Babel sounds
  The blessed angels sing.

Yet with the woes of sin and strife
  The world hath suffered long;
Beneath the angel-strain have rolled
  Two thousand years of wrong;
And man, at war with man, hears not
  The love song which they bring:
O hush the noise, ye men of strife,
  And hear the angels sing.

And ye, beneath life's crushing load,
  Whose forms are bending low,
Who toil along the climbing way
  With painful steps and slow:
Look now! for glad and golden hours
  Come swiftly on the wing;
O rest beside the weary road,
  And hear the angels sing!

For lo! the days are hastening on
  By prophet-bards foretold,
When with the ever-circling years
  Comes round the Age of Gold;
When peace shall over all the earth
  Its ancient splendors fling,
And the whole world send back the song
  Which now the angels sing.

EDMUND HAMILTON SEARS, 1810–1876

TWO FAMOUS CHRISTMAS LYRICS
BY AN AMERICAN

HAD Edmund Hamilton Sears written only one great Christmas lyric, it would have been sufficient to perpetuate his name; but the humble New England minister was actually the author of two. And two lovelier carols than "It came upon a midnight clear" and "Calm on the listening ear of night" have probably never been composed since that holy night when angels sang their "glorious song of old" o'er Bethlehem's starlit plains.

Strange as it may seem, an interval of fifteen years separated the writing of the two hymns. Sears had just graduated from Union College at the age of twenty-four when "Calm on the listening ear of night" was written. It appeared for the first time in the *Boston Observer,* and was immediately recognized as a poem of unusual merit. Oliver Wendell Holmes spoke of it as "one of the finest and most beautiful hymns ever written." It reads:

> Calm on the list'ning ear of night
> Come heaven's melodious strains,
> Where wild Judea stretches forth
> Her silver-mantled plains;
> Celestial choirs from courts above
> Shed sacred glories there;
> And angels, with their sparkling lyres,
> Make music on the air.
>
> The answering hills of Palestine
> Send back the glad reply,
> And greet from all their holy heights
> The Dayspring from on high:
> O'er the blue depths of Galilee
> There comes a holier calm;
> And Sharon waves in solemn praise
> Her silent groves of palm.
>
> "Glory to God!" the lofty strain
> The realm of ether fills;
> How sweeps the song of solemn joy
> O'er Judah's sacred hills!
> "Glory to God!" the sounding skies
> Loud with their anthems ring:
> "Peace on the earth; good will to men,"
> From heaven's eternal King.

517

This day shall Christian tongues be mute,
  And Christian hearts be cold?
O catch the anthem that from heaven
  O'er Judah's mountains rolled,
When burst upon that listening night
  The high and solemn lay,
"Glory to God; on earth be peace":
  Salvation comes today.

Fifteen years elapsed, and then, at Christmas time in 1849, the Christian world was delighted to find in the *Christian Register* another lyric, "It came upon the midnight clear," which many believe is superior to the earlier hymn. With its musical language and its rhythmical lines, it fairly sings itself.

There is a close resemblance between the two hymns, and yet they are different. While the earlier hymn is largely descriptive, the later one is characterized by a note of joyous optimism and triumphant faith. In Sear's *Sermons and Songs,* the one was published at the beginning, and the other at the close, of a Christmas Eve sermon he preached on I Tim. 2.6.

Each of the hymns had five stanzas in its original form. The fourth stanza of the older hymn is usually omitted. It reads:

Light on thy hills, Jerusalem!
  The Saviour now is born;
More bright on Bethlehem's joyous plains
  Breaks the first Christmas morn;
And brighter on Moriah's brow,
  Crowned with her temple-spires,
Which first proclaim the new-born light,
  Clothed with its orient fires.

Sears was a native of New England. Born in Berkshire County, Massachusetts, in 1810, he was a direct lineal descendant of one of the Pilgrim Fathers who had come to Plymouth in 1620. He completed his theological course at Harvard Divinity School in 1837, whereupon he entered the Unitarian Church, serving as a pastor for nearly forty years.

Surprise has often been expressed that a Unitarian could write such marvelous hymns on the nativity; but Sears was a Unitarian in name rather than by conviction. It is said he leaned strongly toward Swedenborgian teachings, and believed implicitly in the deity of Christ. This is particularly evident in his *Sermons and Songs of the Christian Life,* which appeared the year before he died. It was also

518

made clear in a letter to Bishop Bickersteth, the English hymnist, in which Sears wrote:

"Although I was educated in the Unitarian denomination, I believe and preach the Divinity of Christ."

Though highly gifted as a writer, Sears was content to serve obscure parishes the greater part of his life at Wayland, Lancaster and Weston, Mass. In addition to his preaching, he did editorial work for twelve years on the *Monthly Religious Magazine,* and was also the author of a number of works in prose. His books on *Regeneration, Foregleams of Immortality,* and *The Fourth Gospel the Heart of Christ* were widely read in his day. These have now been almost entirely forgotten, but his two great hymns go singing down through the years. Practically every official church hymnal contains "It came upon the midnight clear," and there are many that also include "Calm on the listening ear of night." Sears died at Weston, Mass., January 16, 1876.

Mrs. Stowe's Hymn Masterpiece

Still, still with Thee, when purple morning breaketh,
  When the bird waketh, and the shadows flee;
Fairer than morning, lovelier than the daylight,
  Dawns the sweet consciousness, I am with Thee.

Alone with Thee, amid the mystic shadows,
  The solemn hush of nature newly born;
Alone with Thee, in breathless adoration,
  In the calm dew and freshness of the morn.

Still, still with Thee, as to each newborn morning
  A fresh and solemn splendor still is given,
So does this blesséd consciousness, awaking,
  Breathe each day nearness unto Thee and heaven.

So shall it be at last, in that bright morning,
  When the soul waketh and life's shadows flee;
O in that hour, fairer than daylight dawning,
  Shall rise the glorious thought, I am with Thee!

HARRIET BEECHER STOWE, 1812-1896

HARRIET BEECHER STOWE AND HER HYMNS

THROUGH the fame *Uncle Tom's Cabin* brought her, the name of Harriet Beecher Stowe has become a household word on both sides of the Atlantic. Very few, on the other hand, know of her as a hymn-writer, yet she wrote hymns that are worthy of a place in the best of collections. Indeed, for sheer poetic beauty there is probably not a single American lyric that can excel "Still, still with Thee, when purple morning breaketh."

It was her brother, Henry Ward Beecher, who introduced Mrs. Stowe as a hymn-writer when he included three of her hymns in the *Plymouth Collection,* which he edited in 1865. One of the three was the hymn mentioned above; the other two were "That mystic word of Thine, O sovereign Lord" and "When winds are raging o'er the upper ocean."

Like the Wesley family in England, the Beecher family became one of the most famous in religious literary circles in America. Harriet Beecher was born in Litchfield, Conn., June 14, 1812. Her father was the noted Dr. Lyman Beecher, a distinguished clergyman of his day. Her mother, a very devout Christian, died when Harriet was less than four years of age. Her dying prayer was that her six sons might be called into the ministry. That prayer was answered, and the youngest of them, Henry Ward Beecher, who was only a small lad when the mother died, became one of America's greatest preachers. We do not know what the dying mother's prayer for her daughter may have been, but we do know that Harriet Beecher achieved fame such as comes to few women. Even as a child she revealed a spiritual nature of unusual depth. An earnest sermon preached by the father when she was fourteen made a profound impression on her, and she tells of the experience in these words:

"As soon as my father came home and was seated in his study, I went up to him and fell in his arms, saying, 'Father, I have given myself to Jesus, and He has taken me.' I never shall forget the expression of his face as he looked down into my earnest childish eyes; it was so sweet, so gentle, and like sunlight breaking out upon a landscape. 'Is it so?' he said, holding me silently to his heart, as I felt the hot tears fall on my head. 'Then has a new flower blossomed in the kingdom this day.' "

In 1832 the father removed to Cincinnati, Ohio, where he became president of Lane Theological Seminary. Here Harriet married Prof. Calvin E. Stowe, a member of the faculty. Many misfortunes and sorrows came into her life, but always she was sustained by her strong faith in God, and she bore them with unusual Christian fortitude. In 1849 her infant boy was snatched from her by the dreadful cholera scourge. Her husband, broken in health, was in an Eastern sanatorium at the time, and all the cares and anxieties of the household fell upon the shoulders of the brave young wife. A letter written to her husband, dated June 29, 1849, gives a graphic description of the plague as it was then raging in Cincinnati. She wrote:

"This week has been unusually fatal. The disease in the city has been malignant and virulent. Hearse drivers have scarce been allowed to unharness their horses, while furniture carts and common vehicles are often employed for the removal of the dead. The sable trains which pass our windows, the frequent indications of crowding haste, and the absence of reverent decency have, in many cases, been most painful . . . On Tuesday, one hundred and sixteen deaths from cholera were reported, and that night the air was of that peculiarly oppressive, deathly kind that seems to lie like lead on the brain and soul. As regards your coming home, I am decidedly opposed to it."

Under date of July 26, she wrote again: "At last it is over and our dear little one is gone from us. He is now among the blessed. My Charley—my beautiful, loving, gladsome baby, so loving, so sweet, so full of life, and hope and strength—now lies shrouded, pale and cold, in the room below. . . . I write as though there were no sorrow like my sorrow, yet there has been in this city, as in the land of Egypt, scarce a house without its dead. This heart-break, this anguish, has been everywhere, and when it will end God alone knows."

The succeeding years brought other tragedies to the sorely tried family. In 1857 the eldest son, Henry, pride of his mother's heart, was drowned at the close of his freshman year at Dartmouth College. Then came the Civil War with its bloody battles. At Gettysburg a third son, Fred, was wounded in the head by a piece of shrapnel. Although it did not prove fatal, his mental faculties were permanently impaired.

Through all these afflictions the marvelous faith of Mrs. Stowe remained firm and unshaken. Many years afterwards, in looking back upon these bitter experiences, she wrote, "I thank God there is *one* thing running through all of them from the time I was thirteen years old, and that is the intense unwavering sense of Christ's educating, guiding presence and care."

It was in the midst of these dark tragedies that Mrs. Stowe wrote a hymn entitled "The Secret."

> When winds are raging o'er the upper ocean,
>   And billows wild contend with angry roar,
> 'Tis said, far down, beneath the wild commotion,
>   That peaceful stillness reigneth evermore.
>
> Far, far beneath, the noise of tempests dieth,
>   And silver waves chime ever peacefully;
> And no rude storm, how fierce soe'er it flieth,
>   Disturbs the Sabbath of that deeper sea.
>
> So to the heart that knows Thy love, O Purest!
>   There is a temple sacred evermore,
> And all the babble of life's angry voices
>   Dies in hushed stillness at its sacred door.
>
> Far, far away, the roar of passion dieth,
>   And loving thoughts rise calm and peacefully;
> And no rude storm, how fierce soe'er it flieth,
>   Disturbs that deeper rest, O Lord, in Thee!
>
> O Rest of rests! O Peace serene, eternal!
>   Thou ever livest, and Thou changest never;
> And in the secret of Thy presence dwelleth
>   Fulness of joy, forever and forever.

It was the writing of *Uncle Tom's Cabin* that brought world-wide fame to this unusual mother. The family had moved from Cincinnati to Brunswick, Maine, where Professor Stowe had accepted a position on the faculty of Bowdoin College. There were six children now and her husband's income was meager. In order to help meet the family expenses, Mrs. Stowe began to write articles for a magazine known as the *National Era*. She labored under difficulties. "If I sit by the open fire in the parlor," she wrote, "my back freezes, if I sit in my bedroom and try to write my head and my feet are cold. . . . I can earn four hundred dollars a year by writing, but I don't want to feel that I must, and when weary with teaching the children, and tending the baby, and buying provisions, and mending dresses, and darning stockings, I sit down and write a piece for some paper."

The passage of the Fugitive Slave Act had aroused the deepest resentment among Abolitionists in the North. While living in Cincinnati her family had aided the so-called "underground railway," by which runaway slaves were helped in their efforts to reach the Canadian boundary. Now Mrs. Stowe's spirit burned within her. "I wish," she writes at this period, "some Martin Luther would arise to set this community right."

It was then she conceived the idea of writing *Uncle Tom's Cabin*. In the month of February, 1851, while attending communion service in the college church at Brunswick, the scene of the death of Uncle Tom passed before her mind like the unfolding of a vision. When she returned home she immediately wrote down the mental picture she had seen. Then she gathered her children around her and read what she had written. Two of them broke into violent weeping, the first of many thousands who since have wept over *Uncle Tom's Cabin*.

The first chapter was not completed until the following April, and on June 5 it began to appear in serial form in the *National Era*. She had intended to write a short tale of a few chapters, but as her task progressed the conviction grew on her that she had been entrusted with a holy mission. Afterwards she said: "I could not control the story; it wrote itself." At another time she remarked: "The Lord himself wrote it, and I was but the humblest of instruments in His hand. To Him alone should be given all the praise."

Mrs. Stowe received $300 for her serial story! However, scarcely had the last installment appeared when a Boston publisher made arrangements to print it in book form. Within one year it had passed through 120 editions, and four months after the book was off the press the author had received $10,000 in royalties. Almost in a day Mrs. Stowe had become one of the most famous women in the world, and the specter of poverty had been banished forever. *Uncle Tom's Cabin* exerted a profound influence not only over the American people, but its fame spread to Europe. The year following its publication Jenny Lind came to America. Asked to contribute to a fund Mrs. Stowe was raising for the purpose of purchasing the freedom of a slave family, the "Swedish Nightingale" gladly responded, also writing a letter to Mrs. Stowe in the following prophetic vein: "I have the feeling about *Uncle Tom's Cabin* that great changes will take place by and by, from the impression people receive from it, and that the writer of that book can fall asleep today or tomorrow with the bright, sweet consciousness of having been a strong means in the Creator's hand of having accomplished essential good."

Tributes like this came to Mrs. Stowe from the great and lowly in all parts of the world.

Concerning Jenny Lind's singing, Mrs. Stowe wrote to her husband from New York: "Well, we have heard Jenny Lind, and the affair was a bewildering dream of sweetness and beauty. Her face and movements are full of poetry and feeling. She has the artless grace of a little child, the poetic effect of a wood-nymph."

Mrs. Stowe died in 1896 at the ripe age of eighty-four. Not long before her death she wrote a friend: "I have sometimes had in my sleep strange perceptions of a vivid spiritual life near to and with Christ, and multitudes of holy ones, and the joy of it is like no other joy—it cannot be told in the language of the world. . . . The inconceivable loveliness of Christ! . . . I was saying as I awoke:

> 'Tis joy enough, my All in all,
>   At Thy dear feet to lie.
> Thou wilt not let me lower fall,
>   And none can higher fly."

A Moving Missionary Hymn

Saviour, sprinkle many nations;
    Fruitful let Thy sorrows be;
By Thy pains and consolations
    Draw the Gentiles unto Thee.
Of Thy Cross the wondrous story
    Be it to the nations told;
Let them see Thee in Thy glory,
    And Thy mercy manifold.

Far and wide, though all unknowing,
    Pants for Thee each mortal breast:
Human tears for Thee are flowing,
    Human hearts in Thee would rest.
Thirsting as for dews of even,
    As the new-mown grass for rain,
Thee they seek, as God of heaven,
    Thee as Man, for sinners slain.

Saviour, lo, the isles are waiting,
    Stretched the hand, and strained the sight,
For Thy Spirit, new-creating,
    Love's pure flame, and wisdom's light.
Give the word, and of the preacher
    Speed the foot, and touch the tongue,
Till on earth by every creature,
    Glory to the Lamb be sung.

ARTHUR CLEVELAND COXE, 1818–1896

A HYMN WRITTEN ON TWO SHORES

"SAVIOUR, sprinkle many nations" has been called the "loveliest of missionary hymns." The praise is well merited. All the elements that make a great hymn are present here. Scriptural in language and devotional in spirit, it is fervent and touching in its appeal and exquisitely beautiful in poetic expression. It was given to the Church by Arthur Cleveland Coxe, an American bishop, in 1851, and since that time it has made its victorious progress around the world.

Curiously enough, this beautiful missionary lyric was written on two shores of the Atlantic. It was on Good Friday, in the year 1850, that Bishop Coxe wrote the first stanza at his home in Hartford, Conn. For lack of time, however, or because the needed inspiration did not come to him, the unfinished manuscript was laid aside.

The next year he visited England, and one day, while wandering about the campus of Magdalen College, Oxford, the thought flashed through his mind that he had never completed the hymn. Finding a scrap of paper and a pencil, he sat down to write, and in a few moments the moving words of the two concluding stanzas were composed, and the hymn was sent on its way to touch the heart of the world.

Bishop Coxe was not primarily a hymn-writer. His fame rests chiefly on his religious ballads. In 1840, when a young student of twenty-two, he published his first volume, entitled *Christian Ballads*. These are mostly moral poems, impressive and challenging in character, but not particularly suitable as hymns. One of them, however, bearing the name of "Chelsea," has yielded the famous lyric, "O where are kings and empires now?"

An interesting story is told concerning this hymn. In 1873 the General Conference of the Evangelical Alliance was held in New York City. It was a period when scientific discoveries raised doubts in the minds of many concerning the value of prayer, and anxious souls were fearful that the faith of the Church was being shaken. President Woolsey of Yale University gave the opening address. After he had referred to the wave of skepticism that had swept over the world, he looked out upon the assembly with a quiet, confident smile lighting his features, and then quoted the first stanza of Bishop Coxe's hymn:

> O where are kings and empires now,
>   Of old that went and came?
> But, Lord, Thy Church is praying *yet*,
>   A thousand years the same.

"For a moment," writes an eye-witness, "there was silence. In another moment the full significance of the reference had flashed on every mind, and the response was instantaneous and universal. Shouts, waving of handkerchiefs, clapping of hands, stamping of feet—I never knew anything like it. Round after round continued, until the storm of applause ended in a burst of grateful tears. No one doubted that the Church still believed in prayer and that the tempest had passed without the loss of a sail."

In the same volume of *Christian Ballads* there appears another little poem, most appealing in its simplicity:

> In the silent midnight watches,
>   List—thy bosom door!
> How it knocketh, knocketh, knocketh,
>   Knocketh, evermore!
> Say not 'tis thy pulse is beating:
>   'Tis thy heart of sin;
> 'Tis thy Saviour knocks, and crieth,
>   "Rise, and let me in!"

For a time Coxe gave promise of becoming the "John Keble of America," but after his election as a bishop in the Episcopal Church, pressing duties interfered with his literary work, and in later years he wrote few poems.

Bishop Coxe was the son of a noted Presbyterian minister, the Rev. Samuel H. Cox. He was born in Menham, N. J., in 1818. After his graduation from the University of the City of New York, he decided to leave the Presbyterian Church to enter the Episcopalian fold. At the same time he added an "e" to the end of his name, much to his father's displeasure! He died in 1896 at the age of seventy-eight years.

In 1869, about twenty years after Coxe wrote his famous missionary hymn, the Young Men's Christian Association of Ohio was holding a state convention in the city of Cleveland. Above the platform, letters formed by garlands of evergreens spelled out the convention theme: "Christ for the World, and the World for Christ."

Among those who attended the meetings was a Congregationalist clergyman of the city who at one time had been a missionary to Syria but had been compelled to return to America for reasons of health. His name was Samuel Wolcott. His zeal for foreign missions had never abated, and the sight of convention theme day after day fired his enthusiasm anew. One night, as he was walking home, the words kept ringing in his ears: "Christ for the World, and the World for Christ." Soon they began to take the form of rhythmic pattern, and then came the inspiration. As soon as he reached home, he found a pen and within a few hours a new missionary hymn had been given to the world. Two of its stanzas read:

> Christ for the world we sing;
> The world to Christ we bring
>   With loving zeal;
> The poor and them that mourn,
> The faint and overborne,
> Sin-sick and sorrow-worn,
>   Whom Christ doth heal.
>
> Christ for the world we sing;
> The world to Christ we bring
>   With joyful song;
> The newborn souls, whose days
> Reclaimed from error's ways,
> Inspired with hope and praise,
>   To Christ belong.

Wolcott, who was born in South Windsor, Conn., in 1813, received his education at Yale University and Andover Theological Seminary. After his return from Syria, he served congregations in Providence, Chicago, Cleveland, and Longmeadow, Mass. He had never attempted to write a hymn until he was 56 years old, but after that he composed more than 200! Among the better known are "Father, I own Thy voice," "Lo! the faith which crossed the ocean," and "Pitying Saviour, look with blessing." Wolcott died at Longmeadow on February 24, 1886.

The Hymn of a Saintly Woman

More love to Thee, O Christ,
  More love to Thee!
Hear Thou the prayer I make
  On bended knee;
This is my earnest plea,
More love, O Christ, to Thee,
  More love to Thee.

Once earthly joy I craved,
  Sought peace and rest;
Now Thee alone I seek,
  Give what is best:
This all my prayer shall be,
More love, O Christ, to Thee,
  More love to Thee.

Then shall my latest breath
  Whisper Thy praise;
This be the parting cry
  My heart shall raise;
This still its prayer shall be,
More love, O Christ, to Thee,
  More love to Thee.

ELIZABETH PRENTISS, 1818–1878

A HYMN BORN OF SORROW AND SUFFERING

THE fruits of a sanctified Christian life are often seen long after a believer has ceased from earthly strivings and gone home "to be with Christ." This was true in a very special sense of Elizabeth Payson Prentiss, writer of "More love to Thee, O Christ." Although more than eighty years have passed since she died, her beautiful Christian life still continues to radiate its spirit of trust and hope through her hymns and devotional writings.

As a child she was blessed with an unusual home. Her father, Edward Payson, was a highly esteemed New England clergyman, revered and loved for his saintly life. He was of frail health, however, and died while yet in his prime. It is said that after his death the name of "Edward Payson" was given in baptism to hundreds of children whose parents had been blessed by his ministry.

Elizabeth, who was born in Portland, Me., in 1818, was much like her father. Of a serious mind from childhood, she possessed unusual gifts as a writer. When only sixteen years old she contributed verses and articles to *The Youth's Companion.* Later she taught school until her marriage in 1845 to George L. Prentiss, a Presbyterian minister.

Her home life was beautiful. Those who knew her best described her as "a very bright-eyed little woman, with a keen sense of humor, who cared more to shine in her own happy household than in a wide circle of society."

But all the while she was carrying a heavy burden. Throughout life she was an invalid, and scarcely knew what it meant to be free from pain. Chronic insomnia added to her affliction, as well as intense headaches. While her body languished under physical chastening, however, her spirit rose above all tribulations and grew more radiant and beautiful. She wrote: "I see now that to live for God, whether one is allowed ability to be actively useful or not, is a great thing, and that it is a wonderful mercy to be allowed even to suffer, if thereby one can glorify Him."

It was out of these trying experiences that the famous volume,

531

Stepping Heavenward, was born. The purpose of the book, as she herself explained, was "for strengthening and comforting other souls." It met with instant success, more than 200,000 copies being sold.

Mrs. Prentiss likewise gained fame as a poet and hymn-writer. Her volume, *Religious Poems,* containing 123 lyrics, breathes a spirit of fervent devotion to Christ. "To love Christ more," she said, "is the deepest need, the constant cry of my soul . . . Out in the woods, and on my bed, and out driving, when I am happy and busy, and when I am sad and idle, the whisper keeps going up for more love, more love, more love!"

Her faith and love, however, were destined to undergo a yet severer trial. In 1851 her husband accepted a call to a congregation in New York City, which thenceforth became their home. There they lost a child—the first break in the family circle. Another death soon followed, their youngest child. For weeks the mother was inconsolable, and in her diary she wrote: "Empty hand, empty hands, a worn-out, exhausted body, and unutterable longings to flee from a world that has so many sharp experiences." And then came this touching poem:

> I thought that prattling boys and girls
>   Would fill this empty room;
> That my rich heart would gather flowers
>   From childhood's opening bloom:
> One child and two green graves are mine,
>   This is God's gift to me;
> A bleeding, fainting, broken heart,
>   This is my gift to Thee.

One evening, when the grief-stricken parents had returned home from the cemetery where their two children slept, the emotions of Mrs. Prentiss almost reached the breaking point. She cried:

"Our home is broken up, our lives wrecked, our hopes shattered, our dreams dissolved. Sometimes I don't think I can stand living for another moment, much less a lifetime."

"But it is in times like these that God loves us all the more," replied her husband, "just as we love our own children more when they are sick or troubled or in distress."

While her husband left the house to make some pastoral calls, Mrs. Prentiss took her Bible and read a number of passages. Then she picked up her hymnal, seeking for hymns of comfort and consolation. Coming upon Sarah Adams' "Nearer, my God, to Thee," she read it several times. Impressed by the thought that God met

Jacob in a moment of human sorrow and need, she prayed that she might have a similar experience. As she mused on the words of the hymn, she began to compose in her mind a new hymn in the same metrical pattern:

> More love to Thee, O Christ,
>   More love to Thee;
> Hear Thou the prayer I make,
>   On bended knee.
> This is my earnest plea,
> More love, O Christ, to Thee,
>   More love to Thee.

Following her death in 1878, this verse was found written on the flyleaf of one of her favorite books:

> One hour with Jesus! How its peace outweighs
> The ravishment of earthly love and praise;
> How dearer far, emptied of self to lie
> Low at His feet, and catch, perchance, His eye,
> Alike content when He may give or take,
> The sweet, the bitter, welcome for His sake.

At the time Mrs. Prentiss was writing her hymns and devotional books in New York, two sisters, Alice and Phoebe Cary, were also writing sacred verse in the same city. Both were born on a farm near Cincinnati—Alice in 1820 and Phoebe in 1824. Grown to womanhood, they moved to New York, where they engaged in literary pursuits.

Their lives were greatly influenced by a warm friendship formed with John Greenleaf Whittier. A hymn written by Alice shortly before her death was printed in a number of hymnals. Its opening stanza reads:

> Earth, with its dark and dreadful ills,
>   Recedes and fades away;
> Lift up your heads, ye heavenly hills;
>   Ye gates of death give way!

Phoebe's best known hymn, "One sweetly solemn thought," came into more general use, and is found in many hymnals of today. Written in 1852, it was first published in a hymnbook her pastor was preparing for the Church of the Strangers in New York City. Alice Cary died February 12, 1871, and her sister, broken in health through caring for her, passed away on July 31 of the same year.

A Rally Hymn of the Church

Stand up, stand up for Jesus,
Ye soldiers of the Cross;
Lift high His royal banner,
It must not suffer loss:
From victory unto victory
His army He shall lead,
Till every foe is vanquished,
And Christ is Lord indeed.

Stand up, stand up for Jesus,
The trumpet call obey;
Forth to the mighty conflict
In this His glorious day:
Ye that are men, now serve Him
Against unnumbered foes;
Your courage rise with danger,
And strength to strength oppose.

Stand up, stand up for Jesus,
Stand in His strength alone;
The arm of flesh will fail you,
Ye dare not trust your own:
Put on the gospel armor,
Each piece put on with prayer;
Where duty calls or danger,
Be never wanting there.

Stand up, stand up for Jesus,
The strife will not be long;
This day the noise of battle,
The next the victor's song:
To him that overcometh
A crown of life shall be;
He with the King of glory
Shall reign eternally.

GEORGE DUFFIELD, 1818–1888

534

A TRAGEDY THAT INSPIRED A GREAT HYMN

THE Christian Church has many stirring rally hymns, but none that is more effective when sung by a large assembly than George Duffield's "Stand up, stand up for Jesus." Who has not been moved to the depths of his soul by the inspiring words and resounding music of this unusual hymn?

A tragedy lies in its background. It was in the year 1858, and a great spiritual awakening was gripping the city of Philadelphia. Men referred to this revival afterwards as "the work of God in Philadelphia."

One of the most earnest and zealous leaders in the movement was a young pastor, Dudley A. Tyng, not quite thirty years old. Because of his evangelical convictions and his strong opposition to slavery he had shortly before been compelled to resign as rector of the Church of the Epiphany, and in 1857 he had organized a little congregation that met in a public hall.

In the midst of the revival in 1858 he preached a powerful sermon at a noon-day meeting in Jayne's Hall to a gathering of 5,000 men. His text was Exodus 10. 11: "Go now, ye that are men, and serve the Lord." It is said that the effect was overwhelming, no less than a thousand men giving themselves to Christ.

A few weeks later the young pastor was watching a cornshelling machine when his arm was caught in the machinery and terribly mangled. Though every effort was made to save his life, he died within a few hours. Shortly before the end came he cried to the friends who gathered about him, "Sing, sing, can you not sing?" He himself then began the words of "Rock of Ages," with the others trying to join him in the midst of their grief. When his father, the distinguished clergyman, Stephen H. Tyng, bent over him to ask if he had a last message for his friends, the dying soldier of the Cross whispered:

"Tell them to stand up for Jesus!"

George Duffield, who also was a clergyman and a close friend of the greatly lamented Tyng, felt that the words were too impressive to be lost. On the following Sunday he preached a sermon in his own church on Ephesians 6. 14, "Stand, therefore, having your loins girt about with truth, and having on the breastplate of righteousness." As he concluded his sermon, he read the words of a poem he had written, "Stand up, stand up for Jesus."

Not only did Duffield preserve the dying words of his devoted friend, but it will be noted that the second stanza also contains the challenge of Tyng's last revival sermon: "Go now, ye that are men, and serve the Lord."

The superintendent of Duffield's Sunday school printed the words of the poem for distribution among his scholars. One of these leaflets found its way to a religious periodical, where it was published. Soon it began to appear in hymnbooks, being generally set to a tune composed by George J. Webb a few years earlier. It is said that the first time the author heard it sung outside of his own church was in 1864, when the Christian men in the Army of the James sang it in their camp as they were about to enter into battle.

As originally written, the hymn contained six stanzas. The second and fifth are omitted from most hymnbooks. These stanzas read:

> Stand up, stand up for Jesus,
>   The solemn watchword hear;
> If while ye sleep He suffers,
>   Away with shame and fear;
> Where'er ye meet with evil,
>   Within you or without,
> Charge for the God of Battles,
>   And put the foe to rout.

> Stand up, stand up for Jesus,
>   Each soldier to his post:
> Close up the broken column,
>   And shout through all the host:
> Make good the loss so heavy,
>   In those that still remain,
> And prove to all around you
>   That death itself is gain.

The omission of these lines is really no loss, since they sink far beneath the literary level of the remaining verses. They also carry the military imagery to needless length.

Ten years after Duffield's hymn was written, another lyric was born in the city of Philadelphia, this one with a stirring missionary theme. It came about in this way. The Rev. Daniel March, a pastor in that city, had been invited to preach on October 18, 1868, before the Philadelphia Christian Association. He had chosen as his text the words of Isaiah: "Here am I; send me." At a late hour he had learned that the hymn to be sung after the sermon was not at all in harmony with the theme of his message, wherefore March "at the impulse of the moment" wrote a new hymn, as he states, "in great haste." Thus it was that a group of people who had assembled the following day in a Clinton Street church sang for the first time:

> Hark! the voice of Jesus crying,
> "Who will go and work today?
> Fields are white and harvests waiting,
> Who will b'ear the sheaves away?"
> Loud and long the Master calleth,
> Rich reward He offers free;
> Who will answer, gladly saying,
> "Here am I, send me, send me?"

Very fitting is the comment of Edward S. Ninde: "Little did the preacher think that his carefully prepared sermon would soon be forgotten, but that the fugitive song, product of the passing moment, would live on through the years, to be sung by multitudes then unborn, inspiring many to do their best in the service of the Master."

Another hymn of the evangelistic type which had its birth at this time was "Saviour, Thy dying love." Its author, Sylvanus Dryden Phelps, like March, also was a clergyman. Born at Suffield, Conn., May 15, 1816, he graduated from Brown University and afterwards served churches in New Haven and Providence. He also did editorial work for the *Christian Secretary* and was the author of several poetical works.

The famed composers, Robert Lowry and W. H. Doane, were preparing a collection of Gospel songs about this time, and invited Phelps to contribute some hymns. Among those submitted by the latter was "Saviour, Thy dying love," for which Lowry wrote the tune.

When Phelps celebrated his 70th birthday in 1886, he received a letter from Lowry offering his congratulations. "It is worth living seventy years," he wrote, "even if nothing comes of it but one such hymn as 'Saviour, Thy dying love.'"

A Hymn of Spiritual Yearning

We would see Jesus, for the shadows lengthen
Across this little landscape of our life;
We would see Jesus, our weak faith to strengthen
For the last weariness, the final strife.

We would see Jesus, the great Rock-foundation
Whereon our feet were set by sovereign grace:
Nor life nor death, with all their agitation,
Can thence remove us, if we see His face.

We would see Jesus: other lights are paling,
Which for long years we have rejoiced to see;
The blessings of our pilgrimage are failing:
We would not mourn them, for we go to Thee.

We would see Jesus: this is all we're needing;
Strength, joy, and willingness come with the sight;
We would see Jesus, dying, risen, pleading;
Then welcome day, and farewell, mortal night.

ANNA BARTLETT WARNER, 1821-1915.

A GROUP OF GIFTED WOMEN HYMNISTS

IN the last week of our Saviour's life, a very beautiful and touching incident occured in the city of Jerusalem. The Evangelist John tells the story in the following words:

"Now there were certain Greeks among those that went up to worship at the feast: these therefore came to Philip, who was of Bethsaida of Galilee, and asked him, saying, Sir, we would see Jesus. Philip cometh and telleth Andrew: Andrew cometh, and Philip, and they tell Jesus. And Jesus answereth them, saying, The hour is come, that the Son of man should be glorified."

It was the petition of these Gentile pilgrims from the land of the Spartans and Athenians that inspired an American young woman to write one of our beautiful hymns, "We would see Jesus."

Her name was Anna Bartlett Warner. For almost a century she lived at a beautiful retreat in the Hudson river known as Constitution Island, under the very shadows of the great military academy at West Point. A sister named Susan achieved even greater literary fame than she, but it is Anna's name, after all, that will live on and be cherished for her songs. It is doubtful if there are many children in America during the last century who have not learned to know and to love the little hymn:

> Jesus loves me, this I know,
> For the Bible tells me so.
> Little ones to Him belong,
> They are weak, but He is strong.

Children throughout the world are singing it now, and missionaries tell us that the simplicity of its message makes a wonderful appeal to the newly-converted Christians. This hymn is one of the reasons why the name of Anna Warner will never be forgotten. But this is not all, for she is also the author of that other little gem so dearly loved by children:

> Jesus bids us shine
>   With a clear, pure light,
> Like a little candle
>   Burning in the night;

539

> In the world is darkness,
> So we must shine,
> You in your small corner,
> And I in mine.

Two volumes of sacred song were composed by this gifted young woman. The first, bearing the title, *Hymns of the Church Militant*, was published in 1858. The second, called *Wayfaring Hymns, Original and Translated*, appeared in 1869. "We would see Jesus" was included in the first of these collections. It appears, however, that it was written at least seven years before its publication. An interesting item from her sister Susan's diary, under date of February 8, 1851, tells of the impression the hymn made on her when she first read it. She writes:

"The next day, Sunday, in the afternoon, Anna had been copying off some hymns for Emmelin's book, and left them with me to look over. I had not read two verses of 'We would see Jesus,' when I thought of Anna, and merely casting my eye down, the others so delighted and touched me that I left it for tears and petitions. I wished Anna might prove the author—and after I found she was, I sat by her a little while with my head against her, crying such delicious tears."

Another hymn that has found a place in many hearts bears the title, "The Song of the Tired Servant." It was inspired by a letter received by Miss Warner from a friend who was a pastor, in which he spoke of the weariness he felt after the tasks of an arduous day, but of the joy that his soul experienced in serving the Master. The first stanza reads:

> One more day's work for Jesus,
> One less of life for me!
>   But heaven is nearer,
>   And Christ is dearer
> Than yesterday, to me;
>   His love and light
>   Fill all my soul tonight.

Although the two Warner sisters lived in a secluded corner apart from the busy world, they made their influence felt in widespread circles. They felt a particular responsibility in reference to the many thousands of young men from all parts of the United States who were being trained at West Point for service in the Army, and for many years they conducted a Bible class for the cadets.

Military honors were accorded each of the sisters when they

were buried. Anna Warner was ninety-five years old when she died in 1915.

About the time the Warner sisters were beginning their literary careers, another young woman, Catherine Watterman, was writing verse in Philadelphia. Although she published a volume of poems in 1850, only one of them has the character of a hymn. It is the lovely lyric, "Come unto me, when shadows darkly gather." In a sense, it might be looked upon as the answer to Anna Warner's hymn, "We would see Jesus," and bears a certain resemblance to the latter. One of its stanzas is particularly appealing:

> Large are the mansions in thy Father's dwelling,
>   Glad are the homes that sorrows never dim;
> Sweet are the harps in holy music swelling,
>   Soft are the tones which raise the heavenly hymn.

The hymn was written in 1839, a year before Miss Watterman's marriage to Captain George J. Esling, and it appears in hymnals under the name, Catherine Watterman Esling.

Another woman who composed hymns that have become very dear to the hearts of little children on both sides of the Atlantic was Emily Huntington Miller. The daughter of a Methodist clergyman, Emily was born in Brooklyn, Conn., October 22, 1833. The spiritual and cultural influences of a New England parsonage soon began to reveal themselves when early in youth she began to write.

It was rather uncommon for young women to attend college in those days, but Emily enrolled at Oberlin College and graduated in the class of 1857. Ten years later she became one of the editors of *The Little Corporal,* a popular children's magazine, to which she contributed a poem every month. Like all other contributors, however, she often found it difficult to meet the publication "deadline." One month in 1867 she was handicapped by illness. The final day came, and her poem was not written. When she found sufficient strength for her task, however, the inspiration came all at once, so she tells us, and "in less than fifteen minutes the hymn was written and sent away without any correction." The lyric in question was:

> I love to hear the story
>   Which angel voices tell,
> How once the King of glory
>   Came down on earth to dwell.

I am both weak and sinful,
　But this I surely know,
The Lord came down to save me,
　Because He loved me so.

I'm glad my blessed Saviour
　Was once a child like me,
To show how pure and holy
　His little ones should be;
And if I try to follow
　His footsteps here below,
He never will forget me,
　Because He loves me so,

Almost immediately the hymn attracted notice. In England it was included in the 1875 edition of *Hymns Ancient and Modern,* a very unusual honor, since very few hymns of American origin were admitted to that famous collection. No one was more surprised at the popularity attained by the hymn than the author herself.

Another of her hymns for children, though not so well known as the other one, possesses unusual merit:

Father, while the shadows fall,
With the twilight over all,
Deign to hear my evening prayer,
Make a little child Thy care.
　Take me in Thy holy keeping
　　Till the morning break;
　Guard me thro' the darkness sleeping,
　　Bless me when I wake.

Miss Huntington became the wife of Professor John E. Miller in 1860. After his death she was made dean of the Woman's College of Northwestern University, in which position she exerted a lasting influence over large numbers of young women. She died in 1913.

Another American woman who at this time was writing hymns for children was Mrs. Lydia Baxter. Born at Petersburg, N. Y., September 2, 1809, it seems that she was nearly 50 years old before she began to exercise her gifts as a song writer. Her book of poems, *Gems by the Wayside,* was published in 1855, after which she became a frequent contributor to hymn collections for Sunday schools and evangelistic services. Two of her best known hymns are "Take the Name of Jesus with you" and "There is a gate that stands ajar." Two stanzas of the latter hymn read:

There is a gate that stands ajar,
　And through its portals gleaming,
A radiance from the Cross afar,

> The Saviour's love revealing.
> O depth of mercy! Can it be,
> That gate was left ajar for me?
>
> That gate ajar stands free for all
>   Who seek through it salvation;
> The rich and poor, the great and small,
>   Of every tribe and nation.
> O depth of mercy! Can it be
> That gate was left ajar for me?

Mrs. Baxter may be regarded as one of the forerunners of the Gospel hymn movement of America. Her lyrics fall short of the more exacting standards required in a true hymn, and for this reason few of them have been admitted to the authorized collections of the principal church communions. However, the woman who wrote "Take the Name of Jesus with you" and "There is a gate that stands ajar" will not soon be forgotten by pious Christians, even though the author receives scant notice at the hands of hymnologists. It is significant that in 1937 the Church of Sweden included a translation of the latter hymn in its *Psalmbook*, one of the most conservative hymn collections in Christendom. Mrs. Baxter died in New York, June 22, 1874.

The Divine Pilot

Jesus, Saviour, pilot me
Over life's tempestuous sea;
Unknown waves before me roll,
Hiding rock and treacherous shoal;
Chart and compass come from Thee,
Jesus, Saviour, pilot me.

As a mother stills her child,
Thou canst hush the ocean wild;
Boisterous waves obey Thy will
When Thou sayest to them, "Be still."
Wondrous Sovereign of the sea,
Jesus, Saviour, pilot me.

When at last I near the shore,
And the fearful breakers roar
'Twixt me and the peaceful rest,
Then, while leaning on Thy breast,
May I hear Thee say to me,
"Fear not, I will pilot thee."

EDWARD HOPPER, 1818–1888

A FAMOUS HYMN WRITTEN FOR SAILORS

IT does not surprise us that the writer of "Jesus, Saviour, pilot me" was the pastor of a sailors' church. Edward Hopper, who for many years was minister of the Church of Sea and Land in New York harbor, had in mind the daily life of the seamen attending his church when he wrote his famous lyric. A hymn on the theme of the stormy sea, picturing Jesus as the divine Pilot — this, he felt, would appeal to sailors and be a source of constant comfort and encouragement.

Perhaps Hopper got his idea from Charles Wesley. It was a common practice of the great English hymn-writer to compose hymns that were particularly adapted to the audiences he addressed. For example, when he visited the men who worked in the Portland quarries in England, he wrote the hymn containing the lines:

> Strike with the hammer of Thy Word,
> And break these hearts of stone.

In any event, Hopper's beautiful hymn at once sprang into popular use, not only with sailors, but with Christians everywhere. It appeared for the first time anonymously in *The Sailors' Magazine,* and several hymnbooks adopted it. It was not until 1880, nine years after it was published, however, that the author's name became known. In that year the anniversary of the Seamen's Friend Society was held in Broadway Tabernacle, New York City, and Hopper was asked to write a hymn for the occasion. He responded by producing "Jesus, Saviour, pilot me," and the secret was out.

Hopper wrote several other hymns, but only this one has lived. Like Edward Perronet, the author of "All hail the power of Jesus' Name," he was "a bird of a single song." We could have wished that the fires of inspired genius had continued to burn with both of these men. Nevertheless, "Happy is the man who can produce one song which the world will keep on singing after its author shall have passed away."

The author of "Jesus, Saviour, pilot me" was a child of the city.

545

He was born in America's great metropolis, New York City, in the year 1818. His father was a merchant. His mother was a descendant of the Huguenots, the persecuted French Protestants. He was educated for the ministry, and, after serving several churches in other places, he returned to New York in 1870 to begin his work among the men who go down to the sea in ships. He remained as pastor of the Church of Sea and Land until his death in 1888, and we scarcely need to add that his ministry was singularly successful.

The beautiful prayer in the third stanza of Hopper's hymn was answered in his own passing. He was sitting in his study-chair, pencil in hand, when the final summons came. On the sheet before him were found some freshly written lines on "Heaven." Thus was fulfilled in his own death the beautiful prayer expressed in the final stanza of his hymn:

> When at last I near the shore,
> And the fearful breakers roar
> 'Twixt me and the peaceful rest,
> Then, while leaning on Thy breast,
> May I hear Thee say to me,
> "Fear not, I will pilot thee."

A few years earlier another clergyman had likewise won undying fame by writing a hymn on the theme of God's providential care and guidance. Joseph H. Gilmore was the writer, and his hymn was the well-known Gospel song:

> He leadeth me: O blessed thought!
> O words with heavenly comfort fraught!
> Whate'er I do, where'er I be,
> Still 'tis God's hand that leadeth me.

The author, who was the son of Governor Gilmore of New Hampshire, was born in Boston in 1834. After graduating from Brown University at the head of his class, he became secretary to his father, then served a number of years as a Baptist minister, and finally became professor of English Literature at Rochester University.

It was on March 26, 1862, during the dark days of the Civil War, that Gilmore, who was 28 years old, had been asked to lead mid-week services in the First Baptist Church of Philadelphia, then located on the corner of Broad and Arch Streets. Speaking on the 23rd Psalm, he dwelt at length on how God's guidance is often revealed in the most difficult experiences of life. Following the service, he and his wife were invited to stay at the home of a Deacon Wattson, who resided next door to the church. Still pondering the theme on which he had spoken, Gilmore that night began to compose the verses of his hymn, jotting them down on the back of the note paper on which he had written his sermon. He handed the poem to his wife, and afterwards forgot all about it. The latter, however, sent it to the *Watchman and Reflector,* where it was first published. William Bradbury found it there, and immediately set it to music.

"Three years later," Gilmore relates, "I went to Rochester to preach for the Second Baptist Church. On entering the chapel I took up a hymnbook, thinking, 'I wonder what they sing.' The book opened at 'He leadeth me,' and that was the first time I knew my hymn had found a place among the songs of the Church. I shall never forget the impression made upon me by coming then and there in contact with my own assertion of God's leadership."

In 1926, when the United Gas Improvement Company of Philadelphia erected a modern office building on the site where the First Baptist Church and Deacon Wattson's home had stood, it fastened a bronze tablet on the outside wall of that structure noting the fact that "He leadeth me" had been written at that place. This was done, states the inscription, "in recognition of the beauty and fame of the hymn, and in remembrance of its distinguished author."

A Famous Christmas Carol

O little town of Bethlehem,
How still we see thee lie!
Above thy deep and dreamless sleep
The silent stars go by;
Yet in thy darkness shineth
The everlasting Light;
The hopes and fears of all the years
Are met in thee tonight.

For Christ is born of Mary,
And gathered all above,
While mortals sleep, the angels keep
Their watch of wondering love.
O morning stars, together
Proclaim the holy birth,
And praises sing to God the King,
And peace to men on earth!

How silently, how silently,
The wondrous Gift is given!
So God imparts to human hearts
The blessings of His heaven.
No ear may hear His coming,
But in this world of sin,
Where meek souls will receive Him, still
The dear Christ enters in.

O holy Child of Bethlehem,
Descend to us, we pray;
Cast out our sin, and enter in,
Be born in us today.
We hear the Christmas angels
The great glad tidings tell;
O come to us, abide with us,
Our Lord Immanuel!

PHILLIPS BROOKS, 1835-1893

PHILLIPS BROOKS AND HIS CAROLS

PHILLIPS BROOKS was a great man. Not only was he a giant in stature, but he possessed a great mind and a great heart. Also, he was a great preacher—one of America's greatest—and he just missed being a great poet. Indeed, the flashes of poetic genius revealed in the few verses he wrote indicate that he might have become famous as a hymn-writer had he chosen such a career.

His poetic gift had its roots in childhood. Phillips was brought up in a pious New England home. Every Sunday the children of the Brooks household were required to memorize a hymn, and, when the father conducted the evening devotion on the Lord's day, the children recited their hymns. When Phillips was ready to go to college, he could repeat no less than two hundred hymns from memory. In his later ministry this lyrical treasury proved to be of inestimable value, and he frequently made effective use of hymn quotations in his preaching. But, more than that, the childhood training unconsciously had made of him a poet!

"O little town of Bethlehem," his famous Christmas carol, was written for a Sunday school Christmas festival in 1868, when Brooks was rector of Holy Trinity Episcopal Church in Philadelphia. He was only thirty-two years old at the time. Three years earlier he had visited the Holy Land, and on Christmas Eve he had stood on the star-lit hills where rustic shepherds once had watched their flocks of sheep by night. Below the hills he had gazed on the "little town of Bethlehem," slumbering in the darkness, just as it had done in the night when Jesus was born. Later he had attended midnight worship in the Church of the Nativity in Bethlehem.

He could never entirely forget the impressions of that sublime night, and, when asked to write a Christmas hymn for his Sunday school, he put down on paper the song that long had been ringing in his mind.

The beautiful tune *St. Louis,* to which the hymn is usually sung, also has an interesting story. It was composed by Lewis H. Redner, who was organist and Sunday school superintendent of Dr. Brooks'

549

church. When Brooks asked Redner to write a suitable tune for his Christmas carol, the latter waited for an inspiration that never seemed to come. Christmas Eve arrived and Redner went to sleep without having written the tune. During the night, however, he dreamed of hearing angels singing. He awoke with the melody still sounding in his ears. Quickly he seized a piece of paper, and jotted it down, and when morning came, he filled in the harmony.

Redner always insisted that the hymn tune was "a gift from heaven," and those who have learned to love its exquisite strains are more than willing to believe it.

Phillips Brooks, though he never had a family of his own, possessed a boundless love for children. That, perhaps, is one reason why the Christmas season so fascinated him, and also why he wrote so many Christmas carols for children. One of these is famous for its striking refrain, "Everywhere, everywhere, Christmas tonight." "The voice of the Christ-child" is the title of another Christmas carol. He also wrote a number of Easter carols, among them, "God hath sent His angels." Two of its stanzas read:

> God hath sent His angels to the earth again,
> Bringing joyful tidings to the sons of men;
> They who first, at Christmas, thronged the heavenly way,
> Now beside the tomb-door sit on Easter Day.
> Angels, sing His triumph as you sang His birth,
> "Christ the Lord is risen. Peace, good will on earth."
>
> God has still His angels, helping, at His word,
> All His faithful children, like their faithful Lord;
> Soothing them in sorrow, arming them in strife,
> Opening wide the tomb-doors, leading into life.
> Angels, sing His triumph as you sang His birth,
> "Christ the Lord is risen. Peace, good will on earth."

But Phillips Brooks knew how to appeal to the old and mature as well as to children, and it was not long before people began to realize that a great preacher and prophet had risen among them. There was need of such a spiritual leader, for Unitarianism had threatened to engulf all of New England with its devastating doctrines.

In the beginning, this movement was merely a protest against the stern and forbidding aspects of the Christian religion as it had been exemplified in Puritanism. It constantly grew more and more radical, however, until the deity of Christ was denied.

The old-fashioned religion of "Christ and Him crucified" was all but forgotten in the intellectual circles of New England when a young man thirty-four years of age began preaching in Trinity Church, Boston. He was preaching Jesus Christ, but he was presenting Him in a new and wonderful light. Crowds began to fill the church. Even sedate old Harvard, which had been virtually taken over by the Unitarians, was stirred.

That was the beginning of the work of Phillips Brooks in Boston, a ministry that made him famous throughout the land. It marked a definite turning-point in religious thought in New England, and perhaps was the most potent factor in checking the spread of the Unitarian doctrine. Brooks was later elevated to a bishopric in his Church. He died in 1893.

It is said that when a little girl of five years was told by her mother that Bishop Brooks had "gone to heaven," the child exclaimed, "Oh, mamma, how happy the angels will be!"

A Prayer to the Saviour

Pass me not, O gentle Saviour,
*   Hear my humble cry;*
While on others Thou art calling,
*   Do not pass me by.*

REFRAIN:
Saviour, Saviour, hear my humble cry,
While on others Thou art calling,
Do not pass me by.

Let me at Thy throne of mercy
*   Find a sweet relief;*
Kneeling there in deep contrition,
*   Help my unbelief.*

Trusting only in Thy merit,
*   Would I seek Thy face;*
Heal my wounded, broken spirit,
*   Save me by Thy grace.*

Thou the spring of all my comfort,
*   More than life to me;*
Whom have I on earth beside Thee,
*   Whom in heaven but Thee?*

FANNY JANE CROSBY, 1823-1915

FANNY CROSBY, AMERICA'S BLIND POET

BLINDNESS is not always an affliction. If it serves to give the soul a clearer vision of Christ and of His redeeming love, as it did for Fanny Crosby, it may rather be regarded as a spiritual blessing.

America's best known hymn-writer could never remember having seen the light of day, nevertheless her life was filled with radiance. Always she revealed a cheerful spirit, refusing to be pitied, while she constantly poured out the songs that brought joy and salvation to multitudes.

Born of humble parents at Southeast, N. Y., March 24, 1823, she was only six weeks old when, through the application of a poultice to her eyes, her sight was forever destroyed. Such a disaster would have cast a perpetual gloom over most lives, but not so with Fanny Crosby. Even at the age of eight years she gave evidence not only of her joyous spirit but also of poetic promise by penning the following cheerful lines:

> O what a happy soul am I!
>   Although I cannot see,
> I am resolved that in this world
>   Contented I will be.

> How many blessings I enjoy,
>   That other people don't;
> To weep and sigh because I'm blind,
>   I cannot, and I won't!

When she was fifteen years old she entered the Institution for the Blind in New York City, where she soon began to develop her talent for writing verse. At first she wrote only secular songs. One of these, "Rosalie, the Prairie Flower," brought the blind girl nearly $3,000 in royalties.

Strange to state, it was not until she was forty-one years old that her first hymn was written. In 1864 she met the famous composer, W. B. Bradbury, and it was at his request that she made her initial attempt at hymn-writing. She now felt that she had found her real mission in life, and she wrote that she was "the happiest creature in

553

all the land." Until her death in 1915, hymns flowed from her facile pen in a ceaseless stream. For a long time she was under contract to furnish her publishers with three hymns every week. It has been estimated that no less than 8,000 songs were written by this unusual woman.

Few of her hymns possess high poetic quality. John Julian, the English hymnologist, with his usual candor, declares that "they are, with few exceptions, very weak and poor, their simplicity and earnestness being their redeeming features."

However, the fact remains that few hymns are sung more often than those of Fanny Crosby. And certainly the hymnody of the Christian Church is the richer for "Pass me not, O gentle Saviour," "Safe in the arms of Jesus," "All the way my Saviour leads me," "Jesus is tenderly calling thee home," "I am Thine, O Lord," "Blessed assurance, Jesus is mine," "Jesus, keep me near the Cross," "Some day the silver cord will break" and other simple but inspiring songs by this blind genius.

A strong Scriptural note is heard in most of her hymns. While yet a child, she committed to memory the first four books of the Old Testament, as well as the four Gospels, and this proved a rich treasury from which she drew in later life.

Often the themes of her hymns were suggested by publishers or musical composers. At other times a musician would play a tune and ask her to write for it. It was in 1868 that William H. Doane, the popular hymn composer, came to her one day and said: "Fanny, I have a tune I would like to have you hear." He played it for her, and she exclaimed, "That says 'Safe in the arms of Jesus!'" She went to her room immediately, and within half an hour the words had been written.

Although Fanny Crosby never permitted the fact of her blindness to depress her, there are many touching allusions in her hymns to her affliction. "All the way my Saviour leads me" suggests how much a guiding hand means to the blind. The same thought appears in the song, "God will take care of you," especially in the lines,

> Tenderly watching, and keeping His own,
> He will not leave you to wander alone.

There also are moving passages in her hymns that express the hope that some day the long night of blindness would be ended—in heaven.

> Here let me wait with patience,
> Wait till the night is o'er;
> Wait till I see the morning
> Break on the golden shore.

Nevertheless, she never permitted any one to express sympathy on account of her blindness. Once a Scotch minister remarked to her, "I think it is a great pity that the Master, when He showered so many gifts upon you, did not give you sight."

She answered: "Do you know that, if at birth I had been able to make one petition to my Creator, it would have been that I should be born blind?"

"Why?" asked the surprised clergyman.

"Because, when I get to heaven, the first face that shall ever gladden my sight will be that of my Saviour," was the unexpected reply.

At a summer religious conference in Northfield, Mass., Miss Crosby was sitting on the platform when the evangelist, Dwight L. Moody, asked her for a testmony concerning her Christian experience. At first she hesitated, then quietly rose and said: "There is one hymn I have written which has never been published. I call it my Soul's poem, and sometimes when I am troubled I repeat it to myself, for it brings comfort to my heart." She then recited:

> Some day the silver chord will break,
> And I no more as now shall sing:
> But, O the joy when I shall wake
> Within the palace of the King,
> And I shall see Him face to face,
> And tell the story—Saved by grace!

The sight of her uplifted face, with its wistful expression, made a deep impression upon the vast audience, and many were moved to tears.

In 1858 Miss Crosby married Alexander Van Alstyne, a blind musician, wherefore she is often referred to as Mrs. Frances Jane Van Alstyne. She died on February 12, 1915.

A Soul's Thirst for God

I need Thee every hour,
   Most gracious Lord;
No tender voice like Thine
   Can peace afford.

REFRAIN:
I need Thee, O I need Thee,
Every hour I need Thee;
O bless me now, my Saviour,
I come to Thee.

I need Thee every hour,
   Stay Thou near by;
Temptations lose their power
   When Thou art nigh.

I need Thee every hour,
   In joy or pain;
Come quickly and abide,
   Or life is vain.

I need Thee every hour,
   Teach me Thy will;
And Thy rich promises
   In me fulfill.

I need Thee every hour,
   Most Holy One,
O make me Thine indeed,
   Thou blessed Son.

ANNIE SHERWOOD HAWKS, 1835-1918
Refrain, ROBERT LOWRY, 1826-1899

AMERICA'S EARLIEST GOSPEL SINGERS

OF ALL hymnbooks published during the period following the Civil War to the end of the 19th century, none, perhaps, exerted so great an influence over the American people as the volume known as *Gospel Hymns*. Issued in a series of six editions, it reached such popularity that, in some denominations, it even supplanted the authorized church hymnals.

Philip P. Bliss was the first editor of *Gospel Hymns*. Associated with him in the publication of the first two editions was the renowned Ira D. Sankey, a singer who gained world-wide fame through his participation in the evangelistic campaigns of Dwight L. Moody.

The story of the life of Bliss reads like romance.

Like many a poor lad endowed with love for the artistic, he was compelled to struggle almost all his life for the opportunity that finally came to him. Born at Rome, Pa., in 1838, he early revealed a passion for music, devising crude instruments on which he tried to produce tones.

The story is told how Philip, when a ragged, barefoot boy of ten years, was thrilled one day to hear piano music for the first time in his life. He listened for a while completely entranced, and then stole unbidden into the house from which the music came. When the young woman at the instrument ceased playing, the child who hungered for music cried:

"O lady, play some more!"

Instead of complying with the request, the startled young woman at the piano is said to have invited young Bliss to leave the house forthwith!

Although he received practically no musical education except for occasional attendance at a singing school, he wrote his first song at the age of twenty-six years. It was called "Lora Vale," and, because of its popular reception, Bliss was encouraged to devote all his time to writing songs and giving concerts.

He usually wrote both the words and music of his hymns. His

work was done very quickly, the inspiration for the whole song, text and melody, being born simultaneously.

Any incident of an unusually impressive nature would immediately suggest a theme. He heard the story of a shipwreck. The doomed vessel was abandoned, and the captain ordered the sailors to exert their utmost strength to "pull for the shore." Immediately he wrote his well-known song with the words as a refrain.

One night he listened to a sermon in which the preacher closed with the words, "He who is almost persuaded is almost saved, but to be almost saved is to be entirely lost." He went home from the service and wrote "Almost persuaded," a hymn that is said to have brought more souls to Christ than anything else Bliss ever composed.

In 1870 he heard Major Whittle, an evangelist, tell the story of how the message, "Hold the fort!" was signalled to the besieged garrison at Allatoona Pass. The words suggested the passage from Revelations 2. 25, "That which ye have, hold fast till I come." The result was one of his most famous Gospel songs, the chorus of which runs:

> "Hold the fort, for I am coming,"
>   Jesus signals still,
> Wave the answer back to heaven,—
>   "By Thy grace we will."

Other popular songs by Bliss are "Whosoever heareth, shout, shout the sound," "I am so glad that our Father in heaven," "There's a light in the valley," "Sing them over again to me," "Let the lower lights be burning," "Free from the law, O happy condition," "Down life's dark vale we wander" and "Where hast thou gleaned today?"

These songs, like the greater number of the Gospel hymns, do not possess real literary merit. The most that can be said for them is that they are imaginative and picturesque. As a rule, they are strong in emotional appeal. The same is true of the tunes Bliss composed for them. They are usually very light in character, with a lilt and movement that make them easily singable, but lacking in the rich harmony found in the better hymn-tunes and chorales. No doubt there will always be a certain demand for this type of religious song, and a few of the Gospel hymns will probably live on, but the present trend in all of the principal Christian denominations is toward a higher standard of hymnody.

A terrible tragedy brought the life of the Gospel singer to a close in his thirty-eighth year. He had visited his old childhood home at Rome, Pa., at Christmas time in 1876, and was returning to Chicago in company with his wife when a railroad bridge near Ashtabula, Ohio, collapsed. Their train plunged into a ravine, sixty feet below, where it caught fire, and one hundred passengers perished miserably.

Bliss managed to escape from the wreckage, but crawled back into a window in search of his wife. That was the last seen of him.

The song-writer's first name was originally "Philipp." He disliked the unusual spelling, however, and in later years he used the extra "P" as a middle initial.

The popularity of the *Gospel Hymns* led many American hymn-writers to attempt similar productions. One of these was Will Lamartine Thompson, whose name lives on as the composer of both the words and music of "Softly and tenderly Jesus is calling."

Thompson, who was born in East Liverpool, Ohio, in 1847, revealed unusual gifts as a child. When only 16 years old, he wrote his first song. Ten years later, while studying at the Boston Conservatory of Music, he came out with a popular song titled "Gathering Shells by the Seashore." The song swept the country, and young Thompson reaped a small fortune from its sale. To further his musical education he left for Germany. As soon as he returned he composed two additional popular songs—"My home on the Old Ohio" and "Under the moonlit sky."

Religious convictions at this time seem to have caused the 40-year-old composer to give up writing secular songs and to turn his talent to sacred music. He not only opened a bookstore in East Liverpool, but also established his own publishing house. Moreover, he purchased a wagon and a team of horses and traveled the length and breadth of Ohio, visiting rural homes and singing his hymns. It is said that he even carried a portable piano in his wagon to accompany the singing of such songs as "Lead me gently home, Father," "There's a great day coming," and "Jesus is all the world to me."

Meanwhile the great evangelist, Dwight L. Moody, and his famous singer, Ira D. Sankey, had begun to make use of Thompson's Gospel songs. In both Europe and America, penitents by the thousands streamed down the "sawdust trail" to the pleading voice of Sankey singing "Softly and tenderly Jesus is calling." Indeed, the fame of the hymn spread all over the world.

In December, 1899, when Moody lay dying at his home in Northfield, Mass., Will Thompson hurried from Ohio to pay a last visit to his friend of many years. Despite doctors' orders, when Moody heard that Thompson had come, he insisted that he be admitted to the sickroom. Affectionately clasping Thompson's hand, the dying evangelist whispered, "Will, I would rather have written 'Softly and tenderly Jesus is calling' than anything I have been able to do in my whole life.' Thompson himself died in 1909.

Among others who had a prominent part in the Gospel song movement was Robert Lowry, pastor of a Baptist church in Brooklyn. From childhood he was intensely fond of music, a love that grew stronger with the passing years. Although he had received no training in musical composition, he revealed an extraordinary ability in writing popular hymn tunes. In the sixties he was urged by the music firm of Biglow and Main to prepare a hymnbook for Sunday schools. This was the beginning of a remarkable series of hymnals, among them *Bright Jewels* and *Pure Gold*.

Lowry had few equals in his day as a writer of Gospel tunes. Among hymns for which he composed melodies were "All the way my Saviour leads me," "Saviour, Thy dying love," "One more day's work for Jesus," "We're marching to Zion," and "I need Thee every hour." He also wrote both words and music for a number of songs, of which the best known are "Weeping will not save me," "Where is my wandering boy tonight?" and "Shall we gather at the river?" The latter song is said to have gone around the world.

In Lowry's Brooklyn congregation there was a member by the name of Annie Sherwood Hawks. Born in Hoosick, N. Y., in 1835, she began writing poetry for newspapers when she was only 14 years old. After she married and moved to Brooklyn, Lowry learned of her poetic talent and urged her to write hymns for which he might compose tunes. One day in 1872 she handed him the words of "I need Thee every hour." Although she afterwards wrote a number of other hymns, it is this one lyric that has brought her lasting fame. Late in life she told how it was written:

"I remember well the morning, many years ago, when in the midst of the daily cares of my home, I was so filled with a sense of nearness to my Master that, wondering how one could live without Him either in joy or pain, these words, 'I need Thee every hour,' were flashed into my mind. Seating myself by the open window in the balmy air of the bright June day, I caught up my pencil and the words were soon committed to paper, almost as they are being sung now . . . I did not understand at first why it touched the great throbbing heart of humanity. It was not until long years after, when the shadow fell over my way, the shadow of a great loss, that I understood something of the comforting power in the words which I had been permitted to give out to others in my hours of sweet security and peace."

As indicated above, it was Lowry who wrote the tune for the beautiful hymn, as well as the words of the refrain. The hymn is a universal favorite and has been translated into many languages.

A Song in the Night

What a Friend we have in Jesus,
    All our sins and griefs to bear!
What a privilege to carry
    Everything to God in prayer!
O what peace we often forfeit,
    O what needless pain we bear,
All because we do not carry
    Everything to God in prayer!

Have we trials and temptations?
    Is there trouble anywhere?
We should never be discouraged;
    Take it to the Lord in prayer.
Can we find a friend so faithful,
    Who will all our sorrows share?
Jesus knows our every weakness;
    Take it to the Lord in prayer.

Are we weak and heavy-laden,
    Cumbered with a load of care?
Precious Saviour, still our refuge;
    Take it to the Lord in prayer.
Do thy friends despise, forsake thee?
    Take it to the Lord in prayer;
In His arms He'll take and shield thee,
    Thou wilt find a solace there.

JOSEPH SCRIVEN, 1820–1886

THE SONG OF A KINDLY SOUL

THE LIFE of Joseph Scriven was full of pathos. Born in Dublin, Ireland, in 1820, and a graduate of Trinity College, he was looking forward to a life filled with happiness when tragedy suddenly struck. He was engaged to marry a charming young woman who shared his own ideals in life, but on the day before the wedding her body was found in a pool of water where she had accidentally drowned.

Young Scriven never recovered from the dreadful shock. Eventually he decided to seek new scenes where he might forget his great sorrow. That is why he migrated to Rice Lake in Canada in 1845. But he never forgot. All through life he was known as a melancholy man.

It seems that he made his home with a number of different families around Rice Lake, at times as a guest, and again as a teacher. His sympathy was always with the poor, and at every opportunity he sought to befriend them, particularly in time of trouble and sickness. Sometimes he helped to repair their homes. At other times he sawed wood for them. He even gave away his own clothes. Some people thought him queer.

In 1857 Scriven learned that his mother in far-off Dublin had experienced a great sorrow and was seriously ill. Unable to go to her with the help and comfort he wanted to bring, he wrote a letter instead. And in that letter he enclosed a poem he had composed. Its opening lines read:

> What a Friend we have in Jesus,
>   All our sins and griefs to bear!
> What a privilege to carry
>   Everything to God in prayer!

Scriven never intended that anyone except his mother should ever read the comforting words. However, some time later, when he himself was ill, a friend who came to call on him chanced to see the poem. He read it with much pleasure, and, questioning Scriven, learned the circumstances that had prompted it. Later, when another

563

neighbor asked if it were true that he had composed the hymn, the modest man replied: "The Lord and I did it between us."

Scriven was living at Port Hope, Ont., at the time the hymn was written, but he returned occasionally to Rice Lake. In October, 1886, he was found drowned in a water-run near Rice Lake. Whether his death was accidental or otherwise was never determined, but many noted the strange parallel between his own death and that of his Irish sweetheart more than forty years before.

The people of Port Hope and Lake Rice never forgot the kind man who not only wrote about a divine Friend but who himself had so often proved to be a friend to those who needed help and sympathy. Several years later, on the Port Hope-Peterborough Highway, which runs north from Lake Ontario, they erected a monument on which Scriven's entire hymn is inscribed, and above it these words:

FOUR MILES NORTH, IN PENGELLY's CEMETERY,
LIES THE PHILANTHROPIST
AND AUTHOR OF THE GREAT MASTERPIECE,
WRITTEN AT PORT HOPE, 1857.

The hymn in some strange manner found its way into a little Sunday school song collection called *Silver Wings,* published in Richmond, Va., in 1870. It was discovered there by Ira D. Sankey, who in 1875 had started to prepare *Gospel Hymns No. 1* in collaboration with Philip P. Bliss. Sankey noted that the tune for "What a Friend we have in Jesus" had been written by his friend, Charles C. Converse, wherefore he withdrew one of the latter's compositions in the proposed book and substituted the hymn he had just found. "Thus," Sankey afterwards wrote, "the last hymn that went into the book became one of the first in favor."

Although Scriven's hymn admittedly is not poetry of a very high order, there are probably very few Christian lyrics that have proved as great a source of solace and comfort to distressed and burdened souls as this one. Albert Edward Bailey, after characterizing the hymn as "doggerel," hastens to add: "Our criticism is made harmless by the tremendous service the hymn has rendered. Any unlettered person can understand it, the humblest saint can take its admonitions to heart, practice prayer, find his load more bearable and his spiritual life deepened." And the Scotch hymnologist, James Moffatt, calls the hymn "undoubtedly the most popular Canadian contribution to the hymnody of the Church."

From Canada has come another hymn, more recent in origin, which is finding its way into an increasing number of church hymnals. It is Robert Murray's fine home missions lyric:

> From ocean unto ocean
>   Our land shall own Thee Lord,
> And, filled with true devotion,
>   Obey Thy sovereign word,
> Our prairies and our mountains,
>   Forest and fertile field,
> Our rivers, lakes, and fountains,
>   To Thee shall tribute yield.
>
> O Christ, for Thine own glory,
>   And for our country's weal,
> We humbly plead before Thee,
>   Thyself in us reveal;
> And may we know, Lord Jesus,
>   The touch of Thy dear hand,
> And, healed of our diseases,
>   The tempter's power withstand.
>
> Our Saviour King, defend us,
>   And guide where we should go;
> Forth, with Thy message send us,
>   The love and light to show;
> Till, fired with true devotion,
>   Enkindled by Thy word,
> From ocean unto ocean
>   Our land shall own Thee Lord.

Murray was born in Canada in 1832 of Scottish Highland ancestry. Ordained a minister of the Presbyterian Church in Canada, he served for a number of years in the Maritime Provinces, and then, because of his literary gifts, he became editor of the *Presbyterian Witness,* a position he held for fifty years until his death in 1910. Other hymns from his pen are "Lord, Thou lov'st the cheerful giver" and "Our loved Dominion bless."

565

A Prayer for Divine Guidance

Lead us, O Father, in the paths of peace;
    Without Thy guiding hand we go astray,
And doubts appall, and sorrows still increase;
    Lead us through Christ, the true and living way.

Lead us, O Father, in the paths of truth;
    Unhelped by Thee, in error's maze we grope,
While passion stains and folly dims our youth,
    And age comes on, uncheered by faith or hope.

Lead us, O Father, in the paths of right;
    Blindly we stumble when we walk alone,
Involved in shadows of a darkening night;
    Only with Thee we journey safely on.

Lead us, O Father, to Thy heavenly rest,
    However rough and steep the pathway be,
Through joy or sorrow, as Thou deemest best,
    Until our lives are perfected in Thee.

WILLIAM HENRY BURLEIGH, 1812-1871

HYMNS OF CRUSADING SPIRITS

A MERICA'S great hymn-writers have never looked with indifference upon wrong-doing, whether it be in individual human conduct, in national policies, or even in the life of the Church. Always they have cried out in protest wherever they have discovered injustice, oppression, or lack of Christian love.

We have already pointed out in a previous chapter how the New England poets, particularly Whittier and Lowell, strove mightily to arouse the conscience of the nation to the iniquity of human slavery. We have also indicated the noble part played by two gifted American women in that struggle, namely, Mrs. Harriet Beecher Stowe and Mrs. Julia Ward Howe. Here we need to add the name of another hymnist who fought valiantly to bring an end to this, the darkest chapter in our national history. He was William Henry Burleigh.

A lineal descendant of William Bradford of Mayflower fame, Burleigh was born on a farm near Woodstock, Conn. As a youth he learned the meaning of poverty and the struggle for daily bread. His education was limited to a few years in the public schools of his community. But he was endowed with something of the militant spirit of his stalwart Puritan ancestor, and as he pondered the problems of the day he realized that there were many wrongs that needed to be righted. From early boyhood he had conceived a deep hatred for two national evils—*intemperance* and *slavery*—and he vowed to spend his life in fighting both.

His opportunity came in 1837 when he was apprenticed to a printer in Pittsburgh, Pa. Here he became aware of the power of the printed word, and soon he was publishing *The Christian Witness* and *The Temperance Banner* in a crusade against intemperance. Later he launched his attack on slavery in *The Christian Freeman,* a paper he issued at Hartford, Conn. He also lectured for the American Anti-Slavery Society. Later he became the secretary of the New York State Temperance Society at Syracuse, where he began the publication of *The Prohibitionist.*

Burleigh was imposing in appearance and eloquent as a speaker, and attracted large audiences wherever he spoke. Often he was threatened by mobs, but these gave him little concern. Heartbreaking family bereavements, however, brought much sorrow into his life. It was at this time he wrote his beautiful hymn of faith:

> Still will we trust, though earth seem dark and dreary,
>   And the heart faint beneath His chastening rod;
> Though rough and steep our pathway, worn and weary,
>   Still will we trust in God.
>
> Our eyes see dimly till by faith anointed,
>   And our blind choosing brings us grief and pain;
> Through Him alone who hath our way appointed
>   We find our peace again.

Strangely enough, the British were quicker to discover the unusual merit in Burleigh's hymns than American hymnal editors, and the above lyric soon found its way into the celebrated collection known as *The English Hymnal*.

At the close of the Mexican War, as Burleigh was weighed down by dim forebodings of the approaching struggle over slavery, he penned his greatest hymn, "Lead us, O Father, in the paths of peace." Today there is scarcely a church hymnal in America that does not contain this splendid lyric, and it has also been given an honored place in the British *Songs of Praise*.

The hymn is a prayer for peace, truth and right. In the second stanza Burleigh is believed to have had in mind the seductive sins of youth, particularly intemperance, while in the third stanza he is undoubtedly referring to the cruelty and injustice of human slavery— the two great national evils against which he was fighting so valiantly.

The militant call to warfare against all forms of moral and social wrong is heard even more distinctly in one of Burleigh's less familiar hymns, the first stanza of which reads:

> Abide not in the realm of dreams,
> O man, however fair it seems:
> But with clear eye the present scan,
> And hear the call of God and man.

While Burleigh was crusading against the curse of strong drink as well as the evil of slavery, three New England youths whose social position and education contrasted strangely with the meager opportunities that had been his, graduated from Harvard Divinity School in the Class of 1846. They were Samuel Johnson, Samuel Longfellow and Octavius Brooke Frothingham. Frothingham's name would hardly have been remembered by posterity except for the fact that he composed the graduation hymn for his class. It is one of the few lyrics he ever wrote, but today it is regarded as a classic ordination hymn.

> Thou Lord of Hosts, whose guiding hand
> Has brought us here before Thy face,
> Our spirits wait for Thy command,
> Our silent hearts implore thy peace.
>
> While watching on our arms at night
> We saw Thine angels round us move;
> We heard Thy call, we felt Thy light,
> And followed, trusting to Thy love.
>
> Send us where'er Thou wilt, O Lord!
> Through rugged toil and wearying fight;
> Thy conquering love shall be our sword,
> And faith in Thee our truest might.

All of New England at this time was in the throes of a theological revolution. In the reaction against the stern legalism of Calvinistic Puritanism and its desolating theology, the pendulum had swung far to the left, with the result that for a time it seemed as though all of New England would be lost to Unitarianism. Harvard College was "captured" by the Unitarians as early as 1805, and, although the Divinity School was not established until eleven years later, it too, soon came under the blight of the so-called New Theology.

It was from such an institution as this that Frothingham, Longfellow and Johnson graduated in 1846. Although they have been claimed by the Unitarians, the truth is that all three actually shook off all denominational affiliation and called themselves Independents.

Longfellow and Johnson, it would appear, leaned toward Transcendentalism, which was the peculiar vogue in liberal theology at the time, Ralph Waldo Emerson being its chief exponent. Rejecting the Scriptural teaching of the inherent sinfulness of man and the necessity of redemption, Transcendentalism emphasized the excellence of human nature. It spoke of God as the "universal Soul" who may be known by man as an indwelling experience, transforming all of life. As Emerson put it, "Let man, then, learn the revelation of all nature and all thought to his heart, this, namely, that the Highest dwells in him."

This idea, of course, is not foreign to Christian revelation, for it, too, speaks of an indwelling God. The fatal defect in the above theology lies in the fact that it denies man's need of regeneration, and it completely ignores Christ and His work of redemption.

While they were still seniors at Harvard, Johnson and Longfellow conceived the idea of compiling a new type of hymnbook which would reflect something of the New Theology. They were imbued with a crusading antipathy to slavery, and are credited with being the first to see the hymnic possibilities of the poems of Whittier and of seizing upon them as weapons to fight this monstrous evil. They are believed to have been the first American hymnal editors to include Newman's "Lead, kindly Light" in their collection. However, with characteristic student audacity, they did not hesitate to change the first line, making it read "Send, kindly light," and they edited other traditional hymns so freely that one critic wrote:

> There once were two Sams of Amerique
> Who belonged to profession called cleric;
> They hunted up hymns,
> And cut off their limbs,
> These truculent Sams of Amerique.

Nevertheless, both of the "Sams" developed into hymn-writers who attracted considerable attention on both sides of the Atlantic. Indeed, one of Johnson's hymns has become world famous. Written on the theme of the Church under the Revelation figure of the City of God, it reads in part:

> City of God, how broad and far
> Outspread thy walls sublime!
> The true thy chartered freemen are
> Of every age and clime:
>
> One holy Church, one army strong,
> One steadfast, high intent;
> One working band, one harvest-song,
> One King omnipotent.
>
> In vain the surge's angry shock,
> In vain the drifting sands:
> Unharmed upon the eternal Rock
> The eternal city stands.

Included in *The English Hymnal,* the hymn was sung at the United Nations service in Westminster Abbey in 1935 and at the jubilee service for the 25th anniversary of the coronation of George V. It was also one of seven hymns in a service used throughout England in connection with the coronation of George VI. In 1924, when the new cathedral in Liverpool was consecrated, a massed choir sang it as a climax at that impressive rite. However, as Henry Wilder Foote observes in *Three Centuries of American Hymnody,* "probably most of the congregation attributed the authorship to Samuel Johnson, the eighteenth-century lexicographer, and not to an obscure minister in Lynn, Massachusetts."

Johnson organized and afterwards served an independent congregation at Lynn for seventeen years. He retired in 1870 to devote himself to literary pursuits. He was the author of *Oriental Religions,* one of the first authoritative works in America on the subject of comparative religion. He died at North Andover, Mass., in 1882.

Longfellow, who was a brother of the famous poet, Henry Wadsworth Longfellow, was a more prolific hymn-writer than Johnson. However, there is a surprising similarity in style, as well as a close parallel in thought, in the hymns of the two friends. "I look to Thee in every need," a beautiful hymn of trust, is regarded by many as Longfellow's finest. It is perhaps the first American hymn to emphasize the truth that mental and physical health are closely associated with spiritual health, and that faith in God can dispel the fears and anxieties that often are a basic cause of many ailments of mind and body. The first stanza reads:

> I look to Thee in every need,
>   And never look in vain;
> I feel Thy strong and tender love,
>   And all is well again:
> The thought of Thee is mightier far
> Than sin and pain and sorrow are.

Longfellow was also the author of a number of other hymns that have come into wide use, such as "The summer days are come again," "God of the earth, the sky, the sea," "O Life that maketh all things new," and "Holy Spirit, truth divine."

After serving congregations in Fall River, Mass., Brooklyn, N. Y., and Germantown, Pa., Longfellow resigned from the latter charge in 1886 to write the story of the life of his distinguished brother. He passed away in 1892 at Cambridge, Mass.

In His Footsteps

O Master, let me walk with Thee
In lowly paths of service free;
Tell me Thy secret; help me bear
The strain of toil, the fret of care.

Help me the slow of heart to move
By some clear winning word of love;
Teach me the wayward feet to stay,
And guide them in the homeward way.

Teach me Thy patience; still with Thee
In closer, dearer company,
In work that keeps faith sweet and strong,
In trust that triumphs over wrong;

In hope that sends a shining ray
Far down the future's broadening way,
In peace that only Thou canst give;
With Thee, O Master, let me live.

WASHINGTON GLADDEN, 1836-1918

HYMNS OF CHRISTIAN SERVICE

FOR more than half a century, until his death in 1918, Washington Gladden was known throughout the length and breadth of the country as one of America's most distinguished clergymen. In addition to being a great preacher, he was also a prolific writer, and his books and magazine contributions were widely read.

Like most literary productions, however, his books and pamphlets have already been largely forgotten. It is only a little hymn, written on a moment's inspiration, that seems destined to preserve Gladden's name for posterity. That hymn is "O Master, let me walk with Thee."

The author was born in Pottsgrove, Pa., February 11, 1836. After his graduation from Williams College in 1859, he was called as pastor to a Congregational church in Brooklyn. In 1882 he removed to Columbus, O., where he remained as pastor until 1914, a period of thirty-two years.

During this long pastorate he exerted a profound influence, not only over the city of Columbus, but in much wider circles. Gladden was deeply interested in social reform, believing that it to be the duty of the Christian Church to elevate the masses not only spiritually and morally, but to be concerned about their social and economic welfare as well. By sermons, lectures and writings, he was ever trying to bring about better understanding between employer and employe.

Gladden was often the center of a storm of criticism from those who charged him with liberalism. His beautiful hymn, written in 1879, seems to be in part an answer to these critics. It originally consisted of six stanzas of four lines each. The second and third stanzas, which were omitted when the poem was first published as a hymn, indicate how keenly Gladden felt the condemnation of his opponents:

O Master, let me walk with Thee
Before the taunting Pharisee;
Help me to bear the sting of spite,
The hate of men who hide Thy light,

The sore distrust of souls sincere
Who cannot read Thy judgments clear,
The dulness of the multitude,
Who dimly guess that Thou art good.

573

Dr. Gladden always insisted that he was nothing but a preacher, and he gloried in his high calling. In spite of large, demanding parishes, however, he always found time to give expression to his literary talent. At one time he was a member of the editorial staff of the *New York Independent.* Later he was an editor of the *Sunday Afternoon,* a weekly magazine. It was in this magazine that "O Master, let me walk with Thee" was first published.

The writer had no idea of composing a hymn when it was written, and no one was more surprised than he at its popularity. He himself agreed that the stanzas quoted above were not suitable for worship.

Whatever judgment may be passed on Dr. Gladden's liberal views, it will be agreed that he looked upon Christianity as an intensely practical thing; and, if he underestimated the value of Christian dogma, it was because he emphasized so strongly the necessity of Christian life and practice.

He was always buoyed up by a hopeful spirit, believing implicitly that the Kingdom of Light was gradually overcoming the forces of evil. In one of his last sermons, he said:

"I have never doubted that the Kingdom I have always prayed for is coming; that the Gospel I have preached is true. I believe . . . that the nation is being saved."

Another Congregational minister whose views were quite similar to those of Gladden was John White Chadwick, many of whose hymns were included in the *Pilgrim Hymnal* of 1904. Among these was the exceptionally fine lyric, "Eternal Ruler of the ceaseless round," which is finding its way into many modern hymnals. Three of its splendid stanzas read:

Eternal Ruler of the ceaseless round
  Of circling planets singing on their way,
Guide of the nations from the night profound
  Into the glory of the perfect day:
Rule in our hearts that we may ever be
Guided and strengthened and upheld by Thee.

We are of Thee, the children of Thy love,
  The brothers of Thy well-beloved Son;
Descend, O Holy Spirit, like a dove,
  Into our hearts, that we may be as one;
As one with Thee, to whom we ever tend,
As one with Him, our brother and our friend.

We would be one in hatred of all wrong,
    One in our love of all things sweet and fair,
One with the joy that breaketh into song,
    One with the grief that trembleth into prayer,
One in the power that makes the children free
To follow truth, and thus to follow Thee.

The hymn was written by Chadwick to be sung by his graduating class at Divinity School, Cambridge, in 1864. Among his other hymns are "Another year of setting suns," "O Love Divine of all that is," "O Thou, whose perfect goodness crowns," and "Now sing we a song for the harvest." Chadwick died on December 11, 1904.

Another hymnist of this period who wrote lyrics which pleaded, not only for personal piety and integrity, but also for civic righteousness and national honor, as well as deliverance from ambitious rulers, war and other calamities, was Henry Harbaugh. In his so-called national litany hymn, "Thou, by heavenly hosts adored," occur these arresting stanzas:

From all public sin and shame
From ambition's grasping aim,
From rebellion, war and death,
From the pestilential breath,
From dread famine's awful stroke,
From oppression's galling yoke,
From the judgments of Thy hand:
Spare Thy people, spare our land.

Let our rulers ever be
Men that love and honor Thee;
Let the powers by Thee ordained
Be in righteousness maintained;
In the people's hearts increase
Love and piety and peace;
Thus united, we shall stand
One wide, free, and happy land.

Harbaugh, who was born of Swiss ancestors on a Pennsylvania farm in 1817, became an outstanding theologian and editor of the German Reformed Church. While professor of Theology at Marshall College, he edited the *Guardian* and the *Mercersburg Review*, in which many of his original poems, as well as splendid translations of Latin and German hymns, were first published. In addition to the hymn mentioned above, his best known lyric is "Jesus, I live to Thee." He died at the age of 50 years in 1867.

A Call to Christian Warfare

Lead on, O King eternal,
    The day of march has come;
Henceforth in fields of conquest
    Thy tents shall be our home:
Through days of preparation
    Thy grace has made us strong,
And now, O King eternal,
    We lift our battle song.

Lead on, O King eternal,
    Till sin's fierce war shall cease,
And holiness shall whisper
    The sweet Amen of peace;
For not with swords loud clashing,
    Nor roll of stirring drums,
But deeds of love and mercy,
    The heavenly Kingdom comes.

Lead on, O King eternal:
    We follow, not with fears,
For gladness breaks like morning
    Where'er Thy face appears:
Thy Cross is lifted o'er us;
    We journey in its light;
The crown awaits the conquest;
    Lead on, O God of might.

ERNEST WARBURTON SHURTLEFF, 1862-1917

576

THE SOCIAL GOSPEL IN HYMNODY

URING the latter half of the 19th century, the birth of social consciousness in the Churches of America was quickly reflected in American hymnody. The rapid expansion of the United States, as the flood of migration swept westward to conquer the wilderness, had created many social and political problems. Lust for gold had resulted in vast exploitation of natural resources, as well as widespread corruption in government. The rise of gigantic industries and the growth of large cities, with their attendant evils of sweatshops, child labor, periodic unemployment, slum conditions, poverty, vice and crime, had become a matter of deep concern to thoughtful leaders in the Church as they began to realize more fully the social implications of the Gospel.

Christ's compassion for the weary and heavy-laden, and His proclamation of redemption for the poor and broken-hearted took on a new meaning and soon became the keynote of books and sermons. Men began to speak of a "social Gospel." Then, as the hymn-writers took up the theme, we hear Samuel Wolcott as early as 1869 singing:

> Christ for the world we sing;
> The world to Christ we bring
> With loving zeal;
> The poor and them that mourn,
> The faint and overborne,
> Sin-sick and sorrow-worn,
> Whom Christ doth heal.

Ten years later Washington Gladden, preacher and reformer, composed his moving hymn, "O Master, let me walk with Thee," and a new note had come into American hymnody.

In 1887, when Ernest Warburton Shurtleff graduated from Andover Theological Seminary, he was asked by his classmates to write a hymn for the occasion. He responded with his "Lead on, O King Eternal," a prayer hymn that pictures the consecrated Christian as a soldier of the Cross who follows his Lord in obedient service and love, and thus seeks to bring the Kingdom of God into human experi-

577

ence. The second stanza is particularly fine as an expression of the spirit of ministering love in the Christian religion:

> Lead on, O King eternal,
>   Till sin's fierce war shall cease,
> And holiness shall whisper
>   The sweet Amen of peace;
> For not with swords loud clashing,
>   Nor roll of stirring drums,
> But deeds of love and mercy,
>   The heavenly Kingdom comes.

Following his ordination, Shurtleff served Congregational churches in Palmer and Plymouth, Mass., and in Minneapolis, Minn. In 1905 he went to Europe, where he organized the American Church in Frankfurt, Germany. Later he went to Paris, where he had charge of Students' Atelier Reunions until the outbreak of World War I. During that conflict he and his wife carried on relief work in France, in the midst of which he died on August 24, 1917.

In an earlier chapter we have observed how such New England liberals as Samuel Longfellow and Samuel Johnson began to write hymns which sounded a social note. A much stronger emphasis on the same theme is found in the lyrics of Frederick Lucian Hosmer, who belonged to the same school of theology. The idea of the coming of the Kingdom of God was a constant source of inspiration to Hosmer, as it was to all Transcendentalists. This may be seen particularly in two of his hymns, "Thy Kingdom come, O Lord" and "Thy Kingdom come! on bended knee." The latter is a lyric of rare beauty:

> Thy Kingdom come! on bended knee
>   The passing ages pray;
> And faithful souls have yearned to see
>   On earth that Kingdom's day.
>
> But the slow watches of the night
>   Not less to God belong;
> And for the everlasting right
>   The silent stars are strong.
>
> And lo, already on the hills
>   The flags of dawn appear;
> Gird up your loins, ye prophet souls,
>   Proclaim the day is near:
>
> The day in whose clear-shining light
>   All wrong shall stand revealed,
> When justice shall be throned in might,
>   And every hurt be healed;

578

When knowledge, hand in hand with peace,
   Shall walk the earth abroad;
The day of perfect righteousness,
   The promised day of God.

This is sacred poetry of the highest order. One could only wish that Hosmer had been more specific in making clear in what manner the Kingdom of God is to be realized in this sin-cursed and war-weary world. The final stanza would seem to imply that when man's wisdom and knowledge is increased, the day of peace and perfect righteousness will have dawned. However, had Hosmer lived to witness a second World War and the bombing of Hiroshima, and had he known how the greatest scientific achievement in history would be prostituted to become a threat to all life on our planet and to the world itself, he might have lost something of his confident optimism in the upward climb of the human race.

The believer in a divine Saviour, however, may sing this beautiful hymn with the glorious assurance that He who taught His followers to pray, "Thy Kingdom come!" will also in His own day bring the fulfillment of the promise of "new heavens and a new earth in which dwelleth righteousness."

Hymns by Hosmer on other themes are "O Thou in all Thy might so far," "O Light, from age to age the same," "Not always on the mount may we," "Father, to Thee we look in all our sorrow" and "O Lord of life, where'er they be." The last named is a moving lyric which sets forth the sublime doctrine of the "communion of saints," expressing the confidence that "the faithful" are safe in the keeping of their Maker:

O Lord of life, where'er they be,
Safe in Thine own eternity,
Our dead are living unto Thee.
   Alleluia!

All souls are Thine, and, here or there,
The faithful rest within Thy care;
One providence alike they share.
   Alleluia!

Thy word is true, Thy ways are just;
Above the requiem, "Dust to dust,"
Shall rise our psalm of grateful trust.
   Alleluia!

O happy they in God who rest,
No more by fear and doubt oppressed;
Living or dying, they are blest.
   Alleluia!

Although Hosmer must be regarded as one of America's most gifted hymnists, it is to be deeply regretted that a distinctively Christian note is lacking in his hymns. His references to Christ, which are few indeed, are always quite vague.

Like Longfellow and Johnson, Hosmer was a product of Harvard Divinity School, graduating in the class of 1869. His first parish was in Northboro, Mass., after which he served congregations in Quincy, Ill.; Cleveland, O.; St. Louis, Mo., and Berkeley, Calif. He passed away at the latter place in 1929 at the ripe old age of almost 89 years.

One of the greatest champions of social righteousness among 20th century hymnists is Walter Russell Bowie, an Episcopalian clergyman who in 1939 became a teacher at Union Theological Seminary. In his striking hymn, "O holy city, seen of John," Bowie, after describing the heavenly Jerusalem "where Christ, the Lamb, doth reign," goes on to speak of the squalor and shame of the modern city in burning words like these:

> Hark, how from men whose lives are held
> More cheap than merchandise,
> From women struggling sore for bread,
> From little children's cries,
> There swells the sobbing human plaint
> That bids thy walls arise!
>
> Give us, O God, the strength to build
> The city that hath stood
> Too long a dream, whose laws are love,
> Whose ways are brotherhood,
> And where the sun that shineth is
> God's grace for human good.
>
> Already in the mind of God
> That city riseth fair;
> Lo, how its splendor challenges
> The souls that greatly dare,
> Yea, bids us seize the whole of life
> And build its glory there.

Here is the Christian conscience at its best crying out against such sins as pauper wages, slum tenements, unsanitary living conditions, racial discrimination, and exploitation of the weak and the poor. This is the Christian challenge to every follower of the humble Servant of Jehovah to emulate Him in service and love, to bring something of the joy and blessedness of heaven into the drab days of cheerless human lives, and to begin to build even here on earth the walls of the City of God.

In another striking hymn titled "Lord Christ, when first Thou cam'st to men," Bowie describes how the Christ once came to His own people, offering them His divine love, but how by their rejection of that love they brought doom upon their nation. He then applies the lesson to America in these words:

> New advent of the love of Christ,
>   Shall we again refuse Thee,
> Till in the night of hate and war
>   We perish as we lose Thee?
> From old unfaith our souls release
> To seek the Kingdom of Thy peace,
>   By which alone we choose Thee.
>
> O wounded hands of Jesus, build
>   In us Thy new creation;
> Our pride is dust, our vaunt is stilled,
>   We wait Thy revelation:
> O Love that triumphs over loss,
> We bring our hearts before Thy Cross,
>   To finish Thy salvation.

Bowie, who was born in Richmond, Va., in 1882, received his education in Harvard University and Virginia Theological Seminary, and was ordained in the Episcopal Church in 1908. After serving parishes in Greenwood and Richmond, Va., and New York City, he became professor of Practical Theology in Union Theological Seminary. During World War I he was chaplain of a base hospital in France. For some years he served as editor of the *Southern Churchman.* He was a member of the American Standard Bible Committee which prepared the Revised Standard Version in 1946.

Author of a number of religious works, Bowie was also a contributor to *Christianity Takes a Stand,* issued by the Joint Commission on Social Reconstruction. Described as a man "of great sensitivity and social vision," the *Presbyterian Hymnal Handbook* pays him this tribute: "His ministry is marked by the sympathy and breadth of his churchmanship and his courage in confronting social and industrial situations with the uncompromising standards of the Christian religion."

Chautauqua Vesper Hymn

Day is dying in the west,
Heaven is touching earth with rest;
Wait and worship while the night
Sets her evening lamps alight
    Through all the sky.

REFRAIN:
Holy, holy, holy, Lord God of Hosts!
Heaven and earth are full of Thee,
Heaven and earth are praising Thee,
    O Lord Most High!

Lord of life, beneath the dome
Of the universe, Thy home,
Gather us who seek Thy face
To the fold of Thy embrace,
    For Thou art nigh.

While the deepening shadows fall,
Heart of Love, enfold us all;
Through the glory and the grace
Of the stars that veil Thy face,
    Our hearts ascend.

When forever from our sight
Pass the stars, the day, the night,
Lord of angels, on our eyes
Let eternal morning rise,
    And shadows end.

MARY ARTIMISIA LATHBURY, 1841-1913

THE LYRIST OF CHAUTAUQUA

THOSE who have had the privilege of attending a vesper service in the great Chautauqua Institution auditorium on the shores of beautiful Lake Chautauqua, N. Y., have come away with a holy memory that lingers in after years. It is the singing by the vast assembly of Mary Lathbury's famous vesper hymn, "Day is dying in the west."

This beautiful evening lyric, which was written especially for the Chautauqua vesper hour, has been called by a distinguished critic "one of the finest and most distinctive hymns of modern times," and there are few who will dispute his judgment.

The "lyrist of Chautauqua" was born in Manchester, N. Y., August 10, 1841. As a child she began to reveal artistic tendencies. She developed a special talent in drawing pictures of children, and her illustrations in magazines and periodicals made her name widely known. She also wrote books and poetry, illustrating them with her own sketches.

Very early in life she felt constrained to dedicate her talent in Christian service. She tells how she seemed to hear a voice saying to her: "Remember, my child, that you have a gift of weaving fancies into verse, and a gift with the pencil of producing visions that come to your heart; consecrate these to Me as thoroughly and as definitely as you do your inmost spirit."

An opportunity to serve her Lord in a very definite way came in 1874, when Dr. John H. Vincent, then secretary of the Methodist Sunday School Union, employed her as his assistant. The Chautauqua movement had just been launched the previous year and the formal opening on the shores of the beautiful lake from which the institution has received its name took place on August 4, 1874. Dr. Vincent became the outstanding leader of the movement, and he immediately began to make use of Miss Lathbury's literary talent.

Dr. Jesse Lyman Hurlbut, historian of Chautauqua, writes: "In Dr. Vincent's many-sided nature was a strain of poetry, although I

583

do not know that he ever wrote a verse. Yet he always looked at life and truth through poetic eyes. Who otherwise would have thought of songs for Chautauqua and called upon a poet to write them? Dr. Vincent found in Mary A. Lathbury a poet who could compose fitting verses for the expression of the Chautauqua spirit."

The beautiful evening hymn, "Day is dying in the west," was written in 1880 at Dr. Vincent's request for the vesper services which are still held every evening. It originally consisted of only two stanzas, and it was not until ten years later that Miss Lathbury, at the strong insistence of friends, added the last two stanzas. We are happy that she did so, for the last two lines, with their allusion to the "eternal morning" when "shadows" shall end, bring the hymn to a sublime conclusion.

Another hymn rivaling the fame that has come to her evening hymn is "Break Thou the Bread of life." Its beautiful reference to the Sea of Galilee is made the more interesting when we are reminded that it was written on the shores of lovely Lake Chautauqua. The hymn is particularly adapted for Bible study, and it is said that the great London preacher, G. Campbell Morgan, always announced it before his mid-week discourse. It reads:

> Break Thou the Bread of life,
>   Dear Lord, to me,
> As Thou didst break the loaves
>   Beside the sea;
> Beyond the sacred page
>   I seek Thee, Lord;
> My spirit pants for Thee.
>   O living Word!
>
> Bless Thou the truth, dear Lord,
>   To me, to me,
> As Thou didst bless the bread
>   By Galilee;
> Then shall all bondage cease,
>   All fetters fall;
> And I shall find my peace,
>   My All-in-all!
>
> Thou art the Bread of Life,
>   O Lord, to me,
> Thy holy Word the truth
>   That saveth me;
> Give me to eat and live
>   With Thee above;
> Teach me to love Thy truth,
>   For Thou art love.

O send Thy Spirit, Lord,
　　Now unto me,
That he may touch my eyes,
　　And make me see:
Show me the truth concealed
　　Within Thy Word,
And in Thy Book revealed
　　I see the Lord.

The last two stanzas are not generally included in standard church hymnals.

Miss Lathbury was greatly esteemed, not only for the lovely lyrics which have given inspiration to thousands of souls, but also for her gentle, Christian character. Those who knew her best speak of the indescribable charm of her personality, and tell of the abiding influence she exerted over those who came in contact with her devout and consecrated spirit. She died in New York City in 1913.

A Hymn of the City

Where cross the crowded ways of life,
    Where sound the cries of race and clan,
Above the noise of selfish strife,
    We hear Thy voice, O Son of man!

In haunts of wretchedness and need,
    On shadowed thresholds dark with fears,
From paths where hide the lures of greed,
    We catch the vision of Thy tears.

From tender childhood's helplessness,
    From woman's grief, man's burdened toil,
From famished souls, from sorrow's stress,
    Thy heart has never known recoil.

The cup of water given for Thee
    Still holds the freshness of Thy grace;
Yet long these multitudes to see
    The sweet compassion of Thy face.

O Master, from the mountainside,
    Make haste to heal these hearts of pain;
Among these restless throngs abide,
    O tread the city's streets again,

Till sons of men shall learn Thy love
    And follow where Thy feet have trod;
Till glorious from Thy heaven above
    Shall come the city of our God.

FRANK MASON NORTH, 1850–1935

A HYMN WITH A MODERN MESSAGE

AMONG the more recent hymns that have found their way into the hymnbooks of the Christian Churches in America, there is none that enjoys such popularity and esteem as Frank Mason North's hymn, "Where cross the crowded ways of life." A hymn of the highest order, beautiful in thought and unusually tender in expression, it is typical of the trend in modern hymns to emphasize the Church's mission among the poor, the outcast, the under-privileged, the wayward and the fallen.

From beginning to end this hymn is a picture of the modern city with its sins and sorrows and spiritual hunger. We see the city as the meeting place of all races and tongues; we hear the din and noise of selfish striving; we behold the haunts of poverty and sin and wretchedness; we catch a glimpse of the bleak lives of helpless childhood, of woman's secret griefs and man's ceaseless toil. And all these multitudes are hungering for Christ!

North has, consciously or unconsciously, made a striking distinction between mere social service activity, which aims at the alleviation of human need and suffering, and inner mission work, which seeks to help men spiritually as well as physically. "The cup of water" is never to be despised, but when it is given in Christ's Name it has a double value; for it is Christ himself, after all, that men need, and it is He alone who can truly satisfy. Social service can never take the place of salvation.

What a beautiful prayer is that contained in the fifth stanza, where the Master is entreated to "tread the city's streets again!" And then, as a fitting climax to this whole remarkable poem, comes the triumphant thought expressed in the final lines of the promised coming of the New Jerusalem from above—"the city of our God."

North was well qualified to write such a hymn. He himself was a child of the city, having been born in America's greatest metropolis in 1850. His early education, too, was received in New York City and after his graduation from Wesleyan University in 1872 he served several congregations in the city of his birth. In 1892 he was made corresponding secretary of the New York City Church Extension and Missionary Society and in 1912 he was given the same position with the Methodist Episcopal Board of Foreign Missions. Thus, almost his whole life was devoted to missionary activities at home and abroad. He died on December 17, 1935.

It was in 1905, in response to a request from the Methodist hymnal committee, that North wrote his celebrated hymn. He tells the story in the following words:

"My life was for long years, both by personal choice and official duty, given to the people in all phases of their community life. New York was to me an open book. I spent days and weeks and years in close contact with every phase of the life of the multitudes, and at the morning, noon and evening hours was familiar with the tragedy, as it always seemed to me, of the jostling, moving currents of the life of the people as revealed upon the streets and at great crossings of the avenues; and I have watched them by the hour as they passed, by tens of thousands. This is no more than many another man whose sympathies are with the crowd and with the eager, unsatisfied folk of the world, has done.

"As I recall it, I came to write the hymn itself at the suggestion of Professor C. T. Winchester, who, as a member of the committee on the new hymnal, was struggling with the fact that we have so few modern missionary hymns. He said to me one day, 'Why do you not write us a missionary hymn?' I wrote what was in my thought and feeling . . . That it has found its way into so many of the modern hymnals and by translation into so many of the other languages, is significant not as to the quality of the hymn itself but as to the fact that it is an expression of the tremendous movement of the soul of the Gospel in our times which demands that the follower of Christ must make the interest of the people his own, and must find the heart of the world's need if he is in any way to represent his Master among men."

Another lovely hymn by North, "Jesus, the calm that fills my breast," was written in 1884, but has not come into general use. It is strongly reminiscent of the classic hymn of Bernard of Clairvaux, "Jesus, the very thought of Thee," and was probably inspired by the latter.

It seems fitting to state here that Caleb Thomas Winchester, mentioned above as the one who was instrumental in inducing North to write his famous missionary hymn, is also represented in modern American hymnals by a hymn. Titled "The Lord our God alone is strong," this fine lyric expresses a thought that needs to be re-emphasized in our day of great scientific achievement:

> The Lord our God alone is strong;
> His hands built not for one brief day,
> His wondrous works, through ages long,
> His wisdom and His power display.
>
> His mountains lift their solemn forms,
> To watch in silence o'er the land;
> The rolling ocean, rocked with storms,
> Sleeps in the hollow of His hand.
>
> Thou sovereign God, receive the praise
> Thy willing servants offer Thee;
> Accept the prayers that thousands raise,
> And let these halls Thy temple be.
>
> And let those learn, who here shall meet,
> True wisdom is with reverence crowned,
> And science walks with humble feet
> To seek the God that faith hath found.

The hymn was written for the opening of Orange Judd Hall of Natural Science, Wesleyan University, Middletown, Conn., at which institution Winchester was professor of Rhetoric and English Literature. It first appeared in the Methodist Hymnal of 1878. Winchester died in 1920 at the age of 73 years.

America the Beautiful

O beautiful for spacious skies,
For amber waves of grain,
For purple mountain majesties
Above the fruited plain!
America! America!
God shed His grace on thee,
And crown thy good with brotherhood
From sea to shining sea.

O beautiful for pilgrim feet,
Whose stern, impassioned stress
A thoroughfare for freedom beat
Across the wilderness!
America! America!
God mend thine every flaw,
Confirm thy soul in self-control,
Thy liberty in law.

O beautiful for heroes proved
In liberating strife,
Who more than self their country loved,
And mercy more than life!
America! America!
May God thy gold refine,
Till all success be nobleness,
And every gain divine.

O beautiful for patriot dream
That sees, beyond the years,
Thine alabaster cities gleam,
Undimmed by human tears!
America! America!
God shed His grace on thee,
And crown thy good with brotherhood
From sea to shining sea.

KATHERINE LEE BATES, 1859–1929

590

SINGERS OF NATIONAL SONGS

AMERICA does not lack for patriotic hymns. Francis Scott Key thrilled his countrymen during the War of 1812 with his stirring "Star Spangled Banner." Samuel Francis Smith some twenty years later started them singing the sweet strains of "My country, 'tis of thee." And in the midst of the dark days of the Civil War Julia Ward Howe revived the flagging spirits of the people of the North by putting on their lips the soul-inspiring lines of "Mine eyes have seen the glory of the coming of the Lord."

But none of these, despite official or unofficial recognition, has captured the imagination and the heart of the American people to the extent that Katharine Lee Bates' "America the Beautiful" has done. Ever since the hymn first appeared in the Fourth of July issue of *The Congregationalist* in 1895, it has been steadily growing in popularity, and may be destined eventually to become our accepted national hymn.

The hymn—and because of the deep religious feeling that permeates the entire lyric, it may fittingly be regarded as a hymn—had its birth in a succession of personal experiences of the author in the summer of 1893. Miss Bates, who was born in Falmouth, Mass., in 1859, was the daughter of a Congregational clergyman, William Bates. Her grandfather, Joshua Bates, had served as president of Middlebury College in Vermont. Educated at Wellesley College, she studied in Oxford, England, where she received her Master's degree, and then returned to her alma mater, where she spent the remainder of her life as the distinguished head of the English department.

In company with a group of fellow teachers, she visited the Columbian Exposition in Chicago in 1893. The beauty of the "White City" built around a lagoon made a deep impression on her and was responsible in no small degree for the last stanza of "America the Beautiful," in which she refers with strong patriotic feeling to alabaster cities "undimmed by human tears." She herself has written, "It was with this quickened and deepened sense of America that we

591

went on, my New England eyes delighting in the wind-waved gold of the vast wheatfields."

Colorado was their next stop, and here they experienced the thrill of ascending Pike's Peak and then witnessing the magnificent spectacle of a sunrise from the top of a summit almost three miles above sea-level. Here was born the poetic reference to "purple mountain majesties above the fruited plain." Upon their return to Colorado Springs that evening, the tired but enthusiastic teachers gathered in Miss Bates' room to discuss the glories they had seen. Never before had they been so impressed by the greatness of America. But Miss Bates was in a sober mood, and she is quoted as saying:

"Greatness and goodness are not necessarily synonymous. Rome was great, but she was not good, and for that reason the Roman Empire fell before the assaults of the invader. Her glory consisted in her wealth, her military pomp and splendor, and her reliance upon Roman law. But within the hearts of her citizens, as well as at the very core of the government itself, things were evil. Greatness alone was not enough to save her. The Spanish Empire was a great one also, but as morally rotten as the Roman; consequently the Spanish Empire is no more. Unless we are willing to crown our greatness with goodness, and our bounty with brotherhood, our beloved America may go the same way."

That night the 34-year-old Wellesley teacher could not sleep. Instead, she caught up a pencil and a piece of paper and began to write an immortal hymn. As verse after verse took form, she ended each one of them with a three-line prayer to the God of the Nations to bestow His divine grace on the country she loved — to mend its flaws, to refine its gold, to confirm its soul in self-control, and to crown its good with brotherhood "from sea to shining sea."

For two years she carried the beautiful lyric within her private notebook, and it was not until 1895, when it appeared in *The Congregationalist*, that the American people came to realize that another great national hymn had been born. Soon it was being published everywhere, and numerous composers sought to write music worthy of the noble words. However, it was not until someone in 1912 thought of setting it to Samuel Augustus Ward's magnificent tune *Materna* that the problem was satisfactorily settled. Since that time words and music have been inseparably wedded. And that is why a hymn-tune written in 1882 for the hymn, "O Mother dear, Jerusalem," has

592

gained for an obscure organist and choirmaster of Newark, N. J., undying fame.

As for Miss Bates, she was not satisfied with the words as originally written, and on November 19, 1904, she submitted a revised version to the Boston *Evening Transcript,* and it is in this form the hymn is sung today. Although she wrote a number of other hymns, such as "The Kings of the East are riding," "Dear God and Father, at Thy knee confessing," and "Hosanna to the Son of David," none of these has come into general use. She died at Wellesley on March 29, 1929.

Another national hymn that is growing in favor year by year is Daniel Crane Roberts' stirring anthem:

> God of our fathers, whose almighty hand
> Leads forth in beauty all the starry band
> Of shining worlds in splendor through the skies,
> Our grateful songs before Thy throne arise.
>
> Thy love divine hath led us in the past,
> In this free land by Thee our lot is cast;
> Be Thou our ruler, guardian, guide, and stay;
> Thy word our law, Thy paths our chosen way.
>
> From war's alarms, from deadly pestilence,
> Be Thy strong arm our ever sure defence;
> Thy true religion in our hearts increase,
> Thy bounteous goodness nourish us in peace.
>
> Refresh Thy people on their toilsome way,
> Lead us from night to never-ending day;
> Fill all our lives with love and grace divine,
> And glory, laud, and praise be ever Thine.

Roberts, who was born in Bridge Hampton, Long Island, in 1841, graduated from Kenyon College in 1857. When the Civil War broke out, he enlisted as a private in the 84th Ohio Volunteers and served throughout that dreadful conflict. After being ordained by the Episcopal Church, he became rector of Christ Church, Montpelier, Vermont. He later served parishes in Lowell, Mass.; Brandon, Vermont, and Concord, N. H. The hymn was written at Brandon in 1876 for a local celebration of the Centennial of American Independence, and sung for the first time at that place on the Fourth of July to the tune of the old Russian national anthem. Later it was chosen as the hymn for the observance of the Centennial of the adoption of the Constitution. At that time George William Warren, organist in St. Thomas Episcopal Church, New York City, wrote a new tune, *National Hymn,* to which it has ever since been sung. A few years later it was included in the official hymnal of the Episcopal Church.

Roberts evidently was a very modest man. In 1901 he wrote: "I remain a country Parson, known only within my own small world." And concerning his hymn, he had this to say: "My little hymn has thus had a very flattering official recognition. But that which would really gladden my heart, popular recognition, it has not received."

Before his death, Roberts was honored with a D.D. degree by Norwich University. He also was made president of the New Hampshire Historical Society. His hymn, too, has grown in fame through the years, and today it is found in almost every American church hymnal. He died at Concord, N. H., October 31, 1907.

A third hymn which gives promise of becoming widely used in church services of a national character is William Pierson Merrill's fine lyric, "Not alone for mighty empire." It is particularly suited for Thanksgiving Day observances, its emphasis being on spiritual blessings rather than bountiful harvests and temporal things. According to Merrill, the inspiration for it came out of a Thanksgiving service in 1909 held in the Sixth Presbyterian Church of Chicago, of which he was pastor at the time, when Jenkin Lloyd Jones offered a prayer stressing the spiritual good America has experienced at the hands of God.

"I went home," Merrill afterwards stated, "and wrote a rather diffusive hymn about it, and later made it over into the present one." Here are two of its stirring stanzas:

> Not alone for mighty empire
>   Stretching far o'er land and sea,
> Not alone for bounteous harvests,
>   Lift we up our hearts to Thee:
> Standing in the living present,
>   Memory and hope between,
> Lord, we would with deep thanksgiving
>   Praise Thee most for things unseen.
>
> Not for battleship and fortress,
>   Not for conquests of the sword,
> But for conquests of the spirit
>   Give we thanks to Thee, O Lord;
> For the heritage of freedom,
>   For the home, the church, the school,
> For the open door to manhood
>   In a land the people rule.

Two years after he had written this hymn, Merrill found himself aboard a steamer on Lake Michigan, where he became fascinated by an article he was reading on the subject, "The Church of the Strong Men." Once more he tuned his lyre, and before the trip had ended, he had composed another hymn:

> Rise up, O men of God!
>   Have done with lesser things;
> Give heart and soul and mind and strength
>   To serve the King of kings.
>
> Rise up, O men of God!
>   His Kingdom tarries long;
> Bring in the day of brotherhood,
>   And end the night of wrong.
>
> Rise up, O men of God!
>   The Church for you doth wait,
> Her strength unequal to her task;
>   Rise up and make her great!
>
> Lift high the Cross of Christ!
>   Tread where His feet have trod;
> As brothers of the Son of Man,
>   Rise up, O men of God!

Merrill, who was born in Orange, N. J., January 10, 1867, and received his education at Rutgers College, Union Theological Seminary and Columbia University, became one of the most brilliant scholars of the Presbyterian Church and an outstanding preacher. Following his Chicago pastorate, he was called to the Brick Presbyterian Church in New York City, where he had a long and successful ministry. In 1915 he became president of the trustees of the Church Peace Union. His Lyman Beecher lectures in 1922 were published under the title, *The Freedom of the Preacher*. He died in 1954.

In the Footsteps of the Master

O Thou whose feet have climbed life's hill,
    And trod the path of youth,
Our Saviour and our Brother still,
    Now lead us into truth.

The call is Thine; be Thou the way,
    And give us men to guide;
Let wisdom broaden with the day,
    Let human faith abide.

Who learn of Thee the truth shall find,
    Who follow, gain the goal;
With reverence crown the earnest mind,
    And speak within the soul.

Awake the purpose high which strives,
    And, falling, stands again;
Conform the will of eager lives
    To quit themselves like men:

Thy life the bond of fellowship,
    Thy love the law that rules,
Thy Name, proclaimed by every lip,
    The Master of our schools.

LOUIS FITZGERALD BENSON, 1855-1930

A HYMNOLOGIST WHO WROTE HYMNS

THE NAME of Louis FitzGerald Benson is written in large letters in the annals of Christian hymnody in America. Until his death, October 10, 1930, he was considered the foremost authority in hymnology on this side of the Atlantic. Author of a number of important books on hymnody and the editor of a number of official hymnals for both the Presbyterian and Congregational Churches, he had gathered one of the finest collections of hymnbooks and hymn literature in the world. His library, comprising 25,000 volumes, was bequeathed upon his death to Princeton Theological Seminary, with the provision that it be used for reference only.

"Many of these books," Dr. Benson wrote in his will, "are unique, and more of them can never be replaced."

Because the Presbyterians for centuries followed the Calvinistic tradition in their prejudice against hymns "of human composure," practically no hymn-writers were developed in this segment of American Protestantism until the latter part of the 19th century. What hymnbooks came into use were of an inferior quality and grudgingly accepted. The *Hymnal of the Presbyterian Church,* which appeared in 1866, was virtually a failure. *The Presbyterian Hymnal* of 1874, patterned largely after the English *Hymns Ancient and Modern,* was an improvement, but also met with indifferent success.

It was Benson who finally provided the leadership in his Church, not only to induce Presbyterians to sing hymns, but also to give them a hymnal that truly reflected the spiritual culture of their communion. *The Hymnal* of 1895, which was edited by him, immediately took its place among the foremost hymnbooks of its day, and won instant recognition for its creator as a hymnodist of the first rank. Benson's distinguished service to his Church continued over a period of four decades. In 1911 he was entrusted with the responsibility of revising *The Hymnal,* a task which he completed with consummate skill.

Dr. Benson also edited *The Chapel Hymnal, The School Hymnal,* and was joint editor with Henry van Dyke of *The Book of Common Worship* of the Presbyterian Church in the U.S.A. His books on the subject of hymnody have been extensive, including *The Best Church Hymns, Best Hymns, a Handbook,* and *The English Hymn—Its Development and Use in Worship.* The latter is a monumental work, and is regarded as the authoritative volume in its field.

His original hymns, thirty-two in number, together with sixteen translations from the Latin, were published in 1925 in a little volume called *Hymns, Original and Translated.* Perhaps his best known lyric is "O Thou whose feet have climbed life's hill," which first appeared in *The Hymnal* of 1895. *The Hymnal* of 1933, which was published three years after the distinguished hymnologist's death, contained eight of his hymns, including "For the bread which Thou hast broken," "I name Thy hallowed Name," "The sun is on the land and sea," "O sing a song of Bethlehem," "O Love that lights the eastern sky," "The Light of God is falling," and "O Splendor of God's glory bright." The latter is a translation of the famous Latin hymn by St. Ambrose.

Benson, who was born in Philadelphia in 1855, was trained at the University of Pennsylvania for law, but after seven years of practice decided to enter Princeton Theological Seminary. After his ordination in 1886, he served for six years as pastor of the Church of the Redeemer in Germantown, Philadelphia, but then resigned to devote his life to the study of hymnology and the editing of hymnals for his Church. He also became a lecturer on liturgics at Auburn Theological Seminary and on hymnology at Princeton Seminary.

As indicated above, Benson, in his work of raising worship standards in his own communion, was ably assisted by Henry van Dyke, one of the foremost literary figures in America in the early part of the 20th century. Van Dyke, who was born in Germantown, Pa., in 1852, received his education at Princeton. After serving as a Congregational pastor at Newport, R. I., for four years, he accepted a call to the famous Brick Presbyterian Church in New York City. During his brilliant ministry of seventeen years in that church he became known as one of the most outstanding preachers in America. A member of the Board of Preachers at Harvard, he was also called on to serve other universities as a lecturer.

His own alma mater recognized his literary achievements in 1900 when he was made professor of English Literature at Princeton. However, his tenure of twenty-three years at that institution was frequently interrupted. From 1908 to 1909 he was American lecturer at the Sorbonne in Paris. In 1913, President Woodrow Wilson appointed him United States Minister to the Netherlands and Luxemburg, a position he filled with distinction for four years. When the United States became involved in World War I in 1917, he resigned his post to accept a commission as a chaplain in the Navy.

Van Dyke's works are too well known to require comment here. Mention should be made, however, of his nature book, *Out of Doors in the Holy Land,* and his charming story of the Nativity, *The Other Wise Man.* He was also highly gifted as a poet, and was the author of a number of splendid hymns. He once expressed his ideal of hymn-writing in words that are very apropos today:

"These verses are simple expressions of common Christian feelings and desires in this present time, — hymns of today that may be sung together by people who know the thought of the age, and are not afraid that any truth of science will destroy religion, or any revolution on earth overthrow the kingdom of heaven. Therefore these are hymns of trust and joy and hope."

Perhaps his finest hymn, written to be sung to the music of the "Hymn of Joy," the Finale in Beethoven's Ninth Symphony, was born in 1907 while Van Dyke was on a preaching visit to Williams College. According to the story told by his son, Van Dyke came down to the breakfast table one morning and laid the words of his hymn before the president of the college with the remark: "Here is a hymn for you. Your mountains (the Berkshires) were my inspiration." Regarded as one of the most joyous lyrics in the English language, its first stanza reads:

> Joyful, joyful, we adore Thee,
>   God of glory, Lord of love;
> Hearts unfold like flowers before Thee,
>   Opening to the sun above.
> Melt the clouds of sin and sadness;
>   Drive the clouds of doubt away;
> Giver of immortal gladness,
>   Fill us with the light of day!

Two other hymns that have found their way into recent hymnals are "O Lord our God, Thy mighty hand," a patriotic poem of great virility and noble expression, and "Jesus, Thou divine Companion," a splendid ode on the dignity of honest toil and labor. Van Dyke was a great lover of nature, a trait that is beautifully reflected in another lyric:

599

> Return, dear Lord, to those who look
> With eager eyes, that yearn
> For Thee among the garden flowers;
> After the dark and lonely hours
> As morning light return . . .

Dr. van Dyke retired from his professorship in Princeton in 1923, and was serving as chairman of the Committee of Revision of the Presbyterian *Book of Common Worship* when he passed away on April 10, 1933.

Another Presbyterian minister who added lustre to his Church by his splendid hymns, and who, like Van Dyke, belonged to a long succession of distinguished pastors of Brick Presbyterian Church in New York City, was Maltbie D. Babcock. Born in Syracuse, N. Y., in 1858, he became an outstanding athlete at Syracuse University. E. S. Ninde, in his volume, *The Story of the American Hymn*, gives this graphic description of him:

"A manlier man than Maltbie Davenport Babcock never stood in a Christian pulpit . . . He grew up, tall, broad-shouldered, with muscles of iron, a superb specimen of physical manhood. He was a champion baseball pitcher and swimmer, and at the front in all athletic contests. The young men as well as the boys fairly idolized him, but they all knew where he stood. He was full of fun and mischief as the next man, but some things he would not tolerate. One day when an older fellow was trying to bully one younger than himself, and was indulging in some unsavory language, Babcock quietly seized him by the nape of his neck and the seat of the trousers and with a word of forceful warning pitched him over the fence."

Something of the virile character of Babcock as a preacher is reflected in his well-known lines:

> Be strong!
> We are not here to play, to dream, to drift,
> We have hard work to do, and loads to lift.
> Shun not the struggle; face it. 'Tis God's gift.
>
> Be strong!
> Say not the days are evil—who's to blame?
> And fold the hands and acquiesce—O shame!
> Stand up, speak out, and bravely—in God's Name.
>
> Be strong!
> It matters not how deep intrenched the wrong,
> How hard the battle goes, the day, how long.
> Faint not, fight on! Tomorrow comes the song.

Babcock, like Van Dyke, was a great lover of nature. This is reflected in an evening hymn included in the Presbyterian hymnal of 1933, the opening stana of which reads:

> When the great sun sinks to his rest,
> His golden glories thrilling me,
> And voiceless longings stir my breast,
> They teach me, Lord, to worship Thee.

It is also seen in another poem, from which a cento has been taken to form his best-known hymn:

> This is my Father's world,
> And to my listening ears
> All nature sings, and round me rings
> The music of the spheres.
> This is my Father's world;
> I rest me in the thought
> Of rocks and trees, of skies and seas
> His hand the wonders wrought.

Babcock composed tunes for several of his hymns. By many he was regarded as a musical genius. His extraordinary career was cut short at the age of 43 years. He died at Naples, Italy, in 1901, when he and his wife were returning home from a journey to the Holy Land. Most of his hymns were published after his death.

Another Presbyterian minister who has won recognition in recent years as a hymn-writer is Milton S. Littlefield. Educated at Johns Hopkins University and Union Theological Seminary, he became the editor of two hymnbooks, and wrote a number of lyrics, the best known of which is one that emphasizes the glory of the common task when dedicated to God:

> O Son of Man, Thou madest known,
> Through quiet work in shop and home,
> The sacredness of common things,
> The chance of life that each day brings.
>
> O Workman true, may we fulfill
> In daily life Thy Father's will;
> In duty's call, Thy call we hear
> To fuller life, through work sincere.

Born in New York City, August 21, 1864, Littlefield passed away on June 12, 1934.

A Prayer for the Church

Put forth, O God, Thy Spirit's might,
And bid Thy Church increase,
In breadth and length, in depth and height,
Her unity and peace.

Let works of darkness disappear
Before Thy conquering light;
Let hatred and tormenting fear
Pass with the passing night.

Let what apostles learned of Thee
Be ours from age to age;
Their steadfast faith our unity,
Their peace our heritage.

O Judge divine of human strife,
O vanquisher of pain!
To know Thee is eternal life,
To serve Thee is to reign.

HOWARD CHANDLER ROBBINS, 1876-1952

A GREAT CHURCHMAN AND HIS HYMNAL

NOT very often are so many diversified gifts found in one man as those possessed by the late Canon Charles Winfred Douglas. A distinguished churchman of the Protestant Episcopal Church in the United States, he has been described as a liturgiologist, linguist and musicologist. By the same token, he was an outstanding clergyman, scholar, hymnologist, poet and composer.

Two official hymnbooks of his Church—the *New Hymnal* of 1916 and the *Hymnal 1940*—bear the stamp of his genius. In each instance, he was the musical editor of the volume, but his contribution particularly to the latter hymnal, is also reflected in its literary content.

Douglas from his early youth revealed a deep interest in church music. Born in Oswego, N. Y., in 1867, he studied music at Syracuse University, meanwhile serving as assistant organist in St. Paul's Cathedral in Syracuse. After his graduation with a Bachelor of Music degree in 1891, he became an instructor in voice at his alma mater. Then followed theological studies in St. Andrew's Divinity School. In 1893 he was ordained a deacon and appointed as curate of the Church of the Redeemer in New York City.

Douglas possessed a remarkable physique and while at Syracuse University had played football. However, he had served as curate only a few months before he was stricken with lung trouble and was compelled to leave New York for a dryer climate. He eventually found himself at Evergreen, Colo., where he established the Mission of the Transfiguration. He was ordained as an Episcopal priest in 1899. After two years devoted to the study of church music in Europe, he was appointed director of music for the Community of St. Mary, Peekskill, N. Y., where he applied his theories in plainsong adaptation, in which field he became an acknowledged authority. He became honorary canon of St. John's Cathedral in Denver in 1934, and from 1937 to 1943 he served as vicar of the Mission of Transfiguration in Evergreen. At the latter place he was instrumental in founding the Evergreen Conference, which included a school of church music.

The work of Canon Douglas in the field of liturgy, church music and hymnody is too extensive to be reviewed here. His real monument is *Hymnal 1940,* which contains a large number of his hymn-tune arrangements and original compositions, as well as a dozen beautiful English translations from German, French and Latin sources, some of which were done in collaboration with Arthur W. Farlander and others. Among these are Luther's "From heaven high I come to you," Johann Rist's "O sorrow deep," Gerhardt's "Awake, my heart, and render," and Bogatzky's "Awake, Thou Spirit of the watchmen."

As musical editor of the 1940 hymnal, he was instrumental in encouraging the contribution of a large number of original hymn-tunes by American and Canadian composers. From more than 4,000 manuscripts submitted, forty-eight new tunes were chosen. In addition to Douglas, contemporary musicians who helped to enrich the volume included such well-known organists as Leo Sowerby, David McK.Williams, Thomas Tertius Noble, Horatio W. Parker, Peter Christian Lutkin, and Healey Willan. A considerable number of tunes by such recent English composers as Arthur S. Sullivan, Ralph Vaughan Williams, John Stainer and Martin Shaw were also included. Moreover, Douglas harked back several centuries to revive some fine hymn compositions by Orlando Gibbons and Thomas Tallis.

Canon Douglas did not live to see the 1940 hymnal published. On the day before he died, he returned to the printer final page proofs of his corrections. On the same day he began the composition of an organ prelude based on *Stuttgart,* which was the first tune in the new hymnal. He continued this task on the following day and had just completed it when his death in the evening of January 18, 1944, brought his arduous life's day to a close. Thus, as his biographer states, "He began his career dedicated to the Praise of God. He ended his life with the Praise of God on his mind and pen, and in his heart."

The Episcopalian hymnals of 1916 and 1940 not only marked a significant advance in the standards of American hymnody, but also brought to light a number of gifted hymn-writers who contributed original lyrics of abiding value. Among these were John Henry Hopkins, Jr., Howard Chandler Robbins, Bates Gilbert Burt, Harry Emerson Fosdick, Leigh Mitchell Hodges, Henry Hallam Tweedy and Earl Bowman Marlatt.

John Henry Hopkins, Jr., has won a secure place among American hymnists by his greatly loved Epiphany lyric, "We three kings of Orient are," as well as by his beautiful post-communion hymn, "Come with us, O blessed Jesus." Hopkins, whose father was Episcopal bishop of Vermont and whose mother came from Hamburg, Germany, inherited musical and literary gifts from both parents. Born in Pittsburgh, Pa., October 28, 1820, he received his education in the University of Vermont and General Theological Seminary. Following his ordination by the Episcopal Church he began to give evidence of both poetic and musical talent by writing a number of splendid hymns and hymn-tunes. His *Carols, Hymns, and Songs,* published in 1863, went through four editions.

Hopkins is credited with having been one of the chief exponents of hymnody in the Episcopal Church during the middle of the 19th century, when hymns were first being seriously introduced into that communion. "We three kings of Orient are," with its charming tune, likewise the work of Hopkins, was published in the 1916 hymnal. It also became a part of the 1940 collection, together with his post-communion hymn, which is set to the exquisite Bach harmonization of Johann Schop's tune, *Jesu, joy of man's desiring.* Hopkins died in 1891.

The English version of the jubilant Christmas carol, "Angels we have heard on high," is the work of another American hymnist, Earl Bowman Marlatt. Based on an 18th century French lyric, it was written in 1937 for the *New Church Hymnal* and was subsequently included in the Episcopal hymnal of 1940. Marlatt was a native of Indiana, where he was born at Columbus in 1892. Following his graduation at De Pauw University, he did graduate work at Boston University, Oxford and the University of Berlin. In 1925 he became professor of philosophy and religious education at Boston University, and from 1938 to 1945 was dean of the School of Theology at the same institution. Author of a number of volumes of poetry, he was associate editor of the *American Student Hymnal,* published in 1928.

Harry Emerson Fosdick, who gained nation-wide fame as pastor of Riverside Church, New York City, and as a radio preacher, is the author of the well-known hymn, "God of grace and God of glory." It was written at his Maine summer home in 1930, and was first sung at the opening service of Riverside Church on October 30 of that year. Born in Buffalo, N. Y., in 1878, Fosdick served the First Baptist Church in Montclair, N. J., before becoming pastor of Riverside Church. From 1908 to 1948 he taught at Union Theological Seminary, first as instructor in homiletics and afterwards as professor of practical theology. The above hymn was included in the Episcopal hymnal of 1940, and has found its way into numerous other collections.

"O God of youth, whose Spirit in our hearts is stirring," regarded by many as the most outstanding of contemporary hymns for young people, was written in 1935 to be sung at a high school commencement at Pontiac, Mich. Its author, Bates Gilbert Burt, at the time was rector of All Saints' Church in that city. When it was adopted for the hymnal of 1940, the gifted pastor composed a new tune for the words and called it *Lynne*, after a granddaughter. Burt was born in Wheeling, W. Va., in 1878, and received his education at Kenyon College and Seabury Divinity School. Ordained in 1904, he served in France with the American Army during World War I. He died in 1948 while serving St. Mary's parish in Edgewood, Maryland.

Leigh Mitchell Hodges was one of the few laymen of the Episcopal Church who made a contribution to the 1940 hymnal. In 1939, while serving as corresponding secretary of the Joint Commission on the Revision of the Hymnal, he wrote a confirmation hymn which was accepted for inclusion in that volume. It is titled "As when, in far Samaria." Still later, Hodges wrote a second confirmation lyric which many consider even finer than his first one. It reads:

> Lord of the everlasting light,
> Let shine on these today
> A guiding beam, to lead aright
> Their feet along the way.
>
> O, may they ever turn to Thee
> As Father and as Friend;
> Secure in Thy infinity
> Until the journey's end.
>
> And when, beyond the dusk of time,
> They greet the dawn above,
> O give them, in that blessed clime,
> Thy endlessness of love.

Hodges had an interesting journalistic career. Born in Denver, Colo., in 1876, he worked for a while as a newspaper reporter in Mexico, Mo., and afterwards on the *Kansas City Star*. He then went East, where he became associated with the *Ladies Home Journal* and the *Philadelphia North American*. He also became a contributor to the *New Yorker*, the *Reader's Digest*, and the conductor of a column, "The Optimist," for the *Philadelphia Evening Bulletin*. He holds the unique distinction of having inaugurated the first publicity campaign in 1907 for the Red Cross Christmas Stamp, which later came to be known as the Tuberculosis Christmas Seal. Hodges was the author of a number of books. He passed away in 1954.

The largest number of original hymns in the 1940 hymnal by a contemporary writer came from the pen of Howard Chandler Robbins. A member of the Revision Committee, he contributed no less than five lyrics, namely, "Put forth, O God, Thy Spirit's might," "Now yield we thanks and praise," "Sunset to sunrise changes now," "The Sabbath day was by," "And have the bright immensities," as well as a translation of St. Francis of Assisi's famous *Cantico di frate sole,* "Most High, omnipotent, good Lord." He also composed the tune, *Chelsea Square.*

Robbins, who was born in Philadelphia in 1876, became a national church figure when he was made dean of the Cathedral of St. John the Divine in New York City in 1917, a position he held for twelve years. In 1929 he resigned to become professor of pastoral theology at General Theological Seminary. Robbins was a delegate to the World Conference on Faith and Order in 1937. He retired in 1941, and passed away eleven years later.

The 1940 hymnal was probably one of the first official hymn-books to include Henry Hallam Tweedy's splendid missionary hymn, "Eternal God, whose power upholds." It was written in 1929, being awarded the prize offered that year by the Hymn Society of America for the best new hymn on the theme of missions. A hymn of five verses, each stanza describes a different attribute of God. He is addressed as the God of power, the God of love, the God of truth, the God of beauty, and the God of righteousness and grace. There is a modern note in the hymn, as witness:

> O God of love, whose Spirit wakes
> In every human breast,
> Whom love, and love alone, can know,
> In whom all hearts find rest,
> Help us to spread Thy gracious reign
> Till greed and hate shall cease,
> And kindness dwell in human hearts,
> And all the earth find peace.

Tweedy was a Congregational minister who served parishes in Utica, N. Y., and Bridgeport, Conn., before he was called in 1909 to become professor of Practical Theology in Yale Divinity School. He was made professor emeritus upon his retirement in 1937. In 1939 he edited *Christian Worship and Praise.* He passed away in 1953.

The Saints' Triumph Song

Rise, ye children of salvation,
    All who cleave to Christ the Head;
Wake, awake, O mighty nation,
    Ere the foe on Zion tread;
He draws nigh, and would defy
All the hosts of God most high.

Saints and martyrs long before us
    Firmly on this ground have stood;
See their banner waving o'er us,
    Conquerors through the Saviour's Blood.
Ground we hold, whereon of old
Fought the faithful and the bold.

Fighting, we shall be victorious
    By the Blood of Christ our Lord;
On our foreheads, bright and glorious,
    Shines the witness of His Word;
Spear and shield on battlefield,
His great Name; we cannot yield.

When His servants stand before Him,
    Each receiving his reward,
When His saints in light adore Him,
    Giving glory to the Lord;
"Victory!" our song shall be
Like the thunder of the sea.

JUSTUS FALCKNER, 1672–1723
TR. EMMA FRANCES BEVAN, 1827–1909

LUTHERAN HYMNODY COMES TO AMERICA

THE Lutheran Church traditionally has been known as "The Singing Church." Ever since the Reformation, when Martin Luther in 1524 published his little volume of eight hymns known as the *Achtliederbuch*, the singing of hymns has formed an important part of its stated worship. From Germany congregational singing spread to other European countries where the teachings of the Monk of Wittenberg gained acceptance, and soon a rich native hymnody developed in Sweden, Denmark, Norway, Finland and even in the little Arctic island of Iceland.

It is of historic interest that the first Lutheran pastor to be ordained in America was a hymn-writer. He was Justus Falckner, author of the stirring hymn, "Rise, ye children of salvation."

Falckner, who was born on November 22, 1672, in Langenreinsdorf, Saxony, was the son of a Lutheran pastor at that place. He entered the University of Halle in 1693 as a student of theology under Francke, but for conscientious reasons refused to be ordained when he had completed his studies. Together with his brother Daniel, he instead became associated with the William Penn colony in America, in which capacity he arranged for the sale of 10,000 acres of land to Andreas Rudman, who was the spiritual leader of the Swedish Lutheran colonists along the Delaware.

Through Rudman's influence, Falckner was induced to enter the ministry, and on November 24, 1703, he was ordained in Gloria Dei Lutheran Church at Wicaco, Philadelphia. The ordination service was conducted by the Swedish Lutheran pastors, Rudman, Erik Björk and Andreas Sandel. Falckner thus became the first German Lutheran pastor in America, and also had the distinction of building the first German Lutheran church in the New World—at Falckner's Swamp, New Hanover, Pa. Later he removed to New York, where for twenty years he labored faithfully among the German, Dutch, and Scandinavian settlers in a parish that extended some two hundred miles from Albany to Long Island.

It seems that Falckner's hymn, "Rise, ye children of salvation,"

609

was written while he was a student at Halle. It appeared as early as 1697 in *Geistreiches Gesangbuch,* and in 1704 it was given a place in Freylinghausen's hymnbook. There is no evidence that Falckner ever translated it into English. The present English version is the work of an English woman, Mrs. Emma Frances Bevan, daughter of the late Bishop Philip Shuttleworth of Chichester and the wife of a London banker.

The first Lutherans who crossed the Atlantic to help colonize the New World continued to worship God in their respective mother tongues. To these shores they brought with them not only their Bibles, but also their devotional books, their hymnbooks and their liturgies. This was true of the Swedish Lutherans along the Delaware River, of the German Lutherans of New York and Pennsylvania, and of the later wave of Lutheran immigrants from northern Europe who pushed farther west into the Ohio and Mississippi Valleys.

As new generations arose, however, the demand for hymnbooks in the English language became insistent. The first such Lutheran hymnal was edited in New York City in 1795 by Christopher Kunze.

Each Lutheran church body at first seemed chiefly concerned in preserving in English dress its own distinctive hymn heritage. The work of translation, therefore, completely overshadowed creative writing. The few original hymns that appeared from time to time were not written in English, but in German, Swedish, Norwegian or Danish. A typical example of this is a paraphrase of the 100th Psalm, "O sing, all ye lands, with a jubilant voice," which was written in Norwegian by Ulrik Vilhelm Koren. This man, who was ordained in Norway in 1853, left that year for the United States to become the first Norwegian pastor to settle west of the Mississippi River. Founder of a pioneer congregation at Washington Prairie, Iowa, he eventually became the president of the Norwegian Lutheran Synod. His hymn was rendered into English by Mrs. Harriet Krauth Spaeth of Philadelphia, who devoted many years to the task of translating German and Scandinavian hymns.

Other early pioneers in the work of translation were Mrs. Spaeth's father, Charles Porterfield Krauth, a noted Lutheran theologian and vice-provost of the University of Pennsylvania; Joseph A. Seiss, an outstanding author, preacher and churchman, to whom we are indebted for the English version of "Beautiful Saviour, King of creation," and Charles William Schaeffer, a theologian and church leader who translated Held's "Come, O come, Thou quickening Spirit," Rambach's "Lord, to Thee I now surrender," and Wallin's lovely Swedish lyric, "Where is the Friend for whom I'm ever yearning?"

Among the first Lutheran writers of original hymns in the language of the land was Matthias Loy, at one time president of Capital University, Columbus, O., and also president of the Evangelical Lutheran Synod of Ohio. Loy, who was born of humble parents in the Blue Ridge Mountains of Pennsylvania in 1828, was only nine years old when his mother died. Forced to shift for himself at the age of fourteen when his father married again, he found employment in Harrisburg. Dr. Schaeffer, to whom reference has been made above, learned to know the lad and became deeply interested in him. He suggested to the homeless boy that he prepare himself for the ministry.

Loy eventually found himself in Columbus, O., where he enrolled in Capital University. To support himself, he found employment in the printing office of the *Lutheran Standard,* official organ of the Ohio Synod.

Ordained in 1849 at the age of 21, Loy began his remarkable career as pastor of a congregation in Delaware, O. Eleven years later he was president of the Synod, and four years after that he also became editor of the *Lutheran Standard.* Another year passed and he was called to become professor of theology at his alma mater. In 1878 he resigned as president of the Synod, but two years later he was again chosen as head of his Church as well as president of Capital University. Loy was instrumental in the formation of the Synodical Conference, but in 1881 his own Synod withdrew from that federation. He retired from active service in 1902 and died in 1915.

Loy was one of the most gifted of early Lutheran hymnists. Among his original hymns are "Jesus, Thou art mine forever," "O great High Priest, forget me not," "Give me, O Lord, a spirit lowly," "I thank Thee, Saviour, for the grief," and "Jesus took the babes and blessed them." The latter is a baptismal hymn of unusual tenderness. Loy also translated a number of German hymns, including Selnecker's fine lyric, "Let me be Thine forever."

Henry Eyster Jacobs was another 19th century American Lutheran hymn-writer. His communion hymn, "Lord Jesus Christ, we humbly pray," has been widely used. A penitential hymn, "Forsake me not, my God," is especially poignant in expression. Dissatisfied with the absence of a definite Christian note in Sarah Adams'

"Nearer, my God, to Thee," Jacobs composed another hymn in the same meter, but like all other similar attempts it failed to displace the original.

Jacobs, who was one of the leading theologians produced by the Lutheran Church in America, was born at Gettysburg, Pa., in 1844. He received his education at Gettysburg College and Gettysburg Seminary. After serving as pastor and teacher for a number of years, he became professor of Systematic Theology at the Lutheran Theological Seminary at Philadelphia, a position he held from 1883 until his death in 1993. He also served as dean of the institution.

Later writers of original hymns, as well as translators, were Emanuel Cronenwett, a Lutheran pastor who, after serving several parishes in Ohio, had a pastorate extending over a period of 54 years at Butler, Pa.; Conrad H. L. Schuette, professor of theology at Capital University and later president of the Joint Synod of Ohio, and John Casper Mattes, professor of theology at Wartburg Seminary, Dubuque, Iowa.

No Lutheran group in America has been more zealous in preserving German hymns in English dress than the Lutheran Church — Missouri Synod. Its English District took the initiative in this matter in 1889, when it published a volume under the title, *Evangelical Lutheran Hymn-Book,* containing 400 hymns, many of them translations. It was originally a text edition only. Eventually it developed into a collection of 567 hymns with music, and in 1912 it was designated as the official English hymnal of the Synod.

In 1930 an Intersynodical Committee on Hymnology and Liturgics representing all of the bodies of the Synodical Conference came into being, with the late William Gustave Polack, leading hymnologist of the Missouri Synod, as its chairman. After ten years of labor the group produced the *Lutheran Hymnal,* a volume containing 600 hymns. Of these, 244 were translations from the German, the largest number from that source ever incorporated in an English hymnal.

Polack, who also became the compiler of *The Handbook* to the hymnal, contributed nine translations and three original hymns to the new collection. Among his originals was an anniversary hymn written for the centennial of the Saxon migration to the United States which resulted in the founding of the Missouri Synod. Bearing the title, "God the Father, Son and Spirit," it was sung in nation-wide celebrations on June 19, 1938. One of its stanzas reads:

Thou didst guide our fathers' footsteps
    To this land we hold so dear,
Lengthening the cords and curtains
    Of their habitation here;
Strengthening Thy temple's pillars
    As Thou hast from age to age;
Giving us, their sons and daughters,
    An abiding heritage.

Twenty-three translations of German hymns in the *Lutheran Hymnal* came from the pen of August Crull, for many years a professor of German at Concordia College, Fort Wayne, Ind. William M. Czamanske, a Wisconsin pastor, contributed six translations from the German and one original hymn. Other translators of German hymns included John Theodore Mueller, professor of systematic theology at Concordia Seminary, St. Louis, Mo.; Paul E. Kretzmann, a professor at the same institution; William J. Schaefer, a Wisconsin pastor who was a member of the hymnal committee; Oscar Kaiser, a Milwaukee pastor who also served on the committee; and August F. Zich, a professor in the Lutheran Theological Seminary at Thiensville, Wis.

Two of the original hymns in the *Lutheran Hymnal* came from patriarchs of the Missouri Synod. An Easter lyric, "He's risen, He's risen, Christ Jesus the Lord," was the work of its most distinguished theologian and leader, Carl F. W. Walther. Walther, who arrived in America in the great Saxon migration of 1838, was one of the founders of the Missouri Synod and was chosen its first president. He has been called "the most commanding figure in the Lutheran Church in America during the 19th century." Through his editing of *Lehre und Wehre,* as well as his preaching and writing, his influence has been felt in American Lutheranism for more than a hundred years. Walther's Easter hymn was written while the great church leader was on a journey to Germany in 1860. Above the manuscript text, he had made the notation: "On the First Easter Day, April 8, 1860 on the Ocean." Walther was an accomplished musician as well as an able preacher, theologian and church leader, and also composed the tune to which his hymn is sung.

A missionary hymn, "Rise, Thou Light of Gentile nations," was the other original lyric written by a pioneer pastor. He was Herman Fick, an outstanding poet who came to America from Germany in 1846 and served a large congregation in Detroit for many years. His hymn, as well as Walther's, was written in German.

613

The *American Lutheran Hymnal* of 1930, which was published by the American Lutheran Church, followed the pattern of other Lutheran hymnbooks of this period by including a large number of translated hymns. Hermann Brueckner, a professor at Hebron College, Hebron, Nebr., was represented by seventy translations from the German, three from the French, and four original hymns. Three others who made extensive contributions, in both original and translated hymns, were Paul E. Kretzmann, mentioned above; William H. Lehmann, a home missions executive of the American Lutheran Church, and A. F. Rohr, a pastor of that Church at Fremont, O.

It was not until the turn of the century that various Lutheran groups of Scandinavian origin began the task of translating their hymns into English. One of the earliest attempts was that of the Augustana Lutheran Church, which in 1901 published its first English hymnal. It contained some fifty hymns from the Swedish heritage. A leader in the work was Olof Olsson, at that time president of Augustana College and Theological Seminary at Rock Island, Ill. Among the fine contributions to the book was Olsson's translation of Bishop Franzen's communion hymn, "Thine own, O loving Saviour."

Other professors at the institution who aided in the work were Conrad Emil Lindberg, Victor O. Peterson, Anders O. Bersell, Peter Matthias Lindberg and Claude W. Foss. Foss will be remembered chiefly for his translation of Elizabeth Ehrenborg-Posse's lovely Nativity carol, "When Christmas morn is dawning," as well as Archbishop Wallin's impressive ascension hymn, "To realms of glory in the skies." Augustus Nelson, a pastor in a rural parish in Minnesota, was particularly successful as a translator, and his English versions of Franzen's Advent hymn, "Prepare the way, O Zion," and Arrhenius' fine lyric, "Jesus, Lord and precious Saviour," have found their way into a number of important hymnbooks. Bersell made excellent translations of Rutström's "Come, Saviour dear, with us abide," Lina Sandell's "Jerusalem, Jerusalem, thou city ever blest," and the German hymn by Wilhelm II, Duke of Saxe-Weimar, "O Christ, Thy grace unto us lend."

A layman who had an active part in preparing the 1901 Augustana hymnbook was Ernst William Olson, secretary of literature at Augustana Book Concern. When a new edition of *The Hymnal* was published in 1925, Olson had emerged as the foremost translator of Swedish hymns. Among his English versions that seem destined to live are two of Archbishop Wallin's hymns, "All hail to thee, O blessed morn" and "Ah, how blest is he who knoweth;" as well as a deeply loved lyric by Caroline Sandell Berg, "Children of the heavenly Father." Another layman, Samuel Magnus Hill, professor of history at Luther College, Wahoo, Nebr., translated the first stanza of Wallin's communion hymn, "A voice, a heavenly voice I hear," and Olson translated the last two.

Norwegian and Danish Lutherans were not far behind their Swedish brethren in undertaking a similar task. About fifty years ago three Norwegian synods appointed a joint committee to prepare an English hymnal. Their labors resulted in the publication of the *Lutheran Hymnary* in 1913. Foremost in the group was Carl Doving, an eminent hymnologist, who gave to American worshipers a stirring translation of Grundtvig's immortal hymn, "Built on a rock the Church doth stand." He will also be remembered for his rendering of Boye's "Rejoice, rejoice, this happy morn," as well as Landstad's "To Thee, O Lord, the God of all."

George Alfred Taylor Rygh, another member of the committee, translated Grundtvig's "Peace to soothe our bitter woes," Kingo's "He that believes and is baptized," and Wexels' "O happy day, when we shall stand." A Minnesota pastor, O. H. Smeby, translated Brun's "How blest are they who hear God's Word," and Ole T. (Sanden) Arneson, a Chicago layman, was the writer of an English version of Bruun's "The sun has gone down" and a number of other lyrics. A very fine rendering of Kingo's hymn of thanksgiving, "Praise to Thee and adoration," written to be sung "from Christmas until Candlemas," was made by Kristen Kvamme, a pastor who served congregations in New York City, Washington, D. C., and Salt Lake City, Utah.

During the 1920's two pastors of a Danish synod, J. C. Aaberg of Minneapolis and P. C. Paulsen of Chicago, continued the work of translating the lyrics of Kingo, Grundtvig, Brorson and Ingemann. Aaberg was represented by no less than nineteen translations in the *American Lutheran Hymnal,* and Paulsen by an equal number. The best known of Aaberg's translations is his rendering of Grundtvig's "Print Thine image pure and holy."

615

The Prayer of an Anxious Soul

Now once again for help that never faileth,
We bring our grievous burden unto Thee;
Pour down Thy strength, for nothing else availeth,
Bless Thou the bowing head, the bending knee,

That we may rise and go forth from Thine altar,
To bear the load we could not bear before,
With mind serene, with step that does not falter,
Knowing Thy hand will open every door;

Knowing there will not be so dark a valley
But those who watch may find Thy guiding ray,
Knowing there will not be so blind an alley
But it will open on Thy broad highway.

O Light that led the saints through all the ages,
O Hope that lifted up the martyr's head,
O Comforter of children and of sages,
Lead on, lead on, as Thou hast always led!

MILDRED WHITNEY STILLMAN, 1890–

616

RECENT AMERICAN WOMEN HYMN-WRITERS

ALTHOUGH America has not produced many women hymn-writers comparable to England's Sarah Adams, Charlotte Elliott, Frances Ridley Havergal or Cecil Frances Alexander, the number of women on this side of the Atlantic who are writing Christian lyrics is constantly increasing, and the quality of their hymns is generally very high. Mention has already been made of such writers as Harriet Beecher Stowe, Julia Ward Howe, Elizabeth Payson Prentiss, Mary Artemisia Lathbury, Frances Jane Crosby, Katharine Lee Bates and a number of others. However, we have not done justice to the great contribution that American womanhood has made to the worship life of our nation until we have noted some recent hymnists.

It is not by accident that many of our best Christian hymns have been born in seasons of sorrow and soul travail, or days of deep anxiety and mental distress. It is in such times that the human heart in its helplessness turns instinctively to God, giving utterance to its needs in language that knocks insistently at the portals of heaven.

Such was the experience of a contemporary hymn-writer, Mrs. Mildred Whitney Stillman, from whom we have received the beautiful lyric on prayer, "Now once again for help that never faileth." The circumstances that led to its writing have been described by the author as follows:

"A Cornwall-on-Hudson neighbor of ours, Mrs. Hal Tryon, was staying with us because her young son was at the hospital for a bad mastoid operation. Jimmy was very ill, in danger, and we were heavy with waiting and sadness. One morning in anguish I stepped into St. James Church to pray for Jimmy. As often happens, the prayer came out in rhythm and rhyme. I felt a wonderful assurance that all was well with Jimmy, and soon the crisis passed and he recovered."

Mrs. Stillman, who was born in San Francisco in 1890 and educated at Barnard College, was married to Ernest G. Stillman in 1911, and lives at Cornwall-on-Hudson, N. Y. Herself the mother of six

617

children, she was able fully to share the anxiety of another mother, as a singing of her hymn quickly reveals. Incidentally, it also explains why Mrs. Stillman is a successful writer of books for children. Among her works is a story of Christ, bearing the title, *A Boy of Galilee.*

It was a season of deep mental anxiety also that gave birth to one of our great missionary hymns—"O Zion, haste, thy mission high fulfilling." The author, Mrs. Mary Ann Thomson, was keeping vigil one night in 1868 at the bedside of one of her children who was critically ill of typhoid fever. As she watched prayerfully for any sign of hope that might appear, the words of Faber's beautiful hymn, "Hark, hark my soul! angelic songs are swelling," kept ringing in her ears. Perhaps she made a covenant with God that if He would spare her child, she would consecrate it to His service. Then she felt an impulse to write a missionary hymn to the tune that seemed to haunt her. Undoubtedly she was thinking of her own sick child when she wrote:

> Give of thy sons to bear the message glorious,
>   Give of thy wealth to speed them on their way,
> Pour out thy soul for them in prayer victorious,
>   And haste the coming of the glorious day.
> Publish glad tidings, tidings of peace;
> Tidings of Jesus, redemption and release.

Mrs. Thomson, who was born in London, England, in 1834, came to America as a young girl and spent the remainder of her life in Philadelphia. Her husband, John Thomson, was librarian of the Free Library of that city. Gifted as a writer, she was particularly fond of composing Christian hymns, many of which were published in the *Churchman* and the *Living Church.* Besides her missionary hymn, the best known are "Now the blessed Dayspring" and "O King of saints, we give Thee praise and glory. She passed away in Philadelphia in 1923.

A more recent missionary hymn, and one of our finest, has come from the pen of another American woman, the late Mrs. Laura Scherer Copenhaver, a prominent missionary leader of the United Lutheran Church and at one time professor of English literature in Marion College, Marion, Va. In the sweeping lines of "Heralds of Christ, who bear the king's commands" may be heard not only a stirring call to ambassadors of the Gospel to carry the tidings of redemption to the dark corners of the earth, but also a challenge to the Church to hasten the fulfillment of the promised day

> "When war shall be no more and strife shall cease
> Upon the highway of the Prince of Peace."

Here are the stanzas of her magnificent hymn:

> Heralds of Christ, who bear the King's commands,
> Immortal tidings in your mortal hands,
> Pass on and carry swift the news ye bring:
> Make straight, make straight the highway of the King.
>
> Through desert ways, dark fen, and deep morass,
> Through jungles, sluggish seas, and mountain pass,
> Build ye the road and falter not, nor stay;
> Prepare across the earth the King's highway.
>
> Where once the crooked trail in darkness wound
> Let marching feet and joyous song resound;
> Where burn the funeral pyres, and censers swing,
> Make straight, make straight the highway of the King.
>
> Lord, give us faith and strength the road to build,
> To see the promise of the day fulfilled,
> When war shall be no more and strife shall cease
> Upon the highway of the Prince of Peace.

Mrs. Copenhaver, whose maiden name was Laura Scherer, was a member of a famous Lutheran family in western Virginia. Her father, John Jacob Scherer, was the founder of Marion College and served as its president for some thirty years. A sister, Mary Scherer, was the dean of women at the institution, and another sister, Mrs. E. C. Cronk, became an outstanding writer and missionary leader. A brother, John Scherer, was pastor of a Lutheran church in Richmond, Va., for fifty years.

Laura was born in Marion on August 29, 1868, and spent her whole life in that place. Very early she began to reveal literary talent, and, in addition to becoming a teacher at her alma mater, she was made chairman of the education division of the Women's Missionary Society of the United Lutheran Church.

She was also gifted as a speaker. When she was only twenty years old, her father took her with him to a World Congress of Religions in Chicago. It is said that when she got up to speak at a forum, she held the gathering so spellbound the moderator finally turned the whole session over to the young girl. In later life she was in constant demand as a speaker at missionary conferences in various parts of the country. When illness once prevented her from keeping an engagement in the Middle West, her disappointment was very keen, but she found comfort in composing her famous missionary hymn. She tells the story in these words:

"In writing 'Heralds of Christ' I was moved with a sense of unity with all the builders of the King's highway in other lands and ages. Missionaries and ministers were frequent guests at the college, and the missionaries were especially interesting to me. Romance hung about them."

"Heralds of Christ" was first used at a conference at Northfield, Mass., and later it was published by the Women's Missionary Society of the United Lutheran Church. The missionary program of the women of the Methodist Episcopal Church North for a whole year was built around the hymn. It was used in like manner by the Southern Presbyterian Church in 1934. It was included in the Presbyterian *Hymnal* of 1933, and finally it was adopted by her own Church in the *Service Book and Hymnal* of 1958.

It was through Mrs. Copenhaver's initiative that work was started by the Women's Missionary Society among the mountaineers of the South. She not only encouraged native craftmanship among the mountain people in her own section of Virginia, but also was instrumental in the establishment of an industry in hand-woven rugs. At one time she was urged by the citizens of her district to become their representative in Congress, but declined because she felt she could not do justice to a poltical career and to her family at the same time. She passed away in her Marion home, known as Rosemont, on December 18, 1940. A biographer at that time wrote in *Lutheran Woman's Work:* "To all who enjoyed the hospitality of that home in the Virginia mountains there remains the delightful memory of the unique personality of Laura Scherer Copenhaver."

Closely paralleling the life of Mrs. Copenhaver was the career of Mrs. Margaret Reynolds Seebach, another hymn-writer of the United Lutheran Church. Born in Gettysburg, Pa., in 1875, she was the granddaughter on her mother's side of Charles A. Hay, a professor of Gettysburg Theological Seminary, while her father, John A. Himes, for more than forty years occupied the chair of English in Gettysburg College. One of the first two young women to graduate from the latter institution, she married a classmate, Julius Seebach, who had a distinguished ministry of more than fifty years in Philadelphia.

Mrs. Seebach, like Mrs. Copenhaver, became an outstanding missionary leader in her Church and one of its most brilliant writers. As editor of *Lutheran Woman's Work* from 1918 to 1938, the longest period that anyone served in that position, her editorials were eagerly awaited from month to month. Each one was described as a literary gem, and when she retired in 1938 several were reprinted in booklet form under the title, *As a Woman Thinketh*. She also was the author of a number of books, among them *That Man Donaleitis* and *The Mystery of Jordan Green,* both Rung Prize first awards; as well as *Missionary Milestones, An Eagle in the Wilderness* and *Martin of Mansfield*. Both Gettysburg and Carthage College honored her with the degree of Doctor of Literature. She died on October 20, 1948.

Although her literary achievements were many, Mrs. Seebach will undoubtedly be remembered chiefly for her gripping missionary hymn. Like many other contemporary lyrics written in our generation of world war and strife, it reflects the longing of earnest souls everywhere for the realization of the prayer our Lord has taught us to pray: "Thy Kingdom come; Thy will be done, on earth as it is in heaven."

> Thy Kingdom come! O Father, hear our prayer;
> Shine through the clouds that darken everywhere;
> Thou only light, Thou only life and joy,
> Show us the hope that nothing can destroy.
>
> Stumbling and blind, we strive to do Thy will,
> Trusting the word Thou surely wilt fulfill,
> That men are Thine, however far they roam,
> That love shall triumph, and Thy Kingdom come.
>
> Come, through the faith whereby the Church must live;
> Come, through the word of truth she has to give;
> Come, through her teaching, and her healing, too;
> Come, through the work united hearts can do.
>
> Thy Kingdom come, and come Thy glorious Son;
> O may our task for Him be nobly done!
> Faithful and true let all Thy servants be,
> Till they shall bring all nations home to Thee.

Mrs. Seebach also wrote the refrain for the hymn, "O Christians, leagued together." The stanzas of this hymn, which for more than half a century has been the rally song of the Luther League of America, were written in 1893 by another Lutheran woman, Mrs.

Lillian Weaver Cassaday, and published in the *Luther League Review* in the fall of that year. The following year it was included in the *Luther League Hymnal* and given to the world on Reformation Day. As originally written by Mrs. Cassaday, the refrain reads:

> All hail, our royal colors
>   For kingly lives unfold,
> Beneath our Luther ensign,
>   Black, red, white, blue, and gold.

When the hymn was published in the *Common Service Book* in 1917, Mrs. Seebach changed the refrain to read:

> All hail, our glorious Saviour,
>   We march where Thou hast trod,
> To seek Thy house of triumph,
>   The City of our God.

Mrs. Cassaday, who was born in 1861, in addition to her interest in young people's activities, was also deeply devoted to the work of the Italian Lutheran mission in Philadelphia. She died in 1914.

In 1952, when the Revised Standard Version of the Bible was nearing completion, the Hymn Society of America offered a prize for the best hymn commemorating the event. No less than 550 hymns were submitted, and when the committee had made its choice, it was discovered that a woman was the author of the winning lyric. She was Miss Sarah E. Taylor, who for forty-two years had been a teacher of Latin, English and history in schools at Talladega, Ala.; Richmond, Va., and Central Falls, R. I.

Miss Taylor was born in England in 1883 and came to the United States when she was nine years old. Her father was a minister in the Primitive Methodist Church, and she grew up in a home where the Bible was a daily source of help and inspiration. She started teaching in her father's church school at the age of fifteen. In 1904 she graduated from Brown University, and seven years later received her Master's degree. Her prize hymn, which was sung at services throughout the United States and Canada on September 30, 1952, when the new Bible translation was first introduced, reads:

> O God of Light, Thy Word, a lamp unfailing,
>   Shines through the darkness of our earthly way,
> O'er fear and doubt, o'er black despair prevailing,
>   Guiding our steps to Thine eternal day.

From days of old, through swiftly rolling ages,
  Thou hast revealed Thy will to mortal men,
Speaking to saints, to prophets, kings and sages,
  Who wrote the message with immortal pen.

Undimmed by time, the Word is still revealing
  To sinful men Thy justice and Thy grace;
And questing hearts that long for peace and healing
  See Thy compassion in the Saviour's face.

To all the world the message Thou art sending,
  To every land, to every race and clan;
And myriad tongues, in one great anthem blending,
  Acclaim with joy Thy wondrous gift to man.

When the World Council of Churches in 1954 met for its second Assembly in Evanston, Ill., it adopted as its theme: "Christ, the Hope of the World." Looking forward to that event, which was the first time an international gathering of such magnitude had ever been held on this side of the Atlantic, the Hymn Society of America offered a prize for the best hymn on the stirring assembly theme. When the judges had evaluated the hundreds of lyrics submitted, again it was a woman—Georgia Elma Harkness—who received the award.

Her hymn, which may truly be said to reflect the mood of a war-weary world, torn between hope and despair after two of the most terrible conflicts in human history, pointed anew to a God-given Saviour as the only Light that could lead men out of the darkness of their own sin and folly into the glory and promise of a new day:

Hope of the world, Thou Christ of great compassion,
  Speak to our fearful hearts by conflict rent.
Save us, Thy people, from consuming passion,
  Who by our own false hopes and aims are spent.

Hope of the world, God's gift from highest heaven,
  Bringing to hungry souls the bread of life,
Still let Thy Spirit unto us be given
  To heal earth's wounds and end her bitter strife.

Hope of the world, afoot on dusty highways,
  Showing to wandering souls the path of light;
Walk Thou beside us lest the tempting by-ways
  Lure us away from Thee to endless night.

Hope of the world, who by Thy Cross didst save us
  From death and dark despair, from sin and guilt;
We render back the love Thy mercy gave us;
  Take Thou our lives and use them as Thou wilt.

Hope of the world, O Christ, o'er death victorious,
  Who by this sign didst conquer grief and pain,
We would be faithful to Thy Gospel glorious:
  Thou art our Lord! Thou dost for ever reign!

Miss Harkness, who was born at Harkness, N. Y., in 1891, is undoubtedly America's most outstanding woman theologian of our day. A graduate of Cornell University in 1912, she afterwards studied at Boston, Yale and Harvard Universities, and Union Theological Seminary. She received her Ph.D. from Boston University in 1923, and has since been the recipient of honorary degrees from several institutions. After teaching philosophy and various other courses at Boston University School of Religion, Elmira College, and Mount Holyoke College, she became professor of Applied Theology at Garrett Biblical Institute, a position she held for eleven years. In 1950 she was called to fill a similar chair at the Pacific School of Religion.

Miss Harkness was ordained a minister of the Methodist Church in 1926, and was a delegate of her Church to numerous international church conferences, including Oxford, Madras, Amsterdam, Lund and Evanston. In 1947 she was the recipient of a $7,500 prize as co-winner of the Abingdon-Cokesbury Award for her manuscript, *Understanding the Christian Faith,* which was published the same year. She is also the author of several other important works on religion, including *Prayer and the Common Life, The Gospel and Our World, The Sources of Western Morality, Foundations of Christian Knowledge,* and *Christian Ethics.*

One of the most prolific of 20th century American women hymnwriters was Miss Anna Bernardine Hoppe of Milwaukee, Wis., who during the 1920s and 1930s contributed a large number of hymns to various hymnals. The daughter of German immigrants, she began to compose verse at the age of eleven, when she wrote a poem on angels. Although she had no more than an eighth grade education, and found it necessary to support herself by working in a business office, she continued to cultivate her gift as a writer, and soon began to attract attention by her poetry.

"Many of my hymns," she once wrote, "have been written on my way to and from church, and to and from work. I utilize my lunch hours for typing the hymns and keeping up correspondence. I used to do quite a bit of writing on Sunday afternoons, but now we have a Laymen's Hour in our church at that time, and I do not like to miss it . . . Still I find a minute here and there in which to jot down some verse."

In 1925, no less than twenty-three of Miss Hoppe's hymns were published in *The Hymnal* of the Augustana Lutheran Church, and in

624

1930 eight were included in the *American Lutheran Hymnal.* In 1927, a collection of her lyrics was published under the title, *Hymns of the Church Year.* One of her Lenten hymns, "O'er Jerusalem Thou weepest," has this moving stanza:

> O Thou Lord of my salvation,
>   Grant my soul Thy blood-bought peace.
> By Thy tears of lamentation
>   Bid my faith and love increase.
> Grant me grace to love Thy Word,
> Grace to keep the message heard,
> Grace to own Thee as my Treasure,
> Grace to love Thee without measure.

Other hymns by Miss Hoppe are "The Sower goeth forth to sow," "Rise, arise! Rise, arise!" "Jesus, O precious Name," "Precious Child, so sweetly sleeping," "Thou Lord of life and death," "O Father mine, whose mercies never cease," and "How blest are they who through the power." An Epiphany hymn, "Desire of every nation," is exceptionally fine.

Miss Hoppe also translated a large number of German hymns into English, and at least one Norwegian—Wexel's "O precious thought, some day the mist shall vanish." It was her expressed ambition to write a thousand original Christian lyrics, and she probably composed at least one-half that number. She died in 1941.

An Easter Victory Song

Now let the vault of heaven resound
In praise of Love that doth abound,
   "Christ hath triumphed, Alleluia,"
Sing, choirs of angels, loud and clear,
Repeat their song of glory here,
   "Christ hath triumphed, Christ hath triumphed!"
   Alleluia, Alleluia, Alleluia.

Eternal is the gift He brings,
Wherefore our heart with rapture sings,
   "Christ hath triumphed, Jesus liveth!"
Now doth He come and give us life,
Now doth His presence still all strife
   Through His triumph; Jesus reigneth!
   Alleluia, Alleluia, Alleluia.

O fill us, Lord, with dauntless love;
Set heart and will on things above
   That we conquer through Thy triumph,
Grant grace sufficient for life's day
That by our life we ever say,
   "Christ hath triumphed, and He liveth!"
   Alleluia, Alleluia, Alleluia.

Adoring praises now we bring
And with the heavenly blessed sing,
   "Christ hath triumphed, Alleluia!"
Be to the Father, and our Lord,
To Spirit blest, most holy God,
   Thine the glory never ending!
   Alleluia, Alleluia, Alleluia!

PAUL ZELLER STRODACH, 1876–1947

626

A UNIFYING AMERICAN HYMNAL

IN the year 1783, Henry Melchior Muhlenberg, who has been called "the patriarch of the Lutheran Church in America," wrote to a friend: "It would be a most delightful and advantageous thing if all the Evangelical Lutheran congregations in North America were united with one another; if they all used the same order of service."

Nearly two centuries have passed since Muhlenberg penned those words, but the ideal which he expressed—*One Church and One Book*—has survived to intrigue and challenge all Lutheran groups in the New World.

At one time the Lutheran Church in America was one of the most divided of Protestant communions. Geographical considerations were partly responsible, and there were also some doctrinal controversies. Most of the division, however, was due to differences in language and cultural traditions. As Lutherans from Germany and the Scandinavian countries of northern Europe came to the New World, they brought with them their hymnbooks and liturgies. At first they worshiped God in the language of their fathers. Later, when the demand for English arose, they preserved their respective hymn heritages as well as their liturgies in translation. Each Lutheran body had its own distinctive book of worship.

Through a succession of mergers, however, the number of Lutheran synods in the United States has been gradually reduced, and it now appears that within a short time approximately 95 per cent of all Lutherans in the New World will be found within three large national Churches, namely, The Lutheran Church-Missouri Synod, The American Lutheran Church, and one that will probably bear the name of The United Lutheran Church of America. The latter two, which are still in process of formation, will be composed of eight Lutheran bodies which already work co-operatively in the National Lutheran Council, an agency representing a total membership of five million Lutherans.

Meanwhile, as Muhlenberg's dream of "one Church" is slowly being realized, his idea of "one Book" has also been kept alive. On

627

May 3, 1921, representatives of eight Lutheran synods met in Chicago for the purpose of preparing an intersynodical hymnal. Emmanuel Poppen, who later became president of the American Lutheran Church (one of the constituent units of the proposed merged body to be known as The American Lutheran Church), was chairman of the group. The attempt, however, proved abortive. After nine years of labor, the *American Lutheran Hymnal* was published in 1930, but it was officially adopted only by the American Lutheran Church.

The demand for a common hymnal persisted, however, and the United Lutheran Church in America, at its biennial convention in Minneapolis in the fall of 1944, voted to take the initiative in proposing such a project. All of the bodies of the National Lutheran Council eventually agreed to co-operate. In addition to the United Lutheran Church, they were the American Lutheran Church, the American Evangelical Lutheran Church, the Augustana Lutheran Church, the Evangelical Lutheran Church, the Finnish Evangelical Lutheran Church, the Lutheran Free Church and the United Evangelical Lutheran Church.

The Joint Commission on a Common Hymnal began its work at Pittsburgh, Pa., on June 19, 1945. Eight months later, at the request of the Augustana Lutheran Church, a Joint Commission on a Common Liturgy was likewise constituted. For more than a decade the two commissions labored at their respective tasks, and in 1958 a book of worship bearing the name, *Service Book and Hymnal of the Lutheran Church in America,* came from the presses. Officially adopted by two-thirds of American Lutheranism, Muhlenberg's dream of *One Book* had reached at least partial fulfillment.

The new book of worship has been characterized as perhaps the most unique publication of its kind on this side of the Atlantic. While one of its avowed objectives was to perpetuate in English dress the best of the spiritual and cultural heritages of the several Lutheran lands of Europe, it is thoroughly ecumenical in character, being representative of the noblest worship traditions, both in liturgy and hymnody, of the entire Christian Church. Approximately eighty Greek and Latin hymns are found in it, many of the latter being set to ancient plainsong. About two-thirds of the 602 hymns in the collection had their origin in England or America, including lyrics from the time of the Venerable Bede to those of contemporary writers.

Serving as chairman of both the hymnal and liturgy commissions and directing the work of both was a man who celebrated his 85th birthday shortly before the book was published in 1958. He is Luther D. Reed, who is regarded as the leading liturgical authority in the United States today. Born in a Lutheran parsonage in North Wales, Pa., in 1873, he received his education at Franklin and Marshall College and at Lutheran Theological Seminary, Philadelphia. He also spent a year of study in Leipzig, Germany. After serving parishes in Allegheny and Jeannette, Pa., he became director of Krauth Memorial Library at Lutheran Theological Seminary, a position he held for forty-four years. He also taught liturgics and church art at that institution from 1911 to 1945, and held the office of president from 1939 to 1945. An author and editor of many publications, his principal work is *The Lutheran Liturgy,* published in 1947.

Dr. Reed's contribution to church worship was recognized by the Hymn Society of America when he was elected a vice-president of that organization. For the *Service Book and Hymnal* he composed both the words and music of "O God of wondrous grace and glory," a prayer hymn which sounds a strong national note. The first two stanzas read:

> O God of wondrous grace and glory,
> Whose law is love, whose love is life;
> We worship Thee, we bow before Thee
> In days of calm, in hours of strife.
>   In Thee we trust; bless Thou our land;
>   Our times are in Thy hand.
>
> Strong Son of God, who livest ever,
> Whom death and hell could not contain,
> Who stooped to serve, yet reignest ever;
> Uphold the right; let truth remain.
>   Forgive our sins; our lives command;
>   Our times are in Thy hand.

Paul Zeller Strodach, another distinguished authority on liturgy, hymnody and church art, had served for two years on the commission which produced the *Service Book and Hymnal* when death cut short his labors in 1947. Born in Norristown, Pa., in 1876, Strodach had served parishes in Trenton, N. J.; Easton, Pa.; Washington, Pa.; Canton, O.; Philadelphia and Norristown, Pa., when he was called to become literature editor of the United Lutheran Church Publication House in Philadelphia. He was the author of *A Manual on Worship* as well as a number of other devotional and liturgical works, and the editor of several hymnals. Strodach wrote two lyrics for the *Service*

Book and Hymnal, one for morning worship and the other for Easter. The former, "God of our life, all-glorious Lord," contains this striking stanza:

> Thus may we walk our way with Thee,
> Enabled by Thy grace to be
> A little less unworthy, Lord,
> Of Thee our Friend, our holy God.

His Easter hymn, "Now let the vault of heaven resound," written to be sung to the glorious Cologne tune, *Lasst uns erfreuen,* sounds an exalted note of victory over death. Strodach did not live to see his hymn appear in the new hymnal, but in a very definite sense he has experienced the fulfillment of its final stanza:

> Adoring praises now we bring
> And with the heavenly blessed sing,
> "Christ hath triumphed, Alleluia!"
> Be to the Father, and our Lord,
> To Spirit blest, most holy God,
>   Thine the glory, never ending!
>   Alleluia! Alleluia! Alleluia!

Ernst William Olson, a lay member of the hymnal commission who passed away in Chicago at the age of 88 years shortly after the new hymnal had appeared, contributed a fine hymn bearing the title, "God of peace, in peace preserve us." Written at the close of World War II, it reflects the universal revulsion against war and bloodshed which was felt by all mankind at that time:

> God of peace, in peace preserve us,
>   Hear us, merciful Lord God!
> Let not lust for power swerve us
>   From the way our Master trod.
> Guarded by Thy mighty hand,
> Safe and free our people stand.
>
> God of love, if foemen face us,
>   Armed with weapons forged in hate,
> Let not pride nor greed debase us;
>   All our efforts consecrate
> That the wrong shall be made right
> In Thy Spirit, by Thy might.
>
> God of mercy, bid the terrors
>   Of inhuman strife to cease;
> Overrrule our grievous errors
>   By Thy scepter, Prince of Peace.
> Let Thine angels speak again,
> "Peace on earth, good will toward men."

Olson, whose gifts as a translator of Swedish hymns was mentioned in the preceding chapter, is also represented in the new hymnal by four translations from the Swedish, as well as by a very fine paraphrase of the 121st Psalm, "Mine eyes unto the mountains."

Edward Trail Horn III, another member of the hymnal commission, was the writer of a charming Christmas carol, "Long ago and far away," based on the 15th century German cradle song, *Joseph lieber, Joseph mein.* The latter is a medieval dialogue carol in which Joseph and Mary are represented as alternately addressing each other in song as they watch over the manger cradle. Horn also produced new translations of Luther's "Come, Holy Spirit, God and Lord" and "Out of the depths I cry to Thee," Held's "Come, O come, Thou quickening Spirit," Heerman's "O God, eternal source," as well as a new version of Prudentius' "Despair not, O heart, in thy sorrow."

Pastor of Trinity Church, Germantown, Philadelphia, Horn is an outstanding preacher and lecturer, as well as a student of liturgy and hymnology. He is the author of *Altar and Pew,* comprising addresses given in 1951 in the Knubel-Miller lecture series, as well as other publications. In 1958 he was chosen chairman of the Permanent Commission which has jurisdiction over future editions of the *Service Book and Hymnal* and related publications.

Other members of the hymnal commission* who contributed original hymns to the new collection were George Rise Seltzer, professor of liturgics at the Lutheran Theological Seminary in Philadelphia, and Claus August Wendell, late pastor of Grace Lutheran Church, Minneapolis. Seltzer's "Come, all ye people, come away," a festival lyric particularly appropriate for a church dedication or anniversary, contains these striking stanzas:

---

* The author of this volume, Ernest Edwin Ryden, who was secretary of the Joint Commission on a Common Hymnal, also made extensive contributions to the *Service Book and Hymnal.* His original hymns are "Eternal God, before Thy throne we bend," "The twilight shadows round me fall," "How blessed is this place, O Lord," "With solemn joy we come, dear Lord," "Beyond the everlasting hills," and a number of single stanzas. He also revised several translations of Swedish hymns and translated additional stanzas. Four paraphrases of Finnish hymns, based on previous translations, are from his pen. They are "Arise, my soul, arise," "Lord, as a pilgrim on earth I roam," "Jesus, hear my humble pleading" and "I lift my eyes unto heaven above." For twenty-five years he has been editor of *The Lutheran Companion,* official organ of the Augustana Lutheran Church. He served four years as president of the American Lutheran Conference. *The Story of Our Hymns,* of which this volume is a comprehensive revision, was first published in 1930, and passed through eight editions before being replaced by the present book.—The Publishers.

> O God, to Thee we bring the meed
> Of praise, for help in time of need,
> For mercies given by Thy Son,
> For joys which make our cup o'er-run.
>
> Grant us, throughout our earthly day,
> To love and serve Thee all the way;
> To labor for Thy Kingdom's spread,
> For Christ our Lord, for Christ our Head!

Wendell wrote a singularly strong paraphrase of a portion of the 139th Psalm, "Search me, God, and know my heart," to be sung to an equally virile chorale tune written by the Swedish composer, Gunnar Wennerberg. Wendell, who possessed unusual literary gifts, passed away Sept. 18, 1950, while the hymnbook was still in preparation.

"Under the feeble stable light," a bright Christmas carol from the pen of Arnold F. Keller, was an original contribution to the collection. The author, who also wrote the music for the carol, as well as two other hymn-tunes in the new hymnbook, was pastor of the Redeemer Lutheran Church of Utica, N. Y., for 37 years until he retired in 1958. A leader in both community and church, he was the founder of the Lutheran Laymen's Retreat in the Adirondacks and the originator of the Fellowship of the Open Bible movement. He frequently introduced his carols and hymn-tunes at Christmas festivals in his church.

The 1958 Lutheran hymnal contains an unusually large number of famous Christmas carols of many lands. Among these may be mentioned the exquisite 16th century German lyric, "Lo, how a Rose e'er blooming" (*Es ist ein' Ros' entsprungen*); Dix's "What Child is this?" sung to the haunting English tune, *Greensleeves;* Cecil Cowdrey's delightful translation from the Danish of Ingemann's "Christmas brings joy to every heart"; the traditional English carol, "The first Noel," whose author and composer are both unknown; and the inspiring French carol, "Angels we have heard on high," for which the English words were written by the American, Earl Marlatt.

One of the most unusual hymns in the collection came from an obscure writer in a rural district of Minnesota. William Johnson, who from childhood had lived on a farm near the town of Lindstrom in that state, had never had the benefit of an education beyond the eighth grade, but was passionately fond of poetry, and frequently composed verse. Early in 1953 he submitted a Lenten poem for publication in

The Lutheran Companion, with no thought that it might ever be used as a hymn. However, the editor of that publication, who was a member of the hymnal commission, saw unusual merit in the lyric and proposed it for inclusion in the new collection. Another member of the commission, Leland Bernhard Sateren of Minneapolis, wrote a striking tune for the words, and thus a new hymn was born. Here are the words:

> Deep were His wounds, and red,
>   On cruel Calvary,
> As on the Cross He bled
>   In bitter agony;
> But they whom sin has wounded sore
> Find healing in the wounds He bore.
>
> He suffered shame and scorn,
>   And wretched, dire disgrace;
> Forsaken and forlorn,
>   He hung there in our place
> But such as would from sin be free
> Look to His Cross for victory.
>
> His life, His all, He gave
>   When He was crucified;
> Our burdened souls to save,
>   What fearful death He died!
> But each of us, though dead in sin,
> Through Him eternal life may win.

An important part of the hymnal commission's task was to preserve in English dress the representative hymns of the several Lutheran European traditions. Among commission members who assumed responsibility in the translation of Danish, Norwegian, Swedish or Finnish lyrics were Lawrence N. Field, a professor in Luther Theological Seminary, St. Paul, Minn., and Fred C. M. Hansen, a retired pastor now living in Blair, Nebr. Others who assisted the commission in this work were Samuel V. Autere, a pastor of the Finnish Evangelical Lutheran Church; Mrs. Ida Kaarto Kaskinen of Portland, Ore., and Mrs. Aino Lilja Kantonen-Halkola of Hancock, Mich. A hymn by the 17th century Norwegian hymnist, Peter Dass, was translated into English by none other than Eivind Joef Berggrav, hero bishop in the resistance movement against the Nazis in Norway during World War II. It bears the title, "Mighty God, to Thy dear Name be given."

One of the most unique hymns in the book is "Strengthen for service, Lord, the hands," a metrical paraphrase of a prayer said by a deacon while the people received communion in the Liturgy of

Malabar. This is a 5th century rite still observed in South India by the so-called Thoma Christians, a Church which tradition claims was founded by the Apostle Thomas. The deacon's prayer, as translated by John Mason Neale from the Syriac text, begins with the words: "Strengthen, O Lord, the hands which are stretched out to receive the Holy Thing: vouchsafe that they may daily bring forth fruit to Thy divinity; that they may be worthy of all things which they have sung to Thy praise within the sanctuary, and may ever laud Thee." The prose translation was put into metrical form by the English hymnist, C. W. Humphreys.

Another ancient communion hymn in the collection is "Let all mortal flesh keep silence," which is the Cherubic Hymn in the Liturgy of St. James of Jerusalem, dating from the 5th century. Still celebrated once a year in Jerusalem, the Cherubic Hymn is sung when the sacred elements are brought to the altar at the beginning of the Liturgy of the Faithful.

From Holland the stirring hymn of thanksgiving, "We praise Thee, O God, our Redeemer, Creator," was adopted by the *Service Book and Hymnal*. Written by an unknown poet near the close of the 16th century in celebration of Dutch independence from the Spanish yoke, it was first published in Valerius' *Neder-landtsch Gedencklanck*. The English translation is by Julia Bulkley Cady Cory.

Also in the category of lyrics by unknown hymn-writers is a hymn that made its first appearance in the Congregational *Pilgrim Hymnal* of 1904. Emphasizing the truth that salvation is wholly the work of God, and that it is He who seeks the sinner and not the sinner that seeks God, it is a poetic gem of rare beauty:

> I sought the Lord, and afterward I knew
> He moved my soul to seek Him, seeking me;
> It was not I that found, O Saviour true;
> No, I was found of Thee.
>
> Thou didst reach forth Thy hand and mine enfold;
> I walked, and sank not on the storm-vexed sea;
> 'Twas not so much that I on Thee took hold
> As Thou, dear Lord, on me.
>
> I find, I walk, I love, but O the whole
> Of love is but my answer, Lord, to Thee;
> For Thou wert long beforehand with my soul,
> Always Thou lovedst me.

The poem, it seems, was first published in the early 1880's, but all efforts to discover the identity of the author have proved fruitless.

A very recent hymn in the 1958 Lutheran hymnal is "Thine is the glory," which gained international popularity almost over night when it became the theme song of the constituting Assembly of the World Council of Churches in Amsterdam in 1948. Written in French by Edmond Budry, it was translated into English by Richard Birch Hoyle. It appeared for the first time in *Cantate Domino,* published by the World's Student Christian Federation.

Another of the more unusual hymns in the book is the product of Christian missions in India. It bears the title, "One who is unfit to count," and its last two stanzas read:

> So, Love in human form
>   For love of me He came;
> I cannot look upon His face
>   For shame, for bitter shame.
>
> If there is aught of worth in me,
>   It comes from Thee alone;
> Then keep me safe, for so, O Lord,
>   Thou keepest but Thine own.

The writer was Narayan Vaman Tilak, who was born at Karazgaon, Bombay Presidency, in 1862, of Hindu aristocracy. At the age of 32 he became a Christian, and for twenty-one years thereafter he worked with great zeal in the American Marathi Mission, preaching and teaching. He also employed his unusual poetic gifts in giving to the Marathi Church an indigenous hymnody. Moffatt says: "He produced a great body of spiritual songs, simple, intense, passionate, expressive of the Indian Christian heart in its vision of Christ and its worship of God." Tilak died in 1919. The above hymn was translated into English by Nicol Macnicol, a missionary to India who passed away in 1952.

The growing recognition being given to Negro spirituals by hymnal editors was revealed when the poignant hymn, "Were you there when they crucified my Lord?" was included in the collection. The origin of both the words and music of this deeply moving lyric is hidden in obscurity. One authority on folk-lore contends that a similar song, "Have you heard how they crucified our Lord?" is well known among the whites in the upper Cumberland region of Tennessee. However, the hymn belongs definitely to the Negro spiritual tradition, and is justly regarded as one of the truly great contributions that race has made to American hymnody.

The *Service Book and Hymnal* made it quite clear that Lutherans do not claim that Martin Luther was the writer of "Away in a manger," which for nearly three-fourths of a century has circulated in American hymnbooks as "Luther's Cradle Hymn." The first two stanzas of this little song first appeared in 1885 in a little hymnal for children issued by the General Council of the Lutheran Church. In that book the anonymous character of the words was plainly indicated. Two years later, however, James R. Murray edited a kindergarten song-book for the John Church Company in Cincinnati, designating the song as "Luther's Cradle Hymn" and adding: "Composed by Martin Luther for his children, and still sung by German mothers to their little ones." It was published with a new tune, above which were placed the initials "J.R.M.", which would indicate that Murray composed it. However, the *Service Book and Hymnal* has designated the tune merely as "19th Century, American." The third stanza did not appear until 1892, and is generally credited to a John Thomas McFarland.

Four other anonymous hymns that appear in the collection are "How firm a foundation," "Thee we adore, eternal Lord," "Praise the Lord! ye heavens adore Him," and "Spirit of mercy, truth, and love." The first of these was printed originally in Rippon's *Selection* of 1787, where it appeared with the signature "K—." The names of "Kirkham," "Keith" and "Keen" have been associated with this initial, and modern research seems to indicate that it was the latter who wrote "How firm a foundation." Nothing is known concerning this person, however.

"Thee we adore, eternal Lord,'" which very obviously is a metrical version of the Latin *Te Deum Laudamus* of the 4th or 5th century, appeared in its original English form in the Appendix to Thomas Cotterill's *Selection of Psalms and Hymns*, published in Staffordshire in 1754. Whether the paraphrase was done by Cotterill, or by his friend, James Montgomery, or by some other poet, however, is not known.

"Praise the Lord! ye heavens, adore Him" and "Spirit of mercy, truth, and love" are both from the *London Foundling Hospital Collection*. The former, which is a paraphrase of the 148th Psalm, appeared in the edition of 1796, while the latter was printed in the earlier edition of 1774. Nothing is known concerning the authorship of either.

The same is true of yet another hymn, "The wise may bring their learning," which was first printed in the Congregational Church Hymnal of England in 1887, but without any indication who the writer might be.

The Music Committee of the 1958 hymnbook examined more than 400 original hymn-tunes submitted by contemporary American organists and musicians. Among newer tunes included in the collection are compositions by Ralph P. Lewars, Carl Wilfred Landahl, Arnold Frederick Keller, Clive H. Kilgore, Peter Johnson, Giuseppe Moschetti, Oscar Rudolph Overby, Luther D. Reed, Ralph Alvin Strom, Leland Bernard Sateren, Gerhard T. Alexis, John Victor Bergquist, Charles Winfred Douglas, Thomas Tertius Noble and John Henry Gower. Seven arrangements of plainsong tunes were made by Ernest White.

Recent or contemporary musicians in Europe and Canada whose tunes were adopted include such well-known composers as Ralph Vaughan Williams, Martin Shaw, Gustav T. Holst, Alfred Scott-Gatty, Graham George, Armas Massalo, Otto Emmanuel Olsson, Ernest A. Hagfors, Berndt M. Nyberg and Karl I. N. Wideen. Twenty hymns were set to chorale harmonizations by Johann Sebastian Bach, acknowledged master of all church composers.

Original music or arrangements adopted for the liturgical settings are the work of Harold W. Gilbert, Leo Sowerby, Healy Willan, Charles Winfred Douglas, J. H. Arnold, T. Tertius Noble and Regina H. Fryxell. The second setting of the liturgy was largely adapted by the latter from pre-Reformation plainsong, some of which is in current use in the liturgy of the Church of Sweden.

Mention has been made in earlier chapters of splendid hymns produced as the result of contests sponsored by the Hymn Society of America. The stimulus which this organization has given to creative hymn-writing is exemplified in another hymn in the *Service Book and Hymnal,* titled "Where restless crowds are thronging," which comes from the pen of the late Thomas Curtis Clark. It was one of five "Hymns on the City" obtained by the Hymn Society for use at a convocation on Urban Life in America held under the auspices of the Methodist Church in Columbus, Ohio, in 1954. He had earlier been awarded first prize in a nation-wide hymn competition sponsored by the Society in 1945.

Clark, who was one of America's leading contemporary lyric poets, was born in Vincennes, Ind., in 1877. From 1912 to 1948 he was a member of the editorial staff of the *Christian Century,* and also served as associate editor of *The Pulpit.* In addition to his well-known Lincoln poems, he published numerous volumes of devotional verse. With W. E. Garrison, he was joint author of *One Hundred Poems of Peace* and *One Hundred Poems of Immortality.* He also collaborated with others in the production of anthologies and poetry collections. He passed away in 1953. The above-mentioned hymn reads:

> Where restless crowds are thronging
>   Along the city ways,
> Where pride and greed and turmoil
>   Consume the fevered days,
> Where vain ambitions banish
>   All thoughts of praise and prayer,
> The people's spirits waver:
>   But Thou, O Christ, art there.
>
> In scenes of want and sorrow
>   And haunts of flagrant wrong,
> In homes where kindness falters,
>   And strife and fear are strong,
> In busy street of barter,
>   In lonely thoroughfare,
> The people's spirits languish:
>   But Thou, O Christ, art there.
>
> O Christ, behold Thy people—
>   They press on every hand!
> Bring light to all the cities
>   Of our beloved land.
> May all our bitter striving
>   Give way to visions fair
> Of righteousness and justice:
>   For Thou, O Christ, art there.

ACKNOWLEDGMENTS
and
INDEXES

ACKNOWLEDGMENTS

COPYRIGHT material in this book has been used by permission of, and by special arrangements with, the following publishers and authors, to whom we make grateful acknowledgment for the courtesies granted:

J. Curwen & Sons Ltd.—"Onward, Christian soldiers" by Sabine Baring-Gould, and English translation of Bernhardt Severin Ingemann's "Through the night of doubt and sorrow" by Baring-Gould.

The Macmillan Company—A stanza from John Masefield's "Sing, men and angels, sing."

Abbot of Downside Abbey—Mildred Whitney Stillman's hymn, "Now once again for help that never faileth."

Proprietors of Hymns Ancient and Modern—Cyril A. Alington's hymn, "Good Christian men, rejoice and sing!"

Harper & Brothers—Milton S. Littlefield's hymn, "O Son of Man, Thou madest known," from *Hymns of the Christian Life.*

Mrs. George Bambridge and Doubleday & Co.—Rudyard Kipling's "Recessional" from *The Five Nations* and "The Children's Song" from *Puck of Pook's Hill.*

The Hymn Society of America—Henry Hallam Tweedy's "O God of love, whose Spirit wakes"; Sarah E. Taylor's "O God of Light, Thy Word, a lamp unfailing"; Georgia Harkness' "Hope of the world, Thou Christ of great compassion"; and Thomas Curtis Clark's "Where restless crowds are thronging," the latter from *Five New Hymns on the City.*

Miss Margaret Cropper—Her hymn, "O Christ, whom we may love and know."

Chautauqua Institution—Mary Artemisia Lathbury's "Day is dying in the west" and "Break Thou the Bread of Life."

A. D. Peters, London—A hymn by Clifford Bax, "Turn back, O man, forswear thy foolish ways."

American Tract Society—John Oxenham's hymn, "In Christ there is no East or West," from *Bees in Amber.*

Mrs. F. B. Macnutt—A stanza from "Let all the multitudes of light," a hymn by her husband, Frederick Brodie Macnutt.

Mr. Ernest Merrill—Two hymns by his father, William Pierson Merrill, namely, "Rise up, O men of God" and "Not alone for mighty empire."

Charles Scribner's Sons—Quotations from Henry van Dyke's hymn, "Joyful, joyful we adore thee," and "Return, dear Lord, to those who look," from his *Poems;* also "This is my Father's world," "Be strong," and "When the great sun sinks to his rest" from *Thoughts for Everyday Living* by Maltbie D. Babcock.

Oxford University Press, London—The following hymns from *The English Hymnal*: Catherine Winkworth's translation of "Praise to the Lord, the Almighty," John Athelstan Riley's "Ye watchers and ye holy ones"; translation from the Syriac of "Strengthen for service, Lord"; Dorothy Frances Gurney's "O perfect love, all human thought transcending"; Henry Scott Holland's "Judge eternal, throned in splendor," and Gilbert Keith Chesterton's "O God of earth and altar."

Oxford University Press, London—The following hymns from *Songs of Praise* (Enlarged Edition): William Charter Piggott's "For those we love within the veil" and Percy Dearmer's "Remember all the people," "Book of books, our people's strength," and "Now quit your care."

Oxford University Press, London—The following six translations by Robert Bridges, all of which are from *The Yattendon Hymnal*: "Fear not, thou faithful Christian flock," "The duteous day now closeth," "When morning gilds the skies," "O gladsome light," "O splendor of God's glory bright," and "Ah, holy Jesus, how hast Thou offended."

INDEX OF HYMNS AND SOURCES

AUTHORS, TRANSLATORS, AND GENERAL INDEX

BIBLIOGRAPHY

JOHN JULIAN: *Dictionary of Hymnology*
LOUIS F. BENSON: *The English Hymn*
LOUIS F. BENSON: *Studies in Familiar Hymns*
F. J. GILLMAN: *The Evolution of the English Hymn*
BENJAMIN TERRY: *A History of England*
JOHAN W. BECKMAN: *Försök till Svensk Psalm Historia*
GÖSTA HAGELIN: *Människoöden in Psalmboken*
HENRY WILDER FOOTE: *Three Centuries of American Hymnody*
EDWARD S. NINDE: *The Story of the American Hymn*
EMIL LIEDGREN: *Den Svenska Psalmboken*
E. N. SÖDERBERG: *Den Kristna Psalmen*
WILLIAM LEE HUNTON: *Favorite Hymns*
DANIEL JOSEPH DONAHUE: *Early Christian Hymns*
SAMUEL A. W. DUFFIELD: *English Hymns: Their Authors and History*
EDWIN FRANCIS HATFIELD: *The Poets of the Church*
WILSON T. HOGUE: *Hymns That Are Immortal*
JAMES T. LIGHTWOOD: *Hymn-tunes and Their Story*
CARL FOWLER PRICE: *One Hundred and One Hymn Stories*
JEREMIAH B. REEVES: *The Hymn as Literature*
GEORGE COLE STEBBINS: *Reminiscences and Gospel Hymn Stories*
EDWARD DICKINSON: *Music in the History of the Western Church*
HORATIUS BONAR: *Hymns of Faith and Hope*
MARY SCHALL BACON: *Hymns That Every Child Should Know*
JAMES F. LAMBERT: *Luther's Hymns*
JOHN DAHLE: *Library of Christian Hymns*
ROBERT E. SMITH: *Modern Messages from Great Hymns*
E. J. EKMAN: *Inre Missionens Historia*
SIGFRID LAURIN: *Oscar Ahnfelt*
GEORGE M. STEPHENSON: *Religious Aspects of Swedish Immigration*
J. N. SKAAR: *Norsk Salmehistorie*
DAVID R. BREED: *The History and Use of Hymns and Hymn-tunes*
W. G. POLACK: *The Handbook to the Lutheran Hymnal*
W. G. POLACK: *Hymns from the Harps of God*
HELEN PFATTEICHER: *In Every Corner Sing*
MRS. E. R. PITMAN: *Lady Hymn Writers*

669

MOFFATT AND PATRICK: *Handbook to the Church Hymnary*
PERCY DEARMER: *Songs of Praise Discussed*
PHILIP SCHAFF: *Christ in Song*
KATHLEEN BLANCHARD: *Stories of Popular Hymns*
JOHN MCNAUGHER: *The Psalms in Worship*
JOHN KEBLE: *The Christian Year*
IRA D. SANKEY: *My Life and the Story of the Gospel Hymns*
CAROLINE LEONARD GOODENOUGH: *High Lights on Hymnists*
FARLANDER AND ELLINWOOD: *The Hymnal 1940 Companion*
EMIL LIEDGREN: *Svensk Psalm och Andlig Visa*
AMOS R. WELLS: *A Treasure of Hymns*
CHARLES ARTHUR BOYD: *Stories of Hymns for Creative Living*
RUTH ELLIS MESSENGER: *The Medieval Latin Hymn*
J. M. K.: *Bright Talks on Favourite Hymns*
IVAN H. HAGEDORN: *Stories of Great Hymn Writers*
J. C. AABERG: *Hymns and Hymnwriters of Denmark*
CHARLES VENN PILCHER: *Icelandic Meditations on the Passion*
ERICK BERRY: *The Land and People of Finland*
EDWARD ALBERT BAILEY: *The Gospel in Hymns*
NILS FORSANDER: *Olavus Petri*
CHARLES M. JACOBS: *The Story of the Church*
GILBERT TAIT: *The Hymns of Denmark*
BROWN AND BUTTERWORTH: *The Story of the Hymns and Tunes*
ALFRED H. WELSH: *Development of English Literature and Language*
CATHERINE WINKWORTH: *Lyra Germanica*
JANE BORTHWICK: *Hymns from the Land of Luther*
LAURENCE N. FIELD: *Johann Sebastian Bach*

670